ORCHESTRATION

Cecil Forsyth

With a New Foreword by
WILLIAM BOLCOM
University of Michigan, Ann Arbor

Dover Publications, Inc.
New York

This Dover edition, first published in 1982, is an unabridged republication of the second edition, 1935, as published, within the series "The Musician's Library," by Macmillan and Co., Limited, London, and Stainer and Bell, Limited, London (first edition: Macmillan, 1914). The Foreword to the Dover Edition was specially written for the present edition by William Bolcom.

Library of Congress Cataloging in Publication Data

Forsyth, Cecil, 1876-1941.
Orchestration.

Reprint of: 2nd ed. London : Macmillan, 1935.
1. Instrumentation and orchestration.
MT70.F76 1982 781.6'4 82-7265
ISBN 0-486-24383-4 AACR2

Manufactured in the United States by Courier Corporation
24383412
www.doverpublications.com

FOREWORD TO THE DOVER EDITION

WHEN I was around eleven or twelve years old and growing up in Washington State, I was studying composition with two teachers in Seattle, George Frederick McKay (now deceased) and John Verrall (who is, I am happy to say, very much with us and likely to live to a Eubie Blake-ean great age). The first gave me very general lessons and often upset me; I find, however, that I now teach rather like my memory of Professor McKay, in seeking to disturb my students rather than resolve things for them, which I feel is not my job. However, all students at some point need something more than the wrenching *koans* McKay would pose me; we also need simple skills and discipline in the technical side of music, and this must be taught with as much spirituality as the more transcendental aspects. For this side of my education I am largely indebted to Professor Verrall, who sought and found a balance between the technical and spiritual in music that he could impart to me.

I always bit off more than I could chew, and still do, and so I tried a string quartet. Jack (which I can now call him; I couldn't then) looked at it, and patiently told me that a total of three manuscript pages was not enough to add up to a real quartet, that I must try a larger structure. In order to understand the strings better, he suggested I buy a Forsyth *Orchestration.*

I still have the same copy more than thirty years later, and it is still my bible when I need to refresh my memory about a certain instrument. I have not ever found a subsequent orchestration manual to be anywhere near its equal, and I think the principal reason is that no other book of its genre affords such an insight into the inner workings of the orchestra: namely, a sense of *who the players are.*

In the end, an orchestrator is not writing for instruments as much as for instrumentalists. Every instrument in the modern orchestra has its own history and culture, which is preserved in teaching; gaining a sense of what it is to be a violinist, clarinetist or trombonist is essential in learning to write effectively for the orchestra, and I know of no other book that gives as much insight into this as Forsyth. Not only are the history and evolution of each important instrument fully discussed; the technique and even the players' likes and dislikes *vis-à-vis* what they must play are gone into fully.

One of the special joys of Forsyth, however, and in this I find nothing else remotely like it, is his witty side. The end of the double-bass article (p. 461) not only makes the reader chuckle, it gives a very good general insight in how *not* to write for the bass. Forsyth's articles on obsolete instruments, particularly that on the serpent (p. 286), are replete with quotable zingers. The musical examples (many of them derived, by the way, from those in the Berlioz-Strauss offering of some years earlier) are apposite and (unlike the Berlioz-Strauss) mercifully short and to the point.

A cautionary note: Forsyth's orchestra is the orchestra of before the First World War. There have been numerous developments in instrumental technique on an individual basis since then; one need not remind the reader of the tremendous growth in the percussion family since that time. But much, or most, of what Forsyth says holds today. Since 1914 two major factors have contributed to keeping the orchestra in (I think) a lamentably steady state—up until then the orchestra evolved and added to its numbers as various new instruments gained in players' technique enough to be worthy of it—and those are: (1) the First World War itself, which decimated the ranks of orchestral players dramatically (one need only compare the Stravinsky of *Le Sacre* to that of *L'Histoire du Soldat* to see what that war did to the instrumental ensemble), and (2) the unions. When the American Federation of Musicians decided on the basic complement of winds, brass and strings in the orchestra, that decision effectively eliminated the slow inclusion of instruments like the saxophone into the ranks (no smart orchestrator will use too many instrumentalists that require time-and-a-half pay) or that of any of the electric instruments that now possess a formidable technical culture. Forsyth fully expected these accretions (after all, the previous history of the orchestra had always been in that direction: for proof of Forsyth's feelings on the subject see his late addendum on the saxophone on p. 490), and I am sure he would have been disappointed in the ossification of this wonderful ensemble into the historical monument it now is becoming. Gunther Schuller's famous remarks on the rigidity of the average orchestral musician's attitude today could very well find cause in the vague sense many of these musicians may have that their ensemble may be fading into the past, and themselves with it. Thus it is in a way sad to remark that little need be added to Forsyth's great work in order to make it usable today.

No orchestrally minded composer or orchestrator should rely 100% on any book, of course; much of my subsequent experience in learning about instrumental culture has come from buttonholing and badgering players about their own instruments, and in the end this is the only real way to learn orchestration. A few minor points should, however, be mentioned for the student: for one, Forsyth would today have to list the chromatic harp among the obsolete instruments (the technique died with the last living teacher in the Paris Conservatoire, around World War II); for another, the average tenor trombonist now can reach nearly all the pedal tones Forsyth said were impossible; for a third, most saxophones now possess a B♭ key, extending the bottom range. Similar adjustments that should be made in understanding the scope of each instrument are best accomplished by asking instrumentalists themselves, as I suggested before, and a general check should be made on the same basis of the differences in instrumental ranges (particularly in keyboard percussion instruments like the xylophone) between Forsyth's 1914 British orchestra and the American orchestra of today.

With these cautions I feel that Forsyth is still eminently usable and in fact is very likely the best general textbook on orchestration found today, avoiding as it does the encyclopedic cumbersomeness of the Koechlin and Casella multivolume works and at the same time eschewing the workmanlike humdrumness of most current orchestration manuals. For years I have recommended Forsyth to my students, and I am extremely glad that it will be easily obtainable again.

ANN ARBOR, *1982*

WILLIAM BOLCOM

PREFACE.

In this book an attempt is made first, to describe our modern orchestral instruments, where they sprang from, how they developed, and what they are to-day; next, to trace the types of music which have been reflected in these constructional changes and, in especial, the types most familiar since Beethoven's time. Without some knowledge on these points the student is working in the dark. He is like a Lascar turned loose in a dynamo-house. It is true that one may show him the button, and, if he presses it, he will get a terrific blaze of light. But what is behind the button? How were the wires laid? Why is one type of engine better than another for its own purpose? How is the shop to be run in the most economical way?

All these questions call for answers, and, on the musical side of the analogy, the answers are not difficult to find. For the facts that underlie instrumentation are few and simple: a skin or a metal plate to be beaten; a column of air in a brass or wooden tube with some sort of mouthpiece or embouchure; a string or two—four is a good number—to be bowed, plucked, or struck. These are the essentials and, if the student grasps them, he will soon be brought to see that change comes but slowly and rarely, and that, when it comes, it is more apparent than real. Edward I.'s "Rogero le Troumpour"[1] sounds very ancient in 1914, but he made exactly the same music for his sovereign at Carnarvon as the cavalry trumpeters now make for George V. at Aldershot. And, even if we leave the Long Valley for the more rarefied atmosphere of Queen's Hall, W., we can only record an additional tube or two each with a mechanical air-switch. This is the point for the practical musician. The old persists in the new and, without an understanding of the weapon itself, we cannot wield it.

It is not necessary to enlarge on these topics here. They are all dealt with as they come up in turn for discussion. The main-lines of study concern the original type of instrument, then its modifications.

[1] See page 41.

and last its use in its present-day perfection—or in some cases, one must say, very partial perfection. A good deal of space has been devoted to explaining the String-technique. This is a subject not often studied from the outsider's point of view. It is, however, well worth undertaking as, apart from its inherent musical and scientific interest, its complex and elaborately expressive methods are apt to baffle the student, especially the student who is a professional pianist. For purposes of reference I have begun with a complete list of orchestral instruments, their compasses, and notations; and ended with an index which is also a digest of the work.

Before concluding this preface I wish to acknowledge my obligations to Sir Charles Stanford. To his encouragement this book owes its existence. And, as an old pupil of his, it is with peculiar pleasure that I try to give back a little where I have received much. I hope he will forgive my zoological dissidences on page 461.

To Messrs Boosey and Co. I am indebted for the illustrations which are, I think, an interesting feature of the book. Besides lending me a number of blocks, Messrs Boosey and Co. have allowed me to make photographs from their collection of ancient instruments. Without this courtesy I might not have been able to include such specimens as the Fipple-Flute, Serpent, Cornett, Keyed-Bugle, and Bass-Ophicleide.

Finally I must offer my warmest thanks to Mr. Frank Bridge for his kindness and long labour in reading my proof-sheets. His wide musical knowledge and invincible accuracy have been invaluable to me.

CECIL FORSYTH.

LONDON, *March 7th*, 1914.

NOTE TO SECOND EDITION.

IN the second edition a number of mistakes have been corrected. New facts, that have come to light during the past twenty years, have been incorporated in the text, whenever possible. Some of these are to be found, grouped together under the heading "Addenda," on page 488. With such a deeply rooted, but flourishing, tree as Orchestration, both soil and air have to be watched. And the natural result of this is a certain variety. Our garden-book must include, not only the antique topic of what the Denners did with their primitive chalumeaux, but also the modern question of what students ought to do with their lively saxophones.

C. F.

CONTENTS.

LIST OF PLATES.

ORCHESTRATION

LIST OF INSTRUMENTS.

THE following list is printed here for convenience of reference. The names of the more commonly used instruments are shown in heavy black type. Obsolete instruments[1] are starred thus,— *.

The two semibreve-notes after each instrument give its upward- and downward-compass *in actual sounds.*[2] Extreme notes are shown in crotchet-heads.

The square note that follows the two compass-notes is the note which we should have to write if we wished the instrument to produce the sound middle-C—

It therefore indicates at a glance whether the instrument is a "transposing" or a "non-transposing" instrument and, in the former case, what the transposition is. Thus the square note

appears opposite **BASSOON**, and shows that if we want the Bassoon to sound middle-C we must actually write that note. In other words, it is a non-transposing instrument. On the other hand, the square note

appears opposite **DOUBLE-BASSOON**, and shows that if we want that instrument to sound middle-C we must write a note one octave above that sound. In other words it is a transposing instrument, and it sounds an octave lower than its written part.

It is important to notice that the square note is only a *symbol* which gives the student a ready means of seeing the transposition, that is to say, the method of writing for each instrument. It has nothing to do

[1] Only recently-obsolete instruments, such as the student may possibly come upon in Full Scores, are marshalled above. Schalmeys, Pommers, Bombards, Curtals, Dulcians, Rebecs, Fipple-flutes, Cromornes, and all the rest of the mediæval musical brigade are held in reserve.

[2] This method of defining the compass of transposing-instruments *in actual sounds* is strictly confined to this preliminary list. Throughout the rest of the book the method of mentioning only the *written notes* of the transposing-instruments is adopted. The transposition into actual sound is always understood. This is the plan customary with all orchestral and military-band musicians.

with the instrument's compass. The actual sound, middle-C, may or may not exist on the instrument. That can be found out from the two compass-notes.

In the right-hand column the clefs proper to each instrument are given. For fuller information as to their use and as to the extreme compass-notes the student is referred to the technical details under each instrumental heading.

INSTRUMENT.	COMPASS AND TRANSPOSITION (IF ANY)	CLEF OR CLEFS.
PICCOLO		Treble-clef
* Flageolet	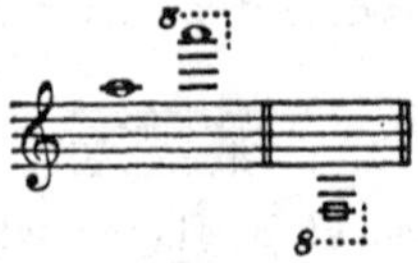	Treble-clef
FLUTE		Treble-clef
Bass-Flute		Treble-clef
Soprano-Oboe in E♭		Treble-clef
OBOE		Treble-clef
Oboe d'Amore		Treble-clef
ENGLISH HORN		Treble-clef
Heckelphon (Baritone Oboe)		Treble-clef

* Musette		Treble-clef
CLARINET in E♭		Treble-clef
CLARINET in D		Treble-clef
* Clarinet in C		Treble-clef
CLARINET in B♭		Treble-clef
CLARINET in A		Treble-clef
Heckelclarind (in B♭)		Treble-clef
BASSETT-HORN (Alto-Clarinet in F)		Treble-clef
Alto-Clarinet in E♭		Treble-clef
BASS-CLARINET in B♭	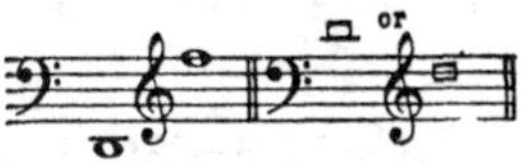	Bass- and treble-clef
Bass-Clarinet in A		Bass- and treble-clef
Pedal-Clarinet in B♭		Bass- or treble-clef

* Tenoroon		Bass- and tenor-clef
BASSOON		Bass- and tenor-clef
DOUBLE-BASSOON		Bass-clef
* Serpent		Bass-clef
Cuckoo-Instrument	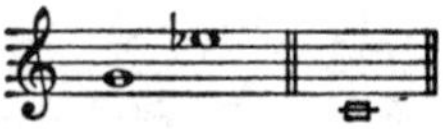	Treble-clef
* Natural-Trumpet	According to crook used. The possible extremes were 	Treble-clef
VALVE-TRUMPET in F		Treble-clef
VALVE-TRUMPET in C		Treble-clef
VALVE-TRUMPET in B♭		Treble-clef
VALVE-TRUMPET in A		Treble-clef
Bass-Trumpet in C		Treble- and bass-clef

CORNET in B♭	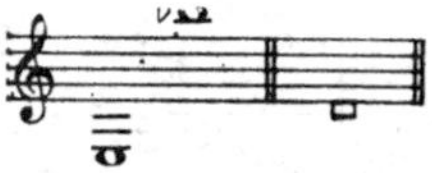	Treble-clef
CORNET in A		Treble-clef
* Natural-Horn	According to crook used. The possible extremes were 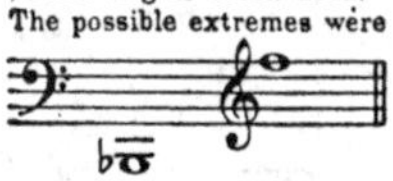	Treble- and bass-clef
VALVE-HORN in F		Treble- and bass-clef
* Zinke. (Known also as *Cornetto* or *Cornet à bouquin*)		Soprano-clef
* Alto-Trombone in E♭		Alto- or bass-clef
TENOR-TROMBONE in B♭	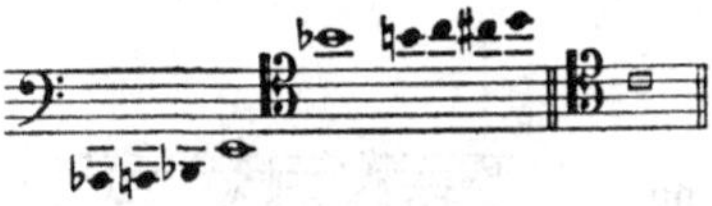	Tenor- or bass-clef
BASS-TROMBONE in G		Bass-clef
BASS-TROMBONE in F		Bass-clef
Bass-Trombone in E♭		Bass-clef
Double-Bass Trombone in B♭		Bass-clef

Valve-Trombone in B♭ (the ordinary 3-valve instrument)

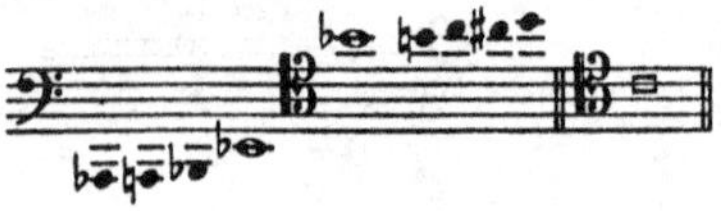

Tenor- or bass-clef

VALVE-TROMBONE in B♭ (with Seven Independent Cylinders)

Tenor- or bass-clef

EUPHONIUM in B♭ (a Tuba with 4 valves)

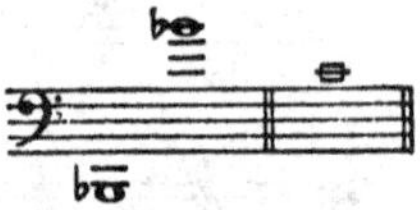

Bass-clef

ORCHESTRAL TUBA in F (with 4 valves)

Bass-clef

E♭ Military Brass-Bass (a Tuba with 4 valves)

Bass-clef

BB♭ Military Brass-Bass (a Tuba with 3 valves)

Bass-clef

More correctly Modified-Horns:

Wagner's "Tenor-Tuba"

Treble-clef

Wagner's "Bass-Tuba"

Treble- or bass-clef

Wagner's "Contrabass-Tuba" (a Tuba with 4 valves)

Bass clef

Sopranino-Saxhorn in E♭ (a "half-tube" instrument)

Treble clef

Soprano-Saxhorn in B♭ (a "half-tube" instrument)

Treble-clef

Alto-Saxhorn in E♭ (a "half-tube" instrument)

Treble-clef

Tenor-Saxhorn in B♭ (a "half-tube" instrument)

Treble-clef

Bass-Saxhorn in B♭ (a "whole-tube" instrument or Tuba)

Treble-clef

Bass-Saxhorn in E♭ (a "whole-tube" instrument or Tuba)

Treble-clef

Contrabass-Saxhorn in B♭ (a "whole-tube" instrument or Tuba)

Treble-clef

The Military Series of Saxophones.

Sopranino-Saxophone in E♭[1]

Treble-clef

Soprano-Saxophone in B♭

Treble-clef

ALTO-SAXOPHONE in E♭

Treble-clef

Tenor-Saxophone in B♭

Treble-clef

Baritone-Saxophone in E♭

Treble-clef

Bass-Saxophone in B♭

Treble-clef

[1] In all the Saxophones the crotchet-head semitone below the lowest compass-note gives the sound which is produced by using the B♭-Key. This extension-key is not in general use in England. See pages 167-8.

The (continental) Orchestral Series of Saxophones.

Sopranino-Saxophone in F

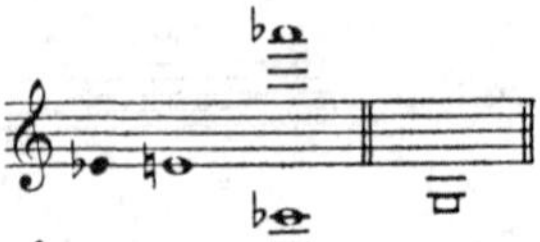

Treble-clef

Soprano-Saxophone in C

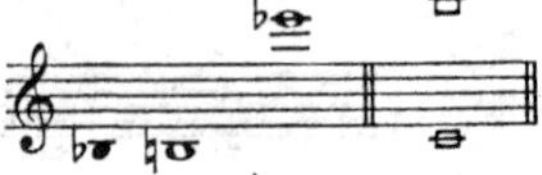

Treble-clef

Alto-Saxophone in F

Treble-clef

Tenor-Saxophone in C

Treble-clef

Baritone-Saxophone in F

Treble-clef

Bass-Saxophone in C

Treble-clef

Soprano-Sarrusophone in B♭

Treble-clef

Contralto-Sarrusophone in E♭

Treble-clef

Tenor-Sarrusophone in B♭

Treble-clef

Baritone-Sarrusophone in E♭

Treble-clef

Bass-Sarrusophone in B♭

Treble-clef

Double-Bass-Sarrusophone in E♭

Treble-clef

THE ORCHESTRAL DOUBLE-BASS-SARRUSOPHONE in C

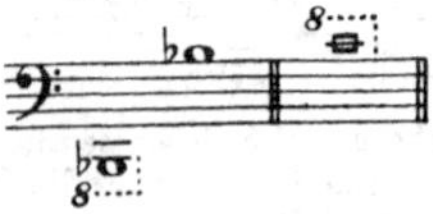

Bass-clef

* Keyed-Bugle in C	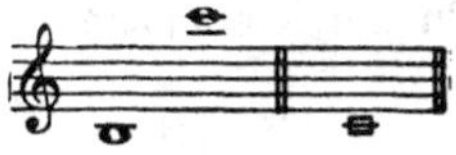	Treble-clef
* Keyed-Bugle in B♭		Treble-clef
* Keyed-Bugle in A		Treble-clef
*Alto-Ophicleide in F		Treble- and bass-clef
* Alto-Ophicleide in E♭		Treble- and bass-clef
* Bass-Ophicleide in C		Bass-clef
* Bass-Ophicleide in B♭		Bass-clef
* Double-Bass-Ophicleide in F		Bass-clef
* Double-Bass-Ophicleide in E♭		Bass-clef
* Russian Bassoon		Bass-clef
SIDE-DRUM	Pitch indeterminate	Conventional treble-clef or a single line
BASS-DRUM	Pitch indeterminate	Conventional bass-clef or a single line

Tenor-Drum	Pitch indeterminate	Conventional bass-clef or a single line
Tabor	Pitch indeterminate	Conventional treble-clef or a single line
TAMBOURINE	Pitch indeterminate	Conventional treble-clef or a single line
TRIANGLE	Pitch indeterminate	Conventional treble clef or a single line
CYMBALS	Pitch indeterminate	Conventional bass-clef or a single line
Ancient Cymbals	 (Any other notes possible according to manufacture.)	Treble-clef
GONG	Pitch indeterminate	Conventional bass-clef or a single line
Castanets	Pitch indeterminate	Conventional treble-clef or a single line
Rattle	Pitch indeterminate	Conventional treble-clef or a single line
Wind-Machine	Pitch indeterminate, but with some variation possible	Conventional bass-clef or a single line
Anvils	Pitch generally indeterminate, but see page 40.	Treble- or bass-clef or a single line
KETTLE-DRUMS -		Bass-clef

Bells (ordinary)		Treble- or bass-clef
BELLS (tubular)		Treble-clef
GLOCKENSPIEL		Treble-clef
* Keyed Harmonica		Treble-clef
CELESTA		Treble- and bass-clef
Dulcitone (or Typophone)		Treble- and bass-clef
XYLOPHONE		Treble-clef

VIOLIN

Treble-clef

VIOLA

Alto- and treble-clef

* Viola d'Amore

Alto- and treble-clef

CELLO

Bass-, tenor-, and treble clef

* Viola da Gamba

Alto-, tenor-, or bass-clef

DOUBLE-BASS

Bass- and tenor-clef

HARP

Treble- and bass-clef

Guitar

Treble-clef

Mandoline

Treble-clef

Dulcimer

Treble- and bass-clef

CLASSIFICATION OF INSTRUMENTS.

ORCHESTRAL instruments are, as a rule, grouped together under the four headings "**Percussion**," "**Brass**," "**Wood**," and "**Strings**." This rough-and-ready arrangement is perhaps quite as good as any other for use in a book mainly devoted to the artistic and historical aspects of Instrumentation. It is, however, by no means a scientific classification.

In the first place, the four groups are not mutually exclusive. A Stringed Instrument, such as the *Dulcimer* or the *Pianoforte*, in which the sound is produced by means of percussion, can be classed in either the first or the last group. In the next place, certain Brass Instruments have all the characteristics of the Wood-Wind, except the actual material of which their tubes are made. For instance, the *Saxophone* is played with a single-beating-reed, very much like that of the Clarinet. It differs from that instrument principally in the fact that its tube is conical, not cylindrical, and made of brass, not of wood. Then, again, we find wooden instruments whose method of tone-production is practically the same as that used on most Brass Instruments. For instance, the obsolete *Serpent* was played with a big cup-mouthpiece somewhat like that of our modern "Tubas." It was, however, always made of wood.[1]

Furthermore, if any one fact is certain with regard to the Wind Instruments, it is that the material of which their tubes are made has very little, if anything, to do with their tone-quality. That seems to depend partly on the bore, shape, and proportions of the tube which contains the air-column, but chiefly on what we may call the "mouthpiece."[2] Now, it is quite obvious that if we adopt the rough classification of "Percussion," "Brass," "Wood," and "Strings," we must be prepared to place such an instrument as the *Saxophone* arbitrarily under the heading "Brass" simply because of the material of its tube. That plan has its advantages. It serves as a mnemonic, and it does not preclude a description of the technical differences of the instrument from the "Wood-Wind" on the one hand, and from the "Brass-Wind" on the other. The student must, however, bear in mind that this is merely a matter of convenience in arrangement. It carries us no distance at all in the direction of a scientific classification.

[1] Gevaert actually classes the Serpent as a ***Brass Instrument played with keys.***

[2] See below, page 286.

It need scarcely be said that History gives us very little help in this respect. Its records are too obscure and confused. We may make a guess that the Kaffir's one-stringed banjo—perhaps first suggested by the thrumming of the hand on the bow-string—was merely the third and last addition to a musical equipment which had served the needs and fulfilled the aspirations of mankind for hundreds or even thousands of years.

Earlier still than this we may imagine man as just emerging from his state of savagery, but emerging with a new and wonderful craving for something more than mere rhythm, a craving which may have been first satisfied by means of a hard blade of grass held between his two thumbs.

Finally, we may suppose a time at the beginning of things when the naked savage squatted down on his native mud, his mind half entranced, passive and vacant to every influence of the wild, but still with a thirst in his nature which could only be quenched by the endless drum-drum-drum of his knuckles on the black earth. Beyond this we can imagine nothing but the animal.

These are, however, only guesses. The order in which we have placed them has been hotly contested, and we have nothing but probabilities on which to found our judgment. We should naturally suppose that musical art began with the least complex and most fundamental thing in human nature, the purely rhythmic. That seems fairly certain. The "percussive" is at the bottom of all things. But it is quite uncertain what we are to put next. It may be the seven oaten straws[1] of the shepherd boy or the stretched string which found its final glory in the Apollo Citharoedus of Greece and the lovely plaything of Cremona.

Nor does it matter much. The array of instruments—ancient, mediæval, and modern—is so bewildering in its variety that historical classification would be out of the question, except in a book specially devoted to that subject. A classification, however, is necessary, and this is only to be found by neglecting the unessential in the instrument. In other words, we must leave out of account its varied forms and the materials of which it is constructed. We must strip it of the complex mass of silver-smithery and brass-smithery in which it is nowadays often embedded. We must come down to essentials.

Now, the essential thing in music is the Series of Vibrations in the air. Until these are set up we can have neither the noise caused by irregular vibrations nor the musical sound caused by regular vibrations. Fortunately, almost all orchestral instruments produce musical sounds. A few, however, produce only noise. We must make our classification so as to include both these groups. It must be of the simplest possible nature, and must give us only the primary methods by which the vibrations can be mechanically set up in the air. We can then subdivide these classes by indicating either fundamental distinctions in the matter of tone-production or integral differences of

[1] The *Syrinx.*

shape. In more concrete language we can show, in the Strings,[1] the various methods by which the strings are set in motion. In the Wind, we can study the effects caused by the varying proportions of the tubes which contain the air-columns and by the different methods of tone-production.

Now all sounds, whether musical or unmusical, are merely sense-impressions caused by longitudinal air-waves[2] of varying shapes and sizes. These air-waves, as far as the art of orchestration goes, are set up in one of three ways:

(1) By the beating of elastic surfaces which are in contact with the air;

(2) By the regular breaking up of air-columns enclosed either in tubes of metal or in pipes of wood;

(3) By the setting in motion of stretched strings which are in contact with the air.

All orchestral instruments are included under this primary classification. We may label the three classes "**Percussion**," "**Wind**," and "**Strings**" respectively.

(1) PERCUSSION INSTRUMENTS.[3]

In the case of the first group, no further subdivision is scientifically necessary. The only subdivision that could be made would depend on the varying degree of elasticity in the beaten surfaces. An artistic subdivision, however, will be made into

(*a*) Those which produce noise but not musical sounds of a definite pitch;

(*b*) Those which produce sounds of definite musical pitch.

(2) WIND INSTRUMENTS.

The second group includes what are commonly known as the Brass- and Wood-Wind. In the case of all these instruments, the air column is contained either in a conical or a cylindrical tube or pipe. As we have already mentioned, this air-column has to be *regularly* broken up before it can produce a musical sound. It is not sufficient

[1] Throughout this book the words "*Strings*," "*Brass*," "*Wood*," are printed with a capital initial when they are used in the orchestral sense of "*Stringed instruments*," "*Brass instruments*," "*Wood instruments*." Without the capital letter, they have their ordinary meaning. The word "Bass," too, is used throughout with a capital in the sense of the instrument, the *Double-Bass*.

[2] In air and in liquids the disturbance is always lengthwise. In solids, such as a rope, we can produce a transverse wave by means of a jerk. See "Sound," by Professor Poynting, in *Encyc. Brit.*, xi. Ed.

[3] For further details, see the preliminary matter before the section devoted to *Percussion Instruments*, page 22. The whole classification in the present chapter is intended merely as an exact groundwork. The names of many instruments, especially *obsolete* instruments, have been omitted here as only likely to confuse the student. In every case the information should be supplemented by a reference to the more detailed study prefixed to each instrumental section—"Percussion," "Brass," "Wood," and "Strings."

merely to blow through one end of the tube or pipe and allow the air to run out at the other. The air-column must be forced to vibrate evenly. This can be done in several ways.

First Method.

By simply blowing across the open end of the pipe, so that the breath strikes the rim. Instruments played in this way are known as **Pipes with neither embouchure nor mouthpiece.** The only representative of this subdivision is the *Syrinx.* No orchestral instruments are blown in this manner. The method has been found too imperfect to allow of musical development. The ancient "*Syrinx*"[1] of the early Hellenic civilization is exactly the same instrument as the modern "*Pan's Pipes*" of the Punch-and-Judy showman.

Second Method.

The second method of setting the air-column in vibration is to direct a stream of wind from the lips across a circular hole bored in the pipe. The wind-stream or "air-reed" strikes the sharp edge of the hole on the side furthest from the player's mouth. Instruments played in this way may be classed as **Pipes without mouthpiece, but with embouchure.** The whole family of *Flutes*[2] belongs to this subdivision.

Third Method.

In the third method a beak- or whistle-mouthpiece is used. The air-reed is directed through this mouthpiece against the sharp edge of a "bevel" cut in the side of the pipe. Instruments played in this way are known as **Pipes with Whistle-mouthpiece.** No orchestral instruments are included in this group. The (orchestrally) obsolete *Flageolet* is the best-known member of the family. But in ancient days a great many instruments were played in this manner. The most familiar of these were the groups of *Recorders* and of *Beak-* or *Fipple-Flutes.* It must be added that the *Flue-Work* of the Modern *Organ* comes strictly into this subdivision.

Fourth Method.

In the fourth method a flexible reed is used. This may be (*a*) a single-reed, or (*b*) a double-reed.

(*a*) If it is a single-reed, it may be either what is known as a "single-beating-reed" or a "free-single-reed." All orchestral single-reed instruments are blown with a beating-reed. This is so arranged that, when set in motion by the player's breath, it beats against the

[1] Gevaert classes the Syrinx, the Bagpipes, and the Organ together, on the ground that each consists of a number of pipes of different lengths, emitting notes of different pitch. He calls them "Polyphonic Wind Instruments," and even suggests that the addition of the air-reservoir in the Bagpipes was "the first improvement" on the Syrinx. The method of tone-production in the three instruments is, however, totally distinct.

[2] Sometimes called Cross-Flutes or *Flauti Traversi.* For further details on this subdivision and on the next two subdivisions, see the preliminary matter before the section devoted to Wood-Wind Instruments, page 177.

"table" at the upper end of the pipe, rapidly opening and closing the aperture. The families of *Clarinets* and *Saxophones* belong to this subdivision, and the subdivision is generally known as one of **Pipes with reed-mouthpieces.** In the case of the "reed-pipes" of the *Organ* the action is very much the same as that described above, but the "reed" itself is simply a strip of flexible metal.

The "free-single-reed" is not used in any orchestral instrument. In fact, the only instrument in which it has been put to practical use is the *Harmonium.* In this instrument the metal "reeds" are "set" in a series of apertures into which they just fit. Sufficient freedom is, however, left for them to vibrate to and fro. The amount of "play" is so adjusted that, while the reed can actually vibrate, it practically closes and opens the aperture at each vibration. It is thus able to communicate the vibratory motion to the enclosed air-space.[1]

In the ancient *Regal*—a small "Positive" as opposed to a "Portative" Organ—the stops were originally reed-stops. The reeds employed were much like those of the Clarinet and Saxophone, "single-beating-reeds." However, like those of the Organ, they were made of metal, not of cane. Scientifically they were quite distinct from the "free-single reeds" of the Harmonium.[2]

(*b*) In the case of the double-reed, two flexible pieces of "cane" are bound *vis-à-vis* in this shape (). The aperture between the upper-ends of the two "canes" is extremely small. The player takes the double-reed between his lips, and, by the pressure of his lips and breath, forces it to vibrate. At each vibration, the narrow aperture between the two "canes" is alternately opened and closed. This, the second section of the subdivision, **Pipes with reed-mouthpieces,** is represented by the ancient *Schalmeys* and *Pommers* and the modern *Oboe* and *Bassoon* families.

The two kinds of Wood-Wind instrument with which we have been dealing, viz. those played with single-beating-reeds and those played with double-reeds, may be conveniently distinguished according to the bore of their pipes, as

(*a*) Cylindrical pipes...(The single-beating-reed *Clarinet* group).
(*b*) Conical pipes........(The double-reed *Oboe* and *Bassoon* group).

This difference in the proportions of the pipes is of fundamental importance in the technique of the reed instruments. The matter will be explained more fully in a later portion of the book,[3] but meanwhile it may be briefly stated that in (*a*), cylindrical pipes, the "fundamental

[1] A special Percussion apparatus is also used in the *Harmonium* to remedy its slowness of speech. At the moment that the air-stream is directed on to the reed a tiny hammer taps it into action.

[2] For the sake of completeness the *Jews' Harp* must be mentioned. In this instrument the air-vibrations are set up by means of a single tongue of flexible metal. The air-space inside the mouth is the resonating-cavity. The shape and size of this cavity are altered by the muscles of the cheeks so as to reinforce the various Harmonics already present in the vibrating metal-tongue. A certain additional prominence can thus be given to any desired note in the Harmonic Series.

[3] See page 178.

scale" can be reproduced (or "overblown") by the player at the interval of a twelfth higher. In (*b*), conical pipes, the "fundamental scale" can be reproduced at an interval of an octave higher. This reproduction is effected by means of an increased pressure of the lips and breath, helped in some cases by the opening of certain holes specially bored for that purpose in the pipe itself.

It is important to notice that the *Saxophones*, though akin to the *Clarinets* in that they both make use of single-beating-reeds, are not cylindrical, but conical instruments. Their technique, therefore, as opposed to their tone-production, is totally distinct from that of the *Clarinets*. A correct classification, according to mere tone-production, would group the following instruments together:

(1) Single-beating-reeds...The *Clarinets*. The *Saxophones*.
(2) Double-reeds............The *Oboes* and *Bassoons*.

A much more scientific classification would, however, be based on the fundamental nature of the instruments; that is to say, on the shapes of their pipes and tubes. We should then group them as follows:

(1) Cylindrical pipes with single-beating-reeds...The *Clarinet* family.
(2) Conical pipes[1] with single-beating-reeds.....The *Saxophone* family.
(3) Conical pipes with double-reeds................The *Oboe* and *Bassoon* families.

Before passing on to the description of the fifth method by which the air-column can be set in vibration, the student should notice that we have already included ALL the methods employed by the modern Wood-Wind. Two obsolete instruments, however, the *Zinke* (or *Cornet à bouquin*) and the *Serpent*, must be mentioned. The first of these was used as the ordinary treble of the *Trombone family*. It was originally made, as its French name suggests, of a ram's horn. Afterwards other materials, such as ivory, bone, and wood, were employed. The *Serpent*, again, was usually associated with the Brass in performance. It was, however, actually made of wood. Both these instruments had a conical-bore and their scales were produced by means of holes pierced laterally. The method of tone-production was, however, quite distinct from that of any Wood-Wind instrument which we have hitherto described. It was, in fact, the cup-mouthpiece-system familiar to us to-day through its universal use on all the heavy Valved-Brass. The student must, however, remember that this association of the cup-mouthpiece with the heavy Brass is, so to speak, only an accident. As we have already pointed out, the material of which the tube is constructed matters very little. The method of tone-production is of the first importance.

[1] The *Saxophones* are actually made of brass. The words "tube" and "pipe" are used consistently to distinguish the Brass- from the Wood-Wind. This is, however, merely a mnemonic. It has no importance as a scientific distinction. As we have already said, the material of the tube or pipe is of no consequence.

Fifth Method.

The fifth method by which the air-column can be set in vibration is, as we have stated, the method now employed by all the Orchestral and Military Brass. A mouthpiece—almost always of metal[1]—is placed at the upper end of the tube. This mouthpiece is either cup-shaped, funnel-shaped, or a mixture of the two. The player's lips stretch across the mouthpiece and themselves act as the vibrating reeds. The shape of the mouthpiece, especially the shape of its lower portion, is the main determining factor in the tone-quality of the instrument.[2] "The shallower the cup the more brilliant the tone."[3] The shallow "cup" is characteristic of the *Trumpet*: the broad deep "cup" of the modern "*Tubas.*" On the other hand, the funnel-shaped mouthpiece is used for the *Horns*. To this they owe their warmer and less incisive tone-colour. A hybrid cup-and-funnel-shaped mouthpiece is used for the *Bugle.*

The group which employs this, the fifth method of tone-production, includes all the Brass, ancient as well as modern, as well as the obsolete *Zinke* and the *Serpent*. It might of course be subdivided according to the shape of mouthpiece used. Such a subdivision, however, would be like that of the Single- and Double-Reeds merely one of tone-colour. It is better, as in the former case, to base the subdivision on the integral characteristics of the tubes themselves. As these tubes, whether they are conical or cylindrical, all produce the same series of notes,[4] we can make our subdivision depend solely on the natural methods of each instrument for altering the length of its air-column. The subdivision will then take the following form:

(1) Tubes of fixed length, which can therefore only produce a single series of notes at a time. The best examples are the *Natural Trumpet*, the *Natural Horn*, and the *Military Bugle.*[5]

(2) Tubes in which the length of the air-column is varied by means of holes pierced laterally. The best examples are the *Keyed-Bugle*, the family of *Ophicleides*, and the *Russian Bassoon.*[6] All of these instruments were made of brass and are now obsolete.

(3) Tubes in which the length of the air-column is varied by means of Valves, or Pistons. The best examples are the *Valve-Trumpets*, the *Cornets*, the *Valve-Horns*, the *Saxhorns*, the *Flügelhorns*, the *Valve-Trombones*, and the modern "*Tubas.*"[7] As will be

[1] Ivory and bone were often used. Even at the present-day ivory mouthpieces are occasionally employed by Tuba-players.

[2] See page 90 for fuller details on this point. [3] Gevaert. [4] See pages 72-3.

[5] For fuller details, see the preliminary matter before the section devoted to *Brass Instruments*.

[6] The *Russian Bassoon* and the *Bass-Horn* were transition-instruments between the *Serpent* and the *Ophicleides*. The student should group together in his mind these six instruments of the "Cup-mouthpiece and laterally-pierced" type in their historical order,—the *Zinke*, the *Serpent*, the *Russian Bassoon*, the *Bass-Horn*, the *Ophicleide*, and the *Keyed-Bugle*. Of these, all but the first two were made of brass.

[7] For a description of the so-called "Wagner Tubas" see page 151 *et seqq.*

explained later,[1] all these instruments are again divisible into what are called "*Whole-tube*" and "*Half-tube*" instruments.

(4) Tubes in which the length of the air-column is varied by means of slides. The only instruments of this subdivision in general use are the *Trombones.*

(3) STRINGED INSTRUMENTS.

We now come to the third group of instruments in our elementary classification. This is the group which sets up vibrations in the air by means of stretched strings. Orchestrally, it is the most complex group and the one that demands the greatest attention from the student. However, from our present purely scientific point of view, it is remarkably simple, and may be easily explained in a few sentences. In every case the stretched strings are of course in contact with the air. They cannot set the air in vibration until they themselves are first put in motion. The only subdivision possible is therefore based on the methods by which the player excites the strings. These methods are three in number.

First Method.

By **plucking.** In these instruments either the finger is used (as in the *Harp* or *Guitar*), or a plectrum (as in the *Mandoline*).[2]

Second Method.

By **striking.** In these instruments a hammer, or a series of hammers, is employed. The *Dulcimer* and the *Pianoforte* are the most familiar examples of this method.

Third Method.

By **contact with a prepared moving surface.** In these instruments either a horse-hair bow is used (as in the *Violin* family), or a wheel-and-handle mechanism (as in the ancient *Organistrum* and the modern *Hurdy-Gurdy*).

We shall now take the four groups of orchestral instruments, beginning with the simplest, the "Percussion," and going on through the "Brass" and the "Wood-Wind" to the most complex, the "Strings." A short preliminary chapter of a general character will be placed before each of these sections. In this chapter the common historical development of the Instrumental group will, whenever possible, be traced. This is not, however, always feasible. It can be done in the case of the Brass instruments and the Violin family. For, though there are exceptions in the general technical development of both these Instrumental groups, these exceptions can easily be explained and brought into line with the rest of the history. For instance, in the "Brass" the general course of progress has been from the Natural outdoor instrument through the era of "crooks" to the

[1] See page 86.

[2] For further details, see the preliminary matter before the section devoted to *Stringed Instruments*, page 290.

period of "valves." The Trombone family is the chief exception. But the Trombones obey just the same physical laws as the other Brass Instruments in the production of their "Harmonics." The slide mechanism is their main differentiating feature. In a preliminary sketch, therefore, they can quite well be treated in company with the Trumpets and Horns.

In the Wood-Wind department, it is scarcely possible to group together these details of technical development. The individual instruments differ so much in the shapes of their pipes and their methods of tone-production that it is better to deal with these points under each instrumental heading.

In any case, only a very brief historical sketch is given. Just sufficient information is supplied to enable the student to understand clearly the origin of the instrument and the principal changes which it has undergone in construction and treatment. Composers too-often look upon orchestral instruments as cleverly manufactured toys springing from nowhere. Most of these instruments, however, have a very respectable family history. And this family history should be of interest, because, in almost every case, the modern instrument, under all its paraphernalia of rings, bolts, and bars, preserves intact the distinctive characteristics of its ancient progenitor. A seventeenth century Horn-player, if we could resuscitate him, would probably be considerably astonished at the Horn-playing which he would hear at a present-day Symphony-concert. But if he were a good Horn-player, it would not be many weeks before he would be quite competent to "make one" in the orchestral quartet.

Under the separate instrumental headings, such as "Violin," "Oboe," and so on, the student will find precise technical details and examples of the orchestral use of the instrument. The technical details, especially in the case of shakes and tremolos, have been presented within the smallest possible space. When printed *in extenso*, they are often enough to make a fair-sized book. Whenever possible, they have been cut down either to a general formula or to the shortest possible list of what is practicable or impracticable, as the case may be. In this way, they can often be reduced to the limits of a few notes.

Some discretion has been used both in quoting and in compressing modern Full Scores. These, again, take up an enormous amount of space. As a rule unessential parts of the Score have been omitted, but these omissions are always clearly pointed out, either in the text or in a foot-note. A certain number of examples have to be selected solely to illustrate the technical capabilities and limitations of the various instruments. But in general an eye has been kept on their artistic value, from the point of view of Scoring. No apology need be made for referring over and over again to some of these quotations.

PERCUSSION INSTRUMENTS.

PRELIMINARY.

A NUMBER of instruments with different mechanical methods of tone-production and of widely varying musical effect must be grouped together under the heading "Percussion" or "Struck" Instruments. They all have this in common however, that, in playing them, the performer sets up vibrations by beating elastic and semi-elastic surfaces which are in contact with the air.

Gevaert subdivides these Percussion Instruments into

(1) Autophonic Instruments.
(2) Membrane Instruments.

In the former he says "the tone is produced by the vibration of solid (metallic or wooden) bodies, of a nature sufficiently elastic to be capable of keeping up the vibratory motion imparted to them, usually by percussion." They include

(a) Instruments of definite pitch, such as *Bells*, *Glockenspiel*, and *Celesta*.
(b) Instruments of indefinite pitch, such as *Triangle*, *Cymbals*, *Gong*, *Castanets*, and so on.

The Membrane Instruments are, in a word, the *Drums*. They include

(a) Instruments of definite pitch, such as the *Kettle-Drums*.
(b) Instruments of indefinite pitch, such as the *Side-Drum*, *Bass-Drum*, *Tenor-Drum*, and *Tambourine*.

This subdivision of the "Percussion" into "Autophonic" and "Membrane" Instruments depends for its logic solely on the degree of elasticity in the struck surface. It seems to be based rather on musical than on scientific considerations. We shall therefore content ourselves by classing all the elastic and semi-elastic beaten surfaces together as "Percussion Instruments." However, a musical subdivision of the whole group must be made. This is not difficult. In some of these instruments the vibrations in the elastic material set up irregular vibrations in the air. These are the "*Unmusical Percussion Instruments.*" Others set up regular vibrations. These are the "*Musical Percussion Instruments.*" The former produce noise, but not sounds of definite musical pitch. The latter produce sounds of definite musical pitch.

UNMUSICAL PERCUSSION INSTRUMENTS.

(1) Side-Drum.
(2) Bass-Drum.
(3) Tenor-Drum.
(4) Tabor.
(5) Tambourine.
(6) Triangle.
(7) Cymbals.
(8) Gong.
(9) Castanets.
(10) "Special-effect" Instruments such as the "Rattle," the "Wind-machine," and the "Anvil."[1]

MUSICAL PERCUSSION INSTRUMENTS.

(11) Kettle-Drums.
(12) Bells.
(13) Glockenspiel.
(14) Celesta.
(15) Dulcitone (Typophone).
(16) Xylophone.

NOTE.—In two other instruments—the Hungarian *Cimbalom* (or *Dulcimer*) and the *Pianoforte*—the sound is produced by means of the percussion of stretched strings by hammers. In the *Cimbalom* the hammers are directly under the control of the player. In the *Pianoforte* there is an intervening mechanism between the player's hand and the strings. In strictness these two instruments belong both to the "*Musical Percussion*" group and to the "*String*" group. However, our present rough orchestral classification is one of "Percussion," "Brass," "Wood," and "Strings." It will therefore be more convenient and more satisfactory from the musical point of view if these two instruments are excluded from the list of "Percussion Instruments" and dealt with under the heading "Stringed Instruments."

We shall now briefly describe the 16 instruments in the above list. Sufficient detail will be given to furnish the student with an adequate knowledge of their mechanism and their compass,—if any. Very few musical examples, however, will be included in this section. There is no very great urgency for special quotations to illustrate the use of Percussion Instruments. But references will be found under each instrument to such examples of its use as are scattered through the book.

No. 1. The Side-Drum.

Fr. *Tambour* (*militaire*) or *Caisse claire*; It. *Tamburo militare*; Ger. *Kleine Trommel.*

This, the smallest orchestral drum,[2] is cylindrical in shape. The "shell" is made of brass. At each end of the shell is a parchment

[1] The *Anvil* is sometimes musical, at other times unmusical. See page 40.

[2] It is curious that the English word *drum*, which one might imagine to be as old as the language itself, is comparatively modern. It first occurs in the *Nottingham Town Records* (iii. 384), "For pleying of hys drome afore Master Mayre...vjd." The date of

"head," that is to say, a circular sheet of prepared sheep-skin. The parchment "heads" are lapped over small hoops, which are themselves pressed down and held in place by means of larger hoops. An arrangement of brass rods and screws or of cords and leathers keeps the "heads" taut. The upper head—that on which the player beats—is called the "*batter-head*": the lower, the "*snare-head*."

Underneath the snare-head—that is to say, at a distance of two parchments and a layer of air from the place where the drum-sticks hit the batter-head—are the *snares*. These are thin pieces, or a single long thin piece, of catgut, not unlike a rough Violin-string. They are stretched to and fro across the snare-head, from a nut on the one side to a screw-hook on the other. The number of snares varies according to the player's taste. They may be only two or three, or as many as a dozen. It is found, however, that the most brilliant effect is to be obtained with a fairly large number of snares. However many are used, it is essential that they should be screwed tight down into close contact with the snare-head.

Two sticks are used. These are made of hard wood, with a small olive-shaped knob at the end. When the player attacks the batter-head its vibrations set up waves in the air which is contained in the shell. These waves are communicated to the snare-head, and so to the snares themselves. The immediate effect is to alter the character of the air-waves and to double the number of the vibrations. The explanation of this "doubling" seems to be that the snares continually impinge on the parchment, and so set up a constant series of "points of nodal contact." In this way the pitch of the snared drum appears to be about an octave higher than that of the same instrument when unsnared. The student should note that it is on these snares that the peculiar quality and brilliance of the Side-Drum depend.

Side-Drum playing is an art in itself, and a very difficult art to acquire. It differs from all other Percussion Instruments in that its technique is founded not on a single stroke, but on double alternate strokes with each hand. Thus, in the "Long-roll" or "Daddy-Mammy," the player strikes the batter-head not Left–Right–Left–Right, but LL–RR–LL–RR. In each pair of strokes the latter becomes, by incessant practice, a sort of controlled rebound stroke.

A word must be said with regard to the notation of the "roll." Two methods are in use, one inaccurate and the other accurate. The in-

this entry is 1541. The word *Drumslade*, with various spellings, is found earlier and is a commoner form in the first half of the 16th century. *Drumslade* is an Anglicized compound-word from the Dutch or Low-German meaning *Drum-beat*. It occurs continually in the State Papers of Henry VIII. For instance,—Under date 1532, "The dayly retinue of fotemen of this towne...wel trymmed and furnished with their dromslades, trompettes, and banerettes"; Under date 1532, "Paied to Hans Pyper and Bartholomew his ffelawe Dromslade for ther lyverages...XLV^{s}"; Under date 1532, "Paied to Xtofer Dromeslade and his ffellawe for ther lyveray cootes...XLV^{s}." The last two quotations are from the *Privy Purse Expenses*.

accurate way is to write out the length of notes required, and to add semiquaver or demisemiquaver strokes, thus,—

This is bad; first of all, because, however many strokes are used, it does not represent the sounds correctly: second, because it sometimes leaves a doubt as to whether the final note should be detached or not. Besides that, the inaccurate way is also the most tiresome to write.

The accurate way to indicate a "roll" on any percussion instrument is to write out the length of notes required, slur them to each other for as long as the roll continues, and add an unbroken "trill line" to the whole, thus,—

Do not write it in this way,—

as it looks like a fresh attack on each bar. If you do not wish a detached stroke at the end, slur right on to the last note. If you do wish it, omit the last slur and see that the ~~~~~~~~~~ comes short of the last note. If you wish a specially strong accent on the last or any other beat, omit the previous slur and mark the accent in the ordinary way, thus,— >.

The above remarks apply generally to all the instruments of the Drum family and will not be repeated. Note, however, that in Side-Drum parts it is practically always necessary to write a detached note on which to finish the roll. The sudden cessation of the roll, except in the faintest *pianissimo*, sounds untidy and does not suit the genius of the instrument. Even if there are musical reasons for not wishing the sound to continue for the extra quaver, it is still better to write the "finishing note" to the roll. In this case, put it back a quaver or a crotchet, according to the rhythm of the piece.

In a very long roll, it is not absolutely necessary to add slurs to all the notes. The drummer will not be tempted to make a fresh attack provided the sign ~~~~~~~~~~ is continued. If you actually want a fresh attack anywhere, end the roll with a detached quaver or semiquaver, followed by a rest. Then begin a new roll.

In addition to the roll there are two other strokes commonly used on the Side-Drum. These are

(1) The **Flam.**

(2) The **Drag.**

The **Flam** consists merely of two notes in this rhythm .

When the first note is on the accented beat of the music it is called an **open flam.**

When the second note is on the accented beat it is called a **closed flam.**

The **Drag** is a series of two, three, four, five, or six strokes fused into a sort of instantaneous roll, and preceding an accented note, thus 

The **Paradiddle** is not really a rhythm, as is often supposed, but a method of arranging the strokes of a rhythm so as to secure an alternate left-handed and right-handed attack on successive principal beats. Thus, if the following simple rhythm  occurred in one single bar only of a Side-Drum part, the player would probably perform it,—| L–R–L–R–L–R–L–R | But if the eight-quaver rhythm were persistent through many bars he would probably play it as a *paradiddle*, so that the attack of any two successive bars would read thus,—| L–R–L–L, R–L–R–R | L–R–L–L, R–L–R–R | In this way he would keep his attention on the alternation of Left and Right, and so secure a stronger rhythmic impulse.

Side-Drum parts are written either on a single line or, conventionally, on a stave in the treble-clef. If the part is combined with any other, such as that of the Bass-Drum, the tails of the Side-Drum part should all be turned upwards, its entry clearly marked with the letters "S.D.," and its exit with a rest.

The quality of the Side-Drum is hard, dry, and bright, with something "perky," obstinate, and combative about it. In the Theatre it has been in continual use since the time of Meyerbeer and Rossini. The opportunities for its employment in Concert-music are fewer. In pieces where some strong characterization is wanted, or where it is desired to call up by association the ideas of war, or of the bustle of military preparation, its use may be appropriate. But even here, unless it is merely intended to keep up a sort of frenzied excitement,

EXAMPLE 1.

the composer must remember that when once he has "shot his bolt" with it there is nothing left to be done. Like almost all the other Percussion Instruments its principal effect is it entry.

In writing Side-Drum parts, remember

(1) That you will always have a tendency to write too few, not too many notes.

(2) That the genius of the instrument is totally opposed to single detached notes. In fact, they should never be written.

(3) That the *drag* and the *flam* are only technical ways of accenting effectively a single beat.

(4) That practically any rhythmic combinations which you can think can be made intelligible on the instrument.

(5) That the *long-roll* continued either for a few beats or for many bars is equally effective *p* or *f*, but that its *crescendo* cannot be spread out over so many bars as that of the Kettle-Drums.

(6) That, in orchestral work at any rate, the composer should write out in full the notes which he wants played. In military bands this is matter partly of tradition, partly of the Drum-major's discretion.

Like the other Drums, the Side-Drum can be muffled. The essential part of the muffling is to remove the snares from contact with the snare-head, and so destroy the peculiar "crackling" tone of the instrument. In funeral-processions this is generally done by means of the "cords" which hang loose from the shell. These are pushed in between the snares and the snare-head. This puts the snares out of action and at the same time damps the air-waves as they reach the lower parchment. Another, but less effective, way is simply to slacken the snares.

No one who has ever been present at a military funeral can have failed to be struck with the indescribably solemn effect of the muffled Side-Drums. The "Drums" that precede the Slow March are usually entrusted to them and to the muffled Bass-Drum. These opening bars are arranged in different ways in different regiments. One of the simplest and most effective is as follows:

EXAMPLE 2.

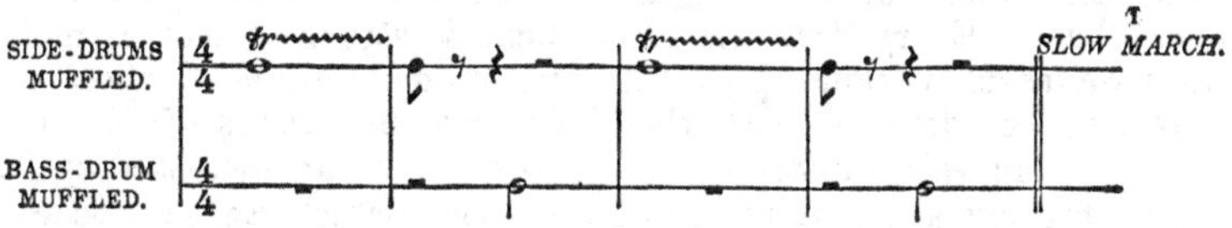

No. 2. The Bass-Drum.

Fr. *Grosse caisse*; It. *Gran cassa, cassa grande*, or simply *cassa*;[2] Ger. *Grosse Trommel.*

The Bass-Drum varies considerably in size from the colossal instrument built for "special concert-effects" to the small single-headed drum which does its humble offensive duty in the Music Hall.

In the standard military and concert pattern, the wooden shell is cylindrical in shape, and its depth is narrow in proportion to its diameter. The parchments are stretched at both ends over hoops, and an arrangement of leather tags or braces working on an endless cord

[1] 3rd Royal Fusiliers.

[2] In old Scores sometimes *Tamburo grande* or *Tamburo grosso.*

gives the player some latitude in tightening and loosening the heads. There are no snares.[1]

The stick used is heavy, with a large knob padded with felt or some other soft material.

The Germans had, or have, a sort of birch-broom, called *Ruthe*, with which to beat the Bass-Drum. There is a part for it in Mozart's *Il Seraglio*, where a good deal of this sort of thing is to be found:

EXAMPLE 3.

The player is evidently meant to beat the quavers with the *Ruthe* and the crotchets with the ordinary Bass-Drum stick. Mahler has revived this method of beating in the 3rd Movement of his 2nd Symphony. Just before "No. 34" a passage occurs in which the Strings, Piccolo and Kettle-Drums (off the beat in a $\frac{3}{8}$ movement) are combined with reiterated semiquavers for the Bass-Drum played with the *Ruthe.*

When the instrument is struck in the ordinary way, slow irregular vibrations are set up which have something of the effect of the deepest 32 ft. pipes of the Organ. In the *pianissimo* they strongly resemble and have often been used to imitate distant artillery and thunder. The instrument has, of course, no definite pitch but it is matter of general observation that the rest of the orchestra and especially the heavy Brass tend to give it definite pitch. This is no more than an illusion and, as it is not of constant occurrence, it is probably explained by the chance coincidence of its strongest vibrations with those of the fundamental bass. Every time the Drum-head is struck it sets in motion sound-waves of various sizes. At any moment some of these may happen to be identical with the definite sound-waves of the more prominent orchestral instruments. The result is an increased sympathetic vibration and a reinforcement of tone which appears to come from the Bass-Drum. We may note in passing that this sympathetic vibration of the partially-slack Drum-head is a matter for consideration in the concert-room. No one who has stood near the Bass-Drum during a concert performance can have failed to notice the places where it begins to sing apparently of its own accord. The result is always unpleasant. To obviate it a cloth should be hung over the head of the Drum when out of action.

The Bass-Drum is muffled by drawing a cover over it, by slackening the head, or by a combination of these two methods.

On such a ponderous instrument, quick rhythmical figures are quite out of place. Indeed, though playable, they are unpractical, for each succeeding note of a quick series merely damps out the preceding

[1] Mediæval Bass-Drums sometimes had a snare which carried a bell or bells; "a refinement of torture," says Mr. Galpin, "which is not found in our modern instruments."

note before it has had time to sound. Single strokes can only follow each other at a moderate speed.

On the other hand, the roll is both practicable and effective. It is played either with the ordinary stick, with a double-headed stick, or, less effectively, with two Kettle-Drum sticks. The Bass-Drum roll has been a favourite *pianissimo* opening with composers for two generations. An early example can be found in the long roll that accompanies the Strings in the opening of Liszt's *Ce qu'on entend sur la montagne.* A similar use of the Bass-Drum roll is quoted below from Strauss's *Also sprach Zarathustra.*[1] In this example, the Bass-Drum is combined with a deep C for Double-Basses *divisi*, Double-Bassoon, and Organ. In both these examples the player is directed to make the roll with two Kettle-Drum sticks.

The Bass-Drum part is conventionally written on a stave in the bass-clef. This is, however, only matter of convenience. A single line may be employed. The Cymbals are usually written on the same stave as the Bass-Drum. The two parts must be distinguished by two sets of tails to the notes. Each entry should be marked with the name of the instrument and its exit by a rest. All that was said above with regard to the notation of the "roll" applies here. There is, however, no necessity to end the roll with a detached stroke. It is as well to remember that the Drum-head vibrates for some little time after a *mf* or *f* stroke. The written note should therefore represent the actual length of sound required. In cases where a specially short note is wanted *f*, the word "damp" should be added to the part.

Apart from the use, or rather the abuse, of the Bass-Drum and Cymbals in Ballet and March music, the former instrument has two main orchestral uses:

(1) To mark the high lights, or the progress and climax of an extended *crescendo.*

(2) To convey a feeling of awe and solemnity by means of its *pp* notes.

In both cases, the instrument is used in a very simple and obvious way. In the first, the Bass-Drum part is confined either to a small series of notes spread out over many bars, and all marked in a carefully calculated *crescendo,* or to a single stroke or group of strokes at the climax of the *crescendo.* This would be difficult to illustrate without somewhat more extended musical quotation than is possible here. Quotation, however, is scarcely necessary. The idea itself is so simple. The student may, however, be warned that he should go through the dynamic scheme of a movement, and select only those few essential places for his Bass-Drum strokes where he feels that the great weight of the instrument is a necessity. In a long concert movement the part is probably right in the one case if there are rests in all but about four bars, and in the other case in all but one.

The *piano* of the Bass-Drum is on a higher artistic level. The mind perhaps from centuries of custom appears to respond instantly to its

[1] See Ex. 274.

appeal as to something fundamental in human nature. A single deep booming stroke is sufficient to produce a sense of farawayness, of solemnity, even of hopeless desolation. It is scarcely possible to find an orchestral *Funeral March* which would not illustrate this point. Here is a particularly happy example of two cunningly placed Bass-Drum notes. It is quoted from Elgar's incidental music to *Grania and Diarmid.*

EXAMPLE 4.

Elgar. *Grania and Diarmid.*

The Bass-Drum, Cymbals, and Triangle—known familiarly in France as the "Batterie," and in England as the "Kitchen"—were first introduced into Operatic music in the eighteenth century. They were originally used merely as what we should call "local-colour instruments." That is to say, they were employed only in distinctly Eastern or Asiatic scenes. As often as not their "parts" were not written out at all. The composer indicated the instruments which he wanted in the Score, and then trusted to the fancy and the muscular development of his players. Even Weber[1] and Beethoven[1] were sometimes content with this haphazard way of doing things. The latter composer uses three Bass-Drums in his *Battle of Vittoria*, one for the orchestra and a couple to represent the cannonade. A painful tribute to the Duke of Wellington, when one thinks of the *Eroica.*

No. 3. The Tenor-Drum.

Fr. *Caisse roulante*; It. *Tamburo rullante*; Ger. *Wirbeltrommel, Rolltrommel,* or *Rührtrommel.*

This is a Drum midway in size between the Side-Drum and the Bass-Drum. Its shell is generally cylindrical in shape, fairly long, and made of ash-wood. There are no snares. In form and musical effect it is probably the most ancient and universal of all Drums.

The quality of the Tenor-Drum, especially when used indoors, is curiously impressive; its flavour sombre and antique. Gluck[2] and Wagner[2] have both written for the instrument. It might with advantage be more often used in the Concert-Room.

[1] In *Preciosa* and the *Ruins of Athens* respectively.

[2] In *Iphigénie en Tauride* and in *Die Walküre* and *Parsifal.* In the concert-room arrangement of the *Ride of the Valkyries* the *Kleine Trommel* (Side-Drum) is substituted in the Score without sufficient reason.

Out of doors one such Drum is used in the "*Drums and Fifes*" of all British infantry regiments, but here its tone cannot as a rule make much effect, particularly when pitted against a full corps of Side-drummers. This is a matter of "balance," however, and not due to any deficiency in the Drum itself. In the Episode of Henry V.'s Funeral at the English Church Pageant of 1909 these Tenor-Drums had a surprising effect. A deep bell was struck every 15 seconds. This was followed immediately by a short heavy "roll" for three or four Tenor-Drums. The combination of Bell and Tenor-Drums was continued as a sort of *ostinato* throughout the entire Episode. At the same time a large number of Male voices sang the *Dies Irae* in procession, while the orchestral Brass played an independent but simultaneous *Requiem pianissimo.*

No. 4. The Tabor.

Fr. *Tambourin (de Provence)*; Ger. *Tambourin.*

The shell of this Drum is very long in proportion to its diameter. It is usually made of walnut-wood carved and ornamented with a conventional pattern. At each end of the shell is a "head" made from the softest calf-skin obtainable. A single snare of catgut, silk, or, more correctly, rough hemp, is passed across the parchment, with which it is kept in close contact by means of a hook. Apparently the snare is not passed across under the snare-head, but above the batter-head. The Drummer plays directly on to the parchment where it is in contact with the snare. Some doubt exists on this point. Widor says categorically that it is "a very long drum, without timbre," *i.e.* snare, "used in Provence." The best authorities seem to favour the other view, and a fine specimen of the instrument[1] now in London has the hempen snare and the hook for its attachment.

A single Drum-stick is used with a top-heavy knob of bone or ivory. In Provence the player generally beats strokes of one time-value with his left-hand while with his right he performs on a sort of primitive Flageolet called *Galoubet*[2] or *Chirula.*

The French always speak of the Tabor as having its origin in Provence. It is however more probable that the universal "pipe and tabor" of the middle-ages had merely found a last refuge there when it was resuscitated and put on the stage by the French composer, Berton, in his opera, *Aline* (1803). However, the instrument is now acknowledged as characteristic of Provence,[3] and at Aubagne (Marseilles) there exists a Society or Guild of Taborers who not only tap unostentatious rhythms with their left hands but also prescribe the

[1] The property of William Wallace, who has introduced the instrument in his symphonic poem *Villon.*

[2] In Béarn the *Galoubet* is accompanied by the *Tambourin du Béarn.* See page 290.

[3] See the delightful account of the drummer Buisson whom Mistral sent up to Paris from Provence with letters of introduction to Théophile Gautier, Alphonse Daudet, and Félicien David, in Daudet's *Trente ans de Paris.*

"ton de Si bémol" as the only legitimate key in which to play with their right.

Bizet has introduced the Tabor into his second Suite *L'Arlésienne*. In the *Pastoral* (*Andantino*) of that work it plays the simple rhythm

for 62 bars on end, while in the *Farandole* it repeats the rhythm

for 83 bars with a *crescendo* from *pppp* to *fff*,—a common French trick.

The typical *English Tabor* was a shallow Drum with a single snare-head. In the 14th century when the corps of Swiss[1] Drums and Fifes became celebrated throughout Europe the instrument was reintroduced to England in an improved and enlarged form. It was no longer held in the left hand and beaten with the right, but "slung" in the modern fashion. At the same time the players were organized into the regular corps of Drums and Fifes which still exist.

No. 5. The Tambourine.

Fr. *Tambour de Basque*; It. *Tamburino*; Ger. *Baskische Trommel*, *Schellentrommel*, or *Tambourin*.[2]

The Tambourine is an instrument of universal distribution. It has practically remained unchanged for the past 2000 years. It consists of a small wooden hoop, on one side of which is a parchment head which can be tightened or loosened by means of brass rods and nuts. The hoop is cut away at intervals to allow the insertion of small tinkling metal plates. These plates, commonly called the *jingles*, hang loose in pairs and are held in position by a wire which passes through their centres.

There are three recognized ways of playing the Tambourine:

(1) By striking the "head" with the knuckles. This gives detached notes and simple rhythmical groups.

(2) By shaking the hoop. This practically gives a "roll" on the *jingles*.

(3) By rubbing the thumb on the "head." This gives a partial *tremolo* made up chiefly of the sound of the *jingles*.

[1] Hence the old Scottish name for the instrument *Swasche*, *Swesche*, or *Swische*. "Item the tent October, 1576, gevin for an swasche...iiij li," from the *Register of the Canongate*. The Scots for Drummer was *Swescher* or *Sweschman*. For an early reference to the English "dromes and fyffes" see page 42 (foot-note).

[2] There is some confusion in the German nomenclature, as *Tambourin* is used both for the Provençal *Long-drum* and for the *Tambourine*. The old English name for the Tambourine was *Tymbyr* (see foot-note, p. 41). In mediæval times it was sometimes furnished with a snare (Fr. *timbre*).

A fourth method may be mentioned, as it has been tried with success in the Theatre. It consists of tuning one of the Kettle-Drums to a drone-bass, placing the Tambourine on the Drum and playing on the Tambourine-head with the Kettle-Drum sticks. The resulting tone has something of the quality of a muffled Drum, but with a sort of "edge" added by the faint sound of the *jingles*.

The notation of the Tambourine is generally on a single line, or conventionally on a stave in the treble-clef.

The sudden unexpected *ff* roll of the Tambourine is effective at moments of rhythmic excitement where a highly-coloured tone-scheme is called for. This is more particularly the case when the orchestra is playing in its upper register. The tone of the instrument, however, soon becomes tiresome. Its proper place is the Theatre.

The *pp* of the Tambourine is less generally useful. It may occasionally be employed with success in dance-rhythms, but it is as well always to bring its notes into direct relationship with the rhythmical pattern of the music. When this is not done the instrument often has the misfortune of sounding like a copyist's mistake.

A good example of the Tambourine used in the real French style with rhythms of this sort

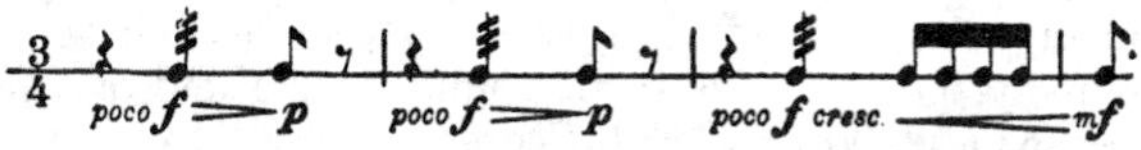

can be found in Berlioz's *Carnaval Romain* Overture. Another excellent example is to be seen on page 37 of the Full Score of Elgar's *Cockaigne*. The Tambourine has crotchets *batutto colla mano* and it is associated with the Bass-Drum, the *pizzicato* of Cellos and *Basses* and a *tenuto* for the 4th Horn.

The following short quotation is from the *Arab Dance* of Tschaikowsky's *Nut-Cracker* Suite. It gives a neat illustration of the "thumb" method.

EXAMPLE 5.

No. 6. The Triangle.

Fr. *Triangle* ; It. *Triangolo* ; Ger. *Triangel.*

This instrument is a small bar of steel bent into the shape of a triangle. It is struck with a beater of the same metal. It should be moderate in size, not so small as to sound " tinkley " nor so large as to acquire a distinct musical note. In tone it should be as clear as crystal.

Simple rhythms, isolated notes and little groups of notes are all possible and effective on the instrument. When a succession of rapid notes are grouped together on a beat thus

Triangle.

it is better to use an odd number of strokes. This enables the player to perform the first and last notes of the series in the same direction, right to left. With an even number of strokes he has to reverse the direction for his accent. As a rule the simpler the rhythms and one might also say the fewer the bars played the more effective will the part be. In this connection the student should look through the whole of the Triangle part in the *Meistersinger* Overture. It is the acme of good taste. Another effective triangle part of precisely the same length—namely one note—is to be found at the end of the 2nd Act of *Siegfried*, page 280 of the Full Score.

The *tremolo* or " roll " is made by beating rapidly to and fro between two sides of the Triangle. Widor picturesquely remarks that " at the climax of a *crescendo*, when the orchestra would seem to have reached its maximum intensity, it suffices to add the Triangle, in order to convert red-heat into white-heat."[1] This type of effect with the Triangle beating either a roll or a strong rhythm is well-known and much practised. In such places the instrument has little difficulty in asserting its tone-quality even in the tutti *ff*. On the other hand its *pp* when used with soft Strings and light Wood-Wind is charming. Single soft strokes mixed with the octave-unison of a Flute, an Oboe, and a Harp (playing in Harmonics) sound delightful. An excellent example of the Triangle *ppp* in combination with the Wood-Wind and the upper Strings is quoted below from Lalo's *Rapsodie*. See Ex. 115.

Another and characteristic use of the Triangle is in starting or, as it were, setting free a new phrase in the orchestra, either at a change of harmony, of melody, or of tone-colour. Of this the passage referred to in the *Meistersinger* Overture is a happy example. But the student must resist the temptation of repeating the stroke on the other first-beats of his succeeding melodic sentences. The notation of the Triangle is either on a single line or conventionally on a stave in the treble-clef. The usual notation for the " roll " is employed[2] Care should be taken with the *p*'s and *f*'s as the Triangle has considerable powers in

[1] *The Technique of the Modern Orchestra*, translated by Edward Suddard.

[2] See page 24.

this direction. As a rule it is well to keep the marking of the Triangle part below the level of the instruments with which it is playing.

Liszt, in his *Pianoforte Concerto in E♭*, has raised the Triangle to the symphonic level of a Solo instrument:

EXAMPLE 6.

No. 7. The Cymbals.[1]

Fr. *Cymbales*; It. *Piatti* or *Cinelli*; Ger. *Becken.*[2]

These are two large circular brass plates of equal size. In the centre of each is a saucer-shaped depression, to the outer side of which a strap is attached. The plates are made, not flat, so that their whole surfaces would touch each other, but slightly tapered so as to secure a contact at the edges only. Their tone varies greatly according to size, weight, and the particular alloy used in their manufacture. When large enough, and of the proper metal, their quality is martial and brilliant in the extreme. But it is to be regretted that makers often turn them out so small in size, and poor in quality, that they add little to the orchestral tone-colour, but a sense of vulgarity and discomfort.

The tone of the Cymbals is produced in four ways:

(1) By clashing them edge-to-edge with a sort of side-ways or brushing movement. This, the two-plate-stroke, is the ordinary method of playing single notes.

(2) By striking a single plate either with a hard Side-Drum stick or with a soft Kettle-Drum stick. The former method can only be satisfactory when used *fortissimo* at moments of wild excitement.[3]

[1] Or *Clashpans*. The English word *Cymbal*, though as old as the 9th century, did not become specialized to its present meaning till the introduction of the "Batterie" in the 18th century. Before that time it was only occasionally used in its modern sense. For instance, "Cymbales be instruments of musick, & be smit together, & soundeth & ringeth" (*Batman upon Bartholome*, 1582). But the student would do well to remember that in old English the word *Cymbal* or *Cimball* is more commonly used for either "Bell," "Dulcimer," or "Psaltery." It is also found as the name of a stop on the *Organ* or *Regal*. The bell-imitation on the former instrument was usually effected by means of mixtures and diapasons, and the controlling stop was always known as the *Cymbal*. The early 17th century *Keyed Carillon* (or, as we should say, the *Glockenspiel*) was known as the *Clavicymbalum*.

[2] The full word is *Schallbecken*. Each plate is known as *Schale* or *Teller*.

[3] But see Ex. 20, where it is used *piano* to reproduce the hard metallic tap of the clapper on the bell.

The latter can be used in any degree of *piano* or *forte*. In the *p* it has a deep gong-like effect. For either of these effects it is customary to write the words "with hard stick" or "with soft stick" above the part.

(3) By agitating the edges of the plates against each other. This is the "two-plate-roll," and it must be marked as such. It can be varied from a rather commonplace and ineffective *pianissimo* to a *fortissimo* of some violence.

(4) By hanging up a single plate and performing a roll on it with two soft Kettle-Drum sticks. This is the "two-stick-roll." It should be written in the ordinary way, and the words "Soft Drum-sticks" or "Timpani sticks" added above the part. In a careless performance a player will sometimes make this roll with only one stick in his right hand. The left is engaged in holding up the plate by its strap. The two-stick-roll, however, when made by an accomplished player, is vastly more effective. In fact, there is no other sound in the orchestra quite so exciting as a long *crescendo* finely performed with two Kettle-Drum sticks. The plate should never be held in the hand. A carpenter can easily make a projecting wooden "arm" to hold the plate. This arm can be fastened to the back of a chair or any other convenient object. The player should then make the roll by beating with the two sticks at opposite sides of the circumference of the plate. In this way the aggravating oscillation that spoils so many cymbal-rolls is prevented. A rapid *diminuendo* can, if necessary, be made by means of the finger-tips without any sticks whatever.

The Cymbals and Bass-Drum are continually associated, though there is no good reason why they should be. In some Comic Opera music, their continual zim-boom in the *tutti* destroys all chance of hearing either the harmony or the melody. This is distressing and inartistic. Furthermore, it defeats its own end, which should be the addition of weight to the music, not the substitution of noise for the music.

The *parts* for Bass-Drum and Cymbals may, however, be conveniently put on one stave, conventionally in the bass-clef, or even on one line. In fact this is usually done. Two sets of tails are used, and the entries of the parts are clearly marked with the abbreviations "B.D." and "Cym." or "G.C." (Grosse Caisse) and "Piatti."

Do not, however, imagine that because the instruments are on one stave they must be used together for safety's sake. They are quite distinct in quality and effect. It is only an unfortunate accident that allows some players to fasten a Cymbal-plate to the shell of the Bass-Drum—incidentally destroying its tone—and to bang away at both instruments with his two hands.

With the exception mentioned above, viz. the stroke with the hard stick, the dynamic range of the Cymbals is anything from *pp* to *fff*. The combination, however, of the soft two-plate-stroke with the *p* notes of the Bass-Drum is, despite Berlioz's liking for it,[1] rather poor and stupid. However, on occasion this sort of bizarrerie can be made

[1] See the *Sanctus* of his Requiem, and elsewhere.

effective. Meyerbeer employs it in his weird accompaniment to Marcel's "War-song."[1] The Full Score of the opening contains nothing but 1 Piccolo, 2 Bassoons in octaves, *pizzicato* Double-Basses without Cellos, and the soft strokes of the Bass-Drum and Cymbals every third beat.

EXAMPLE 7.

In writing a Cymbal part, remember that whether in the two-plate-roll, the two-plate-stroke, or the drum-stick-roll, the vibration continues so long that it is necessary to set down accurately the length of sound required. If you want a minim of sound write a minim and leave it to the player to carry out his instructions. If this is done regularly, and with care, there is no necessity for writing "secco,"[2] "vibrato," and so on. Finally, remember that the effect of the Cymbals is in inverse proportion to their use.

A word must be said as to the *Ancient Cymbals.* These were in common use by the ancient Egyptians, Greeks and Romans. They were, however, much smaller than our modern instruments, and seem

[1] Act I. of *Les Huguenots.* Beethoven has a passage for Kettle-Drums and Piccolo in illustration of the words "Die Trommel gerühret, Das Pfeifchen gespielt" (*Egmont*).

[2] See Ex. 79.

to have been used only by dancing girls. Specimens of Egyptian Cymbals are still in existence. They were made either of brass or of mixed brass and silver, and varied in diameter from $5\frac{1}{2}$ to 7 inches. In shape they closely resembled our modern Cymbals, even to the saucer-shaped depression in the middle. The plates, however, were flat, not tapered as in the modern instruments. There are several sets of Greek Cymbals in the British Museum. One sweet little pair, $3\frac{1}{2}$ inches in diameter, is complete with its tiny chains and rings. It gives out a clear F♯ *in alt.* Round the rim in dots run the words, ΩΑΤΑΣ ΕΙΜΙ, "I belong to Oata."

Berlioz reintroduced these small ancient Cymbals in *Les Troyens* and *Roméo.* In doing so he showed his sound antiquarian taste by having them tuned to a definite pitch—one pair in B♭ and the other in F:

Their effect is charming, but they are better when used in the classical manner, that is to say, played in rhythm by a large number of dancers, than when employed singly in the orchestra.

No. 8. The Gong.

Fr. It. and Ger. *Tam-tam.*

This instrument, as it comes to us from China, is a broad circular plate of thick hammered metal. The edge of the plate is turned over all round the circumference, so that the instrument has the shape of a shallow sieve. Gongs are of course also made in Europe, but the secret of their successful manufacture seems to elude the European. Chinese, Japanese, and Burmese gongs are far superior in size and tone-quality to any which we seem able to make.

The tone of a large Chinese gong, when properly elicited,[1] is strange and imposing. Unfortunately, there is some difficulty in bringing out this tone properly. A single heavy blow produces nothing but a dull unpleasant sound of small power and bad quality. The character of the instrument demands a continual, persistent, and graduated attack. For this reason it cannot be used in the orchestra for much else than a single *p* or *mp* stroke. A stroke of this sort has often a startlingly picturesque effect, but for that very reason it cannot be used more than once in a musical work. A *crescendo* roll *pp* to *ff* might be employed, but there is a danger here. The instrument has associations with the dinner-table.

In the Theatre the Gong has been in constant use from the days of *La Vestale* to those of *Madame Butterfly.* Its effect is by turns solemn, mysterious, and terrifying.

[1] Some of the largest temple-gongs in Japan are set in vibration merely by the moistened thumb of the priest.

A soft Bass-Drum stick is generally used as beater, and the part is usually written on one line without clef. All that was said with regard to the Cymbals' persistent vibration and the consequent necessity of writing notes of accurate length applies with as great force to the Gong. It is, however, somewhat difficult to damp a large gong when once it has been set in vibration.

No. 9. The Castanets.

Fr. *Castagnettes*; It. *Castagnette*; Ger. *Kastagnetten.*

We have already described the brass Cymbals of the Ancient Egyptians. These were occasionally made in miniature, each pair so small that it could be played with the finger and thumb of one hand. Toy-like and insignificant as these instruments were, they appear to have persisted and to have been introduced into Spain by the Moors. There they were made not of brass but of chestnut (*castaña*). Under the name of *Castañuelas* they became the characteristic instruments of the Spanish peasantry, and they have retained their popularity for many hundreds of years. So far, however, they have made little headway outside Spain.

Each pair of Castanets consists of two hollow pieces of hard wood, which can be clicked together by the fingers. The left hand usually plays a simplified rhythm on a larger pair—known as "macho," the male, while the right hand plays the full dance rhythm on a smaller pair—known as "hembra," the female. Several distinctions of variety are noted in Spain, but they are of no great importance.

The characteristic of the Castanet figures is a simple quaver rhythm in triple time, in which the central quaver is split up either into semiquavers, into a semiquaver-triplet, or into demisemiquavers. For instance—

A. 

B. 

C. 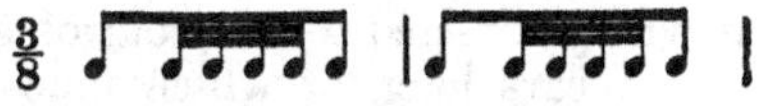

Other varieties of this formula are as follows:

a. 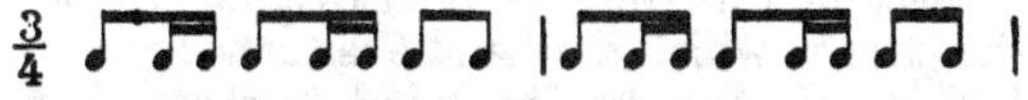

b. 

c. 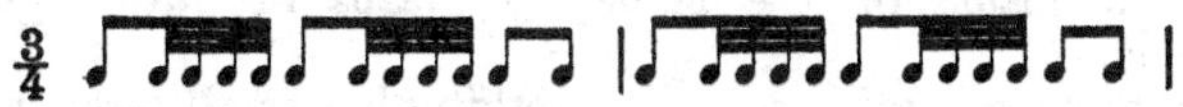

As a rule, the dancers or their companions keep the Castanet-rhythms going throughout the whole dance. During the song, however, they are only used as an interpolation, four bars of Song and four bars of Castanets ad finem et nauseam.

Castanets are sometimes mounted, a pair at each end of an ebony handle, for use in the orchestra and military bands. This is, however, a mere concession on the part of the South to the bloodlessness of the North.

In the Score of *Samson et Dalila* Saint Saëns prescribes the use of Castanets, both of wood and of iron.

No. 10. The Rattle, the Wind-Machine, and the Anvil.

The first two of these instruments are mentioned only because they have recently been used by Richard Strauss; the Rattle ("Knarre") in *Till Eulenspiegel*, and the Wind-Machine ("Windmaschine") in the 7th Variation of the *Don Quixote* set.

The Rattle is of the old Watchman's pattern, a wooden cogwheel which is revolved smartly against a hard flexible spring of wood or metal.

The Wind-Machine is not strictly a Percussion-Instrument at all. On the other hand, it is certainly not a Wind-Instrument, except in a facetious sense. However, it may be conveniently described here, and a few words will suffice for its description.

The sound-producing mechanism in the Wind-Machine is a sort of barrel from which most of the staves are missing. In their place there is a covering of black silk. The barrel is laid on its side in a "bearing" supported by an open "cradle." It is then churned round with a handle, so that the silk comes into contact with a "face" of wood or cardboard.

The instrument is used by Strauss to imitate the wind in the Episode of the Windmills, and the notation employed is a conventional C in the bass-clef, thus,—

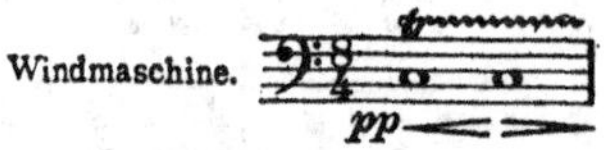

and the player is wisely directed to keep out of sight of the audience. The part is only ten bars long, of which nine are <> bars. These *crescendos* and *diminuendos* represent rather a raising and lowering of the pitch than an actual increase of force. In any case, the whistling effect of the wind as it rises and falls is gained by a variation of the pace at which the handle is turned.

This imitation of the "felon winds" that blow "from off each beaked promonotory" may be itself imitated (*pianissimo*) in the seclusion of the home by means of two fingers and an umbrella.

Orchestral Anvils are really nothing but small steel bars made to imitate the sound of the real anvil as accurately as possible. They can be manufactured so as to produce either a definite musical note or an indefinite unmusical noise. A hard wooden or metal beater is used. The Anvil has been written for by Verdi in *Il Trovatore,* by Berlioz in *Benvenuto Cellini,* by Gounod in *Philémon et Baucis,* and by Goldmark in *The Queen of Sheba.*

The *Rheingold* Anvils as they appear in the Full Score are eighteen in number. Wagner evidently intended them to be of three distinct sizes,—a small, a medium, and a large. They are written in nine parts, three in the treble clef on this note:

and six in the bass-clef on these notes:

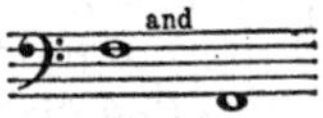

In practice the parts are almost invariably "boiled down." Few Theatres can afford eighteen blacksmiths.

No. 11. The Kettle-Drums.

Fr. *Timbales*; It. *Timpani*;[1] Ger. *Pauken.*

These Drums are of Arabian origin. They were originally quite small—a half-gourd covered with a dressed skin—and could be conveniently held in one hand and played with the other. Introduced into Europe towards the close of the thirteenth century, they were commonly known in England as *Nakers.*[2] In a list of Edward I.'s musicians (1310-11) we have the names of "Rogero le Troumpour, Janino le Nakerer, Menestrallis Regis."[3] The large-sized instrument was first brought to England by that musical enthusiast, Henry VIII., and it is interesting to note that, even at that date, the Kettle-Drums were preeminently at home in the sphere where they still cut such an imposing figure—the cavalry regiment. In a word, Henry VIII. sent

[1] Often mis-spelt with a "y" thus, "Tympani"; but there is no "y" in the Italian alphabet.

[2] From the Arabic *Naqqareh.* The word is still in common use in Hindostan for the state-drums of the Indian Rajahs. "In English the word," i.e. *Naker,* "seems to have had real currency only in the fourteenth century" (Murray). In that century, however, it is continually to be met with. For instance, in an *Alliterative Poem* of the early fourteenth century we read: "Ay þe nakeryn noyse, notes of pipes, Tymbres & tabornes tulket among"; again, in one of Laurence Minot's poems on events in the reign of Edward III. we have, in the account of that monarch's invasion of France:

"Þe princes þat war riche on raw
Gert nakers strike and trumpes blaw"

(before 1352); and, in the last quarter of the century, Chaucer writes: "Pypes, trompes, nakers, and clariounes" (*Knight's Tale,* 1386).

[3] MS. Cott. Nero, c. viii. lf. 87b.

to Hungary for specimens of their cavalry Kettle-Drums[1] and equipped his own mounted drummers with these improved instruments.

The modern Kettle-Drum is the most important of the Percussion Instruments which produce definite musical sounds as opposed to mere noise. It consists of a basin-shaped shell of copper or alloy across which a circular sheet of parchment—the "head"—is stretched. Various skins, such as those of the ass, goat, dog, sheep, and calf, have been used for making this parchment "head," but on the whole calf is found to be the most suitable. Only good skins free from cracks and of an even thickness can be employed, and these have to be prepared with great care. The head is first lapped over a wooden hoop called the "flesh-hoop." That is held in its place by a circular iron ring, which can be slightly raised or lowered by means of screws with T-heads. In this way the player can, within certain narrow limits, adjust the tension of the head so as to produce a succession of definite musical notes. The mechanical action of the screws and the iron ring can be clearly seen in the illustration on Plate I. At the bottom of the shell a hole is pierced in order to lessen the violence of the air-concussion, and so prevent the splitting of the parchment in *fortissimo* passages.

The instrument is played with two sticks. These, in instrumentation books, are made of whale-bone with sponge ends. In real life they are of malacca-tips and have their ends padded with two sorts of pianoforte felting, a hard layer inside and a soft outside. As a rule the Drummer strikes the head at a point about halfway between the rim and the centre. This is, however, varied according to the quality and amount of tone that he wishes to produce.

Drums have always been made in two sizes—a small Drum for the upper series of notes, and a large for the lower. To these a third Drum of intermediate size has now been added, and forms a regular part of every Symphonic and Opera Orchestra. For the present, however, we will leave this third Drum out of account, and describe the size and tunings of the largest and smallest Drums.

Down to and including Beethoven's day two Drums only were used. The smaller of these had a chromatic compass of a perfect fifth from B♭ to F; the larger had a similar chromatic compass from F to C.

[1] The earliest occurrence of the word appears to be in a letter from Sir T. Seymour to Henry VIII. (1548): "The captaynes that your Heynes wolde retayne, the dromes and fyffes, the ketyl dromes." A better-known instance of its use is to be found in Kempe's *Loseley Manuscripts*, under date 1551: "I have provided one to plaie upon a Kettell Drom with his boye and a nother Drome with a fyffe." There is an early example of the word in the interesting Diary of Henry Machyn, Undertaker and Citizen of London. It occurs, under date xxv day of November, 1554, in his account of what we may, without indiscretion, call a royal spree: "The sam day . . . the Kyngs grace and my lord Fuwater and dyvers Spaneards . . . with targets and canes in ther hand . . . and thrumpets . . . and drumes mad of ketylles."

KETTLE DRUM.

By kind permission of Messrs. Boosey & Co.

It will be noticed that the compasses of the two instruments overlap for three semitones. However, as we shall see later, the lowest notes of the small Drum and the highest notes of the large Drum have never been much employed.

Before Beethoven's time the tuning of the Drums was invariable. The small Drum played the tonic, and the large Drum played the dominant a perfect fourth lower. The Drums were therefore limited to those keys which lie chromatically upwards between B♭ and F.

Beethoven did not alter the mechanism, pitch, or compass of the Drums. But he enlarged their scheme of tuning. In the first place, he put the tonic at the bottom whenever he so wished. The Drums were now in a perfect fifth, and this gave him access to various new keys. In the keys of B♭ and F, where it was possible to arrange the Drums either in fourths or fifths, he suited his fancy. He first employed the tuning of a minor sixth (A-F) in the Scherzo of the *7th Symphony*. Finally he invented the octave-tuning F-F of the *8th* and *9th Symphonies*—

EXAMPLE 8.

EXAMPLE 9.

and the diminished fifth tuning of *Fidelio*—

EXAMPLE 10.

The following is the complete list of Drum-tunings as Beethoven left it. As we have already mentioned, none but the tunings in perfect fourths was in use before his day. Even in his time those tunings marked with a + were rarely or never employed. They belong to the extreme keys, D♭, B♮, and F♯.

The Middle Drum, which is now a regular member of the orchestra, is reckoned to have a compass either from A to E or from G to D:

This would give us a theoretical compass for the Three Drums of

The tendency, however, is all in the direction of pushing the playing-register of the Smallest Drum upwards. High F♯'s and even G's are often met with in modern music. By a proper adaptation in the size of the shell and a careful selection of the parchment these notes can be produced. Furthermore, as the composer now has three Drums at his disposal, he rarely needs the wide compass of a perfect fifth. He can keep all his instruments much more in the most useful parts of their register. In fact, he need scarcely go outside the limits of a fourth for any one Drum. It is rather difficult to lay down any law for the student's guidance on this point. But, if he will remember that the two highest semitones on the Small Drum are by no means pleasing to all ears, he may take the following intervals as roughly representative of their modern compass:

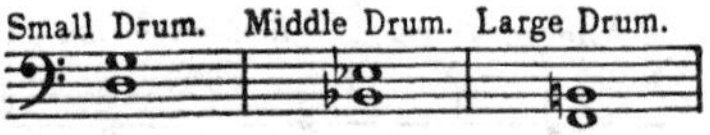

With a little tactful arrangement all Drum-parts can be kept within these limits. The low E♮, however, below the deep F of the Large Drum is fairly often called for.

It may be mentioned in passing that with a sufficiently large shell and a proper "head" Drums *can be made* to give the deep Cello C.

This is, however, only a matter of manufacture,[1] and does not affect the general average of pitch employed in the Orchestra.

The student will see that in forcing the Small Drum upwards the composer has obtained access to two other octave-tunings, F♯-F♯ and G-G. The latter of these has been used by Elgar in his rumbustious Variation *Troyte.* This Variation (No. VII.) is Presto, and the three Drums are tuned to G, C, and G.

EXAMPLE 11.

[1] In a current (1913) Drum-maker's catalogue Drums are advertised and guaranteed for the following pitches:

Before Beethoven's day it was the general but not invariable custom to mark the correct tuning of the Drums at the beginning of the piece and then to write only C's and G's in the part itself. In other words, the Drums were treated as "transposing-instruments." This plan has long since been abandoned, and the universal custom is to indicate the tuning required at the beginning of the Score and then write the actual notes. In the case of notes which have a ♯ or a ♭ it would be correct to mark the ♯ or ♭ every time the note is written. But in practice this is omitted, or at most the accidental is written once only, at its first occurrence. The most logical and satisfactory way is, of course, to give the Drums a key-signature. They deserve as much. In order to prevent any possible doubt as to the tuning of the extreme notes, it is customary not only to name the notes required at the beginning of the Score, but to add the actual notes themselves in small thus:

Timpani in E,C,F.

&c

Except for the fact that the part is always written on a five-line stave, all that was said above about the actual noting-down of the Bass-Drum-part, the clearest way of writing the roll, and the necessity of accuracy with regard to the length of note written, applies equally to the Kettle-Drums. Of the last point it is necessary to be constantly watchful, as the *sostenuto* is quite observable even in a *mf*.

A chord of two notes can of course be taken by one player. Nothing of this sort, however, is of much practical value, except perfect fifths,[1] and, for special effects, diminished fifths. In the case of the smaller intervals, such as major and minor thirds, the two notes, owing to the confusion of their upper partials, only seem to get in each other's way. The minor sixth, unless very accurately tuned and defined in the rest of the orchestra, has a tendency to sound like a fifth gone wrong. The octaves F-F, F♯-F♯, and even G-G, are quite good. Simultaneous octaves, however, never give the heavy "drummy" effect of simultaneous fifths. As both sticks are necessary to the making of a proper roll, simultaneous rolls on two notes can only be satisfactory when performed by two Drummers.

There has been considerable discussion as to the earliest date at which a "Drum solo," in the modern sense of the words, occurs. The honour is generally claimed on behalf of an Opera called *Dido*, produced by its composer Graupner at Hamburg in 1707. This is probably very far from the truth. At any rate one has no difficulty in putting the date back fifteen years to Purcell's Solo Drums at the opening of the Symphony to Act IV. of the *Fairy Queen*:

EXAMPLE 12.

Purcell. *Fairy Queen.*

Kettle-Drums.

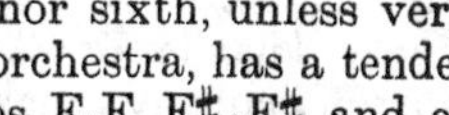

[1] For an instance of this, see below, Ex. 134.

From their earliest introduction the Drums were always used in a conventional manner to play flourishes with the fanfares of the Brass. This style of writing was universal down to the death of Mozart. As we have already mentioned the great innovator in the Drum department was Beethoven. He found the instrument, so to speak, in the kitchen and elevated it to the clouds. With a delicate and truthful perception of its "fundamental" nature he built up its rhythmic-musical sounds into the very substance of his works. It was for this purpose that he enlarged its scope and removed its former restrictions.

With three Drums at his disposal and the concrete example of Beethoven before him the modern composer's only difficulty is to decide to what notes of more than a complete chromatic octave it is best to tune his instruments. No rigid law can be laid down on this point. But speaking generally and without reference to special effects one may say that it is as true now as it was before Beethoven's innovations that two of the Drums should be tuned to the main harmonic notes of the passage in which they are taking part. These notes may be tonic and dominant or they may not.

If the music is so chromatic as to defy every attempt to bring the Drums into its harmonic scheme, it will be better, ninety-nine times out of a hundred, to leave them out altogether. In fact, their character is so vividly opposed to the chromatic, and involves in so special a manner the noble and massive idea of chaining down the harmony,[1] that this difficulty scarcely ever arises. Be it noted, however, that even with three Drums, each with a compass extension of a perfect fifth, a tuning can be arranged that gives a harmony note to each of 18 triads (major and minor) out of a possible 24.

"But," the student may say, "if I want chromatic notes, the Drums can alter their tuning." That is so. And in many modern works the Drummer has to be a particularly quick-change artist. But there are some considerations here. First, we must remember that if the Drummer is continually screwing his parchment up and down, the tension of the head is liable to become uneven and the intonation faulty. Next, no parchment capable of producing a fine Drum-tone will stand this constant racket. The player is therefore likely to save his drum-head at the expense of the intonation. Try therefore to arrange your part so that your Drummer has

(1) Two or three bars at least of 4/4 *Moderato* time in which to make an accurate change of a whole-tone, and consequently a proportionately longer time for a bigger change;

(2) New tunings that involve as small alterations as possible.

The latter point generally admits of a very simple solution. If we omit the two top semitones of the Small Drum altogether, and take the compass of the Middle Drum as from A to E, we shall see that in the thirteen chromatic notes of the normal Drum-stave five are duplicated and three triplicated, thus:

[1] *E.g.* in the opening bars of Brahms's *C minor Symphony*.

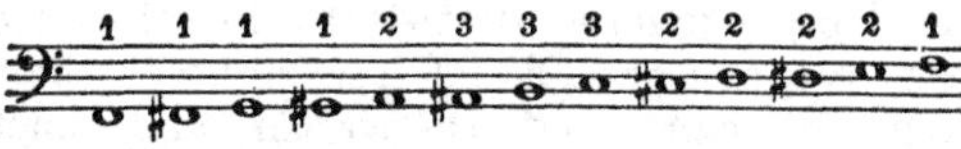

Bearing this in mind the student should have no difficulty in "stage-managing" his Drum-part properly. With a little of the "tactful arrangement" mentioned above he can avoid impossibly big skips, and keep his three instruments mostly midway between their extreme notes.

There may be some few places, especially at a climax where the Drums are to take part in a two- or three-note fragment of a melodic figure. This is no more than an extension of Beethoven's practice. Such a phrase, whether hammered out *ff* or just touched in the *pp*, is equally effective. It may, however, involve some odd tuning and, consequently, a big skip in the alteration. But this limitation of the instrument must be fairly and squarely faced. It is useless to adopt the shabby and unpractical method of writing any notes you fancy and leaving the Drummer to "find out a way" of playing them. Keep in mind the fact that you have got a man standing up in front of three Drums and that, at any given moment, they are tuned to three definite notes. A Drummer *can* make a rapid change of a semitone, or even a tone, but beyond that it is much more satisfactory for him, for yourself, and, be it said, for the audience, to give him time.

When you wish to alter your tuning, mark it clearly in your score thus: "Change F to E, C to C♯, G to A," or, in Italian, "Muta F in E, C in C♯, G in A." This particularizing of the note you wish altered as well as the note to which you wish it altered is the more necessary if you are changing the tuning of only one or two of your Drums.

The question is sure to arise in practice as to how far it is possible to write the Drums on notes that are foreign to the harmony in which they are taking part. Here again no definite answer is possible. It depends on the taste of the writer. Occasionally a Drum can sustain a roll or rhythm with fine effect in a passage which starts "at home," modulates to a distance, and then returns. This does not refer to the sort of passage which might just as well have its pedal-bass written on some of the Wind- or Stringed-Instruments, but to passages where the whole orchestra except the Drums moves away from the original harmony. Sometimes too, in a continuous passage where the Drums are playing, it is of greater artistic value to hear the Drum-tap on a note foreign to the harmony than to miss the rhythm altogether. But however this special problem is presented, it is necessary to write with a consciousness of the fact that you are introducing a foreign harmony-note. You cannot treat the Drum in the way that you would the Triangle,—as a "neutral element" in the orchestra. It always has harmonic value. If you want dissonances, you can get them, but get them with your eyes open and do not pretend that, because the note does not fit your chord, it has suddenly become "neutral" in quality.

The peculiar felicity of the Drum is that it is a wholly rhythmical instrument, and yet has a pure and beautiful tone. A good artist can play and make effective practically any rhythm that a composer can think. Nevertheless, one should not lose sight of the fact that the other bass-instruments can also do the rhythm and something besides. In every passage, therefore, it is matter for consideration whether the heavy "fundamental" tone of the Drum is wanted, and, if so, how much.

Do not be afraid of putting continual *p*'s and *f*'s into your Drum-parts. Mark every entry carefully, and never write a *crescendo* or a *diminuendo* without clearly stating from what level you mean it to come, and to what level you mean it to go. In the following passage

the omitted mark between the < and the > may be anything from *p* to *fff*. Do not think it "fussy" if the part looks like this:[1]

The Drummer has only a few elemental things to do, but they depend for their success on the accuracy of the directions which he receives. One continually comes across passages like this

which appears to be only a *crescendo* from *p* to *mp*, but which is intended by the composer to be a four-bar *crescendo* from *p* to *f* or *mf* (omitted in the fourth bar) and then a dynamic drop down to a slightly higher level than that of the first bar. This means a stoppage at rehearsal or a careless performance.

In this connection the student may be recommended to accept the fact candidly, that, in a long *crescendo*, there is a limit to the powers of gradation of even a Drummer. It is useless to begin with *ppppp*, go on to *pppp*, and scatter the rest of the expression-marks up to *fff* at mathematical distances along the line of action. In practice, about eight bars of *moderato* time at the end of the roll is the limit within which the effect of a *crescendo* or *diminuendo* can be made appreciable to the audience. As a simple example, see the 25-bar roll on B♭ in the *Allegro Vivace* of Beethoven's *4th Symphony*. The first 14 bars are marked "*sempre pp*," then comes an 8-bar *crescendo* to 3 *ff* bars. A similar instance, but on a smaller scale, is to be found at the beginning of the *Allegro con brio* in the *Egmont Overture*.

Do not get into the habit of regarding the Drums as only *forte* instruments. Nothing but the Bass-Drum and Cymbals swamps the

[1] See the Drum-part from letter R onwards to the ***Andante Mosso*** **in the 1st movement of Tschaikowsky's** ***Pathetic Symphony.***

whole orchestra—melody and harmony—so easily. Write the part often *p* when the rest, even the Brass, are playing *mp* and *mf*. In performance note the effect

(1) of steady, persistent rhythms such as the thirty bars of crotchet C's that precede the *crescendo* quavers in the *C minor Symphony* of Beethoven;

(2) of a simple $<$ or $>$ in such rhythms. See, for instance, the pedal D's in Tschaikowsky's *Pathetic Symphony* (letter D of the $\frac{5}{4}$ movement);

(3) of detached Drum-notes, especially when they form part of a pedal-bass. See the examples quoted below from Bizet's *Carmen* and Wagner's *Flying Dutchman*. (Exs. 43, 74);

(4) of a deep roll when the Basses cease playing a tremolo and, as it were, uncover the Drum-roll—

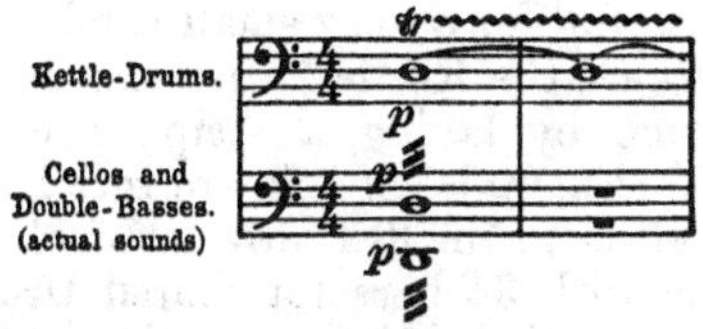

(5) of the precisely opposite arrangement—

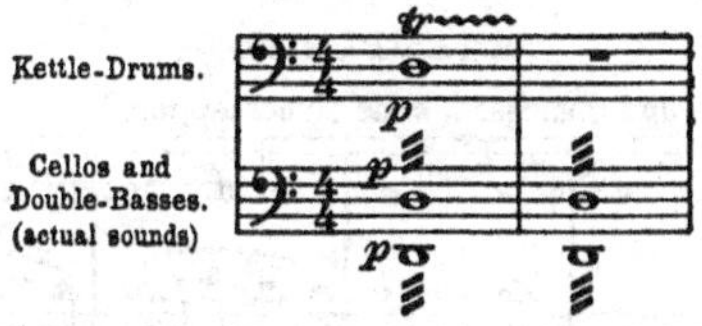

(6) of the Basses and Drums handing on a roll to each other either way without overlapping—

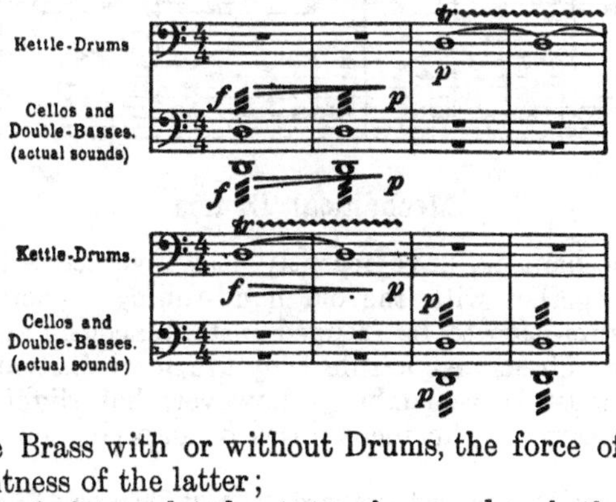

(7) of the Brass with or without Drums, the force of the former and the brightness of the latter;

(8) of a single interpolated note or phrase *solo*, whether *p* or *f*;

(9) of the Drum's *piano solo* notes, the curious feeling which they produce of apprehension or "something to come." See, for instance, the Drum-solo at the first entrance of the Dutchman in Wagner's opera;

(10) of suddenly bringing the Drums and the whole of the orchestra into one simple rhythmical pattern.

There are various "trick" ways of playing the Drums, such as the coins used in Elgar's *Romanza* in the *Enigma Variations*. The best and most useful of them all is the drummer's rapid change of his own sticks from one end to the other. Holding the sticks by the felt, he beats with the cane. The change takes one second.

The Kettle-Drums can be reduced to almost the exact quality of the Side-Drum by simply placing three heavy non-vibrating bodies (such as the T-heads of the screws) on three equidistant points of a circle lying half-way between the outer rim and the centre. This is worth remembering when scoring for a very small band.

Like the other Drums, the Kettle-Drums can be muted or muffled. This is generally done by laying a strip of cloth or some such material on the head. Examples of this are rare in Symphonic music. Mahler has used the effect in the 3rd Movement of his *1st Symphony*. The movement opens with 34 bars for muted Drums. After 2 bars a *solo* Double-Bass, also muted, enters with the subject.

The following are the first few bars:

EXAMPLE 13.

Mechanical Drums.

Several mechanisms have recently been invented with the idea of dispensing altogether with the old hand-tuning. Their object is to enable the Drum-head to be retuned instantaneously and accurately to any note required. As a rule they are more instantaneous than accurate. It must be remembered, however, that slight adjustments rendered necessary by the inequalities or imperfections of the head

[1] Solemn and measured, without dragging.

can be made by hand. These systems are generally worked by means of pedals and levers. Against all of them it is urged that both the tone-quality and the portability of the Drum suffer owing to the necessary heaviness of the frame. The latter objection—the want of portability—is not of much account, as a set of three ordinary Drums always needs a cart or trolley for its transport. The pair of Mechanical Drums weighs very little more. The other objection—the deterioration of the tone-quality—is more serious. It must be allowed that in most Mechanical Drums the tone is notably "tubbier" and less resonant. The difference is most perceptible in the *mf* and the *f*. One needs to get accustomed to it.

There is, however, a simple apparatus known as Potter's Mechanism which has been applied to the Kettle-Drums. It is claimed that the tone of these drums is an actual improvement on that of the old hand-tuned variety. The mechanism consists of an arrangement of rods, screws, and chords. It has the appearance of a Maltese Cross within a circle. It is placed inside the shell of the Drum, and worked from outside by means of a screw. A 28-notched dial corresponds to the greatest possible tension and relaxation of the head, and, in the case of an overstretched parchment, it is possible to secure a still greater tension by beginning again at the first notch.

The question may be asked, "Is the Mechanical Drum wanted?" One may answer this question fairly,—"Yes, if the tone of the instrument is not hurt." It is, however, a matter for the personal consideration and convenience of Drummers. There may be a few places where the mechanism would offer composers an easy way out of a difficulty, especially at the ends and beginnings of consecutive movements in the Theatre. In so far as it helps to solve these and similar difficulties, it is to be welcomed. On the other hand, we must remember that the function of the Drums is not to play scales, portamentos, and melodies.[1] Its elemental nature should never be disregarded.

As we have now dealt with all the more commonly-used Percussion Instruments we may, for the sake of completeness, give a single example of their *forte* combination in the peroration of a Movement. The example selected is from the end of Tschaikowsky's Symphonic Poem, *Francesca da Rimini*. The Percussion Instruments employed are the Kettle-Drums (*timpani*), Cymbals (*piatti*), Bass-Drum (*grosse caisse*), and Gong (*tamtam*). Of these the first and third play a continuous *tremolo*, while the second and fourth are in rhythmical pattern with the rest of the orchestra. Examples of this sort are, of course, common at the end of many concert and operatic works.

[1] According to Strauss, Von Bülow put Beethoven's

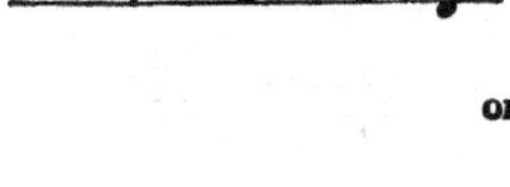

on the Mechanical Drums.

EXAMPLE 14.

Another example of a Percussion ending is quoted below from Dvořák's *Carneval Overture.* The instruments employed are Kettle-Drums, Cymbals, Side-Drum, and Triangle. (See Ex. 79.)

Before leaving this subject the student should look carefully at all the examples in this book which include a Kettle-Drum part. Without very lengthy quotation it is quite impossible to show the relative value of the Drum-parts to the general orchestral texture of a movement. The quotations, however, have been selected when possible to include some illustration of the commonest Drum-effects. They may be found in Exs. 43, 73, 74, 79, 91, 93, 112, 134, 176, 182, 214, 259, 267, 278.

No. 12. Bells.

Fr. *Cloches*; It. *Campane* (or *Campanelle*); Ger. *Glocken.*

There is no need to describe this instrument in detail, but one may say at the outset that the church-steeple variety is never employed in the orchestra. Such a bell, even if it is to produce a note no lower than middle C,

would have to be over twenty tons in weight. This makes it an impossibility in the Concert-room and in the Theatre. The largest theatrical bells in actual use are said to be those at the Paris Opera House. They were cast at Meyerbeer's suggestion to ring the St. Bartholomew's tocsin in *Les Huguenots.* Their pitch is

and Meyerbeer writes their part an octave lower. To the ear, of course, they give the usual bell-illusion of being one or two octaves lower than their real pitch.[1]

Apart from their weight, there are serious obstacles in the way of using real large bells in the orchestra. The difficulty, however, is that the large bell of proper shape and substance is the only one which really "sounds like a bell." Unlike any other instrument, it has two distinct notes, the *tap-note*, which is governed by the disposition and quality of the metal, and gives the actual pitch, and the *hum-note*, which depends principally on the shape of the casting, and gives a note about a major seventh below the tap-note. The unsolvable problem is to get rid of the weight and yet preserve the quality. Unfortunately, the only two partial solutions of this problem which have been made up to the present leave us with a very obvious answer to the question, "When is a bell not a bell?"

The first substitute is the *Saucer-shaped Bell* cast in bronze. This type of bell is fairly satisfactory in the Theatre, where it can be mounted permanently in a massive wooden frame. For concert work, however, it is still far too heavy to have any practical value. When properly struck, it gives a good solid note, but one must remember that it never descends to the deep leger-line bass-notes which composers generally amuse themselves by writing. As we have already mentioned, there is always an illusion in these matters. A composer who writes

will, undoubtedly, get something much nearer

and be quite satisfied that he hears a deep note. The illusion is, of course, caused by the muddled series of notes which make up the hum-note. The ear of the musician dissects these as the higher harmonics of an ordinary musical instrument. He then naturally imagines the deep fundamental note which alone could produce them in a musical instrument.

The second substitute is the *Tubular Bell*. These instruments are made in sets, all of one diameter—either 1 inch, 1¼ inch, 1½ inch, or 2 inches—but of varying length. They are light in weight, and therefore easy to transport. For concert purposes they are usually hung from a wooden bar, supported at each end by a sort of inverted V, thus Λ. The stand folds up and holds the tubes in position for travelling. A damper is attached to the frame and worked by means of a pedal.

[1] See Gevaert, p. 326.

A set of these bells generally consists of a major scale of eight tubes, or a chromatic octave of thirteen. In either case, the tubes are selected from some part of this compass—

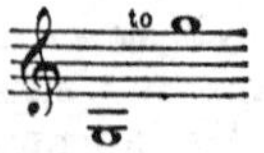

Below the bottom G three semitones are still possible, the G♭, F, and E♮, but these are of doubtful quality. The best tubes are the middle-sized. An E♭ scale of bells,

is a favourite, especially with Military Bands.

Considerable difficulty is experienced in eliminating the hum-notes at the top and bottom of the extreme compass. The makers' object is merely to produce a purely musical sound whose overtones shall have a close analogy to those of any ordinary musical instrument. The awkward point really is, that the more the hum-note is eliminated, that is to say, the more the bell is brought into conformity with our common ideas of musical pitch, the less the Tube sounds like a bell. The dilemma is one from which the composer, at any rate, cannot escape. For heavy cast-bells, however carefully used, always disturb, and in their turn are disturbed by the harmonic scheme of the orchestra. They "sound like bells," it is true, but the pitch-precision of the orchestra is directly opposed to their integral characteristics. The resultant combined sound-quality is generally somewhat uncomfortable. Indeed, in the Theatre the best effect is often to be got by the discreet use of a heavy bell whose tap-note is absolutely removed from the orchestral harmony.

Composers, however, regularly prescribe deep bell-notes whose definite pitch is associated with the harmony of their music. Various attempts have therefore been made to suggest their effect without actually employing heavy bells.

The most elaborate of these attempts is probably the **Bell-Machine** devised by Mottl for the *Parsifal*,—

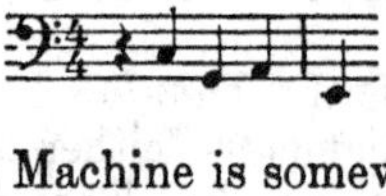

The appearance of this Machine is somewhat startling. It is as if an amateur carpenter had been trying to convert a billiard-table into a grand pianoforte, and in the course of his experiments had left the works outside. There is a deep sounding-board over which are strung heavy pianoforte wires, six for each note required. In each of these sets of six three are tuned to the octave above. The strings are set in vibration by a broad flapper or hammer loosely covered with cotton wool.

How little this sounds like a bell may be judged by the fact that at Bayreuth it was found necessary to employ at the same time four Gongs or Tam-tams, tuned to the pitch of the four notes. Even with this addition, the notes lacked the "ictus" (the *tap*) and the general buzz (the *hum*) of the real bells. A Bass-Tuba was therefore requisitioned and made to play

while a continual roll was performed on a fifth Tam-tam. This instrument has apparently now been abandoned at Bayreuth in favour of a set of Tubes.

A single deep pianoforte-wire strung in a long wooden case is sometimes used for imitating a bell. Indeed, the musical sum-totals of a heavy bell and of a freely-vibrating pianoforte wire are much alike, except in the point of actual force. In this connection we may mention Safonoff's recipe for the *Parsifal* bells. It needs only a grand piano behind the scenes and this music,—

Pianoforte.

No one seems to have suggested trying the class of Bells technically called "clockmaker's gongs." In view of their portability, they might be worth a trial. These "gongs" are lengths of coiled steel-wire. In large clocks they are struck by leather-headed beaters. The Bell-makers say that in opposition to the ordinary Bells which require space, and especially water, for their full effect, these "gongs" must be enclosed. A "gong" of this sort, 9 or 10 feet in length, can be coiled so as to slip into the overcoat pocket. When enclosed in a light glass frame, and struck with a leather-headed beater it will produce a beautifully sonorous and solemn

For orchestral purposes, these "gongs" could be developed from the toy-state in which they are at present. They might be made longer and heavier. A special frame—a cube with one side removed—would have to be designed and mounted on a sound-board.

Mr. Frederick Corder has suggested an ingenious method for reproducing the actual harmonic effect of a bell in the orchestra. It consists of a single

forte and *sostenuto,* played by four Horns and three Trombones in unison. Below it a Cello sounds the B♮ a diminished fifth lower *molto vibrato*; while above it two Flutes hold the chord

This practically gives the tap-note, the hum-note and the confused upper partials of a bell. Simpler schemes for ordinary use include the *mf* unison of Horns, Bassoon and Clarinet on a fairly low note with the addition of a Cello *pizzicato* and a soft-stick-roll on the Cymbal, while a Harp or Glockenspiel sets the note free in the octave above. The addition of *ppp* Brass as a background, with Flutes above, materially helps the illusion. This sort of recipe is, of course, useless, unless the music itself suggests a Carillon-pattern.

Of Bells in musical literature there are not many examples. Two are naively used by Bach in his Cantata for Contralto Voice, *Schlage doch, gewünschte Stunde.* Their pitch notes are B♮ and E♮. The notation of the *Campanella* in this Cantata is as follows:

The actual octave intended by Bach is, of course, quite uncertain nor is it clear why, in writing for the Bells as "transposing instruments in E," he should not have used the obvious notation of G, C. Query, is it merely a mistake of bass- for treble-clef?

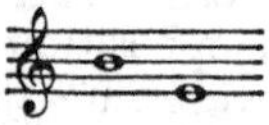

Sullivan employed a set of Bells in the *Golden Legend,*—

EXAMPLE 15.

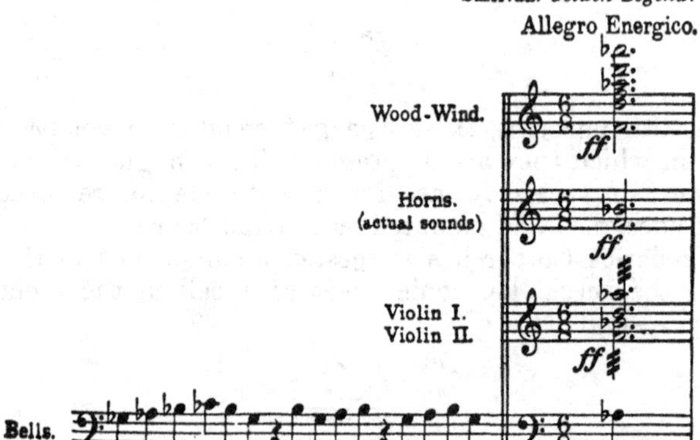

while Stanford has made effective use of a reiterated

in the 3rd Act (the Church Scene) of his opera, *Much Ado about Nothing.*

EXAMPLE 16.

Stanford. *Much Ado about Nothing.*

Very often the composer contents himself with suggesting the "ictus" alone of the bell. This effect, especially when it represents only the striking of a clock-bell, can be obtained by the simplest means. Such is the midnight-chime at the opening of Saint-Saëns's *Danse Macabre*, twelve little "ticks" on the Harp, which an unhappy Harpist has been known to extend to the unlucky number thirteen. The accompaniment is a single Horn "D," with an interrupted *pianissimo* chord for 1st and 2nd Violins and Violas. The composer adds the stage-direction that if there is no Harp the "D" must be struck twelve times on a Bell or Tam-tam, "but *pianissimo*, and not *forte*, as marked for the Harp."

EXAMPLE 17.

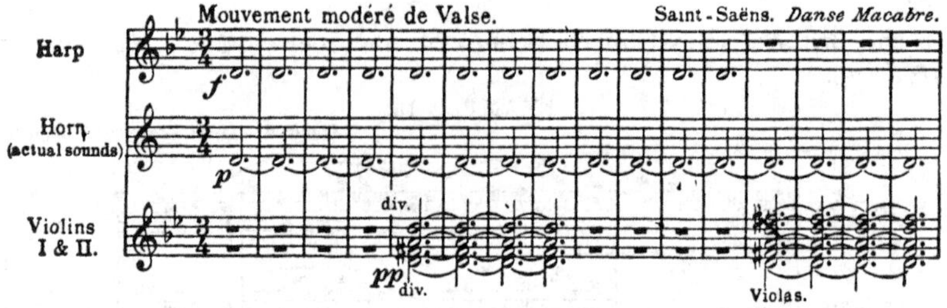

The evening and morning "Seven o'clock's" in Strauss's *Sinfonia Domestica* are merely seven little *p* taps on the Glockenspiel. In the second "Seven o'clock"—quoted below—there is only a miniature accompaniment of three Violins and a Viola, all muted. Here is the passage:

EXAMPLE 18.

It need scarcely be said that bell-like sounds in the orchestra often depend for their effect on the associative ideas called up by the music. Instruments, perhaps sounding very little like a bell, repeat a passage which might well be executed by a peal of bells. The memory of the audience does the rest. Such is the Carillon movement in Bizet's 1st Suite, *L'Arlésienne*. It is founded on the continual bell-like reiteration of the three notes, G♯, E, F♯. The orchestration—four Horns "cuivré"[1] with the *pizzicato* of Harp and Violins, and the energetic repeated notes of the Violas—helps the idea. But the main effect is gained by the iteration, not by the sound-imitation. We can see the truth of this by trying to imagine what our answer would be if we were to hear only the first crotchet of these four bars and were then asked, "What does this represent?"

[1] See pages 113, 129.

EXAMPLE 19.

Allegretto Moderato. Bizet. *L'Arlésienne.*

Another instance of this association of ideas may be seen in Saint-Saëns's song, *La Cloche.* The composer uses a Horn to repeat an A♭ in the last half of several consecutive bars. Now, a Horn sounds very little like a Bell, but the iteration of the note is just such an iteration as one might expect from a single Bell. The words of the song lead the audience to expect a Bell. So that when it actually comes the sound of the Horn is quite satisfactory *as a reminder.*

On the other hand, Wallace's little cracked bells in *Villon* depend for their success chiefly on their direct sound-imitation. The Triangle,

EXAMPLE 20.

Allegretto. ♩= 88. William Wallace. *Villon.*

Cymbal, and Harp give the "ictus," while the false-relation between the Oboe and the unison of Flute and Horn reproduces the confused upper partials. The held three-octave C in the Strings supplies exactly the right orchestral background. This clever piece of scoring deserves detailed examination, the more so because it relies for its vivid effect on a sort of mental jugglery. There are the two sets of notes, the eight at the top of the score and the four in the middle. The mind, accepting them both as sound-imitations, is forced to hover between the two. The artistic deception is only cleared up on a paper analysis.

No. 13. The Glockenspiel.[1]

Fr. *Carillon* (or *Jeu de Timbre*) ; It. *Campanetta.*

This instrument, as Gevaert has pointed out, was originally only a toy-imitation of the Flemish Church-Carillons. Its bells were of the tiniest and lightest, and varied in compass according to the maker's discretion and the composer's requirements. Händel's set in *Saul* has a chromatic compass of

and he writes for them as "transposing instruments" at a fifth below their actual pitch.

EXAMPLE 21.

Carillon.
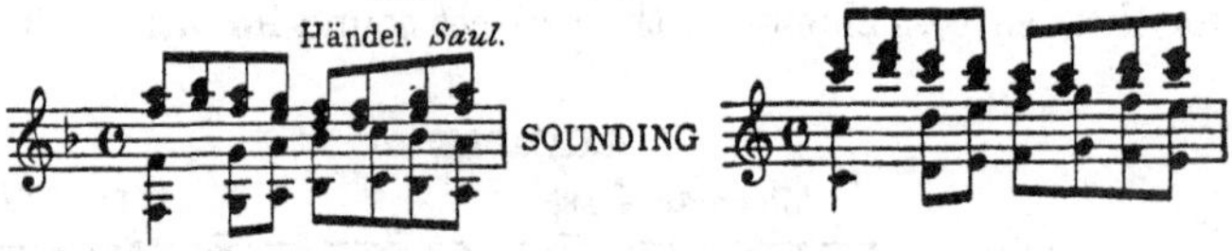

Mozart's set for Papageno's music in the *Zauberflöte* has a chromatic compass from

and he also writes for them as "transposing instruments," but at an octave below their true pitch.

EXAMPLE 22.

Glockenspiel.
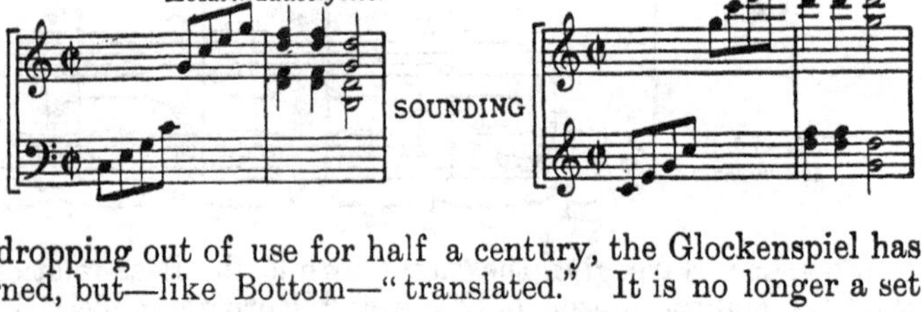

After dropping out of use for half a century, the Glockenspiel has now returned, but—like Bottom—"translated." It is no longer a set

[1] The correct English for Glockenspiel is "Chime-Bells." This might well be revived. Chimes of small bells are represented and described in England from the eleventh century onwards.

of little Bells, but a series of steel plates. Its keyboard is gone and, instead, the player uses a couple of wooden hammers.

The two standard patterns of Glockenspiel in this country are

(1) An instrument of twenty-seven chromatic notes from

(2) An instrument of thirty-seven chromatic notes from

In the best instruments the plates are mounted ladder-wise in two parallel rows on a horizontal surface. Of these two rows the plates making up the diatonic scale of C major from

run in a direct line away from the player on his right-hand side, while the chromatic notes are similarly placed, but on his left. Underneath each plate is an accurately-tuned tubular resonator which very greatly enhances the brilliance of the instrument.

The Glockenspiel-part is written in the treble-clef two octaves below its actual pitch. The following written arpeggio will, therefore, include the whole compass of the smaller instrument (No. 1) described above:

The student is recommended to keep within the compass of the smaller instrument, as the full three-octave Glockenspiel is not found everywhere.

There are, naturally, many varieties in the manufacture of the Glockenspiel. In the *Tubuphone* the plates are replaced by small tubes of metal. These are arranged exactly like a Pianoforte-keyboard with the "black notes" oxidized. The scale is the usual chromatic series of twenty-seven notes.

A charming little Glockenspiel with a fairy-like tone is made of bell-metal plates fitted with resonators. Perhaps the most successful innovation of all is the application of huge watch-case or shell-shaped resonators to the small plates.[1] The latter are at present only made

[1] Known as "Marimba Gongs."

in the diatonic scales of G major and E♭ major, and in various harmonic sets in E♭. A chromatic set made to the standard Glockenspiel pattern would be undoubtedly interesting in the orchestra.

The tone of the Glockenspiel is bright and rather startling. Played, as it usually is in this country, without a keyboard, it is yet capable of a certain rapidity of movement. With a mechanical action it can, of course, be treated as a tiny Pianoforte. But the student should remember that owing to its resonance and extremely high pitch very rapid successions of notes tend to sound "jumbly." Its main use is to "brighten the edges" of a figure or fragment of melody in conjunction with the upper octaves of the orchestra. Strictly speaking, one may say that it combines with nothing. And this is its virtue. When even in a *tutti* it is linked with Piccolo and E♭-Clarinet no further doubling is needed to make the part prominent. The best examples of the Glockenspiel are to be found in the Finale of the *Walküre*, and in the *Waldweben* (*Siegfried*). The following quotation is from the latter work. It shows the Glockenspiel in a three-octave melodic combination with the Piccolo, Oboe and Clarinet. There is a soft "fingered-tremolo"[1] background for Violins in four parts. The part is written according to Wagner's usual method, only one octave below its actual pitch.

EXAMPLE 23.

Wagner. *Siegfried.*

As the Glockenspiel is continually used in the manner shown above, that is to say, in octave-combinations with the Wood-Wind, it may be as well to draw the student's attention to an instructive passage in the

[1] See page 356.

Meistersinger. It occurs in the Waltz-tune (Act III.). The same phrase is played three times by the Glockenspiel, but each time with a slightly different arrangement in the Wood-Wind. The accompaniment, omitted below, is practically the same in all three cases, four Horns *tenuto* with *pizzicato* Strings.[1] The student should examine these three arrangements and then note the difference in performance, especially the difference produced by the high Flute-notes in No. 3.

EXAMPLE 24.

Wagner. *Die Meistersinger.*

EXAMPLE 25.

Wagner. *Ibid.*

EXAMPLE 26.

Wagner. *Ibid.*

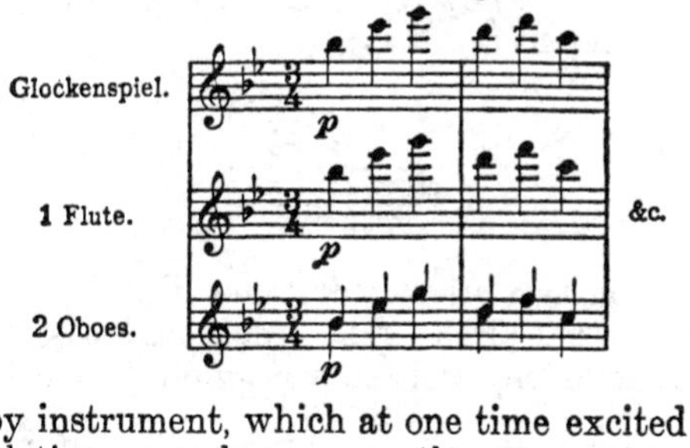

Note. A toy instrument, which at one time excited serious attention and speculation, was known as the **Harmonica**. Originally it consisted either of circular glass plates in a trough of water, or of drinking-glasses partially filled with water. The sound was produced by rubbing the glass with the fingers. The pitch varied according to the size of the glass plates or the amount of water in the drinking-glasses. This toy developed into the **Keyed-Harmonica**, an instrument in

[1] In the first Example the Cellos and Basses are "arco," and there are two Bassoons holding notes. The quotations are from pages 471, 473, and 475 of the Full Score.

which a series of glass plates was struck by light hammers. A simplified Pianoforte-action controlled the hammers, and the compass was from

It was treated as a transposing instrument, and its part was written an octave below the true pitch. Its tone seems to have been something like that of the Celesta, only more flutey.

No. 14. The Celesta.

This instrument was invented by Mustel, and is scientifically interesting as being the first instrument to which the principle of the resonator has been applied.

Some misapprehension seems to exist as to its exact mechanism. Gevaert [1] and Widor [2] make the statement that M. Mustel's Celesta is an arrangement of tuning-forks struck by hammers. This is quite incorrect.

The Celesta consists of a series of small steel bars or plates. These are set in vibration by hammers. And the hammers themselves are set in motion by a simplified Pianoforte-action controlled from an ordinary Pianoforte-keyboard. The peculiar beauty of the tone is partly due to the fact that under each vibrating steel bar is an accurately-tuned resonator of wood. Attached to the instrument is a pedal which materially enhances its sustaining power. The Celesta never goes out of tune.

Originally the instrument was made with a compass of five octaves. The bottom octave has now been abandoned, owing to its unsatisfactory nature. Present compass:

It is written for on two bracketed staves like the Pianoforte, but an octave below its actual pitch. The treble and bass-clefs are used at discretion. The following written arpeggio takes in its full compass:

Celesta. (sounding an octave higher.)

[1] *A New Treatise on Instrumentation.* Translated by E. F. E. Suddard, page 328.

[2] *The Technique of the Modern Orchestra.* Translated by Edward Suddard, page 123.

It is almost unnecessary to say that the instrument is chromatic throughout its entire compass. It can be used in any desired key. The Celesta is perfectly in tune according to the modern tempered scale. Its tone-quality is sweet and clear, with a fairy-like transparence that is delicious. It is equally happy in arpeggios and in chord-work. It is delicious when picking out a fragment of melody with a light accompaniment of Wood-Wind or Strings. When treated thus, however, the melody-notes must not be too long, as the instrument lacks the ordinary orchestral *sostenuto*. The light, the fanciful, and the graceful are best suited to the character of the instrument. In the theatre it is less effective than in the concert-room.

An example of the use of the Celesta is to be found below under the heading, "Bass-Clarinet."[1] In the *Nut-Cracker Suite*, from which it is quoted, Tschaikowsky writes the part at its actual pitch. This is done merely because the Pianoforte is indicated in the Score as a substitute.

No. 15. The Dulcitone (or Typophone).

This is a tiny key-board instrument, quite distinct from the Celesta. The sound-producing medium is a series of steel tuning-forks of graduated size, which are struck by hammers. Dampers are provided for all the notes, and a pedal controls the whole series of dampers. There is a modified Pianoforte-action similar to that of the Celesta.

The instrument is made in three sizes, and these have chromatic compasses as follows:

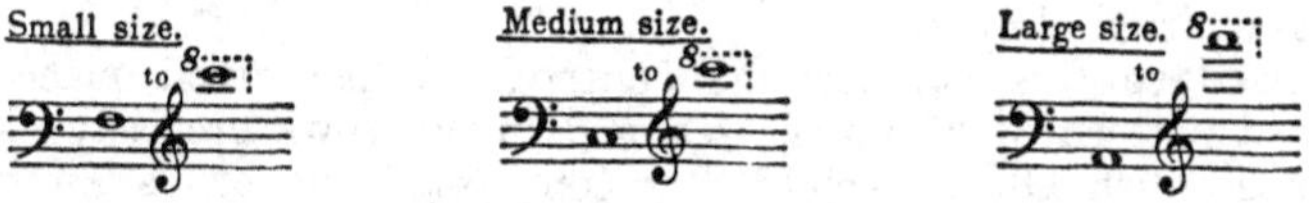

The Dulcitone has a pleasantly sweet tone, bell-like, but not very powerful. It keeps its *sostenuto* fairly evenly right up to the top of its compass. At times it gives one the impression that its sounds are an octave below their actual pitch. A similar illusion is often produced by the bottom note of the Flute. The student should read what is said on that topic below,[2] as the explanation is probably the same in both cases.

The Dulcitone is written for either at its actual pitch or one octave lower, on two bracketed staves. The treble- and bass-clefs are used at discretion. Vincent d'Indy has a part for this instrument (under its Continental name of "Typophone") in his *Chant de la Cloche*.

[1] Ex. 189. [2] See page 186.

No. 16. The Xylophone.[1]

Fr. *Xylophon* (popularly, *Claquebois*); It. *Zilafone*; Ger. *Xylophon, Strohfiedel,* or *Holzharmonika.*

This is an instrument of some antiquity. Till recently it consisted of thirty-six little slabs of hard wood—walnut, rosewood, or box—each one of which had a slightly rounded or domed upper surface. These wooden bars were isolated on long thin bundles of straw and arranged ladder-wise in four interlaced rows. The two beaters were generally spoon-shaped and were cut from willow-wood. In this form the instrument had a compass from

It was, however, awkwardly large, and it had this further imperfection that, for convenience of playing, the bars had to be arranged so as to give the player as clear a diatonic scale of "white notes" as possible in the middle of the ladder. In doing this, it was found necessary to reduplicate the notes

In order to counterbalance this convenience, and also perhaps to prevent too great a degree of pride on the part of the player, the top B♭ was omitted altogether.

Nowadays this cumbersome contrivance has given place to a standard pattern of 27 notes arranged in two rows precisely like the 27-bar English Glockenspiel.[2] Its compass, however, is an octave below that of the latter instrument, namely

This pattern, which omits the ineffective portion of the compass, is perfectly satisfactory for every orchestral purpose. It must, however, be noted that continental Xylophones are still made on the old large pattern. Foreign instrumentation books all give the compass of the Xylophone "in its complete state" as

[1] From the Greek *xulon* = wood and *phone* = voice.

[2] See page 61.

In the best English instruments the bars are made of hard rosewood. They are held loosely on their guides by screws, and have a complete set of resonators accurately tuned to their respective notes. The beaters are light, and are made either of willow, spoon-shaped, or with a rather large globular head of boxwood.

To know what the Xylophone can do one must have heard a good player. Arpeggios, scale-passages, repeated notes, successions of thirds and sixths, and brilliant glissandos are all executed with accuracy and with a lightning-like rapidity. In fact, the technique is very much on the same plane as that of the Hungarian *Cimbalom.*

The Xylophone part is written on one stave in the treble-clef. The best way is to write the part at its true pitch. But, as usages vary in this particular, it is wise to say that you are doing so in your Score. Xylophone players know that its hard dry clatter is most effective between the rough limits of

and therefore generally use their discretion as to octave. Saint-Saëns's well-known

EXAMPLE 27.

Saint-Saëns. *Danse Macabre.*

in the *Danse Macabre* is always put up an octave in performance. Mahler has introduced the Xylophone into Symphonic music. In the 1st Movement of his 6th Symphony there is a part for the instrument with effective repeated notes of this sort:

EXAMPLE 28.

Mahler. *6th Symphony.*

Holbrooke and Grainger have both written for it: the former in *Queen Mab,* the latter in his *Scotch Strathspey and Reel.*

Percussion Notation. A good simple way of distinguishing the four most commonly used instruments to the eye is to write treble G for the Triangle, treble E for the Side-Drum, and bass C for the Bass-Drum and Cymbals, using an upstem for the Bass-Drum and a downstem for the Cymbals, thus:

BRASS INSTRUMENTS.

PRELIMINARY.

BEFORE we begin to study the technical development of the modern Brass Instruments, we must devote a few pages to the early instrumental types from which they sprang. It need scarcely be said that neither the Horn nor the Trumpet began its existence in the comparatively perfect state in which it is usually first presented to the musical student. The beautiful seventeenth century Hunting-Horns and the orchestral Trumpets and Hand-Horns of the eighteenth century had a past. They were not sudden unexpected inventions, like the motor-car or the aeroplane. It is perhaps unnecessary to *detail* this past, but a bare outline of its prominent features will help the student to a better understanding of the various instruments as they appear in modern orchestral history. We shall therefore sketch this outline down to the days of the Hunting-Horn and the Natural Trumpet. From that point onwards we shall take up the subject with greater precision and combine its history with an account of the physical conditions which are common to all the orchestral Brass.

The original type of all the instruments which we are now discussing was undoubtedly an animal's horn or tusk,[1] to the smaller end of which a cup-shaped mouthpiece was fixed. A simple instrument of this sort has been and still is in almost universal use. We must note that from its very nature it is roughly conical in form. It must, however, be remembered that long before the Christian era some metal or other had been substituted for the actual horn or ivory of the original instrument. The model was easily imitated either by a casting in bronze or by means of a thin beaten ribbon of metal wound on a "core." So long as the instrument remained the actual horn of an animal, there was no possibility of musical development. But, with the first manufactured instrument, came the certainty of development. In length, proportions, and smoothness of bore, the player could be studied and variety could be obtained. Thus we find the ancient Romans in the centuries immediately preceding our era with a varied assortment of what we should call "Military Brass."[2]

[1] The "Olifant-Horn" carved from an elephant's tusk was a recognized mediæval instrument of music.

[2] The *Cornu*, *Lituus*, *Buccina*, and *Tuba*.

In mediaeval times, the big metal **Horn** and its model, the Cow-Horn, existed side by side, very similar in shape, and both played with cup-mouthpieces. These were the instruments which were used by Huntsmen, Foresters, and Watchmen. They were often big handsome instruments, and were regularly employed by the mediæval Gilds and Corporations to sound the note of assembly.[1] However, as the manufactured instrument increased in size, it decreased in handiness. It became unmanageable for the Huntsman. This was a serious difficulty in days when layman and even priest had almost no outdoor recreation but the chase.

The difficulty was solved by winding the tube into a complete circle. The Horn was then passed under the player's right arm and the bell projected over his left shoulder. It was, in fact, carried just like a modern "Helicon" or "Circular Bass." One cannot put a date to this improvement, but a guess may be founded on the fact that a Horn-player and his instrument are carved thus on a fourteenth century choir-stall in Worcester Cathedral.[2] It is interesting to note, however, that the English, with their innate conservatism, always preferred the short metal Horn made roughly to the model of the actual animal's horn. This is the Horn that figures in our ballads, folk-lore, and legendary tales as the "bugle." On the Continent the longer form was preferred. In France the *Cor de Chasse* was introduced occasionally in the early part of the eighteenth century to accompany hunting-scenes in Ballets and Operas. It was then, so to speak, re-introduced to England as an orchestral instrument of foreign origin. And "French Horn" it remains with us to this day.

We shall return to the Horn in a moment. But meanwhile we have to consider two other instruments, the **Trumpet** and the **Trombone.** Early in the middle ages there existed two cylindrical brass instruments, the **Claro** (or Clarion) and the **Buysine.** From the eleventh to the fourteenth century[3] these two instruments remained as well-defined types clearly contrasted with each other. The Claro was the ancestor of the Trumpet, the Buysine of the Trombone.

The Claro was originally a *short* straight tube of brass, with a cup-mouthpiece at one end and a bell at the other. As with the Horn, however, an increase of length was demanded for purposes of outdoor effectiveness. With an instrument so constantly used in camp and on the field of battle this necessitated an alteration of shape. And this alteration had to be directed towards greater portability and ease of management. In a word, somewhere towards the end of the thirteenth century the instrument began to be folded up. The folding, however,

[1] Many still exist, and some are even now in use. The Canterbury, Dover, Folkestone, Ripon, and Ipswich Horns are all well known. There are many others. The earliest English reference to the Horn as a musical instrument appears to be in a Psalter in the Cottonian Library at the British Museum. The MS. is interlined with Anglo-Saxon, and its date is about 825. "Singað in fruman monðes horne."

[2] A reproduction of this carving may be seen on page 185 of Rev. F. W. Galpin's *Old English Instruments of Music.*

[3] "Þe ilke orible bosyne him went to þe yeare: 'com to þine dome.'" Dan Michel's *Ayenbite of Inwyt* (Remorse of Conscience), 1340.

was not in the slightest like that of the modern Trumpet. It was a folding in one plane, such as we see in the *Bass-Clarinet* and the larger *Saxophones*. In fact, if the student will take the illustration of the *Alto Saxophone* (No. 3), page 167, and will bring the curve of the bell over so as to form an upside-down letter **U**, he will get a rough architectural plan of the early mediaeval *Clarion*.

A Trumpet of this sort without "stays" was of course liable to continual damage. Accordingly, early in the fifteenth century we find the two curves of the instrument brought together in two planes for mutual support. They were not fixed—merely placed together, and then bound with an ornamental cord. This Trumpet had, however, more or less of our modern shape. At this period the word "Clarion" was more particularly applied to the folded instrument. "Trumpet" was reserved for the old straight instrument.[1] In the last stage of its evolution the folds of the military Trumpet were fastened to each other so as to form practically one rigid whole.

The Buysine was, like the Claro, a straight tube of brass with a cup-mouthpiece at one end and a bell at the other. Unlike the Claro, however, it was *of great length*. We are in complete ignorance as to the manner in which the slide-mechanism was first applied to the Buysine. This is the more surprising when we consider the mechanical complexity of the change and the simple musical perfection of the result. All we know is that the slide was in actual use during the fourteenth century. To the instrument so altered the name **Sackbut**[2] was applied. In Germany, however, the old name was never dropped. The word *Posaune*, formerly *Buzaun*, is merely a collateral form of Buysine.

The Sackbut in its fully developed form was practically a Trombone. Indeed it is quite safe to say that a photograph of a sixteenth century Bass-Sackbut,[3] if included among the Trombones in a modern instrument-maker's catalogue, would scarcely excite the curiosity of even a professional player. It must, however, be added that some difference of opinion exists as to whether the slide mechanism was normally so arranged as to allow of the seven modern "Trombone-positions."[4]

Before taking up the more detailed study of the Brass Instruments as they were in the seventeenth and eighteenth centuries, the student must be informed that the *earliest* device for increasing the scales of the cup-mouthpiece instruments did not depend on any of our modern methods. These methods, which will all be explained presently, are "crooks," "slides," and "valves." The first attempt was merely an

[1] "When, however, the long straight instrument was entirely discarded, the word Trumpet was used indiscriminately for the Clarion and the Field Trumpet, though in the actual performance of music they were distinct, the former, with its smaller bore, taking the higher notes in the fanfares and the latter sounding the lower." Galpin, *Old English Instruments of Music*, page 204. The Thurner Horn was merely a folded Trumpet.

[2] The Spanish word from which Sackbut is derived is used of a pump. It is evidently descriptive of the player's action.

[3] They were made in several sizes from treble downwards. [4] See pp. 83, 134, 139, 140.

analogy from the wooden reed-pipes. In all these instruments the softness of the material made the lateral boring of holes in the pipe easy and practicable. The idea was transferred to the cup-mouthpiece instruments, and it is worth noting that the invention was originally English and was in use as early as the tenth century. None of these "cup-mouthpiece instruments with lateral holes" has survived to the present day, but at one time they played an important part in the history of music.

The most respectable instrument of this family in point of antiquity and length of service was the old **Cornett**,[1] known also as the *Zinke*, *Cornetto*, and *Cornet à bouquin*. This instrument was originally made of horn, bone, or ivory, in three sizes. It afterwards developed into an instrument of wood covered with leather. It had six finger-holes in front and a thumb-hole behind, like that of the *Recorders*.[2] Its usual office was to play the upper part or parts in the Sackbut- or Trombone-harmony. As the Sackbuts generally took the lower part or parts, no pressing need was felt for a Bass-Cornett. Towards the end of the sixteenth century, however, a French priest[3] invented the **Serpent.**[4] This instrument was of wood, pierced laterally with holes. It employed a big cup-mouthpiece, and was the true bass of the Cornett or Zinke family. The Serpent had to give way to the **Bass-Horn**[5] and the **Russian Bassoon,** and these, in their turn, to the **Ophicleide**. They were all cup-mouthpiece instruments with laterally bored holes. The only other instrument which employed this principle was the **Keyed Bugle**, an early nineteenth century invention, which for a few years enjoyed great popularity. Its existence was cut short by the advent of the valve system and the superiority of the modern Military Cornet.

The student is advised to note carefully the peculiarities of the instrumental group just described. It comprises instruments made of brass (such as the Ophicleide) and of other materials (such as the Cornett and Serpent). But they all have a common method of tone-production and of scale-variation. Not only are all the instruments in this group individually obsolete, but the technical method of varying the length of the air-column by means of laterally pierced holes is now unused by any cup-mouthpiece instrument.[6] We shall have occasion to refer to this group once or twice in a later portion of the book. But as no instrument of this type figures in any Score later than Gluck, it will be unnecessary to deal with its general history any more fully.[7]

[1] Of course no connection with the modern valved-Cornet. [2] See page 181.

[3] Guillaume, Canon of Auxerre.

[4] Described more fully on page 286. It is supposed to be identical with the Lysarden, an instrument which occasionally figures in old English inventories.

[5] No connection whatever with the "Horn" in its ordinary musical sense.

[6] It is confined to what we now call the "Wood-Wind."

[7] The technical details of one of these instruments—the Keyed-Bugle—are given with some fulness on pp. 172-4. Shorter articles are devoted to the other instruments. See Index sub "Bass-Horn," "Cornett," "Ophicleide," "Russian Bassoon," and "Serpent."

The appearance of the ancient Cornett and the obsolete Keyed-Bugle can be gathered from the illustrations on Plate II. The former instrument seems innocuous and primitive to the last degree. We must not, however, despise it for that reason. It played a considerable part in the progress of Music, and for a long space of time solved the difficult problem of providing a diatonic compass of sufficient weight in the soprano-octave to balance the Trombones. The Keyed-Bugle had a much shorter and less distinguished career. In tone-colour it came midway between the Horns and the Trumpets. Gevaert laments its disuse and regrets that it is not employed regularly to play the parts of the obsolete Cornett. It is, he says, "the very instrument required to take up the part of the old *Cornetto*, and to serve as a Soprano to the Trombones." The two bass-instruments which correspond to the Cornett and the Keyed-Bugle, namely the Serpent and the Ophicleide, are illustrated later. See Plate VII., p. 174, and Plate XI., p. 287.

We must now resume our study of the Brass Instruments at the place where they became of importance in serious organized music, and the first point to establish is the physical fact which underlies all their various technical methods.

The student is probably aware of the following facts:

(1) That if he takes a length of metal tubing with a mouthpiece at one end, he can, by stretching his lips across the mouthpiece and blowing, cause the air-column inside the tube to vibrate.

(2) That by varying the pressure of his breath and lips—the latter technically called the *embouchure*—he can compel the air-column to vibrate in various ways, perhaps as a whole, in halves, in quarters, and so on, *but*

(3) That he cannot compel the air-column to vibrate in *any* fractions of the whole which he may desire, only in certain unalterable fixed fractions.

(4) That he cannot, by taking a longer or shorter tube, alter these fixed fractional vibrations: that is to say, that he cannot alter the lengths of the air-waves *relative to each other, but*

(5) That, in a longer (or shorter) tube, the whole of the air-waves, retaining their relative lengths to each other, become longer (or shorter).

Combining these five scientific facts into musical terms, we may say

(1) That from an open metal tube we can produce a series of musical notes whose pitch *relative to each other* is always the same.

(2) That the longer the tube the lower will be the pitch of the series; and consequently that the shorter the tube the higher will be the pitch of the series.

This series of notes is commonly known as **The Harmonic Series.** It is of fundamental importance in the technique of all Brass Instruments, because, on them, no notes except members of this Harmonic Series can be produced from any given length of tube. The length of tube may be and is varied mechanically. But, given any length, the player is bound down to this one group of notes.

The intervals of this Harmonic Series are, for a length of tube which would give C as its fundamental note,

FIG. 1.—CORNETT.

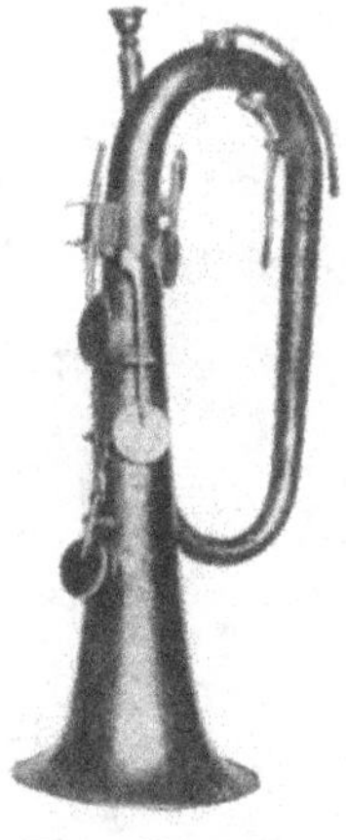

FIG. 2.—KEYED-BUGLE, made by Charles Pace & Son.

By kind permission of Messrs. Boosey & Co.

Of these notes Nos. 7, 11, 13, 14 are, according to our present ideas, out of tune. But this is not all. For, of the three original types of orchestral Brass Instrument, the two most important—the Trumpet and the Horn—could not produce either No. 1 of the Series, or, for any practical purpose, Nos. 17, 18, 19, 20, 21.

We may boil the matter down into a sentence by saying that a player on the old Hunting Horn or the Military Trumpet had a repertoire of 11 healthy and 4 decrepit notes only. Here is the list. The good notes are printed in semibreves and the bad in crotchet-heads:

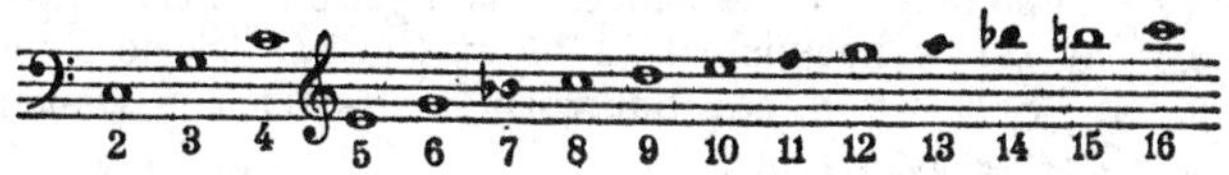

A player on one of these "natural" instruments was like a man continually hopping up and down a ladder, some of whose rungs were so shaky as to be a danger to life and limb. At the bottom they were far apart and badly spaced, while at the top they were set so close together that he had great difficulty in getting his feet on them at all.

A Brass Instrument of the type which has just been described seems strangely imperfect to the musician of to-day. We must not, however, forget that it is the instrument which served, at any rate for out-door purposes, from pre-Christian times down to about the early days of the seventeenth century.[1]

Let us return for a moment to the question of the intervals which our early Brass-player had at his command. The student who appreciates the fact that the player was always perched on some one rung or other of a musical ladder may be inclined to ask this question,—Supposing this musical-workman's ladder were placed half-way up the front-door steps and he wished to get at some part of the wall which he could not reach from any one of his rungs, what did he do? The answer is simple. The "make" of the ladder could not be altered. But its position could. It could be placed one, two, three, or more steps lower down or higher up according to what was wanted. Only there was a limit both ways. It was not much good placing the foot of the ladder out in the road because of the passing traffic, and, if it were put too far up the steps, the workman was liable to break his neck while he was painting the attic window.

Now, in musical terms, the shifting of the ladder—that is of the whole Harmonic Series—was the plan adopted when people began to attempt the improvement of the Brass-Wind. And it was this improve-

[1] The date is only approximate. The first mention of "crooks" appears in 1618. They were first applied to the Trumpets, then tentatively and unsuccessfully to the Trombones, and later still to the Horns.

ment which brought the Horn and Trumpet indoors. Hitherto they had been outdoor instruments, very good for sounding the death of a stag or for "duty-calls" in camps and barracks. But they were too rudimentary to be of any serious use in organized music. The Horn, now that it had at any rate a possibility of development, was unwound from its player's body and coiled to a size convenient for handling. Its "bell" no longer pointed over his head or under his arm, but lay, where it was most wanted, next to his right hand.

A mechanism was found by means of which the Trumpet- or Horn-player was no longer confined to his one series of notes. The pitch of this series had always depended—as it still depends—solely on the length of his tube. Hitherto this length was unalterable. If the tube were of such and such a length he could only produce, let us say, the "C" Series of notes: if it was so much longer he could produce the "F" Series, and so on. The new mechanism gave him the opportunity of blowing any series he wished to blow, the "C" Series, the "B♭" Series, the "A" Series, etc., etc., but with this restriction, that he could blow *only one series at a time.*

This was the first great revolution in Brass instruments, and its results were fairly satisfactory to everyone down to about the year 1835.

The technique of this revolution was remarkably simple. The composer having made up his mind what special series he wished, directed the player to put his instrument into that key. The player, on his part, supplied himself with a complete set of neatly coiled brass tubes, called "crooks,"[1] which he could insert into the main length of his tubing. All these crooks differed in length. No two were the same, and each "crook," therefore, when fixed to the instrument, represented a different key.

Thus, if the composer wished to have the "F" Series of sounds, he marked the Horn-part in his Full Score, "Horn in F." The player then took his "F crook"—a simple piece of coiled brass-tubing about 52½ inches long and fixed it to his Horn. It is true that he could now do no more than he could before, viz. blow the Harmonic Series of 11 good and 4 bad notes, but with his "F crook" on, these now sounded a perfect fifth lower.

But notice here two small points: (1) The blowing with the new crook was not quite the same. The "embouchure," that is to say, the pressure of the lip, varied according to the length of the crook. For a very long (*i.e.* low-pitched) crook the embouchure was very loose: for a very short (*i.e.* high-pitched) crook it was very tight. And this difference became so great between the extremely high and the extremely low crooks that it was almost impossible to jump from one to the other. Furthermore, on the very low crooks the bottom notes of the series demanded a lip looser than any human being could accustom himself to. These low notes, therefore, were unplayable. Similarly the very high crooks called for such a preternaturally tight lip that their top-notes were out of the question.

[1] Called by the Germans *Bogen*, short for *Krummbogen.*

(2) As in the case of the Kettle-Drum, neither composers nor players wanted to see the actual notes which they were sounding. Composers therefore went on writing only the series which was produced from the fundamental note "C." The actual sounds were governed by the direction at the beginning of the Score, "Horn in G," "Horn in D," and so on. The composer wrote, for instance, the notes C-E-G. If he placed the words "Horn in E♭" at the beginning of the part they sounded "E♭-G-B♭." If he wrote "Horn in F" they sounded "F-A-C." In fact, the written notes C-E-G, etc., were no longer pitch-notes at all, but only directions to the player to "blow Harmonics Nos. 4, 5, and 6." The instrument had, in short, become what is known as a Transposing Instrument, and the musical hieroglyphic

Horn in F. 

had come to represent the sounds

This is a type of what was and still is the ordinary notation for all Transposing Instruments. But in the case of the bottom notes of the Horn there was another convention. This convention, which has persisted to our day, consisted in writing them in the bass-clef, *but an octave too low.* There is not a word to be said for this foolish custom. The only reason for adopting the bass-clef at all should be the avoidance of leger-lines. What can one say about a pretended simplification which only adds a complication?[1] However, the student must be prepared to find in all old and in some modern scores such notes as these

Horn in G. 

In order to ascertain the actual sounds he must first put these notes up an octave to rectify the conventional transposition, and then down a perfect fourth to get the crook-transposition. By doing this he will see that the real sounds are

Furthermore, he should notice that, if the first example just given is written in the bass-clef without the alteration of an octave, it does away with the two leger-lines altogether. In his own practice the

[1] See pages 414-5.

student is advised, on the score of logic, that if he uses the bass-clef at all—it is rarely needed—to use it at its proper pitch. If he wants, let us say, this note

on the F Horn he should write

not

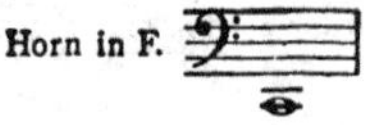

A clef ceases to have any logic at all when its pitch is disregarded.

We must now return to the question of the Horn-mechanism as employed by the classical masters. We have already sufficiently explained how the invention of crooks gave the player the opportunity of producing the Harmonic Series at not one but almost any degree of pitch, and how the player was still bound down to the particular Harmonic Series which was associated with the crook that he was using. But, in addition to that, another change was made in the Horn-technique. The instrument had been included in the first primitive orchestras as an experiment, and was still played with a heavy out-door tone-quality. Its "bell," however, as has been already said, now lay close to the player's right hand. In the course of some experiments made with the object of subduing the instrument's coarse tone it was found[1] that the insertion—or the partial insertion—of the hand in the bell not only stifled the tone, but lowered its pitch anything from a fraction of a semitone to a whole tone.

From this discovery came a new series of notes, totally distinct from, but still dependent on, the old Harmonic Series. These notes were called "hand notes" or "stopped notes," as opposed to the "open notes" of the Harmonic Series. For instance, where the Horn-player was before only able to produce such open notes as

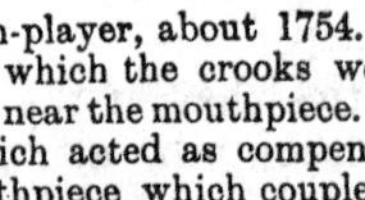

[1] By Hempel, a Dresden Horn-player, about 1754. He it was who brought out the *Inventionshorn*, an instrument in which the crooks were inserted into the body of the instrument, and not merely added near the mouthpiece. This instrument was also the first to have the U-shaped slides which acted as compensators. In 1788 an Englishman, called Clagget, contrived a mouthpiece which coupled together two horns of different pitch. A valve-opening diverted the wind-stream to either instrument at the will of the player, and an additional mechanism gave a lowered pitch on both instruments. The complete mechanism was, in fact, four Horns in one.

he could now take these, as stopped notes, to sound

The Horn had now become partially chromatic. But the student must remember

(1) That the new stopped notes were of a quality so muffled and so different from the open notes that they practically sounded as if played on a different instrument.

(2) That they could, therefore, only be used advantageously (*a*) to humour the notes of the Harmonic Series which were already slightly out of tune; (*b*) as passing notes, where they were only audible for the fraction of a second between two good open notes; (*c*) as "special-effect" notes, where a dull and muted tone-quality was wanted.

(3) That, though these notes were fairly accessible on the Horn, they were absolutely out of the question on the Trumpet. That instrument projected straight out in front of the player. The hand could, therefore, not be inserted in the bell, and only the old Harmonic Series of notes could be sounded. The system of crooks, however, was applied to the Trumpet much as it was to the Horn. Fewer crooks were in general use on the Trumpet, and its favourite crooks were not those most congenial to the Horn. Otherwise the system worked in much the same manner on both instruments.

From a consideration of paragraphs (1) and (2) the student will be able to appreciate the reasons why the use of the stopped notes never became part of the ordinary orchestral routine of the classical masters. Even in Beethoven's music they are the exception, not the rule. One need only glance through a few volumes of his Scores to see that except where the Horn is brought prominently forward as a Solo instrument—and therefore *must* go outside the narrow range of its Harmonic Series—it still sticks to its accustomed C's, E's, G's, and so on. In a word, the stopped notes and the open notes differed so markedly in tone-colour that they could only rarely be brought into action together. Meanwhile the fundamental character of the instrument remained unchanged, and the composer relied primarily on the infinitely purer and more useful series of open notes. Only he now had this additional liberty, that he could switch them into any key by means of the crooks.

The actual number of crooks used in Beethoven's day for the Trumpets and Horns combined was fifteen. In the following complete list a note is placed after each crook to show the actual sound which would be produced by that particular instrument when playing the written note,—

Several other Horn crooks—the C-alto, the B♮-alto, the A♭-alto, the D♭, the B♮-basso and the A-basso—existed as workshop curiosities only. The G♭ (F♯) crook appears to have been used once only,—by Haydn in his *Farewell Symphony*. On the Trumpet no D♭ crook was used nor any higher than F.

In order to make the transpositions of these crooks perfectly clear, six short passages are subjoined. In each case the written notes are given on the left-hand side of the page and the actual sounds on the right.

EXAMPLE 29.

EXAMPLE 30.

EXAMPLE 31.

EXAMPLE 32.

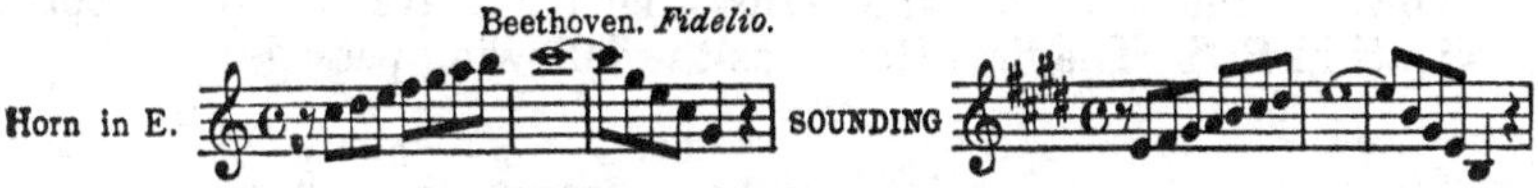

EXAMPLE 33.

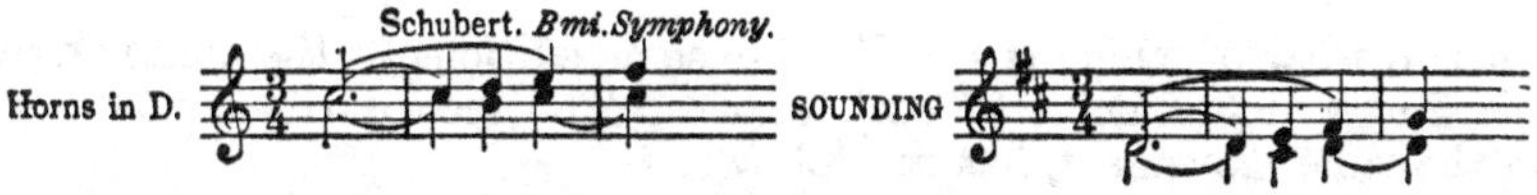

EXAMPLE 34.

Before proceeding further with the history of the Trumpet and Horn, we may be allowed to offer, in parenthesis, the following "crooked" problem, in the solution of which the student may exercise his ingenuity.

There is a Symphony by Haydn sometimes called No. 24 (in Messrs. Breitkopf and Härtel's edition now progressing it is numbered 51).

It was evidently written for two Horn-players of specially brilliant attainments, for (1) the part is marked "Corni obbligati," (2) in an early set of parts at the British Museum the first Horn has the follow-

* "Horn in C" always means "Horn in C-basso" *i.e.* "Horn transposing down an octave." The high C crook was never used. On the other hand, "Trumpet in C" means "Trumpet sounding the written notes in the same octave".

ing passage in the second movement accompanied only by muted strings:

and later the following:

The former passage is altered in one of the published full scores so as to bring its highest notes down an octave. Meanwhile the second Horn has to play such passages as this:

Now, in the "Minuet and Trio," the parts are marked "Corni obbligati in B♭." The first Horn has the following passage:

the third bar of which is simplified in some editions by the omission of the 2nd and 3rd notes of each triplet. The second Horn, however, in the same movement, has the following:

The bass-clef note occurs several times, and in each case the clef is carefully written in and afterwards contradicted. In one edition, however, the bass-clef is omitted each time, leaving a note which does not exist on the hand horn.

Query. Is the crook B♭-alto or B♭-basso?

We may now return to our Trumpet and Horn at the stage where we left them. It was the type of Trumpet and Horn which sufficed for Bach, Händel, Haydn, Mozart, Beethoven, Weber, and Mendelssohn, a type imperfect and limited in scope, but which—especially in the case of the Horn—called for the highest artistry on the part of the player, and gave the composer a series of notes restricted, indeed, in number, but of a purer quality than any to which we are accustomed at the present day.

There is a general disposition to regard the classical masters as always labouring, and consciously labouring, under a terrible handicap in the matter of their orchestral Brass. This is, however, quite wrong We are regarding the matter far to much from our own musically developed point of view. In the first place, up to Beethoven's day music seldom strayed through chromatic chords, and almost never made permanent excursions "far away from home." The Horns and Trumpets in the key of the piece met every emergency. When, in Beethoven's time, the music of a movement began to go further afield, it was possible to write one pair of Horns in the key of the piece and the other pair in the key of the principal modulation. Or, again, a special crook could be used for a special harmonic effect. (Andante in A♭ of the *5th Symphony*, Horns and Trumpets in C. Scherzo in F of the *7th Symphony*, Horns and Trumpets in D.) A change of crook could even be made for an isolated phrase—*Eroica Symphony*, where the first Horn in E♭ takes the F-crook for

Then, again, we must not overlook the fact that the special "harmonic" type of melody was, and is, fundamental to one class of emotional effect. The substitution of a chromatic for a harmonic compass in a Brass Instrument does not affect the psychology of its true appeal in the slightest.

Still, even in Beethoven's later life, there were signs that composers were calling for a more even and a more extended Brass-technique. It was felt as a disadvantage[1] that the orchestral Brass could take very little melodic part in the orchestra unless the tunes were of what we may call the "boy's brigade" type. In the *p* and the *mp*, where nothing but a quiet *sostenuto* was called for, the Brass Instruments were admirable. But when it came to the *f* and the *ff*, they could only blare away at unimportant notes and increase the noise. In fact, their usual business was to "take part in a conventional *tutti*," and, as their notes were often quite subordinate or even opposed to the musical matter in hand, the result was that the real *melos* in the orchestra was lost in a dismal swamp.

Then, again, any harmonic or melodic progression that made a feature of a bad Brass note was impossible. It either had to be dismissed from the composer's thoughts entirely, or else, whatever the dynamic exigencies of the case, played without the Brass. Under these conditions the composer's difficulties were often great, and the resultant Brass parts unbelievably dull. Here is an example of these difficulties. In Beethoven's *Overture to Fidelio* the key-signature is E, and the four Horns are in E. The Trumpets, however, not being able to play stopped notes, have to be crooked in C for the sake of the C major passage in the middle of the overture. The result is that for the rest of the work their part consists of practically one

[1] Mendelssohn is said to have expressed his belief that the valve-system would be perfected and applied to the Horns.

note only, the only one in their series which will fit the key, viz. the note E, which they reiterate more than 150 times.

But, besides the composer, the player had to be considered. We must not think of the substitution of one crook for another as a mere mechanical alteration which did not affect him. A Violinist might tune his E-string down to E♭, and it would make no difference to his fingering. The slackened string, however, would make a considerable difference to his bow-arm if it were lowered to a major ninth below its proper tension. Now, what the bow-arm is to the Violinist, the embouchure is to the Brass-player. There is a difference, however, all in favour of the Violinist. To him his string is an external thing. At a pinch it can be made to vibrate somehow, and the fingering cannot alter. But for a Horn-player, let us say, the vibrating medium is his own lips and breath. He is continually engaged in the delicate task of picking out individual and very slightly differentiated notes from the group of Harmonics that surrounds them. This needs great nicety of physical adjustment. It is, therefore, of the utmost importance that he should have a *standard of lip-tension* which he may correlate with the sounds which he is playing. Under the system of a multitude of crooks no such thing was possible. The note

might mean the production of the sound

with a comparatively high lip-tension on a crook 16 inches long, or the production of the sound

with a low lip-tension on a crook 125 inches long.[1]

All this pointed in the direction of a second revolution in the Brass department.

In 1815 two Prussians—Stölzel and Blümel—impelled perhaps by emulation of their fellow-countrymen who were engaged on a similar errand near Brussels, set out to rescue the Brass from its threatened danger and to fortify it in a position of orchestral safety.

[1] Crooks in B♭-alto and B♭-basso. We must also remember that, in extended works at any rate, the player was compelled at every change of crook to insert a length of *cold* cylindrical tubing into a *warm* conical instrument. This alone was long odds against the player's certainty of attack. In Opera this constant alteration of tube-length became irksome to the last degree. Instead of playing right through a performance on an instrument of one size, he had to make a change every five minutes. The following is the list of crooks in their proper order as prescribed by Mozart for the performance of his Opera, *Don Giovanni*: D, F, E♭, D, G, F, A, B♭, E♭, D, G, B♭, F, C, F, E♭, G, C, G, A, F, C, E♭, G, B♭, C, E♭, E♮, F, D, F, B♭, F, G, D.

We must explain how this was accomplished. The student will have observed that, of the three types of modern orchestral Brass, only two—the Horn and the Trumpet—have been mentioned so far. The third type—the Trombone—gave the cue which led to the second revolution in the Brass department. The Trombone was then what it is now, as far as its mechanism goes. It was not, however, the mechanism of the instrument, that is to say the slide, which was taken as a model by the early experimenters with the "hand-horn" and "natural-trumpet," but the *compass-extension* provided by that mechanism. This *compass-extension* has remained to the present day the fixed type of *compass-extension* for all three-valve Brass Instruments.

We must then glance for a moment at the mechanism of the Tenor Trombone in B♭—the chief member of the Trombone family—and see what its *compass-extension* was. The instrument consists mainly of a "bell-joint" and of two parallel cylindrical tubes over which a third U-shaped tube is drawn. The latter tube—the "slide"—moves up and down the two fixed "legs" of the instrument and, in doing so, alters the length of the vibrating air-column, that is to say, the pitch of its Harmonic Series. In the "1st position," when the slide is held close up so that the air-column is at its shortest, the player can produce the usual Harmonic Series from the fundamental note B♭:

In addition, he can draw the slide down by increasingly large steps, and so can produce six other Harmonic Series from six other fundamental notes. The whole set of seven fundamental notes or positions is then as follows:

and on each of these notes the player can build a Harmonic Series similar to that which was set out above.[1]

In other words, the slide-mechanism gives the player not only a chromatic compass of two octaves upwards from the first fundamental note B♭, but also a *compass-extension* downwards of a diminished fifth. The instrument is built in B♭ and the *compass-extension* is

The student should fix this extension in his mind, as it gives the downward *compass-extension* of practically all modern Brass Instruments.

Now, with the Horn and Trumpet there was no idea of substituting

[1] See pages 134-5 for the "pedal-notes" of the instrument.

a slide mechanism for the crooks. There was, however, an idea, which is now an accomplished fact, of substituting some other mechanism which would give these instruments a purely chromatic compass and incidentally extend that compass downwards a diminished fifth.

The idea, as it gradually took shape, was to adopt a tube of standard length and then to substitute for the crooks additional lengths of tubing welded into the body of the instrument. These additional lengths were to be controlled by a sort of mechanical stop-cocks or valves which would switch the air-current on and off at the discretion of the player.

At first glance this may seem to be a very simple problem, and the student may wonder how it is that only now, after a hundred years of experiment, is the solution at all satisfactory. It is not, however, quite as easy as it looks. In the first place, one scarcely needs to point out that the problem could not be solved by the naïve method of merely placing a dozen crooks and a dozen controlling valves on the instrument. Experiments in this direction were actually made in those early days. Some went so far as to weld together a whole bunch of Horns, bells and all. This type of experiment, in which the underlying idea was to keep the various lengths of tubing associated with each fundamental note absolutely independent, has been resumed in our own day and carried to some success.[1] A hundred years ago, however, it was beyond the reach of any European manufacturer. The complications that resulted in practice were sufficient to put it quite out of the question. The only feasible plan appeared to be this—to weld into the instrument a series of tube-lengths controlled by three valves; to use tube-lengths of such a size that their air-columns, when joined successively and separately to the main air-column, would lower the pitch by a ½ tone, 1 tone, and 1½ tones; and finally, to provide a system of intercommunication between the tube-lengths, so that any combination of them might be thrown into the main air-column.

All this may seem to be only an elementary matter, but there was an inherent difficulty connected with the intercommunication of the valves. Let us state it in broadest outline. Suppose you have a 10-foot tube to produce a given fundamental note and its Harmonic Series. Suppose, again, that you introduce an additional 1 foot of tube which can be switched on by your ½-tone valve, so as to produce the fundamental note and Harmonic Series of one semitone below the pitch of your original fundamental note and produce it *in tune.* What lengths of tube are you to select for your 1-tone and your 1½-tone valves? Are they to bear the correct relative lengths to your original 10-foot tube or to your combined 10+1-foot tube? Whichever you choose, you will get an out-of-tune fundamental note and Harmonic Series for the one which you do not choose. In other words, the problem is to secure truth of intonation when your valves (or pistons) are used in combination.

This is really the one great difficulty which has engaged the

[1] See the description of the Modern Independent-Cylinder Trombone on pages 143-6.

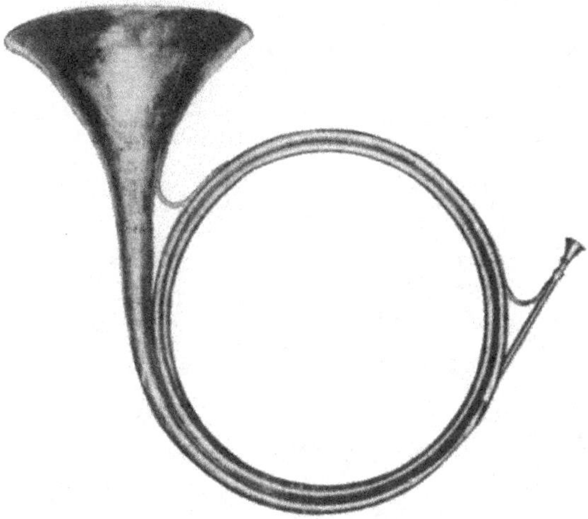

FIG. 1.—HUNTING-HORN.

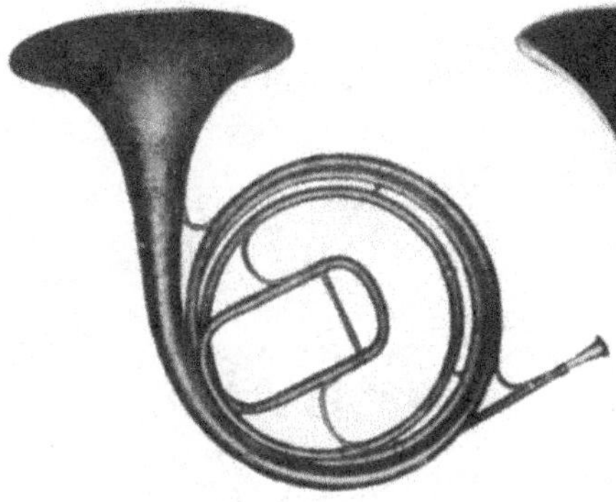

FIG. 2.—HAND-HORN.

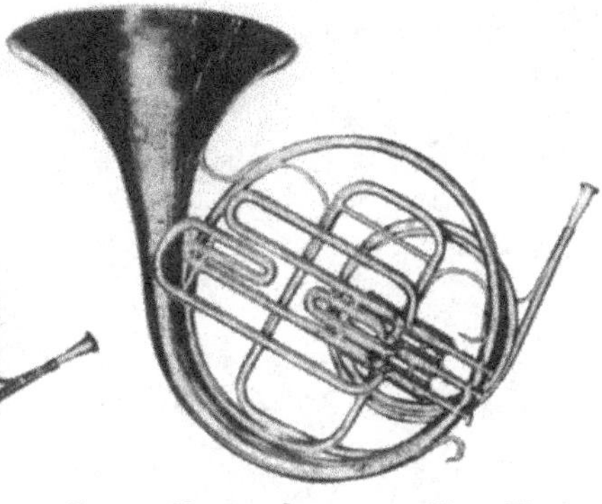

FIG 3.—MODERN ORCHESTRAL VALVE-HORN.

By kind permission of Messrs. Boosey & Co.

attention of manufacturers since the valve system became an artistic possibility. It is impossible even to hint at the many attempts which have been made to solve it. It is sufficient to say that there are now many systems of what are called "compensating pistons," that is to say, of pistons which mechanically correct the error in piston combinations.

The best-known of these are the Boosey *Automatic* invented by Mr. D. J. Blaikley; the Sax *Six-valve Independent* system,[1] which gives a separate length of tube to each descending fundamental; the Besson *Registre*, *Transpositeur*, and *Enharmonic* systems; and the *Rudall-Carte-Klussmann* system, which gives the Horn a conical bore throughout the additional lengths as well as through the original body of the tubing. Any of these systems can be and are applied to the Horn and Trumpet of to-day. Nor do they forbid us still to use the old crooks. However, the integral part of the Horn- and Trumpet-mechanisms of to-day is not the crook, but the series of additional brass tubes controlled by three valves, of which the 1st, 2nd, and 3rd are invariably so arranged that when used separately they lower the pitch of the instrument 1 tone, ½ tone, and 1½ tones. The 1st valve is the whole-tone valve, the 2nd is the half-tone, and the third is the tone-and-a-half.[2]

The three stages in the evolution of the Horn after it became a coiled-instrument are illustrated on Plate III. Fig. 1 is an old French Hunting Horn (cor de chasse) by François Perinet. It is, of course, capable of producing only a single Harmonic Series. Fig. 2 is a Hand-Horn of the type common in the last half of the 18th and the first half of the 19th centuries. The special instrument here photographed was made by Distin for Eugène Léon Vivier, the celebrated Horn-player. He seems to have preferred playing on a Horn-in-E, and that is the key in which this instrument is built. The only mechanism attached is an oblong tuning-slide. Another E-Horn which belonged to Vivier is preserved in Paris. This is the instrument on which he performed before Louis Philippe at the Château d'Eu. Fig. 3 is a modern orchestral Horn crooked in F and furnished with three Automatic Compensating Valves. This instrument is by Messrs. Boosey & Co. In all three illustrations the student will have no difficulty in noting the funnel-shaped mouthpieces.

The modern valve-Trumpets and valve-Horns will be more par-

[1] This system is not applied to what are called the "whole-tube" instruments (see below, page 86). It is probably the nearest *theoretical* approach to the old "crook" system.

[2] Widor states that in France instrument-makers are producing a Horn in which one piston is so modified as to *raise* the pitch a whole tone. In doing this they are compelled to sacrifice one note of the compass altogether:

which sounds on the F-Horn:

ticularly described under their respective headings. Meanwhile we must notice an important discovery which was made during the perfecting of the valve-system. If the student will refer back to page 73 he will see it stated there that neither the Horns nor the Trumpets could produce the 1st note of the Harmonic Series, the deep C or fundamental tone.[1] A Horn, therefore, giving the 8-ft. C of an open 8-ft. organ-pipe had to be 16 ft. long. Half its length was practically useless. This was a well understood fact. However, during the course of the experiments in the application of valves to conical-bore instruments (such as the Horn) it was found that if the calibre of the tube was sufficiently enlarged in proportion to its length, and if a cup-shaped mouthpiece was substituted for one of funnel-shape, the instrument could be relied on to give its fundamental note in all normal circumstances.

The knowledge of this simple fact opened a new era. The Valve-Brass became divisible, according to the German classification, into "half-tube" and "whole-tube" instruments: that is to say, into instruments of comparatively narrow bore, in which the fundamental note was unobtainable, and instruments of wide bore, in which the fundamental note was obtainable.

This is the true distinction between the Saxhorn[2]-Flügelhorn-Trumpet-Horn group and the Tuba group. In the former the lowest open note which the player can produce is the 2nd note of the Harmonic Series. Downwards from that he can do, by means of his three valves, exactly what the Trombone-player can do by means of his seven positions, namely shift his fundamental note semitone by semitone till he arrives at a note which is a diminished fifth below his original fundamental note. And there he stops.

As an example, the lowest open note of the Cornet is its 2nd Harmonic[3]

The additional notes obtained by means of the three valves are

On the other hand, with the true Tuba, whether it is called a

[1] Exceptional Horn-players could and actually can touch this note, even on the F-crook. But for all practical purposes it is useless. A mere grunt. The *sound* on the F-crook would be

[2] More strictly "High Saxhorn." The four upper instruments of the Saxhorn family are "half-tube" instruments, while the three lower are "whole-tube" instruments (see page 164).

[3] Of course, if the Cornet is *crooked* in B♭ this open note and the other six semitones will all *sound* one tone lower; if it is *crooked* in A they will all sound 1½ tones lower.

"Euphonium," an "E♭ Bass," or a "BB♭ Bass," the player can drop from the second Harmonic, whatever it may be, plump down to his fundamental note. It is a mere matter of external furniture as to whether he can fill in the semitones between these two notes. If he has only three valves he can proceed chromatically down through a diminished fifth, and must then skip to his fundamental note. If, on the other hand, he is provided with a 4th valve, lowering the pitch 2½ tones, he is able to fill in these five semitones and so make a complete chromatic descent to his fundamental note. Always provided he has the "lip" to do it.

For instance, the "E♭ Bass"— a four-valve military instrument—can begin from the 2nd note of its Harmonic Series

and proceed downwards by means of its three valves through the following semitones:

Without a 4th valve the player would have to stop there. All he could do would be to take off all his valves and jump to his deep fundamental note

However, by means of his 4th valve he can fill in these intervening semitones:

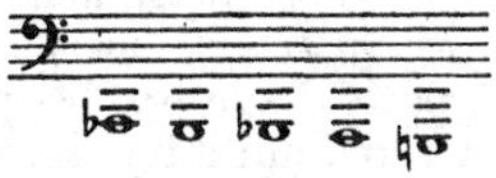

He then takes off all four valves and, with a clear bore, produces the deep fundamental given above.

For the sake of completeness a list of valves and valve-combinations is subjoined. This list shows the alterations in pitch which they effect in any valved Brass Instrument. It is complete as far as the ordinary three-valve system goes. The four-, and even five-valve systems can easily be worked out on the same pattern.

1-semitone-valve - - - -	lowers the pitch ½ tone,
2-semitones-valve - - - -	„ „ „ 1 tone,
3-semitones-valve (or 2-semitones-valve + 1-semitone-valve in combination)	„ „ „ 1½ tones,
3-semitones-valve + 1-semitone-valve in combination - - - -	„ „ „ 2 tones,
3-semitones-valve + 2-semitones-valve in combination - - - -	„ „ „ 2½ tones,
3-semitones-valve + 2-semitones-valve + 1-semitone-valve in combination	„ „ „ 3 tones.

A few words must now be said with regard to the nomenclature of this nineteenth-century invention, the valved whole-tube Brass family. This is a matter of some little difficulty. For, unfortunately, as it gradually became known that a new species of chromatic Brass Instrument was available, and as the growing military system of Europe developed an increased demand for military bands, competitive instrument-makers all over the Continent began a vast manufacture of valved instruments, which were only partially warned off our shores by our musical *Undesirable Aliens Act*,—the difference of pitch.

Simple instruments that should have been standardized under a single name received a dozen different titles in as many countries. Sometimes the name was adopted or modified from that of an earlier instrument: sometimes a purely "fancy"—and often foolish—name was invented: sometimes the instrument was christened after its god-father, the manufacturer. Even such simple words as *alto*, *tenor*, and *bass* were applied with various meanings in various countries.[1]

Hence comes great confusion for the mind of the orchestral student. He knows that when he writes a fiddle part it will be played on a fiddle in Rome, in Dresden, or in London; but he learns with dismay that the instrument which he familiarly calls a "Tuba" is not so called even in the military bands of his own country, and that his "Tuba" part, if it ever travels outside his own study, may possibly be played on a *Pelittone*, a *Bombardon*, a *Flicorno Basso*, or a *Contrabass-Saxhorn*.

In order to throw some light on these dismal obscurities, one may remind the student (1) that though it was Richard Wagner who first installed "the Tuba" in the orchestra, neither his first idea nor its technical expression has ever found general acceptance; (2) that the development of these whole-tube instruments has everywhere been chiefly a development *for military purposes*, and that therefore, wherever deep "Tuba" parts have to be played, the instruments requisitioned are the perfected military instruments either slightly modified in pitch[2] or quite unaltered.

The plan adopted in the following pages will be this: The student will find described and named under the various headings the Brass Instruments as they actually exist and are used to-day in our concert-rooms and theatres. These are often not quite the same instruments as those that existed yesterday, nor the same as those in use abroad. They correspond, however, in a general way to both these groups, and the differences can easily be made plain in the course of each description.

The following simple arrangement of the Brass-Wind is based solely on mechanical differences of method in altering the length of the vibrating air-column. Whatever these mechanical differences, all the instruments named depend for their tone-production only on the

[1] See foot-note to page 163, and page 165.

[2] That is to say, built in a key near to that of the military pattern, but more convenient for orchestral music that does not cling to the flat keys. Of course, besides that, there has to be a second modification in England, owing to the fact that we are still the unfortunate possessors of two pitches, the *high* and the *low*.

notes of the Harmonic Series given above. The names of Obsolete Instruments are given in square brackets after each group.

(1) Tubes in which the length of the air-column is fixed; tubes, therefore, which can only produce one Harmonic Series at a time: the **Natural Horn**, the **Natural Trumpet**, and the **Military Bugle**. Of these the first is practically disused and the second is only used for "duty" purposes in cavalry regiments. [Obsolete: the whole series of ancient military instruments such as the Roman *Buccina*, *Lituus*, *Cornu*, and *Tuba*.[1]]

(2) Tubes in which the length of the air-column is varied by means of holes pierced in the side.[2] [Obsolete in this country: the *Bass-Horn*, the *Russian Bassoon*, the *Keyed-Bugle*, and its bass the *Ophicleide*.]

(3) Tubes in which the length of the air-column is varied by means of valves or pistons:[3] (A) Half-tube instruments: **Valve Trumpets**, **Valve Horns**, **Cornets**, and, rarely used, the four upper **Sax-horns**. (Used in military bands either here or abroad: *Valve Trombones*, *Flügelhorns*, *Tenor-Cors*.) (B) Whole-tube instruments, used regularly in our military bands: the *B♭ Euphonium*, the *E♭ Brass-Bass*, the *BB♭ Brass-Bass*. The last two instruments are also called by the generic name of *Bombardons*. All these three whole-tube instruments figure in a modified form in concert and operatic performances. The *B♭ Euphonium* and the *BB♭ Brass-Bass* appear only rarely as **Tenor-Tuba** and **Contrabass-Tuba**. The *E♭ Brass-Bass* is used constantly in the orchestra. It is as a rule built in the key of F[4] and furnished with four valves. This is the usual instrument on which ordinary orchestral "Tuba" parts are played, in fact the instrument known to civilian composers as the **Bass-Tuba**.

(4) Tubes in which the length of the air-column is varied by means of slides: the **Tenor** and **Bass Trombones**, and, rarely used, the **Contra-bass Trombone**. [Obsolete: the *Alto Trombone*, the *Sackbut*.]

Of the above four groups, the Horns (natural, valve, and tenor) and the "Wagner Tubas" as originally designed are all played with funnel-shaped mouthpieces.

All other Brass-Wind instruments are played with cup-shaped mouthpieces. Exception, the *Bugle*, a hybrid which plays with a mixed cup-and-funnel mouthpiece.

No. 17. The Valve-Trumpet.

Fr. *Trompette à pistons*; It. *Tromba ventile*; Ger. *Ventiltrompete.*

This instrument has replaced the old natural Trumpet. Its bore is mainly narrow and cylindrical. The "bell-joint," however, which

[1] No connection with the modern Tuba.

[2] The hybrid Saxophones and Sarrusophones belong to this group. See pages 166, 170.

[3] The Modified Horns (commonly called Wagner-Tubas) as originally planned belong to this group. See page 151.

[4] Sometimes in C. In this case it is pitched a minor seventh below the Euphonium, *q.v.*

forms something under a quarter of its entire length, is conical. It is furnished with tuning-slides, and has the usual set of three valves described above. The mouthpiece is a hemispherical cup with a rim. In this, as in all other Brass-Wind instruments, the player's lips stretch across the mouthpiece and act as vibrating-reeds. A difference in the tension of the lips, commonly called the *embouchure*, and in the pressure of the breath, serves to produce the various notes of the Harmonic Series.

The material of the Trumpet's tube appears to have no effect whatever on its brilliant incisive quality. This, as far as is known, seems to be due (1) to the exact shape given to the basin of the cup-mouthpiece, and, more especially, to the exact placing of the hole which is bored at the bottom of the cup. The sharper the angle of entry, the more pungent and steely the tone.[1] (2) To the proportion between the bore (or calibre) of the tube and the length of the air-column.

Both the Trumpet and the Horn, though now valve instruments, are played with a crook of some sort. In the case of the Horn the F-crook has supplanted all the others. On the other hand, there is no such uniformity with regard to the Trumpet. In our own orchestras a few players use the F-Trumpet, while the majority use a Trumpet crooked either in C, B♭, or A. The transpositions of all these instruments of course remain the same as they were in the days of the old Natural Trumpet. See page 78 for the full list.

Before we proceed to describe the modern Valve Trumpet in F, the student may be reminded that the ancient Natural Trumpet with its apparatus of crooks is really a totally different instrument from the tiny modern Trumpet in C, B♭, or A. More will be said on this point later. The student should, however, fix firmly in his mind the fact that these differences are not simply differences of external mechanism. The mere addition of the valve apparatus would make no great difference to the instrument, provided the length and bore of tube were roughly maintained. This can be seen in the case of the Horn. With the Trumpet, however, the continual desire for a bright and at the same time less obtrusive tone-colour, and the call for greater flexibility and ease of execution, especially in the top octave, have caused a complete change in the length and bore of the tube itself. It is not merely that the instrument has become chromatic. It has also become, except in name, a different instrument.

The old Natural Trumpet was first employed experimentally by Monteverde. He wrote for five Trumpets—under the names *Clarino*, *Quinto*, *Alto e Basso*, *Vulgano*, *Basso*—in his Opera *Orfeo* (1607). The experiment was not successful. During the greater part of the seventeenth century the Operatic Orchestra consisted mainly of

[1] See the *Encyc. Britt.*, xi. Ed., sub *Trumpet*, for an interesting account of the effect produced by using a shallow "*clarino*" mouthpiece in which the "passage at the bottom of the cup inaugurated by the sharp angle (known as the *grain* in French) is prolonged in *cylindrical* instead of conical bore for a distance of about 10 cm. (4 inches) right into the main tube." This may, perhaps, help to explain the method that was adopted in Bach's day for attacking and overcoming the difficulties of his high Trumpet parts.

Harpsichord and Strings. In the last quarter of the century, however, the Wind began to reappear, and the Trumpet was the first instrument to "make good" under the new régime.[1]

From that time onwards for about a century the instrument was continually employed, chiefly as a Solo instrument, to play all sorts of *bravura* passages, principally in its top register. For this purpose only two crooks were used by Händel and Bach, those in C and D.

About the middle of the eighteenth century something happened to the Trumpet. Nobody knows exactly what it was. Gevaert says: "About 1750 the brilliant technique of the Trumpet suddenly declined; performers lost the habit of playing in the higher octave, the only one which has a continuous scale, and that is, therefore, able to furnish *cantilenas* and melodic figures." It is much more likely that the growing discrimination in matters of orchestral taste developed a horror in the minds of composers for these terrible vocal caricatures. They ceased to write them, and the players therefore lost whatever power they ever had of playing them. It was probably never very great.[2]

The Trumpet now became a much more subservient instrument. It was used much less frequently and much less prominently. It was "warned off" the obbligato ground altogether, and dethroned from the ridiculously false orchestral position which it had hitherto occupied. This was all to the good in the cause of music. Indeed one may say that without this step the development of the Symphony would have been an impossibility. So long as the Trumpet—the most aggressive of all instruments—was allowed to play tunes in its top octave all pleasure in the orchestral ensemble disappeared as far as the unhappy audience was concerned.

New crooks now began to be added. Mozart employed the E♭ as well as the C and D. The B♭, F, and E♮ came next. Later still came the B♮ and A. The instrument thus crooked was employed by all the great Classical Masters, and continued in general use down to the middle of the nineteenth century. Two Trumpets were regularly used in Symphonic music, but in Operatic and even Choral works three and four were quite common.[3]

We may mention in passing that, from time to time, attempts have been made to adapt the slide-mechanism[4] of the Trombone to the Trumpet. In the earliest specimens thus made the instrument was provided with a spring which automatically threw the slide back into its original or "home" position. The spring was soon abandoned as a useless encumbrance, and the slide-Trumpet began to enjoy a somewhat precarious popularity. Outside England, however, it never

[1] In *Eteocle e Polinice*, by Legrenzi (1675). See Gevaert, page 229. Down to about the middle of the 18th century the words *Clarino* and *Principale* were used for the upper and lower Trumpet parts respectively.

[2] But see what is said below, page 120 (foot-note 2).

[3] Haydn, *The Seasons* (three Trumpets in C); Weber, *Euryanthe* and *Oberon* (four Trumpets in D); Mendelssohn, *Midsummer Night's Dream* (three Trumpets in C).

[4] The slide-Trumpet of Bach (*tromba di tirarsi*) was simply a Soprano-Trombone, the successor of the old Treble-Sackbut.

became a recognized instrument, and whatever success it had here was effectually cut short by the advent of the valve-system. Recently some further attempts have been made to reintroduce the slide-Trumpet. These have never been successful, though the instrument is said to have a fine crisp tone.

By 1850 the valve mechanism had been sufficiently tested to enable it to assert its undoubted superiority. A few composers continued to write for the old Natural Trumpet, more as a "platonic kind of protestation"[1] than from any candid examination of the new instrument's capabilities. However, the days of the Natural Instrument were numbered. The most able composers frankly recognized the enormous advantages of the valve system, and the Natural Trumpet now finds itself where it started a great many centuries ago, doing duty in camps and barracks, on the field and the parade-ground.

The Valve-Trumpet in F[2] is in size and build the only representative we now have of the old family of Trumpets, and its tone-quality differs materially from that of the Trumpets in C, B♭, and A.

Theoretically its natural series of Harmonics should range from

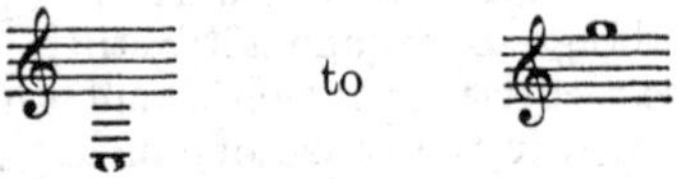

both sounding a perfect fourth higher. Its valve mechanism gives it a complete chromatic compass within these limits, but the four lowest semitones are practically useless. This leaves the instrument with a chromatic compass from

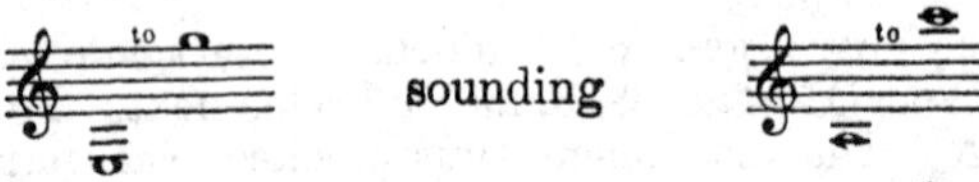

The upper notes above written E, especially the F♯ (sounding B♮), require great certainty of lip, and cannot be taken in anything but the *f*. On the other hand, their effect is as striking as anything in the orchestra.

EXAMPLE 35.[3]

Wagner. *Parsifal.*

Valve Trumpet in F.

In writing for this instrument one cannot be too careful. Indeed the *tessitura* must be as well considered as that of a Soprano voice. Its notes, as they ascend from

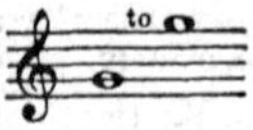

[1] Gevaert. [2] Used in the army in the key of E♭.

[3] In the Full Score there are three Oboes and the 2nd division of the 1st and 2nd Violins in unison with the Trumpet melody.

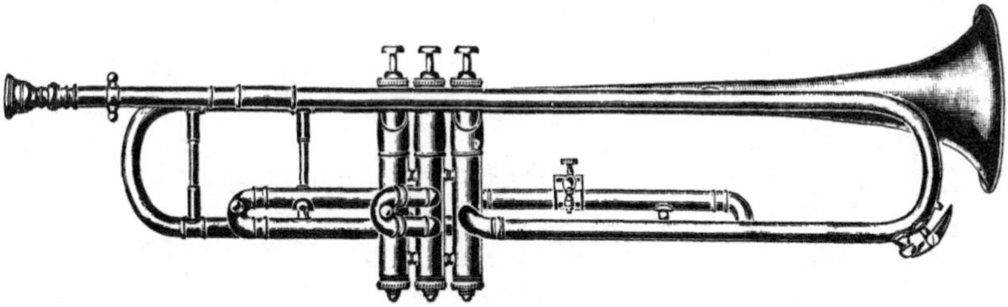

FIG. 1.—VALVE TRUMPET IN F.

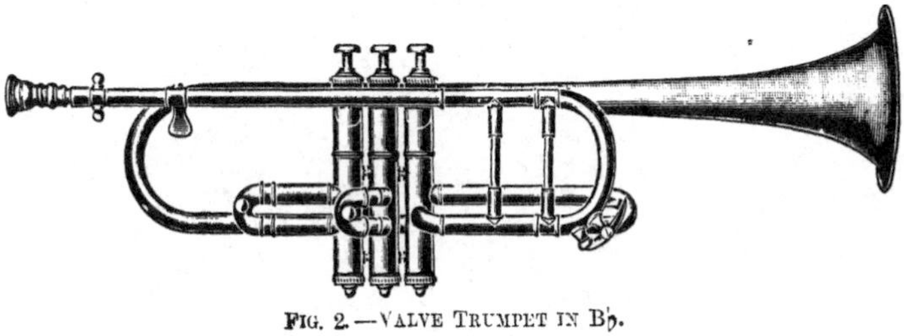

FIG. 2.—VALVE TRUMPET IN B♭.

FIG. 3.—CORNET IN B♭.

By kind permission of Messrs. Boosey & Co.

have an alarming way of detaching themselves more and more from the rest of the orchestra.[1] The best part of its compass is from

An illustration of the instrument will be found on Plate IV.

The F-Trumpet has been alternately praised for its noble and powerful tone and reviled as a "razor-edged antique" and "an out-door instrument borrowed from the military band."[2] One must acknowledge that in actual breadth of tone-colour, especially in its lower notes and in the *p*, it is without a rival. No one who has heard two of these instruments enter *pp* at the 346th bar of Beethoven's *Violin Concerto* can have any doubt on this point.

EXAMPLE 36.

Magical passages like this lose half their intention when played on the small-bore instrument.

It is, however, rather in the *f* and the *ff* that one feels its undoubted brilliance and force to be something of a survival from the days when it was not thought necessary to assimilate the various tone-qualities of the orchestra. Even in the most unimportant passages it appears to be always playing Solos. A certain inflexibility too, due perhaps to the size of its tube, gives the audience additional cause for anxiety.

In the old days its main business was to reiterate single notes *f* and to blare out somewhat conventional flourishes and fanfares "in the *tutti*." On these points there was never any charge against it on the score of ineffectiveness. On the contrary, the objection was then, and is now, that to all its phrases it lends a prominence that sometimes induces almost a sense of physical pain. We must remember too that the difficulties of mastering the instrument are great. It is the undoubted heir of the classical tradition, but our regret at its restricted use is tempered by the reflection that at most one or two players in a generation can make it bearable.

The reasonable view to take on this vexed question seems to be that where the music has been specially designed for this instrument—as it was by the classical masters—it should undoubtedly be called on to perform the parts as written. The heavy cast-iron

[1] The student is reminded that, in speaking of the transposing instruments, one always understands the *written* note without further explanation. This must be borne in mind throughout the following pages.

[2] There seems to be no doubt that the modern Valve-Trumpet in F is heavier and more cumbersome in tone than the old Natural Trumpet. This is said to be due not to the valve mechanism, but to the altered proportions of its tube and mouthpiece.

trumpet parts of ancient days require a massive unyielding tone-colour. Mere weight was nine times out of ten the object of their existence. Played on the puny modern Trumpet in C they sound stupid, undignified, and trivial. On the other hand, in modern music, where the Trumpet-part is woven more cunningly into the tissue of the music, and where a certain flexibility and power of blending are essential, the older instrument might well be dispensed with. Better still, perhaps it might be confined to a single Solo part written so as to turn its qualities to good account.

Very little can be said as to the uses of this instrument in the orchestra, for though it is so dazzlingly effective, its gamut of expression is restricted. Its commonest use is to play the upper parts in the Brass ensemble and to add a climax colour in the general scheme of orchestration. It need scarcely be said that any form of cantilena writing is almost insupportable on an instrument with such a pronounced tone-quality. Certain tunes, however, which appeal either by their imposing and pompous character or by a sort of simple, dignified, direct vigour, come out well enough. Every one who has heard César Franck's *Symphony in D minor* will remember the Trumpet tune in the first Movement. The English Horn here plays with the F-Trumpets, and they are reinforced in the octave above by a brilliant unison of Flutes, Oboes, Clarinets, and 1st and 2nd Violins. A two-part quaver accompaniment for Violas and Cellos, held chords for the Horns, and detached chords for Cornets, Trombones, and Tuba complete the score. The tune with its introductory bars is as follows:

EXAMPLE 37.

César Franck. *Symphony in D minor.*

Another passage to which the Trumpet octaves lend a peculiarly poignant colour can be found just before the 2nd Act curtain in *Tristan.*

EXAMPLE 38.

Wagner. *Tristan und Isolde.*

[1] The mark "à 2" (Italian *à due*, *i.e.* in the manner of two) has two precisely opposite meanings in orchestral scores. When placed over a Wood-Wind or Brass-stave, which is usually devoted to two separate parts, it means that both players are to perform the same part in unison; on the other hand, when placed over a String-stave, which is usually devoted to one single part, it means that the players are to divide and perform the separate parts as written on the stave. The tendency is to confine the expression "à 2" to the Wind-staves and to use the words *divisi* and *unisoni* (abbreviated to *div.* and *unis.*) for the Strings. The Germans usually indicate the String *divisi* when of more than two parts by the words *Dreifach*, *Vierfach*, etc.

The modern instrument which has taken or is taking the place of the old big-bore instrument is still called a Trumpet. It still remains the highest pitched instrument of the Brass ensemble. But beyond that there is not much musical likeness between the two instruments. It seems a pity that a little of the enormous expenditure of energy in nineteenth century Brass-nomenclature was not devoted to coining a name which should clearly differentiate the new from the old instrument. For they are really not the same instrument at all. The student will be able to appreciate this statement when he is told that the Trumpet for which Beethoven wrote the five notes quoted above was 7 feet 8⅛ inches in length, while a modern Trumpet in the same key would measure 3 feet 5¼ inches.

The crooks used for the modern instrument are three. They are

(1) **Crook in C**, which sounds as written,

(2) **Crook in B♭**,[1] which sounds one whole tone *below* the written notes, and which must therefore be written for in the key of one whole tone *above* the music. Its key-signature has two ♭'s less or two ♯'s more than the key-signature of the piece.

(3) **Crook in A**, which sounds one tone and a half *below* the written notes, and which must therefore be written for in the key of one tone and a half *above* that of the music. Its key-signature has three ♭'s more or three ♯'s less than the key-signature of the piece.

This instrument, whatever its crook, has as its bottom open note the 2nd of the Harmonic Series which, with its length of tube, is

Upwards from that it can proceed to the 8th Harmonic

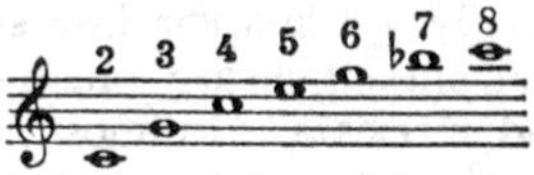

while downwards its three valves take it, as usual, a diminished fifth to low F♯

and also give it a continuous chromatic compass up to the high C. The complete compass therefore is

[1] For an illustration of the Trumpet in B♭, see Plate IV., page 92.

and this compass, on the three crooks mentioned above, sounds

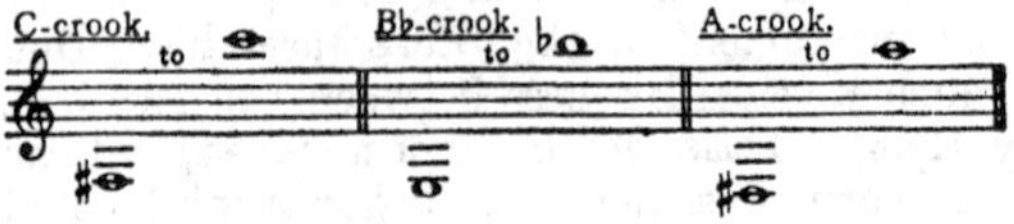

The question now arises: which crook is to be written for? And as precisely the same question arises in the case of some other transposing instruments, a few words may be said on the topic.

In some German, English, and French orchestras—especially in the last—the C-Trumpet alone is used. It does not, however, follow that it is always written for, though the practice is common in France. If it is written for it must, of course, be treated as a non-transposing instrument like the Oboe or Violin. That is to say, the actual sounds required are written in the actual key-signature of the piece. For symphonic work and for work of a chromatic character this plan, which has the advantage of great simplicity, is excellent.

In Operatic work, however, and especially in Comic Opera in this country, players invariably use the B♭- and A-crooks. A non-transposing part would therefore throw on the player the burden of transposition during performance. It is better to avoid this and to choose the crook which will give the player the fewer sharps or flats in the key-signature.

In a key such as E one would naturally write for A-Trumpets in the key of G, not for B♭ Trumpets in the key of F♯.

In a key such as A♭ one would write for B♭-Trumpets in the key of B♭ not for A-Trumpets in the key of C♭. This is only elementary prudence.

Note, however, that it is not worth while changing the crook for a short passage even if it gives a simpler key-signature. Nor is there much difference between one signature and another unless the part is exceptionally quick and intricate. In most cases the player ignores an interpolated change of crook and transposes the part to suit the crook which he has been using. The whole of this question is discussed in full under the heading Cornet, page 103. The student who wishes detailed information on the subject should read the remarks given there.

The student must be warned that, in going through Full Scores, he will continually find a quite different method of writing adopted for the Trumpets and, be it said, for the Horns. This method is to leave the player out of account altogether: to pretend that he is still furnished, as he was in the eighteenth century, with crooks A, B♭, C, D, E♭, E♮, and F: to crook the Trumpets as nearly as possible in the key of the piece: and then to write for him in the key of C. At a change of key in the music the name of a new crook is inserted in the part whether there is time to change it or not. The part proceeds merrily in C as before.

This plan has the high authority of Strauss,[1] and he supports it with four bad reasons. They are

(1) Force of habit.

(2) The Score is easier to read if the Horns and Trumpets are all in C. Their parts detach themselves with a sort of plasticity from the Wood-Wind and String-parts, littered as the two last are with accidentals.

(3) If the composer has sufficient orchestral technique and a sense of tone-colour it does not matter much what key he uses for his Trumpet-parts.

(4) Horn players prefer transposing according to the key of their instrument to reading from a proper F-Horn part full of sharps, flats and so on.

The interest of the first two reasons lies in the fact that they totally ignore the persons most concerned in the matter—the players. Clever as these artists undoubtedly are at transposition, this is surely a burden that should be laid if possible upon the composer in the quiet of his study, not on the player during rehearsal or performance. The fourth reason is curiously unconvincing, for, however much a Horn-player may dislike looking at the nasty sharps and flats, *he has got to play them*, and, with his F-Horn in his hands, he has not only got to play them but first to transpose into them from the simple key in which his part is written.

Gevaert has pointed out how dire would be the result if the player were actually *to take the composer at his word* and use the crooks which he directs. "A crook," he says, "only modifies the length of the main tube, but in no way affects the additional tubes, whose length is calculated for a given pitch. Hence it is evident that the fitting-on of a higher or lower crook upsets the whole tuning of the instrument. True, each additional tube is provided with a little tuning slide, which allows of increasing the length of the air-column to a certain extent, but apart from the fact that such modifications suffice at most to regulate the tuning of a small number of crooks only, they require an accuracy of manipulation which cannot practically be obtained in the orchestra." He adds in a foot-note, "Wagner never takes this practical need into account: he constantly changes the tuning of the Valve-Horns."[2] It is not even certain, as some

[1] In his *Commentaries and Additions* to Berlioz's *Orchestration*. The author commends this method of writing as the "Wagnerian procedure," but no one who has ever spent ten minutes in finding out Wagner's views on the matter, or in reading his Horn, Trumpet, and Tuba parts can doubt that he is the worst possible guide to follow in matters of notation. There is more than one locus classicus of absurdity to be found in his Operas and, even when he gives as his reason for writing 2 B♭-Tubas in E♭ and 2 F-Tubas in B♭ "ease of score-reading," the explanation seems, as Strauss himself suggests, only to add to the mystery. As a fact, Wagner never fairly faced the question of key-signature for his Brass. He was at times quite capable of writing *God Save the King* like this

Trumpet.

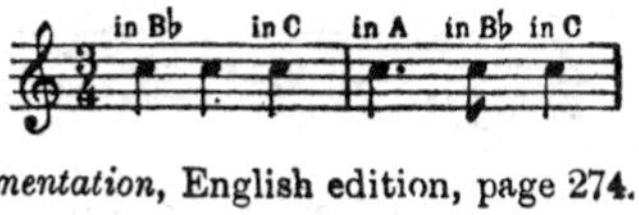

[2] *A New Treatise on Instrumentation*, English edition, page 274.

suppose, that Wagner was always guided in these matters by the desire to employ only those crooks most suitable to the music. There are plenty of examples in his works of actual unison melodies performed by similar instruments playing on different crooks. When one finds a passage in which the Strings are playing "in one sharp" and the Trumpets are crooked Nos. 1 and 2 in E, No. 3 in C and the Bass Trumpet in D...... !

These questions will be alluded to later when we come to deal with the standardization of the Horn. Meanwhile the student may be advised frankly to recognize the fact that players actually play nowadays either on a non-transposing instrument in C or on a transposing instrument furnished with both B♭- and A-crooks. His part will be written with its proper key-signature.[1]

The modern small Trumpet substitutes execution and flexibility for the imposing tone-colour of its predecessor. All sort of figures, arpeggios, and scales diatonic and chromatic can be played with astonishing ease and lightness. Repeated notes are both practicable and effective, but it is well to place them in the middle register of the instrument and to break them up in order to give the player time to breathe. Nothing sounds worse than a series of repeated notes during which the performer has to gasp for breath.

Single-, double-, and triple-tonguing—that is to say the interruption of the wind-stream by the action of the tongue—are all possible even in quick tempos.

The player when single-tonguing *strikes* the note by tonguing on it the letter T, thus

In double-tonguing he makes use of the two letters T-K

while, in triple-tonguing he employs the letters T-K-T

By this method a surprising degree of consonantal distinction is given to the attack.

The Trumpet, unlike the Horn, plays shakes with the pistons only. Good whole-tone shakes are to be had on the following notes:

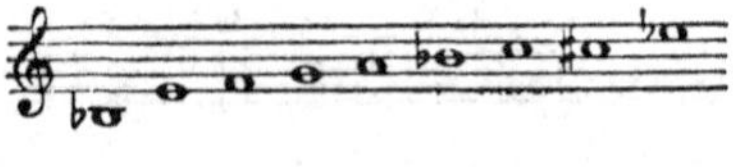

[1] See foot-note on page 105.

and good half-tone shakes on these:

but in general, one may say that shakes are not for Brass Instruments.

There is a curious passage in the last Act of *Götterdämmerung* (full score, page 432), where the ear seems to expect the Trumpet shake on the high G. The shake, however, is actually only superimposed on the Trumpet tone. At the moment when the two Oboes and two Clarinets begin their shake the ear is partially deceived and appears to hear a soft Trumpet-shake. The following is the passage from which the Harp- and String-parts have been omitted.

EXAMPLE 39.

The shortness of the modern Trumpet tube and its comparative smallness of bore combine to give the player an undoubted certainty of grasp over its entire compass. The student is, however, reminded that its extreme notes are not satisfactory. Below

they are uninteresting and lack substance. This is of little consequence, as they can always be adequately replaced by the Trombones and Horns. On the other hand from

they become rather attenuated and "tinny" and, in this octave, there is no other Brass instrument to take their place. It is a good rule never to take them below low C and only for special purposes above high G. A fine example of three Trumpets playing in harmony at the top of their compass is to be found in Strauss's *Ein Heldenleben.* A note in the Full Score directs them to play "Hinter der Scene" and the only other instruments are the 1st Violins, Violas, and Cellos holding an octave B♭ *pp.*

EXAMPLE 40.

A word must be said here with regard to the *Trumpet Mute.* This is a sort of pear-shaped stopper so constructed as not to alter the pitch of the instrument. It is fitted into the "bell" and its effect, when the player blows in the natural manner, is to reduce the tone to a faint echo. On the other hand, by *overblowing,*[1] that is to say by greatly increasing the pressure of the wind-stream, he can disturb and stultify the air waves so as to produce the weird pungent tone-quality which is perhaps a little too familiar to our concert-goers. For these two effects it is only necessary to mark the part *Con sordino p* and *Con sordino f,* adding in the latter case, at discretion, the English equivalent of the French word *cuivré,* "brassy." One may be permitted to mention here that the Trumpet suffers the mute much more gladly than the other brass instruments. In fact it preserves under this indignity an unexpected pliancy and agility. On the other hand, the Horn, perhaps owing to its larger bore and its greater difficulty of intonation, seems to resist partial suffocation. This is to its credit.

Some controversy exists as to the composer who first made use of muted Trumpets in his score. Mozart and Berlioz have both been cited under the First Offenders Act. A recent critic, however, has dug up a queer passage by Scarlatti,[2] in which two muted Trumpets play in thirds at the top of their compass and are answered by two "Trombe Marine"![3] This seems to settle the matter for the present, though of course there is always the possibility of an appeal from the sentence. Whatever the merits of the case, it was Richard Wagner who first found this particular brand of tone-colour where it was lying in

[1] This word *overblowing* is technically used with two different meanings :— (1) As above, the unnatural forcing of a note out of focus by the increased pressure of the wind-stream ; (2) In Wood-Wind instruments the reproduction of the notes forming the lower part of the instrument's compass at a higher part of its compass. This is done by means of increased lip-pressure. For instance, the Oboe is said "to overblow an octave," the Clarinet "to overblow a twelfth." This means that, with the same fingering, the natural scales of these instruments can be reproduced by an alteration of lip-pressure at the distances, respectively, of an octave and a twelfth higher.

[2] In *Mitridate Eupatore,* 1707. See Mr. E. J. Dent's *Alessandro Scarlatti,* page 109.

[3] See page 298.

the dust of the cellar, and brought it upstairs to stimulate the jaded palates of the musical world. The vinegary "tang" of this vintage is well suited to both Mime and Beckmesser.

Since Wagner's day composers have resorted to muted Trumpets on the slightest, or no, provocation. Used with discretion they are capable both in the *f* and the *p* of great effect, but the tone-quality, especially in the *f*, etches itself so deeply into the mind as to become unbearable after a little while.

A striking modern example of the muted Trumpets is to be found in Strauss's *Till Eulenspiegel.* The four-part harmony is arranged for two muted Trumpets and two muted Horns both playing *mf.* Four muted Solo Violins, omitted below, double the four Brass parts and are marked *pp.* They make little difference in performance, but serve to steady, and, so to speak, solidify the Brass harmony. In playing this passage over on the pianoforte the student must not overlook the fact that the transposition of the F-Trumpets is a fourth upwards, that of the F-Horns a fifth downwards.

EXAMPLE 41.

A second and much more elaborate example will be found later under the heading "The Tubas" (Ex. 95). In this quotation (from Strauss's *Don Quixote Variations*) the three Muted Trumpets in D play one of the chief subjects of the work accompanied by Muted Tubas, Oboe, Double-Bassoon and Muted Strings. The student should examine the Trumpet parts of this extract. They give a good idea of the executive capabilities of the modern instrument.

No. 18. The Bass-Trumpet.

Fr. *Trompette Basse*; It. *Tromba Bassa*; Ger. *Basstrompete.*

This Trumpet, as imagined by Richard Wagner for the *Ring,* was to be an instrument of Brobdingnagian length and Brobdingnagian tone-colour, with a compass which extended from the bottom notes of the Tenor Trombone to the topmost notes of the French Horn. The actual notes of the Harmonic Series which it was to employ ranged from the 3rd

to the 19th

It was to be played with three crooks, C, D, and E♭, transposing downwards an octave, a minor seventh, and a major sixth respectively. Its chromatic compass, therefore, with these three crooks was to be

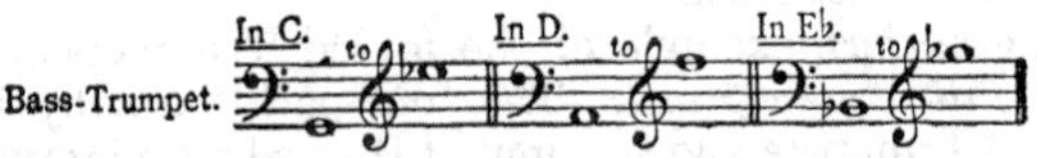

It need not be insisted on that the advantage of having three different crooks on a newly invented valve-instrument was purely a paper advantage. From the player's point of view a single crook would have been infinitely preferable. But over and above this it was found that, with a narrow-bore instrument of such enormous length—viz. 23 ft., nearly the size of a Double-Bass-Trombone—the two lowest Harmonics (Nos. 3 and 4) were poor in quality, while the four top Harmonics (Nos. 16, 17, 18, and 19) were unplayable by human lips.

Wagner's original ideas were therefore thrown overboard, and the Bass-Trumpet was modified into the instrument which we now possess. Its Harmonic Series has been raised an octave, and the player is now asked to produce no Harmonic lower than the 2nd or higher than the 10th

For orchestral use the instrument is built in the key of C-basso only.[1] It has no need of additional crooks. By means of its three valves it has a complete chromatic compass downwards through a diminished fifth to F♯, and upwards to its highest note E.

As in most other Brass Instruments, the extreme notes of its compass upwards and downwards are the most difficult to attack and the least satisfactory to listen to. Its most useful register is therefore from

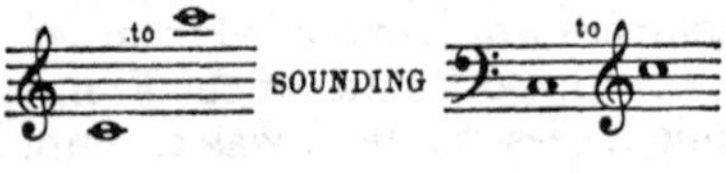

The technique of the instrument is practically the same as that of the standard Trumpet in C, B♭, and A, with this qualification, that its

[1] Bass-Trumpets are also made in B♭ and E♭. These are used in some military bands.

length of tube makes it less facile of execution and much more tiring to the player.

The tube of the Bass-Trumpet is bent into the shape of an ordinary Valve-Trumpet, but apart from that and its name, the instrument is actually a Valve-Trombone half-way in pitch between the Tenor- and the obsolete Alto-Trombone. This is satisfactory enough, as Wagner's parts for the instrument in the *Ring* have exactly the type of melodic outline which suits the Valve-Trombone.

The rarity of its use in this country, of course, militates against its success in performance. However, in the hands of a skilful Trombone player it has an admirable tone, rich and sonorous, both in the *p* and the *f*. Like the other Valve-Trombones, it has considerable powers of *legato* playing.

There is no earthly reason why the Bass-Trumpet should be written for as a *C-basso* instrument an octave above its true pitch. The better way is to write the actual notes in the bass- and treble-clefs at convenience. Being pitched in C, it will, of course, receive the key-signature of the music. For example:

No. 19. The Cornet.

Fr. *Cornet-à-pistons* ; It. *Cornetto* [1] (or *Cornetta*) ; Ger. *Cornett.*

This much-abused instrument is really a military development of the Post-Horn. Its short tube is partly cylindrical and partly conical. The bore is larger than that of the Trumpet, and a cup-shaped mouthpiece is used. The illustration on Plate IV., page 93, gives a good idea of the relative proportions and the general "build" of the B♭-Cornet, the B♭-Trumpet, and the F-Trumpet.

The notes of the Harmonic Series employed are the same as those of the Trumpet in C, viz.:

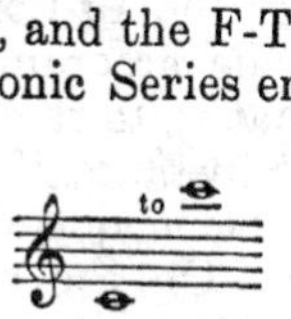

and by means of the three valves the compass is extended chromatically downwards a diminished fifth to low F♯, and made chromatic from that note to top C. The instrument is, however, never played

[1] Not to be confused with the ancient *Cornetto* or *Cornet à bouquin*. See pp. 71-2, 133. The French generally abbreviate the name of the modern Cornet to "*Piston*." With the Italians, on the other hand, the abbreviation "*Pistone*" means the high military *Cornet in E♭*.

in C, but with one of the two crooks B♭ or A. The written chromatic compass, therefore,

sounds, *on the B♭-Cornet,*

and, *on the A-Cornet,*

In quality the difference between the two crooks is negligible. When selecting the crook the composer must therefore be guided by the general considerations given above under the heading "Trumpet." He must endeavour to give the instrument as few sharps or flats as possible in its signature. However, as the Cornet is much more used in short pieces and in light Opera than the Trumpet, a few more words on choice of crook may not be out of place.

The student should first notice that the B♭-crook obviously necessitates a signature two degrees sharper than the signature of the piece. Similarly the A-crook necessitates a signature three degrees flatter.

In major keys, then, the general rule is to use the B♭-Cornet as a corrective to flat keys, and the A-Cornet as a corrective to sharp keys. The crook corrects the sharpness or flatness of the signature of the music.

It is, however, always necessary to use some discretion in this matter when writing for the Cornet, the Trumpet, and, be it said, the Clarinet. Even in the key of C major the choice between the two fairly simple keys, D major for the B♭-Cornet and E♭ major for the A-Cornet, should really be made according as the direction of the modulations is northwards—that is, to the sharp side—or southwards—that is, to the flat side. For instance, if the second section were in E major, the A-Cornets, now in G major, would be preferable to the B♭-Cornets, now in F♯ major. On the other hand, if the second section were in A♭ major, the B♭-Cornets, now in B♭ major, would be preferable to the A-Cornets, now in C♭ (or B♮) major.

The rule, B♭-crook for flat keys and A-crook for sharp keys, will suffice for all the simpler keys and modulations. Notice, however, that when one is dealing with the borderland keys, such as D♭, G♭, F♯, B♮, and with the less simple modulations, it is often wise to modify the general rule and to take advantage of the enharmonic change involved.

Example 1.

The piece begins in D♭ major, and has a second section in A♮ major.

The signatures of the B♭-Cornet will be E♭ major and B♮ major.

The signatures of the A-Cornet will be E♮ (not F♭) major and C major.

Obviously in this case, though it is a flat key, the A-Cornet will be the better, more particularly if it has anything important to do in the second section, 4 accidentals with the A-crook, as opposed to $(3+5)=8$ with the B♭-crook.

Example 2.

The piece begins in D♭ major, and has a second section in F♭ major.

The signatures of the B♭-Cornet will be E♭ major and G♭ major.

The signatures of the A-Cornet will be E♮ (not F♭) major and G♮ (not A♭♭) major.

$(4+1)=5$ accidentals for the A-crook, as opposed to $(3+6)=9$ for the B♭-crook. Here we have a case of extreme flat keys, but for enharmonic reasons the A-Cornet is again more advisable. These questions, however, are not to be solved by rule-of-thumb, but by a consideration of the actual passages which the instrument has to play.

For instance, in the second of the two examples given above, if the Cornets had a really difficult part in the 1st section (D♭ major), and practically nothing in the 2nd section (F♭ major), the balance of probability is that one would use B♭-Cornets (in E♭ to begin with) rather than A-Cornets (in E♮ to begin with). In the 2nd section it would certainly not be worth while to change the crook for a simple part. Even the signature would be better left undisturbed for such a part, and accidentals written into the part instead.[1]

If the student now reverses the supposition, and imagines the Cornets to have very little in the 1st section (D♭ major) and a difficult part in the 2nd section (F♭ major), the chances are that he will use the A-Cornets (in E♮ to begin with) rather than the B♭-Cornets (in E♭ to begin with). Then in the second—the difficult—section he will have his instruments in one of their easiest keys—G♮ major. Finally, if the student supposes that his Cornets have got fairly difficult parts in both sections, he will see that, as stated above, the average of key is in favour of the A-instrument. E♮ major + G♮ major opposed to E♭ major + G♭ major. Five accidentals opposed to nine.

[1] In order to avoid many sharps and flats in the key-signatures of Wind-instruments, it is often wise (1) to avoid the key-signatures of F minor, B♭ minor, E♭ minor, and A♭ minor altogether, and to substitute their tonic major key-signatures; (2) to avoid the key-signatures of E major, B major, and F♯ major, and to substitute their tonic minor key-signatures. In both cases the additional sharps and flats should be written in where necessary as accidentals.

Minor keys are just as easy to deal with, if only one keeps an eye on the modulations and remembers that a transition to the dominant puts one four degrees *to the North.* In flat keys this generally brings one fairly near home (C major); but in sharp keys it lands one near the freezing regions of B♮ major and F♯ major. The direction of the modulations must therefore be taken into account before settling the question of crook, and, as before, the possibilities of enharmonic modulation must not be overlooked.

Example 3.

The piece begins in A minor, and has a second section in E major.
The signatures of the B♭-Cornet will be B♮ minor and F♯ major.
The signatures of the A-Cornet will be C minor and G major.

The A-Cornet is, of course, the better: (2+6)=8 accidentals as opposed to (3+1)=4.

Example 4.

The piece begins in A minor and has a second section in F♯ major.
The signatures of the B♭-Cornet will be B♮ minor and A♭ (not G♯) major.
The signatures of the A-Cornet will be C minor and A♮ major.

There is not much to choose between the two crooks: (2+4)=6 accidentals as opposed to (3+3)=6. The selection will depend on the relative difficulties of the passages in the two sections.

Example 5.

The piece begins in A minor and has a second section in F♮ major.
The signatures of the B♭-Cornet will be B♮ minor and G major.
The signatures of the A-Cornet will be C minor and A♭ major.

Obviously the B♭-instrument is the better: (2+1)=3 accidentals opposed to (3+4)=7.

In a similar way the student may deal on their merits with the other modulations, namely those from major to minor and from minor to minor keys. In a few of these cases he will find extreme modulations where a change of crook is a necessity. For example, from A major (A-crook necessary) to C minor (B♭-crook necessary); or from F minor (B♭-crook necessary) to B♮ minor (A-crook necessary). The student should consider these points carefully, not only because they are of importance when writing for the high Brass—the Trumpets and Cornets—but because when he comes to deal with the more complex instrument, the Clarinet, he will find the same little problems confronting him.

All that was said above with regard to the shakes of the C-Trumpet applies equally to the Cornet. The latter instrument is perhaps freer and easier in this particular than any other Brass Instrument. It is, however, a style of "free and easy" that does not commend itself to everyone's musical tastes.

The *mute* used is similar to that of the Trumpet, but not so effectively acid in the *f*. Occasionally the instrument is fitted with an "echo-attachment," a blind-alley mechanism which reduces its tone to a stifled whisper.

The technique of the Cornet is much easier to acquire than that of the Trumpet. The instrument "speaks" freely, and, except in its very lowest notes, maintains a good even tone-quality throughout its compass. In the hands of even a moderately good artist it is—as far as lightness and agility go—pretty well the equal of the Clarinet. Single-, double-, and triple-tonguing, slurred and detached passages, quick chromatic and diatonic scales, unprepared high notes, arpeggios, and all sorts of mixed figures founded on these various technicalities can be played with extraordinary certainty. Owing to this facility it is indispensable in the military band.

In this country there is an absurd prejudice against the instrument, a prejudice based partly on the fact that it was unknown to the ancient masters, partly on a comparison of its tone with that of the Trumpet when playing Trumpet-passages, partly on a dislike of its repertoire, and principally on ignorance.

True, its tone-quality is not so heroic as that of the old, long, big-bore Trumpet. On the other hand, in nine cases out of ten it is much more pleasant to listen to. Its lowest notes alone, like those of almost all Brass Instruments, are weak and flabby. It is better not to use them at all or to use them at any rate only for helping the Horns or other instruments over a difficult place. Such is their function in this curious unison of low Cornets and high Trombones from Elgar's *Cockaigne*:

EXAMPLE 42.

We must not forget that the contempt which is usually bestowed on the Cornet by those who have never heard it properly played is mainly a contempt because it cannot equal or beat the Trumpet *in Trumpet passages*. These simple straightforward phrases were always consciously designed by the old masters to produce their somewhat oppressive effect by the mere weight of the instrument's tone. In course of time we have come to associate that tone with that type of passage. The Cornet, a youth not yet a hundred years old, is suddenly called on to compete with its hoary rival in the very passages that least suit its *genre.* Naturally it fails, and its failure is gleefully recorded as the culpable failure of a noisy and objectionable upstart. This is hardly fair, for the instruments are quite distinct. It is as if one were to blame the Viola for not being able to characterize the first four notes of the *Tristan* prelude in the way that the Cellos can.

The fact is, that the Cornet when badly played is as bad as the Trumpet or Trombone when played equally badly. But not worse. When played well it is as good, for its own purposes, as these instruments are for theirs. Only it needs a totally distinct style of treatment. In the first place, no other Brass Instrument can touch it in florid music. Its fluent tone-quality, easy diction, and flexible technique, make it the ideal instrument for all those complex passages which need the colour of high-Brass, but which would be spoilt by a too obvious sense of struggle and effort in securing that colour.

It is only in recent years that composers have begun to treat the Cornet otherwise than as a substitute for the Trumpet.[1] Let us accept the fact frankly that a Cornet is a Cornet, not a Trumpet. Then we shall be able to see what can be done with it. Here is one little point. The Cornet more than any other Brass instrument is able to "drop out of sight" at will. It is the only Brass Instrument capable of filling this fifth

for us with quiet unobtrusive sound. This tone-quality is just above the level of the Clarinets. When played *pp* the effect is, in the theatre, often charming. Seconds, thirds, fourths, and fifths, can be either sustained in this quality or repeated in simple rhythms; and quiet two-part chromatic or diatonic passages can be played with a delicacy of poise that will not disturb the vocal equilibrium of even a Comic Opera Soubrette.

The Cornet is often charged with having a "coarse" tone. But the quality of its tone is in the main soft and placid. It lacks pungency and incisiveness. Any coarseness in the Cornet is not so much due to the instrument itself as to the mistaken efforts of injudicious players determined to make their part "stand out" at all costs. As there are hundreds of Cornet players to every Trumpeter, so there must be scores of bad Cornet players to every Trumpeter. And they always remind us of their existence. Players on the F-Trumpet are not heard at street-corners.

One of the most useful features of the Cornet, besides its variety, is its power of combining. Indeed, save in its topmost register, it will "fit in" with almost anything in the orchestra. Bizet, who scored the whole of *Carmen* for Cornets, understood this power of combination well. The tragic theme in the prelude to that opera is assigned to an impressive unison of Cornet, Clarinet, Bassoon and Cellos. The

[1] In France it has always had a certain musical status. It is used there regularly, not only in Comic Opera, but in Symphony and Grand Opera Orchestras.

accompaniment, above the melody, is for Violins and Violas *tremolo*, while the bass notes after each phrase are assigned to Horns (bass-clef, transposing in the old-fashioned way up a tone, not down a seventh), Drums, Harp, and *pizzicato* Basses.

EXAMPLE 43.

No. 20. The Valve-Horn[1] in F.

Fr. *Cor-à-pistons*; It. *Corno Ventile*; Ger. *Ventilhorn*.

Our present-day Valve-Horn consists of a spirally-coiled tube of brass some 7 feet 4 inches long. The F-crook with which it is invariably played in this country adds another 4 feet 4½ inches.[2] The total length of the instrument is therefore 11 feet 8½ inches.

[1] The full English name of the Horn, whether with or without valves, is "French-Horn."

[2] In France the instrument is often built in B♭-Alto. This is much less satisfactory than the medium-pitched key of F. Crooks have to be continually used and, even when the tuning-slides are pulled out, the piston-notes on the lower crooks are all far too sharp. In Germany G is a favourite key for the manufacture of Valve-Horns. The German instruments have very little resemblance to our own. Their tone-quality we should regard as more suitable to the Euphonium. It is somewhat coarse, thick, and "open." In lightness and brilliance they are inferior to the true French Horns. The explanation is to be found in the bore and mouthpiece of the German instruments. It must be added that they are much easier to play. Both tonal and executive control seem to be acquired without much difficulty. The Germans appear to be unaware of the instrument's deficiencies both in elegance and lightness. This is perhaps mainly a matter of custom, though it is surprising that in America some of the finest orchestras should deliberately prefer German to French or English players.

Three valves controlling as many extra lengths of tubing give the instrument the practical advantage of a chromatic compass between

[1]

and the theoretical advantage of a downward extension of compass through a diminished fifth to

Small tuning-slides are attached to the extra lengths of tubing and give the player the opportunity of making some necessary adjustments in pitch. The bore of the Horn is theoretically conical, but, except in one patent valve-system,[2] the extra lengths of tubing are actually cylindrical. The whole tube ends in a parabolically curved bell whose widest diameter is about 1 foot. Unlike most other brass instruments the Horn is played with a small funnel-shaped mouthpiece, which is in shape much like the bore of the instrument itself—a *truncated cone.* The size of this mouthpiece is a matter of convenience to the individual player concerned. As a rule 1st and 3rd Horn-players, being more continually called on to produce the upper Harmonics, use a somewhat shallower mouthpiece than 2nd and 4th players.

In compass the instrument is still practically what it was before the invention of valves. Even in the eighteenth century players were accustomed—or at any rate were required—not only to play the Harmonic Series from high C down through three octaves, but to descend through five further semitones to the low G. These notes were produced with a very loose lip, and were known and disliked as *factitious notes.* An example of their use is to be found in the familiar 4th Horn passage in Beethoven's *Ninth Symphony*. The two bass-clef notes of this passage are, according to the custom of the times, written an octave too low. But, even with that allowance, the second note is five semitones below the true first Harmonic of the Horn.

EXAMPLE 44.

Beethoven. *Choral Symphony.*

These notes, and an additional semitone—the low F♯ (sounding on the F-Horn B♮)—*can* now be produced by means of the valves. But their difficulties both of intonation and emission are great, and their

[1] The student is again reminded that, as this is a transposing instrument, the *written* notes are player's notes only. In every case their *sounds* are a perfect fifth lower.

[2] See page 85.

hoarse grunting quality quite unfits them for general use in the orchestra. For the sake of completeness one must add that an occasional player of genius can just touch the deep C, a note which theoretically does not exist on the instrument at all.

The Horn is now a chromatic valved instrument, and every note can be taken as an open note from a fundamental. The old Horn, however, still persists in the new, and the whole series of "hand" and "stopped" notes with its accompanying variety of tone colour is still available.

The question of the "hand-notes," however, needs a little explanation, as the student will find two diametrically opposed statements on this point in instrumentation books. They are

(1) That the insertion of the hand in the bell *lowers* the pitch of the instrument;

(2) That the insertion of the hand *raises* its pitch.

Incredible as it may seem, both of these statements are right. Let us see what the facts are:

(1) If a Horn is placed in a free position, say on its side on a table, so that no lip-pressure is possible, and if the air-column inside its tube is then set in vibration by the lips a definite note is produced. If the hand is then inserted into the bell a *gradual* or *portamento* flattening of the note is heard. It is important to notice the word *gradual*. Practically every sound between the extreme limits of the two notes is heard successively. Now this is in essence the method of stopping which was practised before the days of the valve, a method which gave the artist, restricted though he was, a great variety of tone-colour.

(2) After the invention of the valve-system it was found that by bringing the hand hard-up into the bell and exerting considerable lip-pressure a totally new series of muffled or stopped notes could be produced one true semitone *above* pitch. This *raising* of the pitch by means of a new technique differs integrally from the old hand-lowering in that any one of the raised series of notes cannot be produced as the highest point of a *portamento* upwards from the lower note. On the contrary it is a definite clear-cut semitone above.

The scientific reason of this curious natural fact is still doubtful. Mr. D. J. Blaikley, the eminent authority on Wind-Instrument acoustics, explains it as being a raising *only to the ear*. The Harmonics are really higher numbers in the Harmonic Series from a disturbed *lower* fundamental. The notes

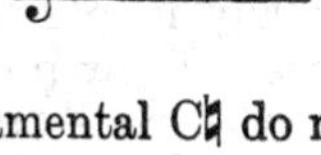

(Nos. 8, 9, 10) from a fundamental C♮ do not become the notes

(Nos. 8, 9, 10) from a higher fundamental C♯. They become the notes

(Nos. 9, 10, 11) from the lower fundamental C♭. From the practical side the very great difference in technique between the old and the modern series of stopped notes makes this explanation appear feasible.

With the new hand-technique the player has now a new series of stopped notes, over all of which he has adequate control. As he has a complete chromatic compass in open sounds, he has—with certain reservations to be mentioned presently—a second complete chromatic compass in stopped sounds. He need only read his part one semitone lower than it is written, and he can reproduce any given passage in muffled notes at its correct pitch. Thus the following passage

when played as hand-notes would be automatically read by the player as

It is interesting to note that, in an art where innovation is looked on as madness or crime, a certain class of player persistently refused to recognize the necessary alteration and extension in technique. This was the more to be regretted as the modern hand-technique gives the player the *certainty* of reproducing his passages in stopped notes, while the attempt to adapt the old hand-technique to the conditions of modern music has always ended in failure.

If the old hand-technique had produced a different quality of stopped note from that obtained by the modern method, one could well understand the reasons for its persistence. But the results to the ear are identical. There is only this difference—that one method is certain, the other uncertain or impossible. Even a simple scale cannot be played in stopped notes by the old method. It is liable at any moment to fizzle-out in a dismal groan. A really brilliant Horn-player of the last generation has been known to hand over a simple stopped passage to a younger and less conservative rival with the remark that it was "not Horn music."

The student will now see that, without the aid of any mechanical mute, the Horn-player is already in possession of a varied system of muffled and half-muffled tones. Their production is a matter for his judgment as an artist. At the same time, the indication of these muffled notes in a Score is *nowadays* a necessity. Before the invention of valves certain notes *had to be played stopped.* Nowadays none need be, but most can be. The composer must, therefore, mark such notes and passages in the part either *stopped* or *con sordino*.[1] In any case when these notes are wanted as "echo-notes" they must be marked *p*. Both the *sfz* and its sign > should be avoided. If the words *con sordino* are used the notes will either be produced as a hand-stopped series or by means of an actual mute. With an instrument so little stereotyped as the Horn the player will use his discretion in the matter.

A mute is, of course, quite commonly used. In former days it was a cardboard or papier-maché affair, which altered the pitch of the instrument, and this alteration had to be allowed for in performance. At the present day it is usually of metal, pear-shaped, and pierced laterally so as to prevent any alteration of pitch. Its effect is to reduce the tone-quality to a distant *pianissimo*. The mute can be inserted by the unemployed right hand either (1) before a passage, (2) in the break between two phrases (for an echo effect), or (3) during the actual performance of a note. In the score it is usually marked *con sordino*. The Germans say *mit dämpfer* or *gedämpft*.

In addition to this purely *p* series of stopped notes there is a second series of overblown notes, that is, of partially or completely hand-stopped notes whose tone-colour is altered by excessive lip-pressure. The quality of the notes varies from a savage bark like that of a wild animal to the dull uncertain sound with which a rout-seat scrapes over a parquet-floor. Before the invention of valves they were, of course, only available on the stopped notes of the Horn's compass. Nowadays, as every open note can be taken stopped, they are available everywhere. There is, however, a certain downward limit to their effectiveness, and this is generally put at

Berlioz and Wagner were the earliest composers to use this effect consciously. Many composers have misused it since.

The usual method of notation in every country is to mark the part *f* with an indication that the note is to be played stopped. The Germans generally put a little + over the note, thus:

Horns. 

with perhaps the word *gestopft* (stopped). They often add some such expression as *Schmetternd* (clanging, shrill) or *Stark anblasen* (blow hard). The French either mark the note *cuivré* or put the words *sons bouchés* over the passage. In this country the best way is to mark the *f* note with the +, and to add the word "brassy."

Complete chords limited only by the number of Horns available and by the "spread" of the notes can be played in this way. When

[1] The resumption of the open notes is usually marked with the word *Naturale*.

not pitched too low, such chords are extremely effective. All overblown notes, however, especially single notes of low pitch, have a tendency to drop out of sight unless they are kept well uncovered by the rest of the orchestra.

It is difficult to select instances of overblown notes from modern Scores, there are so many examples to choose from. The student will find one already quoted (Ex. 41), and, for another he may take the weirdly terrifying passage in Tschaikowsky's Fantasy-Overture *Hamlet*, where the clock strikes twelve on the platform at Elsinore. The composer evidently intends this series of twelve D's to be begun with only a slight "tang" instantly muffled into a toneless whisper. Then from the fifth D onwards each successive note is to be more and more overblown. The first six bars of the passage, with its curious Wood-Wind accompaniment, are as follows:

EXAMPLE 45.

All that was said above with regard to the atavistic crook-notation of the Trumpet applies with equal force to the Horn. There is, however, a difference. Except for one special purpose, which will be mentioned later, the instrument is crooked and played in F. Its habits are thus slightly more regular than those of the Trumpet. As with that instrument, however, composers still keep up the fiction that other crooks are used. It is a useless, even harmful, fiction, in which—as is quite plain—even the composers themselves do not believe.

If the student wishes to see how this fiction works out in practice, he may take the following instance. The quotation is from the *Don Quixote* Variations of Strauss. The composer is writing in the key of F♯ major. He marks his part "*Six Horns in E.*" He writes them with the key-signature of C major, adding the two missing sharps wherever they occur. His second section is in D minor. He marks his part "*Six Horns in F,*" and goes on writing them with the key-signature of C major. But what happens at the junction of these twc sections? Let us look at the first two Horn parts. The composer wishes them to produce these *sounds*:

Their part reads:

EXAMPLE 46.

Strauss. *Don Quixote.*

Horns in E. 

But obviously they cannot change their crooks in this bar-and-a-half. This is where the fiction comes in, for the composer knows this fact and does not expect them to make the change. What actually happens is that the players perform the whole work on the F-crook, and transpose at sight wherever the music is written for another crook. This is what they play:

Horns in F. 

The result, *in sound*, is the same.[1]

The student is not advised to adopt this method, but to write for the instrument on which his music will be played, the Horn in F. There is also no reason nowadays why the Horns should not have a correct key-signature. It is already regularly done in military bands for the E♭-Horn. As we have seen already, whether the key-signature is on the paper in front of him or not, the player who is transposing is compelled to have it in his head. The brain that can master such a difficult instrument up to symphony standard is not likely to be worried by seeing the sharps and flats on the left hand top corner of his music. If you are writing in an extreme sharp key, such as F♯ major—which will not be once in fifty times—make an enharmonic change and give your Horns a flat signature—in this case D♭, not C♯. Do not be afraid to change the signature of the Horn-parts, even if you are writing in accidentals for the Strings and Wood-Wind. Should your music begin in A major (Horn Signature E major) and contain a Horn passage of any importance in F, write-in the key-signature of C major in the Horn part even if you do not alter the signature elsewhere. This plan might often be adopted with advantage in other parts besides those of the Horns. Finally, be once again advised to adopt the plan—which is still far from universal—of using the bass-clef at its proper pitch. The more the clefs and key-signatures are simplified in orchestral music the better for the progress of the art.

[1] See pages 96-8.

In the lower register of the Horn the tone-emission is too slow and heavy to allow of anything but single-articulation. In the medium registers, however, both double- and triple-tonguing can be used with good effect. It is as well to confine such passages within these limits:

Repeated notes for accompanying are so common nowadays as to be scarcely worth quoting. They are almost invariably combined with some form of Wood-Wind, generally Flutes, Clarinets, or Bassoons. The opening of Mendelssohn's *Italian Symphony* and the introductory bars to Elizabeth's "Greeting to the Hall of Song" (*Tannhäuser*, Act II.) are familiar examples of this charming method of accompaniment.

EXAMPLE 47.

EXAMPLE 48.

For shakes, the Horn-player uses his lips only. As may be imagined, they require the greatest nicety in the adjustment of the embouchure. Minor shakes are generally out of the question, and even major shakes can only be made successful in the upper-middle part of the compass, where the Harmonics lie just sufficiently close to each other to be picked out by the player's lips. The somewhat narrow limits between which they may be written are about

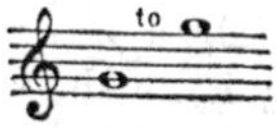

Wagner, whose writing for the Valve-Horn is as classical as that of Mozart for the Hand-Horn, rarely uses shakes at all. There are, however, a few well-known examples, such as the high F♯ shake just before the triplet figure for Strings in the *Siegfried Idyll*,

EXAMPLE 49.

In the Coda of *Till Eulenspiegel* Strauss has a four-part shake for Horns:

EXAMPLE 50.

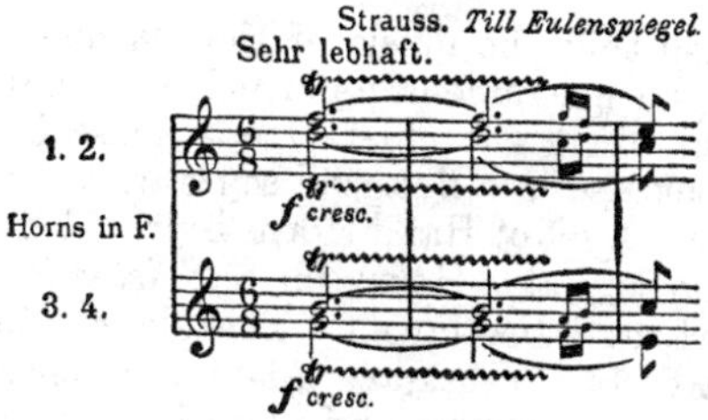

It will be noticed that they are all pitched fairly high, and that of the four shakes three are major. Furthermore, if reference is made to the Full Score it will be seen that they are all pretty well covered up by the heavy Brass and the Strings, and that the whole of the Wood-Wind is trilling at the same time.

From what has been said above, the student will gather that the Horn differs materially from all other Brass instruments. It is, indeed, at a higher artistic level altogether. The player is not a mere "piston-opener." He often has the choice of many methods of execution, and, in order to select the best, he has to keep his lips, his right hand, and his ear, in happy relationship with each other. It would be quite untrue to say that the modern ValveHorn "has replaced" the old Hand-Horn. The latter instrument is incorporated in the former, and is still the foundation of its technique. The player has now the advantage of being able to set and re-set his instrument instantaneously in any key he wishes by means of the pistons, but when once it is so set, his problems of artistic expression, of varied tone-colour, and of technical adjustment, remain much what they were in Beethoven's day.

The question may be asked here, what have we lost in adopting the valve-system for the Horn? Or, again, have we lost anything? The answers to that question vary from the statement that the valve-notes are "slightly more resonant and trombone like" than the open notes, to the opinion that when Beethoven's *Eroica Symphony* is played on the F-Horn instead of the E♭-Horn, for which it was written, "the pile of the velvet is scraped off." Personally, I have not a second's hesitation in agreeing with the latter—Sir Charles Stanford's—opinion. The difference is perhaps not the difference between day and night, but it is the difference between a November and a June day. An experiment which will convince the student on this point once and for ever is easily made. It only needs a double-room with *shut* folding-doors, a Horn-player armed with two crooks, the D and the F, in the other room, and the first three notes of the Oberon overture:

EXAMPLE 51.

One could wish that the music of the old masters should be performed only on the instrument for which it was written, the Hand-Horn. In Berlin, where the chief Opera house is "patronized" not only in a social but also in a financial sense by the reigning monarch, this is the practice. A set of Hand-Horns is provided for orchestral purposes, and the rule is, Valve-Horns on a *Tristan* night, Hand-Horns for Glück, Mozart, and Beethoven. The players there have a fixity of tenure, and a certain necessary amount of leisure, which permit them to nurse their embouchure and adapt it to the varying conditions of performance. In London, where a brilliant artist may be rehearsing a Symphonic Poem of Strauss in the morning, playing a Mozart Symphony in the afternoon, and blaring out pantomime-music in the evening, no such ideal results can be expected. However, nothing comes of grumbling at our conditions. The instrument itself has changed. It has gained something and lost something. The gain is in the direction of added flexibility, and even when we sum up the loss it leaves the instrument still with a tone of great purity, beauty, and nobility.

As might be expected, the music written for an instrument which has undergone two such violent changes as the addition of crooks and valves varies greatly in character. In the very earliest days of its introduction to the orchestra the Horn was scarcely distinguished from the Trumpet. Both were continually associated with the Drums, and were chiefly required to play Hunting-calls and military flourishes. Their type is to be seen in such passages as this:

EXAMPLE 52.

Traditional Hunting-call used by Philidor, Méhul, and Haydn.[1]

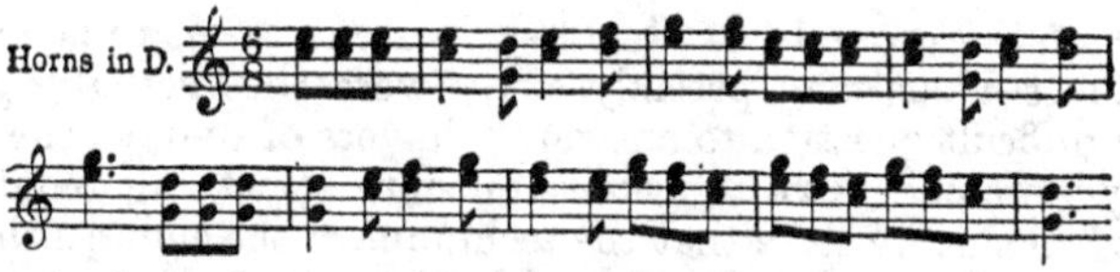

By the beginning of the eighteenth century the quality of the Horn had become continually softer; not so much, however, but that its roughness was still matter of surprised comment on the part of English visitors who first heard it on the Continent. Its music was not now greatly altered in character, but much extended. At all times during its history it has been used for what the French call *remplissage*, but at this time one feels that when the Horns are brought prominently forward in the orchestral scheme it is only to play passages which are a grandly elaborated series of Hunting-calls.[2] In a word, the associated ideas and the restrictions of the instrument govern the composer's technique.

At the same time, with the growth of the purely contrapuntal school, the Horn became involved in a fearful series of difficulties. If the student will turn to the notes of the Harmonic Series on page 73, he will see that the Horn was only a contrapuntal instrument from its seventh Harmonic

upwards. Below that it was "harmonic" only. It had, however, to be brought into the contrapuntal scheme. Hence come all those terrifying eighteenth-century passages in which a descent below the 8th Harmonic comes to both the player and his audience as a heaven-sent boon. In the works of Bach—the most earnest of all men to colour his music by means of purely musical subtlety—the external question of his Horn and Trumpet parts becomes, for players and conductors alike, an acute problem. In such passages as these

EXAMPLE 53.

Bach. *Wie schön leuchtet.*

[1] In *Tom Jones*, *Le Jeune Henri*, and *The Seasons*, respectively.

[2] See, for instance, the elaborate passage for Horns and Strings in Händel's *Alexander's Feast*.

Bach. *Christmas Oratorio.*

Bach. *Mass in B minor. (Credo.)*

the "lay of the ground," as they say in Kent, seems to be all wrong "But," the student may possibly ask, "were they actually played?" This is a difficult question to answer. Players of to-day generally say that they were not. Critics usually murmur something about a "lost tradition," or merely state that the technique of the eighteenth century players was "perfectly astonishing."[1] One thing, however, is quite certain. If they *were* played, they were played in the octave in which they were written, not as we should probably write and play them to-day, in the octave below. A mere glance at the notes of the Harmonic Series—the only notes then available on the Hand-Horn—will prove this assertion.[2]

In the next period, that of Haydn and Mozart, we find two Horns incorporated as a fixed element in the orchestra, but with a clear recognition of their limitations. Except for very special purposes they are confined to unobtrusive but most important holding-notes, to repeated notes, and to simple successions of thirds, sixths, and octaves. To the extreme fastidiousness of his taste in this matter Mozart owed a great deal of his orchestral charm. His Horn-notes always seem to be "placed" in exactly the right spot, at exactly the right pitch, and to be neither one too many nor one too few. The student cannot spend an afternoon better than by going through the Score of *Don Giovanni* from beginning to end, with the object of studying the Horn-parts. It is only rarely that Mozart calls on his Horns to take part in the general melodic scheme. When he does, however, one is occasionally sensible of the *height* at which the parts are necessarily written.

EXAMPLE 54.

Mozart. *Symphony in G minor.*

But this must not be taken in any sense as a general criticism of Mozart's writing. He is the ideal master to study if one wishes to achieve the maximum of effect with the minimum of means.

[1] Gevaert, p. 225.

[2] As far as the Trumpet goes, it is a historical fact that early eighteenth-century instruments were made of a bore and length to facilitate the production of these high notes. The introduction of the Clarinet may have had a good deal to do with the disuse of the top Trumpet-Register. It may be mentioned that the modern "Bach Trumpet" is not by any means the instrument of Bach's day. It is, as Mr. Galpin says, "a return with very modern additions, to the straight Buzine of the Middle Ages."

With the advent of Beethoven, of course, all was changed. Bent as he was on utilizing every instrument to the utmost capacity of its technique and on associating every instrument closely with his musical thought, he soon began to make a sort of strategic rearrangement of the Horns. Adopting early the use of two pairs of Horns[1] as part of his orchestral armament, his philosophical mind began to consider and elaborate both harmonic and melodic schemes into the substance of which he could weld his Horn-parts. They were to be no longer mere subterranean instruments emerging only rarely into the light of day. A place was to be found for them "in the sun." He did not by any means deny them their humble, useful function of "filling-up," but he added to it other functions more brilliant and more poetical. Thus he was able to do for the Horns what he was doing for the Drums and some other instruments: to lift them from a position of servitude to one of equality with, and occasionally even mastery over the other instruments. He not only gives us, in passing, delightful surprises of this sort,

EXAMPLE 55.

but the admirable melodic balance of his mind, inclining equally to the harmonic- and the scale-type of tune, was able to allot many of the former and some of the latter to the Horns. It would be quite outside the scope of this book to give a detailed list of these passages. They are to be found in such works as the *Eroica*, the *C minor*, the *Pastoral*, the *A major*, and the *Choral* Symphonies.

One must, however, notice three points in which Beethoven's enlarged musical demands created a corresponding enlargement in the technique of the instrument.

(1) In the first place, he calls into play a much larger number of stopped notes than had been usual before his time. In a passage of four bars from the *Ruins of Athens*, out of 32 notes 17 have to be artificially flattened with the hand. Similarly, out of 14 notes contained in four bars of the *7th Symphony*, 8 are partially stopped. In the celebrated 4th Horn passage of the *Choral Symphony*, of which a portion was quoted above (Ex. 44), he does not hesitate to write phrases which are poised on such difficult notes as

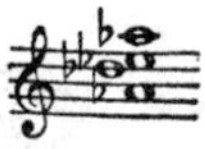

[1] Mozart (in *Idomeneo*) and Cherubini (in *Lodoiska*) were actually the first composers to use four Horns.

In this connection it is interesting to note that Beethoven scarcely ever uses the stopped notes of the Horns when they are merely filling-up or accompanying. When, however, they are brought to the front as *obbligato* instruments, he has no scruple in writing them. It must be remembered that neither Haydn nor Mozart used the stopped notes at all.

(2) In the second place, Beethoven's parts occasionally, not *normally*, have a very wide range. In the passage referred to above the player is asked within the limits of four bars to produce notes varying from the 5th semitone below his first playable Harmonic to the 13th of the Harmonic Series. This is a most important point for the student's consideration, for it is very certain that, whatever is said to the contrary, the lips which can produce the higher Harmonics without hesitation do not pass easily to the immediate production of the lower. There should be no doubt on this matter. It is not that the 1st and 3rd Horns should be kept screaming at the top of their compass while the 2nd and 4th are growling away in the bass. All four of them are, by nature, "middle" instruments, and in the greater part of their compass, let us say from

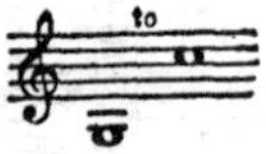

are equally comfortable and happy. On occasion the upper instruments—the 1st and 3rd—can descend the ladder without stumbling to low C

while the lower instruments—the 2nd and 4th—can ascend to high G or even, at a pinch, to A.

But in both cases it is merely humane to approach the extreme notes with discretion. Allow the player reasonable time and he can adjust his embouchure: give him a sudden complete change of *tessitura* and he is done. Hence comes the practice which, in ordinary filling-up parts is nowadays matter of ordinary prudence, the practice of always using the Horns as two pairs, of which Nos. 1 and 3 play the upper parts and Nos. 2 and 4 the lower. To give the simplest instance possible, the normal way of writing out the chord of F major for four Horns is not

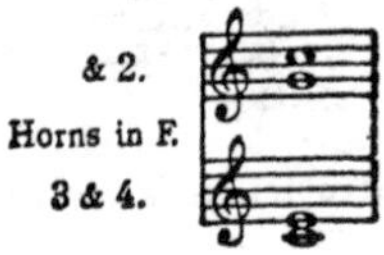

but with the notes of the chord "dove-tailed," thus

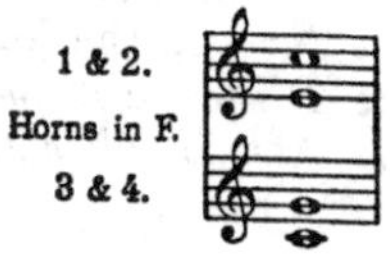

The chord is, of course, merely a symbol. The principle applies in general to all Horn music, whether it be in four-parts or not. To the leaders of each pair are allotted the highest parts. Examples may be found by opening any score at random, or the student may look at the quotation from the *Eroica Symphony* (Ex. 57), where the 3rd Horn is pitched throughout above the 2nd. In the extreme passages that are found in some modern scores it is out of the question to expect 2nd and 4th Horn players, especially the latter, who are generally "low-note specialists," to rise to the occasion. Here is a passage (of thirds reduplicated in the lower octave) which shows the practical advantage of "dove-tailing" the Horn parts. It is quoted from Elgar's Oratorio *The Kingdom*, page 194 of the Full Score:

EXAMPLE 56.

A reference will be made later to the many modern instances where the four Horns play unison phrases that sometimes rise as high as the 12th and 13th Harmonics. As a rule such passages, however dizzy their height, do not cover a greater *range* than that of an octave or a twelfth. This makes all the difference in performance.

(3) The third point that calls for mention with regard to Beethoven's Horn writing is that the 1st Horn part, even when its *range* is not great, occasionally lies very high. It is in such places as these that Horn players are still compelled to use the specified crooks. Let us see the reason for this. It is scarcely necessary to say again that the higher Harmonics are all easier to get on the lower crooks, and the lower Harmonics on the higher crooks. Top C, for instance—unplayable on the B♭-alto-crook—is a perfectly easy note on the C-basso, and easier still on the B♭-basso.[1] Such crooks as these are quite disused for ordinary purposes. Beethoven, however, never writes the highest Harmonics for the high crooks. The modern player, therefore, in attacking these passages, has the option of playing the top notes (1) as a slightly lower series of Harmonics on his medium-pitched

[1] See list of crooks on p. 78.

F-crook, or (2) of taking a very high crook and playing them as a considerably lower series. The latter is the general though not invariable practice. For instance, in the following three examples, of which the first is from the *Eroica Symphony* and the second and third from Leonora's air in Act II. of *Fidelio*:

EXAMPLE 57.

EXAMPLE 58.

EXAMPLE 59.

the topmost notes of the 1st Horn would be, on the F-crook,

while, on the very high crooks B♭-Alto and A-Alto, none of them would rise above the 12th Harmonic (G):

In fact, for a given high *sound*, the higher the crook the more feasible the Harmonic; and conversely, for a given low *sound*, the lower the crook the more feasible the Harmonic. The difference in the height of the Harmonics caused by the choice of crook can be seen at a glance by reading the unison-sounds of the four Horn-parts in Ex. 70.

With the change to valve-mechanism the Horn naturally began to occupy a much more assured position in the orchestra. Halévy was the first composer to introduce both Valve-Trumpets and Valve-Horns into the orchestra. In *La Juive* (1835) he writes for two "*Trompettes à pistons*" and two "*Trompettes ordinaire*" and for two "*Cors à pistons*" and two "*Cors ordinaire.*" The first appearance of the Valve-Trumpets must have caused considerable astonishment. It occurs in a *Drinking Chorus* in Act I., and the instruments start off gallantly with this sort of thing:

EXAMPLE 60.

Later on, however, and, indeed, almost all through the Opera, habit becomes too strong for them, and they revert to their trusty C-E-G style of part. Wagner, in *Rienzi*, was the other early composer to use the method. His plan was at first to write for one pair of Hand-Horns and one pair of Valve-Horns. In a very short time, however, the former instruments found themselves in the ranks of the unemployed. This was only to be expected. Music was undergoing startling changes, and for all the old-fashioned instruments it was "get on or get out." So we come to the new era, in which the progress of the instrument can be traced from *Rienzi*, through the *Flying Dutchman*, *Tannhäuser*, *Lohengrin*, the *Ring*, and the *Meistersinger*, to its latest developments in the *Symphonic Poems* and *Operas* of Strauss.

In this connection attention may be drawn to a few of the more modern uses of the Horns. In the first place, though still possessing their inherent tendency to hold notes, they can now pass easily either by diatonic or chromatic steps, to any other notes. Hence they are available either in the *f* or the *p* for *any* middle part, not merely for a stationary middle part. The effects of such parts,[1] conceived either contrapuntally or chromatically, for one or more Horns, is invariably charming. The tone-colour of the instrument combined with its exquisite smoothness lends a sort of unobtrusive distinction to the part which it is playing. It is scarcely necessary to quote instances of this delightful use of the Horns. They occur in every modern score, and most often in that first of all models, *Die Meistersinger*.

Another modern type of Horn melody is the curiously fascinating alternation of a single note backwards and forwards, perhaps at varying degrees of pitch, with its next-door neighbour. This, perhaps, has its origin in the fact that the Horn has always been able to play such passages when not pitched lower than

It has always been well in the character of the instrument, and hence makes an immediate appeal to our emotions. As an example, the student may refer to the Horn passage in Tschaikowsky's *Romec and Juliet* beginning

EXAMPLE 61.

Horn in F.

and the type receives a sort of apotheosis in the extraordinarily suggestive passage in the 1st Movement of Brahms' *Symphony in D major*, where the Horn struggles up through fourteen bars to a high A♭:

and then returns through eight diminuendo bars to a C:

[1] Not to be confused with that besetting sin of the bad musician, the sin of covering up deficiencies of workmanship by means of a good thick layer of "four-part Horns in the middle."

The first few bars of the passage as as follows:

EXAMPLE 62.

Since the introduction of the valve-system Horn Solos have, of course, become a constant feature of the orchestra.[1] The very natural tendency, however, is to confine such Solos to series of notes characteristic of the Horn technique. By that one does not mean to say that every note should be considered only in the light of its possibilities on the Hand-Horn, but merely that an eye should be kept on the restrictions of the old technique and the valves invoked only to fill up deficiencies. Such Solos as that at the beginning of the *D major Symphony* of Brahms:

EXAMPLE 63.

or the one that appears first at the *Più andante* in the last movement of his *C minor Symphony*:

EXAMPLE 64.

are actually playable, though usually not played, on a valveless Horn. On the other hand, such a subject as this, from Dvořák's *New World Symphony*,

[1] The repeated Horn note in Schubert's *C major Symphony*—a high G for two unison Horns in C—is a magical example of the way in which even a single sound can be turned to account by a genius.

EXAMPLE 65.

contains a note—the B♮—which, if interjected as a stopped note, would make the passage ridiculous. Yet this sounds like and is a characteristically good specimen of Horn-music.

Again, there is the well known Horn-call in the 2nd Act of *Siegfried* (page 221 of the Full Score). In this passage, which is thirty-nine bars long, there is only one note (the

occurring once in Bar 22) which is absolutely unplayable on the Hand-Horn. In addition there are three notes—the F, B, and A—occurring twice in the middle phrase,

EXAMPLE 66.

which would need either complete stopping or slight modification. The rest of the thirty-nine bars is made up of the notes of the Harmonic Series,

and, as far as the actual sounds go, is pure Hand-Horn music. Yet this very passage is specially cited by Gevaert to show the great advantage in "melodic variety" which the Valve-Horn has over the "old hunting horn." And this is quite true, for though, as has been shown, almost all of it is theoretically playable on the Hand-Horn, yet it is a passage that demands the valves for its rapid and smooth delivery, and, as a matter of fact, no player in his senses would dream of performing it on a valveless instrument. In short, it is a happy instance of a Valve-Horn passage preserving almost intact all the characteristic features of the old Hand-Horn music.

A similar but somewhat modified remark might be made about the Horn-opening that succeeds the Introduction to *Till Eulenspiegel*:

EXAMPLE 67.

Here we feel that the first part of the tune is quite naturally built on the open notes

and that the composer is making a legitimate use of the valves to bridge the space chromatically, first between the D and the E, and then between the F and the G. The last three bars are pure Hand-Horn music, and the whole tune, modern as it sounds, is really an excellent example of the new with its feet planted in the old. In the notation of the above example the bass-clef is used in the old-fashioned way an octave below its correct pitch. The extreme *range* of the last three bars is also worth noticing. In performance, as a rule, the Solo player either stops short before the last two notes and hands them over to the 2nd or 4th player or one of the latter enters and helps him out *à 2* with the passage.

There is, of course, another type of Horn Solo, the type which might be played by almost any soft Valved-Brass instrument. In this type the fundamental peculiarities of the Horn and its historical usages are totally ignored, and a purely vocal *cantilena* allotted to the instrument. The long Horn Solo at the beginning of Tschaikowsky's *E Minor Symphony* (slow movement) is a case in point. The short recitative-phrase for muted Horn towards the end of Liszt's *Mazeppa* is another. In the latter case the phrase itself is effective enough, yet one feels that it is not very characteristic of the instrument.

EXAMPLE 68.

It is the commonest thing nowadays to reinforce a single series of Horn-notes by the addition of a 2nd, a 3rd, or a 4th instrument. We have already quoted such a passage (Ex. 19) from Bizet's 1st Suite *L'Arlésienne*. The notation given above is, of course, not the notation in the full score. There the part is written (page 40) as follows:

EXAMPLE 69.

A simple but wonderfully effective passage from Wagner's *Flying Dutchman* Overture is to be found below (Ex. 80). The opening phrase of the overture to this Opera furnishes us with one of the earliest instances of the modern forceful method of writing tunes for

[1] Unaccompanied except for a "diminished seventh" chord on the first note.

four Horns in unison. Here is the melodic passage with the accompanying open fifths omitted:

EXAMPLE 70.

Of a totally different character is the following striking subject from Strauss's *Don Juan.* The four Horns begin this tune to no more accompaniment than a string *tremolo,* Violins on the note G,

EXAMPLE 71.

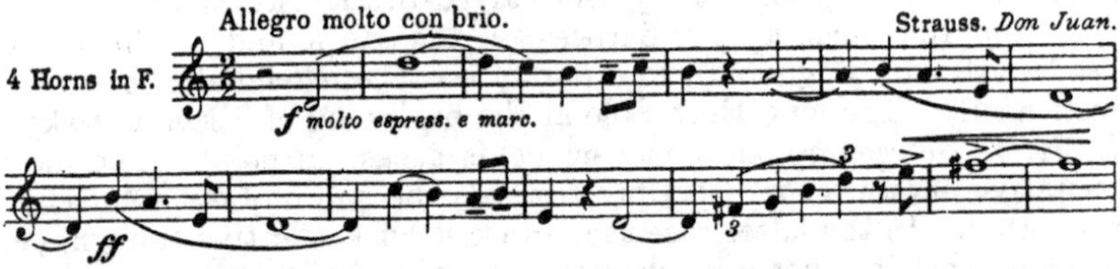

Finally, we may quote a few bars which, for this sort of writing, only just fall within the boundaries of the possible. They occur in Elgar's Oratorio *The Kingdom,* and probably gave their distinguished author some qualms as to their success.

EXAMPLE 72.

However, they are a good example of courage justified in performance. The danger of a passage like this is not its range—a thirteenth—which is easily within the compass of any Horn player, but its height when played by four instrumentalists, two of whom are seldom asked to take high G♯'s and A's. In this special example no very real risks are run by the composer, as his Horns are supported in the unison by Violas, Cellos, and three Trumpets, of which the last-named are directed to play with "subdued tone."

When the Horns are employed in harmony, especially when they are meant to stand well in the foreground, it is often convenient to write their close-harmony in three parts, not four. In such cases if the music be *p* or *mp* three Horns only are employed: in anything from *mf* to *ff*, however, it is usually just as well to double the bottom part. No one who has heard Tschaikowsky's *Fourth Symphony* can forget the effect of the sudden re-entry of the motto-theme on the Trumpets followed by the tremendous rhythmical emphasis of the four Horns. In this case a Clarinet plays in unison with each of the two upper Horn-parts, and two Bassoons with the 3rd and 4th Horns.

EXAMPLE 73.

Another and very impressive use of three-part Horn harmony, this time with a light string accompaniment, is to be found in the second Act of Wagner's *Flying Dutchman* (Erik's Recitative):

EXAMPLE 74.

Here the music is *pp*, and the composer needs only three Horns till the end of Bar 3, where he introduces a 4th to complete his harmony. In this extract the Natural Horns have to be kept to the two upper parts, quite apart from any consideration of their better tone colour—a consideration that constantly weighed with composers in the early days of the Valve-Horn—for the simple reason that, at the minor ninth chord, the only two open notes are those at the top.

Passages for four Horns in harmony, either quite unaccompanied or associated with the Strings or Wood-Wind, have been common from the days of the *Semiramide* and *Freischütz* overtures to that of *Hänsel und Gretel.* The effect is always delightful. In writing such passages unaccompanied one has to be careful not to take the 4th Horn too low. In the bottom fifth of its compass, especially in chromatic music when it is supporting chords other than common chords, it has a tendency to drop out of sight. In cases of this sort it is as well to add a Bassoon or Bass-Clarinet to the 4th part, but this adds a totally new tone-colour, and the better way is to keep the bass, if possible, not too low.

In recent times composers have generally been more inclined to write cunningly constructed chromatic harmony for the Horns, and to mark the parts *Con Sordino.* This gives a delicious tone-colour, but, of course, it can never be what one may call "daily bread" in the orchestra.

Weber introduced eight Horns into his opera *Preciosa* for a special effect, and Wagner even wrote for sixteen in the first Act of *Tannhäuser.* But of these twelve are on the stage; the orchestra has only its usual quartet. In his later work Wagner adopted the eight Horns as part of his ordinary orchestral method. Their use for purposes of increased force, of contrast, and of allowing the players sufficient rest in the long acts of his Music Drama are obvious. Sometimes the whole eight are employed in the theatre orchestra, and sometimes one or more players are detached for service on the stage. Thus, in the second Act of *Tristan,* of the eight Horns, six play the "calls" behind the scenes, while two remain in the orchestra. Since Wagner's day, six or even eight Horns have become almost normal in the concert room for the accompaniment of Choral Music and for Symphonic works of a large size. They are not often used in full eight-part harmony, but rather as a double quartet, whose power of added weight and accentuation can be brought to bear at any desired point.

A very short example of muted Horns in harmony has already been quoted from Elgar's *Grania and Diarmid* (Ex. 4). There the Horn parts were given for the student's convenience in their actual sounds. We may, therefore, give a final example here of the Horns in their transposing notation. (Example 75, p. 133.)

This is a characteristic Wagnerian example of six-part harmony on the muted Horns. The 4th Horn part is to be read a major third higher, not a minor sixth lower. The student would do well to write out these few bars *as they sound,* noting the negligible enharmonic differences between the Horns and the voice.[1]

[1] A few notes for muted Horns may be seen in Ex. 134. They are used merely to fill in the harmony

EXAMPLE 75.

The Trombones.

Fr. *Trombones* ; **It.** *Tromboni* ; **Ger.** *Posaunen.*

PRELIMINARY.

There are four different sizes of Trombone,[1] the *Alto*, the *Tenor*, the *Bass*, and the *Double-* (or *Contra-*) *Bass*—a large family, of which the first is in a state of senile decay and the last only a bawling infant. Under the name of *Sackbuts* they have existed from early times much as they are at present. Indeed, in many pictures of mediæval bands and orchestras it is the familiar slide-mechanism and the characteristic downward slope of the bell-joint in the *Sackbuts* that first attract a modern musician's attention.

In the sixteenth and seventeenth centuries there seems to have been, besides the *Alto*, the *Tenor*, and the *Bass*, a very high *Soprano-Trombone*, in appearance and pitch something like the *Soprano Trumpets* which one sees in Bersaglieri bands. In Bach's day it was the custom at Church-Festivals to give each of the four parts of the chorale to a Trombone in unison with the voices, and it was either to this *Soprano-Trombone* or to the old *Zinke*[2] that the highest part was allotted.

[1] Italian for "big Tromba," *i.e.* big Trumpet.

[2] The extreme compass possible on the Zinke-family was from

This instrument gradually fell into disuse, and, according to Gevaert, showed the last flickering signs of life in Gluck's Viennese production of *Orfeo* (1762). Gevaert adds "Twenty years later, the old instrument having been definitely put aside, Mozart replaced it, in its office of Soprano to the Trombones, by Oboes and Clarinets playing in unison. For more than three-quarters of a century afterwards, the orchestra had no brass instrument able to execute the simplest diatonic scale at the pitch of a woman's voice."

The Soprano instrument soon dropped out of use, leaving the *Alto*, the *Tenor*, and the *Bass* in possession of the field, and this continued to be the usual arrangement down to Beethoven's middle life, when the *Alto-Trombone* began to find itself edged out of the orchestra. This was due to the fact that its tone-quality in the middle and lower registers could not compete successfully with that of the *Tenor-Trombone,* while in its upper register it was at an equal disadvantage with the *Trumpet.* So it had to go. Still, when it went, the orchestral tradition was already firmly fixed of *Three Trombones.* Another *Tenor-Trombone* was, therefore, introduced in its place, and the formula became what it is in most countries at the present day—*Three Trombones,* of which two are Tenors and one Bass. An exception to this tradition is to be found in France. There the *Bass-Trombone* began to be disused about 1830. Since then the French custom has been to write for *Three Trombones,* all Tenors. Finally, in this somewhat uneventful family-history, a deep *Contra-Bass-Trombone* was added by Richard Wagner for the performances of his Music-Drama.

It is to be observed that the changes which have occurred in the arrangement of the Trombone-group are changes of compass only. No essential change has been made in the mechanism of the instrument. Again, one sort of instrument does not vary from any other sort except in size—that is in pitch. A description, therefore, of the most commonly used instrument, the Tenor, will suffice for all.

No. 21. The Tenor (or B♭) Trombone.[1]

Fr. *Trombone ténor* ; It. *Trombone tenore* ; Ger. *Tenorposaune.*

This instrument is played with a cup-mouthpiece, and its peculiar acoustical properties seem to depend on the correct proportion between the lengths of its cylindrical tube and of its conical "bell-joint." The tone and quality of the instrument, however, vary considerably according to the player's method of attack.

We have already described the Slide-Mechanism by means of which the air-column is lengthened so as to produce the seven fundamental notes and their accompanying Harmonic Series. The student is advised to re-read what was said above on this subject (page 83). For the sake of clearness and completeness the whole of the notes which are obtainable in each of the seven positions are now set out in full.

[1] For *Slide-Trombone* the French say *Trombone à coulisse* ; the Italians, *Trombone a tiro* or *Trombone duttile* ; the Germans, *Zugposaune.*

(1) In each of the first two positions two higher notes—the 9th and 10th Harmonics—are playable by means of a strong lip. These are, in the 1st position,

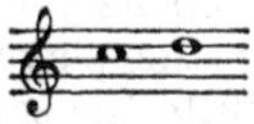

and, in the 2nd position,

The compass of the instrument is therefore four semitones greater than that actually shown in the list of positions. Of course the corresponding 9th and 10th Harmonics are easier to produce in the lower than in the higher positions, but in actual practice they are not used because they merely reduplicate notes which are still more easily obtainable as lower Harmonics from a higher fundamental. The general rule for **all** Brass Instruments is that the difficulty of accurate production increases with the height of the Harmonic Series. It is most important, however, to note that this height is not a height **in pitch** but **in number** (1, 2, 3, etc.). The notes of a 1st Horn part that lies constantly between Harmonics 6 and 13 are, quite apart from any question of pitch, much more difficult to produce accurately than those of a 1st Trombone part which lies mainly between Harmonics 2 and 8. The extreme notes of the Trombone—those above the high B♭—are really not of much use in the orchestra, and it is as well to confine the upward compass to the B♭. Downwards, the last three semitones F♯, F♮, and E♮, are not of such a good quality as the same notes on the Bass-Trombone, though one need not scruple to use them if necessary.

(2) Below the ordinary compass given above are three deep notes shown in square breves. These are the three "Pedal Notes" B♭, A♮, and A♭, all playable with a very loose embouchure. In quality they are somewhat unsatisfactory, rather coarse, and wanting in substance. The highest of these three, the B♭ (1st position), is by far the best, then come in order of demerit the A♮ (2nd position) and the A♭ (3rd position). If they are wanted it is as well to approach them by a drop from the octave above. If that is not possible the player should have a moment's rest in which to adjust his embouchure. It is not wise to skip down to them direct from 6th and 7th Harmonics. Otherwise it may sound like a music-hall comedian's "effect." There are few instances of these pedal-notes to be met in orchestral music. Gevaert quotes 10 bars of held pedal B♭ from the 1st Act Finale of Hérold's *Zampa.* The pedal is allotted to three Tenor Trombones in unison. Berlioz, as every one knows, had a pedal-bee or rather a hive of pedal-bees in his bonnet. Here is a passage from his *Requiem*:

EXAMPLE 76. Berlioz. *Requiem.*

It probably sounds very nasty. Elgar, in his overture *Cockaigne*, has written a three-bar pedal on B♭ for two Tenor-Trombones in unison with a Tuba and a Double-Basoon. He does not even hesitate, earlier in the same overture, to make his 1st Trombone jump down three octaves to the deep pedal A♭. It is true that the player has a moment's grace before his musical dive from the cliff to the sea. This gives him the opportunity of reflecting what it will feel like when he strikes the bottom:

EXAMPLE 77.

If the student will now refer back to the list of Trombone-Harmonics given above, he will see that the majority of them are printed in black crotchet-heads. These are the notes which are reduplicated, the notes which are producible as Harmonics of different Series-numbers from more than one fundamental note. In other words, these are the notes which can be played in more than one position. This reduplication of notes is of considerable advantage to the player, as it helps him to avoid sudden changes of position in quick passages.

The white semibreves are the notes which can be taken in one position only. A caution may be entered here as to their use. The top A and B♭ do not come into the matter, as they are playable from the two closest positions of the slide, the 1st and 2nd. But with regard to the lower notes it must be observed that very rapid sequences of notes involving extreme changes of position, say from the 1st to the 7th, or *vice versa*, are not only awkward but impossible. The slide takes an appreciable time to pass down the two "legs" of the instrument, and has to be pulled away before the instrument has had time to "speak." The result is a sort of ghostly grunt. Imagine what a player *looks like* in trying to play this:

His action is very much that of an energetic cyclist pumping up his tyres against time.

It is a good general rule to avoid quick interchanges of the note

* The numbers above the notes give the positions.

with any of the following:

and of the note

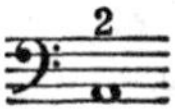

with any of these:

Of course, as the upper pivot note (B♭, A, etc.) becomes lower, or the lower note (E, F, etc.) becomes higher, the junction of the two in a quick succession becomes more feasible. But there are two facts not to be overlooked in this connection. (1) Apart altogether from the question of pivoting one note on another, the three or four deepest semitones of the instrument take an appreciable time to "speak." (2) The actual length through which the slide has to be moved is not the same for all the positions, but increases with the depth of the position. The player therefore in the last three semitones of his ordinary compass has to struggle with a difficulty of tone-production, with a difficulty in the extension of his arm, and with an increased distance between his positions. And finally, as has been already said, the fundamental notes in his 5th, 6th, and 7th positions are all of much better quality on the Bass-Trombone.

Shakes are scarcely worth considering on the Trombone. They are formed with the lips, not with the slide. They can only be made in the upper part of the register where two tones lying next to each other can be blown alternately by a difference of embouchure, but without any alteration of the fundamental note. These whole-tone shakes are *possible* on the following notes:

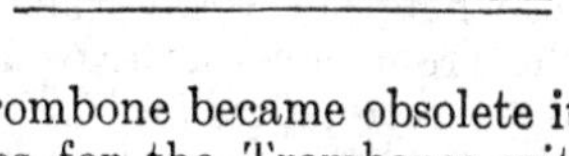

Before the Alto-Trombone became obsolete it was customary either (1) to use three staves for the Trombones with the three clefs alto, tenor, and bass; or (2) to write the first two Trombone parts on one stave with the alto- or tenor-clef, while the Bass-Trombone had a separate bass-clef stave; or (3) to write all three instruments on one line, generally with the bass-clef but occasionally (see below, Ex. 80) with the tenor-clef.

Nowadays the usual plan is to write the two first Trombone parts on one stave. The tenor- or bass-clef is used at convenience. The Bass-Trombone then shares a bass-clef stave with the Tuba. Unless the parts are very simple and similar in outline the practice of crowding three instruments on to one stave is likely to lead to confusion. All three parts have of course to be distinguished by means of tails and rests, and, what with marks of expression, slurs, and so on, a three-part stave generally becomes a muddle. Ease of writing and reading is the object to be aimed at.

The Tenor-Trombone is the first instrument under our notice which, built in a key other than C, is yet not treated as a transposing-instrument. Crooks, though tried on the Trombones, have never "made good" with them. We are therefore in the happy position of being able to write

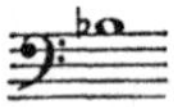

and not

when we want middle B♭.

The method of tone-production and of attack varies greatly in different countries. In England the amount of "tang" and "bite" that is put into the *f* and the *ff* is extraordinary. The player starts the note with a great impetus, and "throws it out into the air." This is well enough in passages that demand the utmost force of delivery. Occasionally, however, the notes themselves seem to disappear and leave nothing but a nerve-splitting edge. The continual call for brilliance in the Brass department has caused such alterations in the instrument's construction that nowadays Tenor-Trombones are made with pretty much the same bore as that of a Cornet. The shape of the cup-mouthpiece is also determined principally with the object of securing the utmost brilliance of attack. In France the most esteemed players have not a tithe of this *bravura*, but their smooth *crescendo*, sounding like an irresistible "head" of water, is something to be remembered. This is partly due to the fact that they usually play with instruments of a wider bore and partly to the fact that they employ a sort of modified funnel-mouthpiece. It must not be overlooked that the special drawback of the present-day Trombone is its aversion from a *forte sostenuto*. The note as a rule barks out and then dwindles down to a *mezzo-piano*. The noble manner of holding a note *forte*, but not so *forte* as to be oppressive, seems to be almost a lost art. This was the majestic *sostenuto* which Mozart and Beethoven always had in their ears when they wrote their Trombone chords. It is certainly worth all the Trombone *bravura*-playing in the world.

There is in general no true *legato* on the Trombone at all. Each note has to be articulated at the moment that the slide changes its position. There is therefore a perceptible moment between each two notes when the air-column is not in vibration. Were this not so we should get a distressing *portamento* between the notes. In the *p* and the *pp* a good player reduces this moment-of-silence to vanishing point, and produces an effect which Widor happily compares with the *sostenuto* of the Violin—a *sostenuto* which is scarcely interrupted by the turning of the bow. When playing a succession of notes from the same fundamental, that is to say, when playing without change of slide-position, the Trombone, of course, enjoys the same advantages of *legato*-playing as any slideless Brass Instrument.

It is worth noting that the Trombone player depends solely on his ear for his correct intonation. This is true of all instrumentalists, but it is true in a special sense of the Trombone-player. He has no mechanical pistons or keys to guide him, nor is he employed, as the Bassoon-player is employed, in correcting the defects of an imperfect instrument. He *makes* his notes just as the String-player makes his. Thus he has the opportunity of a nice accuracy in judgment, and it is only necessary to hear four clever Trombone-players exercising this judgment by playing an "equale" in the pure untempered scale to be made aware how delightfully musical is the essential character of the instrument.[1]

No. 22. The Alto (or E♭) Trombone.

Fr. and It. *Trombone Alto*;[2] Ger. *Altposaune.*

This Trombone is now practically obsolete. It is built in the key of E♭, a perfect fourth higher than the Tenor. Its seven positions, therefore, have as their fundamental notes

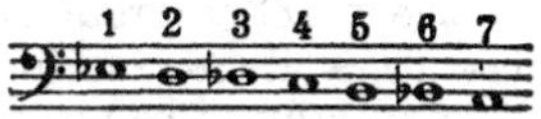

and its highest compass is to

Owing to its narrow bore the notes below

are poor in quality. They are rarely used. The four semitones[3] above

are for all orchestral purposes unplayable. The pedal notes have never been employed, so that the Alto-Trombone is really a two-octave instrument.

Like all the other Trombones, it was written for as a non-transposing instrument. The part was almost invariably written in the alto-clef, but the bass-clef was used occasionally and conveniently for the lowest notes. Nothing further need be said with regard to this instrument, as its technique is merely that of the Tenor-Trombone shifted a perfect fourth upwards.

[1] Some further remarks on the Trombones will be found after the section devoted to the Double-Bass-Trombone, p. 147 *et seqq.*

[2] Sometimes *Trombonino* in Italian. [3] See above, page 135.

No. 23. The Bass (or G) Trombone.

Fr. *Trombone basse* ; It. *Trombone basso* ; Ger. *Bassposaune.*

In this country the Bass-Trombone, both for orchestral and military purposes, is always built in G. Its seven positions have, therefore, for their seven fundamentals, the notes

This leaves a gap of two semitones between the bottom note of the Bass-Trombone and the first pedal-note (the low B♭) of the Tenor-Trombone. On the continent the Bass Trombone has always been built in F, one tone below our standard instrument. Built thus, its seven fundamentals are

and it has always been the practice from Mozart and Beethoven's time till the present day to write down to the low C.[1] Passages where this note occurs have usually to be altered or transposed by our players. This is a disadvantage. On the other hand, our G-instrument—already, perhaps, the most tiring instrument to play in the orchestra—is much more manageable than the continental F-Trombone. This somewhat counterbalances its obvious disadvantages when required to "cry out from the depths." In Germany a Trombone of even greater length, the military Bass-Trombone in E , two whole tones lower than our G-instrument, used to be made. It is now apparently disused, at any rate for orchestral purposes.

The difficulty with regard to the build of the instrument is a rather serious one. If regard is paid solely to its repertoire, it must be in F. On the other hand, if ease of tone-production and flexibility in performance are more studied, G is the better key. The difficulty has been partially solved by the introduction of a mechanism so designed as to give the player the freedom of the smaller instrument together with the possibility of descending below the low C when required. This mechanism consists of an extra length of tubing in the bell-joint, so arranged that it can be switched on or off at will. When the extra length is out of action, the instrument is an ordinary Bass Trombone in G. When, however, the extra length is switched on, the instrument is automatically transposed down a perfect fourth, and becomes a Bass Trombone in D with a descending chromatic compass to

[1] And occasionally to its bottom note, the low B♮. 

that is to say, a perfect fourth below the lowest seventh-position note on the natural instrument in G. The simple mechanism is operated by means of a left-hand thumb-ring. A very slight movement of the thumb throws the extra tubing into or out of action.[1] The tone of the Trombone seems to be unimpaired, and the player not only has the capacity of performing such passages as the one printed below (see Ex. 176), but also the important technical advantage of a new series of the higher Harmonics taken from fundamentals of a low pitch.[2]

The compass of the G-Trombone is from the low C♯ or D♭ (fundamental seventh position) upwards to

Neither the pedal notes below low C♯ nor any notes above the high G are of any practical use in the orchestra.

The Bass-Trombone is written in the bass-clef as a non-transposing instrument. As has been mentioned above, it generally shares a stave with the Bass-Tuba, and is written on the upper part of the stave.[3] This is, however, mere matter of convenience, and may be disregarded if either of the instruments has an important and independent part.

All that was said with regard to the technique[4] of the Tenor-Trombone applies equally to the G-instrument, when allowance is made for the difference of pitch. Shakes are scarcely ever written for the Bass-Trombone. Such as exist may be found by transposing the Tenor-Trombone list down a minor third.

The caution with regard to awkward changes of position is even more necessary in the case of the larger instrument. In fact this point is so important that it will be as well to repeat the warning in its correct transposition. In its new form, and strictly with regard to the Trombone-in-G,[5] it is as follows:

Avoid quick interchanges of the note

with any of the following:

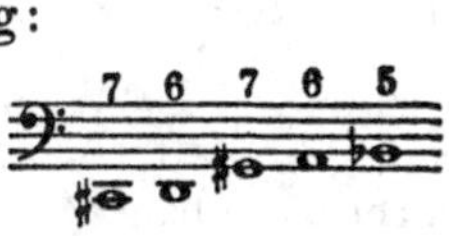

[1] This instrument is used in Sir Henry J. Wood's orchestra by Mr. Gutteridge.

[2] This is practically the German *Tenorbassposaune* with the *Daumenventil* as intended for use in *Die Walküre.*

[3] In *Otello* Verdi omits the Tuba and uses a Bass-Trombone as well as three Tenors.

[4] It need scarcely be mentioned that the slide is not controlled directly by the player's hand, but by a wooden handle fixed to the brass "stay" at the upper end of the slide. Without such a handle the lowest positions could not be reached at all.

[5] The corresponding difficulties on the continental F-Trombone can be easily found by merely transposing the whole series of notes down a whole-tone.

and of the note

with any of these:

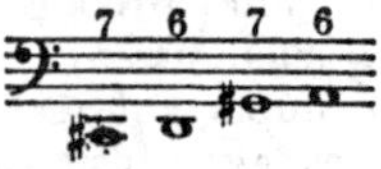

The tone of the Bass-Trombone, when it is not overplayed, is powerful and majestic in the extreme. It is, however, much less capable of execution than the B♭-instrument. The width of its position-changes is greater and its enormous air-column is, especially in the lower positions, less ready to speak. The long continuance of a *f* in the bottom register is most exhausting to the player.[1] Deep held notes, when marked *f*, are quite out of the question. Even after two or three beats of moderate time their volume becomes noticeably less. On the other hand, the *p* and the *pp* of the middle notes are easy to play and delightful to listen to.

This is a question of lungs, and, as it affects both Tenor- and Bass-Trombone players, it may be as well to give the rough serviceable limits within which these instruments should be confined both in the *piano* and in the *forte*:

In the *piano* of each instrument add the three lower semitones for special melodic or harmonic reasons.

No. 24. The Double-Bass-Trombone.

Fr. *Trombone Contre-basse*; It. *Trombone Contra-basso*; Ger. *Kontrabassposaune.*

This instrument was employed by Wagner in the *Ring* with the very sensible object of freeing himself from the continual necessity of associating the Tuba with the Trombones.[2]

[1] This has been recognized for centuries. Indeed in one of the earliest references to the Sackbut—the ancestor of the modern Trombone—its use is advocated not for musical but for medical purposes. "The entrayles, which be underneth the myddreffe, be exercised by blowyng, eyther by constraint, or playeng on shaulmes, or sackbottes, or other lyke instrumentes, which do require moch wynde." The quotation is from Elyot's *Castel of Helthe*, a Tudor system-of-medicine published in 1533. It is hardly necessary to comment either on the practical character of this advice or on the heroic nature of an age which could accept the Bass-Trombone as a medical prescription.

[2] Vincent d'Indy has used the instrument with the same object. In his second Symphony it replaces the Tuba.

As designed by him it was pitched in B♭, an octave below the Tenor Trombone. Its series of fundamentals would therefore be

and he actually calls on the player to produce the deepest of these notes. Upwards it can rise about as far as its 10th Harmonic

but of course its general objective is depth, not height. In England the Double-Bass-Trombone has been built in C. In doing this the special purpose of the instrument, the performance of such parts as these

EXAMPLE 78.

seems to have been overlooked.

Wagner writes the Double-Bass-Trombone in the bass-clef at its true pitch.

With regard to the Double-Bass-Trombone, it may be questioned whether in its manufacture the limits of human lungs and lips have not been overstepped. The difficulties of adequate tone-production, to say nothing of execution, are terrific. If there were really new possibilities in this direction they would probably have been exploited long ago by military-band instrument-makers. In practice, however, it has been found that any possible extension of the Brass-compass downwards must be looked for not from instruments of the Trombone family but from the wide-bore Tubas.

Before passing on to some more general considerations with regard to the use of the Trombones in the orchestra a few words may be spared for the *Valve-Trombones.*[2]

At first sight it would appear that no instrument was less in need of an added mechanism than the Trombone. Its natural habit-of-body is simplicity and perfection itself. Its only technical fault—if fault it be—is a complete inability to play *legato.*

However, the continual modern call is for suppleness and ease of execution, both in diatonic and chromatic music. In this respect a certain stiffness and want of adaptability has been a continual

[1] Two Tenor-Trombones, omitted in the above quotation, play in unison an octave above the Double-Bass-Trombone.

[2] Fr. *Trombones à pistons*; It. *Tromboni a cilindri* or *Tromboni Ventili*; Ger. *Ventil posaunen.*

handicap to the instrument. In order to remedy this and to solve some of the difficulties of compass-extension, several valve systems have been applied to the Trombone.

Of these the ordinary system of *added* tube-lengths under the control of 3 or 4 valves may be put aside as not suitable. The instrument so constructed is really quite different from and inferior to the ordinary slide-Trombone.

However, another system has been seen of recent years in the Queen's Hall orchestra,[1] and, as this system gives the nearest theoretical approach to the old crook-mechanism of the Horn, it will now be briefly described.

The system in question is known as the Seven-Cylinder Independent action.[2] This is a modification of the ordinary Six-Cylinder Independent action, a system which differs completely from all other valve-systems in that the cylinders (or pistons) are used, not to throw in an extra length of tube for each lower fundamental, but to take one off for each higher. It is a system of *cutting off*, not of *addition.* Piston-combination is, therefore, altogether avoided. That is the essence of the system. The Six-Cylinder action answers well enough in ordinary circumstances. When, however, a seventh cylinder is added there are, as we shall see, certain disadvantages.

The modification which was mentioned above, that is to say, the addition of the seventh cylinder, is specially designed for use on the Trombone in order to extend its range downwards without robbing it of its upper register. The first six cylinders and the open cylinderless position control the normal compass of the instrument. The seventh is used for purposes of downward compass-extension. The player is thus presented with an instrument on which he can perform *any* Trombone-part likely to be put before him. In practice a complete length of tube for each of the seven Trombone-positions is provided. This involves a departure from the ordinary *cutting off* system of the Six-Cylinder Independent action; and, in order to make clear the nature of this departure, we shall describe the Six-Cylinder System in a single paragraph and then the precise application of the seventh cylinder.

The Six-Cylinder Independent system was applied by Sax to various Brass Instruments of the "half-tube" family. Its action is normally as follows. The cylinderless position gives the greatest length of tube, three whole-tones below the primary length of tube in which the instrument is built. The action of cylinders Nos. 6, 5, 4, 3, 2, 1, is to cut off in the order named an additional length of tube corresponding to a rise of a semitone in pitch. In other words, the series diminishes in length from 6 to 1, and consequently ascends in pitch. The range of the whole instrument is therefore downwards from No. 1 cylinder (the shortest or primary length of the tube)

[1] Under Sir Henry J. Wood, to whom I am much indebted for the greater part of the above information.

[2] The "Independent" system was due, in the first instance, to Adolphe Sax. The instruments described above were specially built by Messrs. Lebrun of Brussels.

through Nos. 2, 3, 4, 5, 6, to the cylinderless position (the greatest length). We thus get the ordinary downward compass-extension of a diminished fifth, and incidentally a complete chromatic compass throughout the instrument.

The Trombone to which this system has been applied is the ordinary Tenor Trombone built in B♭.

Seven cylinders, however, are provided, and their operation is as follows:

When all the cylinders are "off" the player is actually playing on a B♭ Tenor-Trombone *in the seventh position.* His fundamental note is

and he can only blow the Harmonic Series corresponding to that note.

Now the first six cylinders act in one particular way and the 7th cylinder acts in precisely the opposite way.

Each of the first six cylinders cuts off a portion of the tube. No. 1 cylinder cuts off the greatest amount; No. 2 cuts off a slightly smaller, and so on, as far as and including No. 6. This has already been explained.

In musical language, by putting down cylinders No. 1, 2, 3, 4, 5, 6 in succession, the player obtains the fundamentals of the first six Trombone-positions.

He then "takes off" all the cylinders and, as we saw above, obtains the seventh or lowest Trombone position.

This gives him the complete Tenor-Trombone compass from low E upwards.

But observe, the 7th cylinder is so far unused. Its action is quite distinct from that of the other six. By depressing it a new length of tube is added to the main-line of the instrument, with which we have hitherto dealt, and the whole instrument is shifted down a perfect fourth.

In other words, with the 7th cylinder down the Trombone is now equal to a Bass-Trombone-in-F. The two last semitones below the ordinary Bass-Trombone compass (*viz.* C♮ and B♮) can be produced.

The gap before the first pedal-note (B♭) is thus bridged and the difficulties of playing parts written for the Trombone-in-F vanish. In fact, the seven-cylinder instrument is a Tenor-Trombone and a Bass-Trombone in one. It is only necessary for each player to cultivate his embouchure in the particular type of Trombone part (1st, 2nd or 3rd) which he is accustomed to play.

The principal disadvantage of this instrument is its unwieldiness. This is a failing of the whole Independent-Cylinder System. The extra lengths of tube are heavy, bulky and awkward. In a military band on the march they would be impossible. On the other hand, in the orchestra this is of less importance. One can easily accustom oneself to the unusual sight of three Trombone players apparently tucking sets of brass bagpipes under their arms. It is also to be noted that the special unwieldiness of the seven-cylinder Trombone is principally due, not to the Independent System itself, but to the necessarily great extra tube-length required by the 7th cylinder. In other words, it is due to the fact that the instrument is really a Tenor- and Bass-Trombone in one.

A more serious criticism is connected with the apparent difficulties of intonation. On an instrument of so great a range "truth" is difficult to come by. This is no more than we might expect. So long as the player is employing only cylinders 1 to 6 and the open cylinderless position no special difficulties arise. The trouble begins when he switches on his seventh cylinder. For, of course, though that gives him a Bass-Trombone-in-F, it only gives him one position on that instrument. To secure the advantages of the other positions he should be able to use his six other cylinders in combination with the seventh. This he actually may be compelled to do, though it is completely against the whole theory and practice of the Independent System. Hence come all the practical difficulties of intonation and the necessity of a continual resort to the tuning-slides. In short, the player has to pay the penalty of trying to play two instruments at once.

In tone these Trombones are massive and sonorous. Less biting and seemingly less brilliant than the modern small-bore Tenor, but much more flexible, much better adapted for chromatic work, for *cantabile*, and for unobtrusive part playing. Their apparent want of brilliance is possibly due to the fact that the players, not yet wholly used to the new technique, prefer the slide-instruments for their *bravura* passages.

It is worth noting that the exact correspondence between the old positions and the new cylinders is greatly in favour of the instrument. The B♭-Tenor-Trombone player can pass without serious difficulty from his slide- to his cylinder-instrument. Where he has been used to read his notes as in one of these positions,—

1-2-3-4-5-6-7,

he can now read them as on one of these cylinders,—

1-2-3-4-5-6-0.

Each position, except the lowest, corresponds in number precisely with the number of the cylinder necessary for producing the same Harmonic Series.

It will be interesting to watch whether these instruments establish and maintain their position in our orchestras or whether the slide mechanism, so often threatened throughout its long life, will refuse to "stand and deliver" to the cylinder as it refused before to the crook.

Some of our best Trombone-players—men who have been used to the slide all their lives—think that the addition of a single semitone-valve would solve its orchestral problems. The slide would remain as the main mechanism. Let us hope so! It is not a mere matter of history or tradition. The simple musical perfection of the whole slide-trombone group, both in the orchestra and in the military band, is something not to be sacrificed.

Considering the antiquity and settled technique of the Trombones, the student may be surprised that it is not possible to quote a long series of brilliant passages designed for them. The fact is that they are essentially "group-instruments," that is to say, instruments which make their effects harmonically and their differences of effect by differences of register, of spacing, and of contrasted *piano* and *forte.*

This *general* statement was first made by Berlioz. Strauss, however, quotes a *particular* example from the *Meistersinger* to prove it untrue. But the passage in question—two themes rhythmically contrasted and played simultaneously by the two first Trombones in unison and the third Trombone alone—does not affect Berlioz's *general* remark that "a single Trombone in an orchestra seems always more or less out of place. The instrument needs harmony . . . ," though Wagner's passages may be, as Strauss says, "typical models of the polyphonic style applied to the Brass."

The Harmonic method was, as we have seen, the style of Bach and of his period. It was also the method of Gluck in *Orfeo, Alceste,* and *Iphigénie en Tauride.* It was also mainly the method of Mozart in his Brass accompaniment to *O Isis and Osiris* (*Zauberflöte*), and in the statue and supper scenes of *Don Giovanni.* It was also the method of Beethoven in such works as the *C minor* and *Choral* Symphonies. And the general method in their sanity was the use of simple rhythms and held notes in three-part harmony with carefully thought-out expression marks *p* and *f*, < and >.

Here is a brilliant effect in the last three bars of Dvořák's *Carneval Overture.* The Trombones, in close harmony French-fashion, suddenly "come through" with a flaming chord of A major. Nothing could be simpler on paper: nothing could be more effective in sound.

EXAMPLE 79.

Compare the dynamic range of the three Trombones in this example —that is to say, their actual amount of sound—with the scarcely audible *pianissimo* which they produce at the end of the *Pathetic Symphony* (1st movement, see Ex. 91). Or, again, compare the effect of Tschaikowsky's *pianissimo* close harmony with that of the ideally-spaced last chord of this passage from Wagner's *Flying Dutchman* Overture:

EXAMPLE 80.

In this connection the student should examine the score of Schubert's *Mass in E♭*. It contains a good deal of vocal accompaniment in the old-fashioned German way, and of Trombone part-writing with Horns and Wood-Wind. In particular there is a surprisingly modern stroke at the opening of the *Sanctus*. The key of the movement is E♭. The Chorus repeats the word *Sanctus* on the ascending notes G, B♮, and D, harmonized by chords of E♭ major, B minor and G minor The Trombones enter on the second—the B minor—chord thus:

EXAMPLE 81.

It must be confessed that when not using the Trombones in harmony one runs certain risks. Against Wagner's brilliant "solo" use of the Trombones in the *Tannhäuser* Overture and the Prelude to Act III. of *Lohengrin*, and against Schubert's wonderful solo-passage for three Trombones in unison (*C major Symphony*), one must set the dreadful *Tuba Mirum* of Mozart. Only the first three bars appear to have been written by one who understood the instrument.

EXAMPLE 82.

The rest might better be described as *Tuba dirum spargens sonum.* Here is a sample:

EXAMPLE 83.

Then, again, on the "contra" side, there is the abominable circusy effect in the *Freischütz* Overture

EXAMPLE 84.

In connection with the last example we may note that the *piano* octaves of two Trombones always need caution in treatment. The sound of the instrument is naturally so full of a certain threatening purpose that the slightest variation from the serious, the majestic and the pompous becomes vulgarized almost to the level of a personal insult. Compare the determined semitonic rise of the Trombone-octaves[1] in *Don Giovanni* where the *Commendatore* repeats his words,

[1] Full Score Peters's Edition, pp. 347 and 348. The Trombone-parts in this Finale are said to have been added by Süssmayer, Mozart's pupil.

"Tu m'invitasti a cena," with this sort of thing from Berlioz's *Carnaval Romain.*

EXAMPLE 85.

Halévy, who had a great deal more to answer for than we usually think in this country, was probably the first to write unaccompanied octaves *ff* for the Trombones. In the 4th Act of *La Juive* there is a little eight-note passage which, owing partly to its orchestral novelty and partly to the boldness of its modulation, was looked on in its day (1835) as a surprising stroke, if not of genius, at any rate of theatrical vigour.

EXAMPLE 86.

Stale as this seems to us nowadays, we must remember it as the immediate parent of Wagner's Brass-octaves in *Rienzi* (1842),

EXAMPLE 87.

[1] In unison with the Bass-Trombone there is also an Ophicleide. The latter part is always played nowadays on a Bass-Tuba.

and probably as the original germ of many musically dissimilar passages in his later works.

Tschaikowsky, who, with Weber, may be looked upon as a good model for the ordinary bread-and-butter work of filling in Trombone-parts, rarely uses them as melodic instruments either solo, in the unison, or in octaves. A good example, however, of the last named may be found below (see Example 94).

In his *Commentaries and Additions* to Berlioz's *Orchestration* Strauss points the moral of Berlioz's remark that the effect of reinforcing the Double-Basses with the Trombone is bad. He says, "In big *tuttis* one often finds important bass themes allotted to the trio of Trombones, reinforced also by Bassoons, Cellos, and Double-Basses. Such 'doubling' is perfectly useless.... If one has no filling-up passages or figures to give to the Bassoons, Cellos, and Double-Basses, one should rather let them rest during the *marcatos* of the Trombones unless one has the specific intention of softening the brilliance of these latter instruments."

No. 25. "The Tubas."

The word Tuba has been used loosely to include at any rate two distinct types of Valve-Brass, and it has now acquired so general and vague a meaning that it may be said to refer, not to any existing instrument, but to any bass-part playable by a Valve-Brass instrument. Composers' minds have been confused, partly by Wagner's unfortunate misnomer **Tuben** for a family of instruments only one of which is a true Tuba, and partly by a number of inaccurate descriptions in which the distinction between the whole-tube and the half-tube groups of Valve-Brass has been overlooked. In addition the part has sometimes been mistaken for the whole. Thus, if we speak of "The Tuba (or Euphonium)," it is as if we were to say "The Man (or Nigger)." The composer should, however, understand that the types of instrument vaguely included in the word Tuba have quite definite and distinct characteristics of bore, mouthpiece, length of air-column, and method of attack. It is only his varying demands on the instrument in the way of pitch and execution that have resulted in our present rather unsatisfactory makeshift, the Orchestral Tuba-in-F.

Before proceeding with this subject the student should re-read carefully what was said above (page 86) with regard to the whole-tube and half-tube Valve-Brass.

The orchestral godfather of all this group of instruments was Richard Wagner. His original and successful intention was to introduce a new tone-colour into the orchestra akin to but different from that of the Horns. The new instruments were to be, and actually were, *Modified Horns*. In particular they were to be strong enough to support and contrast with the Trombones and Trumpets and were to have an even compass of about four octaves:

His idea was simply to write eight Horn-parts and so arrange the parts for his new instruments that four of his Horn-players could be turned over at any time to play them.

The instruments were to have a bore slightly larger than that of the Horns, but much less than that of the true Tubas. There were to be four pistons, of which three only were to be necessary for compass-purposes. The 4th piston was to be used in order to secure truth of intonation in the bottom octave. It was to be a sort of "compensating" piston.

The instruments were to be arranged in two pairs, a small high-pitched pair and a large low-pitched pair.

The small pair was to be built in B♭, and was to have a compass, in actual sounds, of

(about that of the Viola or the B♭-alto Horn).

The large pair was to be built in F, and was to have a compass in actual sounds, of

(about that of the Cello or Bassoon).

None of the above is a true Tuba. They are all *Modified Horns*, slender half-tube instruments much like the ordinary French Horn. This is exactly what Wagner intended. However, he *called* them **Tenor-Tuben** and **Bass-Tuben**.

In addition to the above two pairs of *Modified Horns*, Wagner introduced one true Tuba into his orchestra, a large four-valve instrument played with a big cup-mouthpiece and capable of producing its fundamental tone with ease. It was originally built in C, and its part in the *Ring* demands a compass downwards to the low E♭:

Wagner called this instrument the **Kontrabass-Tuba**.

This group, then, of the so-called "Wagner Tubas" was made up of two distinct types of instrument, a quartet of two high and two low *Modified Horns* and one true Tuba. For economy of space, and in order to distinguish the five instruments in the mind of the student, I shall refer to them as

A1 and A2,	- -	(Wagner's "*Tenor-Tuben*").
B1 and B2,	- -	(Wagner's "*Bass-Tuben*").
Z,	- -	(Wagner's "*Kontrabass-Tuba*").

Now, in practice the same thing happened with regard to A1, A2 and

B1, B2 as happened with regard to the Bass-Trumpet.[1] Wagner's intentions with regard to their shape, mechanism, and players were found to be capable of improvement. These intentions were therefore departed from. On the other hand, his intentions with regard to their pitch and quality could not be ignored.

A1, A2 and B1, B2 have therefore been altered. In outward appearance—a small matter—they are no longer the same. Their bells have been turned vertically upwards. They have been drilled, so to speak, into the semblance of military smartness. More important, the French Horn is no longer used as the strict model for their "build." Instead of that, a modified type of *Saxhorn* or *Saxotromba* has been adopted. They still remain half-tube instruments with a conical bore like that of the Horns, not cylindrical like that of the Trumpets and Trombones. The funnel-shaped mouth-piece, somewhat larger than that of the Horns, is still employed, and the instruments themselves have been, in most countries, taken away from the Horn-players and handed over either to military Saxhorn-players or to Trombonists.[2]

In this country there are at any rate three sets of these instruments (A1, A2 and B1, B2). They are all fundamentally of the same pattern, though one set in its desperate anxiety to show the right military swagger has pranked itself up in musically non-effective brass cuirasses.

The tone-quality and attack of these instruments is quite different from that of the true Tuba family. The tone is less "bullocky," quieter, and more "other-worldish." There is less impact in the attack, and the player, owing to the size and shape of the mouthpiece, is unable to *force* the tone. The Wagner parts are not difficult for the instruments, but the instruments themselves need continual careful lip-control in order to secure a beautiful and steadytone.

A few words must be interpolated for the benefit of those who wish to read Wagner's Full Scores. In the *Ring* he adopted two distinct methods of notation. The simplest way of showing what they were and what was the difference between them will be to boil Wagner's principles down and condense them into the space of a single note—the middle C. The student will then be able to refer to this note if, at any time, he is in doubt as to Wagner's meaning.

First Notation.

In the whole of *Das Rheingold* and in the *First Scene of Götterdämmerung*, if Wagner had wished A1, A2 and B1, B2 to sound a four-part unison on the note

[1] See above, pages 101-2.

[2] It need not be said that the Wagner Tuba parts *can* be played on an arrangement of Trumpets (or Cornets), Horns, and Trombones, according to fancy. The resulting orchestral ensemble, however, is a deplorable misrepresentation of the composer's intentions.

in the key of D♭, he would have written

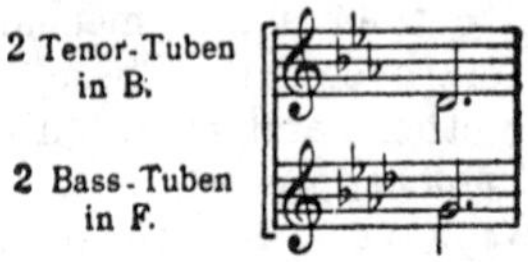

(Transposition as for 2 French-Horns in B♭-alto and 2 French-Horns in F.)

Second Notation.

In *Die Walküre, Siegfried,* and *the whole of Götterdämmerung except the first Scene,* if he had wished A1, A2 and B1, B2 to sound a four-part unison on the note

in the key of D♭, he would have written

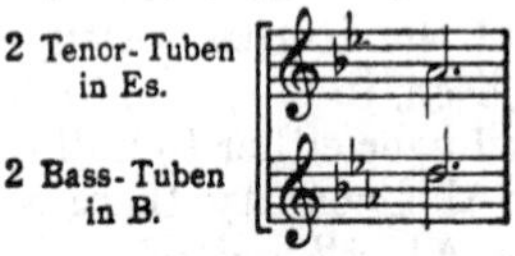

(Transposition as for 2 French-Horns in E♭ and 2 French-Horns in B♭-Basso. Note, however, that when the Composer uses the bass-clef for the two Bass-Tuben he adopts the old Natural-Horn practice of writing the notes an octave too low, so that the actual sounds are then only one whole tone below the written notes.)

In a foot-note prefixed to *Die Walküre* Wagner gives "ease of Score-reading" as his reason for adopting the "Second Notation"! He also directs that in the copying of the parts the keys adopted should be those suitable to the nature of the instruments: that is to say the parts for A1 and A2 should be copied as for transposing instruments in B♭ and the parts for B1 and B2 as for transposing instruments in F. An unholy muddle.

Now, for what players actually do. In this country at any rate A1 and A2 copy out their parts as for the military B♭-*Baritone* in the treble clef, a major ninth above the actual sound.[1] If they want to produce these sounds

they write

B1 and B2 copy out their parts at their actual concert-pitch in the bass-clef throughout.

For playing purposes then the unison

for the four instruments in the key of D♭, would be written thus,

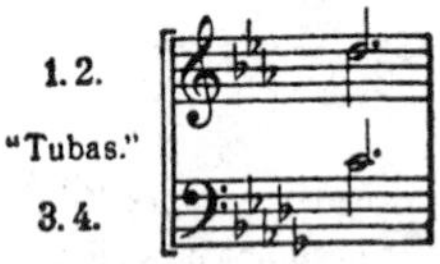

[1] The same transposition as that of the B♭ Bass-Clarinet when written in the treble clef.

Finally, we must mention that for Z Wagner always writes in the bass-clef at its proper pitch, and this is the way it is always read. No alteration is made.

After this digression on Wagner's notation, we must return to our instruments A1, A2, B1, B2. These four, though they look *military*, are really only civilians. They have always (even in Germany!) remained outside the soldier-caste. The Tuba, however, owing to its ponderous tone at once "caught on" all over Europe. It received military rank and began to pad its chest. In a word, every nation began a very successful development of the instrument for outdoor purposes.

It is on a modification of one or other of these military Tubas that Wagner's deepest Tuba-part (Z) and other modern orchestral Tuba-parts are played. However, it is quite impossible to describe in detail one tenth of all these developments. We must then content ourselves with naming the three Tubas which are commonly used wherever the British flag floats. This is fortunately a simple matter. For the sake of associating these Tubas in the mind of the student with Wagner's Z, I shall number them in order of pitch W, X, and Y.

All written for in the bass-clef as non-transposing instruments.

W. The Euphonium. Built in B♭. Cup-mouthpiece. A 4-valve Tuba with a chromatic compass from

X. The E♭-Bass. Built in E♭ a perfect fifth below W. Cup-mouthpiece. A 4-valve Tuba with a chromatic compass from

Y. The BB♭-Bass. Built in B♭ a perfect fourth below X. Cup-mouthpiece. At present only a 3-valve Tuba with a chromatic compass from

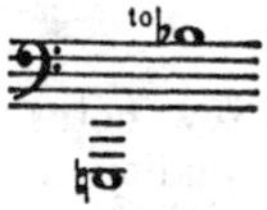

plus its possible but very difficult fundamental note

Of the above three Tubas, W is best and strongest in the upper part of its compass. (See Ex. 296 for W used in the orchestra.)

X is better than Y in the middle part. X is, however, not so good as Y in its bottom octave (E♭ to E♭), though it can actually take the deep E♭ which Y—a deeper-pitched instrument—cannot, owing to the absence of a fourth valve.

X and Y are often called by the generic name of **Bombardons**, and, when curled into circular shape for convenience on the march, **Helicons.**[1]

All three Tubas W, X, and Y are illustrated on Plate V. In the two smaller instruments the 4th valve is to be seen on the side farthest from the mouthpiece. In the Euphonium (Fig. 1) only the lower end of the piston-passage and the little circular finger-plate can be seen: the shape and placing of the valve, however, can be readily made out in the E♭-Bass (Fig. 2). It must be added that, for the sake of lightness on the march, the 3-valve Euphonium is often preferred in the army. In that case the student will understand without further explanation that its downward compass is robbed of all the semitones between its fundamental deep B♭ and the E♮ an augmented fourth above. For orchestral purposes this is, of course, an inferior instrument. The BB♭-Bass (Fig. 3) has no 4th valve at all. In every case valves 1, 2, 3, and 4 run in that order from the mouthpiece.[2]

Unfortunately for the playing of ordinary concert-room "Tuba-parts" in this country, composers as a rule have to be satisfied with a makeshift. This is an instrument derived from the Military E♭-Tuba (X), but built—mainly for reasons of key-convenience to the player—one whole tone higher in F.

This Bass-Tuba in F is not the same as B1 and B2, either in bore build, mouthpiece, method of attack, tone-colour, or compass. It is a true Tuba furnished with four valves, by means of which the player can fill in the eleven semitones below the second note of his Harmonic Series, namely,

He can then take off all his valves, and, with a clear bore, produce his fundamental note

Below this there are some few notes which can be got by means of a very loose lip, but their quality is, as a rule, miserable and their intonation unsatisfactory. Still they are played. The everyday complaint that "the Tuba" gets weakest just in the very place where it should be strongest only means that, for purposes of his general convenience, the player is not using the right instrument. For instance, in the following quotation from Elgar's *Cockaigne* Overture, the last

[1] For a brief description of the mechanism of X see page 87.

[2] For details of the valve-transpositions see page 87.

FIG. 1.—B♭-EUPHONIUM.

FIG. 2.—E♭-BASS.

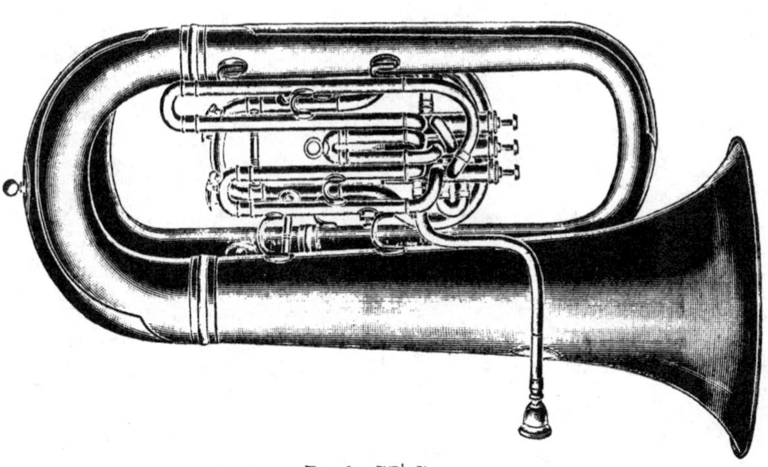

FIG. 3.—BB♭-BASS.

By kind permission of Messrs. Boosey & Co.

three semitones downwards are really not true notes at all when played by a four-valved Tuba-in-F. On a five-valved instrument they could, of course, be produced in a much better quality. It need not be said that in all Tuba parts the actual sounds required are written, and the bass-clef and true key-signature of the piece are employed.

EXAMPLE 88.

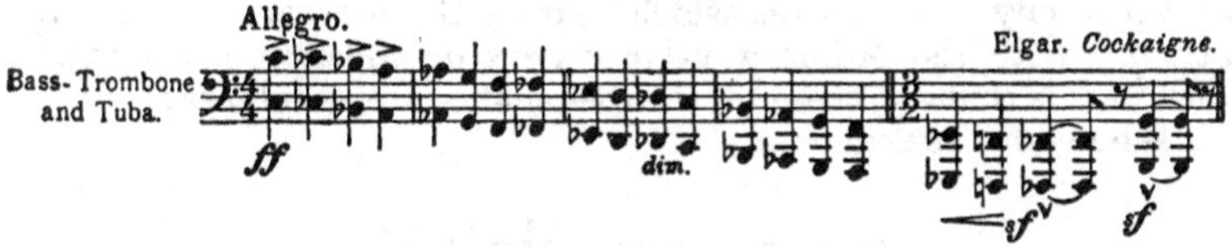

The upward compass depends on the player to a great extent. It may be taken roughly as being

It is, however, just this fact that our orchestral players are continually called upon by composers to play Euphonium (W) and Deep Bass Tuba parts (X and Y) within the limits of a single work that causes the player to adopt an unsatisfactory midway instrument.

It would be far better if he were free to adopt either a five-valve big-bore modification of X, or, better still, a four-valve modification of Y, the finest of all military instruments.[1] The extra weight involved in the addition of the fourth valve[2] would not matter much for concert performances where the player is seated. If this plan were adopted, and expense were no consideration, the higher Tuba parts could be played on W. With regard to the latter parts, this has actually been done when works have been performed in which there is a "Tenor-Tuba" part. Witness the *Don Quixote* Variations of Strauss, in which the Tenor-Tuba solos have been played with admirable and characteristic results on the ordinary Euphonium (W). Here is his first unmuted "solo" entry as written in the Full Score:

EXAMPLE 89.

[1] This would practically be a Contrabass-Saxhorn in B♭. See page 164.

[2] One of our most artistic Tuba-players, Mr. Barlow, plays on a large-bore five-valved Tuba in-F. In his very original system the five valves represent additional tube-lengths of ½, ¾, 1, 2, and 2¾ tones. His results are extraordinarily fine.

The part would be played on W as follows:

All Tuba-shakes are made with the pistons. It is therefore wise to write only those shakes which require the movement of a single piston. With the ordinary valve-system of added tube-lengths, as used in this country, these practicable shakes are as follows:

Whole-tone shakes on

and half-tone shakes on

Of course with the Independent System of *cutting-off* tube-lengths the proviso is merely that both notes can be blown from their two fundamentals as the same No. in the Harmonic Series. In practice this means that any shake whatever can be taken in the middle and upper registers. The only exceptions are the three cases where the lower note of the shake is Harmonic No. 2, while the upper is Harmonic No. 3. These would be, in the continental notation for the Saxhorn-family,[1] the two whole-tone shakes on

and the half-tone shake on

It need scarcely be said that shakes are seldom found in orchestral Tuba parts. A first-class player, however, has no difficulty in producing them with a smooth and satisfactory technique. They are better musically when helped out by some other members of the orchestral ensemble. The Tuba-shake in the *Meistersinger* Overture:

[1] See pp. 164-5 for this treble-clef notation. It is specially used in the above example as the Independent System is more particularly applied to the higher *Saxhorns*, or, as we should say, the *Cornets*, *Althorns*, and *Baritones*.

EXAMPLE 90.

is supported by a shake in the same octave played by the two Bassoons and the Cellos. while the Double-Basses perform the shake an octave lower. The round oily quality of the Tuba-shake, when well made, is by no means unpleasing.

The orchestral results that follow from the association of a single Tuba with the rest of the Brass are not wholly satisfactory in the concert-room. The instrument needs space and the harmony of its own kin. With such harmony it can support and contrast admirably with the rest of the orchestra. Left to itself, its heavy blurting tone, in which there is something elemental, even brutish, is liable to destroy the most cunningly contrived schemes of tone-colour. It is true that in the *pp* it can well sustain the *mf* and the *f* of Horns and Wood-Wind, and in the *f* can take on its shoulder the whole load of the orchestra. Again, in a very large orchestra, it can, when not played above *mp* or at the most *mf*, reinforce without blurring the tone of the Double-Basses. But generally speaking, one may say that as a soloist combining with such harmonic groups as the Trombones and Trumpets—and this is its principal occupation—it is often unsatisfactory.

Composers, however, so continually use the Tuba as a mere means of noise that this is not to be wondered at. If they would only listen to the beautiful *pp legato* and the pizzicato-like *staccato* which the conductor of a first-class military band exacts from his Brass Basses they would not be so much inclined to misuse the instrument.

As an example of the *p* use of the Tuba the student may be referred to the sombre opening of Wagner's *Faust Overture.* The *pianissimo* ending of Tschaikowsky's *Pathetic Symphony* (1st movement) is another case in point. In four-part Trombone chords of this sort it is practically an orchestral routine to give the lowest part to the Tuba. But it is a fair example of what was said above; the results are not quite satisfactory. The fact is that the Tuba is constitutionally compelled to "give himself airs." When sitting at table with the gentlemen of the Trombone family he appears to be something of a stranger who is obviously a "big-bore." In this special instance the Tuba "B" always sounds a trifle above the dynamic level of the three Trombones, not unbearably so, but just sufficient to make one feel that the combination is not ideal.

For this reason it is often better, especially in *p* chords, to associate a Trumpet with the three Trombones, or, if the Trumpet-tone is not desired, to space the three Trombones carefully and introduce a Horn in the middle of the harmony.

EXAMPLE 91.

Tschaikowsky. *Pathetic Symphony.*

The 4th Horn part of the above example is, in the Full Score, written on a separate stave with the 3rd Horn. The B♭ of the 1st Horn is of course merely for A♯. It is difficult to see why it should be written B♭, as it is approached thus:

In the *ff* the Tuba is continually used to support the harmonic mass either of the whole orchestra or of the Brass alone. A good instance of the latter is to be found in the Overture to *Rienzi*. The Tuba, of course, plays the obsolete Ophicleide part. Notice the absence of the Horns from the score. The tone of the Brass is rather more "knife-edged" when they are omitted. This is, however, only possible in an orchestral Brass-tutti when one has plenty of other Brass instruments. For Brass chords need "spreading" if they are to be effective. Notice also that the bass-part is not doubled throughout, as is usual, in the unison or the octave by the Bass Trombone:

EXAMPLE 92.

Wagner. *Rienzi.* [1]

The majestic theme used by Wagner in *Parsifal* furnishes an example of the use of the Tuba and Bass-Trombone in octaves as a bass to the Horns, Trumpets, and Trombones. In this example the Full Score has two separate staves for the Tenor Trombone parts. They are here condensed into one. It may be mentioned in passing that purely Brass passages are uncommon in orchestral music. Even climax passages that sound to the ear as mainly of Brass almost invariably contain high Wood-Wind parts. This adds enormously to the brilliance of the Brass chords by emphasizing their overtones:

EXAMPLE 93.

Wagner. *Parsifal.*

[1] The Oboes, Clarinets, Bassoons, and 2 Horns enter on the 8th bar of this Example in order to support the unison of the heavy Brass.

As an example of the Tuba when playing its Spenserian rôle of the Blatant Beast, the student should look at the end of the last movement of Tschaikowsky's *F minor Symphony* where, after building up his theme in tenths for eight bars on the Trombones and Tuba, he then comes to these octaves:

EXAMPLE 94.

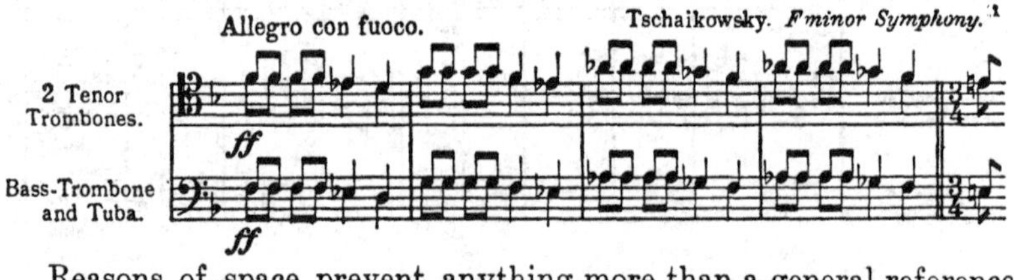

Reasons of space prevent anything more than a general reference to Strauss's use of the instrument. His Tuba parts exhibit a plasticity of treatment quite in advance of anything else in musical literature. The student must examine his Scores at first hand.

A really satisfactory mute has not yet been found for the Tuba. The one in use is a huge pear-shaped stopper like an exaggerated Cornet-mute. Its effect is not ideal either from the point of view of tone-stifling or of intonation. At the Opera, in a work of Stravinsky, the Tuba has been seen to swallow the Harp-cover in default of any better sustenance. There is an extraordinary passage for two muted Tubas in the Introduction to Strauss's *Don Quixote* variations. The two instruments play a weird passage in octaves while three muted Trumpets are busy above them with one of the principal themes of the work. An Oboe, unconscious of the trouble that he is making, holds a low F♯ throughout. The Score also contains parts for Double-Bassoon, muted Violins, and muted Double-Basses. These, however, add nothing essential to the very much condensed extract given below:

EXAMPLE 95.

[1] The Trombone and Tuba parts alone are quoted from the *tutti*.

[2] In the Full Score the 3rd Trumpet occupies a separate stave.

The Tuba is not often asked to perform feats of technical dexterity, at any rate in the concert-room. However, the very best players have a surprising facility and certainty of technique, and, what is almost of more importance, a complete control over their tone-production. This, in an instrument of such great length and of such a wide bore, is a matter of considerable difficulty. It calls for a strong physique, continual practice and experiment, and a nice artistic judgment.

No. 26. The Saxhorns and Flügelhorns.

A few words must be said here with regard to these two groups of instruments, though in this country they have little orchestral significance.

The Saxhorns are a hybrid invention of Adolphe Sax. They are practically an application of the valve-mechanism to instruments of the Bugle-family, but with the difference that, whereas in the Keyed-Bugles and Ophicleides the lateral holes produced an ascending chromatic scale, in the Saxhorns the valves provide a descending scale. They are all played with a cup-mouthpiece.

The Saxhorns are built in *at least* seven pitches, alternately in E♭ and B♭. And in order to associate the lowest three in the student's mind with the three heavy English military Tubas, I shall number them with small letters thus:

(*a*) Sopranino in E♭...[Practically the little E♭-Cornet].
In German the *Piccolo-in-Es.*

(*b*) Soprano in B♭[1]...[Practically the B♭-Cornet].
In German the *Flügelhorn-in-B.*

(*c*) Alto in E♭...[Practically the Althorn].

(*d*) Tenor in B♭...[Practically the B♭-Baritone].
Known in Germany and Austria respectively as the *Tenorhorn-in-B* and the *Bassflügelhorn.*

[1] As an instance of the confusion in the present-day nomenclature of the Brass-Wind, it may be mentioned that the Soprano Saxhorn ("b" in the above list) is known in France as the *Contralto* and in Belgium as the *Tenor Bugle.*

(*w*) Bass in B♭...[Practically the Euphonium (W)].
Known in Germany as the *Euphonion, Baryton* or *Tenor-bass-in-B.*

(*x*) Bass in E♭[1]...[Practically the E♭-Bass (X)].

(*y*) Contrabass in B♭...[Practically the BB♭-Bass (Y), but with a 4th valve filling in the five semitones above the fundamental B♭. Known in Germany as the *Kontrabass Tuba*].

Of the above Saxhorns a, b, c, d are half-tube instruments. Any of them would require 16 feet of tube to produce 8 feet C, where the Euphonium would require only 8 feet. Their conical bore is greater in calibre than that of the French Horn but less than that of the Tubas. Like the Cornet they employ Harmonics 2 to 8

with the usual piston-extension downwards to

w, x, y are true Tubas able to produce their fundamental note, and with the necessary valve furniture to enable the player to reach it chromatically. Theoretically they employ Harmonics 1 to 8

but, in practice, the top fourth on all three instruments is a little difficult to get, and not much needed, while on "y" the lowest seven semitones are unsteady and of doubtful intonation.

The difference between "d" and "w," instruments of the same pitch, is obviously the difference between a half-tube and a whole-tube instrument. "w" is built to produce its fundamental note, while "d" is not.

The student must read the above observations on compass in the light of the fact that all Saxhorns are transposing-instruments. A simple example will show him what these transpositions are without possibility of doubt.

Supposing the seven Saxhorns, beginning with "a" and ending with "y," play this triplet one after the other

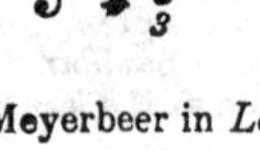

[1] First used by Meyerbeer in *Le Prophète*, 1849.

the actual sounds will be

If the student will now consider these transpositions and see what they mean when applied throughout the whole compass of the seven instruments he will perceive that the Saxhorns give us a practically homogeneous chromatic compass of five octaves and a fourth. In actual sounds:

In French military bands the method still persists of writing all the Saxhorns and Tubas as transposing instruments in the treble-clef. Its only practical advantage, as far as these instruments go, seems to be that the notes, when so written for the E♭-instruments *look like* the real sounds in the bass-clef. See, for instance, the 6th triplet in the 7/4 bar above. Even in such cases as these, however, a mental transposition of an octave or two has sometimes to be made. See the 1st and 3rd triplets of the same bar. However, this system of a cast-iron treble-clef notation has undoubted advantages, as we shall see, when applied to the Saxophones with their complex key-mechanism.

The Flügelhorns are a group of instruments somewhat similar in character to the Saxhorns. They are played with cup-mouthpieces and they have a conical bore. This bore is distinctly larger than the Saxhorn bore and there is a corresponding difference in tone-quality. They are often made with rotary valves and employ the same Series of Harmonics as the Saxhorns. The best known of these instruments are

(1) The B♭-Flügelhorn used by continental military bands for "Cornet parts." It is also used regularly in English Brass Bands. As a rule the number of B♭-Flügels is not more than half or a third that of B♭-Cornets. In compass and method of notation the two instruments are precisely the same. The B♭-Flügel, however, preserves much more the quality of the old Keyed-Bugle. Its tone may be best understood from the statement that the Cornet stands midway in the matter of brightness and mellowness between the Trumpet and the Flügel. The Trumpet is, of course, the most brilliant of the three. Then come the Cornet and the Flügel in an ascending order of richness, but in a descending order of military smartness and "attack."

(2) The Alto-Flügelhorn (or Althorn) in E♭. It is on this instrument that Wagner's "Tuba" parts "A1" and "A2" are sometimes played abroad. As a crying instance of the confusion in military-band nomenclature we may mention that the Germans call our E♭-*Tenor*-Horn an E♭-*Alt*horn; our B♭-*Baritone*, a B♭-*Tenor*horn and our Euphonium, a *Baryton*.

No. 27. The Saxophones.

Fr. *Saxophone*; It. *Sassophone*; Ger. *Saxophon.*

These again are hybrid instruments due to the inventive genius of Adolphe Sax. They employ quite new principles of musical-instrument manufacture, and might be classified either with the Brass or with the Wood-Wind.[1] They have no past history of which to be either proud or ashamed.

Their tubes are of brass and the vibrating-medium is a thickish, flexible, and slightly convex reed secured by a metal ligature to the lower part of the mouthpiece. At its upper end—that is to say at the end nearest the player's lips—the reed lies close to the "table" of the mouthpiece. There is, however, a distinct aperture.

The reed receives its motion from the breath of the player and vibrates to and fro, opening and shutting the gap at a rate which depends on the rate of the air-column vibrations inside the tube. This latter rate of vibration depends, of course, solely on the length of the air-column, and is therefore controllable by means of an elaborate series of holes covered by keys.

Now, a cylindrical pipe when played by a reed has the properties of a "stopped pipe." Its fundamental tone is an octave below that of an "open pipe" of the same length. It also "overblows a twelfth,"[2] that is it reproduces its natural scale at the distance of an octave-and-a-fifth higher.

On the other hand, a conical pipe when played by a reed has the properties of an "open pipe." Its fundamental tone is the same as that of an "open pipe." It "overblows an octave."

The Saxophone family belongs to the latter group, and its scale is therefore reproducible at the distance of an octave higher.[3] This fact differentiates it completely from the Clarinet group.[4]

The fundamental scale of the Saxophone is chromatically from

and therefore the second Series of Harmonics is chromatically from

The last four semitones above the high C are got by means of extra keys. They are "overblown" from fundamentals an octave lower, but these four fundamentals themselves are not used, as they

[1] See pages 13, 18. [2] See page 100 (foot-note).

[3] For a fuller discussion of this "overblowing" see pages 178-9.

[4] See pages 180, 253.

No. 2.

No. 3.

No. 4.

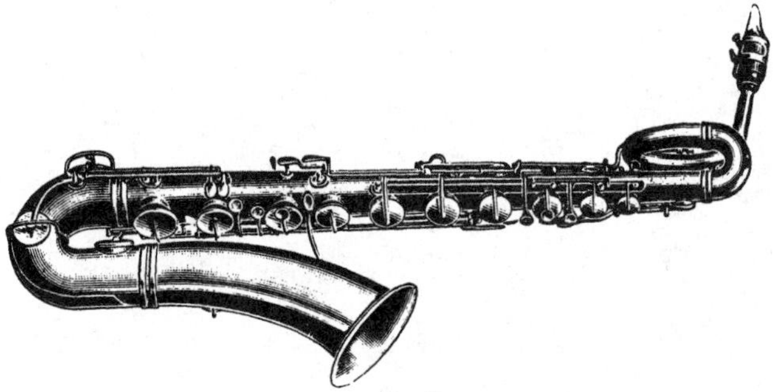

No. 5.

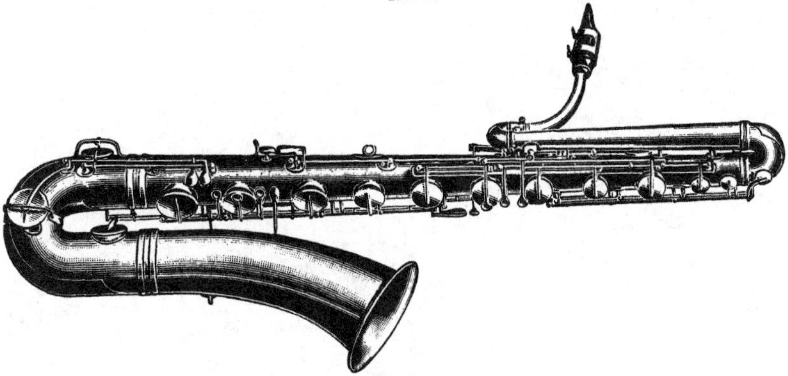

No. 6.

THE SAXOPHONES.

By kind permission of Messrs. Boosey & Co.

merely reduplicate the first four semitones of the first "overblown" octave:

Five varieties of this instrument are made in this country. Like the Saxhorns they are built alternately in E♭ and B♭. These five varieties are, in the list given below, numbered 2, 3, 4, 5, 6. Two other instruments are used in France and Belgium. They are both "extreme" instruments, one in the treble, the other in the bass. We may add them to our list as Nos. 1 and 7. The complete catalogue is then as follows:

[(1) Sopranino in E♭.]
(2) Soprano in B♭.
(3) Alto in E♭.
(4) Tenor in B♭.
(5) Baritone in E♭.
(6) Bass in B♭.
[(7) Contrabass in E♭.]

The whole series of these seven military instruments, alternately in E♭ and B♭, is also reduplicated abroad by orchestral Saxophones alternately in F and C. It must be mentioned, however, that even abroad No. 7 (the "Contrabass") scarcely exists except as a workshop-curiosity. The Bass Saxophone in B♭ (No. 6) is as heavy an instrument as any Wind-player would care to tackle. The "Contrabass," therefore, has been omitted entirely from the list of these instruments given on pages 7 and 8.

The general appearance of the Saxophones can be gathered from the illustration on Plate VI. The five instruments shown on the Plate are numbered to correspond with the list given above. The extreme instruments are therefore the B♭-Soprano (No. 2) and the B♭-Bass (No. 6). The student would do well to note the essential simplicity of all these instruments, despite their elaborate external furniture and their outlandish appearance. If he will imagine the rods and keys removed from the B♭-Soprano (No. 2) he will see what the Saxophone actually is,—a conical tube of metal pierced by holes with a single-beating-reed at the smaller end. The twists and turns in the tubes of the heavier instruments are introduced only for convenience to the player.

In compass, technique, and notation all these instruments are practically identical. The compass of all is from

with this amplification, that when writing for Nos. 3, 4, and 5 one can command two higher semitones still, the E♮ and F *in alt.* These three middle Saxophones—the *Alto, Tenor*, and *Baritone*—are the instruments most used both for solo- and ensemble-work.

A key to give the low B♭

is now regularly fitted to French instruments, but it is not in general use here.

All the above Saxophones are transposing instruments, and a single example (which will include the extreme and rarely-used Nos. 1 and 7) will show what these transpositions are. Let us suppose that the seven Saxophones, beginning with No. 1 and ending with No, 7, play this triplet one after the other:

the actual sounds will be

This petrified system of notation, so dear to the French mind, has one great advantage, that, as the fingering of all the Saxophones is identical a player can with little trouble pass from one instrument to any other. For this reason the Saxophones will probably always remain transposing-instruments with treble-clef parts. On the other hand, the logical absurdity of indicating the note

 by 

is patent.

It would, perhaps, be more satisfactory to use the treble- and bass-clefs at discretion: to leave No. 1 as it is, an instrument transposing upwards a minor third like the E♭-Clarinet: and to write all the other B♭- and E♭-Saxophones in their proper clefs and keys at a distance of a major second or a major sixth respectively above their actual sounds. The treble- and bass-clefs only are necessary.

The technique of the Saxophones is remarkably easy, simple, and regular. Scales, arpeggios, and florid figures are, especially on Nos. 2, 3, and 4, easily played and effective. On Nos. 5 and 6 the characteristic heaviness of the instrument asserts itself more and more.

Shakes are quite easy and extremely effective throughout the whole compass of the Saxophone. The only exceptions are the five whole-tone shakes on these notes,

which are difficult and should be avoided.

The tone of the Saxophone is curious: orchestrally a sort of bridge-quality between that of the Horns and the Wood-Wind. Thicker and heavier than the Clarinet, it has extraordinary powers, especially in the middle and lower registers of *crescendo* and *diminuendo*, of *sostenuto*, and of *cantabile*. When written in four-part harmony it produces at one time the effect of Violas and Cellos *divisi* with added Clarinets and Bassoons, at another the effect of the Organ diapasons. It is, however, less capable than the Clarinets and Bassoons of "dropping out of sight" when required. It always remains a little in evidence. This, of course, only applies to the *p* of the orchestra. On the other side, we must remember that in the *mf* and the *f* of the orchestra it is distinctly below the level of the Horn-quartet.

The Saxophones are principally used as melodic and "background" instruments in foreign military bands. Their tone, so much richer and fuller than that of the Wood-Wind when heard out-of-doors, lends a characteristic colour to such combinations. French and Belgian military bands in particular owe their peculiar flavour to the five or six Saxophones that are always concocted as ingredients in the Full Score. In England one or two at most are used. Of these one is invariably the Alto (No. 3), and it is employed both harmonically and with various effective "doublings" as a solo instrument.

Naturally in those countries where the Saxophone has been officially adopted in the army, and where no difference exists between civil and military pitch, its passage into the orchestra has been easy. At the same time the French orchestral composers do not as a rule get much beyond the idea of writing little tunes for the instrument. It is only lately that Richard Strauss has led the way by introducing a quartet of Saxophones into his *Sinfonia Domestica*. In that work they fill a subsidiary part mainly in enriching the middle harmonies. It must be said, however, that Massenet has used a quartet in much the same manner. In *Fervaal* Vincent d'Indy writes for Nos. 1, 2, 3, and 4, not, however, under their usual names of *Sopranino*, *Soprano*, *Alto*, and *Tenor*, but as *Soprano*, *Contralto*, *Alto*, and *Baritone*. Saint-Saëns uses No. 2, the Soprano-in-B♭, in his Symphonic Poem *La Jeunesse d'Hercule*.

Meyerbeer, Bizet, Massenet, Thomas, and every other French composer who ever put pen to paper, have all written little cantilenas for the E♭-Alto (No. 3), and it is to that instrument that the well known *cantabile* in Bizet's Suite, *L'Arlésienne*, is allotted. This has been so often quoted in instrumentation books and so often played (on the Clarinet) in our concert rooms that it is unnecessary to give the passage here. Instead I shall give a little unaccompanied melodic passage in A minor from Holbrooke's *Apollo and the Seaman*. The quotation, which is purposely chosen for its simplicity, includes Bassoon, Bass Clarinet, Soprano Sarrusophone, Soprano Saxophone, and Tenor Saxophone. The two Saxophones used in this work are those given above as Nos. 2 and 4. Their transpositions are, respectively, a major second and a major ninth downwards.

EXAMPLE 96.

A second Saxophone example from the same work may be found below (Ex. 97). In this latter quotation the Soprano Saxophone (No. 2) and the E♭ Clarinet have a little passage in thirds. The Saxophone plays the upper part.

No. 28. The Sarrusophones.

Fr. *Sarrusophone* ; It. *Sarrusofone* ; Ger. *Sarrusophon.*

These instruments, invented late last century by a French bandmaster named Sarrus, have a brass tube of wide conical bore. The player's breath sets the air in vibration by means of a "double-reed," which consists of two pieces of fine cane bound *vis-a-vis.* The narrow aperture at the mouth end of this reed takes the form (), and it is by the alternate rapid closing and opening of this aperture that the air column inside is set in motion. The Sarrusophone is, in fact, a sort of metal hybrid constructionally based on the Bassoon (*q.v.*). The scale, fingering, and method of tone-production are the same in the two instruments.

French Sarrusophones are made in six sizes, like the Saxophones, alternately in B♭ and E♭. They are as follows:

(1) Soprano in B♭.
(2) Contralto in E♭.
(3) Tenor in B♭.
(4) Baritone in E♭.
(5) Bass in B♭.
(6) Double-Bass in E♭.

They are all written in the treble-clef and they have a uniform chromatic compass from

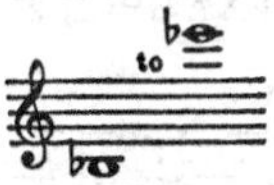

They are all treated as transposing instruments, and their transpositions may be clearly shown by the method which we employed for the Saxhorns and the Saxophones. Suppose that the six Sarrusophones, beginning with No. 1 and ending with No. 6, play this triplet one after the other

The actual sounds will be

The only use of the Sarrusophone in the orchestra seems to be as a rival to the Double-Bassoon, and it is for that reason that French instrument makers have begun to construct a **Double-Bass Sarrusophone in C.** It is written for, like the Double-Bassoon and the Double-Bass, in the bass-clef an octave above its actual sounds. Compass:

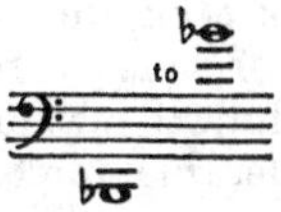

sounding

The top octave is poor and thin in quality. It is, however, only the bottom octaves that are needed in the orchestra, and the instrument is specially constructed to produce these in a heavy powerful quality.

The Sarrusophone has pretty nearly as much agility as the Bassoon. Even shakes and rapid staccato passages are easy. The taste for its tone quality, one thinks, must be acquired. On this point alone it will have difficulty in ousting the Double-Bassoon, now that the construction of that instrument has been so much improved. It is, however, scarcely fair to make comparisons between the two when the former is so rarely heard in this country.

Many French composers have written Double-Bassoon parts for Contrabass Sarrusophone in C, and it now seems to be generally adopted in Paris in place of the Double-Bassoon. In England Holbrooke has written parts for two Sarrusophones in his *Apollo and the Seaman*. He uses No. 2 and No. 6, the former under the name of "Soprano in E♭," instead of the more usual "Contralto in E♭." The

French treble-clef notation is employed. Here is a short extract from the work:

EXAMPLE 97.

No. 29. Obsolete Brass-Wind.

We have already seen[1] that, in one important class of musical instrument, the tone was produced by means of a cup-mouthpiece and the scale by means of the opening and closing of holes bored laterally in the pipe or tube. This family and its technical methods are now obsolete. In its day, however, it had considerable importance, and some of its members are still to be met in old Scores. The *Zinke* has already been sufficiently described: its bass, the *Serpent*, will be dealt with under *Obsolete Wood-Wind*. Both these instruments were of wood. There remain the four Brass instruments, the *Keyed-Bugle*, its bass the *Ophicleide* and the two transition-instruments between the Serpent and the Ophicleide, namely the *Russian Bassoon* and the *Bass-* (or *Keyed-*) *Horn*.[2] Of these by far the most important is the Ophicleide. However, as they are all merely variants of the original type, a few sentences will be devoted to a brief description of that type.

The Keyed-Bugle.

In all the instruments of the Keyed-Bugle family the opening of the holes acted in the same manner as the modern Independent

[1] Pages 70-2.

[2] The student must note that the separation of the *Serpent* from the instrument group under discussion is merely for convenience of reference. All these instruments, whether made of wood or of brass, belong technically and scientifically to the same family.

Cylinder System, that is to say it *cut off* successive lengths of tube and so raised the pitch. The various tube-lengths were in an ascending series. There was, however, a peculiarity here. The key nearest the bell was normally open, not shut like the other keys. In consequence the full vibrating length of the tube could only be got by the closing of this key. The key-technique was therefore irregular. When using none of his keys the player could blow the Harmonic Series from a fundamental

Depressing the first key he had access to the full length of tube with a fundamental

Bringing the second key into action he could blow the Harmonic Series on the fundamental

and so on regularly upwards to the seventh key. The irregularity lay in a reversal of the open-position and the first-key position, and this irregularity was characteristic of the whole Bugle-Ophicleide family. The Harmonic Series used was as follows:

and theoretically the player could blow this Harmonic Series from the seven fundamentals

As a matter of practice, however, any note above

was an impossibility. The instrument was normally built in B♭, occasionally in A, and still more rarely in the high (*sopranino*) key of E♭.[1] The written chromatic compass of the Keyed-Bugle-in-B♭ was therefore

[1] Meyerbeer has used both the "A" and the "B♭" instruments in *Robert le Diable.*

An illustration of the Keyed-Bugle-in-B♭ will be found on Plate II., p. 72. If the student will turn to it he will have no difficulty in making out the first key lying open nearest the bell and the six other keys all closed and placed in an ascending series nearer the mouthpiece.

The Keyed-Bugles and Ophicleides spoke with extreme ease and possessed a power of *legato*-playing unknown to our modern Brass Instruments. Against this must be set the fact that they were shockingly defective in intonation. So long as they were employing only the Harmonics of their three greatest tube-lengths there was not much to complain of. But as the tube-lengths decreased by the successive opening of the holes nearer the mouthpiece so the intonation became more and more imperfect. In fact it was as a partial remedy to this defect that the system of an open 1st-key was introduced. This failing was fatal to the instrument. The early valve-Cornet was by no means a miracle of correct intonation; but compared with the Keyed-Bugle it must have seemed a blessing indeed.[1]

The Bass-Ophicleide.[2]

The Bass-Ophicleide was the bass of the Keyed-Bugle. The two instruments were pitched an octave apart. It was of big bore and coarse, powerful tone. Eleven holes pierced laterally in the tube of the instrument and covered by "cheese-plate" keys gave the performer a complete chromatic compass. A huge cup-shaped mouthpiece was used. The key-technique of the Ophicleide was similar to that of the Keyed-Bugle but, owing to the number of keys, the former instrument had a compass of an octave more than the latter. The Ophicleide was built in two keys, C and B♭, with a compass, in C, from

and, in B♭, from

For orchestral purposes it was always treated as a non-transposing instrument, and its part was written in the bass-clef. All that was said above with regard to the Keyed-Bugle's easy speech and capacity for *legato*-playing applies to the Ophicleide. In intonation, however, the latter instrument was decidedly superior.

Till about the middle of last century it held its place as the chief bass-instrument in all military bands. The parts assigned to it in the orchestra were what we should now call "Tuba-parts." In France it was employed by nearly every composer from Spontini to Meyerbeer. Wagner wrote a part for it in *Rienzi*; Berlioz, in the *Amen Chorus* of his *Faust*, uses two; while Mendelssohn has a well known "clown's" passage for it in the *Midsummer Night's Dream Overture*.

[1] No wonder Mr. Pickwick objected to Mr. Bob Sawyer's classical imitation of the Keyed-Bugle on the top of the coach between Bristol and London.

[2] That is *Keyed-Serpent*, from two Greek words *ophis* and *kleis*, meaning respectively "serpent" and "key."

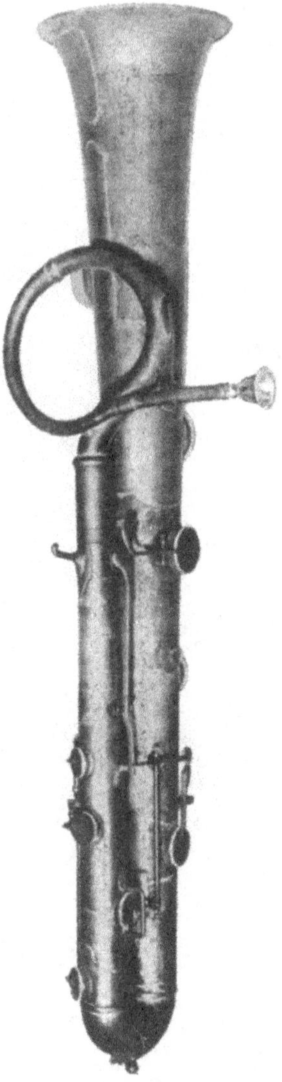

BASS OPHICLEIDE.

By kind permission of Messrs. Boosey & Co.

The general adoption of the milder-toned Tuba in Germany about 1850 led to the gradual disuse of the "bellowing" Ophicleide. It has, however, lingered on in France, where it still figures as a sort of musical hobgoblin in instrument-makers' catalogues. The parts for the instrument are now invariably played on the Tuba. The *Midsummer Night's Dream* passage, however, completely loses its point when so played. The composer's intentions would probably be much more nearly realized if it could be well blown-out on the Double-Bassoon. But reasons of compass forbid this. The Ophicleide parts in Berlioz's *Faust* are usually given to two Trombones, but here again there seems to be some loss of special effect.

Alto-Ophicleides in E♭ and F are mentioned by Berlioz as being used in the "Harmonies" of his day.[1] He even describes a Double Bass-Ophicleide in E♭ with a compass down to

The shape of the Bass-Ophicleide—familiar to all in the hands of the elderly angel on the cover of *Punch*—is shown on Plate VII. The instrument from which the photograph was taken has evidently seen good service, for it has been patched in two or three places. Just visible inside the "O"-curve is the 1st or "open-key." As we have already explained, the other keys lie close over the holes till they are called into action by the depression of the finger-pieces. Their position can be clearly seen in the illustration. The white line under each circular plate is a pad, not an air-space.

The Bass-Horn and the Russian Bassoon.

Very few words need be devoted to either of these instruments. They were both experimental or transitional types which soon lost ground when opposed by the more perfect Ophicleide. Both instruments were made of brass, and employed the principle of laterally-bored holes and a cup-mouthpiece. In both cases the name is somewhat misleading. The only resemblance between the Bass-Horn and the ordinary orchestral Hand-Horn of its time lay in the fact that both were conical in bore. The instrument was also known as the Keyed-Horn; in German, *Klappenhorn* or *Kenthorn.* The latter name was adapted from our own expression *Royal Kent Bugle,* a title bestowed on the Keyed-Bugle in honour of the Duke of Kent. If a fancy name was required for the other instrument, "Russian Bass" would have been better than "Russian Bassoon," for, of course, it had no connection whatever, technical or historical, with the Bassoon.

The Bass-Horn was a conical instrument of big bore terminating in a wide bell that pointed upwards like that of the Ophicleide. The two halves of the tube were bent back upon each other and clumsily

[1] See *Obsolete Wood-Wind,* p. 286, for a description of the *Serpent.*

joined in a metal "butt" something like that of a modern Bassoon. The narrowest end of the tube—that is to say, the end that carried the mouthpiece—was often fantastically curved into an elaborate swan-neck shape in order to reduce the total height of the instrument. As a rule the player merely used his fingers to open and close the holes in the metal tube. In addition, however, an "open-key" was provided as in the Ophicleide and the Keyed-Bugle. The intonation was imperfect, and the tone-quality may be judged from the fact that when the Ophicleide came in the Bass-Horn went out.

The Russian Bassoon was an instrument of similar character. In fact, the description just given will suffice to provide the student with a rough idea of its abilities and disabilities. Like the Bass-Horn, it was scientifically a first-cousin of the Ophicleide, or, to use Berlioz's expression, as translated, "a low instrument of the serpent[1] kind." He gives it a compass of

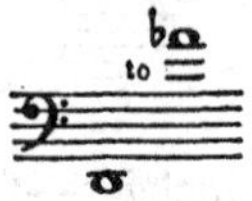

After a short account of its imperfections he makes the ominous remark that "*its two best notes* are D and E♭." No tear has been shed over the disappearance of the *Fagotto à la Russe.*

[1] The compasses of all the Ophicleides may be found on page 9.

WOOD-WIND INSTRUMENTS.

PRELIMINARY.

We now come to an instrumental group which is normally called on to play much more complex passages than any we have hitherto met. As far as the actual *blowing* goes, this group is much less exacting to the executant, but this comparative advantage is counterbalanced by its technical difficulties *of hand*, which are not only much greater but less uniform than those of the Brass.

In all these instruments the tone is produced by the setting in motion of a column of air in one of three ways:

(1) By direct blowing either at the end (e.g. *Flageolet*) or through a hole cut in the side of the pipe (e.g. *Flute*).
(2) By means of a single-beating-reed (e.g. *Clarinet*).
(3) By means of a double-reed (e.g. *Oboe* and *Bassoon*).

There are some difficulties here to be explained. In all tubes and pipes, the pitch depends mainly on these two things: the length of the air-column and the diameter of the openings, whether lateral or at the bell. It depends less on the diameter of the bore. In general, the diameter of a lateral opening must be equal to the diameter of the bore at that point. Now, in all early Wood-Wind instruments, the holes, if properly placed according to exact theoretical requirements, would have been quite *unstoppable* by human fingers. When the key-apparatus was still primitive, makers had recourse to a plan, by which they substituted smaller, *stoppable* holes, placed nearer the mouthpiece.

Another acoustic point. When the diameter of the lateral opening, or of the bell, for that matter, is smaller than that of the bore, the length of the pipe below the open hole—theoretically non-existent—asserts itself, and lowers the pitch of the required note. An excellent example of this is the low-A on the Bassoon, the hole for which is both too high and too small. These are only samples of the difficulties that confront makers when they try to place on an accurately cut reed-pipe a human hand, better fitted to grasp a stone axe or to chip a flint arrow-head.

Various devices to overcome these difficulties were suggested at various times, but they were all superseded by the invention of the Boehm mechanism. This invention allows the pipe to be bored without any reference to the limitations of the human hand. The holes are cut *exactly* where they should be in order to secure a scientifically perfect intonation. For instance, Boehm's mechanism makes it possible to place eleven holes in the pipe of the flute so that their successive opening shortens the air-column in exactly the right proportion for producing the eleven semitones that lie between

At the same time this mechanism gives every Wood-Wind player an apparatus by means of which he can easily stop or unstop any holes or combinations of holes. This is effected by means of a series of padded metal keys fitting closely over the holes, and by an elaborate arrangement of metal trackers, rollers, and finger pieces.

From this short explanation the student will easily see how much more complex are the movements of the Wood-Wind-player's hands than those of the Brass-player's, and therefore how necessary it is to study the peculiarities of the Wood-Wind-player's technique. Passages which are musically very simple—even a single trill which a beginner could play on the Violin—often present quite serious difficulties when attempted on a Wood-Wind instrument. They may involve, perhaps, the sudden rearrangement in position of five or six fingers; and this rearrangement may have to be effected and abandoned within the fourth part of a second. Passages of this sort, even when played by first-class artists accustomed to surmount difficulties, always sound fussy and stupid. Nine times out of ten the player, intent on overcoming the difficulty, has no time to think of the music.

Of course all Wood-Wind instruments, whether they have an external mechanism or not, depend for their compass on the holes pierced laterally in their pipes. They must, therefore, either have a hole for every note required, or make use of the property possessed by columns of air when confined in pipes,—the property of splitting up and vibrating in fractions of their whole length.

As was briefly explained above under *Saxophone*,[1] all pipes whose air-columns are set in vibration by means of a reed may be divided into two classes—

(1) Those whose pipes are cylindrical.
(2) Those whose pipes are conical.

(1) Cylindrical reed-pipes have two properties:

(A) They act in the same way as the stopped pipes of an organ. The air-vibrations have to travel not merely from one end of the pipe to the other, but back again as well. The result is that in the stopped Organ-pipe the note produced is an octave lower than it would be if the pipe were open. Similarly in the cylindrical reed-pipe the note produced is an octave lower than it would be in a conical reed pipe of the same length. This is important, for as Professor Prout has pointed

[1] See page 166.

out, it enables the Clarinet to produce middle C with only one foot of pipe where the Oboe requires two.

(B) They all "overblow a twelfth," that is to say, their fundamental scale is reproducible by means of a difference of embouchure, at a distance of a twelfth upwards.

Example. The Clarinet, a cylindrical reed pipe, needs at least eighteen holes to produce a chromatic compass from

The next octave is not produced by a fresh series of holes but by opening the "speaker-key." This is a little hole pierced in the pipe. When opened it assists the player's embouchure to divide up the vibrations of the air-column and so enables him to reproduce his fundamental scale one twelfth higher. This takes him to top F, and there he stops. Any notes above that he must produce by means of a rearrangement of his keys called "cross-fingering," and by a further increased pressure of embouchure. The explanation of what these top-notes are will be given later under *Clarinet.*[1]

(2) **Conical reed-pipes,** on the other hand, have these two properties:

(A) They act in the same way as the open pipes of the Organ. The air-vibrations have only to travel once through the length of the pipe. The note produced is an octave higher than it would be if the pipe were stopped.

(B) They all "overblow an octave."

Example. The Flute, a conical instrument in which the wind-stream from the player's lips acts as the vibrating-reed, has as its fundamental scale the octave scale of D. After that the player produces his second octave by compelling the vibrating air-column to split up fractionally. In ordinary words, he uses the same fingering but a different embouchure. In the third octave he again overblows from the bottom octave, but this time opens certain of the holes. His object in doing this is the same as the object of the Clarinet player in opening his "speaker-key." He assists his embouchure and helps the air-column to break up into the smaller fractions required. It must be remembered, however, that neither Wood-Wind-, Brass-, nor String-players always do in practice what they might be expected to do in theory.

The student should notice that in the above remarks the term "fundamental scale" is used rather loosely but conveniently. He need not be confused by its use, but he must not imagine that there is anything in a reed-pipe which corresponds at all strictly to the "fundamental notes" in the various Harmonic Series of a Brass Instrument. Any single note in the "fundamental scale" of a reed pipe can be "overblown" at its 8th or 16th, or at its 12th or 24th, according to the shape of the pipe and the convenience of the player. But no Series of

[1] See page 254.

Notes such as the "Harmonic Series" of the Brass can be produced from this single note. This has an important bearing on instrumental performance. In the Brass, while it is by no means always necessary to shift the fundamental for each note played, it is always a slightly cumbersome matter to do so. In the Wood-Wind it is a practical necessity to alter the fundamental for every successive note, but this is compensated by the extreme ease and lightness with which it can be done.

Classification.

The whole family of Wood-Wind instruments may be conveniently divided into five classes,[1] according to their respective methods of tone-production.

(1) *Pipes without embouchure or mouthpiece.* [Obsolete: The *Syrinx*, a little set generally of 7 pipes blown by directing the breath not into but across the open end so that it impinges on the rim. The pipes were stopped at one end, and therefore produced a note an octave lower than they would have if open. There were no lateral holes, and so the rule was "one pipe, one note." They were, however, probably all overblown.]

(2) *Pipes without mouthpiece but with embouchure.* The **Modern Flute**, the **Bass Flute**, the **Piccolo**. [Used only in military bands, the *Fife.*]

(3) *Pipes with whistle-mouthpiece.* [Not used in the orchestra: The *Whistle*, the *Flue-work of the Organ.* Obsolete: The *Recorders.* Obsolete in the orchestra: The *Beak-* or *Fipple-Flutes*, the *Flageolet.*]

(4) *Pipes with reed-mouthpieces*, subdivided into:

(A) *Cylindrical Pipes overblowing a twelfth*: The **E♭-Clarinet**, the **B♭-A-Clarinet**, the **Alto-Clarinet**, the **Bassett-Horn**, the **Bass-Clarinet**. [Rarely used even in military bands: *The Pedal Clarinet.* Obsolete: The Classical *Aulos* and *Tibia*, the mediaeval *Cromornes.*]

(B) *Conical Pipes overblowing an octave*: The **Oboe**, the **Oboe d'Amore**, the **English Horn**, the **Bassoon**, the **Double-Bassoon**. [Rarely used: *The Baritone Oboe.* Obsolete: The mediaeval *Schalmey*, *Pommer*, and *Curtal* (or *Dulcian*). The Saxophones might technically be included here, as they are conical reed-instruments overblowing an octave. As, however, these hybrids embody a new principle, and are actually made of brass, not wood, it has been thought better to describe them in the section devoted to Brass Instruments.

(5) *Pipes of conical bore pierced with lateral hole and played with a cup- or funnel-mouthpiece.* Obsolete: The *Zinke* or *Cornet à bouquin*, its bass the *Serpent.*]

For purposes of modern orchestral classification these five groups can practically be reduced to three:

The Flute-group.
The Oboe-group.
The Clarinet-group.

[1] This is the classification adopted by Miss Schlesinger in the *Encyc. Britt.*, XI. Ed. See sub. "Wind Instruments."

FIG. 1.—EMBOUCHURE (Modern Flute)

FIG. 2.—WHISTLE-MOUTHPIECE (Fipple-Flute).

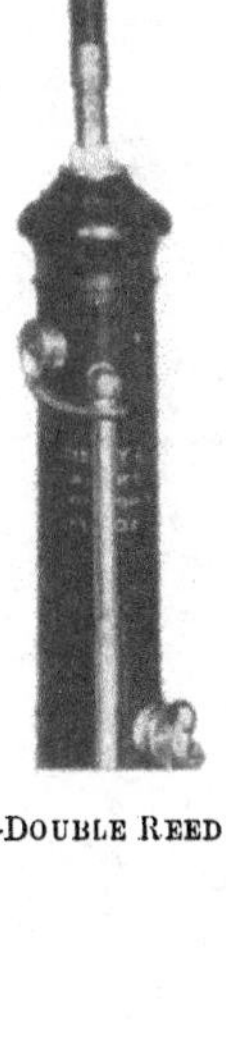

FIG. 3.—DOUBLE REED (Oboe).

FIG. 4.—SINGLE-BEATING-REED (Clarinet).

By kind permission of Messrs. Boosey & Co.

We shall discuss their technical details in that order. But before doing so we must note that, of the five classes mentioned above, only Nos. 2 and 4 furnish us with any modern orchestral instruments. Of the other three classes No. 1 (*pipes without embouchure or mouthpiece*) has no musical significance at all and may be dismissed without further comment. We have already dealt with the principles employed by No. 5 (*pipes with lateral holes and cup-mouthpieces*). The whole series is obsolete, and only a few sentences need be given to the description of the *Serpent*. These will be found under *Obsolete Wood-Wind*. No. 3, however (*pipes with whistle-mouthpiece*), though totally disused in the orchestra, has had some importance in the history of Music, and, as it includes the family of *Fipple-Flutes* and *Recorders*, a few words may be devoted to a description of its technical principles.

In all these instruments the air-column was set in vibration by means of a beak- or whistle-mouthpiece made of bone, ivory, or wood. The air-stream was directed against the sharp edge of a "bevel" cut in the pipe. These were the two characteristic features of the whole family,—the "beak" and the "bevel." They can both be plainly seen in Fig. 2, Plate VIII. The ivory beak projects to the left from the top of the "head." This is a somewhat abnormal position for the mouthpiece, but the illustration has been chosen in order to show the bevel with the utmost clearness. It lies immediately below the ornamental ivory ring that connects the two "joints." A third characteristic feature of this instrumental group was the thumb-hole pierced in the back of the pipe.

The mediæval Recorders were all members of this family. Their size varied from that of a "penny-whistle" to that of a modern Bassoon. Indeed in the Bass-Recorders a crook almost exactly like a Bassoon-crook led from the top of the pipe to the beak, which was in the player's mouth. This was, of course, merely matter of convenience to the instrumentalist. In old pictures the shape of this crook and the apparent likeness of the beak-mouthpiece to a large double-reed may sometimes mislead the student as to the instrument intended. In every case, however, the presence or absence of the bevel decides the question.[1]

The Recorders had a somewhat tame but pleasant, sweet, and woody tone. To the ears of our Tudor forefathers, accustomed to the harsh quality of the double-reeded *Schalmeys* and *Pommers*, they probably afforded the same sort of relief as we get to-day from the Strings in the orchestra.

The only survivor of this ancient family is the *Flageolet*. This instrument may be called a super-acute Recorder. It has the usual whistle-mouthpiece and bevel, but is modified so far as to require two thumb-holes at the back. We owe its introduction to the craze for French fashions which set in at the time of Charles II. The

[1] Double and even triple Fipple-Flutes were at one time fairly common. In pictures and illuminations these often have a certain likeness to the double-pipes of classical times. The integral difference, of course, is that the former were reedless, while the latter were true reed-pipes.

instrument was used by Händel in "Hush, ye pretty warbling quire" (*Acis and Galatea*). It is also in all probability intended in "O ruddier than the cherry," though the Score merely says "Flauto" and a Piccolo is generally employed. Gluck used the instrument in *Die Pilgrime von Mekka*, and Mozart in *Il Seraglio*. The compass was in actual sounds

and it was written for as a transposing-instrument sounding a twelfth above the written notes. For instance

 sounded 

It is worth noticing that the Fipple-Flute, that is to say the Flute blown with a beak-mouthpiece, was the characteristic *English* Flute. It was in common use here in the sixteenth and seventeenth centuries, and was generally known to learned writers as "Fistula Anglica." The opposing instrument, the "Cross-Flute" or "Flauto Traverso," was blown through a hole in the side like a modern orchestral Flute, and was known as "Fistula Germanica." These invaders the Cross-Flutes were actually in evidence from about 1500 onwards, but it was not until much later that they managed to secure a firm foothold in England. Indeed the mouthpiece of the English-Flute[1] represented on Plate VIII., Fig. 2, owes its peculiar right-angled position to a sort of defensive strategy. The player had to hold the instrument horizontally, and appeared to be playing on a German-Flute. In reality he was only blowing into a whistle-mouthpiece,—a much easier task. It was, in fact, a species of "cheat" which has been revived in our own day with some of the Valved-Brass.

No. 30. The Flute.

Fr. *Flûte*; It. *Flauto*; Ger. *Flöte*.

The natural scale of the orchestral Flute is the scale of D major having

as the bottom note of its first octave. Hence, though it is always written for as a non-transposing instrument, it is sometimes called the "Flute in D." This looseness of nomenclature extends to all the non-orchestral Flutes used in military bands.[2]

[1] Bainbridge and Wood's "Patent Chromatic Albion Flute." [2] See page 203.

The compass of the instrument begins nowadays not at the D mentioned above but two semitones lower at middle C. This will be explained later.

The Flute is nominally a "stopped-pipe." The upper end beyond the "embouchure," that is to say beyond the hole into which the player blows, is actually closed. The embouchure itself, however, gives the Flute the properties of an open-pipe.

Originally cylindrical the Flute, about 130 years ago, became conical with a cylindrical head. In this type of instrument the conical bore was so arranged that its smallest diameter was farthest away from the embouchure. Nowadays the Flute is generally cylindrical with a parabolic "head."

The instrument is made up of three pieces or "joints":

(1) The **Head,** about $\frac{1}{3}$ the total length of the instrument, plugged at the end and containing the embouchure or hole for blowing into. It is this portion between the embouchure and the plug—technically called the "stop"—which is now generally of a parabolic shape. An illustration of the "head" with the embouchure-hole will be found on Plate VIII., Fig. 1. The "stop" is the portion upwards (in the illustration) from the hole. The "plug" is at the extreme upper end.

(2) The **Body,** a long joint bored with the holes and carrying the keys necessary to produce the fundamental scale of D. This is a point of theory only, for when

(3) The **Foot-joint** or **Tail-joint** was added and bored to allow of the production of the two bottom semitones C♮ and C♯ it was found desirable to abandon the old D and substitute another playable by opening a key in the Foot-joint.

The instrument is made either of cocus-wood, of ebonite, of silver, or even of gold. Those of wood have the best and most "flutey" tone: those of metal "speak" the most easily.

The Flute is, of course, a reedless instrument. The part played by the reed in such instruments as the Oboe and Clarinet is taken, in the Flute, by the actual air-stream from the player's lips. This air-stream, technically known as the "air-reed," is directed by the player against the sharp edge of the embouchure, and produces the sound-waves in the air-column which is contained in the pipe. The pitch of these sound-waves depends solely on the length of the air-column, and this again is controlled by the opening and shutting of the lateral holes. The effective length of the vibrating air-column is merely the length between the embouchure and the nearest open hole.

The mechanism of the modern Flute not only allows the holes to be bored in their scientifically correct places, but it also enables them to be cut with a sufficiently large diameter. This is an important point. In the days when the holes had to be cut too small, they also had to be placed too near the embouchure. Otherwise the pitch would have been altered and the tone muffled.

The distinctive tone-quality of the Flute appears to be due—slightly—to the material of which it is made and—chiefly—to the shape and position of the stopper and of the air-space between that and the embouchure. Considerable differences of opinion have been expressed as to the reasons for the Flute's "breathe-y" quality in its bottom octave. On the one hand, this has been positively attributed to the paucity of "harmonics" or "overtones" present in these notes. This perhaps explains the fact, familiar to all Flautists, that persons, judging solely by ear and not by any knowledge of the Flute-technique, often suppose them to be playing an octave lower than their actual pitch. On the other hand, precisely opposite and equally positive statements have been made as to the wealth of these lower notes in Harmonics. On the whole, the former opinion seems to be the more satisfactory. One may add that all practical musicians have noticed the curious likeness between these notes and the sounds of the Trumpet when played *piano.*

The compass of the orchestral Flute is chromatically from

Some Flutes appear to have had the low B♮

At any rate, Wagner writes down to that note in *Lohengrin.* On a modern Boehm Flute the addition of this note puts the whole instrument out of tune. It is quite unknown to modern Flute-players. As explained above, the bottom semitones are additional notes playable only by means of holes in the foot-joint. From these upwards we have the natural scale of the instrument, the scale of D major. The second octave D to D is produced by overblowing from the first octave. The technique of this overblowing is merely an alteration in the angle of the air-reed and an increase of wind-pressure. The third octave is obtained in a similar way, but with the help of opening certain of the vent-holes as mentioned above. The top B♮ and C are by no means easy notes to get. They should not be written *piano.* The same caution applies still more strongly to the extreme compass

given by Strauss as possible in the *forte.* Only the most exceptional players can touch them.

Fourteen semitones of its fundamental scale *viz.*:

can be overblown at the twelfth. This gives to the ear a chromatic scale of harmonics from

All these notes are written in the pitch at which they actually sound with the addition of a little "o," thus·

In quality they are thinner and less bodily than the same notes when blown in the ordinary way. They are only mentioned here for the sake of completeness, as they are sometimes to be found in the old style of Flute-music. On the modern Flute the whole series is hopelessly flat.

Although the complete three-octave compass of the Flute can be produced with regularity and smoothness by a good player, there are certain differences of colour as the notes proceed upwards. The temptation for a writer is to make these differences correspond with the three octaves of the scale, but to the ear this is not quite correct.

From bottom C up to about A (a major sixth higher) the Flute has a thick, heavy breathe-y quality, "something," as it has been expressed, "like thick plush." This part of its compass is extremely effective but liable to be easily covered up. The Double-Basses in especial with their wealth of Harmonics seem to have the faculty of blurring the low notes of the Flute. The student should notice how often in the accompaniment of Flute solos they are omitted altogether. Even without the Basses a String *tenuto* needs very delicate playing if it is not to cover up the lower notes of the Flute. A subject like the following from Dvořàk's *New World Symphony*:

EXAMPLE 98.

Dvořàk. *New World Symphony.*

sounds poor and stupid when there is the slightest over-thickness in the accompaniment. Of the emotional, almost exotic sound, of the low Flute no better example can be given than Tschaikowsky's F♯'s in the

Pathetic Symphony (opening of last movement). The effect of this five-part unison of three Flutes and two Bassoons is eerie in the extreme.

EXAMPLE 99.

A charming series of suspended sixths, played by three Flutes in unison in their bottom octave, may be found in Elgar's *Enigma Variations* (*Dorabella*, page 64 of the Full Score).

It has often been observed that the bottom two or three semitones on the Flute have a tendency to sound out of tune. One must confess that in cases where these notes are undoubled and quite uncovered, such as in the charming accompaniment to Gretel's Ballad in Act II. of *Hänsel und Gretel*, there is sometimes a certain uncomfortable feeling about the bottom notes. This is, no doubt, due to their complete want of overtones. The lack of these overtones is not noticed in the upper octaves, but in the very bottom notes one feels their absence, because one is accustomed to hear them in the same notes when played by other instruments. This helps to explain the Flautist's explanation that "the notes are not really out of tune. They only *sound so.*"

EXAMPLE 100.

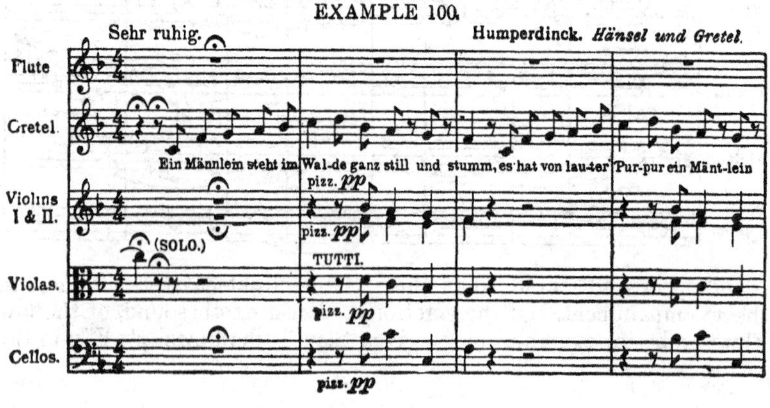

Upwards from A (the sixth above the bottom C) for about a minor seventh to G

the instrument generally loses its thick quality and substitutes a delightfully smooth and silky tone-colour which bears the same analogy to its upper and lower registers as the "A" and "D" strings of the Violin bear to the "E" and "G" strings.

It is in this, not the top, octave that the greater number of lightly accompanied Flute solos are written. In this part of the compass it has a sort of unparalleled ease and serenity. No one who has heard it can forget the delicious moment just before the 2nd Act Curtain in *Die Meistersinger*, where the Flute has these semiquavers accompanied by one Horn and the muted Strings.

EXAMPLE 101.

Another charming example of the Flute in its middle octave is to be found at the opening of the Andante in Tschaikowsky's *B♭ minor*

Pianoforte Concerto. The *cantabile* of the solo instrument is supported only by the *pp pizzicato* of the Strings.

EXAMPLE 102.

The student should also examine the place in the same work where the Flute repeats the little Oboe phrase *in the same octave.* It occurs at the *Poco piu andante*, page 67 of the Full Score.

One of the simplest and most beautiful of these middle-register solos occurs in the 2nd Act of Gluck's *Armide.* The accompaniment is for *pp* Strings with the addition of a single Horn, a single Oboe, or a single Clarinet, etc. The number is in D major, and the Flute part lies mainly between its middle D and the fifth above with an occasional rise to the top D.

Dvořák uses this same register very happily in the Largo of his *New World Symphony*, but lends the Flute-tone a fascinating reediness by the addition of an Oboe in unison. The accompaniment is almost toneless, a *pp* tremolo for Violins and Violas.

EXAMPLE 103.

This tone-colour was a favourite with Dvořák, and he used it to perfection. What can be more charming than the following little tune with its extremely simple but effective accompaniment—a sort of "orchestral five-part" manufactured out of almost nothing?

EXAMPLE 104.

We now come to the top octave of the Flute. From the second G upwards the instrument acquires the bright telling quality which is its most characteristic and useful feature. Of this register there is scarcely any necessity to give examples. The student has only to glance along the top line of any Full Score in order to find instances. These, however, are generally in the *tutti*. When employed purely as a vehicle for accompanied melody the topmost register is not so freely used as might have been thought probable. A certain number of impassioned solos—such as the long and lovely D minor *lento* in Gluck's *Orfeo*—lie in this part of the compass. Their number, however, is not very large. The Gluck passage is too long to quote here. It has already been eloquently analysed by Berlioz. The student should take an opportunity of examining this passage with care, as it shows the utmost artistry in the "placing" of the various phrases to make the greatest possible effect. For a more modern example of the bright top-notes of the instrument he should look at the Introduction (*Più Andante*) to the last movement of Brahms's *C minor Symphony* (page 95, small Full Score). The passage at the opening of the 2nd Act of *Tristan*, beginning

EXAMPLE 105.

is a beautiful example of *legato* Flute writing. It has an accompaniment of Wood-Wind, two Horns, and Strings. Bizet, whose writing for the Wood-Wind is always instinct with a delicate feeling for tone-colour, has written many charming Flute-solos. In its very simple way the following little tune affords a good example of the Flute *legato* in its top octave. The quotation is from *Carmen* (*Entr'Acte* before Act III.), and there is nothing in the Score beyond the Flute and Harps:

EXAMPLE 106.

Bizet. *Carmen.*

We must now return to the purely technical consideration of the Flute. But before dealing with the Shakes and Tremolos it must be said that, for the sake of simplicity and economy of space, the bottom notes only of the tremolos are in most cases given. This applies throughout the Wood-Wind and String sections. A tremolo, whenever mentioned as being "on" a particular note, is regarded as being upward from that note. In performance, of course, a tremolo is just as practicable or impracticable upwards or downwards. The way of writing it—whether upwards or downwards—makes no difference to its technique. Nearly all shakes and tremolos are *possible* on the Flute. However, avoid these:

of which the first four are impossible and the last two excessively difficult. All shakes other than the five given in the above example are practicable. With regard to tremolos, however, some further cautions are necessary. Up to

(regarded as the lower note in the tremolo-combination) avoid all tremolos containing a greater skip than an augmented fourth. Above

confine your tremolo within the limits of a major third except on the notes

where tremolos are possible up to a perfect fourth.

From

upwards the only practicable tremolos, as opposed to major and minor and shakes, are the following:

The above restrictions with regard to tremolos only apply to cases in which the composer actually relies on the instrument to produce its tremolo audibly and unsupported. In passages where the tremolo is being performed by Wood-Wind *tutti* or by Wood-Wind and Strings some licence may be taken without appreciable loss of effect.

In figures and melodic phrases the *legato* of the Flute is practicable throughout its entire compass, and is limited only by the capacity of the player's lungs. It is, however, more in the character of the Flute to break up a long series of notes into its component parts, to interpolate detached notes and groups of notes, and generally to substitute a vivid manner of performance for its more vapid *legato* style.

Single-, double-, and triple-tonguing are the nerves and sinews of the Flute-technique. In single-tongued phrases the Flautist achieves a consonantal clearness and distinction that is more akin to speech-in-song than to anything else. Each note can be made to sound like a falling hailstone or an unstrung pearl. A reasonable degree of speed can be obtained by this means, but for its greatest rapidity of utterance the Flute depends on double and triple-tonguing. These methods of articulation, the T-K, T-K, and the T-K-T, T-K-T, have already been mentioned in connection with the Trumpets and Horns. They are, of course, employed in note-groups which have for their basis the numbers two and three respectively. They are not solely used in groups of *repeated notes*, though they are often so used.

As an example of double-tonguing the student may be referred to the difficult Solo Flute passage in the *Scherzo* of Mendelssohn's *Midsummer Night's Dream*, or to any one of the little introductory scale passages which are so characteristic of Beethoven. The scale, which leads back to the subject in *Leonora No. 3*, is so quick that it would naturally be doubletongued.

EXAMPLE 107.

On the other hand, the passage which depicts the sun breaking through after the storm in the *Pastoral Symphony* is quite slow enough to be single-tongued, and demands that method for its proper emphasis.

EXAMPLE 108.

The quotation from the opening of Mendelssohn's *Italian Symphony* given above (Ex. 47) is a good example of triple-tonguing. In this connection the student may profitably examine the whole of the Flute part in the last movement (*Saltarello-Presto*) of that Symphony. After a few introductory bars the Flutes begin with a subject in thirds, to which they lend exactly the right nimbleness and airiness.

EXAMPLE 109.

This is an effective instance of the Flutes used with a *pp* accompaniment in their quietest register. The student should look at the repetition of this tune that immediately follows in the Full Score. The Clarinets now play the Flute parts, and the latter instruments double them in the octave above.

Besides the species of tonguing already mentioned, Strauss has introduced a method called *Flatterzunge*, or *Flutter-tonguing*. This is applicable to the Flute, and, a good deal less conveniently, to the Oboe and Clarinet. The player, while executing a moderately quick chromatic scale, rolls his tongue thus *d-r-r-r* without touching his lips. Strauss employs this method of delivery throughout the "Windmill" Variation in *Don Quixote*. The bars are all more or less of one pattern, and this is a sample:

EXAMPLE 110.

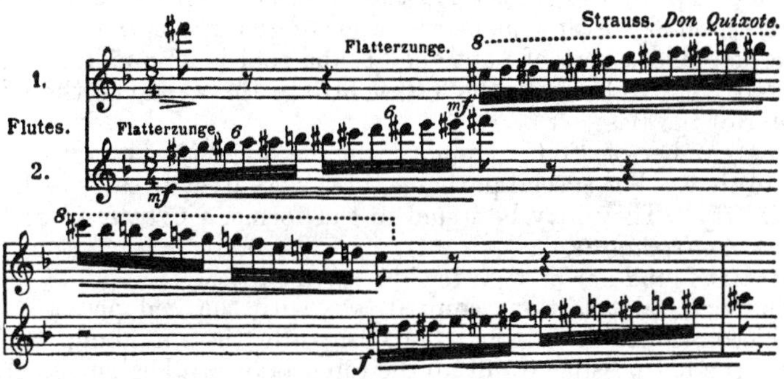

The Flute has no great powers of *sostenuto* or of <>. In its lowest notes especially any idea of an extended *legato* has to be put aside.[1] The length and bore of the pipe are so great that the player has to breathe after every few notes. On the other hand, its nimbleness and general ability to "play anything" have passed into a proverb. This is perhaps crystallized in the answer of the American, who, when asked if he could read a Chinese laundryman's shop sign, said, "No, but I think I could play it if I had my flute."

Staccatos, repeated notes, turns, shakes, skips, arpeggios, scales diatonic and scales chromatic, and all sorts of agile figures founded on such types, are child's play to a good Flautist. Quotations might be given here by the dozen. We shall, however, content ourselves by a reference to one single passage. It occurs in the last Act of *Tristan und Isolde*, where Tristan, seeing Isolde's ship approaching, exclaims, "Es naht! Es naht mit muthiger Hast! Sie weht, sie weht, die Flagge am Mast!" Here the arpeggios of the Flute so often used for trivial purposes conjure up a living picture of what is before the dying man's eyes.

[1] The student should compare the Wood-Wind slur marks in any of Wagner's Scores with what he actually sees and hears the players doing at a performance.

EXAMPLE 111.

Before leaving the Flute one may mention a peculiarity which has often been noticed. No instrument is so much affected by a difference of mode, major or minor. As a rule, its own lack in the matter of natural Harmonics seems to demand the major mode when it is brought prominently forward. At any rate, in its top and middle registers it is much more employed in the major than in the minor mode. In its bottom octave, on the other hand, the substitution of the minor for the major, especially in slow melodies, seems to give it a curious searching tenderness and a sort of "antique" sound that is unique in its octave and only comparable with the lowest fifth of the Viola and the middle register of the Bassoon.

The number of Flutes employed in the orchestra has varied from time to time. For special purposes three were used as early as Haydn and Grétry. They may be found in the former's *Creation*,[1] and the latter's *Andromaque*.

Mozart found one enough for his Symphonies.

The classical tradition required two, with the 2nd player taking the Piccolo when necessary. Two is really the minimum, without which it is not possible to fill-up the top octave at all satisfactorily.

Mendelssohn has made at least one charmingly poetical use of his Flutes. There is a place in his overture "*The Hebrides*" where the upward rush of the two Flutes *after* the *ff* of the rest of the orchestra suggests, in the most picturesque manner, the little crest of spray flung into the air by the huge wave as it breaks. The passage is as simple as it is vivid,—merely an F♯ and a chromatic scale, but as a tiny piece of tone-painting it is quite irresistible. (Ex. 112, p. 195.)

The Symphonic rule to-day is "three flutes." The 3rd player oscillates between Flute and Piccolo like a cherub "'twixt sphere and sphere."

As a matter of prudence, the student should endeavour, in using any three Wood-Wind instruments, not to give the 3rd player a prominent first entry. He has a cold—that is to say, a comparatively flat—instrument to play on. His colleagues have been blowing into theirs all through the piece. And this blowing leads, both in the Wood and the Brass, to all sorts of undesirable "sharp practices" distressing to a "3rd player" with nothing to do.

The artistic success of Example 113, p. 195 (the opening of the *Danse des Mirlitons* from Tschaikowsky's "*Nut-Cracker*" *Suite*),

[1] Part III.

EXAMPLE 112.

Mendelssohn. *The Hebrides Overture.*

depends not on the 1st Flautist but on the ability of the 3rd player to change from Piccolo to Flute in the 10 seconds pause which follows the *Danse Chinoise*, and to blow the bottom part in tune. Incidentally the quotation gives a good example of the light, easy writing which is so effective on three Flutes. The accompaniment is a mere feather-weight:

EXAMPLE 113.

Tschaikowsky. *"Nut-cracker" Suite.*

For reasons of space the String-parts have been compressed onto two staves.

Before passing on to the other orchestral Flutes, a word must be said with regard to the Wood-Wind keys. These will be dealt with when necessary in greater detail under the headings of the various instruments. In general, however, one may say that the fewer sharps and flats there are in the part the better for the player. But this caution need not be taken too seriously, at anyrate for symphonic purposes. With an old 8-keyed Flute, and most of the holes where they ought not to have been, a Flautist might well be excused for shaking his head at D♭ and B♮ major. Times and mechanisms, however, have changed. It is still true to-day that it is easier for a Wood-Wind instrument to play in a key somewhere near its natural scale, whatever that may be, but one need not allow that restriction to become an obsession. Of course if one's favourite orchestral key is F♯ major one deserves to suffer.

No. 31. The Bass-Flute.

Fr. *La Flûte Alto*; It. *Flautone*;[1] Ger. *Altflöte*.

This beautiful instrument should perhaps rather be called by its Continental name the "Alto-Flute." In size and shape it is merely a longer and wider-bored variety of the ordinary Concert-Flute. Like that instrument it is now provided with a Boehm mechanism for orchestral purposes.

The fingering and *written* compass of the two instruments are precisely the same. On the Bass-Flute, however, the written chromatic compass from

sounds a perfect fourth lower

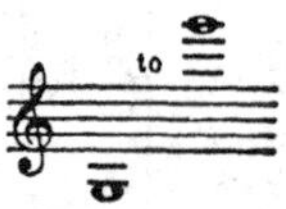

[1] *I.e.* Big flute.

The whole compass of three octaves is producible with ease and certainty. The executive capabilities of the instrument, especially in the middle and top registers, are not much less than those of the ordinary Flute.

The Bass-Flute is, for the player's convenience, treated as a transposing-instrument, and its part is written a fourth higher than the actual sounds required. Its key-signature has a ♭ more or a ♯ less than the key-signature of the piece. The treble-clef only is used.

An eight-keyed "Bass-Flute in B♭" is commonly employed by the "Drums and Fifes" in the army. The key in which it is built gives it facility of fingering for the military flat-keys. For the sake of economizing space on the march the "Head" of this instrument is generally curved back upon itself in the shape of a long narrow letter "U."

It may be mentioned that, from the sixteenth century onwards, many attempts have been made to construct Tenor- and Bass-Flutes with a compass even lower than that of our modern Bass-Flute. The largest of these instruments—a sixteenth century Italian Bass-Flute—has a downward compass to low C, the bottom-string of the Viola. An instrument of this sort, with a bore of an inch and a length of 43 inches, is practically unmanageable by human lungs and lips. It calls for a special race of men, or rather of heroes.

In tone-quality the Bass-Flute is indescribably rich, soft, and velvety. Its characteristic bottom sixth is remarkably strong and sounds almost like a unison of Horn and Bassoon. Above that it has a delightful quality, something like that of the Flute's middle register, but rounder and more tender. The top sixth of its compass though perfectly easy to play has a tendency to sharpness, and is besides not of so good a quality as the same notes on the ordinary Flute. Little is gained, therefore, in writing the instrument above

The relationship of the Bass-Flute to the ordinary Flute in the matter of tone-colour is very much the same as that of the Oboe d' Amore to the Oboe or of the Viola to the Violin. That is to say it is less brilliant and incisive but smoother, mellower, more placid and at times more expressive.

In the orchestra the Bass-Flute has not been used as much as it deserves. Weingartner has written for it in his Symphonic Poem *Das Gefilde der Seligen*, Rimsky Korsakov in *Mlada*, Glazounow in his latest Symphony, and Holbrooke in his Opera *The Children of Don*. The following example of a tender little melody in its bottom register is taken from the 3rd movement—*Sleep*—of Von Holst's Suite *Phantastes*. The effect of the deep, quiet notes of the Bass-Flute with the thrummed accompaniment and the little three-part phrase in the Violins is charmingly representative of the subject. The student should notice the extreme lightness of the accompaniment, twelve stringed-instruments only, all muted

EXAMPLE 114.

No. 32. The Piccolo.[1]

Fr. *Petite flûte* ; It. *Ottavino* ; Ger. *Kleine Flöte.*

This is a small-sized Flute less than half the length of the ordinary Concert-Flute. Its pitch, depending, of course, on the length of the air-column in the pipe, is an octave above that of the Flute. The Piccolo, however, lacks the foot-joint which permits the Flute to produce its two bottom semitones. The compass, therefore, begins

[1] Abbreviation of the Italian words *Flauto Piccolo*, *i.e.* Little Flute. The Italians themselves, however, always use the word *Ottavino*, an abbreviation of *Flauto Ottavino*, *i.e.* Octave Flute. In Germany the regular name is *Kleine Flöte*, but the word *Pickel flöte* also exists.

with the first degree of the natural scale, low D. At the other end the piercing top-C can only be blown in the *fff*; while the semitone below it—B♮—is still more difficult to produce. If needed, for instance, in the brilliant upward rush of a scale supported by the Brass, it can just be played by the instrument and, one may add, tolerated by the audience. In general, it is better to confine the upward compass to the high B♭. This gives it a working compass of

The Piccolo is always written in the treble-clef an octave below its real pitch, so that the compass in actual sounds is

The fingering and indeed the whole technique are exactly the same as those of the Flute.

Bearing in mind, then, the restrictions of the Piccolo with regard to the two semitones at each extreme of its compass, one may say that anything which is effective on the Flute in the way of scales, arpeggios, trills, figures, turns and so on *can be played* on the Piccolo.

One must, however, make two reservations here. In the first place, as the Piccolo reaches the top of its compass, the notes are produced with greater difficulty than the corresponding notes of the Flute, which are pitched an octave lower. The limit-note of a trill in this part of the Piccolo's compass is

In the next place, though the Piccolo *can play* almost anything, there are not many things to which it can lend distinction. There are also some things which it can very effectually spoil.

In this connection we must remember that all the Flute-family is reedless. That is to say the tone-production does not in the slightest resemble the tone-production of the human voice. It, therefore, totally lacks the strong associative appeal which is possessed by the Oboe, the Clarinet, and the Bassoon. The ordinary Concert-Flute substitutes for this appeal a limpid and exquisite clarity. Furthermore, it has this advantage, that for two-thirds of its range it is producing notes within the compass of the Soprano voice. On the other hand, the disabilities of the Piccolo in the way of tone-colour, are accentuated by the fact that it is nearly always playing in a register outside that of any human voice. Consequently the harder, brighter, and more automaton-like the Piccolo part is the better will it suit the instrument. A little phrase like this in which the Piccolo merely "gilt-edges" the notes of the Flute, sounds charming:

EXAMPLE 115.

whereas a fine phrase like this (from the *C minor Symphony*), with its thin twitter at the end, only sounds poor:

EXAMPLE 116.

In the one case it performs a purely mechanical function successfully while in the other it fails to add anything to a passage which is essentially a vocal phrase.

With such limitations as these the Piccolo is most often called on to brighten the upper octaves of the Wood-Wind. It is impossible, within reasonable limits of space, to give examples of these "doublings." They include combinations with practically every possible series of single Wood-Wind notes and with every possible Wood-Wind octave-passage. These may be made up of Flutes, Oboes, English Horn, Clarinets, and Bassoons in any vertical arrangement that may please the composer's fancy.

In these combinations one occasionally finds the middle octave omitted altogether. The Piccolo then doubles the Wood-Wind phrase at the 16th. For instance, in the *Entr'Acte* before Act IV. of *Carmen* the Clarinet has a *pp* semiquaver passage in its middle octave while the Piccolo has the same series of notes *p* two octaves higher. The effect is curiously and characteristically French:

EXAMPLE 117.

In the above example the whole of the accompaniment is omitted. It consists of *pizzicato* Strings, Harp, Tambour de Basque, and a single Oboe "A" held for four bars. The student should also look at the *Chanson Bohême* (opening of Act II. of the same Opera), where there is a somewhat unusual series of sixths between the Flute and the Piccolo.

It is often prudent to double the extreme top notes of the Flutes by the Piccolo *in unison*, not in the octave. This is matter of daily practice. A passage like the following from the Finale of Strauss's *Sinfonia Domestica*

EXAMPLE 118.

is nine times out of ten better arranged as above than with the Piccolo part written to sound an octave above the Flutes. On the other hand, if the Flute-scale had ended about a fifth lower the Piccolo would have added little and would probably have been omitted or written in its upper octave.

Held notes are as a rule ineffective on the instrument. They lack vitality, and if pitched too high approach dangerously near to the scream of a steam-whistle. Even when played *ppp* the upper notes are totally wanting in tenderness and charm. See the passage quoted below (Ex. 238) from the extreme end of Strauss's *Also sprach Zarathustra.* Unless one is very far from the orchestra in a very large hall these harmonies, in which two Piccolos play the top Wind-parts, sound unsatisfactory. Of course in the case of this special example no other Wood-Wind instrument could produce these extremely high notes at all.

Berlioz has pointed out that it is mere matter of prejudice to think that the Piccolo should "always be played loudly." This caution, perhaps more needful in his time, is scarcely called for at the present day, when the art of the orchestral player has been advanced along such artistic lines. It may, however, be repeated here as applicable to every instrument in the orchestra. With regard to the Piccolo in particular the student should examine the extraordinary *piano* use of the instrument at the end of Brahms's *Gesang der Parzen.* The Piccolo part begins with the muted Strings at the words "So sangen die Parzen" sixteen bars from the end of the work. There are not twenty notes to play, and the effect is in inverse proportion to the simplicity of the means used.

One cannot recall any example of the bottom notes of the Piccolo used *solo.* They are weak, and, as Berlioz says, "generally better replaced by their corresponding sounds in the second octave of the large flute." On the other hand, they might well be used in some passage requiring a great peculiarity of characterization. They have a quite distinctive tone-colour; a sort of thin, feeble, disembodied voice, such as might come from a ghost if it had a pip in its throat.

In the middle and top registers the Piccolo is, of course, very much at home. And as it is comparatively an easy instrument, the technique of the player is generally supremely good. The student, however, would be well advised not to keep the instrument continually at the top of its compass. As an average example of writing for the instrument—neither extraordinarily difficult nor yet studiously simple—he should look at such a number as the *Sailors' Chorus* in Act III. of Wagner's *Flying Dutchman,* "*Steuermann! Lass die Wacht!*" In this example the average *tessitura* gravitates round

and has

as its upward limit.

The Piccolo has such marked restrictions that we must not be surprised to find that the early masters only used it on special occasions. Gluck employed a pair in his "*Chorus of Scythians*" in *Iphigénie en Tauride.* Beethoven rarely used the instrument. In the Storm of the *Pastoral Symphony* it has a part, but is mainly used to perform its least effective function, the holding of high notes. In the *Allegro con brio*, at the end of his *Egmont Overture*, there is quite a showy part made up of little flourishes with the Horns, Trumpets and Bassoons. Weber followed Gluck and used two Piccolos in an often quoted passage from the *Freischütz*, while Berlioz has made characteristic use of the same combination in his "*Menuet des Follets*" (*Faust*). Marcel's "War Song" in the *Huguenots*, with its accompaniment of Piccolo, Bassoons, Bass-Drum and Cymbals, and Double-Basses, has already been quoted.[1]

In the modern orchestra one or two Piccolos are used at discretion, not for an entire work but for incidental passages in the work. When three Flutes are employed the 3rd player or the 2nd and 3rd players would take the Piccolo part or parts as required. The actual change from one instrument to another can be made in a single bar of moderate time. In this the Flute and Piccolo have the advantage over all other instruments. They have no reeds or crooks to adjust, and so can be laid down and taken up with ease. It is, however, just as well to remember that in making a rapid change the player has to face some difficulty in the alteration of embouchure. It is, however, only slight, and the difficulties with regard to pitch, already referred to on pages 194-5, are much more important.

It is only necessary to add for the sake of completeness that Military Piccolos in E♭ and Flutes in A♭ and E♭ are used in the "Drums and Fifes" of the army. In addition, D♭ Flutes are commonly used in military bands.

All these instruments are usually spoken of not with reference to the normal pivot-key of C, but with reference to the natural Flute-scale of D. Thus the "E♭ Piccolo" is generally known as an "F Piccolo," the "D♭ Flute" as an "E♭ Flute," and so on. An absurd and spurious piece of archaism.

The ordinary D♭ military Flutes and Piccolos are, of course, written for in the key of a semitone below the pitch of the piece, and, as the usual keys for military music vary from B♭ to D♭, it will be seen that this gives the Flutes a range of four easy keys, A, D, G, and C. In many cases the difference of a semitone in pitch exactly corrects the transposition which is necessary in an arrangement for military band. *Example,*—the *Andante* in the Overture to Rossini's *William Tell.* The brilliant Flute *Obbligato* to the English Horn solo appears in the original Score in G major. On transposition for military band the key of the piece is A♭ major. The flute in D♭ remains in its original key.

[1] See Example 7.

No. 33. The Oboe[1] (or Hautboy).

Fr. *Hautbois*; It. *Oboe*; Ger. *Oboe*.

This is a double-reed instrument of considerable antiquity. Its forefather was the Schalmey, a treble reed-instrument which, with its larger brothers the Pommer and Bombard, formed the principal reed-group in the mediæval Wind-Band.

The Oboe seems to have definitely emerged from its immediate parent, the Discant-Schalmey, in the last quarter of the 17th century. The latter instrument had, as its bottom compass-note, the low D, which is also the original lowest compass-note of the Flute. The first keys which were put on the new instrument gave the whole-tone below this (C♮) and the semitone above (D♯).

The six instruments which comprised the Schalmey-Pommer family were

1. The **High-Schalmey**, [a reed-pipe 17 inches in length.]
2. The **Discant-Schalmey**, [a reed-pipe 26 inches in length.]
3. The **Alto-Pommer**, [a reed-pipe 30½ inches in length.]
4. The four-keyed **Tenor-Pommer**, [a reed-pipe 54 inches in length.]
5. The four-keyed **Bass-Pommer**, [a reed-pipe 72 inches in length.]
6. The four-keyed **Double-Bass-Pommer** or **Bombard** (**Doppelt-Quint-Pommer**), [a reed-pipe 116 inches in length.]

The average pitch of these instruments can be easily remembered, as their lowest compass-notes were respectively the same as the four strings of the modern Viola and the two bottom strings of the Cello:

These were the lowest *natural* notes of the six instruments. But the four keys of Nos. 4, 5, and 6 gave them an extra compass downwards of four notes, so that the actual playing-compass was continued downwards as follows:

It needs something of an effort to imagine what a Band of these coarse, powerful, double-reed instruments must have sounded like. They were used for indoor as well as outdoor purposes, and gave our ancestors a Wind-ensemble with a tone-quality that is simply non-existent to-day.

[1] The English word *Oboe* is from the Italianized form of the French word *Hautbois*. The first mention of the word Hautboy appears to be in Robert Lancham's letter describing the entertainment provided for Queen Elizabeth in 1575 at Kenilworth Castle. The letter, which is also dated 1575, contains this sentence, "This Pageaunt waz clozd vp with a delectable harmony of Hautboiz Shalmz Cornets and such oother looud muzik."

It was from the second highest of this Schalmey-Pommer group that the Oboe sprang. The Discant-Schalmey was, as its name suggests, the main melody-instrument in the old Reed-Bands. It is continually referred to in Elizabethan and Jacobean literature, and, though the musical criticisms of poets and dramatists have to be received with some reserve, we may fairly and charitably sum-up its tone-qualities in Robert Laneham's words "looud muzik."

The Oboe inherited the rough tone and the technical imperfections of the Schalmey, and continued to propagate them down to about the middle of last century. By that time, however, the Oboe had got to be more than the English people could stand indoors. The English Oboist, Barret, suggested various improvements in the instrument, and the technical side of these improvements was worked out by Triébert in Paris. Since then the French and Belgian school of Oboe-playing, aiming as it does at refinement of tone, ease of execution, and suppleness of *nuances*, has been supreme in Europe.

In Germany, however, where they still call any military bandsman an *Oboist* and any military band-master an *Oboe-master*, the instrument is still regarded from the "looud muzik" point of view. It is played as if it were an outdoor-instrument liable to contend with a multitude of Trumpets, Trombones, and Tubas. The reed used is, to our ideas, thick and heavy, while the resulting tone is coarse, unpleasant, and of a terribly predominating quality. Happily, in this country our ideas on tone-colour have always run more nearly parallel with those of the French. Consequently, though the Oboe is perhaps not played so perfectly in England as it is in France and Belgium, we strive towards the same sort of perfection as that which the French have already achieved.

The Oboe is easily described. It is a small conically-bored pipe of cocus, rosewood, or ebonite, terminating at its lower end in a "bell." At its upper end is a short length of metal tubing, called the *staple*, into which the double-reed is fitted. This double-reed is made of two extremely fine and thin pieces of prepared "cane" bound together as described above (page 17). The ()-shaped orifice at the upper end of the canes is very narrow—the merest slit into which a thin piece of paper can just be passed. The position of the two reeds can be clearly seen on Plate VIII., Fig. 3. At the extreme top of the illustration is the ( )-shaped orifice. Below that are the reeds themselves, only one visible. The dark patch that lies immediately underneath that is the waxed-thread lapping that keeps the reeds together. Below that again comes the metal "staple," and then the upper portion of the wooden Oboe-pipe with a couple of metal keys attached. Both these keys are worked from a finger position lower down the pipe by means of metal rods or "trackers." When in use the double-reed is of course actually in the player's mouth and is itself the sound-producer. The air-column inside the pipe acts as a resonating medium, reinforcing the reed-vibrations by synchronized vibrations of its own.

The fundamental scale of the instrument is obtained by the opening and shutting of the holes pierced laterally in the pipe. This is governed in the modern orchestral Oboe by a formidable metal mechanism which often gives the player a choice of means in the production of a note. Two "speaker-keys" are, as a rule, employed in just the same way as the one "speaker" of the Clarinet.[1] The second Oboe "speaker," however, is used only to "vent" the highest notes.

The fundamental scale of the Oboe is chromatic, and begins at middle-C

 but two lower semitones B♮ and B♭ 

are obtained by means of key-extensions. Normally the two holes covered by these keys remain open in playing. The closing of the holes lengthens the air-column and so deepens the pitch.

The instrument being conical overblows an octave, but the first note which in practice is overblown is this D

From there chromatically upwards for a major seventh, that is to

the scale is a reproduction of the lower scale, and is obtained by means of increased wind-pressure. Above that for a diminished fifth, six further semitones are playable to

These notes are 3rd and 4th Harmonics of the fundamental octave. The extreme high notes

are just playable by some artists. However, their poor quality and excessive difficulty render them useless in the orchestra. Even the high F♯ and G are better avoided, though they are both recognized for *piano* production in the French technique. The full orchestral compass of the instrument may then be laid down as chromatically from

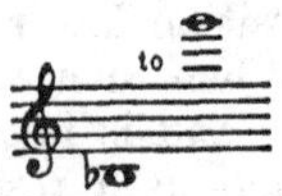

The fingering resembles that of the Flute.

[1] See page 251.

Whole-tone and half-tone shakes are possible on all the notes up to and including the half-tone shake on

Beyond that there are two whole-tone and two half-tone shakes all possible but difficult. They are as follows:

Whole-tone shakes on

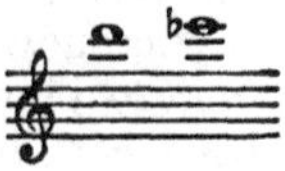

Half-tone shakes on

In both these cases the shake on the lower of the two notes is the more difficult.

The whole-tone shakes on

and the half-tone shakes on

which were difficult or impossible on the old instrument are now, on the modern French Oboe, all practicable.

A certain amount of caution is necessary with regard to the tremolos of the Oboe. Apart altogether from their musical effect, there are eleven in the lower and middle registers which involve such difficulties in the way of cross-fingering and so on as to make them undesirable or impossible. These eleven which should all be avoided are

Upwards from

avoid any tremolos of a greater interval than a perfect fourth.

On

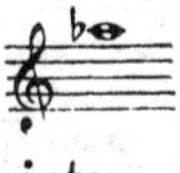

avoid any tremolos of a greater interval than a major third.

Above 

write no tremolos; that is tremolos as opposed to whole-tone and half-tone shakes.

In general, any technical combinations of two notes both of which are either ♯ or ♭ are to be used with caution.

Owing to the position of the reed in the mouth, the Oboe player can use single-tonguing only. This, however, does not in any way interfere with his power of *staccato* playing. Indeed the ease and delicacy with which a good Oboist can deliver a series of rapid light *staccatos* are among the most charming characteristics of the instrument. This capability is not as a rule sufficiently well understood. Composers often hesitate at anything beyond a *legato* melody for the Oboe. It will be as well, then, to give two or three examples which the student is likely to hear in the concert-room. He can then judge for himself how well they suit the instrument when played by a good artist. The fourth example, from Act I. of Rossini's *William Tell*, is included as a rare instance of the quick repeated notes of the Oboe employed in a Solo. It, of course, needs the greatest refinement of execution.

EXAMPLE 119.

EXAMPLE 120.

EXAMPLE 121.

EXAMPLE 122.

Rossini. *William Tell.*

EXAMPLE 123.

Berlioz. *Symphonie Fantastique.*
(Ronde du Sabbat.)

EXAMPLE 124.

Saint-Saëns. *Rouet d'Omphale.*

The Oboe is essentially a *middle-compass* instrument. In that register its tone can be varied by a first-class artist from a beautiful throbbing sweetness in the *forte* to a *piano* so faint as to be almost inaudible. Within this narrow compass of an octave and a fourth

all the best Oboe Solos have been written. Their characteristic remains to-day what it was in the time of Gluck, a touching simplicity which has been happily summed-up by a poet-musician:

> " And then the hautboy played and smiled,
> And sang like any large-eyed child,
> Cool-hearted and all undefiled."

It is scarcely necessary to remind the student of the lovely *Andante* which introduces the Scene of the Departed Spirits in Gluck's *Orfeo,*

EXAMPLE 125.

or of the exquisite little passage just before the Baritone Soloist enters in the *Choral Symphony* of Beethoven,

EXAMPLE 126.

The latter is a happy instance of those short passages in which the Oboe often seems to overhear the conversation of the other instruments and to throw in its own phrase with an added and more intimate delicacy of musical perception.

Schubert wrote many ideal solos for the Oboe. These do not generally take the character of the "Wood-Wind chatter" in which Beethoven delighted. They are usually "solos" in the more formal sense of the word. At the same time their perfect suitability to the instrument, and their enchanting simplicity, make them admirable models. Among these are the opening tune in the Andante of the *C major Symphony*:

EXAMPLE 127.

the beautiful Oboe and Clarinet unison at the beginning of the *Unfinished Symphony*:

[1] *Tutti* on the last quaver of this example.

In the original Full Score the Clarinet part is written on a separate stave for "Clarinet in A" in the key of D minor. (Example 128, p. 211.)

EXAMPLE 128.

and the extended passage for Solo Wood-Wind instruments in the *Andante con Moto* of the same Symphony. A sketch of this example is given below with the accompaniment omitted. The student should look at it from the point of view of the horizontal arrangement of the melody on the three instruments employed. The quotation is from the return of the 2nd Subject.

EXAMPLE 129.

The student must not imagine that the arrangement of a passage such as this is "inevitable." In fact Schubert did not think so. He arranged it differently on its first appearance in the Movement. The difference of arrangement can be found and studied on page 24 of Peters's Full Score. These microscopic differences in the horizontal arrangement of an extended melody are worth careful thought. No rule can ever be laid down on them. Often a composer will almost wilfully adopt a different arrangement for a second appearance of the same subject. If the music is simple it will probably be matter of technical indifference to the instruments concerned. Again, the same subject appearing a second time may necessitate a different instrumental arrangement by reason of its altered pitch. These things, however, are often merely questions of personal preference. Two tone-colours equally good and effective in themselves please two composers in precisely opposite degrees. The only caution that can be given on this point is never to assign a melody on its second appearance to a less effective instrument (or group of instruments) than that employed at its first hearing. The fact that variety is secured *on paper* will not enable one to ride off from the disappointment of one's audience.

Wagner has written some delightful phrases for the Oboe, though it was apparently not one of his favourite instruments. This is generally a point of prudence on the part of the Operatic as opposed to the Symphonic composer. For the Oboe undoubtedly suffers more than any other instrument when shifted from the heights of the concert-platform to the depths of the Theatre orchestra. In his earlier works there is more Oboe solo-playing than in his later. The last notes of the little tune in the *Flying Dutchman* overture are said to have been given to the Flute during rehearsal owing to the fact that the Oboist could not finish the phrase to Wagner's satisfaction. This is the orchestral legend at any rate.

EXAMPLE 130.

In the more significant works of his middle and later life Wagner seems to have used the Oboe less. Isolated phrases of this character

EXAMPLE 131.

are to be found scattered through the *Ring*. When he used it he generally treated it as a purely melodic instrument. But at moments of inspiration he seems to have turned more often to the Clarinet. Perhaps he did not like the German Oboe-players.

With Tschaikowsky the Oboe was a most favoured instrument. As a rule, he wisely confined its Solo-utterances within a very narrow compass. No Oboist could ask for a more effective Solo than the little quaver tune from the *Canzona* of the *F minor Symphony*. The accompaniment is a mere *pizzicato* of Violins, Violas, and Cellos.

EXAMPLE 132.

There is a striking Oboe Solo in the same composer's Fantasy-Overture *Hamlet*. The querulous outline of the melody has a thick reedy accompaniment for Wood-Wind. The "vertical" analysis of this accompaniment will well repay the student. The placing of the high Bassoon notes should be specially noticed.

[1] Accompaniment of Wood-Wind, Horns, and Cellos.

EXAMPLE 133.

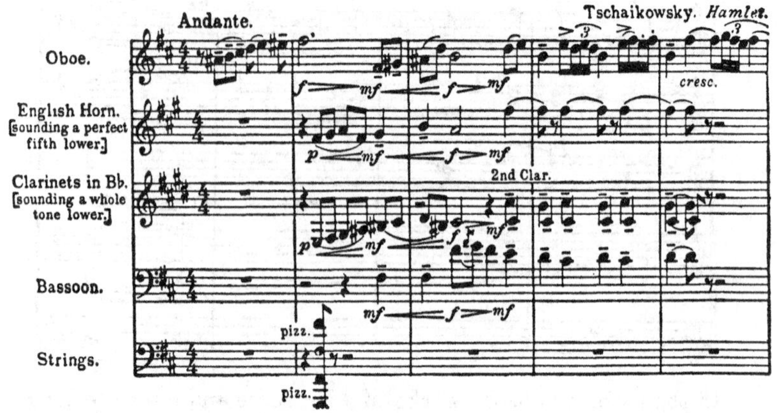

EXAMPLE 134.

Richard Strauss, who has publicly expressed his preference for the French school of Oboe-playing, has allotted more than one delightful Solo to the instrument. The above passage from his *Don Juan* (Ex. 134) is only the beginning of a long Oboe Solo. The student should examine it not only from the point of view of the *cantabile*, but also from that of the very modern and suggestive type of accompaniment employed. It consists mainly of deep four-part chords, held by the muted Double-Basses. The muted Violas and Cellos alternately play a phrase founded on one of the other subjects, and add the upper parts of the Bass chords. The rest is more or less unessential. This example will be referred to again when we come to deal with the Double-Bass.

The whole of the above passage should be looked-at in the Full Score. The Oboe *cantabile* in the introduction to the same composer's *Don Quixote* Variations is an excellent illustration of the charm and fascination which the instrument can impart to a simple tune. The passage fits the Oboe like a glove, and the studied simplicity of the accompaniment only throws the beautiful tone-colour of the solo-instrument into higher relief. It may be added that the Solo part in this example is not generally played at the dead level of *pianissimo* marked in the Full Score.

EXAMPLE 135.

In all the above models one notices not only that the effective compass of the Oboe is somewhat small, but that the type of melody most suited to the instrument is the *vocal* type. In other words, the Oboe makes its main appeal not by means of brilliant figures, arpeggios, and passage work, but by its simple tone-quality. A certain small number of solos are to be found which lie in the top register, and a few passages might be cited where the Oboe, under the dire necessity of musical logic, skips up to its extreme notes. However, these are not models. One may say with confidence that a fiddle E-string melody is not as a rule an Oboe melody. The student will find Solos not of greater effect but of wider range and greater complexity than those given above in the 3rd *Entr'Acte* of Beethoven's *Egmont*, in Berlioz's *Symphonie Fantastique, King Lear*, and *Benvenuto Cellini*, and in the slow movement of Brahms's *C minor Symphony.*

Owing to its penetrating tone-colour the Oboe is peculiarly fitted for purposes of humorous or sardonic characterization. This has been happily used in the little rhythmical figure—two Oboes playing in major seconds—that occurs just after the tragedy of the milk-jug in the 1st Act of *Hänsel und Gretel.* The two Oboes chuckle away with an agitation that is half nervous and half ironical. Meanwhile the Bassoon and Clarinet mimic each other with a fragment of the children's opening song.

EXAMPLE 136.

Humperdinck. *Hänsel und Gretel.*

This faculty which all the Reeds possess of emphasizing the spiteful and the mischievous by means of their dry staccatos has often been used to advantage in modern Scores.[1] In especial the Oboe has a curious un-Oboe like quality in its extreme registers. Its lower fifth particularly, with its somewhat coarse and over-reedy tone-colour, has been often turned to account as a sort of English-Horn effect. One of the earliest examples of the conscious use of this tone-quality is to be found in Act II. Scene IV. of *Lohengrin.* The two Oboes are on their low D in unison and make a *crescendo* to a *fortepiano.*

EXAMPLE 137.

In writing for the Oboe the student must remember that the difficulty of the instrument, as far as the player's lungs are concerned, is precisely the opposite to that of the heavy Brass. In the latter instruments a huge quantity of breath is required to keep the air-column in vibration. A lengthy *sostenuto* is therefore very difficult. On the other hand, with the Oboe almost no breath is required. A *sostenuto*, therefore, can be maintained either *p* or *f* for an indefinite time. These Oboe *sostenutos* are often employed with excellent musical results, even when the rest of the orchestra is playing in some definite rhythmical pattern. Long *sostenutos*, however, make very great demands on the muscles controlling the lungs, chest, and lips. The player is in fact in a continual state of tension. Except when taking breath he can only allow a thin stream of wind to escape through the pipe. The rest of his breathing apparatus is in much the same state as the wind-chest of an organ with the weights atop.

The *sostenuto* should therefore be used with discretion. When the instrument is brought prominently forward for Solo purposes the player may, of course, be called on for some sacrifices in this way, but

[1] See below, page 225.

[2] A crotchet C for 1st Violins is omitted from the first down-beat of this quotation.

when it is only playing a secondary part the composer's rule should be to break up the phrases wherever possible. The player has then opportunity to empty and refill his lungs. Putting solo passages aside, one may say that in order to make its proper effect the pungent Oboe tone requires an average of three or four bars rest at least to every bar of playing. That is to say, in a complete long work the number of bars actually played by the Oboe should not be more than about a quarter the total number of bars in the work.

Every composer, from Lully to the unpronounceable Russians, has used the Oboe, and, as was stated above, there is more similarity of method to be found between the ancient and the modern Oboe parts than between any such parts for Flute, Clarinet, or Bassoon. The standard number of Oboes in Symphony and Opera orchestras is two. In smaller orchestras, such as those in Comic Opera houses, one is ample. In fact the Oboe is peculiarly a Solo instrument. Its tone-colour gives it such prominence that except in purely Wood-Wind ensembles a single instrument answers most purposes. Since the *Ring*, however, composers have written as many as three Oboe parts, with the addition of an English-Horn. This gives the opportunity of more rest to the individual player and leaves the 1st Oboist at liberty to play the Solo passages untired by any exertions in filling-in unimportant parts.

In this connection one may point out that every addition to the Wood-Wind ensemble helps to restore to them at any rate a portion of their ancient power of balancing the Strings. Of this power they have been completely robbed, partly by the increased number of the Strings, but chiefly by the nineteenth century refinements in Wood-Wind manufacture. The constructional changes which were made at that time not only facilitated the technique and partially assimilated the tone-colours of the various instruments, but also deprived them of their former strident power. The student should keep this fact in mind, as he will occasionally find, especially in eighteenth and early nineteenth century Scores, what seem to be ludicrous miscalculations of instrumental balance.

It is true that up to the time when Mozart fixed the Symphony-tradition the instrumental ensemble was not so *static* as it is to-day. But apart from this occasional laxity we sometimes come across a piece of carefully planned orchestral counterpoint by a great master which appears to be an unhappy transference of the Organ-technique to the Orchestra. To our ears it sounds as if the composer had overlooked the fact that he has entrusted simultaneous contrapuntal passages of equal interest to instruments of unequal "telling" power. The balance is all wrong. The passage won't "come off." The explanation often is that the feeble Oboe or Bassoon whose refined notes we hear is only *in name* the instrument for which the passage was written.

No. 34. The Oboe d'Amore.

Fr. *Hautbois d'amour.*

This rarely used instrument is really a mezzo-soprano Oboe. It is built a minor third below the standard instrument, but does not possess the key-extension for producing the low B♭. Its upward range is to high E♮.

The written compass is therefore

which sounds

It is written for as a transposing-instrument in the treble-clef. Its key-signature has of course three ♭'s more or three ♯'s less than the key-signature of the piece. Its best keys, therefore, are the ♯ major keys from G to E and their relative minors. The corresponding easy key-signatures for the Oboe d'Amore are B♭ to G major with their relative minors.

In the eighteenth century the Oboe d'Amore was occasionally written as a non-transposing instrument. Nowadays, on its rare appearances, it is played by an Oboist. The fingerings of the two instruments are the same, and it is therefore more convenient to write a transposing part. Bearing in mind both this point and the restrictions as to compass, one may say in a word that the technique of the Oboe d'Amore is identical with that of the Oboe. Note, however,

(1) That the whole-tone shake on

is impossible, and the half-tone shake on

nearly so;

(2) That no shake is possible beyond the half-tone shake on

In point of tone-colour, however, there is a difference. The lower-pitched instrument lacks something of the Oboe's pungency and distinction. In place of these it has a smooth calmness and serenity which fit it for the expression of simple tenderness and of devotional feeling.

Bach, in his *Christmas Oratorio,* in his *Magnificat in D major,* and in his eighth *Church Cantata,* wrote parts either for a Solo instrument, for two, or for a Quartet of two Oboi d'Amore and two Oboi da caccia.[1] After his time it fell into disuse, but has recently been revived by Richard Strauss for his *Sinfonia Domestica.* In the *Scherzo* of that work (D major) the subject is given to the Oboe d'Amore accompanied by 2nd Violins and Wood-Wind:

EXAMPLE 138.

Perhaps more characteristic of the instrument is the little cantabile in the same work with its high *ppp* accompaniment of 2nd Violins *tremolo*:

EXAMPLE 139.

No. 35. The English-Horn.

Fr. *Cor Anglais*[2] It. *Corno Inglese*; Ger. *Englisches Horn.*

This instrument, which is neither "English" nor a "Horn," is a descendant of the mediæval Alto-Pommer, No. 3 in the Schalmey-Pommer family mentioned on page 204. It may be regarded simply as a Contralto Oboe. Its wooden pipe is wider and longer than that of the Oboe and terminates in a small globular bell. At the upper end the metal *crook* or *staple* which holds the double-reed is generally bent back at an angle with the pipe itself. In old specimens of the instrument this convenient shortening in the total height was secured by bending the whole pipe into a curve. The reed used is larger and thicker than the Oboe-reed and the air-column is much more easily controlled.

[1] The predecessors of the English-Horns (Cors Anglais).

[2] Perhaps for *Cor Anglé, i.e. Bent Horn,* but the first word is difficult to explain. In England the instrument is more commonly spoken of as *Cor Anglais* than as *English Horn.*

The English-Horn is built a perfect fifth below the Oboe, and its part is written nowadays a fifth higher than the key of the piece and with a key-signature of one ♭ less or one ♯ more than the key-signature of the music. Like the Oboe d'Amore, it lacks the key-extension for producing the low B♭. The written compass of these two instruments is exactly the same, two octaves and a fourth,

which sounds on the English-Horn

The fingering of the instrument is practically the same as that of the Oboe. This gave rise to a curious notation which was used in France as late as Halévy's time. The Oboe-player in whose hands the English-Horn was placed had, of course, to finger for

when he wished to produce the sound

The French composer, therefore, satisfied his sense of logic by placing the Mezzo-soprano-clef on the 2nd line and leaving the player to imagine a treble-clef instead. For the sound "Middle C" he wrote "Middle C" in the Mezzo-soprano-clef thus:

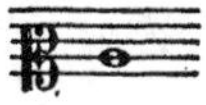 and the player read 

There seems to have been some difference of routine as to key-signatures and accidentals. This perhaps explains what they did at rehearsals in those days.

In Italy composers before Verdi's time adopted the absurd plan of writing the sounds required in the bass-clef an octave below their true pitch.

Bach, in writing for the Oboe da caccia, an instrument similar to the English-Horn, set down the actual sounds required in the Alto-clef on the third line.

The following shows at a glance the three obsolete notations and the now universal modern notation:

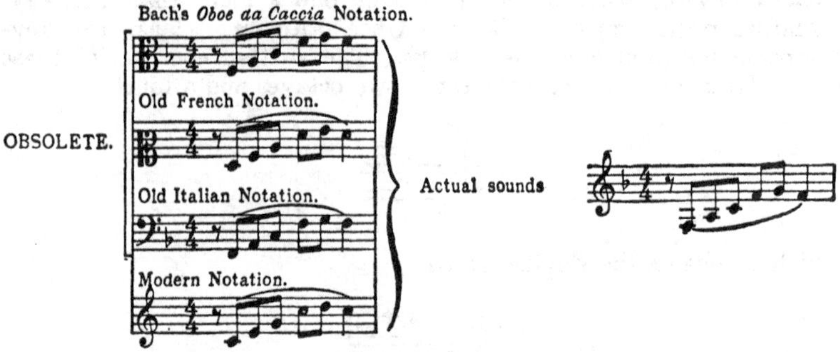

As the fingering is practically the same for the Oboe and the English-Horn the student may transfer all that was said above on the Oboe-technique, its shakes, tremolos, staccatos, legatos, etc., to the compass of the English-Horn.

The restriction with regard to the whole-tone shake on low B♮ and the half-tone shake on low C in the technique of the Oboe d'Amore does not apply to the English-Horn. Both are possible, as follows:

On the other hand, the limitation of the upwards shakes to the half-tone shake on

holds good.

The tone of the English-Horn differs strikingly from that of the Oboe.[1] In its lowest fifth the notes are of a fine quality, slightly hollow but reedy and expressive. Upwards from that it has a smooth richness not unlike that of a Contralto Voice. The notes above

are not much used. Their quality is inferior to the corresponding notes on the Oboe. The whole compass of the English-Horn is tinged with a curious shade of reflection, of sadness, and of melancholy. In expressing ideas of sorrow and regret the instrument seems to have almost more personality than any other in the orchestra. The finest

[1] This is generally supposed to be due to the bell at the end of the pipe.

example of this is the long unaccompanied Solo at the beginning of Act III. of *Tristan.* The passage is, however, too well known and too often played to need quotation. In its place we may cite the beautiful *largo* melody from Dvořák's *New World Symphony.* The accompaniment is for a rich deep ensemble of muted Strings. The Double-Bass part, of course, sounds an octave below the written notes. The A♭ entry in bar nine, therefore, sounds a perfect fifth above the low Cello D♭. The student should notice the curiously empty and sad effect produced by the tenths between the English-Horn and the two Clarinets in bars 5 to 9.

EXAMPLE 140.

The above is an instance of the English-Horn used chiefly in its upper register. As an example of its middle and lower registers the lovely tune from Tschaikowsky's Fantasy-Overture *Romeo and Juliet* may be quoted. Here we have a melody which is doubled in the unison by the muted Violas. The English-Horn is accompanied by quiet syncopated chords for the three French-Horns. The effect is very happy—what one may call the *entente cordiale* in orchestration. The empty bar at the end of the English-Horn part is simply due to the fact that the last note of the tune is out of the instrument's compass. Unless doubled it could not have been assigned to the instrument. In this tune the muted Violas stand out more prominently than the English Horn. The two tone-colours are very similar, but the one stave represents one player and the other stave perhaps a dozen. This is the fate of almost all Wood-Wind instruments when doubling a String-melody in the unison. That is not to say, however, that the plan is of no value. The added richness which the Strings—or, for the matter of that, the French-Horns[1]—acquire is a great factor in the success of the melody. A very experienced orchestral musician of the last generation always used this expression, "A Wood-Wind solidifies a tune on the Strings."

For other examples of the English-Horn the student may examine the *Andante* $\frac{3}{8}$ in the Overture to Rossini's *William Tell*, the *Moderato* $\frac{3}{4}$ passage in Schumann's *Manfred* (page 58) and the *Obbligato* to Meyerbeer's *Robert toi que j'aime*.

EXAMPLE 141.

[1] See, for instance, Ex. 80, where the English-Horn, though contending in the unison with the four French-Horns, undoubtedly adds something to the tone-colour of the high A's.

[2] The Harp-notes are written on the Bassoon stave merely to save space. They have two staves to themselves in the original Score.

The modern tendency with the instrument is not to give it elaborate and funereal solos, but to employ it principally for enriching the middle harmonies of the Wood-Wind. Then again, it has been called upon recently to show an unusual dexterity and nimbleness. This is fortunately not at all beyond its powers. The following passages may be quoted to show its capabilities in this way:

EXAMPLE 142.

Strauss. *Ein Heldenleben.*

English Horn.

EXAMPLE 143.

Strauss. *Ein Heldenleben.*

English-Horn.

In connection with the latter example the student should look at the whole Full Score from which it is quoted—the "Critics" section of the *Heldenleben.* This is, perhaps, the most curiously suggestive and characteristic passage ever written for the Wood-Wind. In particular, the student cannot fail to notice the hard, spiteful, viperine effect produced by means of the *f staccatos* and the little close chromatic passages for the three Oboes, the English-Horn, and the E♭-Clarinet.

The English-Horn, for all its name, owes most of its artistic position to the French. It is true that they were not the first to use the instrument. As early as 1762, says Gevaert, the Orchestra of the Imperial Theatre in Vienna, where there were no Clarinets, possessed two English-Horns. Gluck, on coming to Paris with his *Orfeo* and *Alceste,* had to rearrange his English-Horn parts for Clarinets. For instance, the air, *Plein de trouble et d'effroi,* in Act I. of *Orfeo,* is given in the Paris Full Score of 1774 to two Clarinets-in-C. In those days, and till much more recently, it was usual to write two English-Horn parts—generally simple successions of thirds and sixths—and to employ principally the upper register of the instrument. See, for instance, Gluck's *Orfeo,* Act I. and Halévy's *La Juive,* Act IV.

However, in 1808, the instrument was introduced to the French at the Paris Opera House in a work by Catel, called *Alexandre chez Apelle.* The part was played by Vogt, the 1st Oboist. From that time forward the English-Horn seems to have caught the fancy of every French operatic composer. It became a standard orchestral instrument in all the French compositions of the first half of the nineteenth century. Berlioz wrote for it in his *Symphonie Fantastique.* Meyerbeer not only employed it in *Solo* and *Obbligato* passages but used its middle and bottom registers in *Les Huguenots* to add a warm tone-colour to his accompaniments. This method was copied by Bizet in a charming accompaniment which is well worth quoting. It occurs in Micaëla's song, *Je dis que rien,* in Act III. of *Carmen.*

EXAMPLE 144.

The pattern of the accompaniment consists of successive groups of chords for (1) Wood-Wind supported by the low notes of the English-Horn; (2) Muted Violins divided into four parts, and playing in the upper middle register; (3) *pianissimo* Horns. The tone-colour of each chord is just overlapped on to the tone-colour of the next, so as to prevent any sort of "gap" between the two. The whole series of chords is bound together by a most delightful *arpeggio-figure* for the muted Cellos. Finally, the whole orchestral scheme is subordinate to the beautiful melody in the voice.

In Germany Bach's Oboe da caccia parts, to which reference has already been made, were practically English-Horn parts. Haydn, Mozart, and Beethoven all wrote for the instrument. The last named indeed composed a Trio for two Oboes and English-Horn. But apparently it was never with any of them an instrument of the ordinary orchestral routine. Weber, too, strangely overlooked its possibilities. Beginning with *Lohengrin* (1847), Wagner adopted the instrument in his regular orchestra. It became just as integral to his Double-Reeds as the 2nd Clarinet and Bass-Clarinet to his Single-Reeds.

Nowadays every Symphony and Opera orchestra possesses an English-Horn as well as two Oboes. It is, however, often convenient for a composer to arrange a small lightly-constructed composition so that the 2nd Oboist can take the English-Horn when required. In this case he should allow ten or twenty bars of moderate time in which to make the change.

No. 36. Rarely-used Wood-Wind.

The Musette, Heckelphon, Heckelclarind, Tarogato, and additional Oboes.

Passing mention may be made here of three instruments—the **Musette**, **Heckelphon**, and **Heckelclarind**. Of these the first is obsolete and the last two are only rarely used.

The **Musette** was a two-pipe bagpipe whose natural compass was from

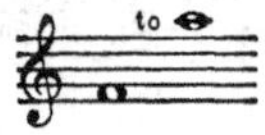

This was occasionally extended by means of keys, a minor second downwards and a minor third upwards. The air was controlled by a bag under the player's arm. The characteristic melody, accompanied by a drone-bass, gave rise to the little instrumental movements fashionable at one time under the name of "*Musettes.*"

The word Musette was also applied to a small Schalmey or keyless-Oboe pitched sometimes in G, sometimes in A♭.

The **Heckelphon** owes its existence to Heckel, the well-known instrument maker of Biberich. It is practically what the French call an "*Hautbois baryton.*" The written compass of the instrument is chromatically from

and this sounds an octave lower:

The instrument has no low B♭ key-extension.

The air-column is set in vibration by means of a double-reed midway in size between that of the English-Horn and of the Bassoon. The finger-technique is the same as that of the Oboe, but the four top semitones of its compass are difficult to produce and only available in the *forte.*

Strauss has made use of the Heckelphon in his Opera *Salome.*

The **Heckelclarind**[1] was invented by Heckel with the express purpose of playing the Solo English-Horn part in Act III. of *Tristan.* It is built in B♭, and possesses a written chromatic compass from

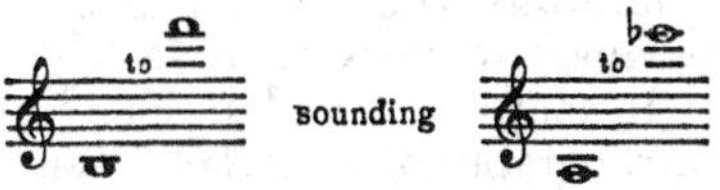

The upper five semitones are practically useless. The air-column is set in vibration by means of a single-reed like that of the Saxophone or Clarinet.[2] It should therefore be included in the Clarinet group. However, the instrument is so little used that for convenience of reference it is mentioned here.

In some Opera-Houses abroad—*e.g.* those of Paris and Brussels—the **Tarogato** ("*Holtztrompete*") has been used, without much success, to play the shepherd's air in *Tristan.* The instrument is a simple conical pipe of wood furnished with a single piston and terminating in a globular bell something like that of the English-Horn. A clarinet-reed is used, and the part is written as for a non-transposing instrument.

A small **Oboe-in-E♭**, transposing upwards a minor third like the Clarinet-in-E♭ (see page 278), is used in some Continental military bands. Its execution is precisely the same as that of the ordinary Oboe.

Attempts have been made within recent years to extend the compass of the Oboe-family downwards by the construction of a Double-Bass-Oboe. These experiments are interesting, first because the Oboe and Flute are the only instruments in the orchestra whose tone-colours are not carried down into the bass-octaves, and next because it is an attempt to revive the sixteenth century Bass-Pommers and Bombards which were reconstructed as Bassoons and, in reconstruction, completely lost all affinity with the Oboes.

No. 37. The Bassoon.

Fr. ***Basson*** **; It.** ***Fagotto*** **; Ger.** ***Fagott.***

The family history of the Bassoon begins in the sixteenth century. Its general outline and its more important details are perfectly well known. Unfortunately the honourable ancestry of the instrument has been besmirched by an event which took place in Italy somewhere before the year 1539,—the invention of the **Phagotus** by Afranio, Canon of Ferrara.

This instrument had no connection whatever either technical or historical with the Bassoon. However, a continental historian and

[1] Or *Clarina-Heckel.*

[2] The Heckelclarind is also made in E♭. This instrument has the same writter compass, but it sounds a minor third higher.

theorist of last century, misled by the name and by an imperfect acquaintance with its mechanism, hailed it as the first attempt to cut up the long pipe of the old Bass-Pommer into two parts, in fact as the original Bassoon. Naturally this claim has been repeated over and over again by subsequent writers until it has almost acquired the sanctity of truth. It may be found, mechanically copied with the original theorist's orthographical mistakes even in our most recent musical works of reference.

No known fact in connection with the Phagotus supports the claim. It is not a conically- but a cylindrically-bored pipe. It is not a double-reed instrument at all, but an instrument of free metal tongues. It is not even blown by the player's breath, but by means of two pairs of bellows. In every essential it differs from the Bassoon; though it must be allowed that there is some slight difficulty in explaining the resemblance between the two names *fagotto* and *phagotus*. However this is not of great importance. The Phagotus itself was, without a shadow of doubt, a development of the ancient *utricular* family of instruments. It was an unsuccessful attempt to elaborate and combine the Organ and the Bagpipes. In fact, if a descriptive name was needed for this unholy hybrid, Valdrighi's expression *quasi-organo* would be more suitable than any other.

Illustrations of the front- and back-view of the Phagotus are to be found at page 488, plate XII. On these the student can exercise his ingenuity and discretion in endeavouring to reconstitute the instrument and its tone. A comparison can also be made with the front- and back-view of the modern Bassoon shown at page 232, plate IX.; for the latter instrument is in essentials just the same as it was in the sixteenth century. In a book of this general character it is not possible to go at all closely into the details of the Phagotus, but for the benefit of those interested in the question a few remarks are added in an Appendix, page 487.

The Bassoon is historically a development of the old Bass-Pommer which in the sixteenth century was the true bass of the Schalmey-family. As we have already mentioned, the Discant- or Treble-Schalmey became changed into our modern Oboe, and this change was effected without any strongly marked alteration of tone-quality. The Bass-Pommer, on the other hand, was so completely transformed between 1550 and 1600 that we are now left with an instrument, the modern Bassoon, which is only a bass to the Oboe-family in the technical sense that it is played with a double-reed. In tone-colour it bears no resemblance at all to either the Oboe, the Oboe d'Amore, or the English-Horn.

The transition-instrument between the Pommer and the modern Bassoon appears to have been the Curtal[1] or Dulcian (Fr. *Douçaine*).

[1] This instrument seems to have enjoyed a certain amount of popularity in the last half of the sixteenth century. Occasional literary references to its employment may be found, *e.g.* "The common bleting musicke is ye Drone, Hobius, and Curtoll." *Batman upon Bartholome* (1582). The word *Bombarde*, with its collateral forms *Bumbarde*, *Pommard*, and *Pommer*, is of course found much more frequently. It occurs as early

This instrument, as originally manufactured, was an adaptation of the Tenor-Pommer-in-C. The main alteration consisted in cutting the whole pipe out of a double-bore block of wood, much in the same way as the double-joint of the Bassoon is now pierced. Hence came its name "Curtal," which simply means "Shortened Pommer." Later on the Double-Curtal was introduced. This instrument was pitched an octave below the (single) Curtal, and, in appearance at any rate, bore some resemblance to the modern Bassoon. Owing to their large size and solid "make," specimens of Pommers, Curtals, and Dulcians are, as such things go, by no means rare. Most museums possess well-preserved examples of these instruments, and there are many in the hands of private collectors.

It will be seen that the alterations which were made in the Pommer towards the end of the sixteenth century were chiefly directed towards a reduction of bore and a greater convenience of shape. The older instrument was of comparatively wide bore and was made in one straight piece over six feet long. The difficulties of "stopping" an instrument of this huge length must have been very great. They were only partially overcome by cutting the pipe into two unequal portions and joining the two in a wooden block provided with a U-shaped piercing. In the new instrument thus made the tone was sweeter and more adaptable to modern needs, but the intonation, depending on a casual, empirical distribution of the holes, was imperfect. And imperfect it remains to the present day. This, however, is no drawback to the instrument. On the contrary, it has thrown on the instrumentalist the same responsibilities in the way of intonation as those incurred by the String-player. The consequence is that a good Bassoon-player is continually on the watch to overcome the natural deficiencies of his instrument, and however uncomfortable this mode of life may be to him, the artistic results are good beyond question.

As we have it now, the Bassoon is a conically-bored pipe doubled back upon itself so as to reduce its length to about four feet. The whole pipe is divided into five pieces which are, in their order from the player's lips, as follows:

(1) The *crook*, a narrow, curved tube of metal to which the double-reed is attached.

(2) The *wing*.

(3) The *double-joint*, at the lower end of which the pipes meet and reverse their direction. The junction is effected, as stated above, by means of a U-shaped piercing in a solid "butt" of wood.

as the end of the fourteenth century, "Such a soune Of bombarde and of clarioune." Gower, *Conf.* (1393). Besides the Curtal there was another intermediate type of Bassoon called from its fat, clumsy appearance the *Sausage-Bassoon* (Fr. *Cervelat*). A second English name for this instrument was the *Racket*. The word appears to be a variant of *Ranket*, from Ger. *ranke* = crooked. Mr. Lindesay G. Langwill, of Edinburgh, kindly furnishes this etymology, which, he informs me, is accepted as correct by Prof. Sachs, of Berlin. The Racket had a cylindrical pipe, with holes bored obliquely, as in the Bassoon. A smaller, alto or tenor, Racket at any rate existed. See illustration on page 7 of Heckel's *Der Fagott*.

(4) The *long* or *bass* joint, which lies next to and extends upwards beyond the *wing*.

(5) The *bell*.

These five pieces together with the double-reed can all be seen in the two views of the Bassoon given on Plate IX. It should also be noted how peculiarly serviceable is the modern system of keys, trackers, and finger-pieces, when applied to an instrument of such great length. Not only does it provide the player with a complete chromatic compass, but it enables the controlling finger-pieces to be arranged conveniently round the two groups of finger-holes in the Wing and the Double-joint. Thus the key-holes can be placed accurately without depriving the player of his technical command over the natural scale of the pipe.

The instrument is held diagonally by the player. The bell points upwards to his left hand, and the double-joint rests against his knee.

The original scale of the Bassoon begins at

but this has always been extended downwards for a perfect fifth to

Originally, however, this extension was not wholly chromatic. This will explain to the student the curious omissions which he is bound to meet in old Scores. As late as 1821 we find Weber writing, in the *Freischütz* Overture:

EXAMPLE 145.

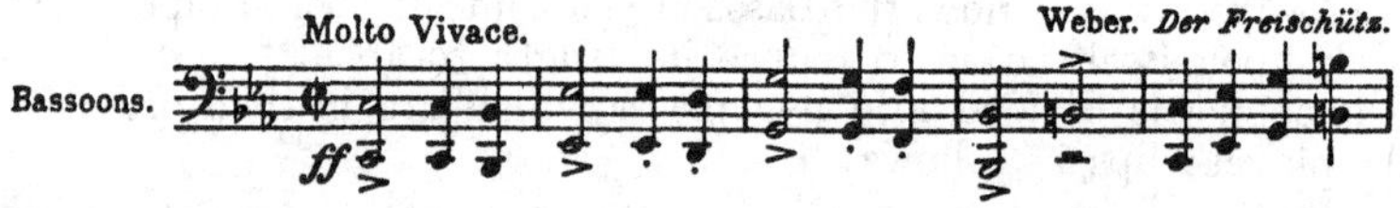

where in the 4th bar the 2nd Bassoon B♮ is omitted simply because that note was not on the player's instrument. This bottom fifth is of course now, like the rest of the instrument, wholly chromatic. Above the first natural octave of the Bassoon (F to F) the second octave to

is produced in the usual manner by overblowing the lower octave. Above that again a complete minor seventh to

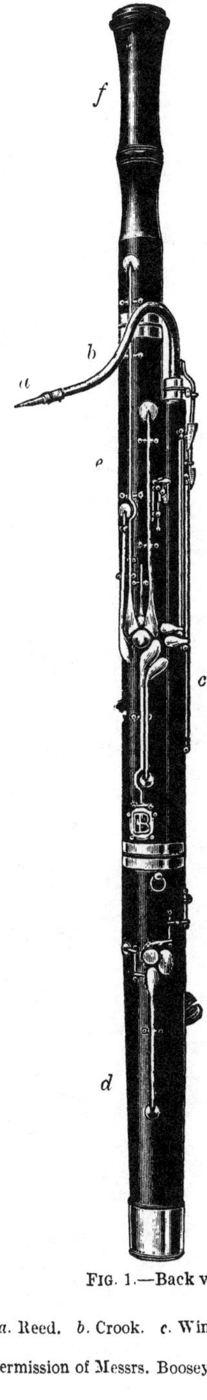

FIG. 1.—Back view.

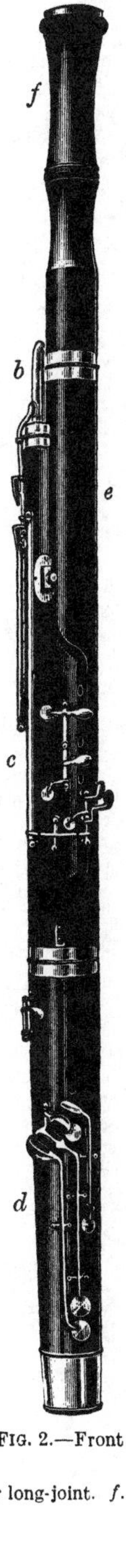

FIG. 2.—Front view.

BASSOON.

a. Reed. *b*. Crook. *c*. Wing. *d*. Double-joint. *e*. Bass- or long-joint. *f*. Bell.

By kind permission of Messrs. Boosey & Co.

is producible by means of overblowing the fundamental octave at the twelfth.

As will be seen, the complete chromatic compass of the Bassoon

is of great length. It must, however, be pointed out that, though it would be easy to produce examples of the use of the extreme upper notes, they have little orchestral value. When well covered up they may be employed to complete the proper contour of a passage, or to characterize a particular musical phrase. But apart altogether from their generally ineffective quality they tend to disturb the player's embouchure. One may give the top B♭

as a good working upper compass for the instrument.[1] At the lower end of the compass Wagner, both in *Tristan* and the *Ring*, writes down to low A♮.

A passage like this from *Die Walküre* (Act I., Scene III.)

EXAMPLE 146.

cannot be circumvented by the mere addition of a key to the instrument. An extra joint or, as the French call it, a "*pavillon de rechange*," has to be fitted on. This is, perhaps, one of the things in which it is better not to imitate Wagner.

The Bassoon shakes are more restricted than those of the Flute, Oboe, or Clarinet.

From

[1] This limit cannot, of course, always be observed. It is merely given as a rough guide to the student. For Bassoon-passages going beyond this note see Exs. 149, 166, and 168. Many others might be quoted from recent Scores.

upwards for two octaves all shakes are *possible*; but avoid whole-tone shakes on the following notes:

Note that for purposes of memory these seven bad whole-tone shakes may be reduced to four by the statement that they are:

(1) The high A♮ shake, and
(2) The shakes on D♭, E♭, G♭, in each of the two octaves.

As the Bassoon is constructed at present, the combination of F♯ and G♯ (or of G♭ and A♭) in any rapid *legato* passage is very difficult. This applies to all three octaves.[1]

Below

whole-tone shakes are only possible on the following notes

and half-tone shakes on

One need scarcely add that the bottom shakes, even when technically possible, are far too strongly marked in character to be of much use.

Tremolos are rarely needed on the Bassoon. The advice with regard to them may be put in a nutshell. As far as possible use only major and minor thirds of which the lower note is any note chromatically upwards from

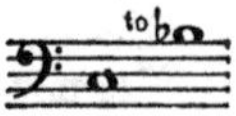

These limits are occasionally exceeded, but it is better for everyone concerned when they are observed.

Strauss employs Bassoon tremolos with considerable freedom in the orchestral *forte* and *mezzo-forte*. As a rule, however, he uses them in such a way that there is very little chance of them being heard. The

[1] An awkward instance can be found in the opening notes of Example 168.

following example of a simple tremolo is from his *Ein Heldenleben* (page 41 of the Full Score):

EXAMPLE 147.

A few pages later on in the same work there are two-part tremolos for Bassoons, and even (on page 49) a three-part tremolo in a very awkward key. The passage is, however, well covered up.

EXAMPLE 148.

A great deal of nonsense has been written about the Bassoon registers. Some authors divide up the whole compass of the instrument into three, others into five distinct parts. There is no necessity for this. From its bottom note upwards for two octaves and a fifth to

the instrument, in the hands of an efficient player, is admirably even and regular. The bottom fifth is of course thicker and reedier than the middle and upper portions, but this is common to all Wood-Wind instruments. The low B♭, in especial when taken *piano*, has a beautiful velvety quality unapproachable by any other orchestral instrument.

The middle-register always figures in instrumentation-books as "weak," "pale," "thin," "cold," "cadaverous," and all the rest of it. This has its origin in Berlioz's remarks with regard to the "*Resurrection of the Nuns*" in Meyerbeer's *Robert le Diable.* As a matter of fact, the octave upwards from

is the very best part of the instrument, capable of a beautiful solemn sonority in slow *legato* melodies, and quite easy to produce and control in quick passages. One must not forget that no other Wind instrument can even faintly suggest the illusion of a Baritone voice in this octave. The Clarinets are too smooth and overcharged with colour in the portion of the octave which they cover; while the Bass-Clarinet is too hollow, windy, and inexpressive.

The real state of the matter is that the Bassoon has a preternatural power of playing *staccato*, and, if it is forced to play passages of a humorous, grotesque, or macabre sort, it easily endows them with a dry *spiccato* quality that is almost toneless. But this is one of the instrument's many virtues. No one would suggest that because the English-Horn can play the stinging semitones at the beginning of the "*Critics*" section of the *Heldenleben* that, therefore, it cannot play the *Largo* of the *New World Symphony*. The less said about Meyerbeer and his rubbishy thirds the better. So much for the middle-register of the Bassoon.

It is only necessary to add that, as the scale progresses above the top tenor F, the absence of the characteristic Harmonics of the lower octaves becomes increasingly noticeable. The result is a somewhat pinched tone-quality as of someone complaining about his poverty. These notes, to be properly effective, must be doubled. If used without doubling they must either be accompanied in the lightest manner possible, or, in harmonic combinations, only pitted against single Wood-Wind "voices." In this connection the student should look at the quotation already given from Tschaikowsky's *Hamlet* (Ex. 133) and the one printed below from the same composer's *Pathetic Symphony* (Ex. 149).

As the double-reed of the Bassoon is between the player's lips he is, of course, precluded from using either double- or triple-tonguing. For all that the executive powers of the instrument are remarkable. Anything in the way of *arpeggio* figures (Exs. 166 and 168), wide *staccato* skips up to and even beyond the limits of a sixteenth (Exs. 163 and 164), diatonic and chromatic scales (Exs. 158, 159, and 165), rapid successions of repeated notes (Ex. 160), of detached and *staccato* notes (Exs. 161 and 162), and passages founded on any combination of these technical methods, are performed with ease and certainty. In the *legato* quick scale passages, if written in any key south of D major or north of A♭ major,[1] are pretty sure to come off and sound well. Like the Oboe, its best slurred skips—that is to say, slurs merely between two notes as opposed to extended *legatos*—are those taken upwards. This point, however, is not of great importance unless the skips are very wide.

A word may be added with regard to the danger of allotting any subject of a serious or poetical nature to the Bassoon if it involves repeated, detached, or *staccato* notes. Such a subject, especially if first heard on the Strings, will appear ludicrously commonplace when heard on the Bassoon. One has only to remember the repeated notes in the slow movement of Mozart's *G Minor Symphony*. On the Bassoon the subject sounds tame, awkward, and mechanical, however good the player. The Bassoon is by no means deficient in seriousness or even

[1] See the caution given above with regard to the notes F♯ and G♯.

in poetry, but, in order to realize these qualities, it needs a certain spacious and somewhat solemn type of *legato* melody.

No instrument is at once so easy and so difficult to illustrate by means of examples as the Bassoon: easy, because any Full Score from Haydn to Strauss has only to be opened at random to provide effective passages for the instrument; difficult, because its uses for melodic purposes, for "filling-up," for figures of accompaniment, and for bass-work are so manifold that fifty pages would not exhaust the possibilities of the subject.

The following skeleton outline from the second Movement of Tschaikowsky's *Pathetic Symphony* contains a good example of a few solo notes for Bassoon at the top of its compass. The melodic phrases are allotted in turn to each of the Wood-Wind instruments and the Horn. The String-accompaniment, omitted here for reasons of space, is throughout marked down to a lower dynamic level than that of the Solo Instruments. It begins *p*, reaches ***mf*** in bar 4, and then *diminuendoes* to *pp* in bar 8.

EXAMPLE 149.

Beethoven's wonderfully effective phrase for Solo Bassoon in the *Più Mosso* of the *Fifth Symphony* (2nd Movement), is accompanied in the lightest manner possible by the Strings. The Basses and Cellos play the low A♭, three *pianissimo* semiquavers on the quaver-beats of each bar, while the Violins and Violas play three *pianissimo* semiquavers "off the beat."

EXAMPLE 150.

The following passage is from the Waltz Movement of Tschaikowsky's *Fifth Symphony*:

EXAMPLE 151.

It affords a very good example of what not to write for the Bassoon. The opening bars present no difficulties, but the big up-and-down *legato* "swoops," of which the last bars consist, need a good deal of nice adjustment in the *tempo* unless they are to sound merely an awkward scramble. Even with a first-class Bassoonist, and with a sympathetic Conductor waiting on him, this passage is liable to sound somewhat unsatisfactory.

Here is another Tschaikowsky passage in the upper register of the Bassoon. It occurs in that composer's *Marche Slave.* The two Bassoons playing in unison with the Violas give exactly the plaintive funereal character which the subject demands.

EXAMPLE 152.

Occasionally in harmonies of Wood-Wind and of Wood-Wind and Horns the composer abandons the normal arrangement in which the 1st Bassoon plays a part lower than that of the Clarinets. This is done with the double object of securing the thick reedy tone of the Clarinets in their "chalumeau"[1] register and of giving greater prominence to the nasal quality of the upper Bassoon notes. An instance of this modern procedure has already been quoted from Tschaikowsky's *Hamlet* (Ex. 133), and a second example in which the accompaniment consists of thick reedy chords and soft Horn notes is quoted in the "String" section of this book from Bridge's *Isabella.*[2] Both these examples are well worth the student's attention from the point of view of the vertical arrangement of the Wind-parts.

[1] See page 361. [2] Ex. 248. See also Ex. 192.

As an instance of the use of the middle register of the Bassoon no better example can be quoted than the subject in the 1st Movement of Tschaikowsky's *Fifth Symphony* as it appears on that instrument "solo." The effect is sombre and melancholy in the extreme. Here are the first few bars of the passage:

EXAMPLE 153.

Wagner occasionally gets an effect of extraordinary desolation and sadness by employing his Bassoons quite alone. No one can forget this little bit of accompanying in *Das Rheingold.*

EXAMPLE 154.

Wagner's terrific slurs that stretch magnificently across his pages like the Rainbow-Bridge of his own imagining are a sheer impossibility except to a race of giants.

The old-fashioned "fun" of making the Bassoon play unexpected, low notes is not in much demand nowadays. On the other hand, the instrument is often called upon to characterize baroque tunes, and this it does very successfully. One has only to imagine the subject of Dukas's *L'Apprenti Sorcier* on any other tone-colour to see how invaluable the Bassoon is in this direction.

EXAMPLE 155.

The most telling examples of the bottom notes of the Bassoon are perhaps to be found on the first page of the *Pathetic Symphony* and in the *Adagio* near the beginning of the last Movement. In the latter of these two examples, both given below, the composer takes the high F♯, which is so striking a feature of the opening, and brings it gradually down in the same tone-colour through two octaves and a fourth. The student should look carefully at the dynamic marks and differentiate in his mind those which apply only to the performance of separate short phrases from those which are integral to the passage as a whole. This whole Symphony is a model in the not unimportant art of phrasing, dynamic marks, balance of expression, and so on.

EXAMPLE 156.

EXAMPLE 157.

Tschaikowsky. *Pathetic Symphony.*

Adagio poco meno che prima. (♩ = 60.)

The following short extracts will give the student some idea of the *legato* and *staccato* technique of the Bassoon. They have already been referred to above (page 236). It must not be supposed that they are special "show" passages. On the contrary, almost any Score which the student may chance to open will provide him with similar phrases of about the same degree of difficulty.

Rapid legatos.

EXAMPLE 158

Presto. Mozart. *Figaro.*

EXAMPLE 159.

Allegro Energico. Beethoven. *Choral Symphony.*

Repeated, detached, and staccato notes in quick tempos.

EXAMPLE 160.

Molto Allegro. Mozart *Don Giovanni.*

EXAMPLE 161.

Allegro ma non troppo. Beethoven. *Symphony No. 4 in Bb.*

EXAMPLE 162.

Wide skips.

EXAMPLE 163.

EXAMPLE 164.

Chromatic scales.

EXAMPLE 165.

Florid passages of wide range.

EXAMPLE 166.

EXAMPLE 167.

EXAMPLE 168.

A good deal of the work which the Bassoon is called on to do in the orchestra consists only of holding-notes in the middle-register, of quietly moving passages in the middle of the harmony, and of unob trusive figures. In dealing with the last-named, its great range often gives it the power of playing a complete figure which, in the String-parts, is split up between two or three groups of instruments. For all these functions the Bassoon is admirably fitted. Its quiet self-effacing tone makes it, like the Clarinet, an ideal "background-instrument" on which to paint the brighter colours of the orchestral palette.

This comparative over-sympathy in its quality sometimes leads to a certain want of distinction. Unless well uncovered the tone-colour is apt to be lost in the surrounding instrumental haze. This is much more often the case when it is compelled to play light staccato notes. It is easily "outwitted," so to speak. For instance, in the *Andantino* of Bizet's 1st *L'Arlésienne* Suite (1st Movement, page 8 of the Full Score) the Cellos play the subject ("*p espress.*"), while two Horns in C play a second part ("*p mais sonore, espress.*"). The Bassoon plays a third contrapuntal part in triplets *staccato* ("*p*"). The orchestral result generally is that the Bassoon-part is almost inaudible. The first bars of the passage are as follows:

EXAMPLE 169.

[1] For a somewhat similar but quite effective passage, see the 1st *Entr' Acte to Carmen*. The two Bassoons begin *Solo* in unison, and a little later the Clarinet has a tune against a descending chromatic passage for Bassoon.

Beethoven, who loved to put in tiny passages for the Bassoon in its middle and top registers, always took care to give the instrument its freedom in this respect. Here is one such example from the *Rondo* of his *Violin Concerto*:

EXAMPLE 170.

Beethoven. *Violin Concerto.*

The E♮ in *Leonora No. 3*, which everybody looks for and nobody has ever missed in performance, is about the best illustration possible of the saying that "you can always hear anything in the orchestra if the composer doesn't prevent you."

EXAMPLE 171.

Beethoven. *Leonora No. 3.*

It has often been pointed out that the Bassoon is continually compelled by its nature to act as the ordinary bass of the Wood-Wind-Horn ensemble. This, in the old scoring, was one of its stereotyped functions. It is unnecessary to quote instances, they occur in every Score. The opening bars of the *Tannhäuser Overture*, of the *Nocturne* in Mendelssohn's *Midsummer Night's Dream*, and of the prelude to *Hänsel und Gretel* will furnish examples.

The student can make an interesting and instructive study merely of the harmonic and melodic "doublings" in which the two Bassoons continually take part. Beginning with a simple "Oboe and Bassoon" octave-unison like this

EXAMPLE 172.

Tschaikowsky. *Symphony in F minor.*

he can note all the single octave-combinations, then go on to the double-octave combinations of this sort,

EXAMPLE 173.

Beethoven. *Choral Symphony.*

and so with the triple-octave combinations. He can then apply the same process to the harmonic combinations, doublings of thirds, of sixths, of fragmentary figures, of held notes, and so forth. The man who either invented or fixed the type of all these combinations was Wolfgang Amadeus Mozart, and if the student will merely write down on a sheet of paper every Bassoon-combination which he can find in the first seven Numbers of *Don Giovanni*, noting each only once on its first appearance, he will probably be considerably astonished.

The Bassoon has been regularly used in the orchestra since the time of Händel. Till Mozart's time, however, it was little else than an instrument for doubling the String-bass. After him Beethoven. He not only understood its possibilities, but brought it sufficiently forward in his orchestral ensemble to compel the Bassoon-players to extend and refine their technique. In the *5th* and *9th Symphonies* especially there are fine Bassoon parts, but, indeed, there are very few of his orchestral works in which at some moment or other the varied capabilities of the instrument are not turned to artistic account. Beethoven wrote for two Bassoons regularly, and this has remained the standard for orchestral music till quite recently.[1]

At the present day there are three Bassoonists in all Symphony orchestras. Of these the 3rd is generally prepared to take either Bassoon or Double-Bassoon as required. In modern times the introduction of the Bass-Clarinet and the Tuba, as well as the perfection of the Valve-Horn mechanism, has contributed to set the Bassoon free from its drudgery as a purely bass-instrument. Hence comes a greater polyphonic independence in the Bassoon parts as well as an undoubtedly increased plasticity in the whole Wood-Wind mass. Among modern composers Strauss and Elgar seem to have lavished the greatest attention on their Bassoon parts. With the latter composer his Bassoon parts, if one may be permitted to say so, always appear to be peculiarly present to his consciousness.[2] The student cannot do better than examine any of his Scores to which he may have access.

No. 38. The Double-Bassoon.

Fr. *Contre-Basson* ; It. *Contrafagotto* ; Ger. *Kontrafagott.*

We have already explained that the Bassoon was a development, or rather an adaptation, of the old Bass-Pommer, an instrument which was the ordinary bass of the Schalmey-Pommer family. The largest and most powerful member of this instrumental group was the four-keyed Double-Bass-Pommer or Bombard (Doppelt-Quint-Pommer). Its length was nearly 10 ft., and its actual compass extended from

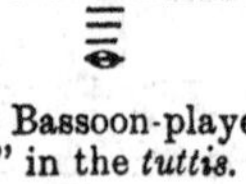

[1] In Gluck's time there were *eight* Bassoon-players at the Paris Opera House. There are now four, two of whom "double" in the *tuttis*.

[2] See, for example, the opening to the 3rd *Pomp and Circumstance* March marked "Fagotti preponderate Also Variations III. and XI. of the *Enigma* set.

From this instrument sprang the Double-Bassoon. In a general sense the last sentence is true, but we must not overlook the fact that the technical development of the Double-Bassoon has always waited on that of the ordinary Bassoon. The object has always been to reproduce the Bassoon-compass and technique one octave lower, but until recently the extreme difficulty of getting the bottom notes has left us with an instrument which lacks the two (or sometimes four) lowest semitones.

Some mention has already been made of Mahillon's attempt to reproduce accurately the tone-quality of the old Double-Bass-Pommer, and to combine it with a modern mechanism and a modern perfection of intonation. This instrument, the *Hautbois-Contrebasse*, has not hitherto figured in orchestral Scores.

Though used orchestrally as early as Händel's day,[1] it cannot be said that the Double-Bassoon had much vogue outside Germany until Beethoven began to write for it. The extreme difficulties of manufacture have resulted in the fact that there is no standard instrument in use all over Europe. Double-Bass-Reed-parts have been continually written for more than a hundred years past, but they have been and are still played in different countries on instruments of diverse makes, compasses, and tone-qualities. These instruments are three in number, and a very brief description of each will at anyrate familiarize the student with their names and general characteristics :

(1) In France, when the Double-Bass-Reed-part is not played on a Sarrusophone, a heavy brass Double-Bassoon is used. This instrument, usually called the "French" or "Belgian" Double-Bassoon, should be more accurately known as the "Austrian Double-Bassoon," since it was invented at Presburg towards the middle of last century. It is commonly known as the **Mahillon-Schöllnast Double-Bassoon.** It is a seventeen-keyed instrument, in appearance not unlike an ordinary military "Brass-Bass." It has a huge conical bore, and the tube, which is about five yards long, ends in a brass "bell" like that of a "Tuba." The tone-quality is coarse and "blurty." The technique is remarkably easy and regular, and the written compass

sounds an octave lower

It will be seen that this Double-Bassoon fails to reproduce the four bottom semitones of the Bassoon compass in the octave below. This instrument is practically unknown to English orchestral players.

(2) The English Double-Bassoon, as designed by Dr. Stone and modified by Alfred Morton and by Haseneier of Coblentz, is a wooden instrument whose conical bore varies from a calibre of ¼ inch at the reed-end to one of four inches at the open end. As in the ordinary Bassoon the open end of the instrument points upwards. There is,

[1] Händel first used a Double-Bassoon in the *Coronation Anthem* (1727). A later Händelian instrument, built by J. Stanesby, jun., and played by F. Lampe (1739), is in the R.C.M. collection.

however, no "bell-joint." The open end is simply finished off with a narrow rim. A heavy double-reed is used, and the compass of the instrument extends from

sounding an octave lower

The two bottom semitones of the ordinary Bassoon compass, B♮ and B♭, cannot be produced in its lower octave. This instrument, commonly known as the **Stone-Morton-Haseneier Double-Bassoon**, is the one which until recently was most familiar in our concert-rooms. It is undoubtedly an easier instrument to play than the "French Double-Bassoon." Its quality, however, in its lower compass—the only part that matters—leaves a great deal to be desired. The impact of the separate vibrations is unpleasantly prominent to the ear. In fact in its bottom fifth there appears to be more "rumble" than note. On the other hand, the instrument, though coarse, must be allowed to have abundant power and the capacity to support a huge volume of orchestral harmony.

The **modern German Double-Bassoon**, which appears likely to oust both the above, owes its improved existence to Heckel of Biberich and his successors. Its conical wooden pipe, of hard Austrian maple, is over 16 ft. long, and is doubled back four times on itself. The peculiarity of its appearance is the metal bell which points downwards. The crook is much like that of an ordinary Bassoon, a narrow curved tube of metal into which the double-reed is fitted. This instrument has two great advantages over any other Double-Bassoon. In the first place its quality is much more refined and much less obtrusive. The vibrations in its lowest fifth are not nearly so apparent to the ear and the tone-colour is homogeneous and practically the same as that of the ordinary Bassoon. In the second place it has a chromatic compass right down to the low B♭. Its written compass is

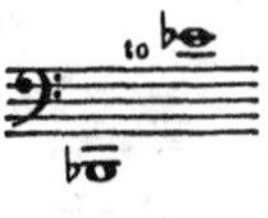

which sounds
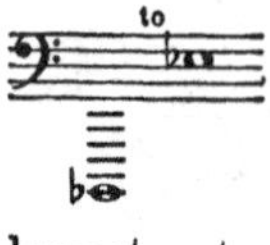

The instrument "speaks" easily even in its very lowest notes.

One need not say that the Double-Bassoon, whatever its make, is fitted only to play heavy bass-parts and bass-passages of a strictly moderate speed. In most Double-Bassoons the notes at both ends of the compass are unsatisfactory. In the *Heckel* instruments the top fourth is undoubtedly bad in quality. This, however, is of no consequence, as the two ordinary Bassoons can always play the parts in this portion of the Reed-compass.

The notation of Double-Bassoon parts is always in the bass-clef and an octave higher than the actual sounds required. There seems to be only one exception to this rule. Wagner writes the instrument at its actual pitch in *Parsifal.*

The orchestral intention of the Double-Bassoon is so obvious and its orchestral outlook so elementary that we need not devote much time to that side of the matter. A few words, however, must be said with regard to the elaborate Double-Bassoon part in the *Finale* of the *Choral Symphony*. This appears to have been written by Beethoven for a smaller and more flexible instrument than the one used at the present day. We have no knowledge that such an instrument existed. On the other hand, it may have been written under a misapprehension of the instrument's limitations. This may perhaps have been caused by his deafness. He employs the instrument continually with the Double-Basses even in the *Prestissimo*, and writes for it up to top A

Its entry at the beginning of the *Allegro assai vivace*, unless very carefully played, only just misses being grotesque. The Score contains nothing for the first eight bars but Bassoons, Double-Bassoon, and Bass Drum:

EXAMPLE 174.

These curious infelicities are all the more remarkable as Beethoven has written at least one striking Double-Bassoon part. The passage occurs in *Fidelio*, where the grave is being dug,

EXAMPLE 175.

Brahms, in his *C minor Symphony*, asks as much from the instrument as Beethoven. Within thirteen bars in the last Movement he uses a written compass of nearly three octaves.

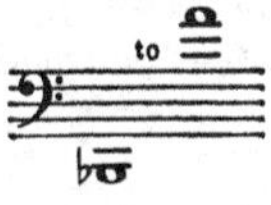

Wide skips up to two octaves and a minor third, notes *in altissimo* attacked without preparation, and difficult passage-work in unison

with the Double-Basses, are all to be found in this Symphony Instead of these, it is perhaps better to quote the simple chorale-subject in the *Più Andante* of the last Movement. In this passage the Double-Bassoon doubles the Bass-Trombone in the octave below. It always "tells" wonderfully in performance.

EXAMPLE 176.

Note. The **Tenoroon**,[2] now obsolete, was a small Bassoon pitched a fifth higher than the standard instrument. Its written chromatic compass

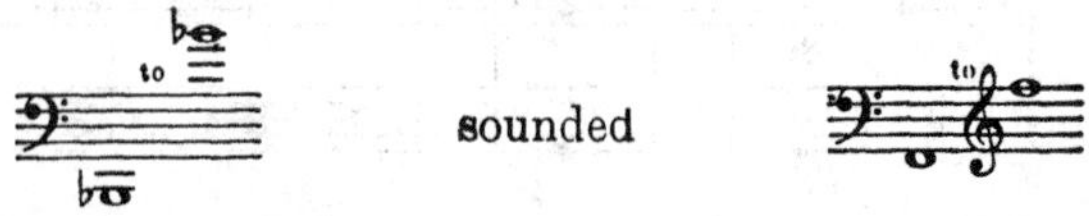

In tone-quality it closely resembled the Bassoon. The superior power of the latter in the lower octaves and the superior tone-colour of the English Horn in the upper have prevented the Tenoroon from acquiring a foothold in the orchestra. The assertion that the English-Horn Solo in Rossini's *William Tell Overture* was originally designed for the Tenoroon is a mistake, based probably on the fact that the part was written in the old Italian Notation;[3] that is to say, in the bass-clef an octave below its proper pitch.

The **Quartfagott**, now obsolete, was a large Bassoon used in Germany. It was pitched a perfect fourth lower than the ordinary Bassoon.

[1] See also the end of this movement, the *Più allegro*, where this subject appears again *ff.*

[2] Fr. *Basson quinte*: It. *Fagottino*: Ger. *Quintfagott* or *Tenorfagott.*

[3] See above, pp. 221-2.

No. 39. The Clarinet.[1]

Fr. *Clarinette*; It. *Clarino* (less usually *Clarinetto*); Ger. *Klarinette.*

The Clarinet is a descendant of a mediæval instrument known as the "Chalumeau." The history of the latter instrument has furnished matter for considerable discussion. Even the existence of such an instrument as a separate and clearly defined type has been denied. Without entering fully into the various arguments that have been brought forward to support one view or the other we may put the probable facts of the case into a few sentences.

The word "Chalumeau" (Schalmey) was used irregularly and loosely to describe not one instrument of special bore and make, but almost any small Wood-Wind instrument. It was a generic name, and as such was applied (*a*) to wooden pipes played with a double-reed, (*b*) to wooden pipes played with a single-reed, (*c*) to the chanters of Bagpipes and Musettes.

(2) One of these early "Chalumeaux" was undoubtedly a small keyless *cylindrical* pipe. It had no "bell" at the end, but was played with a single-beating-reed which was scientifically the same as the modern Clarinet-reed.[2]

This instrument was the precursor of our present-day Clarinet. Its resemblance to the Schalmey, the ancestor of the Oboe, consisted in the fact that both were straight keyless wooden pipes without "bells." Its essential difference from the Schalmey lay in the fact that the former was cylindrical in bore and single-reeded, while the latter was conical in bore and double-reeded.

The fact that the words "Chalumeau" and "Schalmey" were used in a confused manner to describe any small reed-instrument goes some way towards proving that, in their early undeveloped stages, all these instruments had a strong similarity *in sound.* If the difference in tone-colour had been very marked, this looseness of nomenclature would probably not have existed.

However, in the difference of bore and reed lay the possibility of a development which was to take the two instruments farther and farther apart. The stages in the development of the Clarinet from its archetype the cylindrical, single-reeded "Chalumeau" are well known and simple. The first milestone on the road is marked by the name of J. C. Denner (1655-1707), who added the "speaker-key."[3] In doing this, he fixed the type, as it were, and gave the player the opportunity

[1] The word "clarinet" is a diminutive of "*clarino*," the old Italian word for the Trumpet that then played the high parts. "*Clarinetto*"="little trumpet" exactly describes the type of part that the Clarinet had to play when it was introduced orchestrally at the end of the eighteenth century.

[2] The *Pibcorn*, *Swegelhorn*, or *Hornpipe*, cannot be taken into account as the ancestor of the Clarinet for, though it had a single-beating-reed, this was always enclosed in a hollow horn or bone so that the player's lips did not touch the reed itself. The English word Wayte-, Wayghte-, or Wait-pipe (*i.e.* watchman's pipe) appears to have been applied indiscriminately to the early Oboes and Chalumeaux.

[3] See page 179.

of doing with ease what had been before either difficult or impossible. The only method by which an extended scale can be produced in a cylindrical pipe is by overblowing the fundamental scale at the twelfth and in order to split up the vibrations of the air-column into their aliquot parts the assistance of the "speaker" is essential.

It may be mentioned, in passing, that the early instrument to which the "speaker" was first added appears to have had a downward compass to

From there upwards the opening of its nine holes successively gave it a diatonic compass in the key of F to

The history of the Clarinet during the eighteenth century consisted:

(1) In the addition of the "bell" in 1720 and the transference of the "speaker" to a position nearer the mouthpiece. Both these improvements are due to J. Denner, possibly a son of the man who invented the "speaker."

(2) In the gradual addition of metal keys to complete the compass and facilitate the execution. The sixth key was added in 1789 by the brothers Stadler, the celebrated Viennese Clarinettists, for one of whom Mozart wrote his *Clarinet Concerto.*

By 1810 Iwan Müller was making thirteen-keyed Clarinets in Paris. This inventor improved the instrument in many other ways, and his successful experiments form the basis of all modern Clarinet manufacture. In 1842 Klosé applied the Boehm system of moveable rings to the instrument.

The Clarinet as we have it now is a cylindrical pipe of wood or ebonite two feet long, made in either one or more sections. These sections comprise the *mouthpiece*, the *barrel-joint*, the *left-hand* or *top joint*, the *right-hand* or *lower joint*, and the *bell.*

The mouthpiece is usually of wood. With metal mouthpieces the tone becomes clearer and more brilliant, but also harder and less sympathetic. All sorts of experiments have been made in this direction. Strauss states that his 1st Clarinettist in Berlin, Herr Schubert, after trying in turn mouthpieces of marble, of glass, of porcelain, of ebonite, and of gold, came back at last to a wooden mouthpiece as giving the most beautiful tone-quality.

The upper part of the "beak" mouthpiece is flattened to form the "table" which supports the reed, a single piece of carefully prepared "cane." The beating of this reed to and fro sets the air-column in motion. It has, therefore, to be adjusted to the "table" with the greatest care. Neither too large nor too small a space must be left between the reed and the end of the mouthpiece. The reed, which was originally bound on to the mouthpiece with fine twine, has now for over a hundred years been secured in its place by means of a metal "ligature."

A reference to the illustration of a Clarinet-mouthpiece given at page 180 (Plate VIII., Fig. 4) will make these technical details perfectly clear. The mouthpiece there shown is that of an ordinary B♭-Clarinet, but scientifically the illustration holds good of the smaller and the larger Clarinets and of the Saxophones,—in fact of all the single-beating-reed instruments. The principal points to notice in the illustration are (1) the white strip of "cane" held tightly in position by (2) the metal legature, (3) the narrow air-space just visible where the upper edge of the "cane" meets the upper edge of the mouthpiece. This is the essential part of the apparatus; for, as we shall explain presently, it is by means of the combined pressure of his upper lip on the "table" (the portion turned-away in the illustration) and of his lower lip on the reed itself that the player is able to set up regular vibrations in the air-column. It may be added that the upper portion of the reed is quite free to vibrate under the action of the player's lips and breath. If we loosen the two screws of the ligature and withdraw the thin slip of "cane" we find that the "cane" itself completes the pipe at its extreme upper end. In other words the material of the pipe is cut-away on that side, and, when the reed is in position, it lies in contact with the vibrating air-column.

The method of tone-production is as follows. The player takes the mouthpiece between his lips, and, by the pressure of his lips and breath, sets the flexible reed in motion. This beats against the "table" opening and closing the gap at the upper end. The rate of this opening and closing is, of course, solely dependent on the rate of the vibrations set up in the air-column within the pipe. This in its turn is governed by the opening and closing of the holes and keys.

The Clarinet being a cylindrical reed-pipe has the properties of a "stopped-pipe," that is to say, its fundamental note is an octave lower than the corresponding note either of an open-pipe or of a conical reed-pipe of the same length. In addition to that it "overblows a twelfth." The student will see without difficulty that in practice this means that the fingering of the Clarinet differs fundamentally from that of the Flute and Oboe.

The modern Clarinet has seven holes and an elaborate apparatus of keys varying in number from thirteen to nineteen. Into the various systems under which these keys are made—the Barret, Clinton, Boehm, Gomez-Boehm, Buffet, Müller-Bärmann, etc.—it is not necessary to go. Without touching any of these keys or using the thumb-holes the player can open the seven holes in his pipe successively, and if he does this he will produce the natural scale of

Under any of the systems, however, the compass is extended downwards a minor third to

and in practice a fundamental chromatic scale is obtained from

It is only on the

the twelfth above his lowest note that the player begins to overblow and by this means he continues his compass chromatically upwards from

Beyond that seven further semitones are to be got up to high C

These are either fifth harmonics (two octaves and a major third above the fundamental notes) or ninth harmonics (three octaves and a major second above the fundamental notes).

In Mozart's day the Clarinet compass appears to have extended down a major third to low C

He uses that note in *Clemenza di Tito,* and, on the B♭ instrument, for which the passage was written, the *sound* would of course be a whole-tone lower.

During the classical period, and well into the middle of the nineteenth century, orchestral Clarinets were made in three keys:

(1) The Clarinet in C, a non-transposing instrument written for and sounding in the key of the piece.

(2) The Clarinet in B♭,[1] a transposing instrument sounding a major second lower and therefore written for in the key of two ♭'s less, or two ♯'s more than the key of the piece.

(3) The Clarinet in A, a transposing instrument sounding a minor third lower and therefore written for in the key of three ♭'s more or three ♯'s less than the key of the piece.

[1] Mozart uses a B♮ Clarinet in *Cosi fan tutte* and *Idomeneo.* It was pitched a semitone below the C Clarinet, and gave an easy key-signature for very sharp keys. It is quite unknown nowadays.

Of these three Clarinets the first—the non-transposing C-Clarinet—is obsolete. This leaves us the choice of two instruments with the same chromatic compass[1]

which, on the B♭-Clarinet, sounds

and on the A-Clarinet sounds

How then is the choice to be made between the two instruments? In the first place there is said to be a slight difference of quality in favour of the lower-pitched instrument. It is, however, a good deal less than the difference between a Brescian and a Cremonese Violin. In point of fact not even an expert Clarinettist can tell (from its tone-quality) whether a passage is being played in the concert-room on the A- or the B♭-instrument. The difference between the two instruments is more a matter of text-book theory than of practical fact. The student should, therefore, choose the instrument which will give the fewest ♭'s or ♯'s in the Clarinet key-signature. On this point he should read again what was said above with regard to the A- and B-Cornets, as the two cases are exactly parallel.[2] The general rule may be mentioned again: Use B♭-Clarinets for flat keys, A-Clarinets for sharp keys, and remember the possibilities of enharmonically varied key-signatures for the extreme keys. Example: Key 6♯'s, F♯ major = G♭ major. B♭ Clarinets will therefore be in A♭ major (4 flats), and if the modulations are northwards, would of course be preferable to A-Clarinets playing in A major (3 sharps).

In dealing with all these questions, however, the student must bear in mind that the dexterity of the best modern Clarinettists is so great that the question of keys is not of the greatest importance.[3] Mechanisms, again, vary considerably, and what is easy to one player is not so easy to another. Strauss states that his Solo Clarinettist uses a system of fingering which actually makes the key of B♮ major easier than that of B♭ major. He adds that on the Sax-Clarinets sharp keys are the easier, while on the Iwan Müller-Bärmann instruments the flat keys are the more practicable.

[1] The two top semitones, B♮ and C, are excessively difficult. See page 262.

[2] Some composers of the old French Operatic school (Hérold, Chérubini, Spontini, etc.) used to adopt the rather useless method of writing the Clarinet part regularly in the key of the piece. The continual employment of the C-Clarinet was by no means intended. The transposition and choice of proper instruments was merely left to the copyist or player.

[3] See page 196.

The student need not be disturbed by these differences of technique. He should select the instrument which gives as simple a key-signature as possible and then stick to it. Unless for the most urgent reasons, such as, for instance, to avoid giving the Clarinet a prominent and very difficult passage in six sharps, it is better not to change the instrument in the middle of a piece, at any rate in concert-work. The difficulties of correct intonation on a cold instrument generally counterbalance the supposed simplification of key.

We mentioned just now that a third Clarinet—the non-transposing instrument in C—is obsolete. This Clarinet was slightly harder in quality than either of our present instruments, and the statement is always made that composers when they used it did so for the special purpose of utilizing its bright incisive tone-colour. Conductors are therefore adjured to employ this instrument when it is indicated in a Score of the old masters. It is true that in some few instances composers may have used it with this special object in view. But it is a most surprising coincidence that nine times out of ten the desire for this hard tone-quality existed when the key of the piece happened to be C major. There are, of course, some few examples where the composer's apparent intention is to utilize the instrument for the sake of its harder quality. An example of this is perhaps to be found in the *Scherzo* of the *Choral Symphony*, and an analysis of the Clarinet changes in that work may be of interest to the student as showing him the difficulties under which composers laboured at a time when the harmonic schemes of musical works were being much extended, but were still unhelped by the necessary mechanical improvements in the instrument.

Down to the end of Mozart's lifetime these difficulties did not exist. Music was written in short sections and rarely modulated far from "home." A suitable choice of Clarinet was made at the beginning of a piece, and only on the rarest occasions even in Opera was it necessary to change the instrument during the continuance of the music. The same thing holds good to-day. The modulations have gone farther afield, but so has the mechanism of the Clarinet. There was, however, a transition period when the boundaries of musical composition were being widened, but there was no great technical widening on the part of this special instrument. In a work like the *Choral Symphony*, with its many changes of key-signature, a new problem was presented and evidently faced with some hesitation. The following is the analysis. The student should, if possible, read it with the Full Score in front of him:

First Movement in D minor. B♭-Clarinets throughout (written key E minor).

Second Movement in D minor and D major. C-Clarinets throughout (written keys D minor and D major). This choice would appear to have been dictated by reasons of tone-colour, but even here it is at least as probable that the change to C-Clarinets was merely made so as not to frighten the B♭-Clarinet player by a signature of 4♯'s in the D major sections.

Third Movement in B♭. B♭-Clarinets (written key C major). When the signature of the piece changes to 2♯'s and 1♯ (*Andante moderato*) Beethoven prefers to leave the signature of C major in the Clarinet parts rather than risk signatures of 4♯'s and 3♯'s. When the signature of the piece changes to 3♭'s Beethoven writes-in the correct key-signature of 1♭ for the B♭-Clarinets.

Last Movement in D minor. B♭-Clarinets again (written key E minor). When the key-signature of the piece changes to D major (*Allegro assai*) there is no time to change Clarinets. Beethoven continues to use the B♭-instruments for the first 15 bars, but, instead of giving them the correct signature of 4♯'s, leaves their original key-signature of 1♯ and writes-in accidentals.

Fifteen bars later the Clarinets have a long rest; so he changes to A-Clarinets, and writes them with their correct signature of 1♭. The music remains in D major.

The A-Clarinets are used as far as the $\frac{6}{8}$ March Movement, and, as the greater part of the music is in 2♯'s, their signature of 1♭ is generally correct.

At the *Presto*, however, the key-signature of the piece is 1♭. The correct signature of the A-Clarinets would, of course, be 4♭'s, but Beethoven merely writes a single ♭ in the Clarinet-signature, and adds accidentals for the other ♭'s. It is difficult to understand the advantage of this, because the player has to finger and play the A♭'s and D♭'s that occur in his part, whether they are put into the signature or not.

At the *March Movement* (*Allegro assai vivace*) the key of the piece is B♭. The Clarinets have eight silent bars in which to change back to B♭-instruments. Their key-signature is now C major.

At the 163rd bar the key-signature of the piece changes to 2♯'s. The correct key-signature for the Clarinets would be 4♯'s. Beethoven, however, leaves the key-signature of C major, uses the Clarinets as little as possible, and is compelled to write an accidental to almost every note they play. In one place the part vacillates between extreme sharp and extreme flat keys.

After a long rest for the Clarinets the *Andante maestoso* is reached. The key of the piece is G major. Beethoven changes to A-Clarinets, gives them the incorrect signature of 1♭, and adds the E♭ as an accidental.

When the key-signature of the piece changes to 1♭ and (later) to 2♭'s the Clarinets are written, not as they should be, in 4♭'s and 5♭'s, but in 1♭ and 2♭'s, just as if they were C-Clarinets. However, for the principal and constantly recurring key-signature of the piece (2♯'s), the true key-signature of 1♭ is marked in the Clarinets.

At the seven bars of key-signature 5♯'s that come just before the final *Prestissimo* the Clarinets have their correct key-signature of 2♯'s.

The student should note in the above analysis that, in general, where the key-signature is fixed and the music remains near its original tonality, the choice of Clarinets and their key-signatures are quite simple, and practically the same as they would be at the present day. It is only when there is a certain change of key-signature, or when the music is likely to make a distant modulation, that all the confusion of changed instruments and incorrect signatures begins. With modern Clarinet-mechanisms, all this muddle automatically disappears. There is nothing in the whole Symphony to necessitate either an incorrect key-signature or a change of Clarinet when once a Movement has begun.

After this somewhat long digression we must return to our more immediate subject, the modern Clarinet-mechanism. It should be mentioned, first of all, that there are mechanical contrivances for instantaneously altering the B♭-Clarinet to the A-Clarinet. They are, however, not much used. Some few artists actually play everything on a B♭-Clarinet, transposing the part as required. In these cases, it is necessary for the player's instrument to be furnished with an additional key giving the low E♭. This of course produces the sound low D♭ (C♯), the same sound as is produced by the written lowest note

of the A-Clarinet. The practical mechanism of this extra semitone has not yet been perfected to satisfy the majority of players, and the student is therefore warned not to regard it as an integral note in the Clarinet-compass.

Occasionally one finds passages in which the composer specially uses the A-Clarinet in order to take advantage of its lowest note. In the first five bars of the *Largo* of the *New World Symphony* (key D♭ major) Dvořák wishes to use the bottom D♭ in bars 2 and 3. He has to write it for A-Clarinets. The part, however, is only eight notes long, and immediately afterwards he changes to B♭-Clarinets for the passage in tenths with the English-Horn (quoted above, Ex. 140). He therefore does not trouble to give a correct Clarinet-signature for these first five bars. He writes not in the true key of 4♯'s (=8♭'s), but in the key of E♭, the proper signature for the B♭-Clarinets in the rest of the movement. For four out of the eight notes he has to use accidentals. In practice, most symphony players would actually change instruments after these opening bars. A few, however, who use a B♭-Clarinet provided with the low E♭-key would employ that instrument throughout the movement.

Compare this with Beethoven's practice in the three *Leonora Overtures*. All three are in C major. In the 2nd and 3rd Overtures he uses C-Clarinets. For No. 1, however, he uses B♭-Clarinets, and writes, not with the correct signature of 2♯'s, but with that of 1♭. This gives them three accidentals in the main key of the piece, but puts them right for the *Adagio non troppo* section in E♭.

It may be mentioned, in passing, that the technical names for the metal keys on the Clarinet are not those given above for the sake of simplicity. What a layman might call the low "E♮ key" is known by the name of its first overblown note, the "B♮ key." This applies throughout the whole instrument.

From what has been said above it might be supposed that the technique of the Clarinet is somewhat complicated. There are seven holes for the fingers to cover. The right-hand thumb is engaged in holding up the instrument, so that practically only the two little fingers are quite free for key-work. The rest of the fingers have to be used only as opportunity offers. Yet so cleverly contrived are the modern mechanisms that it really becomes a difficulty to make any list at all of "impossible passages." A general warning to the student may take the form of a caution against basing any *prominent* passage on these three notes

the weakest and most intractable on the instrument.

All the old last-century lists of impossible shakes are completely out of date. Nowadays all shakes whole-tone and half-tone are *possible* from the half-tone shake on

 to the half-tone shake on 

In the ordinary routine of orchestration they may all be written and can all be played sufficiently correctly and easily to make their technique a matter of indifference to the composer.

For *Solo passages*, however, there are a few shakes which are neither so easy nor so effective as the rest, and these it is well to avoid. They are the two whole-tone shakes on the bottom F♯'s with their overblown twelfths.

In addition the half-tone shakes on

are either clumsy or ineffective.

These six shakes, all of which are possible in the *tutti*, should not be introduced into any passage where they are likely to be clearly heard.

The Clarinet is one of the very best instruments in the orchestra for tremolo-work. Its restrictions in this kind are few. In general all tremolos up to an octave are possible, provided the upper-note of the two forming the tremolo is not higher than

As with the shakes, however, a few of these tremolos are not so easy and effective as the rest. If the composer does not wish to throw difficulties in the way of the player he will do well to avoid the following

and to remember that it is always practicable and always better to confine the limits of the tremolo to thirds, fourths, and fifths. Finally, though this is not of the greatest importance, he should recall the caution given above with regard to the notes

If he can arrange his tremolo so as to avoid any of these three notes, especially as the *upper-note* of a tremolo, his part will be improved.

Another small point which is worth consideration. Passages based on octave-skips, though congenial to the character of conical instruments, are unnatural to cylindrical instruments. On almost every orchestral instrument—Brass, Wood, and String—the player performs most of his octaves by setting himself in a position from which both the lower and the higher note can be taken. With the Clarinet this is impossible. Indeed out of the sixty Clarinet passages which Berlioz gives as examples of what not to do, only these two

remain as practical impossibilities even with our present-day mechanism.

Different methods of single-tonguing are employed in different countries and schools. They vary from a sharp incisive staccato

 through a sort of half-staccato 

to a delightfully caressing stroke which just articulates the note as it is sounded

The Clarinet approaches nearer than any other instrument to the soft swish of the Violin bow when it sets the strings in motion. The easy charm and delicious refinement of the Clarinet-articulation is of course matter for universal admiration. Naturally it cannot beat the Flute on the Flute's own ground—repeated notes—but still it is capable of a very respectable speed even there. See Exs. 47, 48.

One of the most characteristic features of the instrument is its marked difference of tone-colour in its three registers. Its bottom octave from

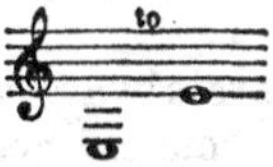

which still goes by the old name of "Chalumeau," has a hollow reedy intensity much admired in orchestration-books and very little used by composers. For special effects this register is excellent. There is, however, a difficulty in treating it. When the orchestra is *tutti mf* or *f* it is not heard, while in thinner passages it is so much overcharged with colour—especially in its bottom fifth—that it upsets the best laid schemes of the composer. Attention has already been drawn to three passages in which skilful use is made of the bottom register. The student should again refer to these extracts (Exs. 133, 192, 248). Mozart, in his *E♭ Symphony* and in the *Finale* to Act I. of *Don Giovanni*, and after him Beethoven, in the *Eroica Symphony*, employed the *chalumeau arpeggios* of the Clarinet. They have a smooth and oily effectiveness. Nowadays, however, this sort of thing is reckoned to be somewhat too much à la "German band."

From

is the very worst part of the instrument, the weakest in quality and technically the most difficult to manage. It has this one virtue that, owing to its unobtrusive and, in the *pp*, almost inaudible quality, it affords an ideal "background" for the brighter orchestral colours. It may be said here, in passing, that no instrument has so complete a command of 𝆒 𝆓 as the Clarinet. This applies to the whole of its compass, and to all the instruments of the Clarinet family. In especial the Clarinet *ppp* is the nearest attainable approach to "nothing at all" in the Wind department.

From

upwards we have the best register of the Clarinet. In the hands of a good artist the tone of this part of its compass is nobly expressive, beautifully clear, pure and even. The best modern players maintain a complete control over the tone-quality right up to the high B♭

After that the two top semitones B♮ and C are just playable. But they are so excessively difficult to produce, and so piercing in quality when produced, that it is better to avoid them altogether, whether in the *solo* or in the *tutti*.

The B♭- and A-Clarinets are always written as transposing instruments in the treble-clef. In some old Scores, however, the Chalumeau notes will be found written in the bass-clef an octave lower than their proper pitch. Wagner occasionally uses the bass-clef (at its proper pitch) for the Chalumeau-register. This is a plan that might be copied. When one is using this register and writing two Clarinet-parts on one stave, the confusion of leger-lines is apt to become a nuisance.

A few words must be said here with regard to the use of the Oboes and Clarinets for what may be called "background passages," that is to say, for subsidiary supporting-harmonies written in the register of the treble voice. The best arrangement for such passages is to interlock the Oboes and Clarinets in the same way that the two pairs of Horns are interlocked.[1] The arrangement downwards would then be:

1st Oboe.
1st Clarinet.
2nd Oboe.
2nd Clarinet.

For ordinary purposes this is a good arrangement, as the 1st Oboe part may roughly coincide with the melodic outline, and, if it does, will add point and brightness.

The clever arrangement of these apparently unimportant parts is really a matter of some importance in the orchestral ensemble. The student should try to imagine for himself the differences of effect produced by slight differences of arrangement and pitch. In scoring for the Theatre, where it is so continually necessary to prevent a sense of emptiness by adding subsidiary parts just underneath the melodic line, these points are well worth careful study.

To find an example of the normal arrangement of Oboes and Clarinets the student need only open any Full Score which he may possess. As an example of the opposite procedure—that is to say, where the Clarinets interlock with the Oboes but play the 1st and 3rd instead of the 2nd and 4th parts—he can take these bars from the 1st Movement of Tschaikowsky's *Fifth Symphony*. It is very unlikely that he will have any difficulty in remembering their *sound*.

[1] See page 123.

EXAMPLE 177.

Tschaikowsky. *Symphony in E.*

In dealing with these little problems the student should keep his mind unbiased by the fact that the Clarinet-parts are always written in the Full Score immediately underneath the Oboes. This is a mere accident, due to the historical priority of the latter instruments. Richard Strauss, than whom there can be no better judge, goes so far as to say that, in ordinary four-part harmonies of Oboes and Clarinets, it is always better to keep both the Clarinets above both the Oboes. In the *tutti* and in the orchestral *mf* where the four-part harmony in question is pretty sure to be pitched fairly high, this practice is undoubtedly to be commended. On the other hand, in the *p* where nothing more than a light background is called for, it has two disadvantages. In the first place, it keeps the 2nd and often the 1st Oboe down in the bottom and worst register. Then, again, it limits the downward compass of the four-part harmony to low B♭, the bottom note of the Oboe. This in itself is not a bad thing, but the bottom semitones of the Oboe are really unpleasant in sound, and the "lay" of the harmony may necessitate an occasional and rather fussy crossing of the parts in order to get low A's and G's.

The point, however, which is of importance for the student is that he should not get in the habit of regarding the Clarinet-parts—especially the 1st Clarinet-part—as being lower in pitch than the Oboe parts. The Clarinets are essentially unlike the Oboes. They are not to be classed as "middle-register" instruments except for the special purpose of securing a neutral background. Their most effective registers are top and bottom registers. Often indeed one finds the 1st Clarinet brought prominently forward and almost detached from the rest of the Wood-Wind. For an example of this style of treatment we may refer to the *Im Garten* Movement of Goldmark's *Ländliche Hochzeit.*

A very simple example of "goldsmithery" in the arrangement of Wood-Wind parts may be found in the second subject of the 1st Movement of Mendelssohn's *Violin Concerto.* The subject is played by the Wood-Wind over a held pedal in the Solo Violin part. On its first appearance the harmonization of the tune is arranged in the following order downwards: 1st Clarinet (melody), 2nd Clarinet, 1st Flute, 2nd Flute. In the second half of the subject where the lowest part passes out of the compass of the 2nd Flute, the 2nd Clarinet skips down to take its place. The 1st Clarinet, however, still goes on with the tune On the return of the 2nd subject (in E major) it is performed by Flutes, Oboes, Clarinets in the order named. In the 2nd half of the subject, however, the 1st Oboe changes place with the 1st Flute and plays the melody. Microscopic studies of this sort can be made with any Symphonic work, and they will always repay the student's attention.

The technique of the Clarinet is so varied that it demands somewhat elaborate illustration. This can happily be presented within reasonable limits owing to the fact that the instrument has been continually used in Chamber Music and in Concertos with orchestral accompaniment. For these purposes it is specially fitted by its expressive quality, its differences of tone-colour, and above all its extraordinary flexibility and variety in "passage-work."[1]

The following quotation from Mozart's *Clarinet Concerto in A major* gives a miniature of the Clarinet technique in his day:

EXAMPLE 178.

Notice the essentials:

A. Quick diatonic scale passages (bars 1 and 2),
B. Arpeggios (bars 3, 4, 5, 6, 7),
C. Figures built on the notes of the scale (bars 8 and 9),
D. And on the notes of a chord (bars 10 and 11),
E. Chromatic scales (bar 12),
F. And shakes (bar 13).

[1] The student should examine the following works: Mozart's *Quintet in A for Clarinet and Strings*, Beethoven's *Clarinet Trio in B♭*, *Quintet for Wood-Wind*, and the *E♭ Septet*, Weber's *2 Concert pieces* and the *Clarinet Quintet* (Op. 34) and the Brahms *Clarinet Quintet.*

The only essential omitted from this highly compressed illustration is the power of the instrument to skip with the maximum of effect from one part of its compass to another. This was well understood by Mozart, as may be seen in the following three bars taken from the same work:[1]

EXAMPLE 179.

Mozart. *Clarinet Concerto in A major.*

The student should now carefully examine the following passage taken from Stanford's *Clarinet Concerto in one Movement.* It gives a brilliant *resumé* of the Clarinet technique at the present day. Notice again the character of the passages, unchanged in essentials, but much enlarged in scope.

EXAMPLE 180.

Andante con moto.

Stanford. *Clarinet Concerto.*

[1] The two quotations from Mozart are printed, as was the custom in those days, with very few indications of nuances, phrasing, and so on.

Here we have examples of

A. Diatonic scale passages *legato* (bars 13, 21),
B. Diatonic scale passages *mezzo-staccato* (bars 17, 18),
C. Arpeggios (bars 1, 3, 5, 6, 10, 20),
D. Melodic figures built on the notes of the scale (bar 22),
E. And on the notes of a chord (bars 14, 15, 19, 20),
F. Chromatic scales (bars 7, 23),
G. Skips up to a width of nearly three octaves (bars 5, 12, 23),

besides passages of a mixed character and a continual juxtaposition of the extreme registers.

The last point is perhaps better illustrated by another quotation from the same work.

EXAMPLE 181.

Stanford. *Clarinet Concerto.*

Passages like those in bars 4-5 and 12-13 must really be heard on the Clarinet to be understood. The ease and certainty with which a first-class artist can execute a brilliant *f* arpeggio and then immediately resume the *p* in a totally different register of his instrument are astonishing.

As a last Solo instance, we will quote from the same work a real piece of *chalumeau* writing with its accompaniment. (Ex. 182.)

Notice in the accompaniment not only its effective simplicity but also the dynamic marking of the parts. The whole passage is *p* both in intention and effect. Yet in bar 3 at the entrance of the Strings we have a *ppp* background for the overhead Strings, a *pp* pizzicato for the Cellos and Basses, a *pp* for the Drums (almost equal in dynamic value to a *mp* of the Strings or Wood-Wind), a *p* for the Oboe in order to lend it a momentary prominence, and a *mf* for the 2nd Horn. The last named instrument is playing a variant of the Solo part, and is also pitched in its ineffective register. In fact its entry is a piece of unblushing orchestral deceit perpetrated in the interests of the Soloist.

Of course an orchestral composer cannot be always writing concerto parts for his Clarinets. That would completely upset the instrumental fitness-of-things. It is only when the instruments are called up for active service that brilliant passage-writing becomes possible. When that does happen the types quoted are excellent models on which to rely. They are all playable and effective.

EXAMPLE 182.

Stanford. *Clarinet Concerto.*

As a happy example of the sudden unexpected prominence of a Clarinet passage, the following bars from the 2nd Act of *Die Meistersinger* are interesting:

EXAMPLE 183.

Wagner. *Die Meistersinger.*

They were intended by Wagner as a sort of aural-optical suggestion of the little eddies of dust and straw that are whirled up by the wind at a street-corner.

The Clarinets were undoubtedly great favourites with Wagner. He understood them thoroughly. Usually he does not give them prominence for many bars at a time, but the total number of bars in which they are prominent is large. An exception to this rule may be found in the music which precedes the 3rd Scene in the 1st Act of *Götterdämmerung*. In this celebrated passage the accompaniment, omitted below, is wholly subordinate, and the Clarinets have the field to themselves for over thirty bars. This is the most heroic example possible of the favourite and effective practice of writing thirds for the two Clarinets.

EXAMPLE 184.

Wagner. *Götterdämmerung.*

A few examples must now be given of the separate Clarinet-registers used orchestrally. Nothing much in the Chalumeau-register is to be found in any of the classical masters. Weber was perhaps the first to employ this tone-colour consciously as a means of orchestral expression. A quotation from his overture to *Der Freischütz* is printed below, Ex. 278. In it the low held notes of two Clarinets are associated with the Kettle-Drums, the String *tremolo*, the *pizzicato* of the Double-Basses, and the high notes of the Cellos. Since Weber's day this has been imitated more than once. As a melodic example, the student should look at the *Andante* subject in the 1st Movement of Tschaikowsky's *Fifth Symphony*. The melody on its first appearance is assigned to two Clarinets in unison. The choice of instrument is undoubtedly happy.[1]

EXAMPLE 185.

In recent years this register has been employed for various effective melodic doublings of Violas, Cellos, and so on. Its use, however, cannot even now be fairly called a regular part of the orchestral routine.

In the middle register there is not much to quote. Weber's subject in the *Oberon Overture*

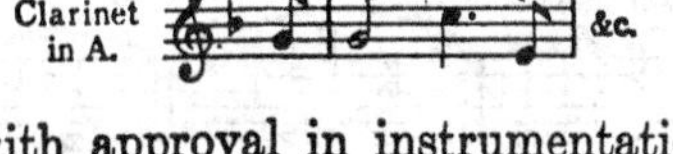

is generally cited with approval in instrumentation books, probably because it is a pretty tune. It always sounds tame owing to the fact that it gravitates round the notes

in the least interesting part of the instrument.

[1] See also Exs. 133, 192, 248.

In the very best register—what one may call the lower-top—there is so much to quote that the difficulty is only one of selection. We must, however, content ourselves with two short examples. In the first, from Tschaikowsky's *Francesca da Rimini*, after a furious *tutti* the music gradually calms down and finally leaves the Clarinet absolutely unaccompanied. The instrument plays a series of simple Cadenza-like passages which ends in the exquisite melody representing Francesca herself.

EXAMPLE 186.

This subject could of course be played by the Flute perfectly well. If this were done, however, the effect would be that the melody would be de-humanized. The impersonal would be substituted for the personal: the neuter for the feminine. It is by means of its capacity to suggest the still, small voice—from which, however, no element of the human is lacking—that the Clarinet often makes its most touching appeal.

A second example of this register, this time varying from *p* to *f*, may be quoted from the 4th Movement of Dvořák's *New World Symphony*:

EXAMPLE 187.

The accompaniment to the above extract consists of a light String *tremolo* of Violins and Violas. The only other melodic feature in the Score is the loud rhythmical interruption of the Clarinet-phrases by the Cellos. The student should note in all the Clarinet examples the large number of dynamic marks,—*p*'s, *f*'s, *crescendos*, and *diminuendos*.

The Clarinet has perhaps more complete control over this form of expression than any other Solo instrument, Wind or String.

Other examples of this register may be found in Weber's *Freischütz Overture* (Peters's Full Score, page 7), Beethoven's *Eighth Symphony* (Trio of the Minuet), Mendelssohn's *Reformation Symphony* (*Andante con Moto*, Full Score, pages 60 and 61), and in Beethoven's *Choral Symphony* (Peters's Full Score, page 151 *et seq.*).

Finally, as a corrective to the somewhat rich elaboration of Clarinet technique served in the above pages, we will quote a tiny passage from Mendelssohn's *Violin Concerto* to prove that effect is not incompatible with the utmost simplicity of means. The phrase is only five notes long, and is easily played at the proper lightning-speed. It sounds like a little jet of water tossed up into the sun.[1]

EXAMPLE 188.

The history of the Clarinet in the orchestra is short and not very eventful. Except for a single isolated instance—a *Mass* written by J. A. J. Faber,[2] and now preserved in Antwerp Cathedral—the instrument was unused before the production of Rameau's *Acante et Céphise* in 1751. Gluck wrote for the old *Chalumeaux* in his earlier works but, becoming acquainted with the Clarinets in Paris, adopted them in place of his former instruments. Later still Mozart wrote for them in his Paris Symphony of 1770, and from then onwards used them in all his Operas. Haydn took them up about the same time. Beethoven adopted them at the outset of his Symphonic career, and from his day they have retained their place as standard orchestral instruments. Gevaert points out that as a matter of orchestral routine, Haydn, Mozart, and Beethoven all consistently avoided the use of the Chalumeau register. As we have mentioned, there are isolated instances to the contrary, and Mozart in his *Clarinet Concerto* uses this register freely.

As a rule two "B♭-A" instruments are employed in the orchestra and, since a Bass-Clarinet and sometimes a small E♭-Clarinet are

[1] See also the two passages earlier in this movement, where the Clarinets play a similar arpeggio phrase in two-parts, while the Solo Violin imitates them on the alternate beats. (Peters's Full Score, pages 52 and 53.)

[2] See Gevaert, page 177.

used as well, this seems sufficient for most purposes. Wagner, however, in his later works, writes for three "B♭-A" instruments as well as the "Bass" and the "E♭. In this he is followed by many modern composers.

The B♭-Clarinets are to the military band what the Violins are to the orchestra. Indeed they are a good deal more, for whereas in the upper register of the orchestra the Wood-Wind instruments can take their proper share of extended figures and melodic passages, in the military band the Clarinets alone can be used to give adequate emphasis to the transliterations of these parts. This important topic scarcely comes within the province of a book devoted to "Orchestration," but if the student be a String-player, and if he will listen closely to the outline and shape of these clever Clarinet-transliterations when played by a good staff-band, he will learn more about the Clarinet "*don'ts*" than can be taught him by a hundred pages of examples.

Besides the standard "B♭-A" instrument four other Clarinets must be briefly mentioned. These are, in the order of their most frequent use in the orchestra:

(1) The **Bass-Clarinet.** In common use both in the orchestra and the military band.

(2) The small **E♭-Clarinet.** Used in the orchestra occasionally and in the military band regularly.

(3) The **Bassett-Horn** and its first cousin the **Alto-Clarinet**. These appear in the orchestra only at the longest intervals, and then chiefly for antiquarian purposes. On the other hand, in (English) military bands the Alto Clarinet is regularly employed.

(4) The **Pedal-Clarinet.** Scarcely ever used even in the largest military bands: in the orchestra almost never.

These four members of the Clarinet family are all adaptations of the standard instrument. They, therefore, have a common technique. Beyond their differences of tone-quality and compass little further description will be necessary.

No. 40. The Bass-Clarinet.

Fr. *Clarinette basse*; It. *Clarone* (sometimes *Clarinetto basso*); Ger. *Bass Klarinette.*

This Clarinet is pitched an octave below the standard instrument, of which it is practically an enlarged replica. Its shape was originally modelled on that of the Clarinet, but this had two disadvantages. In the first place the instrument was cumbersome to manage. In the second the "bell" was within a few inches of the floor. Consequently most of the sound was lost. Berlioz mentions an attempt to overcome the latter difficulty by means of a "concave metallic reflector." Nowadays, however, the problem is solved by introducing two metal curves into the pipe, one at each extremity. The upper of these curved pieces—the one that holds the mouthpiece—is a fairly thick length of metal tubing, in shape something like a Bassoon-crook. The lower is merely a short joint curving back on itself, and ending in a wide metal

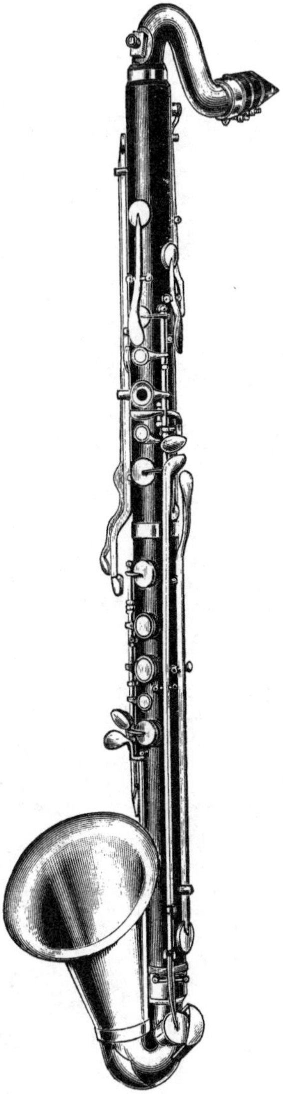

BASS CLARINET.

By kind permission of Messrs. Boosey & Co.

bell that points upwards and outwards. Both these features may be seen in the illustration of a modern Bass-Clarinet-in-B♭ given on Plate X. The single-beating-reed is, of course, invisible in the woodcut. It lies on the lower side of the beak-mouthpiece immediately to the right of the ligature-screws. The student would do well to notice the necessarily great length of the metal rods controlling the lower keys. Apart altogether from the difficulties of regulating the air-column in so long and wide a pipe the player is at a disadvantage in this respect when compared with the standard B♭-Clarinet player.

Bass-Clarinets were formerly built on the analogy of the ordinary Clarinet, both in B♭ and A. The lower-pitched instrument, however, has not proved itself to have any great advantages beyond the possession of the extra low semitone. It has consequently dropped out of use, and, except in Germany, is practically unknown.

We may clear the ground then by saying that "Bass-Clarinet" in almost every instance means "Bass-Clarinet in B♭." We shall therefore proceed to describe that instrument in some detail. But before doing so we may mention

(1) That the compass, key-signature, etc., of the Bass-Clarinet-in-A bear the same relationship to those of the Bass-Clarinet-in-B♭ as the compass, signature, etc., of the ordinary A-Clarinet bear to those of the ordinary B♭-Clarinet.

(2) Parts are occasionally to be found written for "Bass-Clarinet-in-C." This instrument, which may have existed as an orchestral experiment, is nowadays quite obsolete. Its parts, as, for instance, that in Liszt's *Mazeppa*, would be performed on the ordinary Bass-Clarinet in B♭.

As the student will perceive, the written compass of the Bass-Clarinet in B♭

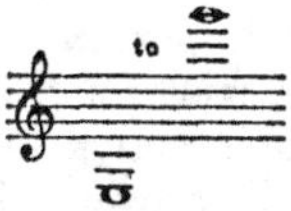

is not so great as that of the ordinary Clarinet. Three octaves and a minor third as opposed to three octaves and a minor sixth. The actual sounds of the Bass-Clarinet compass are an octave and a major second below the written notes, viz.:

The top fifth is scarcely worth writing, except perhaps when, doubled by some other instrument, it is used to complete the contour of a melodic figure.

There are two distinct methods of notation for the Bass-Clarinet.

(1) The part is written in the treble clef and sounds a major ninth below the written notes. This is the **French method**.

(2) The part is written normally in the bass-clef and sounds a major second below the written notes. For the highest notes the treble-clef is employed, but only as a continuation upwards of the bass-clef; that is to say, the sounds are still a major second below the written notes. This is the **German method.**

Whichever notation is adopted the key-signature is 2♭'s less or 2♯'s more than the key-signature of the piece.

In order to make both notations perfectly clear, we shall take a phrase from Meyerbeer's *Les Huguenots*,[1] and write it out both in the French and in the German notation.

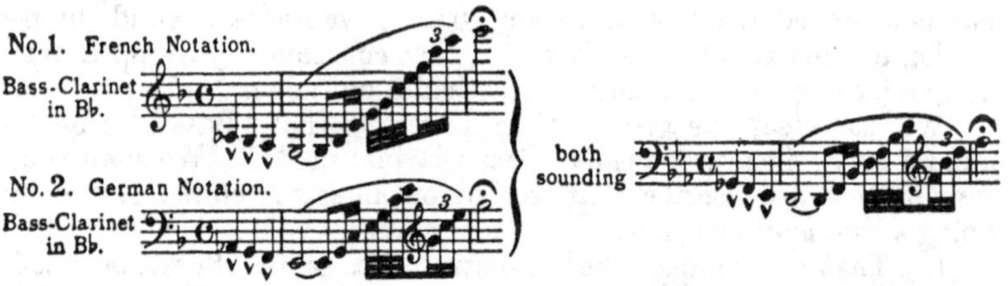

The German method (No. 2) is the more logical and the easier for the Score-reader. On behalf of the French system the intimate association between the fingering and the written notes has been pleaded. This is undoubtedly of importance, in view of the fact that Bass-Clarinet players are all nurtured on the ordinary instrument and that the fingering on the two instruments is the same. A player can pass without difficulty from one instrument to the other. This is certainly an advantage, and would be more so were we to suppose that a knowledge of the bass-clef was one of the supreme attainments of the human mind.[2]

It is not of very great importance which notation the student adopts. It will, however, be wise for him to put a note at the beginning of the part "to sound a major second lower" or "to sound a major ninth lower." This will prevent the possibility of any mistake. It should be done whether the part begins in the treble- or the bass-clef. It may be mentioned, in passing, that army-musicians have actually effected that most difficult of all tasks, a reformed notation. Their Bass-Clarinet players are taught to finger their B♭-instruments in the same way that a Euphonium- or a BB♭-Bass-player would, that is to say, at concert-pitch. The consequence is that, as they are all taught in the bass-clef, the two Bass-Clarinettists in a military band can play and do play off the 1st and 2nd Bassoon parts respectively.

It is a little difficult to describe the tone-colour of the Bass-Clarinet. Only a certain type of smooth *legato* passage is suitable to the instrument, and this has evidently influenced opinion as to its capabilities. Even with regard to its bottom and most characteristic

[1] Quoted below, 4th, 5th, and 6th bars of Example 190.

[2] Widor, in his book *The Technique of the Modern Orchestra*, suggests a musical congress to decide the question of notation for the Bass-Clarinet, the Horn, and the Cello

register diametrically opposed statements have been made by acute observers. "The finest part of the instrument is its rich lower register" (*Prout*). "The tone is hollow and wanting in power, in the lower register particularly" (*Schlesinger*).

As a matter of fact, there is a certain windiness and flabbiness in its tone-quality throughout its entire compass. This and its total want of "ictus" are probably due to its necessarily large bore. In fact, the fancy-title "Bass-goblin" that has been applied to it pretty well describes its musical make-up.

Simple little scale-passages, such as those in Tschaikowsky's Nut-Cracker Suite (*Danse de la Fée Dragée*), come out well on the instrument. Their goblinesque effect is charmingly unexpected.

EXAMPLE 189.

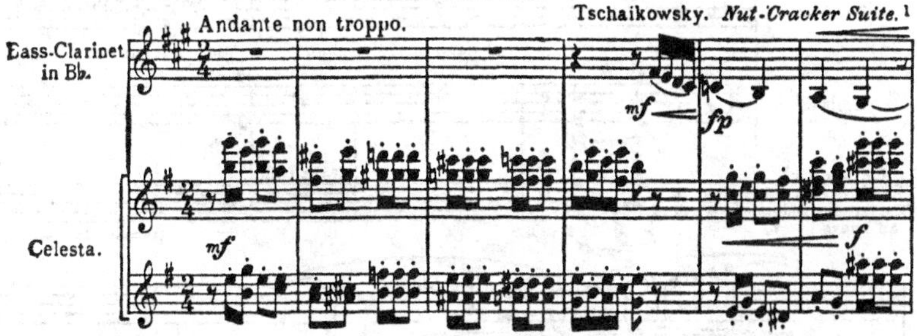

Melodies of a certain unctuous type, such as that quoted above from Strauss's *Don Quixote Variations* (Ex. 89), are undoubtedly effective. Solo subjects, however, which call for strong rhythmic energy or heroic expression, are quite unsuited to the instrument.

EXAMPLE 190.

Meyerbeer was the first to perceive the great possibilities of the Bass-Clarinet in the direction of characterizing certain sombre states of the mind. Examples of this are to be found both in *Le Prophète* (Act IV.) and in *Les Huguenots* (Act V.). In the latter work the

[1] The light string *pizzicato* accompaniment is omitted for reasons of space.

tragic situation of Raoul and Valentine, who are joining their hands at the moment of the St. Bartholomew massacre, is emphasized by an unaccompanied Bass-Clarinet Solo which covers the whole range of the instrument. The passage, which immediately precedes Marcel's address to the two lovers, is written in the French notation and sounds a major ninth lower. For its time and place it is curiously Wagnerian. See the quotation, Example 190.

EXAMPLE 191.

The poignant dramatic moment in Act II. of *Tristan* is characterized by the composer with exactly the same tone-colour. With Wagner of course the element of instrumental display which robs the Meyerbeer passage of some portion of its sincerity is totally absent. The *Obbligato* part in this passage is written for Bass-Clarinet-in-A, and as it touches the bottom note—the low E♮ sounding C♯ (D♭)—needs that instrument for its correct performance. The notation is the ordinary German notation sounding a minor third lower. The full accompaniment is given.

In *Lohengrin* (Act II.) Wagner uses the same dark and immovable tone-colour for the expression of doubt and uneasiness. This time the melody is assigned to an effective octave-unison of Bass-Clarinet and English-Horn. German notation.[1]

EXAMPLE 192.

It is quite unnecessary to give elaborate examples of the Bass-Clarinet technique. It is practically the same as that of the B♭-A-Clarinet, with some limitations of agility, owing to the size of the instrument, its large reed, wide bore, and heavy key-apparatus. In the following extract from Strauss's *Sinfonia Domestica* the chromatic power of the instrument is freely utilized. The student should note that, though this example begins in the treble-clef, the German notation is employed. The transposition downwards is a major second throughout, and the treble-clef is only written for convenience of notation. It is used merely as a continuation upwards of the bass-clef. The two notes A and A♭, where the clefs meet in bar 3, are a semitone apart.

EXAMPLE 193.

[1] Voice part (*Ortrud*) omitted.

To this style of elaborate running-passage the Bass-Clarinet lends a sort of effortless prominence that is most effective. It is, however, rather as a steady bass to the whole Wood-wind group that the instrument proffers its best service to the composer. When used thus it has a happy knack of enriching the harmonies by reinforcing the upper-partials. It is unnecessary to quote instances of this. Any modern Full Score will provide the student with examples. Berlioz's remark that "four or five Bass-Clarinets employed in unison give a rich and excellent sonority to the Wind instruments of the orchestral bass" is not the less true because of its heroic courage and its total disregard of the economics of the concert-room.

Like all the other instruments of its family the Bass-Clarinet has phenomenal powers of < >. Its *ppp* is almost a silence. For this reason the unaccompanied Bassoon Solo that precedes the sudden outburst of the *Allegro Vivo* (*ff*) in the 1st Movement of Tschaikowsky's *Pathetic Symphony*:

EXAMPLE 194.

Tschaikowsky. *Pathetic Symphony.*

is usually transferred to the Bass-Clarinet thus:

with general advantage to the composer, the player, and the audience. The actual sounds of course remain the same. As an example of this power of *pianissimo* carried down to its lowest register the student should refer to the Solo extract already printed from Holbrooke's *Apollo and the Seaman* (Ex. 96).

No. 41. The E♭-Clarinet.

This instrument, which is regularly used in our military bands to brighten and strengthen the top octave, is occasionally heard in the concert-room. In pitch it is a perfect fourth above the standard B♭-

instrument. Its transposition is therefore the same as that of the E♭-Trumpet, viz. a minor third upwards. For instance:

EXAMPLE 195.

Berlioz. *Symphonie Fantastique.*

Clarinet in E♭.

(actual sounds.)

The treble-clef only is used, and the key-signature is three ♭'s less or three ♯'s more than the key-signature of the piece. Music written in the flat keys from B♭ to D♭ is therefore the most suitable for the instrument, as these give key-signatures for the E♭-Clarinet of G, C, F, B♭. In military band music, where everything is in flat keys, this automatically simplifies all the key-signatures of the E♭-Clarinet. But in orchestral music the advantage is not so great. In the middling-sharp keys, such as D major and A major, the E♭-Clarinet has the awkward signatures of B major and F♯ major.

The written compass of the instrument is the same as that of the Bass-Clarinet

but this, on the E♭-Clarinet, sounds

On the former instrument, as was mentioned above, the top fifth is scarcely ever used: on the latter the bottom fifth is equally rarely employed. It is in general better replaced by the ordinary B♭-A Clarinet.

The great advantage of the E♭-Clarinet is its distinctive tone-quality. This, especially in its upper register, is preternaturally hard and biting. The winning feminine charm of the larger instrument is quite wanting, and in its place we have an incisive tone-colour that has much the same relation to the "B♭" as the Piccolo has to the Flute. With regard to the technique, it is sufficient to say that it is the same as that of the B♭-A instrument. It need scarcely be said that for purposes of solo-characterization the melodic types suitable to the larger instrument are often quite unsuitable to the smaller. In particular, the psychological range of the "E♭" is much narrower. It is almost confined either to passage-work of a hard mechanical kind, or to a special sort of mordant humour such, for instance, as is found in Strauss's *Till Eulenspiegel*.[1] For the latter purpose the instrument's great power of what we may call "hail-stone *staccato*" fits it admirably. A good example of this hard biting *staccato* is to be found in the "Critics" section of Strauss's *Ein Heldenleben*. Here is a short extract. It sounds even more offensive than the German direction to the player, "*sehr scharf und spitzig.*"

EXAMPLE 196.

Another short quotation may be given from the "Battle" section of the same work as an example not only of a three-part Clarinet-arpeggio but as an illustration of the fact that it is by no means always necessary or desirable to write Clarinet-arpeggios *legato*.[2]

EXAMPLE 197.

A similar instrument to the above is the little D-Clarinet, for which parts have been written by Gluck in *Echo et Narcisse*, by Liszt in *Mazeppa*, by Wagner in *Die Walküre*, and by Strauss in *Till Eulenspiegel* and the *Sinfonia Domestica*.

This instrument has the same written compass as the E♭-Clarinet, but in this case it gives the sounds, not a minor third, but a major second higher. The highest notes are more easily obtainable on this instrument than on the smaller E♭-Clarinet. An extra semitone or even whole-tone may be employed in that direction. One must not, however, overlook the extraordinarily piercing quality of these notes. See the example below from Strauss's *Till Eulenspiegel* where the high A♭ is written. The treble-clef is used, and the key-signature is that of

[1] Written for the "Clarinet in D," the continental instrument corresponding to our "E♭." See below.

[2] A few bars, in which the E♭-Clarinet has a part, have already been quoted. See Ex. 97. See also Ex. 202.

two ♭'s more or two ♯'s less than the key-signature of the piece. This is a distinct advantage in orchestral sharp keys. There is no difference in technique between the two instruments, and it may be mentioned that, in this country where the D-Clarinet is practically unknown, the parts written for that instrument are almost invariably played on the "E♭."

The following example from a *tutti* in Liszt's *Mazeppa* gives a fair idea of the instrument's use in the old style of scoring:

EXAMPLE 198.

and, for a modern instance covering the whole range of the instrument, we may refer to the extraordinarily vivid passage in *Till Eulenspiegel* where the hero is hanged. The student must take into consideration the peculiar character of the situation and its musical illustration in judging the effect of these extremely high notes:

EXAMPLE 199.

Strauss has pointed out that, in the top orchestral register, we have nothing but the small Clarinets of sufficient weight to counterbalance either an important String-ensemble or a powerful union of Brass-instruments. The Oboes are practically useless in their top register, and the Flutes lack character in the *forte*. This is an important point and well worth consideration in the orchestration of large works. In connection with this point Strauss draws particular attention to the Symphonies of Mahler.

For the sake of completeness it may be added that Clarinets in (high) F, and even in (high) A♭, are occasionally used abroad. The latter instrument is regularly employed in the Austrian military bands.

No. 42. The Bassett-Horn and The Alto-Clarinet.

Fr. *Cor de basset* ; It. *Corno di Bassetto* ;[1] Ger. *Bassethorn.*
Fr. *Clarinette alto* ; It. *Clarinetto alto* ; Ger. *Altklarinette.*

The name of this instrument is only slightly less inaccurate than that of the English-Horn, for though not a Horn at all it *is* Basset. It was first introduced in 1770 by a German maker called Horn. He christened his invention Basset-"Horn," that is to say, "Little Bass (Clarinet made by) Horn." The Italians translated the name "Horn" literally by "Corno." Hence their name *Corno di Bassetto.*

The Basset-Horn is a Tenor-Clarinet. In appearance it is much like a small Bass-Clarinet. It is pitched a fifth below the obsolete Clarinet in C. Its part is therefore written like that of the French-Horn-in-F, a fifth higher than the actual sounds. The treble-clef is used with a key-signature of one ♭ less or one ♯ more than the key-signature of the piece.

In its downward compass the Bassett-Horn possesses the characteristic feature of the old Clarinets of Mozart's time.[2] In other words, its downward compass does not end at

 sounding in this case 

but is continued, by means of four additional keys, to

 sounding 

This gives a written compass of

sounding

The highest notes are of little value, and are better replaced by the corresponding notes on the B♭-A instrument. The middle-and lower-registers are admirable, richer and fuller than those of the ordinary Clarinet, much more interesting and expressive than those of the Bass-Clarinet. Gevaert sums up its tone-quality in two words, "unctuous seriousness." This instrument, or rather its modern equivalent the Alto-Clarinet, is well worth using in large orchestral combinations.

[1] The word *Clarone,* though more strictly used for the *Bass-Clarinet,* is sometimes applied by the Italians to the *Bassett-Horn.*

[2] See above, page 254.

Its placid tone-colour specially fits it for service as a "background-instrument" in those cases where the "more personal colour of the Violas, Bassoons, and Clarinets playing in their lower register" is inappropriate.[1]

The technique of the Bassett-Horn is similar to that of the ordinary Clarinet, and, in the hands of a good player, the instrument can give a good account of brilliant passages founded on arpeggios, diatonic and chromatic scales, broken chords, and so on. It is by no means an instrument whose sole capability is the performance of slow *legato* melodies.

The elaborate *Obbligato* to Vitellia's song, "*Non più di fiori*," in Mozart's *Clemenza di Tito* is still often heard in our concert-rooms. Mozart seems to have had a special affection for this instrument. He uses it either singly or in pairs in the *Adagio* of his *B♭ Serenade*, in the *Nozze di Figaro* (additional number), in the *Zauberflöte*, in *Il Seraglio*, and in the *Requiem*. Beethoven appears to have only written for it once,—in his *Prometheus*. Modern instances are hard to find. The following *Molto Allegro* passage from the Overture to Holbrooke's *Children of Don* is specially chosen for quotation instead of the *cantabile*, which is more conventionally associated with the larger Clarinets.

EXAMPLE 200.

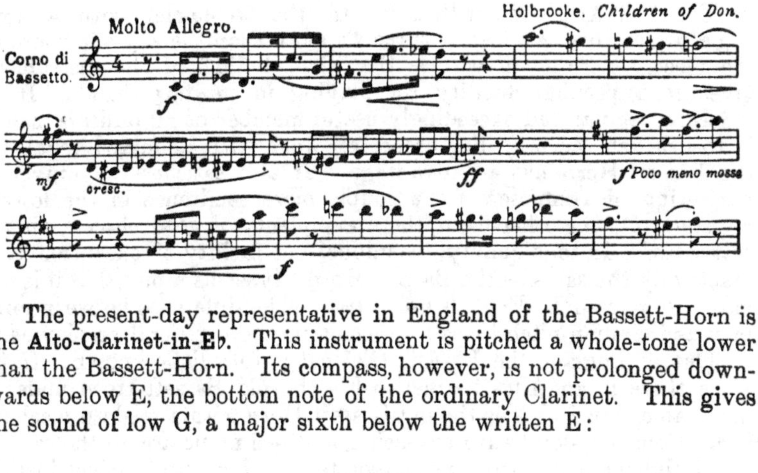

The present-day representative in England of the Bassett-Horn is the **Alto-Clarinet-in-E♭**. This instrument is pitched a whole-tone lower than the Bassett-Horn. Its compass, however, is not prolonged downwards below E, the bottom note of the ordinary Clarinet. This gives the sound of low G, a major sixth below the written E:

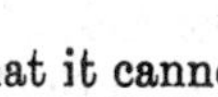

It will therefore be seen that it cannot *sound* the two bottom semitones F♯ and F♮, both possible on the Bassett-Horn.

[1] Strauss.

The difference between the two instruments in downward compass will be made plain by the following example:
Lowest written note of the Bassett-Horn:

sounding

Lowest written note of the E♭-Alto-Clarinet:

sounding

The compass of the "E♭-Alto" is

which sounds a major sixth lower, viz.,

The "E♭-Alto" is written for in the treble-clef with a key-signature of three ♭'s less or three ♯'s more than the key-signature of the piece. Here again we see that the "build" of the instrument gives it a peculiar facility for playing in military bands. It is, indeed, a regular and exceedingly useful member of all military bands in the British service. For orchestral work with its mixed tonalities the Bassett-Horn has an advantage. It also satisfies the universal hankering of composers for a couple more semitones in the lowest register. On the other hand, there are plenty of good players on the "E♭-Alto." In tone-quality, technique, and facility of execution, it is practically the same as the Bassett-Horn. It seems a pity that it is not more often used in English orchestras. The difference between military and civilian pitch helps to prevent its more general employment.

Out of England the E♭-Alto-Clarinet is very little known. In its place there is an Alto-Clarinet-in-F,—the old Bassett-Horn under a new name. In fact it is the old Bassett-Horn with a modern mechanism. Compass, downward extension, and technique are all the same.

Holbrooke has written an elaborate part for Alto-Clarinet-in-F in *Apollo and the Seaman.* Here are two examples. The first is a brilliant passage in octaves with the Bass-Clarinet. The extract is taken from a *tutti* in which the Alto-Clarinet plays in unison with the Violas and the Bass-Clarinet with the Cellos. The two Bassoons and the Double-Bassoon continue the scale downwards at the end of the excerpt. The B♮'s in bar two of the Alto-Clarinet-part are of course enharmonic to the G♭'s in the Bass-Clarinet part.

EXAMPLE 201.

Holbrooke. *Apollo and the Seaman.*

The second example is a rare instance of the employment of the E♭-, B♭-, and Alto-Clarinets without any orchestral background at all. It occurs just before the end of Part III. in the same work.

EXAMPLE 202.

Holbrooke. *Apollo and the Seaman*

No. 43. The Pedal-Clarinet.

Fr. *Clarinette contrebasse* ; It. *Clarino contrabasso* ; Ger. *Kontrabass klarinette.*

The Pedal- or Contrabass-Clarinet, an instrument scarcely known outside the largest military band combinations, is built in B♭ an octave below the Bass-Clarinet. Its tube, over ten feet long, is partly conical and partly cylindrical. At one end it terminates in a huge clumsy Clarinet mouthpiece, and at the other, after four changes in the direction of the air-column, there is a large metal bell upturned like that of the Bass-Clarinet.

The instrument is furnished with thirteen keys and rings, and has the same fingering as the ordinary B♭-Clarinet, except in its top eight semitones. The written compass is from

sounding

The bass-clef is used, and the notation is as for any other B♭-instrument with the key-signature of two ♭'s more or two ♯'s less than the key-signature of the piece. The highest notes, which are rarely used, would more naturally be written in the treble-clef. Another and perhaps simpler plan would be to write the whole compass in the treble-clef, transposing down an octave and a major ninth (two octaves and a whole tone).

In its lowest register the notes are unsatisfactory. They also require a great deal of wind, and can only be used in slow passages. The middle and upper registers are rich and reedy, like the *Chalumeau-notes* of the ordinary Clarinet.

This instrument is undoubtedly capable of improvement, and, if it ever is improved, will be a formidable rival of the Double-Bassoon. In tone-quality it is more vocal and flexible than that instrument. When the proper experiments have been made it should be of service in large orchestral combinations. It would be specially useful in those accompaniments of choral music where the heavy Brass is not desired.

Vincent d'Indy has used a Pedal-Clarinet in *Fervaal*, and during the 1912 season of Promenade Concerts at Queen's Hall two works appeared in which there were Pedal-Clarinet parts. One of these was apparently for a Pedal-Clarinet-in-F, pitched an octave below the Bassett-Horn, but so far as can be gathered no instrument of this pitch exists at present in England.

No. 44. Obsolete Wood-Wind.

The Serpent.

The Serpent, as we have already explained, was the predecessor of the Bass-Horn, the Russian-Bassoon, and the Ophicleide.[1] It was

[1] See pages 18, 19, 71, 72, 172.

THE SERPENT.

By kind permission of Messrs. Boosey & Co.

really the bass of the old *Zinke* or *Cornet à bouquin*, the instrument which supplied the normal treble-part to the mediæval Brass-band. All these instruments, whatever the material of their tubes, employed the same methods of tone-production and of scale-variation—the cup-mouthpiece and the laterally pierced holes.

Originally the Serpent was keyless. It was merely provided with a series of six or eight finger-holes. In the latter part of the eighteenth century, however, two keys were added allowing a slightly better disposition of the holes and consequently improving the intonation; the remaining finger-holes were finished off with brass rims. About this time it secured royal patronage and became a recognized member of the Military Band.

The instrument was normally held vertically in front of the player. This was awkward for an infantry bandsman when marching. He could either play or walk: he could not do both at the same time. Acting on a royal suggestion, however, bandsmen began to carry their instruments sideways, and, though even with this added comfort their mental state cannot have been enviable, the change was reckoned epoch-making.

In England Serpents seem to have been always made on the same model, but in France, where the "*Serpent d'église*" represented our pattern, they had another standard instrument, less cumbrous and therefore more convenient for military use. This instrument was commonly known as the "*Serpent militaire*" or "*Serpent d'harmonie.*"

In the early part of the nineteenth century the instrument's tonal inequalities and its deficiencies of intonation had become more than even the men of Waterloo could stand. The old finger-holes were abandoned; the position of the holes was corrected; and a complete set of huge metal keys like flappers was provided. It is one of these comparatively modern and elaborate Serpents, fit for either military or civilian duty, which is illustrated on Plate XI. The student will have no difficulty, after what has been already said with regard to this special instrumental family, in making out the details of the illustration without further explanation. The material used in the manufacture of the Serpent was wood covered with leather. A large cup-shaped mouthpiece of metal was used, and, as may be seen from the picture, the whole instrument presented the appearance of a dishevelled drain-pipe which was suffering internally.

The Serpent was a B♭-Serpent. Its written chromatic compass from

therefore sounded a whole tone lower: 

In tone it seems to have been an instrument in which the early Christians might have delighted. Berlioz speaks of its "lugubrious poetry" as being fitted for nothing but the plain-song of the Dies Iræ, and mentions its "frigid and abominable blaring" in terms that evidently recall his own early sufferings when he assigned it a part in the *Resurrexit* of a *Mass.*

For years the Serpent was highly popular in French church-circles. It has, however, long since severed that connection, and now leads a respectable secluded life among the mermaids and stuffed alligators of local museums.

No. 45. The Cuckoo-Instrument.

This toy-instrument is one of a somewhat large zoological family which devotes itself to imitating the cries of birds and beasts, generally in outdoor performances.

In construction the "Cuckoo-Instrument" is actually a rudimentary Church-Organ on a very small scale. It consists of two tiny Organ-pipes made of wood and mounted on a pair of miniature bellows. The pipes are stopped, and therefore sound an octave lower than they would if open. The "stop" in each case is a closely fitting plug provided with a knob-handle. This can be pulled out or pushed in at discretion. Consequently, the vibrating air-column can be lengthened or shortened, and this lowers or raises the pitch of the two notes. The utmost range possible is from

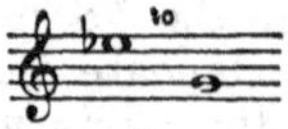

The natural or country-side cuckoo has been observed to sing anything from a major second

to a perfect fifth

but it is well known that the theatrical variety is a military bird, born and bred in the key of B♭ (major or minor).

Humperdinck has employed this instrument in the *Forest Scene* (Act II.) of *Hänsel und Gretel.* Here is a short example in which it is accompanied by a Muted Horn and two Solo Cellos playing in Harmonics:[1]

EXAMPLE 203.

Humperdinck. *Hänsel und Gretel.*

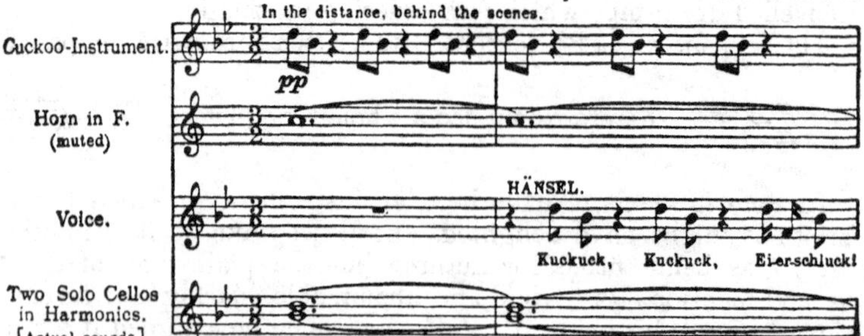

[1] See page 424 for explanation and correct notation.

Beethoven's cuckoo in the *Pastoral Symphony* has the same notes done by two B♭-Clarinets in unison.

EXAMPLE 204.

Beethoven. *Pastoral Symphony.*

STRINGED INSTRUMENTS.

PRELIMINARY.

IN this group of instruments the air-vibrations are set up by means of a stretched string or strings. There are three methods by which the strings themselves are set in motion:

1. By *plucking* either with the finger, as in the modern *Harp*, or with a mechanical instrument, such as a plectrum or quill, as in the ancient *Kithara* or *Lyre*. For musical purposes the latter group may again be divided into

(*a*) Instruments, such as the *Mandoline*, in which the strings are set in motion by a plectrum held in the player's hand.

(*b*) Instruments, such as the *Harpsichord* or *(Clavi)cembalo*, in which the strings are set in motion by a quill not directly under the player's control.

2. By *striking* with a hammer or hammers. This group also may be subdivided into

(*a*) Instruments, such as the *Dulcimer*,[1] in which the strings are set in motion by means of hammers held in the player's hand.

(*b*) Instruments, such as the *Pianoforte*, in which the strings are set in motion by hammers not directly and completely under the player's control.

3. By *contact with a prepared surface*, which is kept in motion while in contact with the strings. This group also may be subdivided into two, each of which has had great influence on the history of music.

(*a*) Those instruments in which the application of the moving surface is not directly and completely under the player's control. The best examples of this type of instrument are the obsolete *Organistrum* and its modern descendant, the *Vielle* or *Hurdy-gurdy*, in both of which the moving surface was a rosined wheel which pressed against the strings and was kept in motion by means of a crank.

(*b*) Those instruments in which the application of the moving surface is directly and completely under the player's control. The

[1] The *Tambourin du Béarn* is a sort of primitive *Dulcimer*. It has seven strings, all tuned to C or G. The player beats these as a sort of drone-bass to the tune of his Galoubet. See page 31.

most familiar examples of these are the old *Rebecs*, the *Minnesinger-Fidels*, the *Viols*, and the modern *Violins*, all played with a "bow."

The development of these groups of *plucked*, *struck*, and *bowed* instruments is to be studied first in existing specimens; second, in theoretical and historical works, and in the surviving ancient music which was performed on them; and third, in the pictures, illuminations and carvings which are to be found scattered all over Europe.

It need not be said that, with the perishable nature of musical instruments, the first method does not take us very far back. Indeed, it is with something of a shock that one comes on an occasional orchestral player who is earning his daily bread on an instrument that was fashioned in Queen Elizabeth's day. Such instruments actually exist, and are sometimes models of great construction; but in general one may say that, save for a stray specimen here and there, all instruments of an earlier date have vanished.

The historian is therefore compelled to rely mainly on illuminations, on carvings in stone, and on historical references. The whole of that field has been, or is being, explored with extraordinary patience and accuracy by various workers, and it is only possible here to hint at the results of their labours.[1] It may be as well, however, to give a very hasty and much compressed account of the three groups of instruments mentioned above.

(1) Plucked Instruments.

This, the simplest form of stringed instruments, is also probably the most ancient. Various legends have attempted to account for its invention, but none has much value in view of the fact that even a savage who possesses a bow for the purposes of war and the chase also possesses a twanging musical instrument. The early developed type of this twanging stringed instrument is the Greek **Kithara**, whose shape is familiar to everyone through its constant representation in Greek statuary, bas-reliefs, and vase-paintings.

It is uncertain when and how this instrument began to develop into what we may call for the sake of shortness a **Lute**, that is to say, into an instrument whose strings were stretched over a vaulted resonating-box. Two facts, however, show that some changes of this sort took place at a very early date.

(1) An actual instrument of distinct Lute-type furnished with a vaulted body and with three pegs in the head was dug up at Herculaneum. Herculaneum was destroyed in A.D. 79.

(2) A four-stringed "**Pandoura**" is represented in a sculpture now in the Mausoleum-Room of the British Museum. This sculpture is

[1] The student who wishes full information on this topic should make himself acquainted with Miss Schlesinger's valuable study, *The Instruments of the Modern Orchestra and Early Records of the Precursors of the Violin Family.* (Reeves, MCMX.) A list of manuscripts, carvings, and paintings from the eighth to the eighteenth century is printed as an *Appendix* to Mr. Galpin's *Old English Instruments of Music* (pp. 301-311). This list, however, refers only to British examples.

of about Hadrian's time, 117-138 A.D., and the instrument in question is clearly being played by plucking. It has something the appearance of a long banjo with a very small body. It differs, however, completely from a banjo in the fact that the body is vaulted like that of a Mandoline and is quite evidently a resonating-box.

It is somewhat doubtful whether these early forms continued to persist through the first centuries of the Christian era and had any true influence on the development of the mediæval *Lutes*. It is known for certain that the early European *Lutes* were based immediately on Arab forms. On the other hand, it is quite possible that these Arab forms themselves were founded on, or at any rate influenced by, the Græco-Roman instruments.[1]

At any rate, we find that the popular instrument in Chaucer's time (fourteenth century) was a boat-shaped **Rebab** which had probably come into Europe during the Crusades. This instrument, which was called a **Cittern** or **Gittern**,[2] was held, not in violin-, but in lute- or guitar-position, and was plucked with a plectrum or sometimes with the fingers of the right hand. The *Gittern* had a flat back and incurved sides much like those of a modern *Guitar*. In this it differed completely from the pear-shaped *Lute* with its vaulted back. When first it came to England the *Gittern* was a simple instrument of four strings tuned either to

Few of these instruments survive. A fourteenth century specimen, however, restored in Queen Elizabeth's reign and bearing the arms of the Earl of Leicester, is preserved at Warwick Castle. The **Citole** was a hybrid-instrument, a mixture of *Gittern* and *Lute*. It combined the flat back of the former with the pear-shape of the latter. From the *Gittern*-type of instrument sprang the whole Lute-family, a large and historically most important group whose services to art only ended in the seventeenth century.

There appear to have been nearly a dozen varieties of *Lute* distinguished from one another by their size, that is to say their pitch, and by their complexity of stringing. The double-necked Bass-Lutes, which in the sixteenth and seventeenth centuries took the place of our present-day Cellos and Basses, were generally known as **Theorbos**. These were strung with 12, 14, or 16 strings tuned in unison-pairs like those of the modern *Mandoline*, and all these strings were

[1] The ancient British *Crwth* was originally a *plucked* not a *bowed* instrument. The principle of the bow was, however, introduced from Asia at an early date and was applied to the *Crwth*. It was played in this manner both in England and Ireland from remote times. In fact the *Bowed-Crwth* is the instrument so often mentioned in mediæval Latin by the name of *Chorus*. The Early English was *coriun*. "Of harpe & of salteriun of fiðele & of coriun" (*Lay*, about 1205). Originally it had neither neck nor fingerboard. The *Rebec*, on the other hand, was imported as a bowed-instrument from Asia.

[2] The *name* alone of the instrument is a debased form of the Greek word *Kithara*.

"stopped" by the fingers of the left hand according to a method somewhat similar to that of the Guitar. On the bass-side there were from 8 to 11 "free-strings." These were never "stopped," that is to say, they were only employed to sound the open note of their greatest length. The largest varieties of *Theorbo* were the **Archlute,** which hailed from Padua, and the **Chittarone** or **Roman Theorbo**, a huge Contrabass which stood as high as a tall man. The early method of notation for all these instruments was by means of "Tablature," a system in which the lines of the stave represented not regular degrees of pitch but the actual strings of the instrument. The fingering was then indicated by the use of letters (A, B, C, etc.) or of figures (1, 2, 3, etc.). Similarly in the Wood-Wind instruments the Tablature-signs represented the holes covered by the player's fingers.

The second type of plucked instrument, that in which the plucking mechanism was not directly and completely under the controlling hand of the player, is represented by the **Harpsichord**. In this instrument a keyboard was used something like that of the *pianoforte*. A mechanism was also provided which was set in motion by the pressure of the finger on the key. This motion was communicated to a series of quills so arranged as to "make contact" with the tense strings. The *Harpsichord* was used in what we may fairly call "modern music," and the nearness of its period to our own times may perhaps cause us to overestimate slightly its importance in the history of the art. Compared with the *Lute*, however, its importance is not great in respect either of its antiquity or of its long continuity of service.[1] Besides the *Harpsichord* there were three other instruments all plucked with mechanically-controlled *plectra* either of quill, leather, metal, or wood. These were the **Virginal**, the **Spinet**, and the **Clavicembalo.**

Of all these plucked instruments the only one which has been galvanized into modern orchestral life is, curiously enough, also one of the oldest—the *Harp*.[2] Several thousand years before the Lute-family began to have its early beginnings in the days of the Græco-Roman civilization the Harp was in use on the banks of the Nile and, apparently, in all its essentials much what it is at the present day. Of course it had neither the large compass nor the chromatic mechanism of the modern instrument; but, if we may judge from the many representations and actual specimens which survive, it was by no means wanting in either power or effectiveness.

(2) Struck Instruments.

These instruments again are, so to speak, "as old as the hills." On the Assyrian sculptures of the time of Sardanapalus, musicians are represented playing what we should call **Dulcimers**, that is to say, instruments in which a series of strings are stretched either on a flat wooden board, or perhaps even on a flat hollow resonating-box,

[1] The earliest instrumental compositions were written either for Organ or for Lute.

[2] But see also what is said below with regard to the *Guitar*, page 479.

and beaten with hammers. This is the instrument which has been mistranslated in the authorized Version of the Scriptures by the word *Psaltery.* "Then an herald cried aloud, To you it is commanded, O people, nations and languages, That at what time ye hear the sound of the cornet, flute, harp, sackbut, psaltery, dulcimer,[1] and all kinds of musick, ye fall down and worship the golden image that Nebuchadnezzar the king hath set up" (*Dan.* iii. 4, 5). It has managed to survive from that day to this, and in Hungary has been elevated to the position of a national instrument—the **Cimbalom**—essential to the performance of the Czardas and other peculiar forms of Magyar music. It can scarcely be called an orchestral instrument, though in small orchestral combinations it has made its way Westward. Even in a London restaurant a Bach fugue on the *Cimbalom* has been heard as an accompaniment to the clatter of knives, forks, and dishes.

The **Clavichord** was not strictly either a plucked- or a struck-instrument. It was a pushed-instrument, and the pushing-mechanism was a small piece of metal called a "tangent." This type of instrument, with its faint elfin tone, only audible in the smallest of rooms, could not compete publicly with the *Harpsichord.*

The modern **Pianoforte** may be said, without disrespect, to be a mechanical variety of the *Dulcimer*, to which it has much the same relationship as the *Harpsichord* to the *Psaltery* or the *Lute.* It is, in fact, an instrument whose stretched strings are set in vibration by means of hammers, between which and the controlling hand of the player there is an elaborate and fixed mechanism. This instrument, again, is scarcely more at home in the orchestra than the *Cimbalom.* As a solo instrument with orchestral accompaniment it, of course, holds the highest place, but as a regular member of the orchestra it has been used only for one of two purposes, either as a substitute for a special instrument such as the *Harp* or *Celesta,* or to eke out the harmony in a poorly equipped band. It may be said that it is not very successful in either capacity. Its poor and slightly unpleasant tone-quality contrasts unfavourably with the beautiful tone-colours of the Strings and Wind, and, in modern pianofortes, the attempt to make a sustaining instrument out of an essentially non-sustaining "box of wires and hammers" has not very happy results.

It must be added that from time to time endeavours have been made to introduce the pianoforte as a purely orchestral instrument. The latest of these are to be found in the scores of Richard Strauss's *Ariadne auf Naxos* and of Scriabine's *Prometheus.*

(3) Bowed Instruments.

To the student of orchestration this is by far the most important group, for it includes the modern string-family of **Violins, Violas, Cellos,**

[1] The word *dulcimer* is here a mistranslation for *bagpipe.* The true *dulcimer* differed from the original *psaltery* as a *struck* instrument differs from one that is *plucked.* The two names, however, are continually confused in early references to these instruments. It is doubtful whether the ancient Irish *timpan* was a *psaltery* or a *dulcimer.*

and **Basses**. These instruments, which are often "taken for granted," really call for considerable historical explanation. Indeed one only needs to take into one's hands a modern Violin and Bow and to examine their perfection to be made aware that they represent merely the last link in a long evolutionary chain. Something is known of this chain throughout the greater part of its length. Alongside of it, however, is another rusty chain whose broken links represent to us the incomplete development of a second family of bowed instruments—the family whose modern descendant is the despised **Hurdy-gurdy**. The links in the latter chain are few in number, but as they had some importance in the history of instrumental music, a few words may well be devoted to them before we deal with the better-known bowed-instruments, the families of Viols and Violins.

The earliest attempt to adapt what one may call "bowed"[1] instruments to the service of Church-music, that is to say, to the service of the only existing organized music, was, by a curious historical inversion, purely mechanical. In every other department of instrumental music the strict order of development has been from instruments directly under the control of the player's hands to instruments in which a controlling mechanism is interposed between the player and the sound-producing medium. Even in the other two groups of Strings—those that are plucked and those that are hammered—this order is strictly observed. With this special instrumental group, however, the first attempt was to set the strings in motion mechanically. It must not be supposed that, at the time when this invention took place, "bowed" instruments in our modern sense of the word did not exist. They existed, but were apparently considered outside the pale of serious art.

A stringed instrument was called for which should be able to accompany the unison choral melodies with those forbidding series of fifths and octaves which satisfied the same craving in the early middle ages as Wagner's harmony satisfied in the nineteenth century. These series of fifths and octaves are known to theorists as "Organum," and the only instrument then existing which could deal satisfactorily with them was the **Pipe-Organ**. The required stringed-instrument was to act as a substitute for the *Pipe-Organ*, and was to possess the advantage of portability.

As far as one can gather from the description of Odo of Cluny and from representations which have come down to our day—for of course no actual specimens exist—the instrument consisted normally of three heavy strings laid parallel to each other over a sound-chest. The three strings were not laid horizontally in one plane, but in the arc of a circle. At one end of the strings a heavy wheel of wood, faced perhaps with leather, and well rosined, pressed against all three strings. A crank, something like the handle of a barrel-organ, was attached, and by that means the wheel could be turned. But observe that the wheel could only grind on the three strings simultaneously.

[1] The word "bowed" is used loosely here to cover the third group of instruments mentioned at the beginning of the chapter.

There was no mechanism for throwing one or two out of gear. In addition to this wheel a series of revolving wooden bridges was provided to "stop" the strings in a limited diatonic scale. These bridges were placed under the strings and were brought into action by means of wooden turn-pins which projected outside the instrument. Like the wheel, these bridges only acted simultaneously on all three strings: indeed their only object was to produce the fearsome series of fifths and octaves which made up the "organum" of those very dark ages.

The instrument described above was not of very large size. It could be rested on the knees of two seated players, and could be easily carried from one place to another. Pictures are in existence showing the two players, one at the crank, the other at the keys, co-operating in much the same harmonious relationship as that which exists between the village organist and the village organ-blower. It is only necessary to add that the instrument was known by the name of **Organistrum.**

With the downfall, or rather the development, of the old system of Church-accompaniment, the necessity for the continual moving drone ceased. A less enterprising instrument than the one under discussion would have been irretrievably beaten by the changed circumstances. The *Organistrum,* however, was quite equal to the new situation, and, much to its credit, at once transmogrified itself into the **Vielle** or **Hurdy-gurdy.**[1]

The old leathered and rosined wheel remained, but the number of the strings was increased first to four, and then to six. The most important change, however, was that the keys no longer pressed the whole series of strings against what we should call the "fingerboard," but only the "chanterelle" or top-string. The other strings were only played "open," that is, in their greatest length, and thus, so long as the wheel was kept turning, they formed an agreeable drone-bass to the chanterelle-melody. One must add that, in the course of time, a complete change was effected in the system of "stopping." The revolving wooden bridges gave place to a series of little upright wooden rods which were originally *pulled* and afterwards *pressed* against the chanterelle. The latter form of instrument can still be seen fairly frequently in the London streets. It generally has four strings. For the two outer—that is to say the "drones"—thick covered Cello-strings are used. The two middle strings—those on which the "stopping" apparatus acts—are like long, thin, Violin E-strings.

It is very easy to make fun of such instruments as the *Organistrum* and *Hurdy-gurdy* in the year 1914, but we must not overlook the fact that these instruments really played a considerable part in music during the thirteenth and fourteenth centuries, and that their services at country merry-makings continued right down to the eighteenth

[1] Known also in France as *Vielle-à-manivelle, Symphonie-* or *Chyfonie-à-roue*; in Germany as *Leier*, combined with some such word as *Dreh-*, *Bauern-*, *Rad-*, *Bettler-*, *Deutsche-*; in Italy as *Lira Tedesca*, *Lira rustica*, or *Lira pagana*.

century. It is by no means a stretch of language to say that the Cello-, Bass-, and Bassoon-pedals, which, even in modern works, are used to accompany dance-rhythms, have their origin in the mechanism of the *Vielle-à-manivelle.*

Naturally many attempts were made to improve an instrument so well known and so widely used. Of these one may mention the *Celestina,* the *Bogen-Clavier,* the *Geigen-Clavicymbal,* the *Geigenwerk* of Hans Hayden described by Praetorius, and the *Bogenflügel.* One may even add the quite recent endeavours of an American inventor to produce a Mechanical Violin, that is to say, a violin—or rather a group of violins—in which the "stopping" should be mechanical, and the exciting-surface an endless horse-hair bow.

The student need scarcely be informed that every attempt to improve the Vielle-family has split on one of two rocks—the difficulty of mechanically varying the application of the force according as the string is stopped into smaller or greater lengths, and the equally serious difficulty of varying the application of the force to the varying necessities of strings of different pitch, that is, of different tension. Were it not for these two insurmountable obstacles, we might all at the present day be playing *Treble-*, *Tenor-*, and *Bass-Hurdy-Gurdies,* instead of *Violins, Violas,* and *Cellos.*

The early history of the Violin family begins in Asia long before the Christian era. With regard to those far-off times there is little precise information to be given beyond the fact that bowed-instruments are mentioned in the Sanskrit classics. The bow, therefore, forms one essential part of a musical instrument of very great antiquity, and it is unlikely that it was a mere development of the plectrum. Neither the bow-half nor the fiddle-half of this musical instrument seems to have formed any part of either the Greek or the Roman civilization. They probably stayed South and South-east of Europe during the early centuries of the Roman Empire. It is difficult to say whether they were introduced into Southern Europe by the Arabs or not, but they first appear there in the form of a pear-shaped **Rebec** or **Gigue**, and a short highly-arched bow. On its first introduction into Europe the Rebec was known by the name which it still bears in Greece, the **Lyra**. No specimens of this instrument are in existence, but, from the carvings and illuminations in which it figures, one can fairly reconstruct it as a two- or three-stringed fiddle which was provided with sound-holes and held somewhat in "fiddle-position." The instrument had no regular neck. The upper part of the body was merely narrowed for the convenience of the player's hand.[1] Nothing certain is known as to the tuning or the compass of the *Rebec*, but, judging

[1] The last relics of this instrument are to be found in the seventeenth and eighteenth century dancing-masters' Kits called *Pochettes* or *Sordinos.* These were very small and extremely narrow fiddles, which could be easily slipped into the pocket. They were usually boat- or truncheon-shaped, without any external resemblance to the Violin. However, as far as the tuning and fitting was concerned, they were merely adaptations of the modern instrument. Many elaborate specimens of these *Pochettes*, made of wood and ivory, still exist in our museums.

from its want of neck, one may conclude that its range was very small, perhaps an octave or slightly more.[1]

To the *Rebec* succeeded the **Troubadour Fidel**, an oval instrument which was used for the accompaniment of men's voices. The historical interest of this instrument lies in the fact that, during the thirteenth century, distinct efforts were made to lengthen its oval form. At about the same time, or a little later, the big **Minnesinger Fiddle** begins to appear. With the advent of this instrument, we first begin to feel that the modern violin is "on the way." The sides are already receiving first a slight, and then a continually greater curve inwards, in order to give freer play to the bow. In one point only it deviates from the path of progress. It begins to adopt a feature which was, in later days, to become characteristic of the Bass-Lute—the free-string hanging clear of the nut and fingerboard, incapable therefore of being fingered, and only useful as a bourdon-bass.

Before passing to the **Viols**, which were the immediate parents of our modern **Violin-Family**, we must pause to describe a once popular bowed stringed-instrument, the **Tromba Marina**. If the reader will imagine a huge wooden metronome case six or seven feet long, of which the base—that is, the part nearest the ground—was about six or seven inches, and the apex about two or three inches wide, he will have some idea of this monstrosity. It had one string only, and this string was stretched down the entire length of the enormous wooden pyramid. Occasionally it was provided with such luxuries as sound-holes and sympathetic strings.[2]

The feature of the instrument, however, was the Bridge or "*Shoe*," as it was called. This was cut on one side so as to form a thick heavy support for the string; on the other it was shaped into a narrow atrophied leg, which neither completely rested on nor completely cleared the sound-board. In fact, it hung loose, just touching the wood below. The result was that every time the player attacked the monochord with his bow, the "game leg" vibrated with a horrid mediæval jar against the wood of the sound-box. The player, as a rule, indulged only in the open harmonics of the string,[3] and the commonest intervals were therefore those usually heard on the trumpet. Hence, say the antiquaries, with an obscurity difficult to penetrate, the name **Marine Trumpet.**[4]

[1] The word *Rebec* also appears continually in the forms *Ribibe*, *Rubybe*, *Rybibe*, *Rebibe*, and *Rubible*. These transformations are a philological mystery, though suggestions have been made that they were due to a confusion or rather a fusion with the word "trible." "In twenty manere koude he trippe and daunce. . . . And pleyen songes on a small Rubible." Chaucer, *Miller's Tale* (1386).

[2] That is to say, strings tuned to the fundamental note and some of the harmonics of the principal string. These strings were, of course, never touched by the bow. They only vibrated "in sympathy" when the "principal-string" was set in motion by the bow. An existing specimen of the Tromba Marina has been described as having no fewer than fifty "sympathetic" strings.

[3] Some lists of "frets," however, give a few other notes.

[4] Another derivation makes *Tromba Marina* equal to *Tromba Mariana*, but this is not convincing. Mr. Galpin suggests a derivation from the name of Marin (or Maurin), a celebrated fifteenth century trumpeter. This seems at least as likely as the other two.

It is hard to believe that this instrument can have been as bad as it seems. On the description, it would appear to have had every vice of which a stringed-instrument is capable—only one string, an over-elongated trunk, a crazy musical constitution, and a "crank" bridge calculated to do everything that a bridge should not do. Yet it enjoyed great popularity, and was written for even by a man of such distinction as Scarlatti.[1] In Germany, where it was commonly known by the names of *Trummscheit*, *Trompetengeige*, and *Tympanischiza*, it was often played by the nuns during the Church services. Hence came its nickname *Nonnengeige* (Nuns' fiddle).[2]

After this short digression we must return to the study of the true fiddle family. We left it at the point where the instruments, under the name of *Minnesinger Fiddles*, were just beginning to assume something of the characteristic violin form. In the course of about two centuries, the efforts which were made to improve the musical character of these fiddles culminated in the **Viols**, a family which occupied in the 15th, 16th, and 17th centuries the same position as that held in our own day by the Violin-group. In shape these Viols were much like the old style of *Double-Bass*[3] familiar to everyone in our concert-rooms and theatres. They had high bridges, very deep ribs, flat backs, and long sloping shoulders. The usual number of strings was six. But one small Viol (the *Lyra-* or *Leero-Viol*) was furnished, early in the 17th century, with an additional set of six "sympathetic" strings. This was possibly an English invention. At any rate, the instrument so strung was at one time popular in this country, and was regarded abroad as a peculiarly English type. Its adoption on the continent produced the Viola d'Amore. One may add that the difficulty of keeping these elaborate sets of strings in tune was always great, and this, combined with the size of the instruments, probably did some service in compelling the players to the utmost nicety of intonation.

Heavy and cumbersome though the Viols were, they yet had a weak and unsatisfactory tone-quality that cannot compare for an instant with that of the modern Violin-family. Some few Viols have been refitted as Violas and even as Cellos. Players, however, find them difficult to manage. The lower strings have a tendency to sound heavy and funereal, while the whole instrument is easily "overplayed." The Viol-players must have adopted what we should consider a quiet, lifeless style of bowing. Under the pressure of a very slight "attack," the instruments cease to do their best. They sulk.

[1] "A rare concert of four Trumpets Marine" was advertised in the London *Gazette* of Feb. 4, 1674, to take place every week-day afternoon at the *Fleece Tavern* in St. James's. The "best places" were one shilling. Quite enough, one would think.

[2] It would be interesting to hear modern-made specimens both of this instrument and of the *Organistrum*. They might well be introduced into non-Operatic plays of the correct periods, and would furnish a very valuable object-lesson in musical history. In particular, the actual sound of the *Organistrum* might help to explain the extreme shortness of early pieces written according to the rules of "Organum." The player could, of course, be insured.

[3] Though this instrument was not an original member of the family.

The original Viol-family consists of three members,

(1) The **Discant-** or **Treble-Viol.**
(2) The **Tenor-Viol** or **Viola-da-Braccio.**[1]
(3) The **Bass-Viol** or **Viola-da-Gamba.**[2]

The tuning of these three instruments was as follows:

The student who is a string-player should look carefully at these tunings and try to imagine for himself the irregularities of technique inseparable from such instruments. The Viola d'Amore with its fourteen strings, of which seven were tuned strictly in the key of **D** major thus

and seven were "sympathetic," is even more impossible from the point of view of the modern String-player.[3]

The intermediate—one might say the experimental—type between the Viols and the Violins is represented by the **Quintons.** These two instruments, **The Treble Quinton** and **The Tenor Quinton,** were furnished with five strings apiece. They are interesting as showing an approach to our modern system, both in the reduction of the number of strings and in the fact that they are actual "half-way instruments." As the student will see from the following tunings

[1] *i.e.* arm-viol, because played in violin position. As showing the extraordinary differences that existed between the methods of various Viol-makers the student may be recommended to look at a Viola-da-Braccio in the *Donaldson Collection* at the Royal College of Music. This instrument, from the general shape of its "bouts" and from the curving of the back and belly, might almost be a modern orchestral Viola. Yet it was made by Karlino in 1452. The "head" is of a very ancient pattern, totally distinct from anything made since the Violin- or even the Viol-settlement. It is provided with seven strings, of which five are on the fingerboard and two are strung *à vide* on the bass-side.

[2] *i.e.* leg-viol, because played in cello-position. Intermediate between the *Viola-da-Braccio* and the *Viola-da-Gamba* came a Viol called *Viola-da-spalla*, *i.e.* shoulder viol. This instrument, something like a very small Cello or a large-sized modern Viola, was held in front of the player in a sort of Cello-position. It was used a great deal in Italy for Church processions, and on these occasions was attached to the player's person by a string or ribbon. For *Viola-da-Gamba* see page 434.

[3] For a full description of this instrument, see below, page 405.

the three lower strings of the *Treble-* and *Tenor-Quintons* are the same respectively as those of the modern Violin and Viola

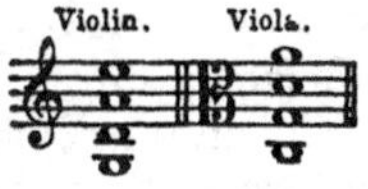

The immediate precursors of our present-day instruments were a set of violins, each of which had much in common with our modern String-group.[1] These were—

(1) The **Tenor-Violin**, a four-stringed instrument which had the same tuning as the modern Viola. (See above.)

(2) The **Bass-Violin**, a four-stringed instrument which had the same tuning as the modern Cello,

(3) The **Double-Bass Violin** or **Basso-da-Camera**,[2] an unwieldy four-stringed Bass which was tuned thus

All these are obsolete, as are also (1) The **Oktargeige**[3] or **Octave-Fiddle**, a small four-stringed Bass standing in pitch between the Viola and Cello,[4] and tuned an Octave below the modern Violin. (2) A small four-stringed Cello tuned the same as the modern instrument. This is apparently the instrument called by Leopold Mozart **Handbassel**, and by Boccherini the **Alto Violoncello**.[5]

The first instrument of the modern family to make its way into serious Church-music was the **Viola**. From that instrument all the others measure their stature. The **Violin**, whose name simply means "small Viola" (Viol-ino), struggled in against much opposition. Objection was taken to its licentious secular character. The name **Violone**,

[1] The true Violins had from the first four strings as opposed to the five or six of the Viols. A well-known Italian chap-book of the middle of the 16th century, *La Violina con la sua riposta*, etc., contains a picture of **La Violina** as its title. This, however, is plainly a small *Viol* of pronounced 15th century type. The Italians from the first used the masculine termination for the Violin, calling it "**Il Violino.**"

[2] This instrument was used occasionally by the great Bass-player Dragonetti.

[3] Not to be confused with Vuillaume's 19th century invention the three-stringed **Octo-Bass**. See Berlioz, page 240.

[4] The early Cello tuning vacillated a good deal between the modern A-D-G-C and a tuning one whole tone lower, G-C-F-B♭.

[5] Similar to this but somewhat smaller was the **Fagotgeige** or **Bassoon-Fiddle** mentioned by Leopold Mozart.

i.e. " big Viola," was given to the **Double-Bass**,[1] and in accordance with the accurate if somewhat limited principles of the Italian language, the intermediate instrument was christened, Red-Indian-fashion, "little big Viola," **Violoncello**.

Into the many and wonderfully subtle improvements which were made, first in changing the Viol into a Violin, and then in perfecting the new instrument, it is impossible to go here. It is sufficient to say that the work was begun in the 16th century by Gaspar da Salo,[2] and ended in the 17th by Stradivarius. All the various instruments had now become standardized. It is, however, necessary to mention three instruments whose names the student may possibly meet in 18th century music. These are

(1) The **Violetta Marina**,
(2) The **Viola Pomposa**,
(3) The **Violino Piccolo** (of Bach).

They were all invented after the final Violin-settlement, rapidly became obsolete, and may now be regarded merely as instruments which "took the wrong turning."

(1) The *Violetta Marina,* for which Händel wrote in *Orlando,* was an eighteenth century atavism. It was an adaptation of the old *Viola d'Amore*[3] with all its paraphernalia of "sympathetic strings." Begotten in the brain of Castrucci, the leader of Händel's Italian Opera orchestra, it died soon after birth.

(2) The *Viola Pomposa* was a small Cello to which a fifth top-string, or chanterelle, had been added. It is probably the "*Violoncello Piccolo*" of Bach's *6th Solo for the Cello,* and is said to have been either invented or suggested by him. There is, however, considerable doubt with regard to both these statements. The instrument was obsolete in Leopold Mozart's day.

(3) The *Violino Piccolo* of Bach stood in the same relationship to the Violin as the E♭-Clarinet to the C-Clarinet. It was in fact a three-quarter sized violin tuned a minor third higher than that instrument. The *Violino Piccolo* had a short and not particularly gay life, and, like the *Viola Pomposa,* was extinct in Leopold Mozart's time.

We must now turn from this short historical study to make ourselves more fully acquainted with the four-bowed instruments which constitute the modern orchestral string-quartet. These are, in their order or pitch downwards, the **Violin**, the **Viola**, the **Violoncello**, and the **Double-Bass**.

[1] Some authority has been found for the assertion that the Double-Bass was actually the first of the modern instruments to receive Violin form. The matter is, however, somewhat doubtful.

[2] Andreas Amati made some very small violins in the 16th century.

[3] One species of Viola d'Amore mentioned by Leopold Mozart bore the poetical name of " The English Violet."

No. 46. The Violin (or Fiddle).[1]

Fr. *Violon*; It. *Violino*; Ger. *Violine* (or *Geige*).

No attempt will be made here to describe accurately the shape of the Violin or the possible relationship of that shape to its exquisite musical qualities. It may suffice to say that the form in which we now have the instrument is apparently beyond improvement. Since Stradivarius's day only non-essential alterations have been made in the instrument, and these consist chiefly in the strengthening of certain parts, such as the bass-bar and in the thinning and lengthening of the neck to meet the demands of the modern left-hand technique.

The violin is made of about seventy separate pieces of wood. Of this number sixty are built permanently into the structure, while the rest are merely "fittings." The belly is made of some such soft wood as pine, the bridge and back are both of hard wood, the former generally maple, the latter either maple or sycamore. The length of the instrument varies slightly according to make. In the finest "Strad" specimens it is, as nearly as possible, fourteen inches. The four strings, tuned[2] to

are, as in all other bowed stringed instruments, numbered downwards. The E (or *chanterelle*) is called the 1st string, the A the 2nd, and so on. These four strings are not arranged exactly parallel to each other, but are slightly "splayed" from the nut to the bridge. The nut[3] itself is a raised bar of ebony at the extreme end of the finger-

[1] Besides these name various cant words have been used in various languages to designate the fiddle, and incidentally to testify to its popularity. In England the most interesting of these is the so-called Romany word *Bosh* (=fiddle; *Boshomengro*=fiddler) which one has heard used as current orchestral jargon. *Bosher* (=fiddler) is also to be found as a proper-name in the London Directory. A secondary meaning of the word *Bosh* appears to have crept into colloquial English as an equivalent of Nonsense or, as one might say, "fiddlesticks." It is only fair to add that Murray traces the latter meaning to a Turkish expression which gained its popularity from the vogue of a nineteenth century novel. In the north of England a word *bosh* is still current in the sense of the *sloping sides* of a blast-furnace or lime-kiln. The essential meaning of this word is the *slope* as opposed to the straight portion of the walls. It would be interesting to enquire whether the Romany word cannot be traced back to the same root. Such a word would well suggest the characteristic sloping sides of the fiddle before it took its present shape. The earliest use of the word "fiddle" appears to be that already given, foot-note 1, page 292.

[2] Ten other tunings have been used at different times by such players as Tartini, Castrucci, Biber, Nardini, Barbella, Campagnoli, Lolli, Ch. de Bériot, Prume, Paganini, and Baillot. None of these has been regularly adopted. Occasionally in modern works one player or the whole group of players is directed to alter a string for a special purpose. This alteration must, of course, take the form of a *lowering* not a *raising* of the pitch, because the tension of the strings is already as great as they will stand. This alteration of tuning is scarcely ever worth doing on the Violin. The results are not sufficient compensation for the tortures of mistuned fiddles which the players and the audience have to suffer during the rest of the programme.

[3] Known in Germany as the *Sattel* (=saddle).

board nearest the scroll. Four small notches are cut in this nut, and the strings lie in these notches on their way to the four pegs which control their tension. The greatest vibrating-length of the four strings, that is to say, the length in which they produce the four open notes E-A-D-G given above, is of course measured by the distance between the nut and the bridge. All four strings are made of very light catgut,[1] and the lowest string of all—the G—is tightly wound with metal filament, generally silver.

[2] The friction of the bow apparently sets up a double vibration in the strings—longitudinal and molecular—and both these series of vibrations pass through the bridge to the soft belly. Connecting this belly and the hard back is a soft wooden soundpost[3] carefully adjusted on the chanterelle-side of the fiddle. The vibrations are carried through this soundpost to the air-space contained by the back, belly, and ribs. If the student will contrast the acoustical process that takes place between the string and the ear with the corresponding processes in the Wood- and Brass-Wind he will see that the former is comparatively complex. The exact action of (1) the hard bridge, (2) the soft belly and soundpost, (3) the hard back, on the air-vibrations initiated by the strings is still a mystery. Apart from this difficult question, the general acoustics of the instrument have never been fully explained. It seems obvious that the wooden air-box can be nothing but a resonator reinforcing the already partially damped vibrations set up by the strings. These consist not of a succession of symmetrical oscillations but of a series of controlled and uncontrolled vibrations. The string is thrown into violent motion when it is engaged by the bow, and then has a period of comparatively free movement as the bow releases its grip. Perhaps the best explanation of the fiddle-quality is connected with the material of which the strings are made. These, owing to their extreme lightness, are rich in harmonics which, in their turn, are quickly damped out by the low elasticity of the catgut. Thus "the ultimate quality of the note" is appreciably softened. No confusion exists. The moment the note stops all harmonics cease.

The method by which the bow attacks the strings will be explained later when we deal with the various "bowings" of the violin. Meanwhile a few words may be devoted to the left-hand technique of the instrument. Outside the four open strings, E-A-D-G, every note on the fiddle has to be produced by one of two methods, either

(1) By *stopping* with one of the four fingers of the left hand, that

[1] Made from the entrails of the sheep. The word *catgut*, however, appears to be not a popular mistake but actually *cat-gut*, that is to say, entrails of the cat. It seems a pity to deprive the cat of this its only title to usefulness, but there is no record that fiddle-strings were ever so made. Murray suggests an alternative humorous derivation from the resemblance between caterwauling and fiddle-playing!

[2] In this article a certain amount of information common to all the orchestral Strings is grouped together. It will not be necessary to repeat this information under the headings "Viola," "Cello," and "Double-Bass."

[3] Known in France as the *âme* or soul of the instrument. The soundpost is generally so placed that its grain is crossed by the grain of the wood forming the belly.

is to say, by pressing down the string against the fingerboard and so shortening its vibrating length, or

(2) By *lightly touching* the string at one of the "nodes," and so assisting the string to vibrate in sections. The notes so produced are known as "harmonics."[1]

Stopped Notes.

The following is the list of notes produced when the left hand is in the 1st or normal position on the neck of the Violin, and when the 1st, 2nd, 3rd, and 4th fingers successively stop the string. The figures 0 1 2 3 4 placed above the stave have nothing whatever to do with the number of the string. They indicate respectively the open string and the string when stopped by the 1st, 2nd, 3rd, or 4th finger.

The student should note

(1) That three of these notes, viz.,

can be played either as open notes or as notes stopped by the fourth finger on the string next below. In practice fiddlers rarely use any open strings except the unavoidable low G

Their tone is too strikingly different from that of the stopped notes.

(2) That this scale is not necessarily a scale of C major. It can just as well be played in, say, four flats throughout, though, in that case, the three reduplicated notes mentioned above would all be flat, and could therefore only be played as stopped notes.

This short scale, however, by no means exhausts the possibilities of the Violin. The whole left-hand can be "shifted" into other positions, that is to say, the hand can be slid along the neck into various degrees

[1] It must be remembered that, even when the string is vibrating as a whole, it is also vibrating in parts. With a good covered G-string it is quite possible to coax out one or two of these harmonics so that they are heard simultaneously with the open note produced by the full-length string. As everyone knows, the quality of the open strings is considerably brighter and harder than that of the same strings when stopped. This is probably due to the fact that, in the former case, the string, vibrating between two sharply defined points of hard wood, is able to vibrate quite freely, not only in its whole length but also in segments. The harmonics which go to make up the bright open-string quality are thus much more clearly audible. With the stopped notes the slightest uncertainty or movement of the fleshy finger-tips tends to damp out these subsidiary vibrations.

of nearness to the bridge. When that is done, and any new position is taken up, the hand then lies still, and the fingers "stop" an entirely new series of notes.

The complete number of these "violin positions" is usually given as seven. It must, however, be stated that for the extreme high notes up to

still higher positions are employed. These higher positions, however, and indeed the upper three of the seven ordinary positions, are of little practical use on the D- and G-strings, except in so far as they enable a player (1) to perform a *legato* melody with the tone-colour of a single string, (2) to remain in or near one position while executing a difficult passage "across the strings." It is as well to notice the fact that the higher the position taken by the hand the closer the fingers have to be set to each other. Naturally this is of more importance on the Violin than on the larger stringed-instruments. The student should bear this in mind with a view to simplifying any passages above top A

In any of the *Seven Positions* mentioned above a series of not more than four notes upwards is producible on each string. In addition to this an extension of the fourth finger upwards allows an extra note a semitone or a tone higher, but this is only used for certain limited purposes. Of course in the first position an extra (open) note *below* the 1st stopped note is always obtainable.

We shall now give a complete list of the Seven Positions on all four strings. The semibreve notes are those on which the first finger rests in each position. The crotchet-head notes are those which are played by the 2nd, 3rd, and 4th fingers. The figures above the notes represent, as usual, the fingering.

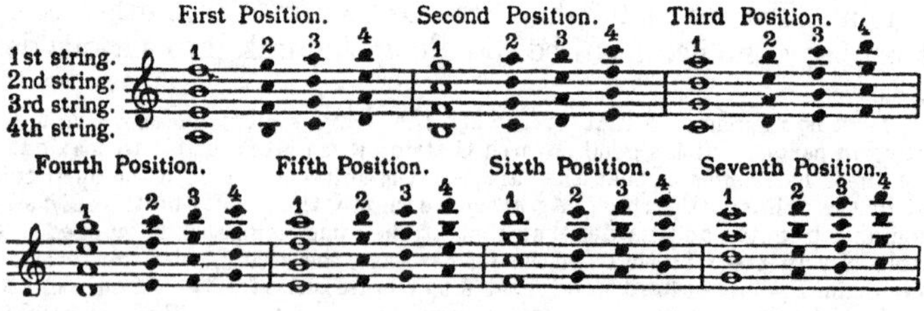

[1] The higher positions—8th, 9th, etc.—can be found by the student for himself They are all formed on the same model.

The student must bear in mind that when the first finger is resting on any of the above (semibreve) notes, the player has access without moving his hand not only to that note and the three notes upwards, but to the corresponding notes *in the same position* on the other three strings. In fact he has practical command not only over his open strings but over the whole series of sixteen notes covered by any one position. These sixteen notes are the four semibreves and the twelve crotchet-heads contained in any one of the above bars. To give a simple instance, it is no more difficult for a good fiddle-player to perform this passage

which all lies "directly under the hand" in the 7th position, than the corresponding passage in the 1st position

This is a most important point, as it is the foundation of all Violin-technique, and the rock on which all pianists split when they come to write Violin-passages. The only slight element of difficulty in this passage consists in the fact that it is "across the strings," that is to say, that the bow and finger have to make a simultaneous jump to the lower string in order to produce the 3rd and 4th notes, then back to the upper string for the 5th and 6th notes, then back to the lower string for the 7th note, and finally back to the upper string for the 8th note. Naturally it is easier to play a passage in one position on one string than a passage in one position on more than one string, and the difficulty increases with the number of strings employed. This is, however, by no means a serious matter to a competent violinist, and the student must fix clearly in his mind the fact that this small difficulty is inherent in the passage itself at whatever altitude it is played. It is no greater in the 7th than in the 1st position.[1]

It is hoped that the student will by now have seized the fact that the Violin-technique is a *technique of position*, and not of notes. Ignorance of this fact is the cause of all the bad fiddle-writing which is too often found in pianists' music. The object, especially in writing fast passage work, should be to keep the player as much as possible in one position, or, at any rate, not to give him passages which involve continual irritating shifts undertaken perhaps merely in order to get single notes. By all means let him shift—a violinist is doing so all the time he is playing—but when he has shifted give him something to play in his new position.

[1] It may be mentioned in passing that the odd-numbered positions (1, 3, 5, etc.) are on the whole more used by violinists than the even-numbered (2, 4, 6, etc.).

There are of course a certain number of passages which, in fiddle player's language, "need looking at," but, when they have been looked at, the result is either that the player can find a position-technique for them, in which case they are probably good fiddle-music, or else that he cannot, in which case they are sure to sound dull, fussy, and ineffective.

The difficulty of taking skips on the Violin, as indeed on all the String- and Wood-Wind-families, has been somewhat exaggerated by the fact that writers always tend to measure these difficulties by the peculiar mechanical standards of the *Pianoforte.* The student therefore, if he be a pianist, should try to rid his mind of all *a priori* views on this point derived from his knowledge of pianoforte-technique. On that instrument a melodic skip of two octaves means an acrobatic swoop of thirteen inches or so. On the Fiddle there is no such thing. The utmost that the hand can move is an inch or two, and skips of even two octaves cannot be more than two positions apart.

A very elementary example will make this clear. In the following passage

the first note must, of course, be taken in the 1st position with the first finger stopping the note "A" on the G-string. The skip that follows is, to the fiddle-player, not a skip from the note "low-A" to the note "high-D," but a skip from the 1st position on the G-string (with his first finger on low-A) to the 3rd position on the E-string (with his first finger *on A* two octaves higher). The player fixes his new position automatically by stopping, but not playing, this high-A, and then instantaneously takes the "high-D" with his fourth finger. The rest of the phrase is merely a "re-entrant curve," that is to say, it is within the limits of his new position. To put it in other words, in playing this passage the first finger merely performs a two-octave skip from

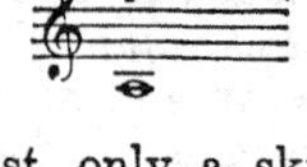

But this is, for the violinist, only a skip from the 1st to the 3rd position, and is in practice no more difficult for the left hand than the skip from

when played, as it can be, in the same two positions, 1st and 3rd. Looked at pianistically, the melodic skip in the above example is wide and difficult. Looked at from the fiddle-player's point of view, it has no difficulty at all. To the pianist such a melodic skip would still be great, if we shifted the first note up a minor third to C. To the violinist, this alteration would obviate any left-hand skip at all. The whole passage would then be in one position—the 3rd—and the difference between the 1st and 2nd notes would be merely a difference of elevation in the bow-arm. All skips, in fact, are to the pianist *skips of notes*; to the violinist they are *skips of position*.

But now alter the last two notes of this passage as follows:

The actual width of the skip between the first two notes remains unaltered, and, to the pianist, the only difference is that he now has to strike the top D with his thumb. To the violinist, however, the skip is now quite different, for the notes which follow are no longer part of a "re-entrant curve" within the limits of the 3rd position. If he were *now* to take the "top D" with his fourth finger, while his first finger rested on the A below in the 3rd position, he would immediately have to slide his little finger forward in order to get the "top G." In fact, he would be in the wrong position for playing the phrase. What he actually has to do is to play the last three notes in their correct position—the sixth.[1] This involves his fixing the "high D" with his first finger, and then playing the last two notes without change of position. The difference then between the two examples given above is that the latter involves a position-skip more than twice the size of the one necessary for the former.

The student must understand that the second of the two passages printed above is not given as an example of excessive difficulty.[2] It is easy to a good violinist, though not so completely easy as the first passage.

The two examples are given only to enforce the lesson that, when the student is considering the possible difficulties of wide skips, it is

[1] The notes could also be taken in the 5th position. In this case the little finger would take the top G as an "extension" in that position. As a matter of theory, the last three notes could also be played in the 1st position as harmonics. (See page 332); but no player would actually do this, unless so directed by a special indication in the part.

[2] In his Primer on "*Instrumentation*," Prout gives a passage containing two wide skips. He states that the performance of the whole passage would involve such a "sudden change in the position of the player's hand, that its correct intonation in the orchestra would be almost impossible." The first of these two skips

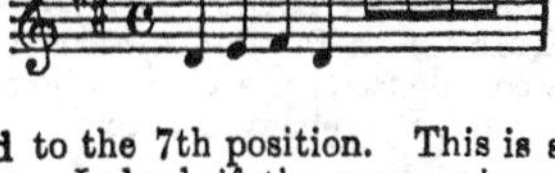

involves a shift from the 3rd to the 7th position. This is something of a difficulty, but by no means an impossibility. Indeed, if the passage is supposed to be in quick time,

only the difficulties *of position*, not *of notes*, that he need take into account. It may also be added that the construction of string-passages based partly on the low (3rd or 4th string) register, and partly on the high (1st string) register, is an integral and well-understood feature of violin music. Here is a passage which, though it only "ducks down" to the *open* strings, fully recognizes this special capacity of the instrument. It was written in 1694.[1]

All the writers of the great Italian Violin School of the eighteenth century exhibit this tendency to treat the instrument in two registers at the same time. Bach made it part of his normal musical armament. Twenty examples might be quoted from the *Solo Violin Sonatas* alone. Here is one taken at random from the Fugue of the *3rd Sonata.*

EXAMPLE 205.

FUGA — Bach: *3rd Violin Sonata.*

A similar and perhaps better example of a tune founded on this method may be seen in the familiar subject in his *Double Violin Concerto*:

EXAMPLE 206.

Bach. *Concerto for two Violins.*

Vivace.

the difficulty of getting the bow neatly across the strings is greater than that of dropping the first finger on to the high E in order to take the fifth note with the second finger. The second of his skips

is actually no skip at all on the Violin. It can all be played in the 3rd position with an "extension" for the note E, and even for the bow-arm it only involves a skip of one string. It may be said with confidence that a player who could not perform the passage at sight would not long remain in a Symphony Orchestra.

[1] From J. J. Walter's *Hortulus Chelicus.*

Beethoven, nearer to the days of the contrapuntal school, and therefore less likely to adopt its method, makes less use of the device. Still, some few examples of this sort are to be found in his writings:

EXAMPLE 207.

Naturally this type of music, founded as it is on a legitimate capability of the instrument, plays a part in all Violin Concertos, and its employment when lit by modern ideas opens out a wide vista for effective passage-construction.

A word must now be said with regard to the question of attacking unprepared high notes on the violin, that is to say, notes that are actually preceded by a rest and not by a low-pitched note. Taking into consideration the advances in modern orchestral-technique, one may assert that any stopped note may be taken unprepared up to about

It is, however, as well to give the player a moment's rest—a beat of *moderato* time will suffice—in which to fix his position with certainty. The following is an example of a high note attacked without preparation. It is quoted from the 1st fiddle part of Holbrooke's Opera *The Children of Don*:

EXAMPLE 208.

The student should now turn back to the list of notes available in the *Seven Positions* (page 306). If he will write out successively the sixteen notes comprised in any one of these seven bars he will see that he has got a diatonic scale of two octaves and a note.[1] This

[1] It is necessary to point out that, though in the example all the notes of the seven positions are given in C major, the question of diatonic sharpness or flatness does not occur. In any of these positions the violinist plays diatonically either in flat- or in sharp-keys with the same finger-technique. In the former case his hand merely rests

is important, because it will show him that the Violin-technique is essentially a diatonic-scale-technique.[1] It is only in a secondary sense either an arpeggio- or a chromatic-scale-technique. Passages founded on the latter systems are both possible and effective—in fact almost everything is possible on the violin—but

(1) The instrument is less well adapted than the Pianoforte or Harp for breaking up wide-spread chords into their component parts.

(2) Chromatic scales have to be played by means of a "fake" in the finger-technique. The result is therefore less sharply semitonic than in the case of the Wood-Wind, where a new key or hole gives individuality to each successive semitone.

In general it will be found that the most effective fiddle-writing is constructed of short scale passages, short arpeggios, combinations in which repeated notes appear, and little figures built round single notes. The last-named are often repeated, with or without joining-passages, on different harmony notes of the same or adjacent chords. Thus they may be regarded as having an arpeggio-basis. This type of passage is much more markedly in the character of the instrument than the ordinary type of Pianoforte-arpeggio.

For chromatic notes the player makes no alteration *of position.* He merely uses one finger twice over at his convenience, advancing it towards the bridge for a chromatically-raised note and drawing it back towards the nut for a chromatically-lowered note. When the chromatic notes have time to sound and are of actual harmonic importance the player distinguishes between the enharmonics, both in the fingering[2] and in the resultant pitch. The correct notes should therefore be written, especially in the case of the larger stringed-instruments such as Violas and Cellos, where the stopping is wider and the enharmonic differences more easily realized. Quick chromatic passing notes which have no harmonic value are generally best written in the simplest form possible. The inclusion of many double-flats in flat-keys and of double-sharps in sharp-keys serves no good purpose.

It is unnecessary to detail the chromatic-technique of the Violin. A single easy example will make the method quite plain:

in what is called a "flat degree of position" and in the latter in a "sharp degree of position." Thus the fingering of the scale of B♮ major is exactly the same as that of B♭ major except for the fact that only one open string—the E—is possible in the former case, while, in the latter, three open strings—the G, D, and A—are available.

[1] The String- and the Trombone-players are now practically the only orchestral musicians who continue to play "by ear" in the old pure scale which has been handed down through countless generations of vocalists and instrumentalists. Even they are being gradually compelled to succumb to the cast-iron tempered pianoforte scale.

[2] The semitone above the open string is, however, of necessity always played with the first finger. In the same way double-flat and double-sharp notes that are enharmonic to the open strings are often actually played on the open strings for convenience in difficult passage-work.

One may draw attention to the fact that, in quick slurred passages, there is necessarily a distinctly audible *portamento* between the notes which are stopped by the same finger. In practice it comes to this, that the pairs of notes are alternately "*portamentoed*" and "*unportamentoed*" except at those places where an open string occurs. The whole effect, however, to the ear has certainly a portamento-character which is not at all represented by the written notes. Richard Strauss has drawn attention to this chromatic indistinctness, which is integral to the Fiddle-technique. In cases where the resultant confusion is evidently not intended by the composer,[1] he prescribes a system of fingering in which each semitone is stopped by a different finger. A String passage from the *Sinfonia Domestica* would then be fingered as follows:

This somewhat exotic type of fingering would not be of great use except in passages mechanically and regularly built up from small phrases each of which was within the compass of three or four semitones. In passing one may mention that "bowed"[2] chromatic scales and passages are, within reasonable limits of speed, quite playable. When pitched on the two upper strings and well performed by a large mass of Violins in unison they have a hard, icy, glittering sound that is strikingly effective.

So far we have dealt only with single-stopped notes. It is possible, however, to play chords and parts of chords made up of two, three, and four notes. These notes, of course, have to be on different strings. In the case of two- and three-part chords the notes are practically sounded together. With three-part chords, however, a distinct pressure has to be put on the middle string of the three in order to bring it into one plane with the other two. Consequently the simultaneous attack of all three notes can only be made *f* or *mf*. In the *p* the chord has to be slightly arpeggioed. With four-part chords an arpeggio from the bottom string to the top has to be made both in the *p* and the *f*.[3]

[1] As opposed to such cases as the chromatic scales in the *Pastoral Symphony* of Beethoven.

[2] That is to say, in which alternate notes are played with alternate "up" and "down" bows. See below, pages 338-9.

[3] The bass notes of suspensions such as those in bars 4 and 9 of the opening *Adagio Sostenuto* of the *Kreutzer Sonata* cannot actually be sustained in the way that they are written. In practice they are just sounded and then rapidly quitted for the upper notes.

Not more than two notes at most can be *sustained* by the bow. It is usual, therefore, in cases where a full chord is taken *tenuto*, to write the lower notes in conventional crotchet-heads, and to indicate the exact length of the *tenuto* in the upper note or notes, thus:

EXAMPLE 209.

Bach. *3rd Violin Sonata.*

EXAMPLE 210.

Bach. *2nd Violin Sonata.*

It may be said in passing that the last chord of the first example given above shows an inversion of Bach's usual practice. He generally writes the underneath notes as separate parts, and adds or omits the correct rests at discretion. This may be seen in the last bar of the second example. Such a chord would nowadays always be written so

An extra part would only be made of the lower notes in those cases where either (A) the *tenuto* note has no tail to be joined to the lower notes, or (B) where confusion would result owing to the fact that the tenuto- or melody-note was already represented by a crotchet-head. In the latter case it of course would not do merely to write the lower notes in crotchet-heads, as they would not be properly distinguished from the melody-note at the top. It would be necessary to write the lower notes as a separate part in order to give them the requisite distinction. The latter necessity rarely arises in orchestral writing, though occasionally, with light arpeggio chords, it will happen that crotchet and quaver upper notes need to be detached in appearance from the lower notes. The following examples of (A) and (B) will arm the student against any of these dreadful emergencies:

EXAMPLE 211.

Beethoven. *Kreutzer Sonata.* [*1st Movement.*]

EXAMPLE 212.

Bach. *2nd Violin Sonata.* [*Sarabanda.*]

EXAMPLE 213.

Bach. *2nd Violin Sonata.* [*Sarabanda.*]

All Violin chord playing, whether of 2, 3, or 4 notes, is usually known as double-, triple-, and quadruple-stopping, even in those cases where unstopped-strings are included in the notes of the chord. Double-stopping is of greater general use in the orchestra than triple: triple than quadruple. The last-named is, except for very special purposes, a little heavy, and not available either in a great variety of chords or keys. With the preliminary observation that all the open strings can be used together or in adjacent pairs and threes, we may proceed to discuss the available

Double-Stops.[1]

These are divisible into

(1) Double-stops in which one note is open,
(2) Double-stops in which no note is open.

In the former case the range of possible chords is almost unlimited.

There is no necessity to keep the hand in one position in order to sound the open note. Any position can therefore be taken on the adjacent string to form the stopped note, and the student should notice that this stopped note can not only be any one of a chromatically ascending series on the upper string but also any one of a chromatically ascending series on the lower string. This sometimes results in the violinist playing on the lower string a stopped note higher in pitch than the open note of the upper string. The only limit to either of these series is set by the fact that, when the stopped note attains a certain degree of nearness to the bridge, the difference in bowing necessary to secure a good quality on the two strings—one very short and the other open in its full length—becomes so great that the resultant chord sounds dull and lifeless.

[1] The invention of Violin double-stopping is generally credited to Carlo Farina, a violinist who was born at Mantua towards the end of the sixteenth century. He was a kind of early Paganini, and made all sorts of experiments in Fiddle-technique. His *Capriccio Stravagante* was published at Dresden in 1627 while he was Court-Violinist in Saxony.

(1) Double-stops in which one note is open.[1]

The following are available for orchestral use:

Combinations of the open note

with any semitone on the 3rd-string from

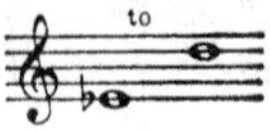

Combinations of the open note

with any semitone on the 4th-string from

and with any semitone on the 2nd-string from

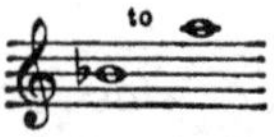

Combinations of the open note

with any semitone on the 3rd-string from

and with any semitone on the 1st-string from

[1] Combinations of purely open strings, whether in 2, 3, or 4 parts, are omitted in the following pages. They are, of course, all perfectly easy.

Note.—The unison combinations of a stopped and an open E, A, or D are in common use for purposes of increased force. They must always be written either with two notes or with two tails to a single note, so as to show clearly what is intended, thus

The two notes can, of course, be alternated with each other. This is generally done under a slur to produce a wavy tremulant effect, thus :

In this case the odd-numbered notes would be played stopped on the A string, while the even-numbered notes would be taken on the open E. The alternate use of an open and a stopped string for the same note is common in cases like the following

where distinction of part-writing is called for.

(2) Double-stops in which no note is open.

The following are all quite easy and playable:

(*A*) All major and minor sixths of which the lower note is any semitone from

(*B*) All major and minor thirds of which the lower note is any semitone from

The following are not so completely easy but are still quite playable:

(*C*) All perfect and augmented fourths of which the lower note is any semitone from

[1] The low G is not included in this list, as it occurs with its combinations under the previous heading, "*Double-stops in which one note is open.*" This extension of the list must be kept in mind throughout. For instance, in (*B*) (major and minor thirds), besides the series given above, the major third on low B♭ containing the open note D♮ is also available.

(*D*) All perfect, augmented, and diminished fifths of which the lower note is any semitone from

All perfect fifths are difficult. They have, of course, to be stopped with one finger directly across the strings, and the slightest sharpness or flatness of either of the strings precludes correct intonation.

(*E*) All octaves of which the lower note is any semitone from

The intonation of octaves is not so difficult as that of fifths. They are stopped with two fingers, the 1st and 4th; some adjustment can therefore be made if the strings are not quite in tune. [The 12 **very** easy **octaves** which can be played in any place or at any time are those whose lower notes are as follows:

Of course successions of octaves such as those that occur in Concertos are quite out of the question unless they form part of the above short series.]

(*F*) The only major seconds worth considering for orchestral purposes are those whose lower notes are any one of the following:

[Major seconds on

can of course be played with either one note open or both stopped. In the former case the upper note is played in the 3rd position on the lower string: in the latter case both notes are played in the 1st position.]

(*G*) The only minor seconds worth considering are those whose lower notes are any one of the following:

[The remark made above with regard to the performance of major seconds on D, A, and E applies also to the minor seconds on these notes.

Furthermore, the student should observe that, besides the above six minor seconds, there are only three others available, viz. those on

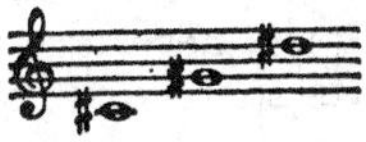

These are omitted from the first list because they are played with the upper note open. The complete list of all the available minor seconds is therefore as follows:

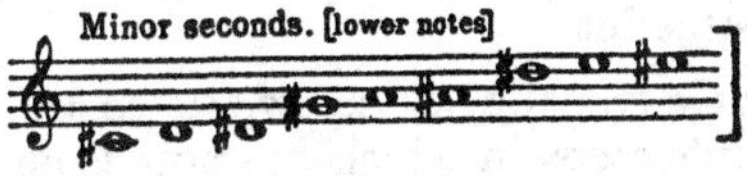

The above is a fairly complete list of all the double-stops which the student may write without fear of the consequences. Quick successions of double-stops are always to be avoided. One may, however, make an exception in favour of such short successions of sixths, of thirds, or of mixed sixths and thirds as can be played without moving the hand in either the 1st or the 3rd position. If these two positions are mixed it is as well to confine the passage to the same two strings throughout. The student will find this a very safe rule, and, if he conforms to it, he need not hesitate to write thirds and sixths in his Violin-parts. Into such passages he can interpolate any simple double-stops, especially double-stops in which one note is open, provided they do not require violent changes of position. On this point there is rarely any difficulty, for, as the student will doubtless have observed, a good many double-stops can be played in more than one way. The player chooses the easiest one.

It is as well to confine successions of double-stops as far as possible to pairs of adjacent strings, which have one string in common. If the character of the music forbids this, the double-stops should not be written in quicker notes than *moderato* crotchets.

Everything that was said above with regard to the position-technique of the Fiddle applies equally to wide skips from low to high double-stops. Little difficulty, however, will be encountered on this score, as double-stops above the 3rd position are practically unknown in the orchestra. The student must use his judgment in all these matters. Even so trustworthy a guide as Gevaert cites the following

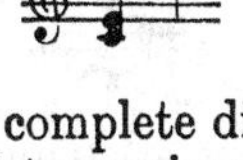

as involving "a sudden and complete displacing of the hand," and as being "extremely difficult, not to say impossible." As a matter of fact, it involves no movement of the hand at all, only of the fingers. It is all in the 1st position, and a child could play it.

In this connection it may be mentioned that, as far as the bow-arm is concerned, it is easier to get over from a double-stop on the two lower strings to a double-stop on the two upper strings, or *vice versa*, than to get over from a single bottom-string note to a single top-string note, or *vice versa.* In the latter case the bow is compelled to detach the first note in order to obtain the necessary moment-of-silence in which to pass over the intermediate strings: in the former case it pivots on these intermediate strings, and, whether a new stroke of the bow is taken or not, can engage the second chord immediately.

Triple Stops.

These are divisible into

(1) Triple-stops in which two notes are open,
(2) Triple-stops in which one note is open,
(3) Triple-stops in which no note is open.

(1) Triple-stops in which two notes are open.

The following are available:
Combinations of the two open notes

with any semitone on the second string from

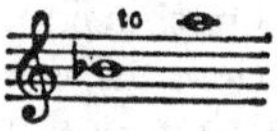

Combinations of the two open notes

with any semitone on the 1st string from

and with any semitone on the 4th string up to

Combinations of the two open strings

[1] As already mentioned, combinations of purely open strings do not occur in this list.

with any semitone on the 3rd string up to

(2) Triple-stops in which one note is open.

Combinations of the open note

with any perfect or augmented fifth, and with any sixth, seventh, or octave of which the lower note is any one of the following:

Combinations of the open note

with any perfect or augmented fifth, and with any sixth, seventh, or octave of which the lower note is any one of the following:

In combinations of the open note

the two *stopped notes* of the chord are on the 3rd and 4th strings. The only chords which have any orchestral value are the following:

In combinations of the open note

the two *stopped notes* of the chord are on the 2nd and 3rd strings The only chords which have any orchestral value are the following:

(3) Triple-stops in which no note is open.

Practically only major and minor triads and a few augmented fifths are available. They must be arranged either (1) with the fifth at the top and the sixth at the bottom, or (2) with the sixth at the top and the fifth at the bottom, or (3) with a sixth both at the top and the bottom. For examples the student should consult the general lists of orchestral chords given below.[1]

Quadruple-Stops.

Quadruple-stops in which three notes are open are almost useless. The combination of the three lower open strings practically ties the part down to the tonic and dominant of the keys of G major and minor. If required these three open strings could be written in conjunction with such notes as

The combination of the three open top strings with a stopped note on the lowest string is scarcely worth considering, though the low A might be arpeggioed with them. The other Quadruple-stops are divisible into

(1) Quadruple-stops in which two notes are open,
(2) Quadruple-stops in which one note is open,
(3) Quadruple stops in which no note is open.

(1) Quadruple-stops in which two notes are open.

The following are available:
Combinations of the two open notes

with any simple sixths and fifths on the two top strings, such as

[1] Pages 324-6.

but the topmost of the four notes should not be allowed to rise above

Notice that combinations of the two open top strings with two stopped notes on the bottom strings are little used. The following may be of occasional service in the orchestra:

(2) Quadruple-stops in which one note is open.

Practically only a few major and minor triads and augmented fifths are available, all built on one or other of these two patterns,

but the topmost of the four notes should not be allowed to rise above

(See the lists of chords given below.)

(3) Quadruple-stops in which no note is open.

Of these chords few are possible and still fewer advisable. They are practically confined to this formula:

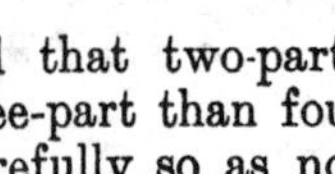

with the same restriction upwards as was imposed in the case of the other quadruple-stops.

We have already said that two-part chords are better on the Violin than three-part, three-part than four-part. Three-part chords, however, when written carefully so as not to be difficult and when played with vigour by a large body of violinists, are slashingly effective. In setting-out these chords, especially for *tutti* Strings, the composer who has an eye for orchestral effect will throw overboard all ideas of writing complete harmonic chords for each instrument. Good keys near C, G, and D (all major or minor), and easy fingering, are the two necessities.

The student will now wish to see the above general rules embodied in the more concrete form of the most serviceable chords for orchestral use. It would be the easiest thing in the world to compile a complete list of all the chords playable on the Violin at a pinch, or rather at several pinches. Such a list would include nearly 1500 different chords. A very large number of them, however, are absolutely useless in the orchestra. They involve such cranky fingerings[1] that a wise composer would not write them even in a Fiddle Concerto.

The following list contains practically every chord that can be wanted for orchestral composition. It is confined to three-part and four-part chords for the reason that almost all simple two-part chords are playable on the violin. The student may easily manufacture them for himself from the general rules given above. In his choice of three-part and four-part chords the composer is, of course, restricted by the particular pitch at which he wishes to take them. Otherwise he should be guided by the advice (1) that three-part chords are generally preferable to four-part, and (2) that open strings in the middle of a chord are usually to be avoided. Very few such chords are printed below.

Chords of the Tonic and of the Dominant Seventh.

The following groups of chords are arranged under their key-signatures, thus: The first and second bars give respectively three-part and four-part chords of the dominant seventh, then, after the double bar, the third and fourth bars give respectively three-part and four-part chords of the Tonic. Almost all the tonic chords are available in both the major and minor modes. In those few cases where a chord is only available in one mode an accidental is placed before the chord to show the only form in which it can be used. The student must bear this in mind, as, in this case, the accidental is used with a meaning slightly out of the ordinary. Of course, whenever an accidental is used, it refers only to the one note before which it is placed. It does not affect that note in succeeding chords. Thus the 22nd and 24th chords in the following list are available only in the major mode, but the 23rd and 26th are available in both modes.

[1] For the "normal spread" of the fingers in String-chord-playing the student should see page 422. The remarks there apply just as much to the Violin and Viola as to the Cello.

Chords of the "Diminished Seventh."

In the following chords and parts-of-chords of the diminished seventh the easiest notation is adopted. Any enharmonic variations of these chords can, of course, be used.

Chords of the Major and Minor Ninth.

The following are the only chords and parts-of-chords of the major and minor ninth that are likely to be of any practical use in the orchestra.

Chords of the Augmented Fifth.

These are scarcely worth writing in four parts. Confined to three parts they should be restricted within these limits:

and should all be written on this simple model.

Any of the chords given above may be broken up into arpeggios. In the simpler keys a fair number of spread chords are available in comparatively easy stoppings, and this type of formula is often used for making up String-backgrounds. Such passages when formed of groups of stringed-instruments are not to be looked at too closely from the part-writing point of view. If this is done the result is often to write an effective and simple arpeggio for the 1st Violins and awkward arpeggios for the 2nd Violins and Violas. At most the outside notes of the arpeggios need be considered, and even that is often unnecessary. In the following passage from Act I. Scene 3 of *Die Walküre*

EXAMPLE 214.

Mässig schnell. Wagner. *Die Walküre.*

the object is obviously to secure the complete three-part chord at each end of the arpeggio. It would, however, make practically no difference to the effect, and would be more in the Violin-way of writing if the 2nd Violin passages were written to be played in the 3rd position, so:

and the Viola passages, so:

It is a fair general rule that the String technique should be the first

[1] This example is much compressed. The two Harp-parts are omitted as well as the entry of the Bass Trumpet on the last crotchet of Bar 2. All the Wood-Wind and Brass notes are written *as they sound.* In the original score the 4 Horns are in E, 1st and 2nd Trumpets are in E, 3rd Trumpet in C, Bass Trumpet in D.

consideration in such cases. In the example just given the Brass *ff* covers up everything, and it is therefore easy to arrange the arpeggios with a single eye to the String technique. On the other hand, if, in *p* passages, the harmonic basis of the music is only to be apprehended from the outline of the arpeggios, the Strings may reasonably be asked to bate something of their technical demands.

Before leaving the subject of chords the student's attention may be drawn to an important point. Quick successions of chords are made no easier on the Violin by being broken up. In order to make a judgment as to their practicability they must be considered as unbroken. So far as the Fiddle-player's left hand goes the following two passages from Mendelssohn's *Violin Concerto*

EXAMPLE 215.

EXAMPLE 216.

are simply

and

Natural Harmonics.

Hitherto we have only dealt with that series of stopped notes which is produced by pressing the string tightly against the fingerboard. Two other series of notes, however, exist. Of these the first is the Series of Natural Harmonics.[1] They are obtained by lightly touching

[1] These Harmonics were probably known even to the earliest string-players. Their use, however, as a regular part of the Violin technique was first studied by J. J. C. de Mondonville in his book of Violin Sonatas with Basso-continuo, called *Les Sons Harmoniques*, etc. This work was published at Paris in the first half of the eighteenth century. Leopold Mozart characterizes harmonic-playing as trick work only fit for mummers at Carnival time. It appears to have been first used in the orchestra by Philidor in his Opera *Tom Jones* (1765).

the string at any one of those nodes where it naturally breaks up into subsidiary vibrations. The action of the finger destroys the vibration of the complete string-length and compels the string to vibrate only in segments.[1]

The actual physical process may be illustrated by an example. If we touch the open string E half-way between the nut and the bridge the note E an octave above the pitch of the open string is sounded. The reason is that by touching the string midway we prevent it vibrating as a whole. The principal vibrating lengths are now the two halves of the string, and these, of course, each sound an octave higher than the original string-length. Theoretically it is of no consequence whether we draw the bow on the nut-side or on the bridge-side of the finger.

The intonation of the Natural Harmonics depends solely on the correct tuning of the open string, and is therefore outside the violinist's control at the moment of playing.

All the Natural Harmonics are of a light "flutey"[2] quality, very different from that of the stopped notes. It follows that, except in quick passage-work where they sometimes materially facilitate the execution, they should never be used by the player unless they are actually indicated in the part. Occasionally such notes can be introduced both into quiet *legato* melodies and into vigorous passages, but this needs some judgment.[3] They are more often used in groups of all the upper Strings to produce special ethereal effects. Double-,[4] triple- and quadruple-stopping are all quite out of the question in writing Harmonics.

On each string of the Violin, five Natural Harmonics can be produced. These give a portion of the ascending Harmonic Series[5] with which the student is already familiar. He will have no difficulty in remembering the notes of this Series, as they give a regularly diminishing set of intervals from the open string upwards,—an octave, a perfect fifth, a perfect fourth, a major third, a minor third.

In the following list of Natural Harmonics the Open String is represented by a semibreve and marked 1, while the 5 Harmonics are represented by crotchets and marked 2, 3, 4, 5, 6, respectively. The numbers have, of course, nothing to do with the fingering.

[1] See above, page 305.

[2] They are commonly known on the Continent as "Flageolet notes," and their use is often prescribed by the words *flautato* or *flautando*.

[3] See Ex. 18 (Solo Viola-part) and Ex. 247 (last bar of Viola-part).

[4] See below, page 331, for the only available chords.

[5] See page 73.

In each of these four groups of Natural Harmonics,

No. 2 is obtained by lightly touching the string half-way between the nut and the bridge at the place where the ordinary stopping would produce the same note.

No. 3 can be obtained in two different ways.: (A) By lightly touching the string $\frac{1}{3}$ of its length from the nut and $\frac{2}{3}$ of its length from the bridge at the place where the ordinary stopping would produce the perfect fifth above the open string, (B) by lightly touching the string $\frac{2}{3}$ of its length from the nut and $\frac{1}{3}$ of its length from the bridge at the place where the ordinary stopping would produce the same note.

No. 4 can be obtained in two different ways: (A) By lightly touching the string $\frac{1}{4}$ of its length from the nut and $\frac{3}{4}$ of its length from the bridge at the place where the ordinary stopping would produce the perfect fourth above the open string, (B) by lightly touching the string $\frac{3}{4}$ of its length from the nut and $\frac{1}{4}$ of its length from the bridge at the place where the ordinary stopping would produce the same note.

No. 5[1] can be obtained in four different ways: (A) By lightly touching the string $\frac{1}{5}$ of its length from the nut and $\frac{4}{5}$ of its length from the bridge at the place where the ordinary stopping would produce the major third above the open string, (B) by lightly touching the string $\frac{2}{5}$ of its length from the nut and $\frac{3}{5}$ of its length from the bridge at the place where the ordinary stopping would produce the major sixth above the open string, (C) by lightly touching the string $\frac{3}{5}$ of its length from the nut and $\frac{2}{5}$ of its length from the bridge at the place where the ordinary stopping would produce the major tenth above the open string, (D) by lightly touching the string $\frac{4}{5}$ of its length from the nut and $\frac{1}{5}$ of its length from the bridge at the place where the ordinary stopping would produce the same note. [Of these four ways only Nos. 1 and 2 are actually employed in the orchestra.]

No. 6 can be obtained in two different ways: (A) By lightly touching the string $\frac{1}{6}$ of its length from the nut and $\frac{5}{6}$ of its length from the bridge at the place where the ordinary stopping would produce the minor third above the open string, (B) by lightly touching the string $\frac{5}{6}$ of its length from the nut and $\frac{1}{6}$ of its length from the bridge at the place where the ordinary stopping would produce the same note. [This Harmonic, however produced, is of no practical use.]

The student should notice that, in each of the groups of Harmonics on the three lower strings, Nos. 2 and 6 are reduplicated in the series on the next higher string. Theoretically it is necessary to indicate in the part how the harmonic is to be taken. This is done by using the Italian words "Sul II," "Sul III," etc., that is to say, "Played on the 2nd string," "Played on the 3rd string," and so on. However, this sort of direction, unless given by a skilled violinist, is not of great use. So much depends upon the technique of any given passage, and upon

[1] This Harmonic is, on all stringed-instruments, distinctly out of tune with the similar note in the tempered scale. The note is sharp, about $\frac{1}{10}$ of a tone above the tempered note.

the position in which the player's hand happens to be lying. As a rule, then, the choice of method in performing those harmonics which are playable in more than one way may be left to the violinist's discretion.

In practice, as we have already said, Harmonic No. 6 is not used at all. It can be produced more easily and with a better tone as No. 4 in the series on the next higher string. On the top (E) string practically only Nos. 2, 3, and 4 are used. These are all excellent notes.

The Notation of the Natural Harmonics is simplicity itself. A little round "o" is placed above each note that is to be taken as a Harmonic. Here is an example of the high Violin-Harmonics. It forms the connecting link between the *Sanctus* and the *Benedictus* in Stanford's *Requiem*. The Violins are *divisi* for the first five bars, and then unison for the rest of the passage.

EXAMPLE 217.

A charming little example has already been quoted of a single harmonic note held *ppp* above a melody for Flute and Oboe in unison (see Ex. 104), and other instances have been given in the short quotation from Strauss's *Sinfonia Domestica* (Ex. 18). Further examples can be found under the headings "Viola," "Cello," and "Double-Bass."

Chords in Natural Harmonics are only possible in two parts, and then only when both notes can be taken as No. 2 on adjacent strings. In other words, they are limited to these three

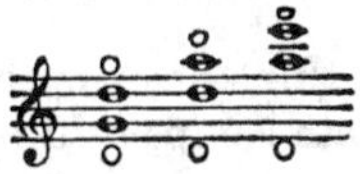

However, unless the number of instrumentalists is very small, it is better even in these cases to write the chords *divisi*.

Gevaert has pointed out that when a Harmonic cannot be made to sound on the Violin this is usually due to a fault, not in the string, but in the bow. The simple reason is that "a string set in vibration at any given point cannot sound any harmonic for which the said point is a node." In other words, the bow is "standing in its own light," and if it be shifted a trifle nearer either to the bridge or to the nut the desired harmonic will "come out."

Artificial Harmonics.

If the student will now turn back and read the description of the two different ways in which No. 4 can be obtained he will see that, by the first method, the string is lightly touched at the place where the ordinary stopping would produce the *perfect fourth* above the open string. The harmonic obtained by this method sounds two octaves above the open string. It is, however, obvious that when the 1st and 4th fingers are laid upon the fingerboard in any position they are normally just a *perfect fourth* apart. It is, therefore, always possible to use the 1st finger as a sort of moveable nut; to stop the string hard with this finger and lightly to touch the perfect fourth above it with the outstretched 4th finger. The resulting note will, of course, be two octaves above the actual note which the first finger is stopping. This 1st finger, however, can stop any note within reason in the lower positions, and can be slid about from position to position while the 4th finger is all the time lightly touching the perfect fourth above. The consequence will be that, whatever series of notes the 1st finger is stopping will be reproduced *to the ear* two octaves higher.

These notes are known as *Artificial Harmonics.*

They begin on the lowest semitone A♭ (G♯) which can be stopped by the 1st finger on the 4th string. This produces the *sound*

Upwards they may be continued chromatically for about two octaves and a semitone.

Now the whole compass of the violin in *Natural* Harmonics is

Therefore, if we add to this the compass in *Artificial* Harmonics we get the following complete compass in both Natural and Artificial Harmonics:

The first three notes of this complete Harmonic-Compass can only be played in Natural Harmonics. The rest can all be played in Artificial Harmonics, while those notes which are marked with a + can be taken both ways.

The notation of Artificial Harmonics presents no difficulty. The passage is simply written out in notes of the desired time-value two octaves lower than the required sound. This gives the player the correct stopping for his 1st finger. To each note is then added a conventional diamond-shaped note a perfect fourth above the pitch of the stopped note. This gives the player the "light stopping" for his 4th finger. If one wishes the following phrase played in Artificial Harmonics:

one writes:

It may be as well to mention that, if in writing a series of artificial harmonics one needs to use Natural Harmonic No. 4, that is to say, to substitute the actual nut for the 1st finger, it is usual to take a certain licence and write the note as an Artificial Harmonic. This applies to all four strings. Thus, in the example just given, no player in his senses would dream of taking the last note by jumping over to the G string and stopping the note D with his 1st finger and the note G lightly with his 4th. The result would be doubtful. In place of that he simply takes up the 1st finger and remains in position on the D string, using the nut in place of his 1st finger and lightly stopping the perfect fourth above with his 3rd finger.

There is no need, when using artificial harmonics, to write the actual sounds produced. This old-fashioned method involves the composer in the labour of writing three notes for every single sound required. Conductors and players who do not know the meaning and effect of these little diamond-shaped notes are now extinct.

Occasionally, however, composers write out a complete passage at its actual sounding-pitch and mark the part "to be played in harmonics," or simply "harmonics." This is a lazy way which leads to much conversation at rehearsals, and generally results in the separate players doing what the composer should have done in the first instance—writing out the passage in its correct Harmonic Notation. Single Artificial Harmonics can never be interpolated into quick passages. Their accurate stopping needs a little time and caution. In *moderato* time, however, such single notes might possibly be used for special effects provided they did not necessitate a skip of position. This happy conjunction of circumstances, however, is unlikely to occur, as their use naturally involves an upward skip of two octaves.

On the other hand, single notes in Natural Harmonics can often be interpolated with happy effect into passage-writing. Opportunities for this sort of thing occur more frequently at the ends of phrases. The Harmonics which sound the octave, the double-octave, and the twelfth above the open string, can be used almost anywhere.

It may be necessary to add that, in writing complete Harmonic-chords for the Strings, no effort need be made to keep the notes rigidly to one sort of Harmonic, natural or artificial. The two kinds are so nearly alike to the ear that they may be indiscriminately mixed. It is, however, as well (1) so to arrange the parts that there may be as many Natural Harmonics as possible. This steadies the intonation and gives greater firmness and clearness to the chords. (2) To avoid as far as possible any but the simplest position-skips in writing a series of Artificial Harmonics.

Examples of String-Harmonics are so common in modern orchestral composition that it is scarcely necessary to quote any of them. As an illustration of their use for extending the "spread" of the String-parts the student may refer to the *tenuto* "A" in seven octaves at the opening of Mahler's *First Symphony.* This passage is laid out for Violins and 1st and 2nd Violas, and for Cellos and Basses each in three parts.

As an illustration of the use of the Artificial Harmonics for continuing a subject upwards beyond the range of any other orchestral instruments no happier example could be quoted than the extreme end of the *Scherzo* in Glazounow's *Fourth Symphony.* The quotation below is much compressed, but nothing is omitted. The rising fragment of melody is confined to one line. In the lowest octave it is played by the Violas, then in the next octave by four desks of Violins, then in the highest octave by two desks of Violins playing in Artificial Harmonics. At the same time the soft String-chords are carried upwards by the omission first of the Basses and then of the Cellos. A rippling quaver-figure on the Clarinets and the Flute follows the upward trend of the music. Finally there is a tiny *piano* chord for Wood-Wind alone, followed by a String-*pizzicato.* Apart altogether from its technical interest this passage is well worth quoting as a most charming example of those little roguish Scherzo-endings which are so delightful when scored with the light but certain "touch" of a master.[1]

EXAMPLE 218.

[1] For other examples of Harmonics, see Exs. 18, 104, 235, 247.

Having dealt with the left-hand technique of the Violin we must now turn to its complement, the bow-arm technique. It is not necessary to describe in detail the evolution of the modern bow, but one may mention that the Violin technique has always originated from and been dependent on the shape of the bow, not of the Violin. Furthermore, the bow, as we have it now, was perfected long after the Violin, and its evolution, though occupying a great space in length of years, has been simple.

The original bow of the mediæval Fiddle consisted of a hank of horse-hair uniting the ends of a more or less flexible wooden stick. This stick was arched *upwards* from the horse-hair, and, if we are to trust the representations that have come down to us, the arching was often so great that its height nearly equalled the length of the horse-hair.

The first long stage in the evolution of the bow consisted merely of a series of attempts to lower this arch and to bring the horse-hair more into line with the bow. Other minor improvements were, of course, introduced from time to time, but if we look at the pictures of even so recent a work as Leopold Mozart's *Versuch einer gründlichen Violinschule* we cannot fail to see that the violinist is playing with what might be described to-day as a long, light, old-fashioned Double-Bass bow. From the nut to within ⅓ of the point of the bow the stick and the hair run nearly parallel. Then, in the upper ⅓ of the bow the stick gradually and awkwardly curves down till it reaches the place where the hair is attached.

This style of bow was undoubtedly a vast artistic improvement on the mediæval type, whose shape reminds us only of a boy's bird-trap ready set. Still, if any of the older orchestral players were armed with this weapon at the celebrated rehearsal when Schubert's *C major Symphony* was condemned as impossible, we must offer them our respectful sympathy.

During the second stage of its history the arch of the bow was gradually turned round the other way, so that its natural curve was inwards towards the hair and not outwards away from the hair. With this type of bow almost anything is possible on the Violin. It has been adapted to the use of all the stringed-instruments. Even the Basses have during the past twenty years or so acknowledged its undoubtedly greater technical powers.

The violin-bow as perfected by Tourte is a shade over 29 inches long. The stick is made of a very light but highly elastic wood called *Pernambuco.* At the upper end or "point" the original block from which the stick has been cut is brought round in a characteristic curve to receive the horse-hair. At the lower- or "nut"-end the hair is firmly fixed in a holder which is not itself part of the bow-stick. Underneath this holder is a ring through which a screw-thread is cut. When the holder is in position this ring lies in a slot cut out of the solid bow-stick. At the extreme lower end of the stick a long screw passes for an inch or so through a hole bored lengthwise in the bow-stick. On its way this screw passes through the ring. The two screws are thus engaged, and the player, by turning the ornamental head of the long screw can draw back the holder and so tighten the hair. The curve of the bow-stick is inwards towards the hair, and its nearest approach to the hair should be exactly midway between the nut and the point. The hair itself is simply a bundle made up of between 100 and 150 hairs taken from the tails of white horses. Before use the hair is rubbed on a specially prepared fine rosin[1] to give it a grip on the strings.

The strings are set in vibration by the bow at a point between the bridge and the end of the fingerboard. This point, however, is varied slightly according to the quality of the tone required. In the centre the tone is clearest and most supple. As the bow approaches nearer to the bridge the difficulty of setting the strings in motion appreciably increases, with a corresponding marked hardness in the quality. Finally, when it is drawn close up to the bridge, a painfully glassy and unpleasant quality is produced. This special tone-colour is occasionally demanded by composers, and is indicated in the score by the Italian words *sul ponticello* (on the bridge), or simply *ponticello.*[2] If, on the other hand, a very light feathery quality is needed, the bow is drawn somewhat nearer to or actually above the fingerboard. This

[1] Called also Colophonium (Fr. *Colophane*; It. *Colofonia*).

[2] See below, pages 355-6.

effect, though delightful, is less often prescribed in orchestral works. It is, as a rule, left to the judgment of the conductor. The indication in the score generally takes the form of the French or Italian words for "on the fingerboard," viz. *sur la touche,* or *sul tasto.* The student may find an example of its employment in the *pp* repeated demisemiquavers for 2nd Violins and Violas at bar 14 in Act I. of Debussy's *Pelléas et Mélisande.*

The top of the bridge is convex but not regular in its slope. On the E-side it is cut down very low, and rises to its highest point at the D-string. Midway between these two is the A-string. Thus the three strings, E, A, D, all lie in a slope upwards. From the D the bridge slopes slightly down again, but it is not cut to so low a level as that of the E-string side. About ⅜ down this slope the G-string lies almost on a level with the A. This peculiar shape makes for ease in the technique. The bow is always strictly in one of four planes, according as the player wishes to set the E, the A, the D, or the G string in vibration. Each of these four planes from the E-plane to the G-plane is reached by means of a simple upward movement of the right elbow. Hence the name "elevations," by which they are known. When the correct elevation has been taken by the back-arm and elbow, the wrist—the real controlling force in the bow-arm technique—remains unaltered relatively to the bow.[1]

The method of attacking the strings with the bow is interesting, because it explains in great part the peculiarly soft and swishing effect so characteristic of the string tone. The technique is as follows: The bow is first turned so that, while its whole length remains at right angles to the strings, the stick is slightly nearer than the hair to the player's *left* hand. Only a portion of the hair engages the string at the first moment of attack. The rest of the hair is gradually brought into play with a soft "cleaving" action. During the progress of the bow-stroke the string is kept vibrating with greater or less amplitude according as (1) the pressure of the fingers on the bow is increased or decreased, (2) the bow is moved more quickly or more slowly over the string. The "cleaving" method of attack soon becomes so completely automatic with violin-players that some of them forget its very existence. However, one has only to listen to the hard perpendicular "bite" with which a beginner attacks the string to become aware of its importance.

When the bow is turned, that is to say, when a stroke is to be made in the opposite direction, the pressure of the fingers on the bow-stick is relaxed. In other words, the bow is "lightened." At that instant the bow is turned and a second (reverse) stroke is begun in exactly the same manner as the first. It must be said that, though at the moment of lightening the bow the pressure is completely removed and no sound can therefore come from the instrument, this moment can be made by the most ordinary fiddler so minute in duration as to be inappreciable to the ear.

[1] In setting more than one string in vibration at the same time an elevation midway between those of the two strings is taken.

This is the true *bowed legato* of the Strings, the most perfect and satisfying method of instrumental tone-production in existence. In this point the strings are differentiated from all the other orchestral instruments. The Trombone-*sostenuto* alone partially reproduces this feature.

It is necessary for the student to grasp the importance of the above remarks. *A change of bow does not necessarily mean an absence of legato.* On the other hand, the amount of "lightening" *can* be extended in duration so that every note is isolated from its fellows. And this can be done not only at either end of the bow—at the "heel" or the "point"—before it is turned, but in the middle of the bow before resuming for a second stroke in the same direction. Furthermore, when the bow is being drawn from point to heel—"up-bow," as it is called—this stoppage may take place any number of times in reason. When drawn from heel to point—"down-bow," that is to say—these stoppages are less easily controlled by the player, and therefore less used by the composer.

Here we must mention a second method of attack, called the *sforzando.* This attack when performed—but not overperformed—by large bodies of Strings is highly effective. The technique is as follows: At the commencement of the stroke the player overpresses the bow for an instant, and in doing so first sets the string in motion and then immediately damps out or "spoils" the musical vibrations. This gives the initial "bite" to the note, and the unmusical sound thus produced lasts only for about $\frac{1}{10}$ of a second or less. Immediately afterwards the bow is made to travel on with the normal "cleaving" motion described above. This gives the actual musical sound required. The *sforzando* is indicated in the score either by the letters *sf* or *sfz*, or by a little accent mark thus >. It is equally effective in the *p* and the *f*, and violin-players are quite accustomed to graduate the "bite" on the note according to the dynamic requirements of the music. The following example of the *pp sforzando* is from the *fugato* in Weber's *Euryanthe Overture.* The whole passage is played at a dead *pianissimo,* the four minims only just bitten into prominence.[1]

EXAMPLE 219.

Before proceeding to describe the various *coups d'archet* which are, so to speak, standardized all over Europe, it may be as well to say that, with the exception of the *sforzando,* they are all performed with the same initial attack, even when the strokes are so minute in point of time as to appear to be merely a dancing of the bow on the strings They differ among themselves only

(1) In the length, force, and pace of bow allotted to each note,

[1] For other *sforzando* see Exs. 74, 99, 112, 137, 156, 230, 241, 245, 248, 278.

(2) In the length of the stoppages between consecutive notes taken either with the same bow-stroke or with alternate bow-strokes,

(3) In the pressure exerted on the bow by the fingers of the right hand during any part of the bow-stroke,

(4) In the *part* of the bow—upper or lower half, upper, middle, or lower third—used for the stroke.

Notation. The signs ⊓ and V are used to indicate "down bow" and "up-bow" respectively. The ⊓ and V are called in French *Tiré* and *Poussé*; in German, *Herabstrich* (or *Herunterstrich*) and *Aufstrich*.

The long curved line drawn over extended phrases as an indication that their component notes are conceived as parts of a whole has no existence in violin music.

Neighbouring notes, if unconnected by a slur, are played with alternate "down" and "up" bows. Successions of these unslurred notes are always spoken of simply as being "bowed." In such passages the length of stoppage between the ⊓ and the V is determined by the character of the music. As was explained above, it varies from an inappreciable fraction of time to a fraction which is perceptible as a distinct gap between each pair of notes. The "silence" in the latter case is, of course, robbed from the end, not from the beginning of the note.

The various bow-strokes or *coups d'archet*[1] are generally known in England by their French names. The principal of these are:

(1) The **Détaché**[2] (sometimes called the *Grand Détaché*). This is a "long bow" stroke. The bow is drawn rapidly and with considerable force through as great a part of its length as the duration of the written notes will allow. In this style of bowing, despite its name, the bow is kept well on the string for as long as possible. The individual notes receive only a slight articulation from the swift turning of the bow. Its use is practically confined to *f* and *mf* "bowed" passages needing a fair amount of vigour. Anything much quicker than *allegro* quavers cannot well be played with the true *détaché*. No special indication beyond the general character of the music is in general use for this style of bowing.[3] If, however, these long-bows are required with the addition of a distinct isolation of each note it is usual to write simple dots (unslurred) over the passage, thus:

EXAMPLE 220.

Beethoven. *Choral Symphony.*

In English orchestras the words *long bows* are sometimes written as a direction for *Détaché* bowing. This seems a sensible plan worthy of general adoption.

[1] German, *Bogenstrich*. [2] *Sciolto* in Italian.

[3] Spohr, in his *Violin School*, says "this bowing is at all times understood when no marks for bowing are given."

(The French also distinguish a **Détaché moyen** and a **Petit Détaché**, both used in the more rapid tempos. Both of these are played with the same smooth and even stroke, but the former is restricted to the upper $\frac{1}{3}$ and the latter to the point.)

If the utmost degree of detachment is required for the successive notes of a *f* phrase, these can all be played ⊓. In this case the player lifts the bow bodily from the strings after each stroke and replaces it at the heel. It is not wise to continue this style of bowing for more than about half a dozen notes, and these must not be too rapid. The student must remember that the player has to make a silent up-bow stroke in the air between each pair of down-bows, and this requires a distinct interval of time. The effect, especially on the bottom string, is ferocious in the extreme. In the following passage from Tschaikowsky's *Fifth Symphony* the first four String-chords come out admirably. If, however, the quavers in bar 2 are all played ⊓, as indeed they are marked in some of the parts, the players (preoccupied with the necessity of making a series of silent up-bow strokes for which no time is allowed) can only perform the passage by means of a series of perpendicular and ineffective scratches on the strings. The passage, from which the Wood-Wind and Drums have been omitted, is as follows:

EXAMPLE 221.

The student will notice that there is an obvious omission of a ⊓ from the second note of the second bar in each of the four upper String-parts. The first of the quavers must, of, course, be attacked ⊓.

Another and even better example of consecutive down-bows is to be found in the familiar passage from Tschaikowsky's *Pathetic Symphony*. (Ex. 222.) Successions of *up-bows* of a character corresponding to the passages given are wholly unknown to the String-technique.

(2) The **Martelé** [1] or hammer-stroke is done at the point of the bow. The actual stroke is a quick alternate push and pull, not too short, but with an abrupt termination that instantly checks the vibration of the string. In effect it is hard and mechanical, like the strokes of a hammer on an anvil.

[1] Italian, *Martellato*. The French also call this stroke *Détaché sec* (dry détaché).

EXAMPLE 222.

The notation for the ordinary *Martelé* bowing is generally a series of little upright strokes, like the tops of exclamation marks. To these it is usual to add the word *point,* or the Italian words *a punta d'arco,* so that no mistake can arise.

The *Martelé* is equally suited to both the *p* and the *f.* Less usually it is done at the heel of the bow. When so played the sound is quite different from the true *Martelé* "*a punta d'arco.*" A little of it is tremendously effective in the orchestra. It should be indicated by the little upright *Martelé* dashes,[2] with the addition of the word *talon* or *heel,* thus:

EXAMPLE 223.

(3) The **Sautillé**[3] is a middle-bow stroke. It is done by letting the bow rebound quietly on the strings. At each stroke it just "picks up" the string and sets it in vibration. This style of playing is really the daily bread-and-butter of all orchestral players for light passages. It is the style adopted for all those hundred and one phrases usually called by non-string-players "*p* staccatos." Its notation is merely the staccato dot over each of the notes. The student has only to open any score which he may possess to find instances of this bowing.[4] Its total lack of strength precludes its use at any dynamic level above *mp.*

(4) The **Jeté** is a species of *Sautillé* in which the bow is thrown on to the strings and at each rebound picks up a little rhythmical group of notes. The effect is light and airy in the extreme. The bow actually

[1] The Wood-Wind and 2nd Horn parts are omitted from the above quotation.

[2] Spohr uses this sign in a rather confusing manner for both the *Martelé* and the *Détaché.*

[3] Italian, *Saltato,* sometimes *Saltando.*

[4] See, for instance, the last six notes of the Viola and Cello parts in Ex. 222.

dances on the strings in what seems to be a series of little perpendicular jumps that are scarcely either up-bow or down-bow. This stroke is much more effective when executed with precision by a large body of violinists than when employed by a single player. The notation for the *Jeté* is a slur over the whole rhythmical group with a dot over each note of which the group is composed. This style of playing is frequently miscalled *Sautillé.* It is often found in Spanish and other national dance-measures where rhythms of this kind predominate:

An example may be found in the *Moderato Mosso* of Tschaikowsky's *Pathetic Symphony.*

EXAMPLE 224.

Tschaikowsky. *Pathetic Symphony.*

[1] In the above example the 1st and 2nd Violins are written with only one set of tails, in order to show the notation of the bowing more clearly. In the Full Score they naturally occupy separate lines.

(5) The **Slur**, though not strictly a bow-stroke at all, is included here for the sake of convenience. Any number of notes within reason may be included under a ⌒, and so long as the slur continues the player will not change the direction of the bow. It should be noted, however, that (A) only notes on the same string or on adjacent strings can be slurred, (B) the more notes that are included in the slur the slower the bow has to travel, and therefore the weaker becomes the tone. Long *f* slurs are an absolute impossibility. In any case the eking-out of a long *p* slur at the end of an V (that is to say, at the extreme heel of the bow—its strongest part) is unsatisfactory. Similarly the eking-out of a long *f* slur at the end of a ⊓ (that is to say, at the extreme point of the bow—its weakest part) is ineffective. *Pianissimo* held notes or slurs consisting of a few long notes bound together can be performed up to a maximum of about 4 bars of $\frac{4}{4}$ *moderato* time. In this case the string has only just to be kept moving. If, however, the slur includes a large number of notes, such as scales or figures, a certain amount of "way" has to be kept on the bow in order to give each note its requisite impetus. In this case the maximum number of bars mentioned above must be about halved. This is a fairly good general rule.

The next three bow-strokes are mixed strokes, that is to say, they may be regarded as slurs in so far as the bow performs more than one note when proceeding in the same direction. On the other hand, a distinct stoppage of the bow, and therefore of the sound, is made after each note, so that the musical effect is of a series of more or less detached notes.

(6) The **Louré** is a characteristic V stroke, though it can also on occasion be performed ⊓. It is used only in the *cantabile* for the purpose of giving the utmost intensity of feeling to a group of unslurred notes. In making this stroke the player exerts a strong pressure with the fingers of the right hand on each of the notes composing the group. The stoppage of the bow after each note is reduced to a minimum. Consequently the effect is that of a series of "pushes." By increasing or decreasing the length of bow used, a very effective *crescendo* or *diminuendo* can be secured.

The notation of the *Louré* is a slur under or above the group, with a little horizontal line thus – under or above each note of which it is composed.

It need scarcely be pointed out that, as the object of the stroke is to give the maximum *cantabile* effect combined with a certain amount of detachment to each note, the bow is compelled to travel a considerable distance while "singing" each note. In this point it is precisely opposite to the *Staccato,* in which the bow only just engages the string for each note sounded. It is, therefore, impossible to include a large number of notes under one *Louré* slur. Six, perhaps, would be the maximum: half that number the most effective. The opening of

"Comfort ye" in *The Messiah* gives an excellent example of the *Louré*.

EXAMPLE 225.

Notes written this way are commonly called in English orchestras "one-line-crotchets," "one-line-quavers," etc. The student should note that the type of tone which is indicated by the slurs and dashes can also be secured by using separate bows. The essential point is that the *Louré* is a slightly detached *cantabile*, in which each note receives a definite pressure from the bow. If a modern Score, such as that of the *Pathetic Symphony*, is read through it will be seen that a very large number of *Louré* notes occur either (1) as isolated notes with separate bows, (2) as successions of "one-line-crotchets" and "one-line-quavers," or (3) as single notes bracketed in *Louré* with other notes. In all these cases the effect is precisely what has been described above—a detached emotional *cantabile*.

A good example of a few *Louré* strokes cunningly interpolated here and there in order to secure a maximum of effect may be found in the Viola melody quoted below from Bridge's *Isabella*.[1] A second excellent example is to be seen in the excerpt from Vaughan Williams's *String Fantasia*.[2] In this quotation the melody is played *con molto espressione* by 2nd Violins, Violas, and one division of the Cellos. Almost every note has a *Louré* stroke. A third example may be found in the section devoted to the Violin *pizzicato*. In the quotation from the slow movement of Tschaikowsky's *Fifth Symphony* the *Louré* is used in the 1st Violin melody to detach the last note of the up-beat triplet from the preceding notes.[3]

(7) The true **Violin Staccato** is scarcely ever used in the orchestra. It is done by taking a rapid group of notes—generally an upward but sometimes a downward diatonic scale—with the upper half of a single up-bow. After each note a distinct stoppage of the bow is made, but the whole scale is bracketted together, so to speak, into one brilliant whole. Naturally this stroke demands very great skill on the part of the player. The capacity for its execution is, as Spohr says, "in some degree a natural gift." The Violin Schools of Bohemia, Hungary, and the Latin countries, excel in this species of bowing, but in mixed orchestras the dangers in the way of securing a proper ensemble practically forbid its use. However, three or four *Staccato* notes before a down beat can safely be hazarded anywhere.

The notation of the *Staccato* is a slur over the whole scale-passage with a dot above each note of which it is composed. Here is an example from Spohr's *Ninth Concerto*:

[1] See Ex. 248. [2] See Ex. 277. [3] See Ex. 241.

EXAMPLE 226.

Down-bow *Staccatos* are very rarely used, even in Solos. In the orchestra they are quite out of the question.

Simple passages across the strings of this sort

can easily and effectively be played with a light staccato-like effect provided the notes of the arpeggios are arranged so as to be practicable *as chords.* This type of *staccato,* however, has nothing technically in common with the true *Violin Staccato.* The latter is done solely with the wrist. The former merely consists of throwing the bow backwards and forwards across the strings with the lightest possible pressure of the fingers of the right hand. Perhaps it would be truer to say, " with no pressure at all except that which is exerted by the weight of the bow itself." Arpeggios played in this manner have less tone and quality than they would have if they were merely slurred. In the latter case they can be performed at any dynamic level from *pp* to *ff.*

Though the true *Violin Staccato* is little used in the orchestra, a simplified and curtailed variety is continually employed by all String players. It is essentially a system of grouping together little sets of not more than two or three notes for convenience of phrasing. These notes, however, are not grouped together so as to give the effect of slightly detached *legatos*—as in the case of the *Louré*—but so as to give the effect of a *staccato* in the ordinary sense of the word. Though this system of staccato-grouping is in daily use in every orchestra all over Europe, it unfortunately has never received a name. For convenience of reference it may be called

(8) The **Group-Staccato.** (A) Its notation in the case of notes of equal length is the same as that of the true *Staccato,* a slur with dots over each note. (B) In the case of notes of unequal length the notation is conventional—a slur over the two notes and a dot over the second, thus

The first of these (A) is merely an abbreviation of the true *Staccato.* It is solely an V stroke, and can be equally well used for repeated notes, scales, or arpeggios.

Except when interpolated into a rapid passage for the sake of "getting the bowing right" its want of strength precludes its use *f.*

The second of these *Group-Staccatos* (B)

demands a little more attention. The student should notice that the dot under the second note of each pair is merely a convention. The shortening is a shortening of the first note. The second note is played strictly in time but clearly detached from the first note. In fact, the time robbed from the first note gives the characteristic detachment to the group. The second note is attacked at its strictly correct place in the time-scheme of the bar, and is not shortened. The effect of the rhythm

 when so bowed is 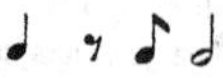 not 

Occasionally the detached character of these string rhythms is emphasized by means of rests, thus:

This is satisfactory, except that a bracket ⌴ under the notes would be more logical than a slur. However, if the notes are written out thus at their true time-values there is little need to add dots under the notes. It is somewhat difficult to understand the reason for these dots in an *allegro* rhythm such as that in the *Finale* of Beethoven's *Fifth Symphony.* The written rhythm

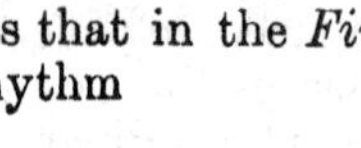

would appear to demand the sound

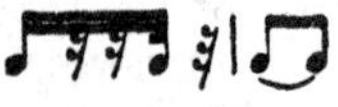

but this is meaningless in so quick a movement. These dots seem to be often put in merely to terrify the player into a *staccatissimo* frame of mind and muscle.

The second species of *Group-staccato* can be used equally well *p* or *f*, ⊓ or V. When played ⊓ with the 2nd note bitten out hard at the point of the bow it is immensely effective. The V *Group-staccato* is also continually used, but it is slightly less in the character of the Fiddle, owing to the fact that it is less easy to check an V decisively and to bite out the 2nd note at the heel of the bow. Gevaert says that "this bowing is commonly used when not expressly prescribed by the composer, for certain rhythmic combinations, particularly for groups of two notes, of which the second is short and unaccented." Such notes, however, ought *always* to be grouped by the composer, except in those cases where he actually wants the rhythm played with alternate bows. The latter method of playing them—possible either ⊓ V at the head of the bow or V ⊓ at the point—secures a great degree of rhythmical detachment and vigour. It is, however, a little fussy and tiring to the player. The reason of this is that, in a series of such groups, the player has to keep to the same portion of his bow, and is therefore compelled to draw very strong and rapid strokes for each of the second (the short) notes, in order to get back again for the first (the long) notes.

To sum up, the composer should remember that the written rhythm

represents, on every stringed-instrument, a perfectly clear detachment of the first two notes, and not a sort of semi-slur. If, in his most "rumbustious" passages, he wants this type of rhythm played ⊓ V he should omit both the dots and the slurs. This, however, will probably not happen more than once in a hundred times.

There are a number of other bow-strokes associated with the names of the great Fiddle-masters who first employed them. These are known by such names as the *coup d'archet de Viotti, coup d'archet de Kreutzer*, and so on. For the most part they consist merely of different combinations or arrangements of the strokes already given. The Viotti-bowing, however—consisting as it does of alternate groups of two ⊓ and two V staccatos, all played with the upper $\frac{1}{3}$ of the bow, thus:

deserves to be excepted from this category.

Shakes.

Very little need be said with regard to the Violin shakes. They are playable both whole-tone and half-tone practically throughout the whole compass of the instrument. There are, however, two restrictions to be borne in mind.

(1) Violinists never shake on an open string. The whole-tone and half-tone shakes on low G, therefore, cannot be, or rather are not, used.[1] The shakes on the three other open strings are performed either in the 3rd or the 4th position on the next lower string.

(2) At the extreme upper end of the compass the shortness and high tension of the E-string combine to destroy the "freedom" of the shakes. The limit of top G

should not, as a rule, be exceeded.

These are the only restrictions to be observed in writing Violin shakes. Their *effect* must be studied in the concert-room. It is exquisitely musical, and, of course, wholly different in sound from that hard mechanical "purr" which is represented by the same sign in pianoforte-music.

The notation of the Violin shake is the ordinary trill sign *tr*~~~, and the student should be careful to slur together those notes which he wishes played with the same bow. This is a most important point. The new attack on the same or on a different shake makes a strong appeal both to the ear and to the eye. In very long shakes which exceed the possible limits of a single bow-stroke the players will, if the whole shake is slurred, change the bow at discretion. This secures a uniform quality in the shake.

The Tremolo.

As early as the time of Monteverde efforts were made to give a dramatic intensity to String-backgrounds by substituting a quick trembling movement of the bow for the ordinary *tenuto* stroke. In the earliest known examples the device adopted was merely to fill up the required space of time by writing repeated notes of a smaller time-unit. These note-groups were presumably performed with rhythmical regularity by the players. The result was a sort of *bastard tremolo*, new and surprising at the time when it was invented, but still not a true *tremolo* in our sense of the word. This *tremolo*, which, in quick tempos, approaches the effect of a modern *tremolo*, is commonly known as **The Measured Tremolo.** It appears to have been first used by Claudio Monteverde at the beginning of the seventeenth century. The following excerpt from his Opera *Il Combattimento di Tancredi* (1624) is quoted from Vol. II. of Reissmann's *Geschichte der Musik.* The Italian Direction in the 7th bar "to leave the bow and pull the strings with two fingers" is of course equivalent to our modern word *pizzicato.*

[1] The whole-tone and half-tone fingered-tremolos on low G are, in effect, nothing but shakes.

EXAMPLE 227.

Monteverde. *Il Combattimento di Tancredi.*[1]

This is the earliest form of the *tremolo*,—a characteristically awkward repetition of a single String-chord as an accompaniment to a vocalist. Monteverde's experiments in this kind did not, however, meet with any general acceptance, and it was not until Gluck's time that the real *tremolo* became a recognized method of tone-production for all the Strings.

[1] See foot-note, p. 395.

In discussing the various sorts of *tremolo* we may leave out of account this early *Measured Tremolo.* It was merely the rapid reiteration of a note or notes in which the strict rhythmical values were observed. Undoubtedly this often has a tremulous effect, but it cannot be properly classed as a *tremolo*, for the simple reason that no rule can be given as to the pace at which it either becomes or ceases to be a *tremolo*.

Besides this *Measured Tremolo* there are four sorts of true *tremolo* which either have been or are now used in the orchestra. These are

(1) The obsolete **Undulating Tremolo.**
(2) The **Bowed Tremolo.**
(3) The **Fingered Tremolo.**
(4) The **Bowed-and-fingered Tremolo.**

(1) The Obsolete Undulating Tremolo.

This variety as used by Gluck is traditionally supposed to have been done by means of a series of pressures exerted by the fingers of the right hand on the bow during the progress of a long *legato* bow-stroke. The fingers alternately exert and relax the pressure as the bow proceeds on its course. A certain—or, to be accurate, a very uncertain—undulating effect is thus produced. This is the tradition. But it must be said that, unless violinists have wholly lost the art of this particular stroke, the result is disappointing and futile in the extreme. Perhaps the best proof that the *Undulating Tremolo* was performed in this way is to be found in the fact that it has been totally abandoned for more than a century.

It is difficult, however, to believe that a composer of Gluck's eminence could really have been satisfied with a *tremolo* so uncharacteristic of all the String-group. A suggestion has been made that it was not done as a *legato* bow-stroke at all but as a series of little dancing strokes or *jetés*. In this case the players would simply throw the bow on the strings continually till the value of the written note was exhausted and, if this were done by a large body of players all making the stroke without rhythmical collusion, the total result would probably be effective. The shape and weight of the bow as used in Gluck's time were certainly well-fitted for this style of playing. The light incurved bows of to-day are much more flexible and yielding, and they are consequently less adapted for this hard rapping method of attack.

The notation of the *Undulating Tremolo* was not uniform. Sometimes the note was written at its full value with the addition of a series of quaver dots combined under one slur, thus:

Sometimes the quavers were written out thus:

and sometimes a little wavy line was placed under the note, thus:

It is not known whether this difference of notation indicated an intentional difference of effect or not.

The following example of the *Undulating Tremolo* is quoted from the 1776 edition of Gluck's *Alceste.* It occurs in the air of Alcestis, *Arbitres du sort,* etc., Act 1, Scene 5.

EXAMPLE 228.

(2) The Bowed Tremolo.

This, the most commonly used orchestral *tremolo,* is performed by rapidly reiterating a single note or at most a two-part chord formed of notes on adjacent strings. In the latter case the two notes composing the chord are not alternated but reiterated simultaneously. To be effective this *tremolo* must be very *close,* that is to say the individual players must perform as great a number of strokes as possible on each note. This is often difficult to achieve in the orchestra. The player's attention, when confined to so mechanical a task, is liable to wander and his muscles to flag. Still it makes all the difference in the effect. Perhaps the best way to ensure a good close *tremolo* is not to continue its use in one part beyond a dozen bars or so.

The notation of the *Bowed Tremolo* is simply a number of slanting strokes drawn through the tail of the note, if it has one, or placed above the note if it has not:

Less than three strokes should not be used and, in very slow tempos where demisemiquavers would clearly be played as rhythmical constituents of the bar, the abbreviation *trem.* should, for safety's sake, be added above the stave.[1] The overlooking of this word in a score has on more than one occasion produced absurd results. The converse of this proposition must also be kept in mind. If too many strokes are added to a rapid series of notes in quick tempo a *tremolo* will result when not intended. The Fiddle cadenza towards the end of the *Flying Dutchman* overture is a case in point. The sound of this passage is always more or less of a fussy *tremolo*. In this instance it might be just possible, by means of careful rehearsal, to secure an intelligible ⊓ V attack on each note. However, it is difficult to recall a performance in which this nicety has received the proper attention.

EXAMPLE 229.

The only nuances possible in the *tremolo* are the <, the >, and the extraordinarily effective *sforzando* written thus:

The latter is performed exactly like the ordinary Violin *sforzando*, except that immediately after the bow has taken the preliminary "bite" on the strings it is moved rapidly to and fro. The *sfz* can be taken at any dynamic level of *p* or *f*. In the *f* it is usual for players to emphasize the note by taking an extremely rapid bowed note (⊓) immediately after the "bite" and before beginning the *tremolo* proper.

The effect of the *Bowed Tremolo*, especially of the full *tremolo* harmony for strings, varies very greatly according as it is used in the *f* or the *p*, and in the lower, middle, or upper registers of the different instruments. In the lower registers it has a sombre, threatening effect. As it rises upwards to the top string it gradually loses its gloom and becomes more and more ethereal. On the top-string "it seems," in Gevaert's words, "to sparkle." It would be impossible except at great length to give adequate examples of the many *p* and *f* *tremolo*-combinations of Violins, Violas, Cellos, and Basses. They must

[1] See below, p. 358, for the ordinary notation of the *Bowed Tremolo* in notes whose time-values vary from the semibreve to the semiquaver.

be studied by the composer in the concert-room and the theatre An example of a low *tremolo* for *tutti* Strings is given below.[1] For the sake of contrast we shall give here a medium-register *tremolo* for Violins only in four parts.

EXAMPLE 230.

In this passage the magical effect of the E major chord, which is left as it were trembling in the air, is much enhanced by the strongly contrasting tone-colours of the two previous bars. This familiar example prompts an observation which is well worth the student's attention. All *Bowed Tremolos*, whether *p* or *f*, have *much less sound* in them than the corresponding *legatos* or *Fingered Tremolos* (No. 3). This statement, which is directly contradicted in some orchestration books,[3] is undoubtedly true. In the *Bowed Tremolo* the amplitude of the string-vibrations is very small, and, with every turn of the bow, the sound is damped. Even the greatest *crescendo* possible, provided it remain a true *tremolo*,[4] never approaches the dynamic level of an

[1] Example 231. [2] From Act III. [3] See *Widor*, page 165.

[4] The practical application of this can be seen in any big "*Trem. cresc. to ff.*" In such passages the String-players always tend to increase the length and to diminish the number of the bow-strokes. This is done to make a more perceptible dynamic difference between the two ends of the *Crescendo*.

ordinary *legato* or bowed *fortissimo.* These facts, which are within the knowledge of all conductors and players, can be demonstrated scientifically or they can be judged roughly by listening *with the eyes shut*, and then contrasting the two types of sound. The mistake on this point has indisputably arisen from the fact that the *tremolo* is *more exciting* to the hearer, and this added excitement is mistaken for increased sound.

The *Bowed Tremolo* need not of course always be employed only with *tutti* Strings. It is more often written for middle parts, such as 2nd Violins and Violas, Violas and Cellos, or for the lowest parts, such as Cellos and Basses, or Basses alone. When tempted to employ this method of expression in the middle parts, the student should *occasionally* pause and consider whether it is not a rather too easy "refuge for the destitute."

Unaccompanied solo *tremolo* passages are rare. When not too definitely melodic, and when played *pp* very "close" on the top string of the Violin, they have a charming character. The effect is that of a tiny, thin, wandering thread of sound. This type of *tremolo* can be usefully employed to give colour-contrast to the upper of two contrapuntal phrases where the lower is not too loud, and where it is some distance away.

A few examples of the *Bowed Tremolo* have already been given under various Brass and Wood-Wind headings. It is therefore unnecessary to give any further extracts here. The student should refer to those already printed. They are as follows:

(1) Exs. 67 and 139. Two high *tremolos,* one in four parts for 1st and 2nd Violins *divisi,* the other in three parts for three desks of 2nd Violins. In both cases the melody is placed below the accompaniment. Note that, though both the String-accompaniments *look* much the same, in the case of the Horn—the stronger and more telling instrument—about thirty-two Violins are employed *pp*; in the case of the Oboe d'Amore there are only six players in all, and their parts are marked *ppp.* Furthermore, the Oboe d'Amore probably plays at a slightly higher dynamic level than *pp.* Also notice that the String-accompaniment to the Horn solo is really one of those *Measured Tremolos* to which reference was made above. Each of the quavers enjoys its exact time-value. A similar instance may be found in the open fifths for 2nd Violins and Cellos (semiquaver triplets) at the beginning of the *Choral Symphony*. See also Ex. 15.

(2) Exs. 43 and 103. Two middle compass *tremolos,* one *ff* in three parts forming the background to a thick unison of Clarinet, Cornet, Bassoon, and Cellos, the other *pp* in two parts forming a very light accompaniment to the Flute and Oboe unison. In the former case the accompaniment is above, in the latter case below the melody. In the Example from Carmen the three *tremolo* String parts could of course be laid out differently.

(3) Ex. 74. A lower but still not very low *Bowed Tremolo* for Violins and Violas supporting *sostenuto* of the Horns. Note the effective *pp sforzando* on the minor ninth, the last chord.

(4) Ex. 191. A deep *Bowed-Tremolo* for Violas, Cellos, and Basses (bars 1 and 5).

The following examples occur later in this book:

(5) Ex. 274. A low octave *tremolo* for Double Basses, accompanied by a roll on the Bass Drum and a held note on the Double Bassoon and the Pedal-Organ.

(6) Ex. 278. A three-part *tremolo* on the lowest strings of the Violins and Violas. The passage is too familiar to need comment.

(7) Ex. 277. A high two-part *tremolo* for 1st Violins accompanying a melody some distance below it. The accompaniment is comparatively weak: the melody is played by a rich String-unison. This type of accompaniment is a favourite one in modern music. It is always effective and interesting, and is capable of considerably varied treatment. As a rule, a high *tremolo* accompaniment of this sort is best in three parts, neither more nor less.

For the sake of completeness a short example will be given of a low *tremolo* for *tutti* Strings. The excerpt is from Act I. Scene III. of Wagner's *Die Walküre.* Notice the sudden cessation of sound secured, in Bar 3, by the omission of the Cellos and Basses, and by the substitution of the *fp* in the upper strings for the previous *ff.* On the word *Schwert* the Horns, Bassoons, and Drums enter with an octave F, omitted in the quotation. Further reference is made below (page 362) to this passage and to the bars that follow it in the score.

EXAMPLE 231.

For the sake of an occasional, and especially dramatic effect, the composer sometimes writes the word *ponticello*,[1] above his *Bowed Tremolo.* As was explained on page 336, this effect is produced

[1] Italian for "bridge." The French say *au chevalet*, and the Germans *am steg.*

by drawing the bow across the strings close to the bridge. The result—a sort of core of sound covered up by a thick layer of "scrape"—is not very pleasant. It may, however, be used once and again with advantage. In playing the *Bowed Tremolo sul ponticello* the violinist uses exactly the same technique as he would for the ordinary *tremolo.*

Pressure on the strings, however, is almost out of the question, and he is therefore able to concentrate all his attention on keeping afloat the right side of the bridge. An excellent example of *ponticello* is to be found near the beginning of the 2nd Act of *Tristan* (full score, page 139, bar 3 onwards). It occurs just after Brangäne's words "*Noch sind sie nah';—deutlich tönts daher,*" and is laid out for Violins, Violas, and Cellos, against which the ascending Clarinet passage stands out in strong relief.

The *ponticello* effect is practically confined to the *Bowed Tremolo.* It has occasionally been written for the ordinary bowing, with detestable results. In the Scherzo of Beethoven's *C♯ minor Quartet* there is an ordinary bowed String passage marked *ponticello.* However, from the nature of the passage in question, and from other considerations, the composer's exact intention is more than doubtful. It may have been meant merely to secure an almost toneless *piano.* Another Beethoven *ponticello* which Gevaert cites with high approval occurs in the choral portion of the *Ninth Symphony.* At the words *Ueber Sternen muss er wohnen* the whole of the strings have a *pp Measured Tremolo*—semiquavers in $\frac{3}{2}$ time—against the crotchet triplets of the Wood-wind. Gevaert quotes this passage with the addition of the words *sul ponticello* under each of the String-parts, but there seems to be no authority for this addition, and, in Sir Henry J. Wood's words, "certainly Bülow, Richter, Mahler, Levi, Steinbach, and Nikisch never allowed it to be played in the manner suggested."

(3) The Fingered Tremolo.

This *tremolo,* sometimes called the *Slurred Tremolo,* consists of the rapid alternation of one note with another by means of the fingers of the left hand. The player firmly stops the lower of the two notes with his 1st, or 2nd, or 3rd finger, and then quickly stops and unstops the upper note with his 2nd, 3rd, or 4th finger, as the case may be. Each time the upper note is unstopped the lower note "sounds through," and this gives the alternation of the two notes. The bow continues to be drawn in a smooth *legato* stroke across the string. It has no part in producing the *tremolo* or in increasing its rapidity. The only influence that it brings to bear is a dynamic influence. On this point a word will be said later.

For this kind of *tremolo* the limits of an augmented fourth should not be exceeded. In the case of a fifth the player is compelled either (1) to use an open and a stopped note alternately—a not very satisfactory method—or (2) to use two stopped notes on adjacent strings. In this case the two fingers merely hold the notes as if they were the notes of a chord, while the bow undulates from one string to another during the progress of a *legato* stroke. This produces a somewhat shabby and ineffective *tremolo.* But for its comparative rarity it might be placed in a class by itself. For all intervals wider than an augmented fourth this method is the only one that can be adopted, but, as was said above, it is much better to restrict the width of the *tremolo* so that it can be performed on one string.[1]

The notation of the *Fingered Tremolo* is as follows: The two notes on which the *tremolo* is to be made are reckoned as sounding simultaneously. The time-length of only one of them is taken as an integral portion of the bar. In other words, their united written time-length is always twice the actual time-length in sound. If we wish to fill a bar of $\frac{3}{4}$ time with a *Fingered Tremolo* on the notes B and D, we write as follows:

If only two beats of the bar are to be occupied by this *tremolo* the crotchet rest is put in its proper place, and we write:

In any case the total *written* time-value of the two notes must be halved to get the actual time-length in sound.

At least three conventional demisemiquaver strokes are added to the notes in order to indicate the *tremolo,* and a slur is always drawn above the two notes.

The student however should notice that, in dealing with notes of different time-values—semibreves, minims, etc.—slightly different notations have to be adopted in order to distinguish clearly the *tremolos* from the *non-tremolos.*

(1) In the case of semibreves (dotted and undotted) the demisemiquaver strokes are simply drawn above or below, according to convenience, but are not attached to the notes. See Ex. 232, Bar 5.

(2) In the case of minims (dotted and undotted) the tails of the two notes are joined together by the demisemiquaver strokes. See Ex. 232, Bars 1 and 4.

(3) In the case of crotchets (dotted and undotted) the tails of course cannot be joined by the demisemiquaver strokes, otherwise they would make merely a group of two demisemiquavers. The two crotchets are therefore placed next to each other, and the demisemiquaver strokes are drawn between the two tails so as not to touch either of them. See Ex. 232, Bars 2, 3, and 4.

[1] It may be mentioned in passing that the utmost stretch possible between the 1st and 4th fingers on the same string is an augmented fourth. When the 1st finger is on one string and the 4th finger is on the next higher string, the corresponding interval becomes a minor ninth. This latter stretch, however, should be used with caution, and not employed if the chord or *tremolo* can be obtained by any other arrangement. These restrictions with regard to finger-stretches apply only to the lower positions.

(4) In the case of quavers the tails of the two notes are joined by a single quaver stroke, and the two extra strokes are inserted so as not to touch either of the tails. See Ex. 232, Bars 2 and 3. When, however, the quavers are followed or preceded by semiquavers to form a single crochet unit, the whole is usually written out. See Ex. 232, last beat of Bar 3. For a series of quavers, this plan could not be adopted. See Ex. 232, first 2 beats of Bar 3.

(5) In the case of all units smaller than quavers, the notes of the *tremolo* are usually written out in full. Thus the following

would be represented in *Fingered Tremolo* by

with perhaps the addition, in a very slow tempo, of the word *trem.* above.[1]

The logic of these *tremolos* is very simple, and a single example, including all time-values from semibreves to semiquavers, will make it perfectly clear. Suppose we wish to write the following series of two-part chords as a *Fingered-Tremolo,*

the correct notation would be:

EXAMPLE 232.

If the same passage had to be written out as a *Bowed Tremolo* in double stopping, its notation would be:

The extra stroke through the tail of the last semiquaver in Bar 3, though strictly necessary to conventionalize the time-value, would be omitted nine times out of ten and the player trusted not to break the *tremolo.*

[1] Demisemiquavers *must* of course be written out in full. Semiquavers might be written so  but in practice they are generally written out.

Written for two Violin parts, each in single stopping, the passage would appear thus:

The student should notice

(1) That the usual convention of putting in a fresh slur every time the two notes of the *Fingered Tremolo* change is unnecessary and illogical. So long as the *tremolo* is on one string or on adjacent strings, the player can go on slurring it exactly as if it were an ordinary *legato* phrase. The change of finger does not necessarily call for a change of bow. The composer should therefore slur the passage to suit the phrasing. If the *tremolo* is, as often happens, *piano*, fairly long slurs are a good insurance against the ubiquitous and much-dreaded *orchestral mezzo-forte.* If, however, the *tremolo* is *ff*, long slurs should be avoided. In the latter case, even when the same harmony persists for many beats, it is often as well to break up the *tremolo* into smaller units. If each of these units be slurred, and the first two marked ⊓ V, they may be made strikingly effective. At the opposite extreme, if a mere *p background-tremolo* is required, it is as well to use the longest possible slurs, and to leave the players to change their bows without rhythmical collusion according to their individual styles.

(2) With the *Fingered Tremolo* the player has just the same powers of < and > as in the ordinary *legato* bow-strokes; that is to say, anything between *ppp* and *fff* is both possible and effective.

(3) A *Fingered Tremolo* is often *crossed* with itself. One part is written upwards and one downwards. This can be done either by dividing up any one of the String groups (1st or 2nd Violins, Violas, Cellos, or, more rarely, Basses), and writing the part thus:

or by giving one complete group the upward *tremolo* and another the downward, in this way:

Both these divisions of the *tremolo* into two parts are merely pretty arrangements for the eye of the score-reader. Violin players make no difference in the performance. They set the lower finger and beat with the upper in any case. Furthermore, no accent—unless specially prescribed—is given by the player to the first written note. The effect of the upward and downward *Fingered Tremolo* is therefore precisely the same. If of 16 1st Fiddle-players 8 are directed to make the *tremolo* one way and 8 the other, the effect is the same as if all 16 were playing it in one direction. The *addition*, however, of 16 other players performing the same *Fingered Tremolo* on the same notes, whatever the notation, makes a sensible difference in the thickness of the *tremolo*. It must be said that *Fingered Tremolos* are often crossed with the object of confining the *tremolo* within narrow limits. As each *tremolo* necessitates the use of two harmonic notes, the chord is sometimes liable to spread too far unless this plan is adopted.

(4) *Fingered Tremolos* of a major and minor second are, of course, nothing but shakes, and are often so written in the middle of *tremolo* passages.

(5) *Bowed- and Fingered-Tremolos* can be combined in different parts. The effect, which is curiously elusive and fascinating, may be obtained by arranging the two sorts of *tremolo* in different parts, so that different notes or parts of chords are played by different methods. In this case it is matter of choice which sort of *tremolo* should occupy the extreme or middle positions in the harmony. Still more elusive to the ear is the actual superposition of the one *tremolo* on the other in this sort of way

Of course it is not necessary that the whole of a String-group should be employed on each part. Such a passage can, as a rule, be well done by a single group—1st Violins, 2nd Violins, Violas, etc.—*divisi.*

EXAMPLE 233.

Debussy. *Pelléas et Mélisande.*

¹ For an explanation of the Harp-part see below, page 466.

A single example of the *Fingered Tremolo* has already been quoted from *Lohengrin.*[1] The student should notice carefully how it is written, as it is a good type of all such *tremolos.* Nowhere is the player asked to exceed the limits of a major third. This is a "middle-register" example. Such *tremolos* are very rarely used in the lowest octaves, as some confusion is likely to result in the bass. The Measured *Fingered Tremolo,* however, in which the notes are written out in full and executed at their proper time-values, is often used by Wagner in the Basses and Cellos. The student can easily find examples of these in *The Ring.* There are many in *Siegfried.* Instances of the *Fingered Tremolo* in the upper octaves are so common nowadays that the difficulty of quotation is merely one of selection. A charming example occurs in *Pelléas et Mélisande* (Act II. Scene 1) at the moment when the ring drops in the water.[2] The *pianissimo Fingered Tremolo* passing down through two octaves with the descending Wood-Wind and the deep *pp* of the Cellos and Basses brings to

[1] See Ex. 137, also Ex. 23. [2] See above, Ex. 233.

the mind a vivid picture of the gurgling water and the gradual obliteration of the widening circles on its surface.

It is interesting to notice the different mental effects produced by the various sorts of *String-tremolo.* These are not often to be found in close proximity to one another, but there is an instructive example in Act I. Scene 3 of *Die Walküre.* The passage begins on page 45 of the full score with *ff* and *p* *Bowed Tremolos* all written in the lower register.[1] Six bars later the *tremolo* changes and we have high *Fingered Tremolos* for 1st and 2nd Violins, each in two parts. Fourteen bars later, without altering the pitch, the composer changes back to a *Bowed Tremolo.* Any of these *tremolos* might have been written precisely the other way round, and the student cannot do better than examine the whole passage in the score and then note, in performance, the important mental differences implied by the differences in technique.

(4) The Bowed-and-Fingered-Tremolo.

This type of *tremolo*, sometimes called the *Broken Tremolo,* is as old as Gluck.[2] It can be performed by setting the two fingers in position on adjacent strings and then bowing the notes in rapid alternation with a series of *tremolo* ⊓ and V strokes, thus

or by making the ordinary *Fingered Tremolo* on a single string and at the same time making a *tremolo* bow-stroke,

In either case a little more bow and right arm attack is necessary than in the ordinary *Bowed Tremolo.* This *tremolo* has not been much used, though it offers great scope for effect. When played *f* on the upper strings it has a hard brilliant sound, something like a shower of hail-stones. It should be written just like the *Fingered Tremolo,* but with the omission of the slurs. The word *stacc.* should be added above the part. The effect may be practically shown by an illustration from Act III. Scene 3 of Wagner's *Götterdämmerung.* It is true that here the notes are written out at their strict rhythmical values, and, in so far as that goes, the passage may be regarded as a *Measured Tremolo.* But that does not make a great difference to the sum total of the String-effect. The sound of the Strings here immediately strikes the imagination, and will be recalled by everyone who has heard the passage. It may be mentioned that the String-parts begin two bars earlier than the quotation given below, and that they are there marked *staccato.*

[1] These opening bars have already been quoted above. See Ex. 231.

[2] *Iphigénie en Tauride,* Act III. Scene 4.

EXAMPLE 234.

The Col Legno.

Besides playing with the hair of the bow, String-players are occasionally directed to strum the strings with the bow-stick itself This not very legitimate effect is usually indicated by the Italian words *col legno* (or *col ligno*), that is to say "with the wood." In executing this stroke the player throws the bow-stick on to the strings with a hard mechanical tap in which there is a good deal more wood than music. The bow is not *drawn* at all either ⊓ or V. It follows that no *legato* is possible. Isolated notes, small *staccato* phrases, and little rhythmical groups in the style of the *jeté* are all that can be attempted with the *legno*. As a rule players perform the stroke with a rather bad grace, preferring to keep the varnish on their fiddle-sticks and the hair on their strings—both where they should be.

The *col legno* is little used in serious music. Familiar examples, however, are to be found in the *Danse Macabre* of Saint Saëns, in Liszt's *Mazeppa*, and in the Second Act of *Siegfried* (Full score, page 257). In more modern times Strauss has introduced a *Violin-tremolo* played with the wood of the bow. The passage which occurs in his Symphonic Poem, *Also sprach Zarathustra*, is here reproduced with the omission of the Wood-Wind-, Harp-, and Trumpet-parts.

EXAMPLE 235.

The effect is curious and perhaps unique. In reading the Artificial Harmonics the student should remember what was said above, viz. that if in writing a series of Artificial Harmonics one needs to use Natural Harmonic No. 4—that is to substitute the actual nut for the 1st finger—it is usual to take a certain licence and write the note as an Artificial Harmonic. The above excerpt affords a good example of this licence, for, though the fingering $\frac{4}{1}$ is scattered in a mechanical and somewhat haphazard manner throughout the passage, it would not always be used when written. For instance in the last bar (3rd and 4th desks of Violas) the note might be played according to the directions as an Artificial Harmonic in the 4th position on the bottom string according to the fingering. It would, however, more probably be played as Natural Harmonic No. 4 on the 3rd string merely by touching the note C lightly with the 3rd finger. Again, in the 1st violin part, the first two notes do not exist on the instrument as Artificial Harmonics. They *must* be played as Natural Harmonic No. 4 in the 1st position on the G string. The omission of the fingering in certain cases is probably only accidental. On the other hand, the stopping of the note G with the 3rd finger (last note, 5th and 6th desks of Violas), while the 1st finger is stopping the 4th below, is simply an impossibility

The Portamento.

Before leaving the bow- and finger-technique of the Violin it must be mentioned that String players alone in the orchestra employ the *portamento.*[1] Not every *legato* phrase can be treated in this way. However, it would probably only confuse the student if full details were given on this point. Roughly speaking, one may say that if the interval is small, and if both its notes can be conveniently played with a single finger, the finger is slid along the string from one note to the other. All the intermediate connecting intervals between the two notes are thus heard in rapid succession.

If the interval is larger, and if both its notes are not conveniently playable with one finger, a species of "cheat" is practised on the ear. The finger that stops the lower note is slid forward in a true *portamento* until it reaches the position in which the upper note can be stopped by another finger. When it has arrived in that position the other finger instantaneously stops the higher note, leaving a gap, so to speak, in which there is no *portamento.* For instance, in making the portamento from B to G on the 2nd string, the 1st finger slides forward, as explained, from B to D (not G). The 1st finger is then in its place in the 3rd position, and the 4th finger snaps down on to the G. The actual *portamento* is from B to D. Between that note and the top G there is no *portamento* whatever. The process may be graphically represented thus:

[1] The Trombone, of course, has a terrific power of *portamento.* However, except for humorous military-band pieces and pantomime-effects, it can scarcely be said to be used.

The latter portion of the operation is performed so swiftly that the ear of any but a String-player is quite deceived.[1]

The *portamento* is not used except between slurred notes on the same string. It *could* be used on adjacent strings by means of a somewhat similar technique to that described above. The moment, however, of changing the bow from one string to another makes the gap a little too obvious.

The Pizzicato.

In place of the bow, String-players occasionally pluck the strings with a finger or fingers of the right hand. This mode of execution is indicated by the Italian word for "pinched" or "plucked," *pizzicato*, or its abbreviation, *pizz.* When the bow is to be resumed the Italian word *arco* ("bow") is inserted in the part.

For short *pizz* passages the player retains the bow in his hand, doubling it up against the palm with the 2nd, 3rd, and 4th fingers. He then rests the thumb against the fingerboard and plucks the string with the fleshy tip of his first finger. Occasionally in prolonged *pizzicatos* he lays the bow down on the desk. But this can only be done if time is allowed him both at the beginning and at the end of the *pizz.* A single isolated *pizz* note or chord of this sort

can be interpolated even into a quick *arco* passage. In such a case the player does not take up the usual *pizz* position at the fingerboard, but merely thrums the chord with the 1st finger while the bow remains practically in its playing position with regard to the right hand. An interpolated *pizz* note or chord is, of course, easier if the previous bow-stroke is V not ⊓. The V brings the fingers of the right hand somewhere near the fingerboard, and the player has to make less of a swoop in order to get the *pizz.*

Very little time is required in which to pass from *arco* to *pizz*, especially if the last note or group of notes in the *arco* can be arranged to come V. A phrase of this sort is quite easy and playable.

[1] It is interesting to contrast this partial *portamento* with the ordinary vocal *portamento*. This is theoretically a true *portamento*, containing all the intervals between the two extreme notes. In practice, however, the majority of singers seem unable to make this extensive *portamento* with the necessary neatness. Their practice is just the opposite to that of the string-player. The sounds which they omit are those nearest to the "taking-off" note, that is to say they generally jump a portion of the gap at the beginning, pick up the sound somewhere near the final note, and then perform a true *portamento* till it is reached.

On the other hand, it is not so easy to get the bow back into its proper position for playing, as it is merely to throw it out of action for the *pizz.* About half a second by the watch must be allowed. Nothing beyond quavers in *allegro* time can be attempted at the place where the *pizz* changes to *arco.* The following, from the *pizzicato* movement in *Sylvia* (Delibes) is only just possible. Indeed if the *animando* is done as it should be, either the last *pizz* note has to be scamped or the first *arco* note has not its proper force and precision.

EXAMPLE 236.

Players, as a rule, give little study to *pizzicato* playing, and therefore the maximum speed possible is not great. Widor gives semiquavers when ♩=104 as the limit. This should certainly not be exceeded. It would not be possible beyond one or two bars of $\frac{4}{4}$ time at most. The better technique of the rapid *pizz* by means of alternate 1st and 2nd fingers certainly deserves the closer attention of orchestral players.

Chords which can be struck with the bow can naturally be arpeggioed *pizzicato* at any speed. If they are written out they must be spread from the bottom note upwards only, thus:

It need scarcely be said that, as no prolongation in the tone of the *pizz* is practicable, the part is generally written with as few rests as possible. The crotchet *pizz* sounds the same as the quaver or the semiquaver. A passage written so:

sounds to the ear thus:

On all the Stringed-instruments the *pizz* is more sonorous and satisfactory for general purposes of accompaniment when used on the two bottom strings. On the upper strings, and especially on the top-string, it is harder and drier, with less of a musical and more of an explosive quality. On the Violin the note

may be kept in mind as being roughly the upward limit for *pizzicato.* Much higher than this it is not advisable to go. The plucking of a very short and very tense string produces only poor musical results.

It must not, however, be supposed that the *pizz* should be kept rigidly to the bottom strings. That register is merely the most useful for ordinary purposes. On the other hand, a *f* chord written on the top strings will sometimes come out with the force of a pistol-shot. Witness the passage in the *finale* of Mendelssohn's *Violin Concerto,* where the Violins and Violas interrupt the running Fiddle-passages with a snap-chord *pizz sf*:

EXAMPLE 237.

Examples of the *pizz* are to be found in almost every orchestral work. Beethoven often makes the happiest use of it. The student should look at the opening bar of his *Fourth Symphony,* where the *pizzicato* B♭ of the Strings seems to set free the held note for Flute, Clarinets, Bassoons, and Horns. A somewhat similar instance has already been quoted from Mendelssohn.[1] In these, the opening bars of the *Italian Symphony,* the *f pizz* chord for the strings acts in the same way for the reiterated triple notes in the Wood-Wind and Horns. In the *Scherzo* (*allegro,* $\frac{3}{4}$) of Beethoven's *Fifth Symphony,* there is an effective *pizz* Fiddle-part in crotchets, and in the *Violin Concerto* the student should examine the little bit of *pizz* accompaniment in the slow movement. (Peters's Score, pp. 54 and 55.) The three *pp pizz* C's with which the *Coriolanus* Overture ends offers another good example of Beethoven's originality. This, again, may be compared with the striking ending to Strauss's *Also sprach Zarathustra,* where the repeated chords of B major in the Violins and higher Wood-Wind are answered by the *pizz* C's in the lower Strings.

[1] See Example 47.

EXAMPLE 238.

A few examples of the ordinary use of the *pizz* accompaniment have already been given.[1] If the student wishes to find an instance of the *pizz* used in a more heroic way, he should take an opportunity of hearing either one of the complete *pizzicato* movements which have become popular in Ballet since the production of *Sylvia* or the extraordinary *Scherzo* in Tschaikowsky's *F minor Symphony*. The latter movement may be said to be the high-water mark of the *pizzicato*. The whole Scherzo is well worth detailed examination.

Before leaving this subject, it must be mentioned that when the *pizz* is used in conjunction with the whole or a portion of the Wind, it occasionally has a higher function than that of mere support or accompaniment. In such cases, where it is pitted contrapuntally against either the Brass or the Wood-wind, or both, it is almost always best to employ the whole of the strings in three octaves. It is not of course necessary that the *pizz* should be *f*, though it may be so if desired. The solemn ending to the first movement of Tschaikowsky's *Pathetic Symphony*, where the strings reiterate the downward scale of B major against the *legato* phrases of the Wind, is a case in point.[2] Even when the bass alone is to be made specially prominent, this plan

[1] In the *p*, see Exs. 4, 6, 7, 91, 100, 102, 113, 114, 115, 128, 133, 154, 155, 186, 227 in the *f*, see Exs. 19, 43, 47, 296.

[2] See above, Ex. 91.

can be recommended. The mere *pizz* of Cellos and Basses, which will be dealt with later, of course gives "point" to the bass; but if a special effect of this sort is required, the whole of the Strings can quite well be used. See Beethoven's Overture *King Stephen* (85th bar of the Second Presto). See also Ex. 133.

The student should familiarize himself with the very marked difference between the *pizzicato,* in which each group of instrumentalists plays only one note, and that in which each group plays whenever possible in double- and triple-stopping. Contrast any of the *p* and *pp* single-note *pizzicatos* given in this book (*e.g.* Exs. 100, 102) with the Guitar-like thrum of the Violas and Cellos accompanying the Bass-Flute melody in Ex. 114. Furthermore, as the point is sure to crop up in practice, the student should take every opportunity of contrasting in the concert-room the *pizz* of the Strings with that of the Harp. The two sounds are quite distinct. It would, however, be difficult to put the distinction into words, and perhaps more difficult to give any but a dynamic reason for a preference in any individual passage. A very little attention to the mental effect produced by the two tone-qualities will soon give the student an instinctive appreciation of their differences.

As most of the examples given above have been of quiet *pizzicatos,* the following three short quotations will illustrate the use of the *pizz* *f.* The first, from Act I. of Humperdinck's *Hänsel und Gretel,* shows a very effective series of loud *pizz* chords accompanying the Soprano voice. The chords in the 2nd Violin part are marked in the score to be played "together"; that is to say, each player is to play both notes. They are all very simple.

EXAMPLE 239.

Poco più allegro. Humperdinck. *Hänsel und Gretel.*

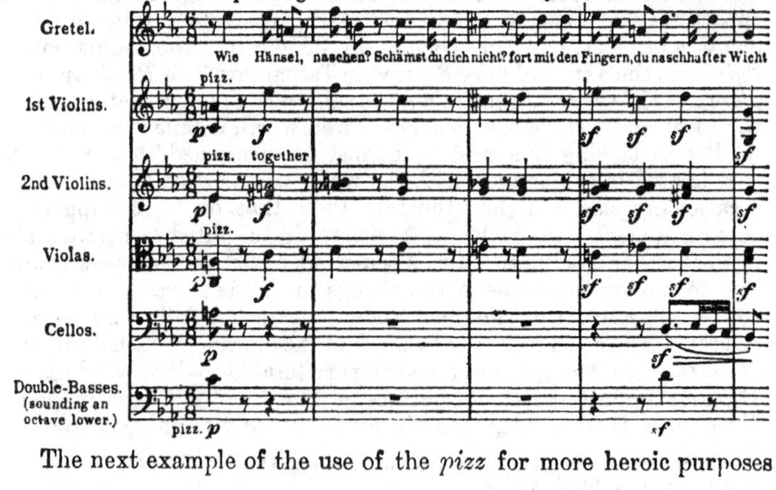

The next example of the use of the *pizz* for more heroic purposes

[1] Two Horns and a Clarinet, omitted above, enter on the note D with the Basses in the fourth bar.

is to be found during the final *fortissimo* of Berlioz's *King Lear* Overture. The noise and flare of the full orchestra is suddenly interrupted by a *f pizz* for *tutti* Strings: a moment later there is a second string chord *pizz* but *p*. This picturesque piece of orchestration has been cited by Strauss as a stroke of genius in the employment of the *pizzicato*. He says, "This passage gives me at every hearing the impression of a fibre breaking in the heart of Lear—or, in a more realistic sense, of a blood-vessel bursting in the brain of the mad King." The two *pizzicatos* are quoted below, but, in order to appreciate their effect, one really needs to see what is on the left and on the right-hand side of these six bars.

EXAMPLE 240.

The next example is musically perhaps more surprising, and again relies for its full effect on its contrast with what has gone before. It occurs most unexpectedly after the big *ff* climax in the slow movement of Tschaikowsky's *Fifth Symphony*. The effect of the big thrummed chords is startling and impressive in the extreme. It may be mentioned that these chords are generally taken *ff*, or at least *f*—not *mf* as marked—with a *diminuendo* in the 3rd and 4th bars to allow the effective entry of the 1st Violin melody. See Ex. 241, page 372.

In the *Cadenza Accompagnata* of his *Violin Concerto* Elgar has introduced a new form of *pizzicato*—the *pizzicato tremolando*. The effect is obtained, not by means of the quick iteration of a single note, but by thrumming the notes of a spread chord Guitar-fashion. This thrumming is, of course, done without any rhythmical collusion on the part of the players. The result is a curious species of *tenuto*. The ear is conscious of the continual movement of the players' fingers, but it does not "dissect out" the individual chords any more than it distinguishes the separate strokes of the hammers in listening to a Dulcimer.

EXAMPLE 241.

The quotation (Example 242, page 373) from the *Cadenza* in question will make the method perfectly clear. It should be said that the bowed quaver played by the 1st division of the Strings at the beginning of this bar is omitted in order to save space.

The Mute.

The use of the Mute for deadening the quality of the Violin seems to have been known from very early times. Mersenne, in his *Harmonie Universelle*, draws attention to the fact that, if a key or some such object be attached to the bridge, the instrument loses its usual tone-quality. Keys are not employed nowadays for this purpose, though pennies and half-crowns have been pushed in between the strings on the tail-side of the bridge as a poor substitute for the proper mute.

EXAMPLE 242.

The scientific object of the mute is to damp out a portion of the vibrations as they pass from the strings through the bridge to the sound-chest. This is effected by placing temporarily on the bridge a little three-pronged, comb-shaped apparatus made of wood, ivory, or metal. The prongs are split and are made—or rather should be made —to clutch the bridge firmly. Only in this way can the vibrations be properly damped. Unfortunately a satisfactory mute has yet to be evolved by the Fiddle-makers. It should be heavy, and should not merely be cast or cut in a straight piece, but made to fit the contour of each individual bridge with accuracy. The difference in tone-colour produced by a heavy well-fitting mute, and one that is light and ill-fitting, is simply astonishing. This is more especially the case with the Violas, Cellos, and Basses;[1] but it applies also to the Violins.

Unhappily the mutes remain something of a problem on the mechanical side of concert-room organization. When they are required the noise and fuss is most distressing, and, as these moments always occur when a *pp* is approaching, the musical attention of the audience is completely distracted. About fifty or sixty players all rattle their bows down on their desks in order to be free to search their waistcoat-pockets. When the mutes have been dragged out they are fitted to the bridges with a studied and elaborate caution which may be necessary to preserve the bridges from injury, but which gives an impression that the players are taking part in a solemn cabbalistic

× The *pizz. tremolando* should be "thrummed" with the soft part of three or four fingers across the strings. (Composer's note in the Full Score).

[1] Corder gives 2 lb. as the necessary minimum weight of a Double-Bass mute.

rite. And all this occurs in 1914 when inventors are as thick as bulls in Bashan.

Some conductors have endeavoured to get over these difficulties by adopting little spring-mutes which can be instantly and silently clipped on to the bridge, and, after use, clipped on to the desk. The idea is good, but hitherto these mutes have been made so that only the extreme points of the prongs clutch the bridge. This is not good enough. The result, even when the six points actually touch the bridge as they are meant to, is ineffective. The damping is so slight, especially in the case of the Violas, Cellos, and Basses, as to be almost useless. It is to be hoped that someone will devise a heavy noiseless mute, in which by the action of a spring the whole inside surface of the split prongs will be firmly clasped against the bridge.[1]

The general effect of the mute is to attenuate the string-tone to a sort of weird thinness, which, in the *pp*, is about as near to nothing as is orchestrally possible. Of course all the varied bow- and finger-technique can be put in practice just as readily with as without the mute. A couple of bars at least of moderate $\frac{4}{4}$ time must be allowed for fixing the mute. A slightly shorter time will suffice for snatching it off. Occasionally it happens that by no ingenuity can the proper rest be given just before[2] the muted passage. In this case the part is marked some eight or a dozen bars earlier *poco a poco con sordino.* This means that the players in turn cease playing for a bar or two in order to put on their mutes. When this is properly arranged and carried out the result is a gradual "infusion," so to speak, of the muted tone-quality. More often its actual result is that, at the critical moment, nobody is found to have his mute fixed. The ordinary indications in the score for the use and disuse of the mutes are, in Italian, *con sord,*[3] or *senza sord,* or, in English, *mutes* (*on*) and *mutes off.*

Early examples of the effect to be obtained from muting and unmuting the strings have been quoted in instrumentation books from such works as Lully's *Armide* (Act II. *Plus j'observe ces lieux*) and Haydn's *Creation* (*And God said, Let there be light*). One of the earliest and most interesting to Englishmen is the beautiful muted String music in Act II. of Purcell's *Fairy Queen* (*See, even night*). The student will probably prefer to see the opening bars of this

[1] Several attempts have been made to produce a mute which should be a permanent fixture on the violin, switchable on and off at pleasure. The general objection to this sort of contraption is that, when out of action, it slightly alters the tone of the instrument.

[2] Or after. The converse of course holds true. This method of gradually substituting the muted for the natural tone-colour might well be employed under proper control, not merely as a makeshift, but as a legitimate orchestral effect.

[3] Abbreviation of *sordino*, a mute. The word is also used in the feminine *sordina*, plural *sordine*. See below, Ex. 279. In Italian scores one often finds *sordini levati* or *sordini alzati* for mutes off. The French either use the Italian words or *avec* (*sans*) *les sourdines*. For "mutes on" the Germans say either *Gedämpft*, *Dämpfer*, or *Dämpfer auf*. For "mutes off" either *Dämpfer weg*, *Dämpfer fort*, *Dämpfer ab*, or *Ohne Dämpfer*.

passage rather than the more often quoted examples from Lully and Haydn. It is, of course, printed in the usual seventeenth century fashion without nuances of any sort. For modern performance it would have to be carefully slurred, as its character is clearly a *legato cantabile.*

EXAMPLE 243.

In the above example it will be noticed that the Violins alone are muted. This practice continued to be fairly general down to and including Beethoven's day. The reason was simply that makers would not produce mutes of sufficient weight to damp the Violas, Cellos, and Basses properly. It was therefore said that mutes—it should be *inadequate mutes*—made little difference to their tone. The converse is true. Nowadays the invariable rule is "mutes for none" or "for all." The possible exception is to be found in the union of the upper Strings *arco con sord,* with the Cellos and Basses *pizz.* In this case the *pizz* stands out more firmly and pointedly if the mutes are omitted from the *pizzicato* parts.[1]

A beautiful example of the sudden "hush" produced by the muted Strings is to be found in the Second Act of *Tristan.* It occurs just before the words *O sink' hernieder,* etc., on the exquisite rhythm

and is well worth attention, as being an instance of the truly artistic as opposed to the merely sensational use of the muted Strings. The passage is too long to quote here.

A number of examples have already been given of the muted Strings as employed in modern music. The student should now refer back to them. They may be conveniently grouped together here in their order of pitch downwards. The student should, in each case, refer to the example already printed.

(1) Ex. 144. A *pp* series of four-part chords for 1st and 2nd Violins, each group of which is divided into two parts. The effect is delightful, and the chords just serve with the Cello arpeggios to lock together the Horn- and Wood-Wind-chords.

(2) Ex. 5. An ordinary middle-compass example of muted Strings.[2] Note that, with the mutes on, the two upper melody parts

[1] See for instance Ex. 264. [2] See also Ex. 101 (muted Strings, Horn, and Flute).

cannot get anything like the dynamic distinction of the unmuted *f*. If all the strings were unmuted and the two lower parts marked as they are, an *mp* or at most an *mf* would be enough in the Violins.

(3) Ex. 135. For muted Violins in their lowest register (middle orchestral compass) accompanying a Wood-wind melody. The effect of these held chords is particularly charming, when each part is performed by one player only. Chords of this sort can be disposed in any part of the Violin compass. The quality of tone is so thin that a Wood-Wind melody will come through even when the accompanying chords are at a higher or—most doubtful of all—at the same pitch.

(4) Ex. 141. The Violas *tutti*, playing a *cantabile* mainly on their two middle strings. The English-Horn in unison with them. Soft accompaniment for the Horns. (See also Ex. 295.)

(5) Ex. 140. A good example of a *ppp* muted String background used at the lowest pitch possible, lowest, that is to say, if the Violins and Violas are retained in the score. The 2nd Cellos play the bass most of the time. The effect would be slightly heavier if the Basses took this part. In that case the Cellos would not be divided, but would all play the lowest part but one. If they did that either the characteristic Violin harmony on the 4th string (in bars 5 and 8) would be lost, or, more naturally, the Cellos and Basses would play in unison for these bars. Note the unusual "placing" of the Basses in the 9th bar on the A♭ sounding a fifth above the Cello part. In the score the String parts are, of course, engraved on the usual five lines.

(6) Ex. 134. A characteristic example of Strauss's method. The Basses divide into four groups all muted. The soft downy effect of these chords would be a good deal disturbed if the third of the chord were written in at so low a pitch. The Violas and Cellos, also muted, fill in the harmony and play in octaves a portion of another subject against the Oboe tune. The *tenuto* of the actual bass-note is strengthened by the deep G of the Double-Bassoon. The effect of the passage when properly performed is one of great depth, richness, and softness.

(7) Ex. 186. An example of the muted Strings *pizzicato* accompanying a *legato* Clarinet melody. The Basses have, somewhat unusually, a semi-independent part.[1]

The following three examples occur later in the book:

(8) A very light middle-register passage for muted Violins in four parts, with a tonic-and-dominant pedal for *divisi* muted Violas. Ex. 252.

(9) A four-part rhythmical accompaniment for muted 1st and 2nd Violins playing in double-stopping. *Pizzicato* on the second half of each bar for *divisi* muted Violas. Cellos and Basses *pizzicato* unmuted. Ex. 264.

(10) Three-part *pp* harmony for 1st and 2nd Violins and Violas (all muted) in their highest and most ethereal register. Muted Solo-Basses beginning in the lowest part of their compass. Ex. 279.

[1] For other easily accessible examples of muted Strings the student may refer to Haydn (Tenor air in Part 2 of *The Seasons*), Beethoven (Duet in *Fidelio* and *Larghetto* of the *Violin Concerto*), Weber (*Largo* in the *Euryanthe Overture*, and "Leise, leise," in *Der Freischütz*), Berlioz (*Queen Mab Scherzo*).

A few words must be said here with regard to the tone-quality [1] of the Violin. To describe adequately the extraordinary beauty of this, the most perfect of all musical colours, would require a volume, not of prose, but of poetry. The peculiar felicity of the instrument lies in the fact that, though each of its strings has a particular character of its own, and though each seems to possess—for its own register—the most exquisite colour conceivable, yet they all "carry over" into each other without the slightest unevenness.

The 4th string alone, covered as it is with metal filament and reinforced by the "bass-bar" glued underneath the belly, has a slightly harsh and penetrating tone-quality. *Legato* melodies executed on this string by the 1st Violins, or by the 1st and 2nd Violins in unison, are always effective. In compass they are quite safe up to

 or even 

If this tone-colour is needed for any passage, long or short, rising above the low fiddle D♭, the part should, of course, be marked *Sul IV.* or *Sul G*,[2] and, unless it is rendered quite unnecessary by the shape of the phrase, a dotted line thus .... should indicate how long this stage-direction is to remain in force. In general, the natural tendency of String players is to confine *legato* passages as far as possible to one string. This applies all over the whole instrument.

When attacked *ff* with the heel of the bow, the 4th string is harsh and savage in the extreme. Such a phrase as this from the 1st movement of Tschaikowsky's *Pathetic Symphony*:[3]

EXAMPLE 244.

Allegro Vivo. Tschaikowsky. *Pathetic Symphony.*

1st Violins. 

&c.

furnishes a good instance of this ferocious method of expression.[4]

[1] The tone-quality of the Violin, like that of all other instruments, depends, not on the amplitude or frequency of the wave-lengths set up in the air, but on the *shape* of the waves themselves. These wave-forms, in the case of the Violin, take the shape of a succession of gables, in which the left half of each gable is considerably longer than the right. This shape appears to be the nearest instrumental approach to the ideal evenly-undulating line which is the wave-form of the tuning-fork and the human voice.

[2] Dog-Italian for *Sopra* or *Sulla 4ta* (*corda* understood). It may be mentioned in passing that the directions *Sul II.* and *Sul III.* are only rarely used in Scores, and then only as a hint to the player not to use the upper string for a particular phrase. Nobody, of course, writes *Sul I.* for a passage in the topmost octave.

[3] A fragmentary example of a Violin melody *Sul G* has already been given above, Ex. 241.

[4] With regard to the bowing of the above passage the student should notice the somewhat illogical way in which the down-bow marks are scattered through the part. Four down-bow marks only are necessary to secure the proper attack in this passage. They should be placed on the 1st, 4th, 5th, and 10th notes.

Nor does it need, for its full effect, the detestable rattle of the G-string against the fingerboard, which is permitted in some orchestras.

The two middle-strings of the Violin may be conveniently classed together. Of the two the D-string is the sweeter. In fact, a fine *p cantabile* played on this string by a dozen or twenty good fiddlers takes one as near heaven as it is possible to go with the aid of music alone. The quality of the 2nd string is somewhat similar. It is, however, a little more placid and flute-like, "well adapted," in Gevaert's words, "for rendering a soft ideal melody."

The E-string or *chanterelle* is more penetrating than the two middle-strings. The *f* and *mf cantabile* on this string are full of passion and earnestness, while the *p* and *pp* are capable of expressing the most ethereal ideas. In anything approaching a *tutti* or even an orchestral *mezzo-forte* the greater part of the 1st Fiddle music must, of course, lie mainly on the top-string.

Before leaving this topic the student's attention must be drawn to the fact that the tone-colour of a number of Violins playing in unison —what one may call the 16-Fiddle-quality—is quite different from that of a Solo-Violin. It is not a mere augmentation of the Solo-Violin tone, but something different, something sweeter and more softened.[1] This can only be due to the slight differences in intonation which must always exist even when the music is performed by a group of first-class executants. In a Violin-concerto it undoubtedly gives the soloist a somewhat greater chance of "standing out" from the String-ensemble, though, on occasion, the repetition of a simple solo phrase by the orchestral Violins has had an almost comic effect, as if they were saying "this is how it ought really to sound."

The Violins are for orchestral purposes always divided into two main-groups of "1st" and "2nd" Violins, and their parts occupy two lines in the score. In most of the examples quoted above these two parts have been engraved on one stave merely to save space. This abbreviation is never used either in manuscript or in printed Full-Scores.

The number of Violinists employed in a first-class Symphony Orchestra averages 16 to each part; but it must be remembered that, in many orchestras, the 2nd Violins, sitting on the conductor's right hand, hold their instruments with the sound-holes turned away from the audience. That is to say, they are in a position of maximum inefficiency. The result is that dynamically they are about equal to half the number of 1st Violins, and their part, however skilfully written and performed, makes its chief appeal to the Wind-Players at the back of the orchestra. This question of "placing" the strings on a platform is a real difficulty, and there are many things to be said about it from several points of view. However, it cannot be dealt with here. The student must merely note the fact that he cannot, as

[1] See Sir Charles Villiers Stanford's *Musical Composition* (in this series), page 114: "It is well known that the sound of a single Violin is far preferable to that of two Violins playing in unison, and that it is not till the number reaches at least four that the collective effect in unison is satisfactory."

a rule, rely on the same melodic distinction from the two Violin groups.

It is scarcely necessary to say that the 1st and 2nd Violins are occasionally united in a unison, and that, in the upper register, this unison gives the composer one of the most powerful and striking melodic effects at his command. In the bottom register the quality of this unison can be augmented by Violas and Cellos, as in the forceful opening to Bizet's *Arlésienne Suite* (a *ff* unison of 1st and 2nd Violins, Violas, Cellos, English-Horn, two Clarinets, two Bassoons, one Saxophone, and two Horns), in Tschaikowsky's *Fifth Symphony*, Full Score, page 211, and in the well-known $\frac{6}{8}$ tune in E major at the beginning of Act III., Scene II., of Humperdinck's *Hänsel und Gretel* (a unison of 1st and 2nd Violins, Violas and Cellos, with a held Bass-part and an accompaniment of Bassoons *tenuto*, with four Horns and Harp). Naturally this heroic method of procedure is not for all tunes, as it involves the sacrifice of more than half the players in the orchestra to a single part.

Unaccompanied melodic passages are, of course, to be found in profusion in modern music. Perhaps the finest and most elaborate of all occurs at the awakening of Brünnhilde in Wagner's *Siegfried* (beginning of Act III., Scene III.). The whole passage, which may be seen on page 365 of the Full-Score, is assigned to the 1st Violins alone. It ranges through the whole compass of the instrument three octaves, and an augmented fourth upwards from the bottom G, and, except for the two interpolated Trombone-chords, is unaccompanied throughout.

Besides these two main divisions, it is often necessary to divide up again the 1st, or the 2nd, or both the Violin parts. If it is merely a case of a few incidental notes a second stave is not usually employed. The parts are written on the one stave, are differentiated by upward and downward tails, and are marked *div.* Short series of notes, double-stoppings, etc., which cannot possibly be performed by one player, are naturally divided up as they occur. On the other hand, if they can be performed by each player, but, for reasons of smoothness or softness, are not to be so performed, the composer must mark the *divisi* clearly in the part. In the more elaborate *divisis*, where from six to a dozen separate Violin parts are written, it is as well to write not more than two parts on a single stave. An additional cunning is often given nowadays to these divisions, and especially to the employment of a few solo Violins in harmony by writing for special desks of players[1] either near the leader (Nos. 1, 2, etc.) or in the body of the orchestra (Nos. 6, 7, 8, etc.). In the latter case the place from which the sound is coming is much less apparent to the audience.

The elaborate String divisions in which the modern musician delights are much more for the purpose of quiet backgrounds than for actual melodic effects. They are a perfectly legitimate form of expression, but the student should keep well in his mind that every time he divides a part he halves the number of players, and therefore the dynamic efficiency of the constituent parts. Furthermore, he

[1] See Example 135.

should try to avoid the besetting sin of the amateur orchestrator,—writing for the eye and not for the ear. Some composers will blossom out into five or six Violin-lines on the slightest or no provocation. It makes their pages look so grand and imposing, and the existence of a couple of *divisi* notes in any bar is, to them, sufficient justification for their folly. The best cure would be to make them pay for the engraving of their scores.

There is nothing to be said against the use of a quartet of solo Violins, Violas, or Cellos, or against the use of a mixed Solo Quartet.[1] The tone-quality is, for a few moments, a delightful relief, and more than one example has been already given of this exquisite method of accompanying a Wood-Wind solo.[2] On the other hand, when no special effect of this sort is intended, the continual littering of the String-parts with "2 desks only," "3 desks only," and so on is merely a confession of orchestral incompetence. The old String-players' rule "one or all" was not so bad after all.

The use of a single Violin playing an independent passage requires a little caution. One has to consider and provide for the differences between the 1-Fiddle and the 16-Fiddle tone-quality. The Solo-Violin, in fact, needs special treatment, and it can scarcely be pitted with advantage against any thick, spread mass of sound. Almost any scores of Richard Strauss will afford examples of the lightness and thinness which are necessary in order to secure a proper effect from a solo Violin.

The student need not worry much with regard to suitable keys for the Violin. Except for the most difficult and florid passages the technique is sufficiently pliable to meet all demands. Even the extreme keys are less to be avoided than sudden changes of chord and irregularities during the progress of what should be symmetrical figures. There is, however, no getting away from the fact that, owing to its tuning, the Violin is happiest in simple sharp keys, that is to say in G major and D major and in those keys that are nearest to them.[3] For the orchestral composer this is scarcely more than a "counsel of perfection." However, it is just as well to remember that the most crooked passages become surprisingly straight when there is the possibility of an occasional open-string or Harmonic.

All major keys from E♭ to E♮ and all minor keys from C to B♮ may be looked upon as easy.

Slightly more awkward are the major keys of A♭ and B♮ and the minor keys of F♮ and F♯.

The most difficult major keys are D♭, G♭, C♭, F♯, C♯, and the most difficult minor keys, B♭, E♭, A♭, C♯, G♯, D♯.

[1] This style of accompaniment was common at the end of the seventeenth and the beginning of the eighteenth century. At the Paris Opera House the solo trio of two Violins and one Cello was a regular institution. It was known as *petit choeur*, while the rest of the Strings were called the *grand choeur*. See *Gevaert*, page 44.

[2] See, for instance, Example 135.

[3] E major is commonly spoken of as the "Violin-key" by all except those who play the instrument.

The following complete list of keys shows their comparative difficulty at a glance. The large, middle-sized, and small types are used respectively for the easiest, the less easy, and the most difficult keys:

Major.

C♭, G♭, D♭, A♭, E♭, B♭, F, C, G, D, A, E, B♮, F♯

Minor.

A♭, E♭, B♭, F, C, G, D, A, E, B, F♯, C♯, G♯, D♯.

The character of the Violin is so varied that it is not possible to give within the limits of an instrumentation book a series of passages which would adequately illustrate its technical possibilities. A knowledge of this technique is an important part of a composer's equipment, but it is only to be gained by a first-hand acquaintance with the instrument, by a diligent perusal of Full-Scores, and by study in the Theatre and Concert-room. These studies it is hoped the student will undertake aided by a knowledge of the rough general principles of Violin playing, which have been given above.

It goes without saying that practice in String-quartet writing is an essential preliminary to the acquisition of ease and suppleness in the treatment of the orchestral Strings. The two things are not identical. In writing for the orchestra a great many facts have to be considered that can be neglected in writing for a quartet of evenly balanced "voices." These questions of contrast, balance, and variety cannot be dealt with here; but it is in their proper solution that the secret of successful orchestration lies.

No. 47. The Viola (or Tenor).

Fr. *Alto*, It. *Viola*, Ger. *Bratsche.*

The Viola is not merely "a big Violin." It is a Viola. If it were called "a big but not quite big enough Violin" that would be a better description, for though its four strings are tuned

a perfect fifth below those of the Violin, its size by no means corresponds to the increased depth of pitch. A similar remark holds true of the Cello, but in that instrument the deficiency in size is compensated by extreme depth of ribs and height of bridge. On the Viola, however, these compensations are impracticable. Nor can the general size of the instrument be increased so as to be in correct proportion to its pitch. In either case we should get an instrument too small to be played satisfactorily in the Cello-position and far too large to be properly played in the Violin-position. The result of these discrepancies between size and pitch is our present Viola, a betwixt-and-between instrument imperfect in construction, "difficult" and somewhat uneven in tone-quality,[1] and undeniably clumsy to manage

In actual size the instrument shows a much greater percentage of difference than any other member of the String-group. The corresponding differences in ease-of-management between, let us say, a huge sixteenth-century Gaspar and a modern French Viola are so great that it is difficult to class the two, except in pitch, as the same instrument. There is, therefore, considerable latitude for the player in the choice of an instrument. On this point there are many divergent opinions, but on the whole it may be said that the first necessity of the Viola above all other stringed-instruments is warmth and depth of tone-colour. Without size this appears to be an impossibility. The resulting difficulty in handling the instrument has to be faced by players, but the difficulty of this position can easily be "turned" if composers would steadily refuse to treat the instrument as a *Violon manqué*, and if players would as steadily refrain from practising Fiddle-studies on the Viola in public.

In fitting and general appearance the Viola differs from the Violin in only one particular. The two bottom strings—the C and G—are both covered; that is to say, they are "spun" with metal filament in order to secure the necessary weight without undue thickness.

The Viola-technique is, in theory, precisely the same as that of the Violin. All that was said above with regard to the Violin fingering, positions, shakes, *tremolos*, Natural and Artificial Harmonics, double-, triple-, and quadruple-stopping, bow-strokes, lists of keys, and so on, applies equally to the Viola when transposed down a perfect fifth. It is therefore unnecessary to repeat these details. A few slight differences, however, due to the pitch, the greater size, and the consequent more clumsy build of the instrument, may be mentioned.

Chromatic technique.

This is precisely the same as on the Violin. In each case a single finger is used to play both the natural and the chromatic note. Chromatic passages, however, are somewhat easier in execution and clearer in effect when played on the Viola. This is due to the greater length of its strings as compared with those of the Violin. The finger has more room in which to move. The intonation of the semitones is more easily precise, and enharmonic differences are more apparent to the ear. The greater chromatic freedom of the Viola, however, must be taken in a comparative sense only. The instrument is no more purely chromatic in its technique than the Violin.

Short chromatic passages in the middle and bottom registers are always orchestrally effective. Care should be taken that each of these

[1] The Viola more than any other stringed-instrument is liable to have some one or two *wolf notes* in its compass. In fact very few Violas are wholly free from this defect. The opposite disease, commonly known as *sleep*, seems to affect it less. Perhaps its constitution, inured for centuries to sleepy passages, has by now become immune to the microbe of sleeping-sickness.

passages is not too long. Furthermore, they are much more effective slurred than bowed. This may be taken in a general sense for both fast and slow passages. In particular, very fast bowed chromatic scales are almost impossible. This is not due to any defect in the left-hand technique, but to the constitutional unreadiness of the instrument to speak.

The alto- or C-clef (𝄡) on the third line is used normally for all Viola-music. For the highest notes the G- or Violin-clef (𝄞) on the second line is employed. As a rule the former clef would be written for all passages up to about

The 𝄞 is scarcely worth using, except in those rare cases where a complete passage lies in the top octave, say from

 upwards.

Continual change of clef is worrying to the player. Even in the case of a passage which is mainly in the highest register and must therefore be written in the 𝄞 it is as well not to interpolate the 𝄡 simply because the passage happens to descend for a moment. For instance, in the extract given below from Strauss's *Ein Heldenleben*,[1] the use of the 𝄡 at bar 4 would certainly save a leger line. The notation, however, is clearer as it stands.

Upward Compass.

It is unwise to go beyond

in the orchestra.[2] Indeed the last three or four semitones of this compass can, in the ordinary orchestral routine, be dispensed with. This leaves the instrument with a three-octave compass, sufficient for most purposes, one would think. In dealing with the top-register it must not be forgotten that, owing to the size of his instrument, the Viola-player has much more difficulty in fingering his notes than the violinist. The upper curves of his instrument are large. They therefore offer a much greater obstacle to his left hand. He has however

[1] See Ex. 245.

[2] With of course the Natural Harmonic A a fourth higher. See below, page 389, for its Harmonic compass.

no "thumb position"[1] like the Cellist. He has to rely solely on the Violin-technique, and has to apply it in disadvantageous circumstances. So long as he is not called upon to rise beyond the 5th position on the 1st string, the technique suffices; but, beyond that, the fundamental deficiencies of a "too large and too small" instrument begin to assert themselves, and the technique, except with the most brilliant players, "peters out."

It does not follow, then, that the Viola can be regarded in its top register as merely a Violin tuned a fifth lower. Any good violinist is much more at his ease between

than the correspondingly good Viola-player between

Indeed it might almost be said that, in judging the relative difficulty of Viola-passages *in alt*, it is safer to class them with similar Violin-passages an octave higher.

Another reason for using the upper Viola-register with some caution is to be found in the fact that Viola-players are not continually playing in that register. Attention has been already drawn to this point in the section devoted to the Horn. It applies less to a stringed-instrument, but, even here, if a composer allots 99 per cent. of his Viola-music to its two lower octaves he must be prepared to find that the player inevitably loses a certain portion of freedom in the extreme top-register.

A Viola-passage like the following, the last five bars of which are included not as an example but as a warning, can only be made orchestrally tolerable in very special circumstances. Here it forms part of a tremendous melodic String-unison supported by the whole orchestra. The Violins really pull the passage through. The circumstances may justify this special case, but one would not like to be asked to name the orchestra whose Violas could play these bars neatly with only a light *pizzicato* accompaniment.

EXAMPLE 245.

Sehr lebhaft. **Strauss.** ***Ein Heldenleben.***

[1] See page 411.

The above remarks must not be taken as pointing backwards to the bad old days when Viola players were selected merely because they were too wicked or too senile to play the Violin. Those days are happily gone for ever. The path of progress lies in the direction of writing for the instrument with all the freedom possible in this age of study and specialization, but with a knowledge of the instrument's limitations.

Like all the middle-compass instruments, the Viola has to take its share of "filling-up." This is not a drawback. In a way it is a peculiar felicity for the orchestral composer. With perhaps a single exception, every "voice" which he is at liberty to call upon for musical utterance is in itself beautiful. Simple phrases, therefore, which lack interest when exhibited in an imperfect and mechanical medium—such as the *pianoforte*—acquire, on the orchestral instruments, a *beauty of sound* second only to that of human voices. This point is worth keeping in mind when the temptation arises to write wild, crooked, pianistic passages for the Viola.

Chords.

The available double-, triple-, and quadruple-stops may be taken in a body from the list of Violin chords given on pages 315 to 328. For the Viola they must, of course, be all transposed down a perfect fifth. In general it is the lower parts of the Violin-chords (transposed) which are most serviceable on the Viola. The nasal twang of the top string gives a certain unevenness and emptiness to big spread chords.

In laying out chords for the Viola it must be remembered that there is an added heaviness in the triple- and quadruple-stops. They should only be used in fairly simple keys where there are opportunities for the employment of the open strings. As a rule, the triple-stops are of greatest orchestral service when written for the three bottom strings.

It is necessary to mention these reservations explicitly, but the student must not forget that the principal object of orchestration is the enforcing of musical ideas by means of suitable tone-colour. He should not be too ready to throw away the more striking tone-colours of the Strings on *any* musical passage; nor to risk spoiling his musical idea by so doing. He should reserve the right quality for the right idea. The peculiar "hulking" quality of the Viola chords is a strong weapon in his hand, but a weapon that should only be used at the right moment. When associated with the chords of the Cellos and with the notes of the Basses its effect varies, according to the character of the music, from a rich, organ-like placidity to a sombre and sometimes almost painful savagery.

Simple double-stops are more continually used and more smoothly effective on the Viola than on any other stringed-instrument. Indeed, in many modern works the Violas are constantly playing in two parts. This must not be taken to mean two parts each of which has a clear contrapuntal outline, but merely two "filling-up" parts. Naturally the three lower strings are more often employed for this sort of work than the top string.

In such unobtrusive passages cases often occur where an isolated chord or two cannot be performed by each separate player. Both notes, for instance, may lie on the bottom string. It is unnecessary always to mark these chords *div.* The players will instinctively divide at such places. An example can be seen in the extract printed below, page 413, from the 3rd Movement of the *Choral Symphony.* In the last bar but one of the Viola part the first two chords are quite easy and natural to play. The third chord—low D and F♯—is an impossibility, as both notes lie on the bottom string. The players, therefore, divide for that chord only, and resume the unison on the next quaver. See also Bar 2 of the *Freischütz* Example printed below,[1] where the same thing occurs.

On the other hand, if the composer wishes the whole passage divided he must mark it clearly in his score. See, for instance, the Example quoted below[2] from Strauss's *Don Juan.* The last bar, both in the 1st and 2nd Violin parts, could quite easily be played in double-stopping, but it is specially marked *div* in both cases. The result is, of course, an actual halving of the amount of tone on each part.

A consideration arises here which is of general application. All two-part writing for single stringed-instruments is less pure and flexible than the same two-part writing when played *divisi.* This has been matter of general observation, though the reason has, one thinks, not been mentioned. The explanation is simple and purely physical. In order to produce the maximum resonance, whether in the *p* or the *f*, a certain speed and pressure of bow-stroke has to be used. This speed and pressure differ materially as between any two of the four strings. When, therefore, the bow is setting any two neighbouring strings in vibration, a certain compromise speed-and-pressure has to be adopted. This accommodation of the bow, while satisfactory for most practical purposes, suits neither of the strings perfectly. The result is a certain loss in the purity and flexibility of the tone, and this loss is orchestrally less noticeable in the *p* than in the *f*.

As on the Violin, chords can be arranged in any form of arpeggio, and either slurred or bowed. For purposes of quiet accompaniment the former method is usually the more convenient. Such passages are perhaps more common on the Viola than on the other stringed-instruments, as its pitch and tone-quality tends to throw them into the required shadow. This style of quiet arpeggio may be illustrated by an excerpt from Act I. Scene 3 of *Die Walküre.* The student should notice that, except for the first arpeggio, which has to be played in the 2nd position, all the chords lie easily under the hand in the 1st position, and, where possible, make use of at least one open string in each chord. The last bar is a little awkward, as in it the fingers cannot be laid on the strings in their natural position, viz., in the

[1] Example 278. [2] Example 247.

order 1st finger, 2nd finger, 3rd finger, at increasing distances from the nut. The substitution of a B♮ for A, the second note of the arpeggio, would simplify the passage from the player's point of view.

EXAMPLE 246.

Natural Harmonics.

The technique, notation, and available list of Natural Harmonics is exactly the same for the Viola as for the Violin. The list given above, pp. 328-9, has therefore only to be transposed down a perfect fifth.

Artificial Harmonics.

A similar remark applies here. However, owing to the imperfections of the instrument, it cannot be said that the Artificial Harmonics come out as well on the Viola as on the Violin. This is more particularly the case with those Artificial Harmonics which must be taken on the C-string. Nevertheless they are practicable, and as the great orchestral difficulty in writing Artificial-Harmonic-chords is to keep their pitch low enough for intelligibility, the compass and resources of the Viola in this direction are not to be overlooked.

An example of these Artificial Harmonics (for Violas divided into three parts) has already been quoted above[1] from Strauss's *Also sprach Zarathustra.* If the student wishes to see a more elaborate example he should examine the Viola parts at "No. 18" in the same work. In this passage the composer, beginning with a single high G♯,

gradually adds parts till he has a complete five-part Harmonic-chord played by six groups of Violas. The bottom part is doubled, and the whole series of notes is played *tremolo.*

The following is the complete compass of the Viola in both Natural- and Artificial-Harmonics:

Of these notes the first three can only be played in Natural Harmonics. The rest can all be played in Artificial Harmonics, and those notes which are marked with a + can be taken both ways.

The Viola Bow

is precisely similar in shape to the Violin bow, but it is a good deal heavier and rather less elastic. All the *coups d'archet* which are practicable on the Violin are also practicable on the Viola. The lighter strokes, however, such as the V *staccato* and the *jeté,* are considerably less effective on the latter instrument. This is due partly to the greater weight of the Viola bow, but principally to the fact that not one Viola in a hundred will "speak" with the readiness of an ordinary Violin. The instrument needs a certain continual nursing and coaxing with the bow-arm. Consequently the heavier strokes, such as the *f détaché,* the *sforzando,* and the *legato* slur are much more in its character. The last point is worthy of particular attention, for a good deal of the "chippiness" of effect with which the Viola has been charged is really due to want of proper phrasing.

[1] Example 235.

It should be remembered that the Viola bow has to be kept moving at a fair pace in order to produce a good steady tone. Consequently the number of notes that may be included in a single ⊓ or V is somewhat curtailed. Even in the *p* and *mp* this point must be borne in mind. In the *f* and *ff* two or three crotchets in *moderato* time are about the limit. This applies equally to the Cello. The following passage is from Strauss's *Don Juan*. The melody for Violas and Cellos is marked *f molto appass.*, and contains three *nuance crescendos* in the first three bars.

EXAMPLE 247.

Phrased as written there is an inevitable hardness and tightness of the tone in bars 2 and 3. If bar 2 is taken *détaché* throughout, or at most with the last two notes under one slur, and if bar 3 is split up into two slurs over the 1st and 2nd halves of the bar respectively, a very much better and more vigorous result is obtained. It is always depressing to watch the Cellists and Viola-players in an orchestra straining to get tone, and yet not daring to adopt the only means by which it can be got,—plenty of bow. As a rule in this country conductors pay far too little attention to the necessary refinements of String-phrasing. They rely on the infallibility of the composer, and play his parts as printed or copied. More often they save time by putting the whole matter aside and leaving it to chance. In a recent

[1] The entrance of the Flute, 3rd and 4th Horns, and Timpani is omitted from the last bar of the example.

performance of the passage printed above each one of the Cellists and Viola players adopted a phrasing to suit his own individual taste. The result to the ears of the audience is of course no phrasing at all,—mud instead of rhythm.

Tremolos.

The only difference to be noted here occurs in the case of the Fingered-Tremolo. It was stated that in the Fingered-Tremolo of the Violin the utmost stretch possible between the 1st and 4th fingers on the same string was an augmented fourth, while, with the 1st finger on one string and the 4th finger on the next higher string, the maximum stretch was a minor ninth.

Owing to its greater length of string these limits, in the case of the Viola, have to be reduced respectively to a perfect fourth and an octave.

The caution to keep the notes of the Fingered-Tremolo as close as possible applies with even greater force to the larger instrument.

Nothing more need be said here with regard to the different "fancy" methods of tone-variation. The *Ponticello*, the *Sul Tasto*, and the *Col Legno* have already been sufficiently described in the section devoted to the Violin. It is to be noted, however, as a general statement that the *Pizzicato* becomes more resonant as it descends through the String-groups from the Violins to the Basses.

Mutes are regularly used nowadays on the Violas when that quality of tone is required. As we have already seen, the ancient composers' reluctance to use muted Violas, and the ancient theorists' explanation of that reluctance on the ground that their tone was already "sufficiently veiled by nature," have their common origin in the fact that the then existing mutes did not adequately damp the vibrations. No stringed-instrument answers so well to the mute as the Viola. Its strings, already struggling against the difficulties of a too-small sound-box, reduce their utterance, under the mastery of a heavy close-fitting mute, to a weird mystical thinness. In especial the two outer strings undergo a transformation that has the curious effect of at once attenuating their tone and intensifying their characteristics. Under these conditions the top-string becomes over-nasalized to the quality of a far-off double-reed instrument, while the bottom-string suffers a C-change which muffles and, at the same time, accentuates its tragic quality.

Tone Quality.

This is an important feature of the Viola. The discrepancies between the size and the pitch of the instrument have already been referred to. It is these discrepancies which produce its characteristic flavour of sombre antiquity.

The top-string is perhaps the most affected. Its quality has something nasal and piercing; something suffering, even unpleasant. A prominent melody on this string becomes unbearable after a short time.[1] In the *p* it appears to great disadvantage if contrasted with the lovely Violin-tone of the same register. On the other hand a tearing *forte* subject, if not too much prolonged, is immensely effective. Such a passage has already been quoted above[2] from Strauss's *Don Juan.* The student should notice, in the last bars of that extract, the curiously good and telling effect of the Violas with the Wood-Wind. This peculiarity of the instrument has been well known almost since orchestral composition began. Indeed it is one of the strong characteristics of the Viola that, while its melodic effects with String accompaniment leave something to be desired, each of its strings exhibits an affinity with some one or other of the Wind-groups. The top-string in particular not only combines well with the Wood-Wind, but shows in a degree remarkable for a stringed-instrument certain likenesses to the heavy Brass. In this register it can be quite well combined with the *p* or *mp* of the Trombones and Trumpets. This was known to Berlioz, and it has often been practised since his day.

The two middle strings are at once the least characteristic and the most sympathetic. Lacking the piercing unhappy quality of the top-string, they combine well with almost anything in the orchestra,—with the other Strings, with high or low Wood-Wind, and with Horns. It is on these two strings that the Viola does most of the accompanying and filling-up work, to which a great part of its existence is devoted. It is quite unnecessary to quote examples of such passages as they abound in every Score. The instrument, however, is often entrusted with melodic passages in this middle register, and no better example could be given than the beautiful subject already quoted from Tschaikowsky's *Romeo and Juliet.*[3]

A remark may be interpolated here with regard to the striking emphasis which the Viola quality lends to the minor-mode. This may be merely associative. It may be a half-conscious mental linking of its antique tone-colour with the dark hues of the ancient Dorian mode. Whether this be so or not, it is a fact that a large number of effective melodic passages in the minor-mode have been assigned to the instrument. In place of quoting any of the well-known classical examples, an extract will be given here from Bridge's Symphonic Poem *Isabella.* This excerpt has already been referred to[4] as an example of cleverly contrived bowing. The sixteen bars of which it consists give both an excellent example of the Viola used melodically chiefly on its two upper strings, and of the peculiar lamenting quality with which it can invest the minor-mode. It must be said that in the Score the 3rd Horn (the 2nd highest of the four Horn-parts) occupies a line to itself. These three Horn-parts are here compressed on to one

[1] Berlioz commends this string for use in "scenes of religious and antique character," and instances Spontini's *La Vestale* as the first work in which it was so employed. Since his day this type of characterization has become common. See, for instance, the *Andante con Moto*—the so-called "Pilgrims' March"—in Mendelssohn's *Italian Symphony.* Wagner has employed the instrument with the same object both in *Tannhäuser* and *Lohengrin.*

[2] Example 247. [3] Example 141. [4] Page 344.

stave for reasons of space. The 4th Horn-part in the bass-clef transposes downwards in the way usual in modern Scores. The vertical arrangement of the Wood-Wind parts,[1] the momentary introduction of the Oboes on the two climax-bars of the tune (bars 8 and 16), and the phrasing of the String *cantabile* are all worth attention.

EXAMPLE 248.

[1] See also the arrangement of the Wood-Wind in the short extract from Wagner's *Lohengrin* given under "Bass-Clarinet," Example 192.

The bottom-string[1] of the Viola is the most characteristic of all. In fact, to the average concert-goer the Viola is only a Viola when it is on its bottom-string. "Sombre, austere, sometimes even forbidding,"[2] its mere sound, even in the simplest phrases, is sufficient to conjure up the image of Tragedy. Indeed, the simpler and more persistent the phrase the greater its effect when played on the Viola. Gevaert mentions the impressive effect produced in Act III. of *Robert le Diable* by these few Viola notes:

EXAMPLE 249.

They could be played either in the 1st position on the 3rd and 4th strings or in the 3rd position on the 4th string. Even simpler is the rhythmically-complex reiterated note assigned to the Violas in Rebecca's song, "*Lord of our chosen race*" (Sullivan's *Ivanhoe*, Act II., Scene III.).

EXAMPLE 250.

In the Full Score these notes combine with a String *pizzicato*, Harp-chords, and a *tenuto* for English-Horn in supporting the Vocal-

[1] It need scarcely be said that, in every stringed-instrument, the bottom (open) string is regularly used for its enharmonic equivalent. Thus the notes:

are continually written in Violin- and Viola-parts respectively.

[2] Gevaert. See also the reiterated Viola "D" in Ex. 154.

Melody. They give a curiously restless and tragic colour to the song. This type of expression so characteristic of the instrument is as old as the time of Gluck. Berlioz quotes with eloquent admiration from that master's *Iphigénie en Tauride* the air of Orestes, in which the Violas play a continual throbbing syncopated middle-part. The whole Viola part has only a compass of a minor third—G to B♭—and out of sixty bars fifty contain merely repetitions of the note A. Berlioz claims this "fearful and persevering mutter of the violas" as an "unspeakably fine piece of inspiration."

The student should accustom himself to listen carefully to the quality of the Viola bottom-octave, and especially to differentiate between its mental effect and the effect of the same notes when played mainly on the 2nd string of the Cello. On this point it is impossible to give any rule. Probably any passage will be as playable on the one instrument as on the other. A little experience is needed here in order to ensure a correct decision between Viola, Cello, and Viola-and-Cello unison.

The Viola has perhaps suffered the ups and downs of musical treatment more than any other stringed-instrument. In the late sixteenth and early seventeenth century it held much the same position in the orchestra that the 1st and 2nd Violins occupy to-day. We have only to remember that fact in order to realize how sombre, melancholy, and unbending must have been the quality of the String-ensemble in those times.[1] The Violin, however, with its higher pitch and its more exquisite tone-colour, was continually "knocking at the door," and the Viola found itself servant where once it had been master.

So long as Music was developing along the polyphonic lines, which we now associate with the name of Bach, this meant little decrease in its dignity. The instrumental family which joined its voices in the elaboration of fugues and fugatos was a happy family, the members of which differed among themselves only in the matter of pitch, not of importance. With the downfall of the old polyphony, however, all was changed. The family had now got one master—the top-line melody—and it is easy to understand the feeling of relief with which men's minds turned to this new and agreeable species of music. The bustle and confusion of four or five real parts was now replaced, except for the most special occasions, by a straightforward tune, supported by a modest tinkle of accompaniment.

If we turn now to the Scores that represent this period—that is to say the Haydn-, Mozart-, and even early Beethoven-Scores—we feel that the Viola is often merely a source of anxiety to the composer. We feel that he must have regarded its existence as something in the nature of a prehistoric survival. The instrument was there and had to be written for. Interesting but subordinate contrapuntal middle-parts were, however, still a thing of the future. The Viola, therefore, either did nothing or something which by the ingenuity of the composer was

[1] See, for instance, the extract quoted above from Monteverde's *Il Combattimento di Tancredi*. Example 227. The three top parts, Viola da brazzo I^{ma}, II^{da}, and III^{a}, are for the *Tenor-Viol* or *Viola-da-Braccio* mentioned on page 300.

made to appear as much like nothing as possible. If all else failed it could always play the bass, and, though this often resulted in an unnecessary and uncomfortable three-octave-bass, it was better than filling the part with rests.

Then Beethoven began to develop his style. In his quartets and symphonies he soon began to find out ways in which the Viola might be more individualized from the rest of the Strings. Occasional melodic unisons with the Cellos—such as those in Symphonies No. 5 (*Andante con Moto*), No. 6 (*Andante molto mosso* and *Allegretto*), No. 7 (*Allegretto*), and No. 9[1] (*Allegro assai*): Solo passages—such as that in the E♭ Quartet (Op. 127)—and new groupings, such as that solemn association of Viola- and Cello-harmonies in the *Finale* of the *Choral Symphony* are to be met with in the works of his middle and third periods.

On the whole, however, it cannot be said that Beethoven exalted the Viola in the same way that he exalted some of the other orchestral instruments. His main contribution consisted of this, that he found a way in which he could always give the Violas a wholly independent yet subordinate middle part. In his music they are always "doing something," perhaps not very interesting, but still something which materially adds to the general orchestral prosperity.

Berlioz was perhaps the first person to undertake the serious study of the Viola from the composer's point of view. His researches on this point are embodied in his elaborate work, *Harold in Italy*. Unfortunately a good deal of this work is monumentally dull, while in many places the composer shows only an imperfect acquaintance with the instrument's possibilities. The result usually is that one hearing of *Harold in Italy* is quite enough to put the listener off the Viola for the rest of his life.

With the advent of Wagner the Viola began to be written for as it deserved. Its patience was no longer tried, and the edge of its qualities blunted by a continual subservience to the caprices of the other Strings. Wagner never experimentalized with the Violas in the way that Brahms did. The latter composer did not hesitate at such an atavism[2] as a Symphonic work in which the top String-line throughout was assigned to the Violas. In his other works too one continually "feels" the presence of the Viola-tone as something rather too prominent and sometimes even unpleasant. Occasionally there is an apparent disregard of the peculiar tone-quality with which they are sure to endow their phrases. Hence comes a certain sombre effect, a somewhat unnatural air of lumbering solemnity. Wagner never did this. He had

[1] See also the forceful unison of Violas, Cellos, and two Bassoons at the end of the *Egmont Overture*, beginning at Bar 4, page 71 (Peters's Ed.).

[2] Under the influence of the early nineteenth century Ossianic movement Méhul wrote a complete Opera—*Uthal*—with this instrumentation (Violas in place of Violins). According to Berlioz Grétry's criticism on this procedure was conveyed in the remark, "I'd give a guinea to hear a *first string*." Other composers, such as Cherubini in his *C minor Requiem*, have omitted the Violins from a complete movement in order to secure a special tone-colour throughout. Bach's interesting experiments in String-writing without Violins are rarely heard nowadays in our concert-rooms.

the true orchestral "sense" that is content to subordinate or omit colour till its prominence is called for in order to enforce the musical idea. His Violas have to play acres of "filling-up" stuff, but their prominence when it comes, is a prominence urgently demanded by the special character of the music.

In more modern times still the composer has begun to ask of the Viola-player much the same extension and perfection of technique as he asks of the Cellist or the Violinist. Strauss in particular treats the instrument with a freedom and plasticity quite unknown before his day. It cannot perhaps be said that the elaborate Viola *obbligato* in the *Don Quixote Variations*—however cleverly characteristic of its subject, Sancho Panza—adds much to the dignity or technique of the instrument. Example 251, taken from the Sancho Panza section of the *Introduction*, gives a fair idea both of Strauss's whimsical treatment of the Viola and of his typical style of orchestral accompaniment. The Bass-Clarinet is of course to be read as sounding a major ninth lower, and the Tenor-Tuba a major second lower. Their phrase in the 11th Bar is therefore a unison, whose first note is a major third above the 3rd Bassoon part.

It has already been mentioned that the Violas are more often divided than either of the groups of Violins. This remark should, however, be qualified by the statement that, whereas the simple two-part *divisi* which makes up the hack-work of harmony is common on the Viola, the elaborate Violin-subdivisions which are perhaps too common in modern Scores are less often found in the Viola-parts. Such an elaboration as the twelve-part-*divisi* (eight-part shakes and four-part Bowed-Tremolos) in Variation II. of Strauss's *Don Quixote* is only of the rarest occurrence.

EXAMPLE 251.

Another point which cannot fail to be noticed in the perusal of modern Scores is that the Viola, being a midway instrument as far as pitch is concerned, is associated (1) as a middle-part with the general orchestral ensemble, (2) as a lower-part with the upper strings and Wood-wind, and (3) as an upper-part with the lower portions of the orchestra. The result of this is that the Viola-part of any modern orchestral work is as a rule longer than even the 1st Fiddle-part.

With regard to (1) nothing need be added to what has already been said.

With regard to (2) it is obvious that where the compass permits and only a very light String-bass is wanted the Violas can be used for that purpose. A well-known example of this method is to be found in the opening *Adagio* of the air *Softly sighs* (Act II. Scene II. of Weber's Opera *Der Freischütz*). This has been quoted so often that the student will probably prefer to see a more modern instance, the fascinating String-passage in Tschaikowsky's *Romeo and Juliet* that follows the Viola-melody already quoted above.[1] In this example the muted Violas repeat the tonic and dominant pedal, while the muted Violins in four-parts play the curiously wavering and attractive harmonies in their soft middle register.

EXAMPLE 252.

The two pedal parts in the above extract could of course be played by Cellos *divisi* or by Cellos and Violas. It is just on this point that the student should try to cultivate his orchestral cunning so as to distinguish the subtle differences of the three methods.

With regard to (3) the first thing to notice is the constant use of the Viola-and-Cello-unison for melodic purposes. This method of reinforcing the String tone in the tenor-octave was first practised as a part of his ordinary orchestral routine by Beethoven. A reference has already been made to a number of his works in which this procedure is adopted. Mozart also occasionally uses this unison, but he generally does so, not for a full-dress melody, but in order to give momentary prominence to a short isolated phrase. See for instance the 3rd and 4th bars of the Introduction to Zerlina's song *Vedrai carino* in Act II. of *Don Giovanni*.

The important point for the student to notice is that while the Violas add a good deal to the power and weight of a subject so arranged, they rob the Cello top-string of a good deal of its clarity and "bite," and substitute a certain velvety thickness and richness. The distinction can be grasped in a moment by listening carefully to the opening bars of the *Tristan* prelude as played by the Cellos alone:

[1] Example 141.

EXAMPLE 253.

Wagner. *Tristan.*

and then contrasting the effect with the similar passage towards the end of the prelude:

EXAMPLE 254.

Wagner. *Tristan.*

The Schumann *Pianoforte Concerto in A minor* is another work in which these differences can be observed with ease. In the *Intermezzo* of that work the Cellos alone play the subject:

EXAMPLE 255.

Schumann. *Pfte Concerto.*

Later on the Violas are added thus:

EXAMPLE 256.

Schumann. *Pfte. Concerto.*

This instance, though less in the modern style than the Wagner excerpt, is perhaps more instructive, as the compass is so much greater. The student should especially note, at a performance of this work, the tone-quality on the top C, B, and A. Here the Violas themselves are on their top-string, and, so far from dulling and smoothing the Cello-tone, they add enormously to its pungency. Indeed, within the very narrow available limits of pitch there is nothing in the orchestra so poignant and irresistible as the unison of Cellos and Violas, both playing on their top-strings.

Attention must however be principally directed towards the harmonic- not the melodic-union of Violas with Cellos. With this union the Basses are, especially in the theatre, often associated. Occasionally too the Bassoons, Horns, and *p* Trombones are added. Whatever the arrangement of this sonorous ensemble, its basis is almost invariably a *divisi* harmony of Violas and Cellos. The quality of tone so produced is, when *legato*, rich and somewhat organ-like: when detached and *forte*, impressively crude and sometimes almost savage. In most cases of this sort the top line, or even the two upper parts, *can be* arranged for Violins. The substitution of the *divisi* Violas, however, gives a quite different character to the music, a character perhaps not often desirable, but, when desired, strikingly effective.

So many examples of this type of orchestration are familiar to all that it is scarcely necessary to give any quotations. Among the best-known are

(1) The accompaniment to Wolfram's address at the beginning of the *Sängerkrieg* in Tannhäuser. The key is E♭, and the whole passage is over a hundred bars long. The accompaniment consists of nothing but Violas and Cellos (*divisi*, according to circumstances), and a Harp playing in simple arpeggios and chords. This is a good example of the long continuance of one tone-colour, quite appropriate and effective in Opera, but lacking variety when transferred to the Concert-room.

(2) The short passage in *Lohengrin's Narration*, in which the Viola and Cello harmonies are supported and reinforced by the Trumpet, Trombones, and Tuba. (Full Score, bottom of page 357.)

(3) The far-off organ effect in Act III. of *Die Meistersinger*. Here both the Violas and Cellos are divided into two-parts, each of which plays in double-stopping, that is to say, eight notes in all. (Full Score, page 355, beginning at Bar 7.)

(4) Act I., Scene II., of *Tristan*, just after Kurwenal's words "Darf ich die Antwort sagen." (Passage begins in the Full Score at the bottom of page 34 and continues as far as page 37, bar 5.) This is a *locus classicus*. The student should by no means omit to examine the passage.

The above list might very easily be added to, and other composers —German, French, Russian,[1] and English—might be drawn upon for purposes of quotation. Wagner, however, exhibits such a certain and subtle "touch" in this matter that it is quite satisfactory to confine the illustrations to his works.

In this country Elgar[2] continually shows a keen appreciation of the instrument's capabilities and limitations. In particular he has the faculty of writing passages and melodic subjects which are not only orchestrally effective, but which *must* be played on the instrument for reasons of compass. This is an important point. So many composers when writing for the Viola think in climaxes that are far too high

[1] *E.g.* the *Allegro non troppo* at the beginning of Tschaikowsky's *Pathetic Symphony.*

[2] See for instance his variations *Dorabella* (con sord.), *Ysobel*, and *Troyte* (Violas in octaves), and the unexpected high unison of Violas and 2nd Violins in *Pomp and Circumstance, No. I.* (Full Score, page 4).

for the instrument. They are also apt to neglect the bottom string entirely. The instrument labours under the disadvantage of not being sufficiently individualized in composers' minds. There is, however, no getting beyond a phrase like this. It must be either Violas or nothing.

EXAMPLE 257.

Elgar. *Enigma Variations.*[1]

The neglect of the bottom string seems to be often due to the fear that its use will make the music thick and heavy. But this fear is groundless. The orchestral sound of the instrument on that string, especially in the *p* and *mp*, has nothing of the tubby effect of the same notes on the *Pianoforte.* Owing to the relative shortness of its string and the consequent difference in its harmonics, the Viola is much less likely than the Cello to overweight a passage in that register.

Occasionally a single Viola is employed as a solo instrument. In the old school of opera this usually meant a full-dress Obbligato made up of little scale-passages and arpeggios, both of which the Viola does in a nicely sympathetic and not too obtrusive manner.[2] Nowadays this sort of thing is scarcely *à la mode.* The interest of adding a fussy nothing to something is questioned. Also it takes a Mozart to save such a musical situation. The Viola Soloist has, therefore, less space nowadays in which to move about. On the other hand, he generally has something much better to do. It is usually melodic, and the melody may vary from the half-dozen effective unaccompanied *C*-string notes in Max Bruch's *Ave Maria* to the beautiful tune which

[1] From No. VII. of the set (*Ysobel*). A crotchet, C-G-E for 1st Violins and 2nd and 3rd Trombones, is omitted from the first beat of the example.

[2] See, for instance, the Viola *obbligato* to Annette's song in Act III., Scene III., of *Der Freischütz.* Berlioz's Viola phrases in the *King of Thule* song (*Faust*) are much more direct and satisfactory in every way. The *obbligato* in Meyerbeer's *Plus blanche que la blanche hermine* is undoubtedly designed for the *Viola d'Amore.* It is quite true that the part is merely marked in the printed score, "*Un Alto Solo,*" but the laying-out of the double-stopping and the *Harmonic* writing are quite conclusive on the point.

Elgar assigns to the instrument in his overture, *In the South.*[1] The expressive soaring passage which proclaims the might of the Love-potion in *Tristan* (Act I., Scene III.) gives a happy example in a single phrase, both of the Viola used as a solo instrument, and of the accompanying harmonies of Violas and Cellos. The long slur in the Solo Viola part is, of course, only an advertisement to the player that the passage is one phrase. It could not be played in a single bow.

EXAMPLE 258.

Berlioz, in his *Treatise on Modern Instrumentation*, gives it as his opinion that in cases where great energy is required, and the 2nd Violins are to play the same melody as the 1st Violins, they should play in the unison and not in the octave below. In such cases he says "it is preferable, if the Viola part cannot be made prominent, to employ it in augmenting the sound of the Violoncellos, taking care to put them together (as much as the low compass of the instrument will permit) in the unison and not in the octave." In support of this, he quotes the well-known peroration in Beethoven's *C minor Symphony*. The following tabloid-version of the first five bars will enable the student to see the force of Berlioz's remarks:

EXAMPLE 259.

[1] Full score, page 56.

They amount to this, that when the passage is meant to sound clear and strong, the addition of the Violas 8va below the Violins, merely darkens the tone-colour without adding anything material to the force and vigour of the passage. This is very true and, as Strauss observes, it is no less applicable to the similar case of the Trumpets and Horns. Circumstances, however, alter cases. To soft melancholy melodies of a precisely opposite character, this curious shadowy darkening may be highly appropriate.[1] A few notes sung by a Soprano or Contralto often gain enormously in pathetic appeal by the judicious addition of the Violas on octave lower.

In this connection it may be mentioned that nothing needs such gingerly handling as the orchestral use of Violas and Cellos in octaves. There is sometimes a temptation to fall back on this when "nothing better can be found for the Violas to do." As a rule rests are better. For special subjects of a vigorous type,[2] or for deep quiet *p* effects when the harmony is simple and very clearly defined by the other instruments, the combination may be effective. But its haphazard interpolation into a musical ensemble where the other parts are merely in single notes, not octaves, produces a feeling of emptiness in the alto- and tenor-registers. Nine times out of ten the passage will gain strength if "8va" is written above the Cello line. If this is impossible from the nature of the music the Violas can be omitted.

An attempt has been made by Professor Ritter to regularize the qualities and to extend the upward compass of the Viola; the instrument which has been produced under his direction is known as the Ritter *Viola-alta.*

His two main objects were (1) to enlarge the instrument up to a size that should be theoretically in proper proportion to its pitch, and (2) to ease the technical difficulties in the top register by the addition of a 5th string tuned to Violin-E.

Theoretically, the instrument is a success. Top-string shifting is—save on the rarest occasions—done away with; the tone is big, fine, and free. Yet the Viola-alta, at any rate in this country, is scarcely ever used. The reason is not far to seek. While the Viola can be easily increased in length, depth, and girth, the human frame cannot be. The management of the ordinary Viola was already something of a puzzle to human arms and fingers: in its new plethoric form, one fears that it must remain a forbidden joy to all but musical Jack Johnsons. Other experimental Violas, such as the *Violotta* manufactured by Stelzner of Dresden, have been designed with the object of extending the downward compass of the instrument. There seems, however, to be very little orchestral necessity for this type of "improvement."

[1] A few bars in which the Violins and Violas play in octaves above a moving bass for Cellos and Basses is quoted below. Example 282.

[2] See Exs. 134, 247. For a *p* quotation see Ex. 287.

No. 48. The Viola d'Amore.

Fr. *Viole d'amour* ; Ger. *Liebesgeige.*

This semi-obsolete instrument, a modification of the old Tenor-Violin,[1] need only be briefly mentioned here because of its use by Bach[2] and Meyerbeer, and its occasional appearance at antiquarian concerts.

Of its seven "principal" strings the three lowest are "covered" like the bottom strings of the Viola. The tuning is strictly in the key of D major,

and the practical compass[3] is about three octaves and a fifth.

As with the Viola the alto- and treble-clefs are used at discretion.

The characteristic feature of the instrument is its apparatus of "sympathetic-strings." This, according to Gevaert, was a seventeenth-century innovation based on the study of certain Asiatic instruments. Made of steel wire, each of the seven sympathetic-strings lies just above the belly of the instrument, and directly underneath the string with which it sympathizes. The exact tuning of these seven strings is not quite constant; that is to say, different players have at various times adopted different systems of tuning. But in any case the tuning is kept strictly to the chord of D major. Excessive accuracy in the tuning of the strings is an absolute necessity. This is a source of continual anxiety to the player.[4] If either of the sets of strings deviates in the slightest degree from truth they cease to be sympathetic one with another. The sympathetic-strings are of course out of reach of the bow, and are merely excited into a faint tinkling murmur by the vibrations set up in the air by their "principals." The effect is rather more curious and toy-like than musical.

The instrument is larger, heavier, less manageable, and less responsive than the ordinary Viola. It has two fundamental defects: first, the defect of all the old Viol-family, an irregularly-spaced system of tuning which precludes a regular and adequate left-hand technique,

[1] See above, pages 299, 301.

[2] There are two Viola d'Amore parts in the Bass solo, '*Betrachte meine Seel*' (St. John Passion), and in the Tenor air that follows it. Bach writes both in the alto- and bass-clefs for the instrument.

[3] Without Harmonics, see below, page 406.

[4] It used to be said facetiously at Covent Garden that when the *Huguenots* was put on, the Viola d'Amore player was always to be found in the theatre soon after lunch *trying to get in tune.*

and, second, a system of tuning too definitely attached to one key.[1] The instrument is, as it were, stamped or hall-marked with a key-signature. Its path is marked out for it before it begins to play. It is a musical chained-dog. When it strays out of the back-yard it is not merely bad-tempered and difficult to control, but it loses its snarl—the chief virtue of a watch-dog. In other words, when it is compelled to play in flat or in very sharp keys—that is to say, in keys where open D's, A's, and F♯'s do not abound—the sympathetic-strings are either not heard at all or else only occasionally make their presence felt. In the latter case the unexpected reminder of their existence is often extremely irritating to the musical sense.

In a word, the Viola d'Amore belongs to a school whose doom was preordained when the first modern Viola was strung. It has now only the interest of the unusual. However, its quiet tone-quality might still be used to characterize antiquarian melodies or stage-scenes. In the key of D major, and in the sharp major keys immediately surrounding D, it has very great ease in playing chords, arpeggios, and simple passages founded on arpeggios. Indeed, when on its own ground, so to speak, it has much greater variety of method and fingering than the Violin or Viola. Only it must be on its own half-acre of ground. If the student will remember the tuning, and the fact that the stretch of the fingers on the neck of the Viola d'Amore is about the same as on that of a large orchestral Viola, he will have no difficulty in writing practicable chords and arpeggios.

One of the chief features of the instrument is its power of playing groups of Natural Harmonics in the sharp keys. The Harmonics employed are Nos. 2, 3, 4, and 5. These are the Harmonics produced on touching the string lightly at the place where the ordinary stopping would give the octave, the fifth, the fourth, and the major third. They can be taken on any of the "principal" strings, and the resulting sounds are as follows:

[In the above example the two "8vas" refer to *all* the notes below them, fourteen notes in all, and not merely to the top note of each group. The first of the above four bars contains the series of Octave-Harmonics (No. 2) produced from each of the seven strings.

The second bar contains the series of notes produced as Harmonic No. 3 from each of the seven strings, and so on with the other bars.

It follows that the four Harmonics possible on the bottom-string are to be found by reading the four lowest notes of the above chords from left to right. Similarly, the Harmonics of all the other separate strings may be dissected out from the chords.]

With regard to these Harmonics the student cannot fail to notice

[1] As a way out of this difficulty Berlioz suggested sets of instruments tuned in different keys, such as C major and D♭ major.

that some of them are duplicated or even triplicated on more than one string. This point has already been touched on in dealing with the Violin.[1] It is, however, of much greater importance on an instrument like the Viola d'Amore, part of whose normal equipment is the Harmonic-technique. It may be as well then to warn the student not to confuse in his mind these two facts:

(1) On all stringed-instruments, including the Viola d'Amore, every Harmonic except No. 2 (the octave-Harmonic) can be produced on the same string in at least two ways.

(2) On the special instrument under discussion, the Viola d'Amore, its cast-iron system of tuning gives the player considerable latitude in the *choice of string*. He can often get the same sound by taking it as a differently-numbered Harmonic on a different string.[2] This choice of string is a quite different thing from the *choice of method* in taking the same Harmonic in different ways on the same string.

To give a concrete instance on the Viola d'Amore, the note

can be taken, by only one method, as the octave-harmonic (No. 2) on the 2nd string. It can, however, also be taken by two different methods, as Harmonic No. 3 on the 4th string; or, again, by two different methods, as Harmonic No. 4 on the 5th string.

The choice both of method and of string is a matter for the player. In writing Harmonic-arpeggios, however, when this choice exists it is generally safest to confine them where possible to a single Harmonic Series (No. 2 or No. 3, etc.) This has been done in the short example given below.

The best notation for all these Harmonics is to write the open string in the length of note required, and to add a conventional diamond-shaped note at the place where the finger is to touch the string. Thus, if we suppose that a note one crotchet long is required by the music, the bottom notes of each of the four groups of Harmonics printed above, page 406, would be represented by

If this method is not adopted the passage should be written out at its proper pitch and the sign o placed above each note. In this case the bottom notes of each of the four groups of Harmonics printed on page 406 would be represented by

[1] See page 406.

[2] Very much in the same manner that a Brass-player can often produce the same sound in various ways as Harmonics of a different number from different "fundamentals."

Both notations will be made quite plain by the following example

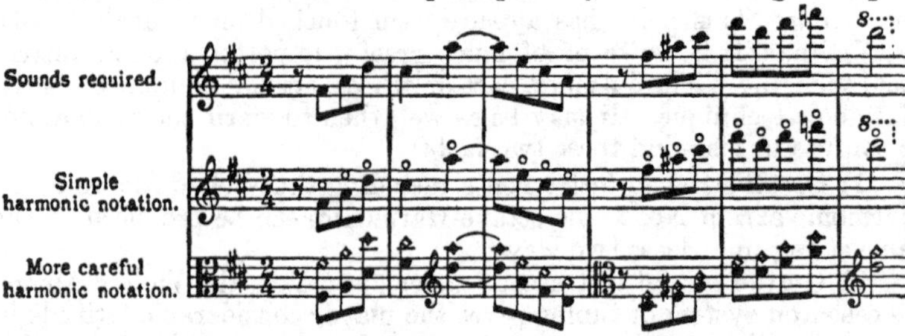

but the student is advised to adopt the plan of indicating the fingering by means of the diamond-shaped notes. If he does this he will keep more in touch with the difficulties which he is setting before the player.

Note.—In Berlioz's quotation from Raoul's *Romance*[1] the three bars of Harmonics with which the passage concludes appears thus:

This is confusing and inaccurate. With the exception of the last two notes of the first bar these notes, *if read in the treble clef*, give one of the correct fingerings of the passage, but they do not indicate the string on which to finger. The correct notation and the actual sounds are as follows:

The high *F*♯ which occurs five times in the first bar can, of course, be produced in four different ways as a Harmonic on the 4th string,

Of these only two enter the sphere of practical politics, viz.,

 and 

Gevaert, in citing the passage, writes the note thus:

[1] *Les Huguenots*, Act I.

which is quite accurate and represents what a modern Violin- or Viola-player would probably do in the circumstances. But it is just on these rare occasions that the possession of his *F*♯ strings is an undoubted advantage to the Viola d'Amore player, and he would certainly prefer to play the note as a No. 4 Harmonic on an *F*♯-string rather than as a No. 5 Harmonic on a *D*-string.[1]

No. 49. The Cello.[2]

Fr. *Violoncelle*; It. *Violoncello*; Ger. *Violoncell.*

The Cello is in pitch an octave below the Viola. Its four strings, of which the lower two are "covered," are tuned

Its fittings are very much the same as those of the Violin and Viola with the addition of a long metal "peg" or "rest," so arranged at the lower extremity that it can be slid through a hole into or out from the body of the instrument. In the latter case it is used by the performer as a firm support when playing: in either position it is held tight by a metal screw-head.

Theoretically the Cello shares with the Viola the disadvantage of being too small for its pitch, but this disadvantage, as we have already seen, is counterbalanced by the great height of its ribs and bridge. This difference in construction is only made possible by the player's use of the sitting-position. And it is worth noting that this position has the effect of reversing the bow-attack, which is now normally from the bass-side of the instrument upwards and not, as in the Violin and Viola, from the treble-side downwards.

The result of these differences in construction is an instrument which is acoustically nearly as perfect as the Violin, and much more perfect than the Viola. Occasionally, in instruments of a poor quality, there may be some note or notes of a "*wolfy*" quality. This, however, is by no means a characteristic feature of the instrument. Widor remarks that the four semitones,

[1] There is a further mistake in Berlioz's quotation. The note immediately preceding the three bars printed above is given by him as

It should be an octave higher.

[2] See page 302. The full word *Violoncello* is practically non-existent in this country as a spoken word, and even when used it seems to be always mispronounced Violincello. The shred of a word, *Cello*, though convenient, is no more logical than *Bone* or *Nett* would be as abbreviations of *Trombone* and *Clarinetto*.

when played on the 3rd string are "bad notes . . . their tone is rough, harsh, incongruous, and uncertain; this is equally true of all Violoncellos used for orchestral purposes, whoever may be the maker." This seems rather too sweeping unless indeed the French orchestral cellist uses a type of instrument to which we are unaccustomed in this country.

Diatonic Left-hand technique.

This is quite different from the Violin-technique. The vibrating-length of string in the Cello is nearly double that of the Violin-string. Therefore, when playing in the lower positions near the nut, the cellist can stretch at most a tone from 1st finger to 2nd, and a semitone from 2nd to 3rd, and from 3rd to 4th. Thus he is forced to adopt a fingering not quite so regular as that of the violinist. It may be formulated as follows:

Three ascending notes, each of which is a whole tone from its neighbour, are fingered 1, 2, 4. Example:

Three ascending notes, of which the first two are divided by a semitone and the last two by a whole tone, are fingered 1, 2, 4. Example:

Three ascending notes, of which the first two are divided by a whole tone and the last two by a semitone, are fingered 1, 3, 4. Example:

As will be seen, this involves a certain amount of irregularity. In the first example the 2nd finger stretches the whole tone, from B♭ to C, while, in the last example, it is the 3rd finger which stretches the whole tone. This, however, is by no means a source of weakness to the cellist.

The student will easily perceive that, as the fingers can stretch no more than a fourth above the open strings, the only diatonic scales practicable without shifting are those in which the open strings are employed. That is to say, in any other keys than B♭ major, F major, C major, G major and minor, and D major and minor, shifting must be used. Furthermore, all scales and passages that rise above

require shifting.

The student may be inclined to ask whether this endless moving of the left hand does not infer a cumbersome and angular technique little adapted to elaborate passage-work. The answer to this is a plain "No." The best methods of taking the shifts have long ago been perfected and standardized, and capable players employ them in a way that quite evades observation. Also it must not be forgotten that, after a cellist has assumed any position, he has much better technical command in that position than the violinist has in his corresponding position. For diatonic purposes he has four fingers to serve three notes: the violinist has only four fingers for four notes. For chromatic purposes the cellist's four fingers have to cover only five semitones: with the violinist the ratio is four fingers to at least six semitones. The important limitation with regard to this part of the Cello-technique is that at any given moment the cellist has command of a compass of only a major third.

Skips of a fourth can, of course, be used when necessary in passage-writing, but the student should earnestly endeavour to avoid:

(1) Phrases—even slow *cantabile* phrases—which are continually skipping a fourth to-and-fro.

(2) Elaborate figures whose component parts are clearly founded on the interval of a fourth.

No. 2 is the more important point, and the point on which the beginner is more likely to go astray. Quick middle-register passages which a second- or even a seventy-second-rate fiddler can play with ease, whatever his position, by merely stretching out his little finger to take the perfect fourth, may present a quite unnecessary degree of difficulty, or at any rate of awkwardness, to the cellist. A tiny group of rapid notes may involve two quick shifts up and down during its performance.

No. 1 is not so important, but even here it is surprising how few good Violin-melodies make good Cello-tunes, whatever the cunning with which they are transposed either in pitch or key.

In both cases—Nos. 1 and 2—the point to keep in mind is the position of the player's hand at the beginning of the note-group. This is really a simple matter, and any thought expended in the improvement of phrases and their adaptation to the needs of the instrument will be well repaid in a more finished performance.

The technique as described above is employed as far as the high A one octave above the first open string. Above that the string-length between the various intervals is so much shortened that the cellist is able to use the ordinary Violin finger technique.

In the highest register the thumb is withdrawn from its usual position on the bass-side of the neck and is placed firmly across and at right-angles to the string as a sort of artificial nut. These "thumb-positions" are a necessity for passages that lie above the high B,

Their use is generally indicated by the sign ♀ placed above the note on which the thumb is to rest, thus:

In orchestral music it is scarcely necessary to bother about this, as the players will find out the technique best adapted to their individual requirements. Some discretion, however, must be used in *mixing* the high thumb-positions promiscuously with the lower positions. There is considerable difficulty in jumping[1] to the thumb-position and accurately fixing it, though, when once it is fixed, other thumb-positions can be taken with comparative ease. Even here, however, there are ways out of the difficulty. A series of note-groups that involve a continual shifting of the register up and down can be played across the strings without any shifting, provided the lowest note of the upper group is not more than a fifth above the lowest note of the lower group. This is, of course, obvious. The difficulties, however, become serious when a player is asked to play a note-group in a high thumb-position near the bridge, then to swoop down for a few notes to his 1st or 2nd position; and, immediately afterwards, to make a wild dash for his thumb-position again. That way madness lies.

Besides its use in the top-register technique the thumb is employed for stopping the lower note of those octaves whose lower note cannot be taken as an open string. For instance

This is not of great importance to the composer, for all *octave-passages* on the Cello are really too risky for orchestral use. Occasional isolated double-stopped octaves may, however, quite well be used if not taken too hastily. The following example, from which the whole of the Wood-Wind has been omitted, will illustrate this point. The passage occurs at Bar 25, 3rd movement, of Beethoven's *Choral Symphony*. The interpolated note D in the Cello part (Bar 8 of the extract) needs no change of position, as it merely involves lifting the third finger and sounding the open string. The finger is then replaced and the octaves resumed in the original position.

[1] When the thumb-note jumped-to "happens to be the first harmonic of an open string . . the danger is minimized, because this first harmonic will come out, even if the position of the finger is not mathematically correct."—*Widor*. By "first harmonic" the octave above the open string is meant. The expression "position of the finger" would be more correctly "position of the thumb."

EXAMPLE 260.

Andante Moderato. Beethoven. *Choral Symphony.*

The three octaves in which the lower note is an open string, viz.

can, of course, be used with freedom in the orchestra, but anything in the nature of octave passages had better be avoided. Even brilliant soloists, though they play such passages regularly in public, never seem able to play them "dead in tune."

Chromatic Left-Hand Technique.

Cellists have a very simple and regular chromatic technique. It consists in filling up the six semitones which occur between any two open strings with a repetition of the fingering 1, 2, 3. This is applicable to all the strings and all the keys. The differences of ♭ or ♯ cause no alteration in the fingering.

It will be seen that this technique is much more satisfactory than that of the Violin and Viola. Each separate note has a separate finger, and even ordinary players are able to obviate the bad effect that might be supposed to be inseparable from passages where there is so much shifting. Furthermore, this system of separate fingers gives to each individual semitone a clear-cut consonantal distinction. There is an absence of that blurred *portamento* effect which is inevitable on the Violin when two adjacent semitones are produced by sliding one finger backwards or forwards on the string. It only remains to add that the chromatic technique is applicable from the low C (4th string) to the A one octave above the 1st string. Above that it is as well to avoid chromatic *passage-work* altogether. To be effective and even possible in that register chromatic passages must be quite short and simple. Lengthy chromatic scales and figures which have an elaborate chromatic contour are best transferred to the Violas.

Three clefs are used for Cello music—

The bass-clef is employed for the lower- and middle-registers, the tenor-clef for the next higher register, and the treble-clef for the top-most notes of all. All these three clefs are used nowadays with their proper pitch-significance. It is quite obvious that the use of the tenor-clef is something of an anachronism. The sole object in using more than one clef is to avoid leger-lines. The treble-clef, however, owes its general acceptance principally to the fact that it follows the bass-clef with only an interval of a single leger-line common to both. Almost all Cello-music, therefore, could quite as well be written in the treble- and bass-clefs; and all high Cello-passages are best when written in the latter clef. In a few Cello-passages, however—those which lie somewhere in this register

—the employment of the tenor-clef obviates the use of leger-lines. Passages, therefore, which lie in and near this register, let us say, between A and A,

are generally written in that clef. Anything that lies *continually* above middle C is much better confined to the treble clef.

The convenience of using the treble-clef for the top register of the Cello was quite understood by the classical German masters. However, the medicine-man's primitive idea of surrounding his craft with as much mystery as possible was too much for their good intentions. Having adopted the clef for the sake of its *convenience*, they wrote their passages in that clef an octave too high. This prevented it becoming *too convenient.* Consequently these few simple notes

appear in Beethoven's *E♭ Quartet* thus:

Sixteen leger lines used where none is necessary. Any argument which justifies the good sense of writing the passage an octave higher will also justify the better sense of writing it two octaves higher.

Upward Compass.

The note

may be suggested as a reasonable upward-limit for orchestral writing, but it is difficult to lay down a hard and fast rule on this point. One must remember that cellists play with comparative ease in the higher positions on their top-string. This is by no means a recently acquired accomplishment on their part. Haydn[2] writes for the mass of his Cellos as high as

and Beethoven does not hesitate to take a Solo Cellist a fourth higher. This is the phrase in his own step-ladder notation:

EXAMPLE 261.

Beethoven. *Prometheus, Act II.*

Passages written in these lofty nipping altitudes are fairly common in the most modern school of orchestration. On the other hand, it must not be overlooked that such passages, if they are really to come off when played by a dozen instrumentalists, must have a certain simplicity and suitability of outline. Cellists as a body are excellent

[1] As in the Viola, the *Natural Harmonic* A a fourth higher may be included in its normal upward compass.

[2] Largo of *Symphony in G* (No. 13, B. and H.).

technicians, but a passage which a single player can ease to his own requirements in the topmost register will probably sound doubtful under the rigorous conditions of a big unison-ensemble. For instance, it would need a very rare group of executants to perform satisfactorily Strauss's solo-phrase which portrays the last struggle and aspirations of the dying Knight.

EXAMPLE 262.

Strauss. *Don Quixote Variations.*

Chords.

Owing to the length of the strings and the consequent difficulty in stopping groups of notes with the fingers, the number of Cello-chords is a good deal smaller than those available on the Violin or Viola.

Double-Stops.

Needless to say all combinations of adjacent open strings are possible. Furthermore, it is unnecessary to detail all the double-stops in which one of the two strings is open. They follow the same general rules as were given under the heading "Violin."

Double-stops in which no note is open.

The best general rule to give here is that all perfect fifths, minor and major sixths, diminished and minor sevenths, may be used provided the top note is not higher than

(1) Avoid all major sevenths. Their stretch is too great.
(2) Perfect fifths are more satisfactory, and may be used with less apprehension on the Cello than on the Violin and Viola.

Triple-stops in which two notes are open.

These follow the same general rules as those applicable to the Violin. See page 320.

Triple-stops in which one note is open.

The following are available:

Combinations of the open note

with any kind of fifth or sixth of which the lower note is either of the following:

Also these three chords

Combinations of the open note

with any kind of fifth or sixth of which the lower note is any of the following:

In combinations of the open note

the two-stopped notes of the chord are of course on the 3rd and 4th strings. The only chords which have any orchestral value are these three:

In combinations of the open note

the two-stopped notes of the chord are on the 2nd and 3rd strings. The only chords which have any orchestral value are these three:

Triple-stops in which no note is open.

The general rule here is the same as that for the Violin. See and read it on page 322. There are, however, these two added limitations:

(1) No chord may contain any sort of seventh.
(2) The topmost note must not go higher than

Quadruple-stops in which three notes are open.

The rule is the same as that for the Violin. See page 322.

Quadruple-stops in which two notes are open.

Combinations of the two open notes

with any simple fifths and sixths on the two upper strings built on this pattern:

The upper parts of the chords must not go beyond

Quadruple-stops in which one note is open.

Practically only those in which the three upper parts are arranged on this model

The upper parts of the chords must not go beyond

Quadruple stops in which no note is open.

Practically only those in which the four parts are arranged on this model

The upper parts of the chords must not go beyond

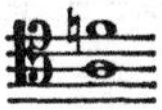

The above are the general rules, stated as concisely as possible. The following is a list of the most serviceable chords for orchestral use. They are grouped first as simple two-part intervals, and then as three-part and four-part chords.

Two-Part Intervals.

Seconds.

Only those which contain an open-string—viz.,

The following are less satisfactory:

In these cases the lower (open) note is played on the upper string, while the upper (stopped) note is played on the lower string.

Thirds.

The following are possible:

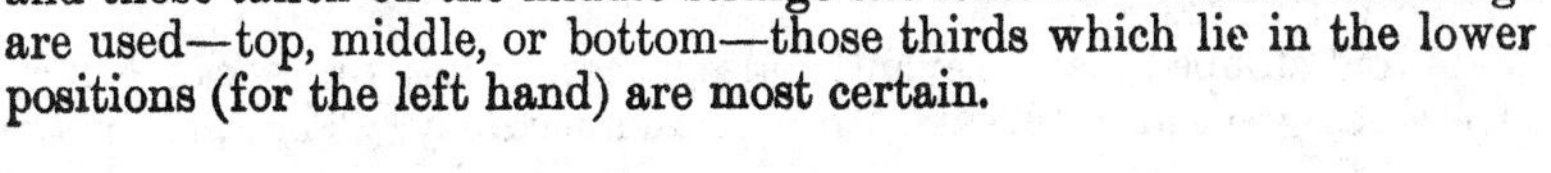

But note that those taken on the top strings are the most satisfactory, and those taken on the middle strings the least so. Whichever strings are used—top, middle, or bottom—those thirds which lie in the lower positions (for the left hand) are most certain.

Fourths.

In addition to the augmented fourth on the low D♭

all perfect and augmented fourths are possible, provided the lower note is any note chromatically from

Fifths.

All perfect fifths chromatically upwards from

Augmented fifths may be regarded for purposes of technique simply as minor sixths.

Sixths.

All minor and major sixths chromatically upwards from

Sevenths.

Minor sevenths are as well avoided unless the lower of the two notes is an open string,

All other minor sevenths are somewhat uncertain in the orchestra. However, they have to be used occasionally when writing for the Strings alone. If no other arrangement of the seventh can be made, they may be used at a pinch. In that case the limits of

should not be exceeded.

Avoid stopped major sevenths altogether. Only rarely can cellists stretch so great an interval with ease and accuracy. The three major sevenths which involve no stretch—viz., those which have an open string as their lower note,

can be employed freely.

Three-Part and Four-Part Chords.

Triads and their inversions.

All major and minor triads and their first and second inversions, provided the note

is not exceeded as the top note in any chord. There is only one pattern for each group of these chords, and that pattern, in three-part and four-part harmony, is as follows:—

Triads:

First inversions:

Second inversions:

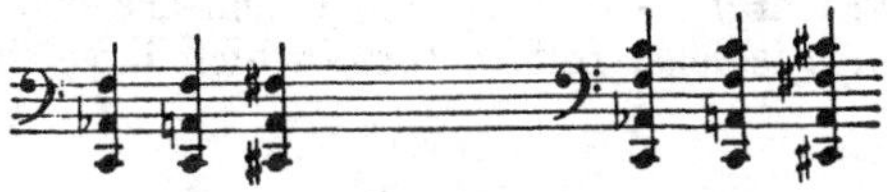

Dominant Sevenths.

These chords, which can be obtained in a practicable form in most keys on the Violin and Viola, are scarcely worth using on the Cello. In three-parts only six are worth considering—viz., those in the keys of F, G♭, G♮, C, D♭, D♮. They are as follows:

In four-parts, only this chord in the key of F is of any use:

All the other four-part dominant sevenths are impracticable in the orchestra, for a simple reason. The bass-note and fifth have to be stopped by the 1st finger on the two bottom strings. The natural method of playing a four-part string chord is then to stop the 2nd string with the 2nd (or 3rd) finger slightly farther away from the nut, and to stop the top string with the 3rd or 4th finger still farther away. This is the normal "spread" of the fingers on all stringed instruments. It cannot, however, be adopted in the case of a dominant seventh. The third of the key-note is higher on the 2nd string than the minor seventh is on the 1st string. The notes of the chord have therefore to be taken in an awkward and unnatural position. In reference to their nearness to the nut, the bass note and fifth come first: then comes the dominant seventh (on the top string): then the major third (on the 2nd string). This artificial placing of the fingers is *possible* as well on the Cello as on the Violin and Viola. At the same time, it is not congenial to their nature. Chords so arranged are never very effective in performance.

Dominant Ninths.

None possible but these two:

and, for reasons given above, these are better avoided.

Parts of "Diminished Sevenths."

In three-parts these may be used at a pinch, but they almost all involve the awkwardness of fingering which has just been described. The awkwardness is least felt in those which have an open string as bass-note

When the 1st finger has to be used to stop the bass-note the chords are much more crooked and tiresome to play. If they cannot possibly be avoided, they may be written on the pattern given above. The upward limit should be top G

In four-parts all "diminished sevenths" are out of the question.

Augmented fifths.

These are quite practicable in three-parts. In four-parts all, except the lowest possible chord which has open C (4th string) for its bass-note, require a certain amount of time. The player has to adjust each of his four fingers on the four strings in an ascending semitonic degree of sharpness. He must therefore have the opportunity of fairly fixing the chord before playing it. Otherwise it will tend to sound like two two-part chords broken in the middle. The upward limit for the top notes of these chords is the same as that for the triad and its inversions—high G—and the only models on which they should be written are

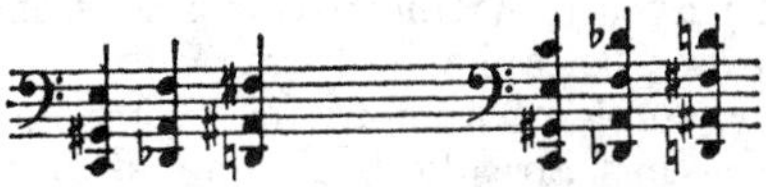

Chords built up on any of the three following models must be avoided altogether:

Any playable chords can be taken in arpeggio; but harmonic accompaniments built up in this way, though by no means unknown, are less common on the Cello than on the Violin and Viola. This is partly due to their weight, and partly to the almost necessarily wide downward spread of the chords. Still they are quite practicable, and, especially in the *mf* and *f*, very effective.

Natural Harmonics.

The technique, notation, and available list of Natural-Harmonics is exactly the same on the Cello as on the Violin and Viola. All that was said above under the heading "Violin"[1] can therefore be read of the Cello, if transposed down a twelfth.

Artificial Harmonics.

The technique is the same as on the Violin and Viola. The compass, however, is a little more extended. On the Violin and Viola the upward limits are about

[1] Page 328.

On the Cello the limit may fairly be extended to

The complete Harmonic compass of the Cello in both Natural and Artificial Harmonics is therefore

Of these notes the first three can only be played in Natural Harmonics. The rest can all be played in Artificial Harmonics, and the notes which are marked thus + can be taken both ways.

A very simple example of a chord for two Solo Cellos playing in Artificial Harmonics has already been quoted from Humperdinck's *Hänsel und Gretel.*[1] The notation in the Full Score is of course not the one printed above, but this:

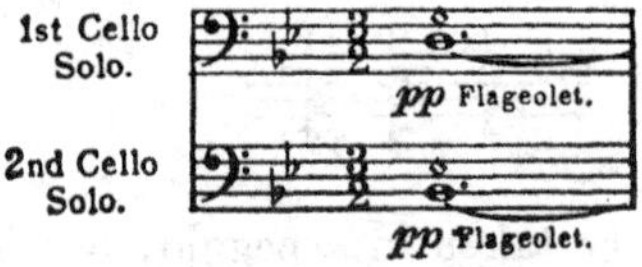

The upper of these two parts is another example of the license mentioned above.[2] The sound two octaves above the open string is actually performed as a Natural Harmonic. The second Cello-part can only be played as an Artificial Harmonic.

Shakes.

As with the Violin and Viola, shakes, both whole-tone and half-tone, may be employed through practically the whole of the playing compass. As the pitch descends, however, the slowness of the vibrations produces, on the Cello, a somewhat tubby effect. This applies in some degree to the bottom string of the Viola also. On the Cello it is as well to avoid, except for a particular effect, shakes on the C string.

The Cello Bow.

The Cello Bow is shorter, heavier, and less elastic than the Violin Bow. It can, however, perform with finish and distinction all the Violin *coups d'archet.* The greater constructional perfection of the Cello gives it an advantage over the Viola. All the bow-strokes, not merely the heavier bow-strokes, are quite congenial to its easy, free-speaking nature. Nevertheless it shares with the Viola its antipathy to lengthy slurs. In the *f* and *mf* especially these should be dealt out

[1] Example 203. [2] Page 333.

with a somewhat niggardly hand.[1] More particularly in cases where an appreciable melodic *crescendo* is called for, the player is handicapped by long slurs. He is compelled either to alter the phrasing or to harden and tighten the tone. If the composer breaks up the phrases and remembers (1) that the point and the nut are respectively the weak and the strong parts of the bow, and (2) that therefore the V is the best *crescendo* stroke, he will secure an accurate ensemble in the phrasing and a better melodic effect.

In a more general way it may be repeated that the careful adjustment of slur-lengths to tone required is an insurance against careless orchestral playing. In *p* and *pp* passages the judicious lengthening of the slurs makes a *crescendo* or an "orchestral mezzo-forte" a practical impossibility. Then, when a *crescendo* is required, the breaking up of the slurs gives the String-players a surprising ease and freedom of movement. Attention to small points of differences, such as this, meets its due reward at rehearsal.

Tremolos.

Both Bowed- and Fingered-Tremolos are in common use, and there is little to add to what has been already said on the subject.[2] Bowed tremolos in the upper register are naturally not often allotted to the Cellos. In the middle-orchestral-register, even if the Violins are not at liberty to make the tremolo, it is generally better to secure the chord by a division of the Violas rather than by employing the Cellos for that purpose. Lower still, in the bottom- and lower-middle-register of the Cello, tremolos are often written for special purposes.

In arranging Fingered-Tremolos for the Cellos it is important to notice that the utmost stretch possible between the 1st and 4th fingers on the same string is only a major third: with the 1st finger on one string and the 4th finger on the next higher string the maximum stretch for most players is a minor seventh. A point to be kept in mind with regard to the Cello tremolo is that it is something more of a "fact," something slightly more present to the consciousness than the tremolo of the upper stringed instruments.

Everything that has been said already with regard to the *ponticello*, the *sul tasto*, the *col legno* applies as much to the Cello as to the Violin. The *Mute* is in regular use. It must, however, be confessed that one rarely hears a group of orchestral Cellos adequately muted. The little "clip" mutes scarcely veil the tone at all. In fact they rob the instrument of its romantic tone-colour, and do not substitute for it the proper mysterious muted quality. Then, again, light wooden mutes without sufficient substance are often chosen so that their loose clutch shall not harm the bridge. In either case the result is disappointing. The lower strings are enfeebled without being much altered, while the tone-colour of the top-string changes, not from one kind of poetry to another, but from poetry to prose.

[1] See what was said on this subject above, page 390.

[2] For Cello-tremolos, see Exs. 86, 191, 231, 234, 275.

The Pizzicato.

A special word must be said with regard to the Cello *pizzicato* for, besides its stereotyped usefulness as the ordinary bass of the String *pizzicato*, it possesses exactly the right mixture of suppleness and resonance for playing what may be called left-hand pianoforte arpeggios. Used thus, it gives a delightful piquancy and a sort of subordinate prominence to its part. It is happiest when contrasted in a quiet ensemble with the bowed upper Strings or with the Wood-Wind. A Cello part of this sort generally lies, especially in the lighter forms of music, somewhere between the 3rd string and the note D one twelfth above. It usually includes a statement of the true bass at the beginning of each bar followed by an easy and not too rapid arpeggio on the two upper strings. These *pizzicato* parts never stray very far outside the bounds of a somewhat severe simplicity. Broken chords that lie well under the hand and short, easily-played scale passages are the most effective. In this medium even the simple alternation of tonic and dominant sounds charming. Here are the first four bars from the *Opening Chorus* of *The Mikado* (Act II.).

EXAMPLE 263.

Sullivan. *The Mikado.*

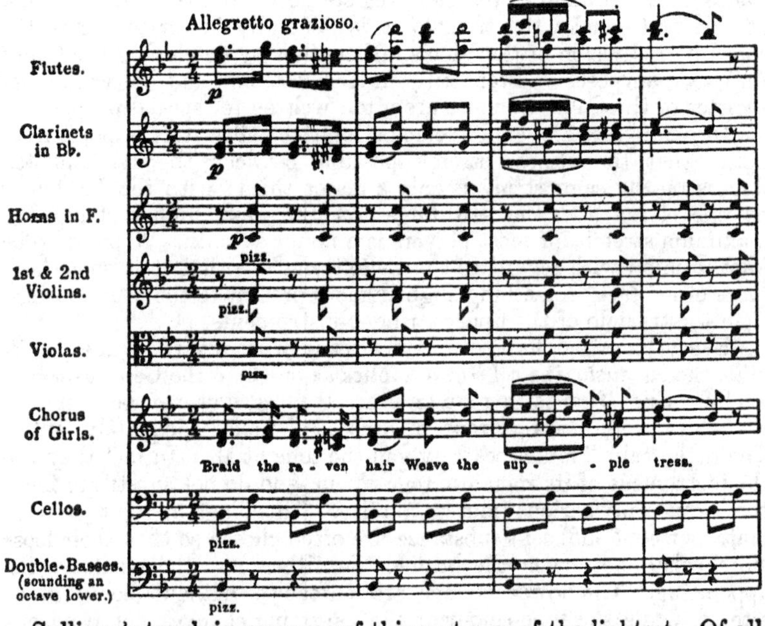

Sullivan's touch in passages of this sort was of the lightest. Of all the accompaniments in his Comic Operas perhaps the most graceful is that to Phoebe's song, *Were I thy bride*, in Act I. of *The Yeomen of the Guard*. It is simplicity itself, merely repeated chords on the muted

EXAMPLE 268.

The bottom (covered) strings of the Cello bear some analogy to those of the Viola, but their tone is more "straightforward" and less unexpected. In solo passages they have a certain mingled smoothness and austerity which fits them for the performance of very serious and deeply-felt passages. An excellent example covering the range of the three bottom strings is to be found in the familiar Cello passage with which the 3rd Act of *Die Meistersinger* opens. Another and even better instance may be quoted here from the 2nd Act of *Lohengrin.*

EXAMPLE 269.

In the above example the long slurs, so characteristic of Wagner, are, of course, absolutely impracticable as far as the orchestral player goes. They are, in fact, not bow marks at all, but merely vague directions that a *legato* performance is required. The phrasing is left to the conductor. In nine cases out of ten the deplorable result is that the players adopt a bowing each at his own sweet will. Fortunately it is quite easy to break up a passage like this into its component bow-phrases. Even in the first long *legato,* which extends for six bars and a crotchet, it is quite obvious that a new bow *must* be used for the repeated C♯ at the beginning of bar 4. Similarly the second crotchets of bars 5 and 9 would be naturally played with new bow-strokes. Nor are these the only places where this long *legato* can be broken up to suit the exigencies of the String-technique. The student may profitably examine any of Wagner's colossal slurs from this point of view, always remembering that the breaking up of a *cantabile* into its necessary bow-phrasing does not destroy its *legato* character, and that the difference between the two ways of writing involves the difference between personal accuracy and the merely haphazard.

It need hardly be said that one of the principal functions of the Cellos, in their middle and bottom registers, is to play the bass, and this they do quite efficiently, provided there are enough of them in the orchestra. "Remember that violoncellos supply a perfectly adequate and sonorous bass without any double basses at all, and that the double basses are only an adjunct to them in this capacity for purposes of reinforcement and not *vice versa*."[1] This is true in a general sense, but more particularly with regard to the String *legato*, as can be seen from the many pages in *Die Meistersinger* where the Basses are omitted. In other cases even when the Cellos are the main support of the harmony an occasional *pizzicato* for the Basses helps the Cellos without robbing them of their dignified task.

As more and more Wood-Wind is added to the orchestral mass the addition of the Basses becomes more imperative, and when the weight of the Horns is superadded, they cannot be dispensed with, even in the concert-room. On the other hand, in those theatres which are devoted to light Opera—that is to say, in the vast majority of Houses—where the orchestra averages about 35, the Cellos are, except on the rare occasions of quiet *legato* String-harmony, a not sufficiently solid foundation. The Basses, therefore, have to be used much more continually, though, even when both are playing the bass, in a manner different from that appropriate to the Cellos.

One may note that, in those cases where the Cellos alone are supporting the weight of the other strings, they do so more satisfactorily when their notes are fairly near the rest of the harmony. When, in these circumstances, they descend to their bottom-string, a certain hollowness becomes apparent. This may be an acoustic fact or it may be due only to our ideas which associate this type of passage with the Double-Bass, and so call for its solidity of utterance and its easy power of reinforcing the harmonies with its own wealth of upper-partials.

The union of the Violas and Cellos as a separate tone-group has already been discussed under "Viola." Nothing more need be said on that point. Two other combinations may be mentioned.

(1) The union of Cellos with Basses in a low-pitched harmonic or contrapuntal combination. In passages of this sort, provided the String-quality is called for, there is usually only a choice in the arrangement of parts. If there are not more than two of these the arrangement is obvious. The Cellos take the upper and the Basses the lower part. In three parts it is usually better to divide the Cellos, and, if necessary, to reduce the number of Basses. The Cello *divisi* is better than double-stopping even when the latter is practicable. This applies more especially to the *p* and the *mp*. In the rare cases where there are more than three parts and the top-part cannot be played by the Violas, it is, as a rule, better to subdivide the Cellos again. However, if the two lower parts are merely playing in fifths and octaves, there is not so much danger of the unpleasant clash of overtones resulting from the divided Bass-parts. If the Basses are divided it is always better for safety's sake to indicate the use of more Bass-players on the bottom part.

(2) The Cello *Divisi*. This highly effective combination is occasionally used to form a rich harmony accompanying the 1st Cello. The chords are generally well spread in four or five parts so that the two top Cellos at least are playing on their A-string. In arrangements of this sort a Solo Cello usually plays the melody, while each of the

[1] Stanford, *Musical Composition*, in this Series, page 106.

middle parts is assigned to two players; a couple of Basses doubles the bass-part either in the unison or the octave below. See the well-known introduction to Rossini's *William Tell* overture and the passage at the beginning of *Die Walküre*, where Siegmund drinks (full score, page 11). It may be mentioned that though this Cello *divisi* is generally used in a sort of full-dress way, it is highly interesting when employed merely as a passing effect. The rich sound of three or four Cellos playing in harmony on their top-string makes a delightful change from the eternal Horn-harmony. In smaller combinations and in arrangements from larger works it can, of course, be used to represent the Horns, and, in doing so, it often throws a new light on the orchestral prospect.

Up to the end of the eighteenth century the Cello in the orchestra was, like the Double-Bass, merely a bass-player. The two instruments ran together, a stag and an elephant in double-harness. Haydn and Mozart,[1] asking only for a quiet uneventful journey, drove the pair well enough. So long as the ground was smooth and the pace easy the arrangement answered admirably. When, however, the musical coach was enlarged, rebuilt, and furiously driven by Beethoven, the old ruts and the old yoke-fellows were found unsatisfactory. Beethoven unyoked his pair. He saw that, except when every solid ounce of strength was needed for collar-work on a heavy road, the lighter animal would do better in a light cart of its own. In other words, he recognized the possibilities and the greater individuality of the smaller instrument. And his curriculum in these matters can be followed easily step by step from its first starting-point in the *Eroica Symphony* to its goal in the *C minor* and *Choral* Symphonies. Reference has already been made to the numerous places in his Symphonic works where he detaches the Cellos for purely melodic purposes.[2] On such occasions he usually doubles them either with a Bassoon, with the Violas, or with both. But his reformation is not merely the discovery of the Cello as a vehicle for orchestral melody. He also discovered the fact that the Cello demands a sort of writing different from that of the Double-Bass. If the student will take a Score of the *Choral Symphony*, and, turning the pages quickly, will follow the bottom two lines, he will see at once many places where the outline of the upper part is distinct from that of the lower. Greater freedom and range is allowed to the lighter instrument. In a Mozart work these differences scarcely exist. In a Beethoven work they do exist. Of course it would be an exaggeration to say that they show the same width of divergence as would be normal in a modern work. But the patent—in this case of nobility—goes to the inventor.

[1] "Mozart hardly ever gives the Violoncellos a separate part; Haydn does so somewhat oftener."—*Gevaert.* It is to be noted that the old masters all knew the capabilities of the Cello *as a solo instrument*, but hesitated to employ them with any freedom in the orchestra. Haydn's *Concerto in D* is still reckoned a difficult work by cellists, and Mozart occasionally wrote florid passages for the instrument, for instance in the obbligato to Zerlina's song, *Batti, batti* (*Don Giovanni, Act I.*).

[2] See pages 396, 399.

The Cello then is bequeathed to modern orchestral music in a three-fold capacity:

(1) **As a plastic bass-instrument**, either alone, in unison, or in octaves with the Double-Basses. (See the Storm at the beginning of *Die Walküre*, where for the first sixteen bars the Cellos and Basses are in actual unison and afterwards in octaves.) This use is, in modern music, rather more strictly confined to the quieter modes of expression.

(2) **As a melodic vehicle.** (See any modern score, for instance the top part of the Cello *divisi* in Act I. of *Die Walküre* or the *Preislied* phrases in Act III. of *Die Meistersinger.*) In this use the Cello may be said to stand to-day very much where Beethoven left it. The character of its tunes is altered, and their upward range a good deal extended, but otherwise there is little difference.

(3) **As a medium for elaborate passage- and figure-playing.** It is in this particular that the modern Cello writing differs most from the ancient. Beethoven foreshadowed the change, but did not bring it bodily forward. If, however, we open any score of to-day, say Strauss's *Don Juan* or *Ein Heldenleben*, we shall be at once struck by the fact that for a considerable portion of the time the Cellos are wholly detached from the Basses, and are playing difficult complex passages which have comparatively a much greater value in the general orchestral ensemble than is apparent in the classical style of Cello-writing. It is not merely that the compass is extended, but that the whole outlook on the instrument's capabilities and its proper place in the orchestra is enlarged. To illustrate this point adequately one would need to print a dozen or twenty pages of brilliant passage-work from the most modern Scores. That is impossible in a book of this size. The student, however, can *hear* its importance by attending any concert where a late eighteenth century work is brought into juxtaposition with one of the late nineteenth or early twentieth century.

No. 50. The Viola da Gamba.

Fr. *Viole de Gambe*; Ger. *Gambe.*

This instrument, commonly known as the Bass-Viol, is mentioned merely because of its occasional appearances at antiquarian concerts and because John Sebastian Bach provided it with parts in the *St. John Passion* and the Actus Tragicus *Gottes Zeit ist die allerbeste Zeit.*

The tuning has already been given on page 300. As the student will see, it divides the instrument into two halves: a lower and an upper half, each of three strings tuned in fourths. Between these two halves there is an interval, not of a fourth, but of a major third.[1] The notation was generally in the F-clef, but occasionally the C-clef was employed.

No instrument had a greater popularity than the Bass-Viol. It was to the sixteenth and seventeenth century amateur what the Cello is at the present day.[2] It provided him with an easy recreation. Its

[1] An additional (7th) string was added about 1700. This was tuned to low A, a perfect fourth below the then existing bottom-string, D.

[2] Sir Toby Belch's highest praise of Sir Andrew Aguecheek is "he plays o' the viol de-gamboys, and speaks three or four languages word for word without book."

pleasant, ambling *cantabile* called for a minimum of technical dexterity. Like all the other members of the Viol-family it was charmingly inlaid with "frets," and these contributed not only to its handsome appearance, but also to its player's security of finger and peace of mind.

When Bach employs the Gamba he generally writes for it in two separate parts, using the alto-clef for the upper part and the tenor- or bass-clef for the lower. As the *St. John Passion* is so well known, it will perhaps be better to quote an example from his Church-Cantata *Gottes Zeit ist die allerbeste Zeit.* This work is scored throughout for Flutes and Gambas. The impressive *Adagio* opening to the Cantata begins as follows:

EXAMPLE 270.

No. 51. The Double-Bass.[1]

Fr. *Contre basse*; It. *Contrabasso*;[2] Ger. *Kontrabass.*

This instrument, the lowest and heaviest of the entire String-group, has only recently been standardized in pitch. In the seventeenth and eighteenth centuries various types and sizes of Bass were in use, and it may almost be said that, in the matter of stringing and tuning, each player did what was good in his own eyes.

The instrument which had emerged in the latter half of the eighteenth century as fittest to survive was a three-stringer. It was generally tuned thus

[3]

but, less commonly,

This was the Bass for which Beethoven wrote, the Bass which still remains the most characteristic in tone-colour and the most powerful in tone-quality. Up to Beethoven's day, however, little attempt was made by composers either to study the Bass as an independent instrument or to provide it with parts suitable to its nature. This laxity extended in particular to questions of downward compass. A single part was written for the Cellos and Basses. Provided the written notes lay no lower than the 3rd Cello-string the result was, of course, a bass-part sounding in octaves throughout. The upper line of the octave-part sounded on the Cellos as written: the lower part sounded on the Basses an octave lower.

EXAMPLE 271.

Composers, however, did not always confine this single-stave double-part within the necessary limits. Consequently, passages continually occurred which the Cellos could play at their written pitch on their

[1] Or, more simply "The Bass." The student is reminded that the word *Bass* when used in the sense of *Double-Bass* is printed with a capital.

[2] The older Italian word *Violone* is now practically obsolete.

[3] It must be clearly understood that the Bass is always a transposing-instrument. The actual sounds are an octave below the written notes. All the examples, references to tuning, and so on, must be read by the student with that provision in his mind.

4th string, but which the Basses could not play so as to sound an octave below that.[1] In these cases it was common until quite recently to allow the Bass-players discretion in the rearrangement of the passages to suit their instruments. They made a jump into their upper octave wherever they found it convenient. With players of judgment and experience the result in the concert-room was probably not so haphazard and confusing as it would seem on paper. Still the plan lacked the artistic nicety and exactitude which we now regard as essential to fine orchestral playing. It has therefore become a necessity to rearrange these passages whenever their range is outside that of our modern four-stringed Bass. The result in performance is a proper unison of the Bass-players throughout, though of course the original outline in the lower octave of the single-stave double-part is disturbed.

Somewhere about the beginning of the nineteenth century a 4th string began to be employed on the regular orchestral Bass. The tuning then became what it remains to the present day—a system of fourths,

This type of instrument, which is practically the only one now used in our theatres and concert halls, was indisputably known as early as 1802.[2] However, its undoubted deficiencies in tone and attack as compared with the old three-stringer were held insufficient to counterbalance its advantages of compass. It struggled into the orchestra only very gradually. Two factors, however, were strongly in its favour. First, the modern demand—initiated by Wagner—for the lowest possible notes in the orchestral ensemble. Second, the improvements in the lowest Brass- and Wood-Wind. When these improvements began to be generally recognised and adopted, the necessity for the heavy jagging notes of the powerful three-stringer was no longer felt. A smoother and less obstinate tone-quality was preferred. People began to say that the instrument always made its part sound "like a Händel bass." The same reason which had preserved its existence in the first half of the century hastened its downfall in the second. It has now more or less completely lost caste, and is scarcely ever seen in our concert-rooms. There is, however, a good deal to be said for the instrument in one way or another, and some reference to its capabilities will be made later.

[1] It has often been asserted that the existence of these passages presupposes the instruments on which they could be played. There is, however, no necessity to split logic on the point, for we know as a fact that the instruments in general use at that time were the ordinary three-stringers. These instruments were occasionally tuned in fifths, A, D, G, downwards. This was more especially the case in France. The difficulties of technique, however, were always in favour of the tuning in fourths. A few enormous church-Basses are still in existence. These might well have been tuned down to the low E or even to C. But there is no ground for supposing that they ever were so tuned.

[2] It is mentioned by N. W. Koch in his *Musikalisches Lexikon*, 1802. See *Widor*, p. 185.

The general adoption of the four-stringed Bass only partially solves the difficulties of the old classical one-stave two-part passages. So long as they do not go below the low E, they can now be played by the Cellos and Basses so as to sound throughout in the two intended octaves. But these parts sometimes go down lower still to the D, and frequently make use of the bottom-string Cello C. As far as such passages go, the disabilities of a century ago remain unchanged. The Bass-part has to be re-arranged either by the player or by the conductor.

In this connection Gevaert quotes the passage from the *Choral Symphony*, where a regular figure is established, having for its bottom note the low Cello D.[1]

EXAMPLE 272.

Here it is quite obvious that the mere raising of the third quaver by an octave would defeat the composer's intentions. The only way of securing the pedal D effect on the second half of each bar is to adopt this formula for each bar. The Cello part, of course, remains unaltered.

It must not be imagined that the effect of these unintended unisons between Cellos and Basses was always disastrous. In nine cases out of ten they have no orchestral significance at all. Even in the solo opening of Schubert's *Unfinished Symphony*:

EXAMPLE 273.

it is doubtful if any one has ever felt much perturbed by the sudden unison in bar 5. This unison is intended and foreseen by the composer. The consideration of this typical passage, however, involves a point which is sure to bother the student. He will probably ask for

[1] The Cellos here have the same written notes, but they perform them in measured demisemiquaver tremolo.

[2] If the *Peters* score of this Symphony is correct, the Bass-part was undoubtedly written for an instrument possessing the low E. See the corresponding passage immediately after the double-bar. The Basses descend with the Cellos to the low E. The Cellos then continue downwards to D and C♮ (open string), but the Basses jump up a seventh before taking these notes. In several other places the Basses have the low E.

some rule-of-thumb by which he can assure himself that his descending passages will have the effect of descent, while at the same time they remain within the compass of the instrument.

The point is of less artistic importance than one would suppose from the statement of its logic. In ordinary detached basses, even when the "lay" of the part is clearly downwards, it matters very little. By reading the Bass-part back for a few bars a convenient place can always be found in which to jump to the upper octave. Purely melodic passages rarely occur in these depths. But when they do occur, especially when they are solo passages with or without the Cellos, they must be treated rigorously with regard to pitch as one would treat melodic passages on any other instrument. Sequence-patterns, however, occur continually in Bass-parts, and, if these be in descending-sequence, it is often a little troublesome, especially if the notes be long and heavy or the *tempo* slow, to secure the continual feeling of descent. In these cases, if the end of the sequential-passage lies below the low *E*, it is often wise to begin the whole Bass-passage an octave higher. The notes will then sound in unison with those of the Cellos. It may be added that there is no greater pitfall for the young composer than the use of the bottom register of the Bass. The analogy from the added resonance of the lowest *pianoforte* notes is absolutely false. The rule should be "keep the Basses up." They then have some chance of practising their peculiar virtue, the reinforcement of the upper-partials in the Strings and Wood-Wind. Confined to the dismal profundities of their bottom strings they merely sound like a herd of unwieldy "hippos" stirring up the mud on the river-bed.

The above recommendation to "keep the Basses up" must be taken as only applying to the general orchestral ensemble. Cases occur where for special effects excessively deep notes are necessary. And it is this necessity which has created the demand for a Bass whose compass extends still lower than the low *E*.

This necessity has been met in four ways.

(1) By the invention of the five-stringed Bass, whose tuning is the same as that of the ordinary four-stringer, but with the addition of a fifth (bottom) string tuned to *C*. This instrument has the fundamental technical disability of an irregular tuning. It has the further disadvantages of increased size and increased length of string,—both important matters in such a formidable monster as the Bass. These five-stringed Basses are used in French and Belgian orchestras. They have been tried here, but not with any general success. However, one must add that some solution of the difficulty has been found by the recent introduction in this country of a five-stringer whose bottom string is tuned to B♮. Under this system the tuning remains a perfectly regular series of fourths, and the player has the further advantage of an additional semitone in his downward compass.

(2) By the lengthening of the ordinary bottom string (the *E*) and the addition of a mechanism. In this case the *E*-string is prolonged to the length necessary for producing the deep *C*. In ordinary circum

stances the mechanism remains out of action, and the string retains its vibrating-length as an *E*-string. By a simple pressure of the thumb the mechanism can be switched-on, and, by the addition of the upper string length, the four lower semitones *E*♭, *D*, *D*♭, *C* can be obtained.

(3) By a temporary alteration in the tuning. The player alters his string to suit the depth of the passage before him. This is the Wagnerian procedure. In the *E*♭ pedal at the beginning of *Das Rheingold* half the Basses are instructed to tune their bottom-strings down one semitone. This plan is unsatisfactory. The system of fingering is disturbed; the vibrating-length of the string becomes incorrect; it is difficult to retune the string to its proper pitch. The inconveniences to the player are so obvious as to be scarcely worth pointing out. However, if the plan of a casual misfit-tuning is adopted, it is better at the beginning than in the middle of a work. In either case time must be allowed for the tuning and the retuning of the string.

(4) By a permanent difference in tuning. Some players have adopted the low *D* tuning for the bottom string. Their strings then run upwards *D-A-D-A*.[1] This innovation is by no means generally accepted among Bass-players. It involves the old disadvantages of an irregular tuning, and therefore an irregular finger-technique. Furthermore, it does not give the low *C*. Of all these methods that of the five-stringer tuned in perfect fourths appears to be open to the fewest objections. The student must, however, be warned that none is regularly available in this country. Players do not, as a rule, possess five-stringed Basses or mechanically controlled bottom-strings. Furthermore, it is monstrous to expect them to tune down a tone or more in any chance two-bar rest. The difficulties of accurate tuning and recovery are great. The fingering, founded as it is on a series of fourths, is thrown out of gear. The other stringed-instruments are practically never called on for this sacrifice. Why then the Basses? More than any others they demand help in order to secure an accurate intonation. The whole "truth" of the String ensemble depends on them. Is it not then better for the composer to make up his mind that the lowest *String-sound* at his disposal is at present

One would hesitate to ask this question if it could be shown that the addition of a semitone or two downwards added materially to the sonority or the sense of depth in the orchestra. This is, however, very far from being the case, and as we possess many fine Bass-players who perform on the E-A-D-G instrument, it is surely the wisest course to regard that instrument as it should be regarded, viz. as clearly standardized in its tuning as the Violin or the Cello.

[1] Occasionally also *D-A-D-G*. This is practically the old three-stringer tuned in fourths, with the addition of a bottom-string tuned in fifths with the third-string.

It must not be forgotten that this question of tuning is not a question "in the air" for Bass-players. It is a question that intimately concerns their technique. On that point a few words will be said later.

Before leaving this topic it is interesting to quote the very great authority of Richard Strauss in favour of the combined use in the same orchestra of Basses of different systems. In especial the distin guished composer recommends the inclusion of "the 3-string Italian Double Bass" for the sake of its great *cantabile* powers. This is practically a return to the method universal in English orchestras twenty-five or thirty years ago. The undoubted advantage lies in the extraordinary tonal strength of the old three-stringer. But the system was abandoned owing to the serious lack of uniformity which resulted in the Bass-department. A group of players, half of whom were compelled to stop playing when the music descended below *G*, was a source of some anxiety to conductor and composer alike.

Diatonic Technique.

The fingering of the Bass is something like that of the Cello. The proportion between the vibrating string-lengths of the two instruments, however, is as 2 to 1. It therefore follows that the distance between the adjacent semitones is twice as great on the Bass as on the Cello. When the hand is closest to the nut the maximum stretch between the 1st and 4th fingers is only a whole-tone, and, of individual pairs of fingers, the 1st and 2nd alone can be separated sufficiently to produce a true semitone. If the instrument were tuned in fifths, like the Cello, the simplest scale passages would involve continual shifting. Tuned in fourths, however, the instrument is, so to speak, readjusted to the human hand. The necessity for excessive shifting is obviated, and in this respect the difficulties of the instrument are not much greater than those of the Cello.

It is unnecessary to go very fully into the fingering. In the lower registers it is a system by means of which the fingering 1-4 is used for adjacent ascending whole-tones and 2-4 for adjacent ascending semitones. In those keys where the open strings are not wholly available —that is to say, in keys north of D and south of F[1]—a simple position-technique is adopted. This technique furnishes a method of performing a series of four notes on a single string by means of a shift taken between the 2nd and 3rd notes of the series. The fingering used is either 1-4 or 2-4, according to the stretch involved. In the higher parts of the compass, as the vibrating string-length diminishes the distance between the notes becomes correspondingly smaller. The fingering adopted is then very similar to that of the Cello.

[1] The two keys B♭ major and A major are transition-keys partly playable by the one method, partly by the other.

Chromatic Technique.

The chromatic technique is simple. Each series of four upward semitones between any open string and its neighbour is produced by a repetition of the fingering 2-4. The following example will make this quite plain:

This system is used regularly in the two lower octaves of the instrument. Upwards from

the 1st finger is brought into play.

The above much-compressed account of the left-hand technique will be sufficient to show the student that the Bass is as fairly chained down to a tuning in fourths as are the other stringed-instruments to a tuning in fifths. Any disturbance of this tuning must therefore be adopted with a knowledge of the risks run. The bottom-string of the Bass is not a vaguely indefinite note whose alteration is matter of indifference to the player. It is the note E as definitely to its technique as the note G is to the Violin-technique.

Notation.

The bass-clef is regularly employed for Bass-parts. The highest register, however, is usually written in the tenor-clef on the fourth line

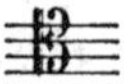

Whatever the register or clef the written part remains an octave above the actual sounds. A rare exception to this procedure is sometimes found in the case of the Natural Harmonics.[1] These may be written at their actual pitch. For the higher of these Harmonics the treble clef is occasionally used.

Upward Compass.

Of late years, under the influence of the modern German school of music, our Bass-players have been compelled to acquire such a degree

[1] See below, page 443.

of virtuosity that it is a little difficult to set any upward limit to their capabilities. Perhaps

may be suggested. Above that the notes and the execution are in an ensemble unsatisfactory.

Chords.

A certain number of two-part chords are *possible*, but very few are advisable. In fact chords are not worth writing for the orchestral Basses, unless either both notes are open or one of the notes is an open string and the other clearly playable as a stopped note on the adjacent string. This may be taken as applying theoretically to all thirds, fourths, fifths, sixths, sevenths, and octaves. In practice, however, all Bass-chords, even when possible as double-stops, are better written in two parts *divisi*. A narrow exception may be made in favour of those fifths and octaves which have one open string. The list is as follows:

Natural Harmonics.

These are particularly easy on the Bass. Hitherto, however, they have not been much used in the orchestra, perhaps because the instrument is usually fulfilling other functions. As a general rule the higher the string the more satisfactory the Harmonic. On the bottom-string only two are worth using: on each of the other strings there are at least five.

A word must be said with regard to their notation. Owing to the fact that the upper Harmonics lie high up in the treble-register it would be necessary, if the part were still to be written as a transposing-part, to use the treble-clef and a great many leger lines. Therefore, in this case only, it is as well to treat the Bass as a non-transposing instrument: to write the harmonics at their actual pitch, adding the direction "*actual sounds*": and to place the usual harmonic sign o above each note.

It is scarcely worth while giving the theoretical list of Harmonics possible on each string. In practice they may be reduced to these

It will be noticed that the lowest Harmonics are not available on the E-string. As a matter of fact, all Harmonics on that string are

somewhat thick in utterance, and their avoidance only involves the loss of one note (the G♯), as the lower note (E) is obtainable in a better quality on the A-string. Furthermore, the highest Harmonic given on the two top strings—viz., the high C on the 2nd string and the high F on the first string—is a little difficult to produce. It is not absolutely impossible, but it should be avoided.

The rest of the Harmonics given in the above list are by no means theoretical notes. They are all obtainable in a good sound quality, and can be employed either in *tenutos* or in chord-combinations for *divisi*-Basses. Their restrictions in the way of key are, of course, obvious. Provided the composer marks the notes clearly as Harmonics and as "actual sounds," the use of the treble- or tenor-clef for the highest notes is a matter of indifference.

In the well-known passage in Act III. of Verdi's *Aïda,* where the *divisi* Cellos and the Basses hold a harmonic G in three octaves,[1] thus—

[Actual Sounds.] 

the Basses play the lowest of the three notes. This is the third Harmonic given in the list of 1st-string Harmonics above. In the Full Score Verdi writes the note thus—

Double-Basses. 

Harmonics.

This is the old-fashioned way, adopted in order to show the player the proper fingering. The bottom note indicates the string; the middle note the fingering; and the top note the actual sound. The "8........" only applies to the top note, and is necessary here because the notation is not in actual sounds, but in the usual Bass convention of an octave above true pitch. It is not of much importance which method the composer adopts, provided he makes his meaning clear. The notation in actual sounds seems to be simpler from the composer's point of view, as it involves the writing of only one note instead of three. Nowadays there is little need to instruct players in the technique of their Harmonics.

Artificial Harmonics.

As it is impossible in the lower positions to stop a perfect fourth with the 1st and 4th fingers on the same string, the whole of this series is ruled out of court. The complete Harmonic compass of the instrument is therefore merely the list of natural Harmonics already

[1] The two upper notes are played by *divisi* Cellos in artificial Harmonics. The student will have no difficulty in writing those out for himself in the correct notation. In each case he has only to write a note two octaves below the actual sound and to add the diamond-shaped note a perfect fourth higher.

given. For the sake of accuracy it must be said that, with the very finest Bass soloists an elaborate Harmonic-technique, both Natural and (in the top register) Artificial, is available. It is not, however, for general orchestral use.

Shakes.

Both major and minor shakes are quite playable on the Bass, but on the lower strings their effect is generally rather grumbly and unsatisfactory. Even on the top string they must be employed with some caution. When used merely in passing they often come out surprisingly well, but unless a very special effect is intended, it is wise not to persist with them too long. They are better when backed up by some other tone-colours, such as those of the Bassoons or Tuba. A reference has already been made to a shake of this kind.[1]

The Bass Bow.

The old Bass bow associated with the name of *Dragonetti* is now practically obsolete. Right down to our own day it preserved the type of ancient bow which was at one time in general use for instruments of the Viol family. Attacked by this bow, the Bass became an engine of desolation, dealing out destruction to all the finer tone-colours of the orchestra. The modern bow commonly called the *Bottesini* is modelled on the Cello bow. It is, however, larger, heavier, and shorter, and is provided with black hair of a coarser quality. Its use gives the player a much greater variety and ease than was possible with the old type of bow. The instrument is brought more into line with the other Strings. The old "hacking" Bass-tone disappears, and in its place we have a smoothness of tone-production and a plasticity of phrasing that was undreamt of by the older generation of Bass-players.

The extreme shortness of the Bass bow as compared with the length of the string which it has to set in vibration makes a long *tenuto* an impossibility. Even in the *p* the bow must be changed every three or four seconds. That is not a caution against writing a single long-held note *p*, for the players will change their bows at discretion, and so secure the *tenuto* effect. But in the case of a long *legato* phrase it is absolutely essential that the bowing should be broken up. If this is not done, each player will phrase his part for himself, and places may occur where the whole of the players will accidentally give an undesired prominence to an unintended phraseology.

It is better to face the fact fairly and squarely that the Bass part must be phrased to suit the instrument rather than to join up the whole of the *legato* with a long slur that is an impossibility in performance. When we come to the *f* and the *mf* the necessity of

[1] See pages 158-9.

continual change of bow is still more pressing. Here even a single long *tenuto* note is unsatisfactory. The continual aimless and unrhythmical change of the bows has a rather stupid effect. It is far better either to divide the Basses and give them two parts on the one note, so that each part alternately covers up the change of bow in the other part, or to write a rhythm in fairly short notes. The latter method is the best possible, provided it falls in with the musical scheme of the work. Nothing gives so great an impression of power as a simple rhythm, even on a single note, consigned to the Basses.

At the opening of the *C minor Symphony* of Brahms the pedal C is entrusted to 2 Horns *f tenuto* and to the Drums, Double-Bassoon and Basses in quavers. The Bass part appears thus—

Contrabasso.

and the slur underneath the six notes merely indicates that the composer wishes each quaver prolonged so far as is consistent with the heavy throbbing rhythm. It is probably not a bow-mark from which the *louré* lines have been omitted, but only a caution against this sort of attack—

The desired effect could perhaps best be obtained by the *louré*, but under the conditions (*f pesante, un poco sostenuto*) it would probably be necessary to split the slurs up thus—

The Bowed-Tremolo.

The Bowed-Tremolo is of course in constant use from *fff* to *ppp*, especially in the middle- and lower-registers of the instrument. Alone, associated with the Cellos, with the rest of the Strings, with the Wood-wind or with the Drums[1] it is always effective. So familiar are these tone-combinations that it is scarcely necessary to quote examples. However, the following four bars with which Strauss's *Also sprach Zarathustra* opens may be of especial interest. The deep pedal is laid out for *divisi* Basses *tremolo*, supported by the Organ *tenuto* and the Double-Bassoon. A roll on the Bass-Drum, performed with kettle drum sticks, completes the score.

[1] See page 49

EXAMPLE 274.

In the above example the Bass *divisi* presumes a certain number of five-stringers in the orchestra. It may be mentioned that, though the Bass-part looks so effective on paper, it adds little but scratch and excitement to the ensemble. The weight of the tone comes principally from the Organ Pedal and the Double-Bassoon. And here the student may again be reminded of what was said above[1] with regard to the general want of tone in all bowed-tremolos. It applies with particular force to the Basses and, whenever a great accession of quality is wanted, it always pays to change the bowed-tremolo to a simple rhythm. However many *crescendo* signs and *fortes* are put into such a part, the tone only becomes more scratchy, not much greater in volume. If the *tremolo* be changed to a short-note rhythm on which the player can use the full length of his short bow, the increase in energy is astonishing.

The classical masters employed the bowed-tremolo of the Basses only sparingly. Even when they clearly required what we should call "a tremolo effect," their almost invariable routine was to write a measured-tremolo consisting of fairly rapid reiterations of the same note. On the heavy thickly-strung Bass this is good and effective. The rhythmical collusion of the players is distinctly less tame than it would be in the higher Strings. Indeed, in a true bowed-tremolo Bass-players are unable to change the bow as rapidly as Violinists and Cellists. Instances of this partial tremolo may be found in such places as the First Movement[2] of the *Choral Symphony* (bowed demi-semiquavers *ff*, supported by the Drums in $\frac{2}{4}$ *Allegro ma non troppo* time): and in the Last Movement[3] of the same work (bowed semi-quavers in $\frac{3}{2}$ *Adagio ma non troppo* time). The beginning of the Storm in the *Pastoral Symphony* is also a case in point. The unexpected measured *tremolo* of the Cellos and Basses which interrupts the easy gaiety of the previous *Allegro* is a landmark in the history of orchestral daring. The effect of the passage can most readily be

[1] Page 353. [2] Peters's Score, page 37.

[3] Peters's Score, page 239. See also the quotation from Halévy's *La Juive*, Ex. 86

seen by quoting it in the manner in which it should be quoted—as an interruption. The student will then have no difficulty in perceiving wherein lies the virtue of the orchestral technique—in the rests that are to be found on the right-hand side of the double-bar. The score is a little compressed. The Flutes and Oboes and the 1st and 2nd Violins are each grouped together on a single stave.

EXAMPLE 275.

The Fingered-Tremolo.

Owing to the great length of the strings on the Bass practically only one fingered-tremolo is possible, the minor third. Even this is too great a stretch when the player's hand is near the nut. It only becomes possible when the lower note of the *tremolo* is at least a major third above the open string. A list of fingered-tremolos, fairly complete for all orchestral purposes, would consist of all the minor thirds whose lower notes are any of the following:

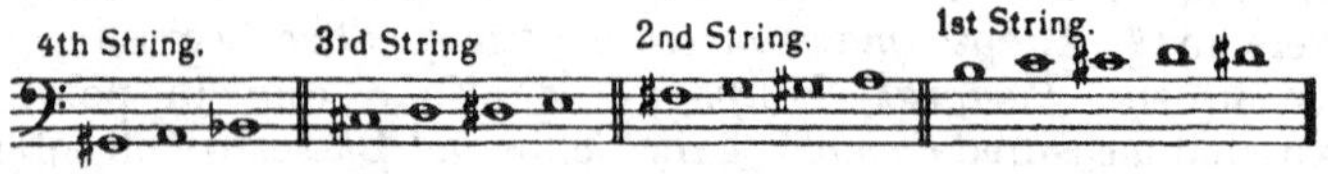

On the lower strings these tremolos can only be of the rarest use in certain deep mysterious *piano* passages. On the upper-strings, however, and especially on the top-string, they come out well, and might be highly effective in a *mf* or *f* ensemble of an agitated character.

The *ponticello* and *col legno* are both used on the Bass, and when properly played are perhaps more effective than on any other stringed-instrument.

It is customary nowadays to *mute* the Basses whenever that muffled quality is called for in the String-ensemble. Cases, of course, occur where muting is only required in one special department of the Strings. That is a matter of practical judgment in orchestration. If, however, the general intention is the deadening of the Strings, it is best not to omit the mutes from the Bass-parts. All the difficulties mentioned above with regard to the proper weight of the mutes become still more serious in the case of the Bass. The solidity of the bridge, the amplitude of the string-vibrations, and the immense resonance of the sound-box, all join in producing a series of air-vibrations which can only be effectively damped by a very heavy close-fitting mute.[1]

The Pizzicato.

The *Pizzicato* is continually employed. So common is it that some Bass-parts have nearly as much *pizz* as *arco.* Almost invariably the Basses play with the Cellos, both *pizzicato.* Occasionally the Cellos play a *legato* version of the bass *col arco,* and the Basses play the essential notes of the bass *pizzicato.* This is a capital plan for lightening the general weight of the orchestra. It relieves the stodginess of a persistent unimportant Bass-part and at the same time leaves the Cellos to support the harmony with the necessary orchestral *tenuto.*

Here are two short instances of the Bass *pizzicato.* The first is a characteristically English example of a simple tune harmonized for the Horns and Wood-Wind, and supported by the *pizzicato* of both Cellos and Basses.

EXAMPLE 276.

In the second, from Vaughan Williams's String Fantasia, the Basses

[1] For an instance of solo muted Basses see the extract given below from the last Act of Verdi's *Otello* (Ex. 279). For an example of Basses doing a persistent moving *pizzicato,* without Cellos, see the 2nd movement of Dvořák's *New World Symphony.*

are *pizzicato* while the 2nd division of the Cellos play *col arco.* The two are at one time mainly in octaves with an occasional unison necessitated by the pitch (bars 1-4), at another mainly in unison with occasional octaves (bars 5-8). In fact these few bars give a good general idea of the routine employed in associating Cellos *arco* with Basses *pizzicato.* In this work the composer writes regularly for the Basses down to the low D. The unison on the first three notes of bar 5 is therefore clearly employed for musical reasons, not for reasons of pitch. The other interesting feature of this quotation is the expressive melodic unison of Violins, Violas, and Cellos, all playing with the emotional *louré* bow-stroke.[1] The very modern spacing of the three constituent parts of this passage—the two-part *tremolo* in the 1st Violins, the melody and the bass—is also worthy of notice.[2]

EXAMPLE 277.

Bass *pizzicatos* are playable up to a fairly rapid *tempo,* but successions of quick notes should not be continued too long. Apart from the musical confusion resulting in such cases there are instrumental difficulties. The string-vibrations are necessarily so ample that some time must be allowed if each note is not to be damped by its successor. In addition to that, rapid *pizzicato* playing in the *f* and the *ff* is an exhausting physical exercise, and some consideration should be shown to the player on that point.

As with all the other stringed instruments, the most resonant *pizzicatos* are to be found on the lower strings. But it must be remarked that in the bottom-register pace is musically out of the question. These notes have a tendency to "drag." In other words, they prolong their sound in a manner that one might consider not quite proper in a *pizzicato.* Still, the player is able to control

[1] See above, page 343.

[2] For a few notes of *pizzicato* Basses see Exs. 141, 144, 155, 182, 224, 238, 278, 296

this to some extent. *Pizzicatos* are written right up to the top of the Bass compass. In these altitudes, however, the notes become dry and snappy.

may fairly be taken as a working upward limit, though for most practical purposes even that height is unnecessary.

The student should try to cultivate an "eye" for putting in Bass *pizzicato* notes. This is a matter which is largely concerned with his feeling for the rhythm that underlies his design. It is often surprising how few Bass *pizzicatos* are absolutely necessary in an orchestral ensemble. Yet the omission of those few notes, or the substitution of a *tenuto* Bass-part *col arco*, will often befog the whole passage. The *pizzicato* Bass not only lightens the weight of the whole orchestra but it also adds a sense of "point," of "movement," of "something doing." Even a single Bass note played *pizzicato* in the proper place can be eloquent and even poetical. Strauss has drawn attention to the *pizzicato* G of the Basses, which, in the 1st Act of *Tristan* just touches the word *blau* (blue) with colour. The passage may be seen on page 32 of the Full Score. Another happy instance of two simple *pizzicato* notes has already been quoted from Bridge's *Isabella.*[1] In this example the composer's intention is, of course, not the illustration of an external idea. The cleverly placed *pizzicato* is, however, none the less delightful from a musical point of view.

EXAMPLE 278.

[1] See Example 248.

[2] The chord for four Horns is omitted from the 1st Bar of this Example.

Within the present limits of space it is impossible to illustrate adequately the curious psychological effect produced at times by the *pizzicato* of the Basses. The student must seek these for himself in the concert-room and the theatre. The simplest and possibly the earliest attempt to utilize this tone-colour for the sudden realization of Drama is to be found in Weber's familiar passage on page 451. Here the means is the simplest: the result, the most magical. The essence of the orchestration is the contrast between the mass of held Harmony above and the lugubrious mechanical stroke of the Basses and Drums below. The colour in the low Clarinet-notes, in the *tremolo* Strings, and even in the high Cello melody, is less essential to the tragedy. Since the days of *Der Freischütz* this kind of orchestral effect has been used again and again often in a much more elaborate form. The type, however, always remains the same, a mass of *tremolo* harmony, with a *pizzicato* underneath.

Tone-Quality.

The tone-quality of the Bass differs markedly from that of all the other Strings. Owing to its pitch it cannot invoke the aid of any association with the human voice. Hence comes its somewhat strange and "unearthly" character. Fortunately this demoniacal quality only becomes apparent when the instrument is forced to the front dissociated from other softer tone-colours. In the general run of its parts the Bass remains unobtrusively efficient in the background. Yet there are moments when the unique quality of its tone might well be used for purposes of orchestral characterization. The first to perceive this was probably Mozart. In the 2nd Act of *Don Giovanni*, where the statue intones the words *Di rider finirai pria dell' aurora . . . Ribaldo audace! lascia a' morti la pace*, the composer adds the Basses to the solemn chords for Trombones and Wood-wind. The effect, though often omitted in performance, is "astonishly fantastic."[1]

Another passage whose effect the student should not fail to note occurs in the accompaniment to Wotan's recitative in Act II. of *Die Walküre* (Full Score, page 163). This is indeed a *locus classicus*, for though the part is excessively simple from the player's point of view, the effect of the never-ending Bass *pianissimo* associated in turn with the Bass Clarinet, the Horns, and the Trombones is weirdly powerful.[2]

A third instance may be referred to, this time from the inimitable Verdi. No one can forget the extraordinary moment in the last act of *Otello* after the *Ave Maria*. The etherial notes of Desdemona's prayer have scarcely floated away when the Moor appears silently and murderously at the back of the stage. At that moment the muted Basses attack their deep open 4th string and begin a slow heavily-moving *cantabile* as Othello paces into the bedroom. The savagery and raw brutality of their notes exactly express the stage-picture, and

[1] Strauss.

[2] See also Example 7 (the opening of Marcel's "War-Song" in *Les Huguenots*) for an instance of the Basses employed *pizzicato* without the Cellos.

one may say with confidence that, as a master-stroke of orchestration, their first bar alone would be hard to beat. The following is the complete Full-Score without abbreviation. The first six bars are the concluding portion of the *Ave Maria*. Othello enters at the *poco più mosso*.

EXAMPLE 279.

The student should notice in this example the meticulous care with which every phrase is bowed. Nothing is left to chance. The indication, "I soli Contrabassi a 4 corde," is explained by the fact that even when *Otello* was written the three-stringed Bass was still in general use all through Italy. Verdi probably had a single desk of four-stringers, and they made the entry on the low E♮. The rest entered at the 7th bar (marked "Tutti un poco marc." The footnote, "Vedi diteggiatura segnata," *i.e.* "see the fingering marked (in the part)" refers merely to the indications under the stave ("3ª corda," etc.) of the correct strings. It may be added that, in this country at any rate, the first entry of the Basses is not made *pp*, but with a heavy mournful *sforzando*. This is perhaps a tradition from the first performance under Verdi's direction.

It is, however, rather in the use of its top-string *cantabile* that the Bass may be a somewhat new weapon in the hand of the composer. This cannot effectively be done for the same type of music or in the same simple way as that which suits the other Strings. It needs a definite breadth and dignity of character in the melody and a certain fulness of ensemble for its support. As a lengthy full-dress solo it

* Vedi diteggiatura segnata (Composer's note in the Full Score).

would be unbearable. When employed, however, only as an incident appearing and disappearing from the colour-screen, the unnatural insistent quality of the tone makes a strong impression on the listener. The actual unison of Basses and Cellos, or of both, with the Bassoon softens without obscuring the characteristic Bass quality. In such cases the Bassoon and Cello parts must be written an octave below the pitch of the written Bass notes. A unison of this sort, when kept well up in the higher registers of the instruments, is one of the most suggestive in the orchestra. Its psychological significance should not be confused with that of the big melodic passages for *tutti* Strings which are to be found in many modern works.

The historical use of the Bass in the orchestra need not detain us long. Down to Beethoven's day its parts were of the simplest. Even in Mozart's best work there is little appreciation of the fact that the individuality of the instrument could be used as a vehicle for musical expression.[1] In consequence, performers lacked technique. Very hard things have been said about these early Bass players. They have been called "hewers of wood."[2] The fact, however, remains that whenever composers have made calls for an extended technique Bass-players have always answered the call. In this country especially there have always been capable and earnest players. At the present day one may assert with confidence that our best orchestras owe their rich quality mainly to the exceptional powers of tone and attack which are to be found in the Bass-department. This is a gratifying feature, and, if one may be allowed to adapt Canova's remark into musical terms, one might say that it would be well worth a journey from Italy to London to hear a dozen fine English Bass-players deliver the noble recitatives in the *Choral Symphony*, or some of the massive melodic passages in *Ein Heldenleben*.

Bass-players were not always thus. Before Beethoven's day they were accustomed mainly to an easy-going sepulchral kind of plidge-plodge. Very little technique existed, and any good Cellist could have learned to play their parts in a week. Then came Beethoven asking from them variety of expression. They were compelled to practise and to play with accuracy vital passages such as this,

EXAMPLE 280.

and this,

EXAMPLE 281.

[1] There are occasional exceptions, but the statement is generally true.

[2] It might perhaps be added "and drawers of water" from the eyes of their unfortunate audiences.

Rapid *pianissimos* in the bottom register with very little to cover them up,

EXAMPLE 282.

sudden skips to their top octave,

EXAMPLE 283.

and expressive phrases, such as those in *Fidelio,* which sound like the utterance of some huge monster toiling underground,

EXAMPLE 284.

All these and many others were demanded of the Basses. In the *Choral Symphony* they receive what we may call their final apotheosis, for there they are selected to be the representative voice of the orchestra through which it utters its pleading, its remonstrances, and its contentment.

EXAMPLE 285.

[1] In this example the harmony is held by a thick ensemble of Oboes, Clarinets, Bassoons, Horns, and Trombones, while the other Strings play repeated notes (triplets to each crotchet). The Violins and Violas are muted.

From a perusal of the above passages the student will see that though Beethoven treated the instrument with an unexampled freedom, and indeed elevated it to the position which accorded with its merits, yet he generally associates it with other instruments. As a rule, it is not allowed to shine alone. The Cellos or Bassoons share its dignity. This point has already been treated as far as it deals with the joint playing of actual Bass-parts. A little qualification, however, is needed

True there are some instances, especially in the composer's latest works, where he foreshadowed the modern dissociation of the Cellos and Basses, some instances where he treats the latter instruments not merely as the lower part of an octave-combination. Such passages are among the most interesting in his works, for they clearly point the way to our modern developments. They are, however, in a great minority, and it was Beethoven's peculiar gift to this department of orchestral technique that he first recognized the combination of Cellos and Basses, not merely as a smoothly satisfactory Bass, but as a plastic medium for musical expression.

It would be impossible without elaborate quotation to establish this fact in detail. It is, however, well understood that the general "cunning" of present-day Bass-parts is a legacy from Beethoven, and though the extent and proportions of this craft have been much enlarged since his day, they had their origin in his brain.

The smoothly-running *legato* passages written for facility of utterance on the top-strings: the strenuously attacked groups of bowed quavers and semiquavers: the immensely effective little scales of three or four notes running up to a top-note: these with others too numerous to mention were first standardized by him as an integral part of the Bass-routine. In especial he recognized the fact that *continual moderate movement* is a necessity of the instrument: that when it stands still it becomes stodgy. We are all too much inclined to take these niceties of technique for granted. They did not, however, drop out of the skies—unless, indeed, Beethoven was the Saint who drew them down.

Since Beethoven's time the development of the Bass has been mainly in the direction of its dissociation from the Cellos and Bassoons, both of which instrumental groups are used nowadays in a more plastic and less stereotyped manner than they were in the old Scores. It must be understood that the Cellos and Basses still form what may be called the routine orchestral Bass. But there are many passages where the former instruments must be detached for passage-work in their upper-register. Again, there are many other passages where the mixed colours of Wood-Wind and Horns need the support either of all or of some of the Basses.[1] Furthermore, the amount of movement and figure allowable to the Cello middle-octave often sounds heavy and tiresome when reduplicated by the Basses in the octave below. Orchestral confusion can, if desired, be readily obtained by this simple means. But for general orchestral purposes a totally different method has to be employed, a method which leaves both the Cellos and the Basses free to play the passages most congenial to their separate natures.

A caution must be added here. The above remarks do not in any way indicate the old-style of so-called "simplified Bass-parts"—a nervously apologetic system of writing in which the Cellos were directed to play what the composer wanted and the Basses were left to play what he didn't. These perished with Mendelssohn's popularity. On the other hand, they do refer to the many modern passages where the inclusion of the two instrumental groups in an octave-combination would falsify the musical value of the phrases allotted to one.

There is another class of Cello-and-Bass-passage peculiar to the modern school. In type these passages invariably consist of brilliant contrapuntal phrases or harmonic figures played in octave combination right up to the top register. They are often of excessive technical difficulty. Indeed fifty years ago a composer would hardly have written them even for the Cellos alone. Some objection has been taken to this form of Bass writing. However, it may be legitimately urged that its use introduces a wholly new sound-effect into the orchestra. In fact, one may say with confidence that nothing so clearly differentiates the old from the new as this type of Bass-passage. Its surging tumultuous quality brooks no denial. The listener is shot off his feet and upward into the air. It is an earthquake followed by a volcano.

The Basses are less commonly divided than any other of the String-groups. Occasionally, but very rarely, a single instrument is detached for the purposes of Solo playing. An instance of this from Mahler's *First Symphony* has already been quoted.[2] It is, however, a very rare effect, only employed for special purposes of characterization, and it is merely mentioned here for the sake of completeness. Brilliant passage-work and imposing *cantabiles* are by no means beyond the powers of the finest artists. But in order to write such passages, the

[1] "In passages given exclusively to the Wind it is an excellent effect to double the lower parts of the Bassoons, Bass-Clarinets, or deep Horns, even of the Trombones or Bass-Tubas, by one or more desks of Double-Basses. . . ."—*Strauss.*

[2] Example 13.

composer needs an intimate acquaintance with the instrument, and in particular, a familiarity with its elaborate system of Harmonic-playing in the highest register. The *Bottesini Concertos* show the capabilities of the Bass in their widest extent. These works, however, are rarely heard in public.[1]

It has already been mentioned that a desk or two of Basses is often detached to give solidity to an ensemble of Wood-Wind, of Wood-Wind and Horns, of Violas and Cellos, or of *divisi* Cellos. This is a common procedure nowadays. It is of special value in the theatre, where the difficulty of securing a firm Bass is notorious. One may say in passing that the Basses as a whole need to be much more continually employed there than in the concert-room. It does not follow that they require constant *legato* passages. Indeed that is rather the wrong style to adopt. But owing to the position of the orchestra in a theatre, and the restricted resonance of the floor on which they are placed, they are continually needed to *outline* the Bass of the harmony. This may not apply so fully to those theatres where the orchestra is either blessed with a strong battalion of Cellos, or placed on a resonating double-floor. It is, however, none the less true as a general proposition. The continued absence of the Basses from the general orchestral ensemble in the theatre robs the orchestra of its "body" and quality.

One occasionally finds in modern scores that when the Cellos are "employed upstairs" the Basses are playing *divisi* in octaves. This is not, as a rule, very satisfactory. The Bass *octave-divisi* does not really represent the Cello-and-Bass octave-combination. This is probably not due to the fact that the Basses are likely to play out of tune, though this explanation has been offered more than once. It is rather caused by a confusion in the upper harmonics. The Basses are greatly virtuous in their power of reinforcing these upper partials, and, if they are written in octaves, the one set of harmonics blots out the other. In most cases, especially if strength is looked for, it would be better to add a low Horn, a Bass-Clarinet, a Double-Bassoon, or even a Bassoon. All the Basses would then play in unison probably in the lower octave of the octave-combination, but this is a matter for the composer's discretion. In the *p* and the *pp* the splitting-up of the Basses into two octave-parts does not matter so much. Even here, however, the effect can generally be got better by some other means.

The Bass *divisi* is not often used for harmonic or contrapuntal purposes. For its purpose, however, it is highly effective. Rossini, in his *William Tell* Overture, and Meyerbeer in Act V. of *Le Prophète*,

[1] Mr. Claude Hobday played the Bottesini Concerto in F♯ minor at a Philharmonic Concert on March 24, 1904. It may be of interest to mention that, for this particular work, the artist retunes his instrument, raising each string one whole tone. The compass of the *Concerto* as written is from

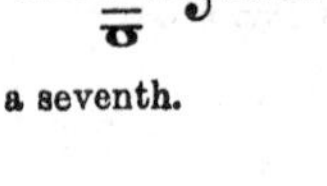

and the soloist transposes his part a seventh.

each made some rather timid experiments in this direction. In the Meyerbeer example the Basses are arranged in two and three parts as an accompaniment to the recitative of Fidès. The Cellos are omitted from the quotation. In the Full Score they double the Bass-parts in the unison, and are therefore written in the octave below.

EXAMPLE 286.

Recitative. Meyerbeer. *Le Prophete.*

In his Cantata, "*The 5th of May, or, The Emperor's death,*" Berlioz has divided his Basses into four parts "with a view of expressing a lugubrious silence." As this Score contains a part for the unusual orchestral instrument, "*Distant Cannon,*" the student may care to see an extract

EXAMPLE 287.

Moderato. Berlioz. *The Fifth of May.*

It must be admitted that this example has something of the Berliozian taint. Its orchestration appears to be prompted not only by a genuine musical impulse, but also by a delight in "the glory of the boast." It is nevertheless a remarkable foreshadowing of modern orchestral methods. In the Full Score the two Clarinets in C and the two Bassoons double the Viola and Cello parts respectively. The 2nd and 4th Horns (omitted above) help the two top Bass-parts in Bar 2 only.

A portion of the striking accompaniment to the long Oboe Solo in Strauss's *Don Juan* has already been quoted on page 214. The student should notice here how carefully the chords are restricted. There are no "diminished-sevenths" and "Six-four-two's" as in the Berlioz example. This is in the interests of lightness and clarity. Furthermore, he should notice in performance how intensely soft and almost woolly is the sound of these *divisi* Basses. This again is clearly an instance of intentional tonal weakness produced by the clash of upper partials.

The opening and closing bars of the *Pathetic* Symphony are familiar to all. A few bars of the former have already been quoted on page 240. Both passages are good models of the harmonic simplicity which is almost a necessity in dealing with these very deep sounds. Far more complex and interesting from the technical point of view is the extraordinary Fugue in Strauss's *Also sprach Zarathustra* ("*Von der Wissenschaft*" section).

EXAMPLE 288.

Strauss. *Also sprach Zarathustra.*

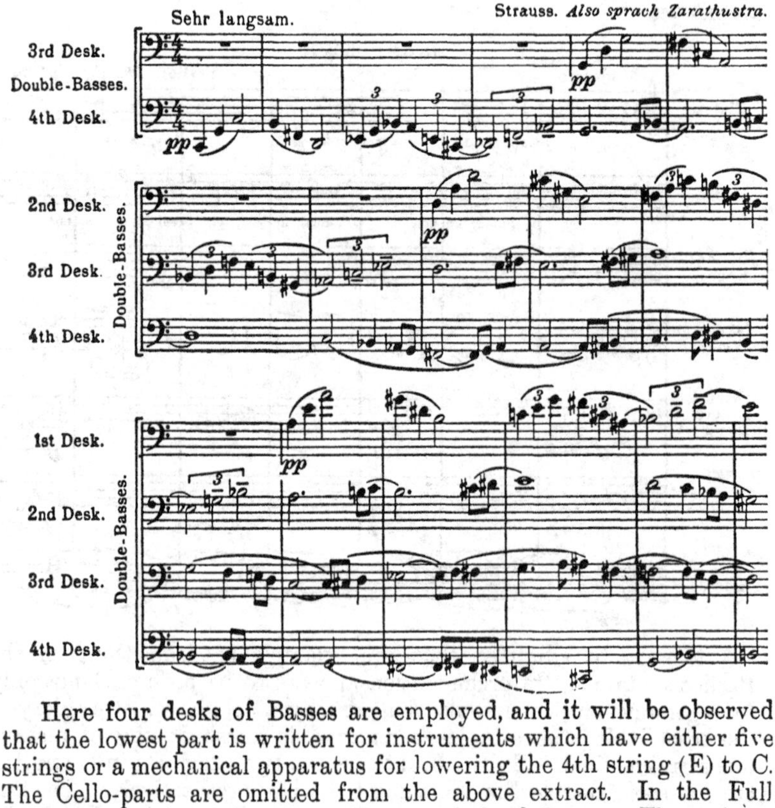

Here four desks of Basses are employed, and it will be observed that the lowest part is written for instruments which have either five strings or a mechanical apparatus for lowering the 4th string (E) to C. The Cello-parts are omitted from the above extract. In the Full Score a desk of Cellos plays with each desk of Basses. The written notes are the same, and it therefore doubles the Bass-melody in the octave above.

In his chapter on "Colour,"[1] Sir Charles Stanford calls the Bass a "dangerous rogue-elephant." This is rather cruel. It is so long since he was corralled and shut up in the Government Keddahs that he has by now become docile. Such a huge brute can indeed still be mighty unpleasant, if he is ill-treated. It is therefore *safer* to treat him well. Then he will show his true elephantine nature in not withholding his skill from the humblest "chores" or his strength from the most burdensome tasks. Humour him a little. Don't let him stand about, perhaps catching cold, and probably getting in everyone's way. Give him a certain amount of freedom, air, and exercise. Above all don't stable him in the cellar.

No. 52. The Harp.

Fr. *La Harpe*; It. *Arpa*; Ger. *Harfe.*

This beautiful instrument should have a special place of honour. Alone of all the ancient "plucked" instruments it survives in daily orchestral use. Furthermore, with the possible exception of the Drum, it was probably the earliest instrument to be elaborated in the service of organized music. Indeed, it would be no stretch of language to say that, if we could awaken a mummied Pharaoh of the thirteenth century B.C. in a modern concert-hall, he would recognize practically nothing but the sound of the harp-parts.[2] What his ears heard in Thebes thirty-two centuries ago we hear to-day in London.

As far as Western Europe is concerned the Harp seems to have first installed itself in England and Scandinavia about the twelfth century. The term *Cythara Anglica* (*i.e.* English Harp) was in common European use, and was employed to distinguish the Harp from the *Cythara Teutonica* (*i.e.* the old quadrilateral *Rote*). From England the Harp appears to have passed to Ireland where, under the name of *Clarsech*, it was beautified, elaborated, and finally elevated to the position of a national instrument. Introduced into Wales in the fourteenth century the Harp became to all intents and purposes chromatic. Its strings were arranged in three rows, of which the two outer rows were tuned in unison-pairs generally diatonically in the key of G, while the middle row gave the additional chromatic notes.

[1] *Musical Composition*, in this Series, page 108.

[2] The thirteenth century (B.C.) wall-painting of two harpists was discovered by Bruce. The instruments—one bow-shaped and the other three-cornered—are as tall as a tall man. A species of Guitar called *Nefer* appears to have been used in Egypt from very early times. The same may be said of the *Nanga*, a sort of cross between Harp and Guitar. The ordinary bow-shaped Harp was a familiar Egyptian musical instrument for many centuries. Its simple form was subtlely perfect for its object—the stretching of a series of strings all differing in length. The Egyptians had also sistra, small cymbals, and small flute-like pipes in common use. They appear to have been much more familiar with the use of small Bells than were the ancient Greeks. In the Egyptian Gallery at the British Museum there are no fewer than fifteen of these ancient diminutive Bells.

Harps of this sort with nearly 100 strings seem to have actually existed, but the elaboration of their manufacture and the awkwardness of their technique practically forbade their general employment even in Wales.

The Harp, then, has existed from very early times, and, in essentials, it is still unchanged. It has always consisted of a series of stretched strings, all differing in length and in pitch. The strings have always been set in vibration by the plucking action of the fingers of both hands, and each separate string has normally been employed to sound only one note—the open note of its full vibrating-length.

Until comparatively recent times these musical "essentials" remained unaltered. It is true that, in various parts of Europe, Harps existed which were tuned and strung in various ways. These differences, however, of stringing—that is to say, of pitch and compass—left the musical character of the instrument unchanged. It was a purely diatonic instrument capable of sounding only the series of notes to which its strings were tuned. On the other hand, the character of the framework which supported the strings was considerably altered from time to time. These alterations, however, more particularly engage the student's attention in connection with the first attempts which were made to enlarge the Harp's radius of action. They will therefore be considered later.

It need scarcely be said that an instrument so rigid and inelastic could not hope to secure a firm foothold in the orchestra without improvement. An instrument which could only play one set series of notes was on a par with the old Hunting-Horn before the discovery of crooks. A mechanism had to be invented in order to bring the instrument into line with musical progress. This mechanism became standardized in an instrument which was, until 1810, in general use all over Europe—the (now) obsolete *Single Action Harp in E♭*.

This instrument had a diatonic compass in the key of E♭ from

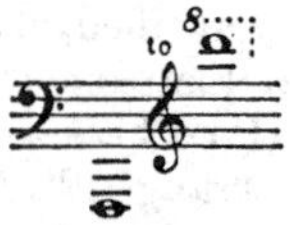

Furthermore, each string was provided with a simple but efficient apparatus by means of which its vibrating-length could be shortened, and this shortening was so adjusted that the pitch of each string was raised one semitone, neither more nor less. But this was not all, for each group of mechanisms shortening those strings which had the same name (A, B, etc.) was circuited on to a single rod controlled by a single pedal.[1] The player, therefore, had seven chromatic pedals at his disposal, and by using these seven pedals he could "naturalize"

[1] The invention of the Harp-pedal has been credited to various persons. Among others the name of Hochbrucher, Gaiffre, Simon, and Goepffert have been mentioned. The date of the invention was somewhere in the first half of the eighteenth century.

each of the three flat notes in his compass (viz. E♭, B♭, and A♭), and sharpen each of the four natural notes (viz. F, G, C, D).

But observe that if he used any one pedal, say the E-pedal, he mechanically altered *all* the E♭-strings in his compass to E♮. He could not raise the pitch of one selected string and leave its octave-strings unraised. That would have necessitated forty-one pedals.

The instrument thus became chromatic, but chromatic only in a doubly restricted sense. In the first place, no octave-notes named by the same letter could be chromatic to each other; and, in the second place, when once the strings were "set" by means of the pedals in any desired tuning that series of notes was immovable without further resort to the pedals.

There can be no doubt that this type of Harp was a great advance on anything that had gone before. Provided its music lay, without much modulation, in one of the simpler keys it answered its purpose admirably. It had, however, some fundamental deficiencies. In order to see what these were the student should go to the *Pianoforte* key-board and attempt the formation of various scales and chords from the diatonic notes of E♭ major. His only license is that he may raise any note one semitone. But he must remember that, if he does so raise any note, *the lower note has vanished* and cannot be used in that or in any other octave. He will then begin to find out the restrictions of the E♭-Harp. Such a simple chord as a minor ninth in the key of E♭ is impossible. The B♭-string has to be raised a semitone to give the ninth (C♭ = B♮). But when it is thus raised the B♭ itself disappears. The full chord becomes an impossibility.

Furthermore, even for the playing of simple scales the instrument can only be "set"—that is to say, its strings can only be arranged by the pedals—to give a regular technique in the eight keys of E♭, B♭, F, C, G, D, A, E. If this limit is exceeded in either direction the technical difficulties become insurmountable. Let us suppose that the Harpist wishes to play the first five notes of the scale of A♭ major. The first two notes, A♭ and B♭, offer no difficulties. For the third note (C) the C-string is plucked. The C-pedal has then to be rapidly depressed in order to raise the string to C♯ (= D♭). The finger has then to pluck the same string again in its shortened form to get the D♭. This is in itself awkward. The D♮-string, however, still remains in its place. The finger has therefore to skip this string and resume on the dominant (E♭). In keys such as D♭, G♭, and B♮, all these difficulties were intensified. The two former keys were, as Berlioz suggests, "nearly inaccessible."

The student must not compare the old *Single Action Harp in E♭* with our modern instrument by saying that the former was less chromatic than the latter. The Harp has never been a chromatic instrument. It always has been and possibly always will be *an instrument of harmonic formulae.* The deficiency of the old instrument as compared with the new is to be sought in the fact that the former instrument could be less freely set to any required sequence of notes. The modern Harp can be set almost as one chooses. Its radius of action is great. Once set, however, it is nearly as much bound to its formula as was the E♭-Harp. The formula itself is capable of wider variation. It can be executed even in its most grotesque forms. Try to change it, however, and all the old mechanical difficulties of pedalling begin to reappear.

The Harp as we have it at the present day is due to the inventive genius of Sébastien Erard. In 1810-1811 he produced his *Double Action Harp*, an instrument whose mechanism still remains the model for manufacturers. Besides minor improvements Erard made two capital innovations. In the first place, he saw the necessity of developing the mechanism so that each string and its octaves might be shortened at will by two different lengths so as to raise the pitch either a semitone or a whole tone. Furthermore, he perceived the fact that, if this development was to be musically effective, there was only one key in which the instrument could be tuned. That key was not E♭, but C♭. When so tuned the whole series of strings could be raised by the single- or double-action of the pedals respectively to the diatonic scales of C♮ and C♯. Whatever the arrangement of the pedals might be, the fingering, the technique, and the actual correspondence between the written note and the string played remained unaltered.

The main features in the framework of *Erard's Triple Action Harp* are the *Vertical Pillar*, the gracefully curved *Neck* with the *Comb* which conceals the mechanical stopping-apparatus, the diagonal semi-conical *Soundboard* of polished Swiss pine, and the *Pedal Box*. Of its forty-seven strings the eleven longest are "covered," the rest are of simple catgut. The uncovered C-strings are, as a rule, stained red, and the F-strings blue. In performance the Harpist rests the instrument against his right shoulder, and, it need scarcely be said, plays from the treble side.

The Modern Harp, then, stands normally in the key of C♭. It has a normal diatonic compass in that key[1] from

Its music is written, as for the *Pianoforte*, on two bracketted staves, and the treble and bass clefs are used at discretion.

As in the old E♭-Harp, seven transposing pedals are provided, each one of which acts simultaneously on all the strings of the same name. The seven pedals are arranged three on the left-hand side of the player and four on the right. On the left-hand side the B-, C-, and D-pedals, and on the right the E-, F-, G-, and A-pedals radiate outwards from the player in the order named. The B-, and E-pedals, therefore, are next to the player on his left and right hand respectively. In the centre between these two groups of pedals an eighth pedal is generally provided for dynamic purposes. This is known as the *forte pedal*. It has

[1] The top note of which can be mechanically raised to G♮ or G♯.

no connection with the seven mechanical pedals, and does not affect the pitch of the strings.

Each of the seven transposing pedals is provided with a couple of notches cut in the framework of the pedal-box. The depression of any one pedal into the first notch raises all the strings of its name by one semitone. A further depression into the second notch raises them another semitone, that is to say, one whole tone above their original pitch. The depression into either notch requires a small but appreciable fraction of time, and is not always free from noise. When released from either notch and also relieved from the pressure of the feet, the pedals are thrown back and held in their original position by the concealed action of spiral springs. The highly ingenious and smoothly-working mechanism for shortening the vibrating length of the strings need not occupy the student's attention. A glance at the neck of a Harp when in action will tell him more than a paragraph of explanation.

An important point now arises which demands some consideration. It is plain that, as the Harp is tuned diatonically to a major scale, no two adjacent strings can differ in pitch by more than a whole tone. The use of the pedal, then, on the lower of these two adjacent strings will bring it *into enharmonic-unison* with the upper string.

Thus, in the normal (unpedalled) scale of the instrument, the two notes B♭ and C♭ lie next to each other. If the B-pedal be fixed in the first notch the B♭ string is raised a semitone, and we get B♮. The two strings are now in enharmonic-unison B♮-C♭. The only other enharmonic unison obtainable on the Harp when one string is unpedalled and its next lower neighbour pedalled in the first notch is the combination E♮-F♭.

Five further enharmonic unisons, however, are obtainable by means of an unpedalled upper string and a lower string pedalled in the second notch. These are A♯-B♭, G♯-A♭, F♯-G♭, D♯-E♭, C♯-D♭.

Besides the above seven enharmonic-unison, two others can be produced by pedalling the lower string into the second notch and the upper string into the first notch. These combinations are the E♯-F♮ and the B♯-C♮. They can, of course, only be taken on those strings which in their normal (unpedalled) condition are one semitone apart.

We can now set out a complete list of the nine available enharmonic-unisons, noting that the small figures ^{0}, ^{1}, and ^{2}, placed above the names of the notes, represent respectively the open unpedalled string, the string pedalled in the first notch and the string pedalled in the second notch:

$$\overset{2}{\mathrm{B}\sharp}\text{-}\overset{1}{\mathrm{C}\natural},\ \overset{2}{\mathrm{C}\sharp}\text{-}\overset{0}{\mathrm{D}\flat},\ \overset{2}{\mathrm{D}\sharp}\text{-}\overset{0}{\mathrm{E}\flat},\ \overset{1}{\mathrm{E}\natural}\text{-}\overset{0}{\mathrm{F}\flat},\ \overset{2}{\mathrm{E}\sharp}\text{-}\overset{1}{\mathrm{F}\natural},\ \overset{2}{\mathrm{F}\sharp}\text{-}\overset{0}{\mathrm{G}\flat},\ \overset{2}{\mathrm{G}\sharp}\text{-}\overset{0}{\mathrm{A}\flat},\ \overset{2}{\mathrm{A}\sharp}\text{-}\overset{0}{\mathrm{B}\flat},\ \overset{1}{\mathrm{B}\natural}\text{-}\overset{0}{\mathrm{C}\flat}.$$

These nine enharmonic-unisons are frequently called *homophones* (=same sounds). They have also been christened *synonyms*, but a more inaccurate word could scarcely be found, for synonyms are essentially "things of the same name," and this is exactly what the strings are not. They are strings of different names tuned to what is practically the same sound. The word homophone is convenient and accurate. The longer expression, enharmonic unison, is perhaps better as an explanation.

A very simple example of the use of an enharmonic-unison has already been quoted from Debussy's *Pelléas et Mélisande*.[1] In this passage the E♭-string is raised to E♮, and the F♭ string remains unpedalled. It may be mentioned that, even if the composer had adopted the notation of two E♮'s or two F♭'s, the harpist would still play the rhythm on two strings. The reason is that quick reiterations of the same string are rather awkward. The string needs to be plucked a fair distance out of the vertical if it is to produce a good tone. Furthermore, its vibrations have a certain amplitude, sufficient, in the lower and middle registers, to be quite visible. Quick repetitions, therefore, *of the same string* are unsatisfactory. Each plucked note damps out its predecessor. Reiterations *of the same sound*, however, are quite in the character of the Harp, and are produced with ease, as in the example under discussion, on adjacent strings.

If we now recur to the list of enharmonic-unisons given above, we notice that, whereas our octave is made up of twelve chromatic notes, only nine of these can be taken as homophones. On reading the list of these nine carefully, we see that the notes D♮, G♮, and A♮ are missing. The reason is obvious. It is impossible to raise either the C♭, the F♭, or the G♭ string by three semitones so as to make the necessary unison with the string above. That would require a Triple Action Harp which does not exist.

A second point calls for our attention. Under this system of "tuning in pairs," the new series of intervals is "set" on the Harp and becomes technically to the player merely a scale. It does not matter how grotesque or unlike a scale the series looks when placed on paper. Its intervals mechanically replace the ordinary intervals of the scale, and can therefore be treated with the same freedom.

For instance, a Harpist can make a rapid *glissando* over the whole or a portion of his compass. This he does at pleasure upwards or downwards by drawing his finger quickly over the strings. If the pedals are not used at all, the *glissando* will be a diatonic *glissando* in the key of C♭ major. If all the pedals are used in the 1st notch, the *glissando* will be in C♮ major. Similarly, by using only a portion of the pedal apparatus, all the other scales can be set.

Suppose, however, that some of the strings are tuned in pairs of enharmonic-unisons. The player's finger still touches each string, but a certain number of the *sounds* of the scale have been eliminated. Now this elimination can be so arranged as to leave only the notes of definite musical chords.

The most commonly used of these chords are the parts of minor ninth chords usually known as "diminished sevenths," but dominant sevenths and the upper portions of major ninths and elevenths are also available. In the following list the notes which are taken as enharmonic-unisons are printed as minims. Each of these notes is of

[1] See Example 233. See also Example 20.

course sounded twice in quick succession by two separate strings. The notes printed in black crotchet-heads are taken only on one string.

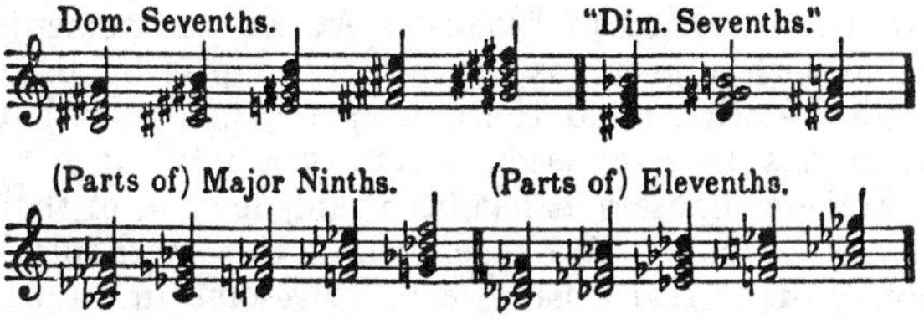

The Harp can be set for any of these chords, so that they become mere scale passages playable at will, *glissando* or otherwise.

It need scarcely be said that all these chords are used "enharmonically" in the ordinary sense of the word. The dominant sevenths are used as augmented sixths: the sharp and flat nomenclatures are used at discretion to represent each other in sound.

It is important to notice that no *glissando* can possibly be used unless all seven of the strings in each octave can be associated in the desired chord-setting. The omission of a single string would involve the necessity of a skip of the finger, and this would totally destroy the *glissando*-effect. If the student will look carefully at the above last example, he will see that in each of the chords there are three minims and one crotchet-head. Now, each minim represents an enharmonic-unison of two strings: each crotchet-head represents a single string. The simple sum, $3 \times 2 = 6 + 1 = 7$, will show him that in every case all of the seven strings are brought into action.

In order that there may be no mistake whatever with regard to the technique of the *glissando*, an example will be given which puts the matter in a nutshell. If the first of the three "diminished sevenths" in the above list, viz.,

occurred as a portion of an upward *glissando* in a Harp-part, the actual strings which would be touched by the player's fingers would be

The passage which, from the point of view of the *Pianoforte*-technique, is essentially a chord made up of repeated notes with skips, can be arranged on the Harp *as a scale*. It can therefore be played as a *glissando*. A few words on the less technical side of the question may be interpolated here. There can be no doubt that the scale-*glissando* with strings paired to form either definite chords or one of those ingenious combinations[1] which give so elusive a character to modern Harp-music is an effective weapon in the armoury of the composer. It can be taken *f* or *p*, upwards or downwards, and its length can be increased by the insertion of "loops." At certain moments its effect in conjunction with almost any orchestral group is brilliant and even exciting. On the other hand, there is equally no doubt that this form of expression has been abused of late years till it has become a nuisance. Some composers, it has been said, demand of their Harpists not fingers, but brooms. The repetition of this mechanical sweeping sound at every orchestral crisis becomes tiresome in the extreme. It is, however, a quite legitimate means of expression, if used with discretion and reserve.

Notation.

Of course no one ever actually writes out the correct nomenclature of all the strings touched by the Harpist's fingers in a *glissando*. Life is too short. The nearest approach to that logical ideal is the method of writing each pair of enharmonic-unisons as a repeated note of the same name, thus:

EXAMPLE 289.

This procedure, showing clearly not only those notes which are taken as enharmonic-unisons on two strings, but also the note which has no homophone, is quite sufficient for all purposes. Indeed, it is too elaborate for ordinary everyday use. It would be quite enough to indicate the tuning clearly by a series of single notes confined to one octave.[2] If the limit of the *glissando* upwards or downwards, as the case may be, is then shown by an additional note at the other extremity, the Harpist can have no doubt as to what is wanted. This is really all that is necessary, for there is only one way of "setting" the Harp for any given *glissando*. The labour of writing out Harp-parts is always so great that any form of abbreviation is a blessing.

[1] Widor instances the following

[2] The quotation from Liszt's *Mephisto-Walzer* (Ex. 289) gives only the first seven notes of the *glissando*. In the Full Score Liszt writes the whole passage out in full for four octaves. Each octave after the first is of course only a repetition of the notes in the preceding octave.

Here is an ordinary example of an abbreviated *glissando* from Variation VII. of Strauss's *Don Quixote* set:

EXAMPLE 290.

The student will notice that a single complete octave of notes is written in each case, and that they are disposed at each end of the *glissando*. This ensures accuracy. The notes on the descending side of the *glissando* are, however, added more for symmetry of appearance than for any other reason. On that side the top and bottom notes would be quite sufficient for all practical purposes. It is more usual to write the single complete octave of notes at the beginning of the passage. Strauss's method, however, is clear and logical. It might well be made a standard for such passages.

With regard to the length of *glissandos* anything less than about four or five octaves is liable to sound tame. The player can easily get over the whole of his compass in one second of time, and, if the *glissando* is written too short, he is forced either to insert a "loop" or to perform it in an ineffectively deliberate manner.

For all *glissandos* the Harpist must be given a few beats or bars—according to the changes involved—in which to "set" his instrument. When the composer has satisfied his mind as to possibility of the required setting, he should then see what alterations it necessitates from the preceding setting. In this way he can form a fairly accurate idea as to the necessary rests.

From the above remarks, it is hoped that both the general subject of the setting of the Harp and the more particular subject of the *glissando* will be quite clear. *Glissandos*, however, are only one and a not very important part of the Harp-technique. A point should be mentioned here with regard to the general Harp-notation as opposed to the special notation of the *glissando*. Some composers write into their parts all the required alterations in tuning. This is generally done by enclosing the directions for pedal-alterations in square brackets wherever required. Thus a change from the key of B♭ major to that of G major would be indicated by [B♮, E♮, F♯].

There is no actual necessity for undertaking a task which the Harpist usually performs at or before rehearsal. On the other hand, it is a perfectly satisfactory and by no means difficult method. Furthermore, it compels the composer to understand the medium in which he is writing, and to foresee the harmonic difficulties which he imposes on the player. If this plan is adopted, its logical outcome is really the abandonment of key-signatures altogether. There is of course a certain redundancy in employing the ordinary key-signatures and at the same time indicating the correct pedalling. Strict necessity requires only the correct setting of the strings, and then merely the *names* of the notes to be plucked. Their pitch—that is to say, their ♯ness, ♭ness, or ♮ness—is unalterable at the moment, and is governed by the previously indicated "setting."

Harmonics.[1]

The only Harmonic used on the Harp is No. 2. This is the harmonic produced by stopping the string lightly at a point equidistant from its two extremities. The resultant note is an octave above the open string. In order to obtain this Harmonic on the Harp, the string is lightly stopped by the lower part of the hand, while it is simultaneously plucked by the fingers of the same hand. This requires some little care and deliberation. Neither the highest nor the lowest portion of the Harp compass can be used for these harmonic notes. They should be confined to the seventeen strings from

Within these limits Harmonic No. 2 can be taken on any note ♭, ♮, or ♯. The effect *in sound* is of course an octave higher. The universal modern notation is to write the note required an octave below its sounding-pitch, with the addition of the sign o. Thus the following written passage

sounds

"Double-action Harps allow of sounding two, three, sometimes even four simultaneous harmonics with the left hand, on condition that the intervals are small, and require no extension of the fingers. The right can never play more than one harmonic at a time."[2]

It should be added that, in old Scores, the Harmonic-notes are often written at their actual sounding-pitch with the addition of the o above each note. The player in this case takes each note on the string an octave below the written note. The practice of the old masters was not, however, invariable on this point, and there is often considerable doubt as to their intentions.

[1] Boïeldieu in *La Dame Blanche* (1826) was the first to make serious orchestral use of these sounds.

[2] Widor, *The Technique of the Modern Orchestra.*

In using the Harmonics the student should remember that (1) any form of elaborate passage writing or arpeggio is quite out of the question. The fewer and the more deliberate the notes employed, the better will be the effect. (2) The tone is so etherial and fairy-like as to be inaudible, unless unaccompanied or accompanied at most by the *pp* of some one orchestral group.[1]

Two other methods of plucking the strings may be mentioned here for the sake of completeness. These are

(1) The method of stopping the string as soon as the note is uttered. The sounds so produced are known in France as *sons étouffés*, and are, in quality, something like a short dry String-*pizzicato*. They differ strikingly in effect from the usual warm vibrant notes of the instrument. In the Score they may be indicated either by the French term given above or by the English word *stopped*. The resumption of the ordinary technique is usually indicated in French Harp music by the words *laissez vibrer*. A dotted line, however, clearly showing the required limits of the stopped passage is quite sufficient for all ordinary purposes. Here is a brief example of this style of tone-production:

EXAMPLE 291.

Th. Dubois. *Ronde des Archers.* *(Transcription de Mlle L. Delcourt.)*

(2) The method of plucking the strings close to the sounding-board. The sounds so produced are generally known to French Harpists as *Sons près de la table*. The effect is metallic and somewhat more like a Guitar or Banjo. The following short quotation[2] gives an example both of these sounds and of the ordinary Harp-Harmonics. "M.D." and "M.G." of course mean right- and left-hand respectively.

EXAMPLE 292.

Jean Risler. *Petite Fantaisie.*

[1] Good examples are Berlioz's *Valse des Sylphes* and Charpentier's *Louise* (towards the end of Act I).

[2] From Jean Risler's *Petite Fantaisie pour Harpe Chromatique.*

Shakes and Tremolos.

Shakes and *tremolos*, as a rule, sound rather stupid on the Harp. They are both played by means of a double-handed technique. Each group of notes making up the shake or *tremolo* is performed rapidly and alternately by the right and left hands, thus:

Neither is worth doing in anything but a *pianissimo*, scarcely even then. The *tremolo* has only recently been introduced into orchestral music as a sort of murmuring ("bisbigliando") accompaniment. It is not often met with, but an example may be found on page 67 of Strauss's *Sinfonia Domestica*,

EXAMPLE 293.

With the old masters, from Händel onwards, the Harp was used more especially to give an appropriate "tang" to those subjects which demanded a flavour of antiquity. This particularly suited the taste of the French under the First Empire. Macpherson and the Classics were then all the vogue, and the Harp became firmly established in Parisian orchestras as an interpreter of the pseudo-classical culture and of the vaporous days of Ossian. From France its orchestral use spread through Germany to the rest of Europe. Nowadays every Symphony and Opera orchestra has at least a couple of Harps. Its fine poetical qualities have become better understood. Its power of characterization—varying according to its music from the fairy-like to the grandly heroic—is now employed on more general topics. It is still occasionally used to produce the illusion of antiquity, but that side of its musical character tends to become of less importance.

A list of those arpeggios which have been found practical and effective is scarcely worth giving. Owing to the nature of the case it would occupy an enormous amount of space. Furthermore, the type is familiar to all and varies mainly with the momentary necessities of the harmonic progressions. A certain number of quotations have already been made in which the Harp figures in a subsidiary manner. The student should now refer to these. They include examples of

(1) Single repeated-notes: opening of Saint-Saëns's *Danse Macabre.* Example 17.

(2) Enharmonic-unisons, where (A) both strings are plucked at the same time: the "bell-effect" in Wallace's *Villon.* Example 20. (B) The two strings are used separately as repeated notes: the passage already referred to in Debussy's *Pelléas et Mélisande.* Example 233. In the former example (A) the

Harp.

is one of the two enharmonic-unisons produced[1] by pedalling the lower string into the 2nd notch and the upper string into the 1st notch. The unison is actually B♯—C♮ on the B♭ and C♭ strings.

(3) Melody-notes where the Harp-part is merely added to give the ictus of the bell: Bizet's *Carillon.* Example 19.

(4) Simple arpeggio-accompaniments: Tschaikowsky's *Romeo and Juliet,* Example 141, and Bizet's *Carmen,* Example 106.

(5) Simple chord-accompaniments in the lower-middle register: the two quotations from Strauss's *Don Juan* and *Don Quixote.* Examples 134 and 135.

(6) Bass-octaves, occasionally useful in quiet passages, but generally needing either support or thin orchestration: Bizet's *Carmen.* Example 43.

As it is not possible to give elaborate quotations of Harp-parts here, a few detached observations will be made on the writing of these parts. The student should then take any modern Full Scores to which he has access and see how these general rules work out in practice.

(1) The Harp is the only instrument whose particular technique has given a generic word—*arpeggio*—to the rest of the instrumental force. It is unnecessary to dwell on the point that nine-tenths of all orchestral Harp-music must be "*in arpeggio.*"[2] That does not preclude the occasional use of individual detached notes, short prominent melodic figures, and so on. These are often found nowadays in the quieter parts of compositions. Their effect is generally in inverse ratio to the number of notes written.

(2) In laying out Harp-chords and arpeggios remember that the

[1] See page 465.

[2] For a very happy example of the arpeggios suddenly "coming through" the rest of the orchestra, see the 52nd bar from the end of Wagner's Overture to the *Flying Dutchman.* The heavy Brass is taken off and the Harp-part has only to contend with the Wood-wind, the Horns, and a light *pizzicato.*

Harpist uses only the thumb and first three fingers. The little finger remains idle. Five-note chords and arpeggios for either hand are therefore *impossible.*

(3) The Harp-octave, though controlled by only four fingers, consists merely of seven strings, and these are fairly close together. The Pianoforte-octave controlled by five fingers consists of twelve notes. The advantage in ease of mechanism lies clearly with the Harp. The scale is more "under the hand." Stretches up to and even beyond a tenth are normal for the Harpist. Indeed, that interval—the tenth—may be said to correspond on the Harp to the pianist's octave-stretch.

(4) In general, the more notes and the closer they are placed in an arpeggio or chord the better the effect.

(5) The Harpist always "spreads" his chords slightly. If the composer wants a short *pizzicato* effect he must take care to write only notes that lie well under the fingers of the two hands. The chord is then marked with some such expression as *short* or *struck.* The French word *sec* (dry) is often used for this purpose.

(6) Don't let the centre of your arpeggio figures lie either too high or too low. Spread them well, and, except for special effects, keep to the most sonorous part of the instrument between

(7) In two-part arpeggios do not ask the fingers of one hand to pluck those strings which have just been quitted by the other hand. In other words, do not let the two arpeggios overlap too closely. It is equally important that the two should not lie at opposite ends of the instrument. Otherwise the effect is jejune, and poverty-stricken. Keep the hands fairly close, but don't let them overlap. Keep the harmony going in the middle part of the instrument.

(8) Very long arpeggios can only be written *in one part.* Each hand plays at most four notes of the arpeggio alternately, and then changes position to take up the arpeggio after the other hand.

(9) You cannot get away from the non-chromatic nature of the instrument. There is always that restriction. It is by no means necessary that the Harp should stop playing at every slight modulation. The pedals can be employed during performance or in any momentary rest. But of course when they are employed the string or strings on which they are used must be for the moment out of-action. A little understanding and ingenuity in laying out the Harp-part so as to avoid the chromatic note or notes is amply repaid by ease of performance and enhanced effect. If there are distinct pauses between the chords or arpeggios the instrument can be reset for each new attack. This is, however, somewhat out of the character of the Harp.

(10) If the harmony is of a wildly chromatic character either omit the Harp altogether or write for two. In the latter case divide up the

passages so as to give the minimum of pedalling to each of the players. Quite apart from chromatic necessities the Harp-part gains enormously by an increase in the number of players. Reasons of expense, however, often lead, in the performance of even the greatest works, to the "boiling down" of the Harp-parts.

(11) When two or more Harps are employed and it is not necessary for chromatic reasons to cut-up the Harp-parts, richness of effect is rather secured by writing additional separate parts than by reduplication of the same part. This must, however, be interpreted with discretion. A 2nd, 3rd, or 4th Harp-part that is merely filling in the notes which the 1st Harp happens not to be playing at the moment is apt to sound unsatisfactory. With straightforward arpeggios, however, this difficulty will seldom arise.

(12) Repeated *notes* on different *strings* are possible at any pace. Repeated *strings*, however, are less easy. Except in quite slow tempos they are better avoided.

(13) In the very ♯ keys, such as B♮, F♯, and C♯, it is better to write the Harp-part in the corresponding enharmonic flat keys, C♭, G♭, and D♭. It gives a greater vibrating-length for the strings.

(14) Be careful where you "place" your Harp-chords in the music. If the instrument is merely adding the mechanical tinkle of its arpeggios to the general orchestral ensemble, the "placing" does not much matter. In any other circumstances it is well to think the matter over carefully, and "plant" the chords wherever they derive the greatest force from the harmonic-scheme of the music. In extended arpeggios you must face the necessary toil of writing a great many notes. On the other hand, a few cunningly-placed chords, or even isolated notes, are occasionally strikingly effective.

(15) Some of the great masters have written without much understanding for the Harp. The detailed technique of the instrument can be studied in the works of such specialists as Parish Alvars, Oberthur, Zabel, Dubois, etc. In studying serious modern orchestral composers you cannot do better than make yourself acquainted with Granville Bantock's Scores. His Harp parts are models of refinement and happy effect.

(16) In translating from Pianoforte to Orchestra you will often find that the music of the original is enclosed and defined by means of a series of arpeggio-like passages. This is the nature of the Pianoforte. The mere transliteration and rearrangement of these Pianoforte passages for Harp against an orchestral background is rarely satisfactory. The Pianoforte passage *is* the music: the Harp part merely gives the effect of *an addition* to the music.

No. 53. The Chromatic Harp.[1]

The Chromatic-Harp is little seen in English concert-rooms. It is, however, an interesting instrument, whose usefulness is bound to increase with the continued development of chromatic-harmony. A few words with regard to its mechanism and capabilities may therefore not be out of place.

The Chromatic-Harp abandons the Pedal-action altogether, and substitutes a string for each semitone throughout the entire compass. The arrangement of strings adopted is, curiously enough, by no means new. In fact a primitive instrument on this system is to be seen in the South Kensington Museum. It is a Scottish Harp of the fifteenth century.

The main difficulty in producing a Chromatic-Harp, of course, lies in the fact that, as there is a string for each semitone, the total number of strings is nearly doubled. And the ancient system which has been revived to solve this difficulty consists in using a double series of strings.

The first series runs from the right-hand side of the "comb" to the left-hand side of the sound-board; the second series runs from the left-hand side of the "comb" to the right-hand side of the sound-board. The strings are therefore in two distinct planes which bisect each other at an acute interior angle. Their position may be roughly represented by two hair-combs so locked together that each pair of adjacent teeth forms the capital letter X.

With this instrument a completely new finger-technique is demanded from the Harpist, and this undoubtedly militates against its artistic progress. One must therefore be chary of condemning an instrument against whose introduction the interests of a great many living Harpists combine. On the musical side it may be said with confidence that, as far as the chromatic side of the matter goes, any music playable on the Pianoforte is also playable on the Chromatic-Harp. If space permitted, this assertion might be supported by endless examples taken from the works of the modern French school. This is naturally the instrument's special title to the musician's respect and sympathy, though, it must be candidly admitted that the general opinion of Harpists and Harp-makers is against the Chromatic-Harp on the score both of its technique and its poor tone. The instrument, however, has some minor advantages, of which two may be mentioned here.

(1) There are no pedals. There is therefore no unmusical noise. The player is free to devote himself entirely to what should be his proper task, the control of the strings by his hands.

(2) The strings are not being continually shortened and lengthened.

[1] Invented by Lyon, and adopted by the Parisian firm of Pleyel. The instrument is known in France as the *Harpe Pleyel "Chromatique sans pédales," Système G. Lyon.* The earliest re-introduction of the cross-strung Harp, however, appears to have been made by Pape in 1845.

They last longer,—a serious advantage to the player. Their intonation is more stable.

Against these advantages it has been objected:

(1) That it is not in the nature of the Harp to be chromatic. This sort of criticism, which has probably been directed against every advance in instrumental-construction, is sufficiently answered by putting the statement in its more correct form, "that it is not in the nature of the old Pedal-Harp to be chromatic."

(2) That the Chromatic-Harp cannot perform the *glissandos* which exist everywhere in the modern repertoire of the Pedal-Harp. This may possibly be good news to the frequenters of our concert-halls. It may dispose many of them to look with a friendly eye on the new Chromatic-Harp. It involves, however, an interesting and unique point. Every musical instrument at the successive phases of its evolution has invariably incorporated the resources and the technique of its predecessor, and has added some new facility, some greater scope for musical expression. The Chromatic-Harp alone seems to be an exception to this rule. It is true that its harmonic radius is far greater than that of the Double-Action Pedal-Harp. On the other hand, it has been compelled by its very nature to abandon the system of setting its scales into fixed harmonic patterns. The *glissando* as a standing dish has to disappear from the Harp menu.

It need scarcely be said that, putting aside its advantages in the way of chromatic passage-work and its disadvantages in the way of *glissando*-chords, one can treat the instrument orchestrally very much as if it were an ordinary Double-Action Pedal-Harp.

The student will be interested to see a specially written passage embodying chromatic features which could not possibly be played on the ordinary instrument. The following quotation is from a work composed for the Chromatic-Harp. If the student will merely write out the pedalling necessary for the performance of these four bars on the Double-Action Pedal-Harp he will see how widely different are the mechanical conditions of the two instruments. No one in his wildest moments would write such a passage for the older instrument, and, if he did, it would sound anything but *vif et gai* when performed.

EXAMPLE 294.

E.-M. Delaborde. *Scherzetto.*

It may be said that the special literature for the Chromatic-Harp is at present small. It tends, however, to increase in quantity.

No. 54. The Mandoline.[1]

Fr. *Mandoline*; It. *Mandolino*; Ger. *Mandoline.*

This is a small pear-shaped instrument with a fretted neck. It is furnished with eight wire-strings tuned in pairs. The actual tuning as now standardized by the Neapolitan makers is the same as that of the Violin:

In the best makes a simple "machine-head" with screws and ivory thumb-pieces is used to tighten and loosen the strings.

The peculiarity of the instrument is that, in its method of tone-production, it employs the ancient and now almost disused *plectrum.* As manufactured for the Mandolinist, this consists of a small flat piece of tortoiseshell, bone, or ivory, in shape a pointed oval. It is used not merely to produce single *staccato* notes, but also a sort of tremulous *tenuto.* This is accomplished by a rapid iteration of the plectrum to and fro on any pair of strings. The resultant *sostenuto* is the chief characteristic of the instrument. The fingering is the same as that of the Violin, and it has a working compass from its low G (4th string) of about two octaves and a major sixth.

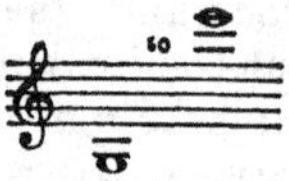

The Mandoline-part is written in the treble-clef at its actual sounding-pitch. The poor tinkley tone-quality and the imperfect method of tone-production preclude the instrument from taking a serious place in music.

In the theatre the Mandoline has been used by Mozart in *Don Giovanni,* by Grétry in *L'amant jaloux* and by Verdi in *Otello.* The well-known serenade in Act II. of *Don Giovanni—Deh vieni alla finestra*—has an *obbligato* part marked in the Full Score "Mandolin." In view of the specially *staccato* nature of this *obbligato*—mostly semiquavers in a $\frac{6}{8}$ *Allegretto*—and of the admitted indefiniteness in the nomenclature of the less commonly used instruments, Mozart's intention has been questioned more than once. It has been suggested that, if he had really wished the ordinary Neapolitan Mandoline, he would have written phrases more characteristic of its special method —the reiterated *tenuto.* A decision on this point is difficult, though if the Mandoline was not intended it is not easy to see what *staccato*-instrument could supply its place in this Number. It must be added that in practice the whole *obbligato* is played, nine times out of ten, by the 1st Violins *pizzicato.*

[1] Diminutive of *Mandora* or *Mandola.* The modern Italian *Mandola* is a large *Tenor-Mandoline.* See what has been already said with regard to the early *Pandoura,* page 291.

No. 55. The Guitar.

Fr. *Guitare*; It. *Chitarra*; Ger. *Guitarre.*

The Guitar can scarcely be regarded as a regular orchestral instrument, though its occasional appearance in the theatre or concert-hall makes a brief description necessary.

In shape its incurved sound-box recalls some of the early stages in the development of the Fiddle-family. It is provided with a fretted neck, and of its six strings the three lowest are "covered" or "spun" with silver wire, while the three highest are of plain catgut.

In pitch the instrument stands between the Viola and the Cello. Its tuning, a series of perfect fourths broken between the 2nd and 3rd strings by a major third, perpetuates the old vicious tradition of the irregular lute system.

The strings are plucked by the thumb and four fingers of the right hand,[1] while the four fingers of the left hand stop the notes on the fretted neck. A peculiarity of the left hand technique is the use of the *barré*. As the number of strings is six, and the number of left-hand fingers only four, certain chords would be impossible unless 2, 3, or 4 strings were stopped by the same finger. On the Violin the stopping of a perfect fifth on two adjacent strings is accomplished by means of the ordinary technique; that is to say, only the point of the finger is used. In the case of the Guitar, however, the breadth of the neck would prevent such a stopping of three or four strings. The *barré*, therefore, is used. The first finger is laid flat across the strings, and acts, in Berlioz's words, "as a temporary fret."

Natural Harmonics 2, 3, 4, and 5 are employed upon the Guitar, and there is a regular and peculiar technique for the production of Artificial Harmonics. It consists mainly of stopping the note with one of the fingers of the left hand. The first finger of the right hand is then used to touch the string lightly at the proper "node." At the same time the string is plucked by the thumb of the right hand.

The Guitar is always written-for in the treble-clef an octave above the actual sounds required. Though little used nowadays, it has occasionally been introduced into Opera mainly for the purpose of giving "local colour" to Spanish scenes. Examples of its use may be found in Act I. of Rossini's *Il Barbiere*, and in Act I. of Weber's *Oberon*. Broad spread chords of a simple nature, arpeggios founded on these chords, and easy figures in arpeggio, best suit the character of the instrument.

The Guitar has recently received a new lease of life through the exertions and enthusiasm of Mr. Percy Grainger. He has written

[1] But see below, page 481.

some Guitar accompaniments to vocal music. In some of these accompaniments the Guitar is treated and tuned in the orthodox style. A few bars from his charming setting of "Willow willow" will serve as a specimen of this simple reserved style. It must be mentioned that "Middle Fiddle" and "1st and 2nd Bass Fiddles" are *Graingerese* for "Viola" and "1st and 2nd Cellos." The horizontal lines above the Guitar part show how long the strings should be held down and allowed to go on vibrating.

EXAMPLE 295.

Greater interest, however, attaches to Mr. Grainger's innovations in the Guitar-technique. They constitute quite a new departure. In his setting of the Faeroe Island Dancing Ballad, "*Father and Daughter*," he has employed "Five Men's Single Voices, Double Chorus, Strings, Brass, Percussion, and Mandoline and Guitar band."[1] Mr. Grainger's innovations mainly consist in the recognition of the fact that the Guitar is by its tuning limited to only a few well-ascertained chords. He therefore alters the tuning, splits up his Guitar-band into sections, and allots to each section only easily played chords. This not only gives him the possibility of some harmonic variety, but leaves his Guitarists free to perform all sorts of mechanical evolutions with their right hands. On this point it is perhaps better to allow Mr. Grainger to speak for himself. He says:

"I have written mostly for Guitars to be played in what I call the 'Australian' way. . . . This consists of tuning the Guitars to any complete chord, such as

(but generally a *major* chord), using the left hand mostly to stop straight across the six strings at once, and using the right hand in various ways, with a plectrum, or hitting the strings with a paper-knife, or in various Spanish ways ('nails,' etc.), but *chiefly* using the right hand in thrumming backwards and forwards *with the thumb*; thrumming with the *flesh* when travelling from low strings towards high strings, with the *nail* when travelling in the other direction.

As to the left hand: If the Guitar is tuned,

right across the fifth fret would give

sixth fret would give

[1] First performed with forty Guitars and Mandolines at a Balfour-Gardiner Symphony Concert, and afterwards by the London Choral Society.

seventh fret would give

and so on, chromatically, from

On such a tuning, plenty of other chords can be easily got: any minor chords between * and †, and such as the following chromatically:

and several others. The left-hand work being easy in the way of playing, and able to shift very quickly (as there are no elaborate finger-changings), the right hand can undertake all sorts of complicated rhythms and contrasts of playing of which the '*Father and Daughter*'[1] parts only offer a very primitive example."

In the "*Father and Daughter*" four separate groups of Guitars are employed. They are required to tune as follows:

The 1st and 2nd Guitar parts have only four different chords to play in the work: the 3rd and 4th have only three. Altogether, the players have easy access in various positions to chords of F major, D minor, B♭ major, E♭ major, and C minor.

The actual parts are written out in a sort of musical shorthand. Only one double-tailed note is employed to represent each spread chord. At the top of the part the tuning is indicated for each of the Guitar-groups, and the technical method of playing each chord is explained. For instance, the 1st Guitar has to play four chords (F major, D minor, B♭ major, and E♭ major), of which three will be found in the Full-Score-quotation given below. The four double-tailed notes,

[1] Mr. Grainger has also written a "Scotch Strathspey and Reel" for four voices, four Wood-wind, Xylophone, English Concertina, Guitars and Strings.

are used as a conventional representation of these four chords. Thus the 1st Guitar part in the extract given below figures *in the part* as follows:

The chords in the Full Score represent the actual sounds played, but not the technical method by which these sounds can be obtained. Thus, in the 1st Guitar part, though no chord has six notes in it, all are "six-string-chords." These are obtained in various clever ways. For instance, if we represent the open-strings by diamond-headed notes, the four double-tailed conventional notes would actually be performed as the four following chords:

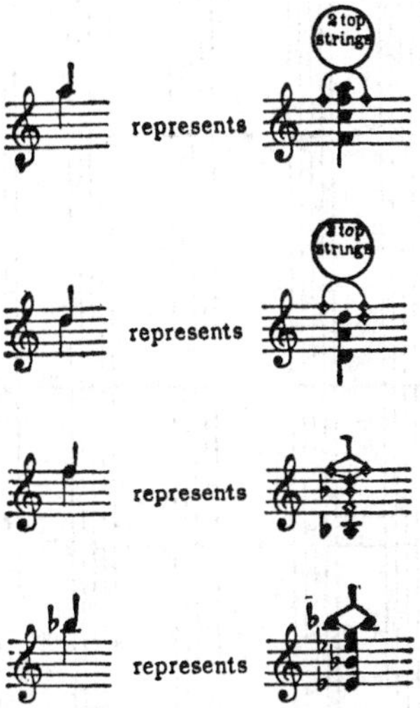

Similarly with all the other three Guitar-parts. Each has a special tuning, a conventional notation, and easy access to a few cunningly devised "six-string-chords." Finally, a certain number of chords are marked * "to be played with the left hand in the 'upside down' position; with the palm of the hand *downwards,* much as in grasping an oar, not upwards, as in the usual guitar or violin position."

The following seven-bar quotation from the Full Score will give some idea of this interesting work:

EXAMPLE 296.

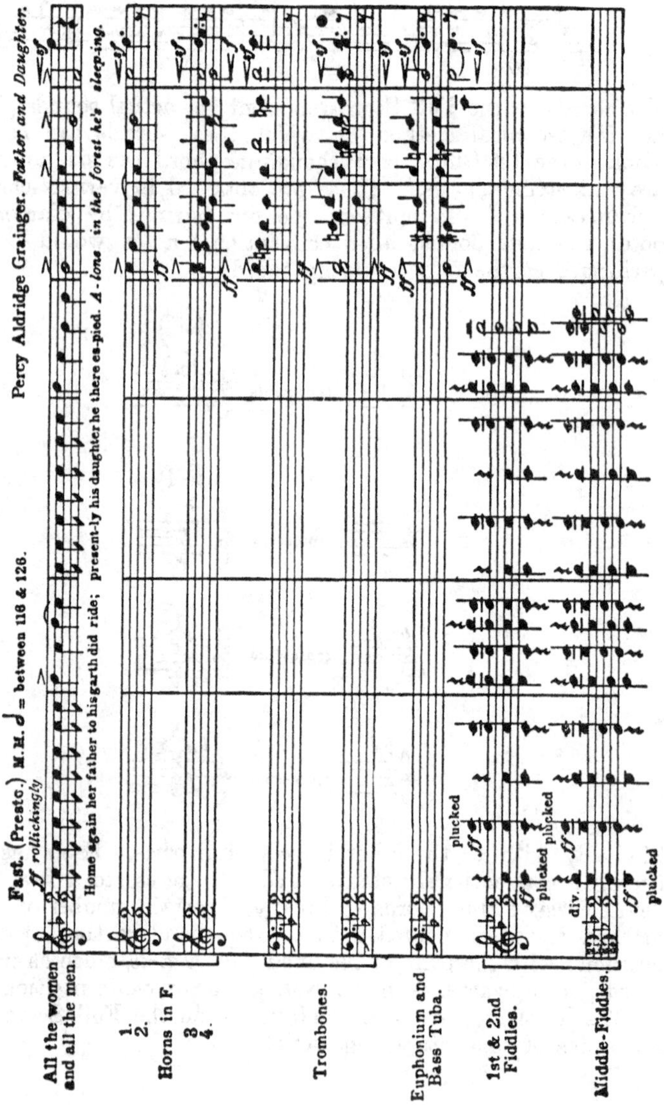
Percy Aldridge Grainger. Father and Daughter.
Fast. (Presto.) M.M. 𝅗𝅥 = between 116 & 126.
ff rollickingly
Home again her father to his garth did ride; present-ly his daughter he there es-pied. A-lone in the forest he's sleep-ing.
All the women and all the men.
1. 2. Horns in F. 3. 4.
Trombones.
Euphonium and Bass Tuba.
1st & 2nd Fiddles.
Middle-Fiddles.
plucked
div.
ff
sf

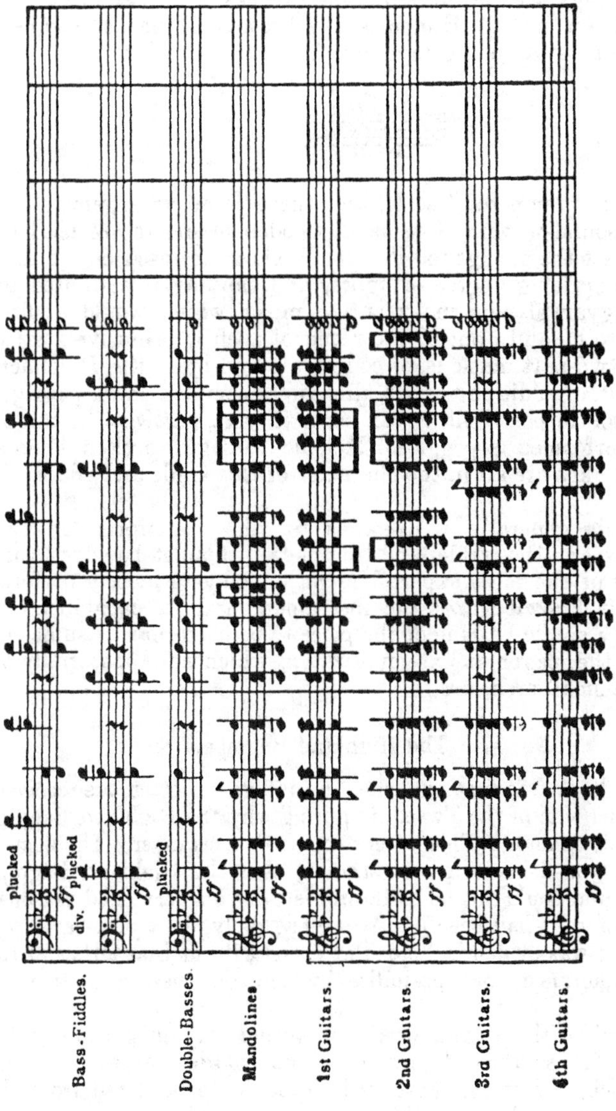
Bass-Fiddles.
div.
plucked
ff
Double-Basses.
Mandolines.
1st Guitars.
2nd Guitars.
3rd Guitars.
4th Guitars.

No. 56. The Dulcimer (or Cimbalom).[1]

The Dulcimer is, like the Pianoforte, a percussion instrument in which the strings are set in vibration by means of hammers. As manufactured for use in Hungarian orchestras, it has a complete chromatic compass of four octaves from

The scale is a "tempered" scale, and there is an arrangement for damping the sound-waves. Two small wooden hammers are used by the player to set the strings in vibration. These are used one in each hand, and a surprising degree of agility and cunning is exhibited by the finest Magyar players in executing music which would at first sight appear to be quite out of the reach of such a primitive instrument. True two-part music is, of course, a stand-by in the Dulcimer-technique; but, in addition to that, all sorts of complex chord passages and even elaborate part-writing can be, as it were, *outlined* by means of rapidly performed arpeggios. Melodic passages, broken chords, figures, and shakes are all in the character of this facile and adaptable instrument.

The part is generally written, as for the Pianoforte, on two bracketed staves in the treble- and bass-clefs. It must be added that a great many of the most expert Hungarian players merely perform by ear. Their knowledge of the instrument and its capabilities is complete, and a single hearing of the piece to be performed is sufficient to suggest to the player an extemporization which adds materially to the effect of a small orchestra.

No. 57. The Highland Bagpipe.

When this book was first published, an indignant letter was received, from the sterner side of the Tweed, inquiring why the Highland Bagpipe had been totally ignored. This letter came from a stranger. The answer was that this was a book on *orchestration*, that the Highland Bagpipe was not used, and could not be used, orchestrally for very good reasons; and that therefore it had been omitted. The reply, on a post-card, was that the author was evidently "good at excuses," but that either of the two words "ignorance" or "prejudice" would come nearer the truth of the matter.

With regard to the "ignorance," the author was quite comfortable in his mind. The southron "prejudice" was harder to swallow. By the oddest trick of fate this post-card happened to be dated from the very street in which the author's father and grandfather were born—Alva Street, Edinburgh. There was, and is, no orchestral justice in in-

[1] Ger. *Cimbal* or *Hackbrett.*

cluding the pipes. But ancestral memories may temper that justice by a brief note on the instrument.

The standard Highland Bagpipe has four pipes, one of which is the "chanter," bored with holes, on which the melody is played. The other three are the "drones," which skirl a continuous bass-accompaniment to the melody. The reed of the chanter is a double-reed, something like that of the Oboe, but broader and stiffer. In the drones, the ancient single-reed—long, thin, and tubular—is still employed. Except in the Bagpipe, this reed is now obsolete. The Bagpipe, too, is now the only indirectly-blown instrument in existence. The player has a sloping wooden tube in his mouth. Through this he blows. And the action of his arm on the bag keeps the drones sounding. Normally, there is at least a foot and a half between his lips and the reed of the chanter. But, provided the many mechanical details of the Bagpipe are fitted snugly, the whole scale of the chanter can be obtained in this indirect fashion.

The chanter has only a short compass; produced, of course, by opening and closing the bored holes of the pipe. The whole scale is the following nine "white notes" of the Piano:

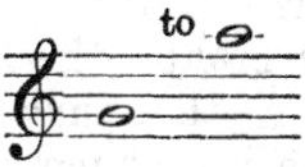

The above statement is not strictly true. The Bagpipe notes are not all precisely the same as the notes on the Piano. In the pipe-scale, the "C," between B and D, and the "F," between E and G, are bored exactly midway in pitch between the two outer notes. To our ears, accustomed to the modern tempered scale, they both sound about a quarter of a tone sharp. The barbaric, or Oriental, sound of the Highland Bagpipe is mainly due to this one fact. It is for this reason that it cannot be used seriously in any orchestral combinations.

Long may it flourish out of doors! For, no laboratory dabblings in quarter-tones are ever likely to be a satisfactory substitute for this genuine relic of primitive melody. One feels that Nero would have appreciated it: what he would have done to the quarter-tonists need not be mentioned.

The tuning of the drones is not altogether agreed on. The balance of opinion is in favour of "A's," with "G's" and a "B" as a second choice. Naturally, with the fixed scale of the chanter, an alteration in the bass has considerable effect on the *character* of the tunes that are played above it. The accepted tunings for the drones are as follows:

A. J. Ellis. David Glen.

Angus Mackay.

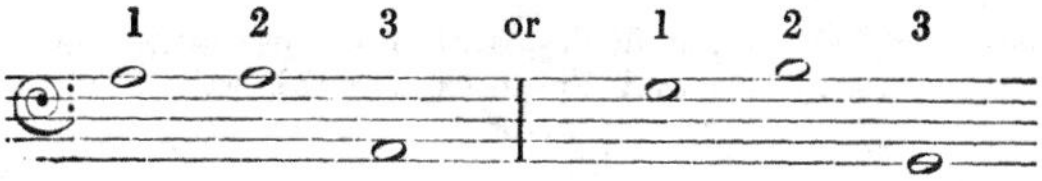

ADDENDA.

A Note on Genealogy.

SOME misconceptions with regard to the ancient *keyless*-Bugle seem to persist. Let it be said, then, that this instrument was the ancestor of two distinct lines of musical children.

The first line consisted of the *keyed* instruments, the Royal Kent Bugle and the Ophicleide.

The second line consisted only of *valved* instruments, and included the whole of our modern valved-brass: the Cornets, E♭-Horns, B♭-Tenor Horns, Euphonium, and Tubas.

The popularity of the first group—the keyed-Bugles and Ophicleides—rose to its climax in 1856. At that time the Royal Artillery possessed a complete Bugle Band. The instruments on which they played were known as "Halliday's Keyed Bugles," from the name of their inventor, Joseph Halliday. This Halliday was an Irishman who had given lessons to Balfe in Waterford in 1815. He was bandmaster of the Cavan Militia and took out his patent for the key-mechanism in 1810.[1] It held the military field against all comers for half a century. Adopted in the Royal Artillery and other regiments, it was superseded by the Cornopean, a sort of early two-valved Cornet, which in its turn gave place to the regular Cornet now in use. It was the addition of valves to the Royal Artillery band by their bandmaster, Trumpet-Major James Lawson, that began the modern military band movement in England.

One of the military results of this movement was that the Drum, which during the whole of the eighteenth century was the regular duty and signal instrument for infantry, was abandoned. The keyless-Bugle took its place in all infantry regiments, and the keyless-Trumpet in the cavalry.

So far for history. It is obvious that tradition supports our special way of treating the Cornets as the regular melodic instrument in a band, with an occasional Trumpet (in F or E♭) as an extra. But modern Trumpets have valves; and their mechanism is no more difficult to control than that of the Cornet. Why then have we not abandoned our Cornets long ago in favour of Trumpets?

The answer is that the Cornet is at least twice as easy *to blow*. And that makes for considerable peace of mind on the part of our far-flung

[1] Two of these post-1810 keyed-Bugles, with fake inscriptions attaching them to George Washington (Brandywine and Fraunces Tavern), were sold quite recently in New York.

Cornet-players and of the bandmasters who have to teach them. It is a matter of convenience. In place of the pungent, military aristocracy of the Trumpet we have the placid, plebeian ease of the Cornet. And, as we are all quite used to this second-best, nobody notices it. A very friendly foreign critic put it to the writer thus :

" When I hear your superb English Trombones and Tubas, I always feel that your top-line men ought to be in mufti."

The Harp that (perhaps) once.

There is a statement on page 461 that " as far as Western Europe is concerned the Harp seems to have first installed itself in England and Scandinavia about the twelfth century. The term *Cythara Anglica* (*i.e.* English Harp) was in common European use. . . . From England the Harp appears to have passed to Ireland," etc.

An Irish critic challenges this statement vigorously. He points out that the existence of the term *Cythara Anglica* only proves that certain European peoples knew what was the Harp's immediate source *for them*. He adds that England herself received it from Ireland, where it had been in use for at least 400 years, from the sixth to the tenth century.

The author has many Irish friends but no Irish forefathers. No call of the blood is there to cajole him into acting unfairly by the Harp. His only wish is to hold the scales evenly balanced. *Fiat justitia, ruat coelum.* The Irish critic's point with regard to the name *Cythara Anglica* has weight. Even to-day the huge quantities of Bulgarian tobacco that find their way annually to England are known as Turkish tobacco because we receive them directly from Turkey.

On the other side of the argument is the fact that there is no record of the English, of that date, ever having called the Harp the Irish Harp (*Cythara Hibernica*). They probably would have done so if they had received it as a developed, national instrument from Ireland. Furthermore, even with the small sailing vessels of that day, there was plenty of communication between the Continent and both Ireland and England. Ireland was then much more completely different from England than she is to-day. She spoke Erse solely : she had a different civilization. We must suppose that people on the Continent would easily distinguish the two types. If the Harp had come from Ireland originally, they would have been told so in England. There was no way of keeping it a secret. On this point the author's judgment is that the Irish critic's plea is " not proven."

The other matter, the existence of the Harp in Ireland from the sixth to the tenth century, is still more nebulous. The reader should be warned that almost everything about the early history of the Harp is guesswork. We do not know, to a century, when it first appeared in England. How should we ? Where are the records ? " Records " here can only mean statements in MSS., pictures in missals, and sculptures in churches. The difficulties only increase when we come to examine the Irish claim. For the four centuries, over which we have to throw a mental searchlight backwards, are the centuries 1100 to 700.

The author would not lose a moment's sleep if he heard that an undoubted triple-action Harp of the tenth century had been dug up in Ireland. He would be surprised—but delighted to hear the news. To that honest statement of his national impartiality he would add that the most he can subscribe to is the fact that the Harp *may have been* in Ireland centuries before it was known in England.

Edward I. is a long, long distance from George V.; but, when you come to consider it, it is about the same as the distance that separated Edward I. from sixth-century Ireland. History deals in these vast spaces. And as the author, a little against his will, has had to discuss controversial matters on the origin of the Harp, he would like to reprint here two excerpts from *The Book of Household Expenses* of Edward I. Historically, they are both unchallengeable. And they both concern harpists: one of whom is shown in a practical rôle that anticipates by many centuries our use of music in hospitals; the other in a more poetical rôle, which, we fear, would not be encouraged in our modern churches and cathedrals. However, one is not sure. Some optimistic harpist might make the experiment at the Abbey.

"To Melioro the harper of Sir John Matravers for playing on the harp when the King was bled . . . . xx^s."

"To Walter Luvel the harper of Chichester whom the King found playing the harp before the tomb of S. Richard . . . vi^s viii^d."

The sardonic remark has been made that these two entries, when compared with each other, show that the king valued the practical (20/-) man at thrice the poetical (6/8) man. This does Edward I. an injustice. Probably he was only recognizing a difference in artistic standing. Walter Luvel was obviously a local·nobody, born on the spot. A man with Melioro's name must have been a great foreign artist. And, as all great foreign artists disguise their names freely, our pet theory is that *he was an Irishman.* The king wanted the best anaesthetic possible—and was ready to pay for it.

Saxophones and their Notation.

Since the first publication of this book Saxophones have been made by the thousand, perhaps by the million. To-day the instrument is as familiar as the Cello. Still, even to-day and in America, no Saxophone-group is a regular member of a first-class symphony orchestra. In the ordinary routine there are no parts available. Outside the field of jazz and dance music, where the Saxophone-*soloist* is master, these instruments are called for mostly in large orchestral combinations which have to cope with long, solid works. Whether for the purpose of variety or of strength this is a legitimate sphere of action. The writer has heard many such combinations, and wishes to state a few elementary conditions that apply to the use of Saxophones with the orchestra.

The main point is that, for orchestral purposes, the Soprano in B♭ is useless. The Clarinet, with its infinitely superior tone-colour, always kills it. Unless the "lay" of the music is such that the use of this instrument cannot be dodged, it should be avoided. In ninety-nine cases out of a hundred, two Altos, a Tenor, and a Baritone are the best combination for orchestral use. It gives enormous solidity, particularly if there is a chorus to be taken into account. Saxophone-players, by and large, are technically proficient. Even the sharp key-signatures, that are sometimes necessary in the orchestra, do not disturb them much. So that the main thing that an orchestrator has to decide is when he wants them and when he doesn't.

The remarks on page 168 about notation need modifying. The matter is not quite on all fours with the question of the Bass-Clarinet notation. The practical fact is that first-class saxophonists possess, play, and are ready to play in public, two or three different Saxophones. The writer has heard such a player give an astonishingly brilliant technical exhibition in public on the Tenor-Saxophone—and then, with no more than six or eight bars rest, give a still more brilliant performance on the Baritone. For this reason the author favours the use of the strictly French notation, without adding any difficulties of the eye to the player's difficulties of breath, lip, and finger. The objection has been often heard that the Saxophone-lines in the score all " look like second soprano parts." This look of sameness is unfortunate, but unavoidable. It is necessary always to study and memorize the first page of the score, where the *names* of the instruments dictate the *pitch*.

One word more, in amplification of the remark above that an orchestrator's main task is to decide when he wants his Saxophones and when he doesn't. The Saxophones are certainly not a substitute for the Horns. In a long work, especially in the theatre, they may alternate with the Horns. They offer nothing to replace the fine poetry and passion of the solo 1st Horn in his top octave. But they *do* offer a completely new tone-colour, a colour which is not only an ensemble in itself, when so desired, but capable of all sorts of effective doublings with Clarinets, Bassoons, Horns, Violas, and Cellos. The Saxophone-lines may *look* rather thin in the score, but by keeping a wary eye on whether the Saxophones themselves are in unison, two-part, three-part, or four-part, endless variety *of sound* can be secured. Furthermore, this sort of lively alternation, with rests between, is exactly in the Saxophone-character.

In the matter of solid chords—a thing every orchestrator must have when he wants them—the Saxophones have great value. I don't know if anybody has ever heard the full Wood-Wind of a symphony orchestra playing spread harmony without Strings or Brass, and has been able to lay his hand on his heart and declare that what he heard was satisfactory. I have not. The tone-colours of the individual instruments are too heterogeneous. Add four Saxophones, and you bind them together in a much more satisfactory mass. With this addition, composers can at last resume their ancient practice, *so long cautiously discontinued*, of allowing the audience to hear the full Wood-Wind, without Brass or Strings. And it will *not* sound like a chance family gathering of colour-specialists, who are not on speaking terms with each other.

Within the limits of this short additional note, it is only possible to suggest a few general ideas.

The Saxophones are only *occasionally* valuable as soloists. Four are necessary, if they are to be worth using.

Their four-part harmony, with no other colour to help it out, comes through satisfactorily. It blends well with Strings or Wood-Wind or both together—rather too well with the Horns. So that, except in the *tutti*, these two groups, when used merely as a background, can be alternated.

In the solo field, my judgment is that a certain type of extended, vigorous tune best suits the instrument. Bizet's tameness and the banalities of the worse sort of jazz are second-bests. Serious, energetic rhythm is the necessity.

Finally, it is absolutely useless for a student, who wants to learn the possibilities and the limits of the Saxophones, to go and hear the many works, such as Strauss's *Sinfonia Domestica*, in which the instruments are, it is true, in the full score, but all carefully doubled everywhere with other instruments, so that their absence will not prevent a performance of the work. The first performance in London of the above-named work had Saxophones: the second had none. It made little difference. It ought to have made much.

NOTE.—An easy, students' mnemonic for the B♭- and E♭-Saxophones, with the usual extension-key at the bottom, is that they are all two-octaves-and-a-semitone instruments, with a few extra semitones possible upwards. The lowest *sounds* are all D's and A's. For the four most commonly used instruments—the Soprano, Alto, Tenor, and Baritone—these are:

Pizzicato.

An early example of *pizzicato* is given on page 349, Monteverde's *Il Combattimento di Tancredi*, where the direction to the players is "to leave the bow and pull the strings with two fingers." This was not quoted as *the* earliest example of *pizzicato*, only as *an* early one; for the reason that any fiddler, with a Fiddle in his hands, can pluck it as easily as he can bow it. Nay, much more easily; for a beginner, at his first lesson, can pluck the strings without difficulty. Yet the control of the bow may be still a matter of the distant future for him. In other words, granted a Fiddle, and you have the certainty of *pizzicato*. The date of its first appearance *in print* is a matter of mere chance.

However, it seems that this chance has favoured England. The first printed example has been found in a number called "Hark! Hark!" one of a collection of Ayres for the "Viola da Gambo, by Tobias Hume, Gentleman." This collection was printed by "John Winder, dwelling at the Signe of the Crosse Keyes, at Powles Wharfe, 1605." It contains the two following directions, which anticipate Monteverde's "here leave the bow," etc., and mean the same thing:

(1) "Play nine letters with your finger" ["letters"=notes].
(2) "Your finger as before."

Later on in this piece there is a direction, "Drum this with the back of your Bow"—a horrible suggestion to a String-player, quite unworthy of Tobias Hume, Gentleman.

Let us jump two or three centuries from archaeology to the practical politics of orchestration. The author has been asked more than once for a statement as to the correct manuscript notation for *pizzicato*. There is so much dog-work to be done in writing a score, that even the smallest abbreviation of labour in a single bar, when multiplied many times, means great saving.

The author's view is that the only logical way is to accept the fact that the *pizzicato* notation is only a convention. The position of the note in the bar represents the moment at which the string must be plucked: the length of the written note does not, and should not, represent the length of the sound at all. If composers were to attempt any such foolish practice, they would get themselves into all sorts of difficulties. They must accept the convention.

Cleverly designed *pizzicato* parts are by no means as easy of achievement as the beginner is apt to imagine. They need cool and broad judgment. The author advises looking through a passage very carefully before putting in *pizzicatos*. Then the exact notes must be decided on, with careful attention to the dynamic marks. Often the Basses, or the Basses and Cellos, will be so used with Wood-Wind or Brass; and the *pizzicatos* have to be marked up a bit; otherwise, they would lose their point.

Any score will show the student that Basses, Cellos, Violas, and Violins are used, in that order of frequency, in the *pizzicatos* that they have to play. The *pizzicato* Bass can be easily overdone. Even in the most modern work there are sure to be places where the good old-fashioned crotchet-Bass, *arco*, once or twice in a bar, is the best Bass to write.

But if the Bass has to be *pizzicato*, and your piece is in $\frac{3}{4}$ time, nobody but a madman (or a highly leisured amateur) would waste his life writing out the crotchet rests. He would write the easiest *correct* notation for the part—dotted minims, with *pizz* above them. In other words, he would accept the convention, and if he had to write a *pizzicato* on the down-beats of a passage in $\frac{5}{4}$ time, he would write as follows:

Vibrato.

No writers on orchestration have ever uttered a word about vibrato. It is a matter of taste, they say. You start with taste, and probably you will have to end with it. Taste is respectable—we all have it. It is a sort of Feminine of Genius, as FitzGerald said. So why not leave it at that? After all, there is no notation for vibrato. The composer must put up with what he gets.

It happens that the only instrument which is a wholesale dealer in vibrato is outside the scope of this book—the Organ. The author has heard plenty of bad tremolo stops and tremolo combinations. But his observation is that continued use in churches breeds weariness—and then refinement. Another point. All vibratos except that of the Organ are made by fallible human bodies. The Organ has an elaborate mechanism for a purely mechanical task. There is plenty of money to spend on preliminary experiments and later adjustments; so that the results are as near perfection as can be hoped for.

When we come to the orchestra it is a different matter. On the unmuted Brass there is no way of making a vibrato. The instruments have to be muted, and muted with a specially bored mute that has a fine airway pierced through it. Over this the player flip-flaps his closed fingers so as to interrupt the air-stream. If this can be done within the limits of good taste, the present writer has never heard it. Often, with the ancient representative of threatening majesty, the Trombone, the effect has the gaiety of a sick and drunken funeral party.

On the Wood-Wind vibrato is made by lightly beating the air, with a disengaged finger, at an open hole. It is made naturally and easily. But of course it can only be used on certain notes. The drawback to it is that it is not always as audible as could be wished. The Oboe, playing solo passages *forte*, has the best chance of making its "throb" come through. The exquisite loveliness of the late Mr. Lalande's Oboe-vibrato is a thing to treasure in the memory.

A casual reader might suppose that, when we come to the Strings, there is nothing to be said. Far from it. The Strings had to fight for centuries before they were allowed to use vibrato without question. It was regarded as a disreputable way that bad fiddlers had of *making music sound emotional.* Everybody protested against it, tooth and nail, as a circus-clown's way of playing. Leopold Mozart, Spohr, and Courvoisier all took this view. Molique actually went through the whole of his career without ever using it. Clear bowing was the thing they wanted, and a nice variety in dynamics. Vibrato was taboo.

However, curses did not kill it. Both the beautiful sort and the sort that resembles a nanny-goat in distress continue to be heard in our midst.

On a stringed instrument vibrato is, scientifically, a slight wavering of the finger below pitch, with an instant return of the finger to true pitch. Of course, it can only be used on a single stopped note. But it ought to be available in every part of a String-player's compass and technique. It should always be beautiful. And it should be added by the player as an emotional embellishment of those notes only that call for it. Even in the simplest melodic passages it may add great charm to the music.

The difference between a vibratoed and an unvibratoed note is a real, though subtle, one. The warmth and vitality that a fine vibrato gives can be instantly appreciated by pre-arranging a phrase with a friendly fiddler and then listening to both versions with the eyes shut.

In the orchestra vibrato is left to chance. If a player feels like making it on a note, he does; if not, he doesn't. The conductor as a rule does not interfere. The most he can do, when he has plenty of time at rehearsal, is to say, of a phrase, " I want plenty of vibrato on this," or " No vibrato here."

We come back to where we started. It is all a matter of taste. And the only way, in the orchestra, is to hope for the occasional appearance of a super-FitzGeraldy melodic conscience.

Händel's Wood-Wind.

Händel's general practice seems to have been always to engage a large squad of Wood-Wind players for his performances. He would have four Oboes and four Bassoons, with as many Flutes and Fipple-Flutes as he could lay his hands on, sometimes as many as five of each. Nowadays people roll their eyes upwards at Tschaikowsky's three Flutes and three Bassoons in unison. No doubt, if we could revive Händel, with his strong sense of the Organ and of mammoth showmanship, and ask him *his* verdict on the passage, he would say : " Very thin and tame."

In Händel's nomenclature " flauto " always means " fipple-flute." He calls the ordinary Flute " traverso," " traversa," or " traversiera " ; rarely " flauto traverso." As both types of instrument were orchestrally abundant in his day, he practically always decides beforehand which he wants, specifying it in the score. Apparently, only in a single instance (*Parnasso in Festa*) does he leave the decision to the choice of the player.

" Flauto Piccolo," with Händel, means " Octave Fipple-Flute." In the Flute-trio for the letting loose of the birds in *Rinaldo* the three parts in the printed score are named " Flauto Piccolo, Flauto I, Flauto II." But in Händel's autograph score the word used for the first instrument is " Flageolett."

A word must be added about Händel's most celebrated " Flauto," the " Flauto " in " O Ruddier than the Cherry." In this obbligato the instrument, which imitates the ancient Greek syrinx, is a Fipple-Flute. It was played on a Fipple-*Piccolo* with the sanction of the composer. He may have forgotten to add the word " Piccolo " to his " Flauto " in the score ; or, more likely, he may have found the octave instrument so much brighter at rehearsal that it was worth making the change. Even if it had not been an octave instrument, it would still be a Fipple-, not a Lip-Flute. At the Concerts of Antient Music this obbligato was always played on a Flageolet. Now everybody plays it on a Piccolo. The Fipple-Flutes, of which the Flageolet was one, have had their day. Their *tameness* sealed their doom.

The above details are taken mainly from Welch's *Six Lectures on the Recorder*, which interesting volume is heartily recommended to the student in search of fuller details on the subject.

The First Use of Four Horns.

The statement, in a footnote to page 121, that Mozart (in *Idomeneo*) and Cherubini (in *Lodoiska*) were the first composers to use four Horns, needs correction. Händel (in *Giulio Cesare*) undoubtedly preceded them.

Incidentally, the date of the first appearance of *any* Horns in the orchestra has been put back to 1705, in which year Reinhard Keiser introduced two " Cornes de chasse " into his opera *Octavia* at Hamburg.

Händel uses his four Horns first in the introductory chorus to Act I, *Viva il nostro Alcide.* The music is in A major, Horns 1 and 2 are in A, 3 and 4 in D. This is a " Non troppo Allegro." There is plenty of movement in the Horns, of the usual eighteenth-century type. Even the third Horn has to face high A and a trill on high G♯. Then comes an elaborate part for one Horn in F: the music also is in F. This occurs in Cesare's air in Act I, *Va tacito e nascosto.* The part hardly ever gets below C in the third space; while it constantly goes up to top A and top C, with running passages, arpeggios, and all the other florid embellishments. Again, in the *Sinfonia* to Act III, there are four Horn-parts. Here the music is in G; Horns 1 and 2 in G, 3 and 4 in D. This number actually ends with four bars of Adagio, unaccompanied, for the two pairs of Horns, thus:

Händel uses his four Horns again in the Final Chorus of Act III, *Ritorni ormai.* Here the music is in G; Horns 1 and 2 in G, 3 and 4 in D. Simple, broad chords, well-up, are the feature of the movement, with occasional top A's and a couple of shakes for the first Horn.

Composers who may be inclined to nightmare, brought on by the remembrance of Händel's Horn-parts, may care to know that, for special altitude-scaling, a modern Horn in F, with three rotary valves and a piston, is occasionally used in Germany and America. The piston is worked by the thumb. Its effect is to shorten the tubing so that the Horn, when the piston is in use, is a Horn in (high) B♭. It gives much more ease of production and fingering in the top register. But the quality is *not* a scarlet joy. To be complete, one should add that Horns are being built, and used, in Germany in high B♭. These the writer has not heard. But, even for *them*, Händel's 1st Horn top C, printed above, would be a top A!

Apparently the eighteenth century is not to be too easily swallowed by the twentieth. The nineteenth century had its " Bach Trumpet," really a Cornet in A, with an antique make-up and modern, military insides: it also had certain wicked dissimulations with the Tuba, to hoodwink conductors and audiences. The only malpractice left for the makers to perpetrate would be to camouflage a high E♭-Cornet inside a Bassoon, and to put it on the market as the " Soprano Monteverde Zinke."

Mediæval Loud and Soft.

In the mediæval Brass-ensembles, that were used mainly, but not altogether, out of doors, the two contrasting groups of instruments were (1) a loud group of Trumpets and Horns, (2) a soft group of Sackbuts, with a Cornett at the top. It needs a certain effort of the mind for us to grasp the fact that the Horns were in the loud group. But there they were. The ideal, set before themselves by the Sackbut-players and the Cornettists, was to make their group sound as much like a big, rich, smooth choir of human voices as possible. To attain this, especially in the case of the Cornett, needed enormous strength and hardness of lip. But we have ample evidence that it was attained.

The main factor that made the Cornett obsolete was the development of the Chalumeau into a Clarinet. With its advent, the terrific " labour of the lips and lungs," of which we read so much, ceased. No doubt, the intruding Clarinet had a less solid tone. But that improved as the instrument was perfected. And with regard to ease and pliability, even the earlier forms of the Clarinet were superior to the Cornett.

We may add that, in the mediæval Wood-Wind ensembles, there were exactly the same two contrasting groups—what Chaucer calls the " Dulcet " and the " Reed." " Dulcet," of course, is the soft group of Fipple-Flutes and Recorders, corresponding to the Sackbuts and Cornetts of the Brass-ensemble. " Reed " is the strident, nasal group of Shawms and Pommers, corresponding to the brassy Trumpets and Horns.

The Chalumeau and the Clarinet.

All through the Middle Ages there existed a primitive reed-pipe. It was made of wood, was keyless, of cylindrical bore, and was blown by a single-reed, bound to the upper end of the pipe with twine. This instrument was known as " the reed " (chalumeau = Greek *kalamos*). Its compass was the 10 notes of the diatonic scale of F major, with no addition whatever.

Till the end of the seventeenth century the Chalumeau remained in this primitive condition. The first improvements may have been started in Nürnberg. At any rate, by the beginning of the eighteenth century, 3-keyed instruments were fairly common. Several specimens still exist.

The addition of the 4th and 5th keys (F♯-C♯ and G♯-D♯) gives us the 5-keyed instrument used in Mozart's day.

The addition of the 6th key (C♯-G♯) gives us the instrument used by Beethoven.

All through the eighteenth century the reed remained in its original, " chalumeau " position on the upper side of the mouthpiece. The instrument played parts that were, in pitch and character, much like the ordinary florid Trumpet-parts of the period. Hence the name " clarinetto " = " little trumpet." For the greater part of the century the name " chalumeau " continued to exist. Obviously, the new-comer was not realized by musicians as a distinct orchestral instrument.

The elder Denner is generally credited with having " invented the speaker." This is not likely. No specimen of the earliest Chalumeau is known to exist. But it is plain that a primitive, 10-note instrument, using only a fundamental, non-overblown scale, must have had at least nine finger-holes. Eight of these would naturally be in front covered by the eight fingers. Is it not more than probable that the ninth was behind covered by one of the thumbs, and so furnishing the idea of the speaker ? This speaker, introducing an easy way of overblowing at the twelfth, was well known to and practised by the ancient Greeks in the manufacture of the Aulos. To claim the *invention* of such an antique device as the speaker for the elder Denner seems unwarranted. But he may have revived it for practical use ; and his son certainly improved its position.[1]

It was only in the eighteenth century that the transference of the reed from front to back and the invention of the present Clarinet mouthpiece gave the instrument promise of a brilliant orchestral future.

The earliest Clarinet parts, actually so named in full scores, are Arne's *Artaxerxes* (1762), in which C-clarinets are used, and J. C. Bach's *Orione* (1763), in which B♭- and D-clarinets are used. As both these works were produced in London, it is certain that these instruments must have been in ordinary orchestral use there at that date.

In France, Gossec claimed to have used Clarinets in 1757 ; Rameau, even earlier, in 1751. At any rate, from the date of Gluck's Paris *Orfée* onwards (1774) they were regularly employed in French orchestras.

It is not quite certain when the Mannheim and Dresden orchestras acquired Clarinets, though the two dates 1767 and 1786 have been given. The facts are not beyond dispute.

There is a point on which the author has often been asked questions. Briefly put, it is this. If the Clarinet was so far developed in 1762 that it was an ordinary orchestral instrument in London, why did not the post-Händelian composers, who actually christened it " little trumpet," transfer their Trumpet passages to it ?

The answer to this naive, archaeological question is the simple, practical one that, though these passages could all have been played, they would have been inaudible, and therefore useless. The comparative tonal weight of the two instruments then was the same as it is now. For a generation and a half the Trumpet was the only soprano instrument which could make a serious difference in an orchestral *tutti*.

However, there were still no valves. " Tune," therefore, meant to the trumpeter " high tune." He always had to be a prima donna ; but a desperately unhappy prima donna, whose part never went below C in the third space.

There *was* an alternative. And that was for composers to turn him out of his prima donna's position, and to employ him as a loud " super "

[1] It was the son who gave clarinettists their low-E.

in the performance, making as much noise as he could " off." If they did this, they often had to shut their ears to the fact that much of his noise and shouting had very little to do with the musical business in hand.

Some of them were acutely conscious of this difficulty. It was a bad second-best, and they knew it. But the thing in humanity which then could only be expressed by the loud blastings of the Trumpet was an artistic necessity. It still is. But *we* have much easier and more pliable ways of expressing it. The post-Händelians had to put up with their primitive means and make the best of a bad job.

And the pity of it is that the post-Händelians, referred to in the last sentence, included everybody from Haydn onwards, right down to the moment when the Valve Fairy appeared and, with a wave of her wand, effected such a magical Transformation Scene in the Realms of Music.

APPENDIX.

The Phagotus of Afranio.

As we have already mentioned on page 229, this instrument has been claimed as embodying for the first time the essential features of the Bassoon. These features are, roughly, the rearrangement of a conical wooden pipe whose air-column is set in vibration by means of a double-reed held between the player's lips. For reasons already given, the claim cannot be conceded. The instrument, however, is so curious that a few more words may be devoted to its history and chief characteristics.

In the early part of the sixteenth century there lived a man called Afranio. He belonged to the house of the Counts Palatine of Albonese, and, according to the fashion of the times, was known as Afranio degli Albonesi, or, in Latin, Afranius Albonesius. He was a native of Pavia, a canon of Ferrara, and, though not strictly an instrument-maker, at any rate an enthusiastic musical amateur and an indefatigable collector of instruments. This man invented or perfected the instrument in question. If he did not actually christen it *phagotus*, he knew it by that name.

Very little more would probably have been heard of the Phagotus in musical history but for the fact that he had a nephew who combined the best elements of Paganism and Christianity in his imposing name of Teseo Ambrogio degli Albonesi (Theseus Ambrosius Albonesius) This nephew was, like his uncle, a priest. He was also a celebrated jurisconsult, a canon of the Lateran, and professor of Syriac and Chaldaic in the University of Bologna. In 1539 he published at Pavia what we should call an advanced text-book on the Chaldaic and Syriac languages, with mystical and cabbalistic interpretations and notes thereon.[1]

The greater part of this work is naturally devoted to linguistic and philological studies. On folio 33, however, having taken the root *phag* as far as the Greek word φαγότα, he suddenly drags in "my uncle Afranio's singular instrument, the Phagotus," with the remark that its name is probably derived from the same root. After a fantastic and rubbishy justification of this statement, he abandons his Chaldaic studies, and, spurred on by laudable family zeal, launches out into a very long, childish, and somewhat inflated description of the instrument. This odd proceeding, which would be looked on as a sign of madness in a twentieth century Professor of Oriental Languages, is, of course, in the best manner of the minor literature of the sixteenth century. After this surprising digression, he then drops the topic and resumes his Chaldaic and cabbalistic investigations. No more is heard of the Phagotus till folio 179, where he suddenly confronts his readers with two engravings of the instrument—"Phagoti pars anterior," front-view of the phagotus, "Et pars posterior," and back-view. He also adds a few short remarks on the subject.

[1] *Introductio in Chaldaicam linguam.*

PHAGOTI PARS ANTERIOR ET PARS POSTERIOR

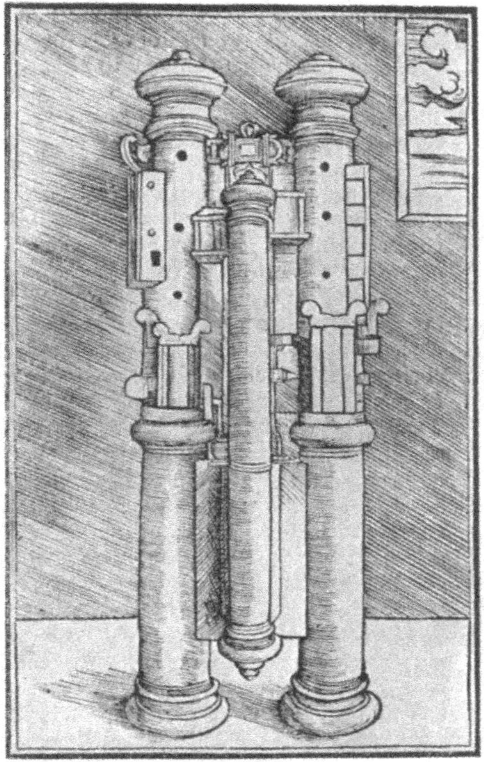

1. Front View.

2. Back View.

These two engravings are reproduced in small on Plate XII. The description given in the early part of Theseus Ambrosius Albonesius's book certainly deserves reprinting, but unfortunately it is far too long for inclusion here. An attempt, however, will be made to summarize its main points. This is not a very easy task, as, apart from his infamous dog-Latin and his strong leaning towards the mythological, the author is vague on those very details which demand precision. However, those points on which there is any doubt will be noted as they occur.

Afranio was, if not the inventor, at any rate the perfector of the instrument (*vel inventore aut certe perfectore*). He tried unsuccessfully to get it manufactured abroad. After more than one attempt, he fell in with one Giambattista Ravilio, a celebrated mechanician and instrument-maker of Ferrara. Ravilio evidently put his patron's ideas into practical shape. The instrument consisted of hollow resonating tubes or pipes (*columnæ*) with ornamental capitals, and bases turned on the lathe out of boxwood. The two small additional tubes (of unequal length), which are seen in each view between the two main tubes, had no musical value. They were beautifications, not necessities. The smaller of these two, however—that which is seen in the back-view between the two main tubes—was used as an air-passage. Apparently only the upper portions of the two main tubes acted strictly as resonating-chambers, so that, of the whole monster, only about one-sixth or one-seventh was "practicable." The size of the tubes is given in one sentence of doubtful meaning. The author speaks of them as *vix ad medii cubiti longitudinem protensas*, where "medii" may mean "middle" or "middling-sized," and "cubiti" may be either "elbow" or "cubit." The most probable meaning is "scarcely as long as a cubit of moderate size."

The tubes were bored with two sorts of holes: the round open holes which were directly controlled by the fingers, and the square holes which were covered by keys plated with silver. The one set of holes was open, the other closed. The author, however, states that some of the apparently open holes were really closed, and "*versa vice*." The open finger-holes were used for producing the notes of the natural scale from the second to the octave above the fundamental note. It is just possible that the closed-keys gave access to a lower octave altogether. This is not definitely stated by the author, but he seems to imply it from one of his comparisons, and indeed makes a distinct statement that the instrument could descend below the ten-foot reeds[1] of the Organ.

Ravilio's share in the instrument lay in the provision of two tongues of metal—the one of silver, the other of brass. The author further describes them by using the Italian word *piva*, which means a bagpipe, sometimes the reed of a bagpipe-chanter (*geminas linguas sive ut vocant pivas fabrefecit*). These flexible metal-reeds were placed one in each of the two tubes. They differed in disposition and shape, and, from a consideration of these differences and of their actual material, we may fairly conclude that they were the sound-producers for the treble- and bass-octaves respectively. The principal claim made for Ravilio is that, by means of ten additional holes, he turned the Phagotus "from an instrument of twelve imperfect notes into one of twenty-two very perfect and clear notes" (*a duodecim imperfectis vocibus ad duas et viginti perfectissimas candidissimasque reduxit voces*).

[1] The old method of measurement. "Eight-foot reeds" according to our modern nomenclature.

Two pairs of bellows were needed. These may be seen, lying on the floor detached from the instrument, in Plate XII., back-view. The pair on the left was of stitched skin about the size of a bladder or a shepherd's wallet This we may call the "wind-sack." It had two small attachments or wind-passages. These also may be clearly seen in the engraving. One of these was the ingoing, the other the outgoing wind-passage. The pair of bellows on the right was made of skin and provided with two small wooden boards. This we may call the bellows proper.

Elaborate directions are given for the fixing of the wind-sack and the bellows under the two arm-pits of the player. When he had securely strapped them to his person, he attached the ingoing wind-passage of the wind-sack to the bellows. He then removed the ornamental cover from the smaller of the two additional tubes and fastened the outgoing wind-passage to an attachment there. Next, he took the Phagotus in his hands, sat down, and held it upright against his thigh, keeping the round open finger-holes in front. His next move was to pump the bellows with his right arm. This filled the wind-sack under his left arm, and by pressure on that he could maintain a steady air-stream into the resonating chambers. He then had to employ his disengaged faculties (if any) in the production of music by means of the various holes and keys.

But before he could do this he had to turn on the air-stream in the instrument itself: for a "cut-off" key was provided in the upper part of the Phagotus. This is apparently the large curved key seen on the right-hand side of the back-view and the left-hand side of the front-view. Until this key was brought into action the air-stream could not enter the resonating chamber. Theseus Ambrosius Albonesius takes immense delight in drawing attention to this subtlety. Apparently its only object was to prevent an ignorant person from playing the instrument. This precaution seems unnecessary. Even a mediæval Italian would scarcely have had the necessary mixture of cunning and hardihood to make the attempt.

The conclusions with regard to the total want of connection between the Phagotus and the Bassoon have already been drawn. They can be referred to on page 230. It may be added that the Phagotus was never in general use. Indeed, so far as is known, only one specimen ever existed. There is nothing to show definitely that the elementary idea of cutting up the long Bass-Pommer was suggested by Afranio's "freak."

Finally, it is curious to notice that on the one point which Theseus Ambrosius Albonesius sets out to illustrate—namely, the philological question—we are still in the dark. The word *fagotto* is usually derived from the likeness of the Bassoon to a fagot of sticks. How then comes it that an instrument "invented or perfected" just prior to the invention of the Bassoon came to be called *phagotus*? It can hardly be an accident, and the author's ridiculous explanation as to the Phagotus *eating*[1] and digesting the wind, and then vomiting it forth in sound, has no value except as humour. It is to be noted that he does not say that his uncle invented the word. He merely gives what seems to him a probable derivation. Of course the Latinizing of a vulgar word, and the subsequent invention of a far-fetched explanation, is a commonplace of sixteenth-century philology.

A modern study of the Phagotus has been made by Luigi Francesco Valdrighi in his brochure *Il Phagotus di Afranio* (Milano, 1881).

[1] φάγω.

INDEX.

Compositions and works are entered under the author's or composer's name.
Unless otherwise stated all numbers refer to pages.

A CATALOG OF SELECTED

DOVER BOOKS

IN ALL FIELDS OF INTEREST

A CATALOG OF SELECTED DOVER BOOKS IN ALL FIELDS OF INTEREST

ALICE'S ADVENTURES IN WONDERLAND, Lewis Carroll. Beloved classic about a little girl lost in a topsy-turvy land and her encounters with the White Rabbit, March Hare, Mad Hatter, Cheshire Cat, and other delightfully improbable characters. 42 illustrations by Sir John Tenniel. 96pp. 5³⁄₁₆ x 8¼. 0-486-27543-4

AMERICA'S LIGHTHOUSES: An Illustrated History, Francis Ross Holland. Profusely illustrated fact-filled survey of American lighthouses since 1716. Over 200 stations — East, Gulf, and West coasts, Great Lakes, Hawaii, Alaska, Puerto Rico, the Virgin Islands, and the Mississippi and St. Lawrence Rivers. 240pp. 8 x 10¾. 0-486-25576-X

AN ENCYCLOPEDIA OF THE VIOLIN, Alberto Bachmann. Translated by Frederick H. Martens. Introduction by Eugene Ysaye. First published in 1925, this renowned reference remains unsurpassed as a source of essential information, from construction and evolution to repertoire and technique. Includes a glossary and 73 illustrations. 496pp. 6⅛ x 9¼. 0-486-46618-3

ANIMALS: 1,419 Copyright-Free Illustrations of Mammals, Birds, Fish, Insects, etc., Selected by Jim Harter. Selected for its visual impact and ease of use, this outstanding collection of wood engravings presents over 1,000 species of animals in extremely lifelike poses. Includes mammals, birds, reptiles, amphibians, fish, insects, and other invertebrates. 284pp. 9 x 12. 0-486-23766-4

THE ANNALS, Tacitus. Translated by Alfred John Church and William Jackson Brodribb. This vital chronicle of Imperial Rome, written by the era's great historian, spans A.D. 14-68 and paints incisive psychological portraits of major figures, from Tiberius to Nero. 416pp. 5³⁄₁₆ x 8¼. 0-486-45236-0

ANTIGONE, Sophocles. Filled with passionate speeches and sensitive probing of moral and philosophical issues, this powerful and often-performed Greek drama reveals the grim fate that befalls the children of Oedipus. Footnotes. 64pp. 5³⁄₁₆ x 8 ¼. 0-486-27804-2

ART DECO DECORATIVE PATTERNS IN FULL COLOR, Christian Stoll. Reprinted from a rare 1910 portfolio, 160 sensuous and exotic images depict a breathtaking array of florals, geometrics, and abstracts — all elegant in their stark simplicity. 64pp. 8⅜ x 11. 0-486-44862-2

THE ARTHUR RACKHAM TREASURY: 86 Full-Color Illustrations, Arthur Rackham. Selected and Edited by Jeff A. Menges. A stunning treasury of 86 full-page plates span the famed English artist's career, from *Rip Van Winkle* (1905) to masterworks such as *Undine, A Midsummer Night's Dream,* and *Wind in the Willows* (1939). 96pp. 8⅜ x 11. 0-486-44685-9

THE AUTHENTIC GILBERT & SULLIVAN SONGBOOK, W. S. Gilbert and A. S. Sullivan. The most comprehensive collection available, this songbook includes selections from every one of Gilbert and Sullivan's light operas. Ninety-two numbers are presented uncut and unedited, and in their original keys. 410pp. 9 x 12. 0-486-23482-7

THE AWAKENING, Kate Chopin. First published in 1899, this controversial novel of a New Orleans wife's search for love outside a stifling marriage shocked readers. Today, it remains a first-rate narrative with superb characterization. New introductory Note. 128pp. 5³⁄₁₆ x 8¼. 0-486-27786-0

BASIC DRAWING, Louis Priscilla. Beginning with perspective, this commonsense manual progresses to the figure in movement, light and shade, anatomy, drapery, composition, trees and landscape, and outdoor sketching. Black-and-white illustrations throughout. 128pp. 8⅜ x 11. 0-486-45815-6

DOOMED SHIPS: Great Ocean Liner Disasters, William H. Miller, Jr. Nearly 200 photographs, many from private collections, highlight tales of some of the vessels whose pleasure cruises ended in catastrophe: the *Morro Castle, Normandie, Andrea Doria, Europa,* and many others. 128pp. 8⅜ x 11¾. 0-486-45366-9

THE DORÉ BIBLE ILLUSTRATIONS, Gustave Doré. Detailed plates from the Bible: the Creation scenes, Adam and Eve, horrifying visions of the Flood, the battle sequences with their monumental crowds, depictions of the life of Jesus, 241 plates in all. 241pp. 9 x 12. 0-486-23004-X

DRAWING DRAPERY FROM HEAD TO TOE, Cliff Young. Expert guidance on how to draw shirts, pants, skirts, gloves, hats, and coats on the human figure, including folds in relation to the body, pull and crush, action folds, creases, more. Over 200 drawings. 48pp. 8¼ x 11. 0-486-45591-2

DUBLINERS, James Joyce. A fine and accessible introduction to the work of one of the 20th century's most influential writers, this collection features 15 tales, including a masterpiece of the short-story genre, "The Dead." 160pp. 5$\frac{3}{16}$ x 8¼. 0-486-26870-5

EASY-TO-MAKE POP-UPS, Joan Irvine. Illustrated by Barbara Reid. Dozens of wonderful ideas for three-dimensional paper fun — from holiday greeting cards with moving parts to a pop-up menagerie. Easy-to-follow, illustrated instructions for more than 30 projects. 299 black-and-white illustrations. 96pp. 8⅝ x 11. 0-486-44622-0

EASY-TO-MAKE STORYBOOK DOLLS: A "Novel" Approach to Cloth Dollmaking, Sherralyn St. Clair. Favorite fictional characters come alive in this unique beginner's dollmaking guide. Includes patterns for Pollyanna, Dorothy from *The Wonderful Wizard of Oz,* Mary of *The Secret Garden,* plus easy-to-follow instructions, 263 black-and-white illustrations, and an 8-page color insert. 112pp. 8¼ x 11. 0-486-47360-0

EINSTEIN'S ESSAYS IN SCIENCE, Albert Einstein. Speeches and essays in accessible, everyday language profile influential physicists such as Niels Bohr and Isaac Newton. They also explore areas of physics to which the author made major contributions. 128pp. 5 x 8. 0-486-47011-3

EL DORADO: Further Adventures of the Scarlet Pimpernel, Baroness Orczy. A popular sequel to *The Scarlet Pimpernel,* this suspenseful story recounts the Pimpernel's attempts to rescue the Dauphin from imprisonment during the French Revolution. An irresistible blend of intrigue, period detail, and vibrant characterizations. 352pp. 5$\frac{3}{16}$ x 8¼. 0-486-44026-5

ELEGANT SMALL HOMES OF THE TWENTIES: 99 Designs from a Competition, Chicago Tribune. Nearly 100 designs for five- and six-room houses feature New England and Southern colonials, Normandy cottages, stately Italianate dwellings, and other fascinating snapshots of American domestic architecture of the 1920s. 112pp. 9 x 12. 0-486-46910-7

THE ELEMENTS OF STYLE: The Original Edition, William Strunk, Jr. This is the book that generations of writers have relied upon for timeless advice on grammar, diction, syntax, and other essentials. In concise terms, it identifies the principal requirements of proper style and common errors. 64pp. 5⅜ x 8½. 0-486-44798-7

THE ELUSIVE PIMPERNEL, Baroness Orczy. Robespierre's revolutionaries find their wicked schemes thwarted by the heroic Pimpernel — Sir Percival Blakeney. In this thrilling sequel, Chauvelin devises a plot to eliminate the Pimpernel and his wife. 272pp. 5$\frac{3}{16}$ x 8¼. 0-486-45464-9

AN ENCYCLOPEDIA OF BATTLES: Accounts of Over 1,560 Battles from 1479 B.C. to the Present, David Eggenberger. Essential details of every major battle in recorded history from the first battle of Megiddo in 1479 B.C. to Grenada in 1984. List of battle maps. 99 illustrations. 544pp. 6½ x 9¼. 0-486-24913-1

ENCYCLOPEDIA OF EMBROIDERY STITCHES, INCLUDING CREWEL, Marion Nichols. Precise explanations and instructions, clearly illustrated, on how to work chain, back, cross, knotted, woven stitches, and many more — 178 in all, including Cable Outline, Whipped Satin, and Eyelet Buttonhole. Over 1400 illustrations. 219pp. 8⅜ x 11¼. 0-486-22929-7

ENTER JEEVES: 15 Early Stories, P. G. Wodehouse. Splendid collection contains first 8 stories featuring Bertie Wooster, the deliciously dim aristocrat and Jeeves, his brainy, imperturbable manservant. Also, the complete Reggie Pepper (Bertie's prototype) series. 288pp. 5⅜ x 8½. 0-486-29717-9

ERIC SLOANE'S AMERICA: Paintings in Oil, Michael Wigley. With a Foreword by Mimi Sloane. Eric Sloane's evocative oils of America's landscape and material culture shimmer with immense historical and nostalgic appeal. This original hardcover collection gathers nearly a hundred of his finest paintings, with subjects ranging from New England to the American Southwest. 128pp. 10⅝ x 9. 0-486-46525-X

ETHAN FROME, Edith Wharton. Classic story of wasted lives, set against a bleak New England background. Superbly delineated characters in a hauntingly grim tale of thwarted love. Considered by many to be Wharton's masterpiece. 96pp. 5³⁄₁₆ x 8 ¼. 0-486-26690-7

THE EVERLASTING MAN, G. K. Chesterton. Chesterton's view of Christianity — as a blend of philosophy and mythology, satisfying intellect and spirit — applies to his brilliant book, which appeals to readers' heads as well as their hearts. 288pp. 5⅜ x 8½. 0-486-46036-3

THE FIELD AND FOREST HANDY BOOK, Daniel Beard. Written by a co-founder of the Boy Scouts, this appealing guide offers illustrated instructions for building kites, birdhouses, boats, igloos, and other fun projects, plus numerous helpful tips for campers. 448pp. 5³⁄₁₆ x 8¼. 0-486-46191-2

FINDING YOUR WAY WITHOUT MAP OR COMPASS, Harold Gatty. Useful, instructive manual shows would-be explorers, hikers, bikers, scouts, sailors, and survivalists how to find their way outdoors by observing animals, weather patterns, shifting sands, and other elements of nature. 288pp. 5⅜ x 8½. 0-486-40613-X

FIRST FRENCH READER: A Beginner's Dual-Language Book, Edited and Translated by Stanley Appelbaum. This anthology introduces 50 legendary writers — Voltaire, Balzac, Baudelaire, Proust, more — through passages from *The Red and the Black, Les Misérables, Madame Bovary,* and other classics. Original French text plus English translation on facing pages. 240pp. 5⅜ x 8½. 0-486-46178-5

FIRST GERMAN READER: A Beginner's Dual-Language Book, Edited by Harry Steinhauer. Specially chosen for their power to evoke German life and culture, these short, simple readings include poems, stories, essays, and anecdotes by Goethe, Hesse, Heine, Schiller, and others. 224pp. 5⅜ x 8½. 0-486-46179-3

FIRST SPANISH READER: A Beginner's Dual-Language Book, Angel Flores. Delightful stories, other material based on works of Don Juan Manuel, Luis Taboada, Ricardo Palma, other noted writers. Complete faithful English translations on facing pages. Exercises. 176pp. 5⅜ x 8½. 0-486-25810-6

THE JUNGLE, Upton Sinclair. 1906 bestseller shockingly reveals intolerable labor practices and working conditions in the Chicago stockyards as it tells the grim story of a Slavic family that emigrates to America full of optimism but soon faces despair. 320pp. 5³⁄₁₆ x 8¼. 0-486-41923-1

THE KINGDOM OF GOD IS WITHIN YOU, Leo Tolstoy. The soul-searching book that inspired Gandhi to embrace the concept of passive resistance, Tolstoy's 1894 polemic clearly outlines a radical, well-reasoned revision of traditional Christian thinking. 352pp. 5³⁄₁₆ x 8¼. 0-486-45138-0

THE LADY OR THE TIGER?: and Other Logic Puzzles, Raymond M. Smullyan. Created by a renowned puzzle master, these whimsically themed challenges involve paradoxes about probability, time, and change; metapuzzles; and self-referentiality. Nineteen chapters advance in difficulty from relatively simple to highly complex. 1982 edition. 240pp. 5⅜ x 8½. 0-486-47027-X

LEAVES OF GRASS: The Original 1855 Edition, Walt Whitman. Whitman's immortal collection includes some of the greatest poems of modern times, including his masterpiece, "Song of Myself." Shattering standard conventions, it stands as an unabashed celebration of body and nature. 128pp. 5³⁄₁₆ x 8¼. 0-486-45676-5

LES MISÉRABLES, Victor Hugo. Translated by Charles E. Wilbour. Abridged by James K. Robinson. A convict's heroic struggle for justice and redemption plays out against a fiery backdrop of the Napoleonic wars. This edition features the excellent original translation and a sensitive abridgment. 304pp. 6⅛ x 9¼. 0-486-45789-3

LILITH: A Romance, George MacDonald. In this novel by the father of fantasy literature, a man travels through time to meet Adam and Eve and to explore humanity's fall from grace and ultimate redemption. 240pp. 5⅜ x 8½. 0-486-46818-6

THE LOST LANGUAGE OF SYMBOLISM, Harold Bayley. This remarkable book reveals the hidden meaning behind familiar images and words, from the origins of Santa Claus to the fleur-de-lys, drawing from mythology, folklore, religious texts, and fairy tales. 1,418 illustrations. 784pp. 5⅜ x 8½. 0-486-44787-1

MACBETH, William Shakespeare. A Scottish nobleman murders the king in order to succeed to the throne. Tortured by his conscience and fearful of discovery, he becomes tangled in a web of treachery and deceit that ultimately spells his doom. 96pp. 5³⁄₁₆ x 8¼. 0-486-27802-6

MAKING AUTHENTIC CRAFTSMAN FURNITURE: Instructions and Plans for 62 Projects, Gustav Stickley. Make authentic reproductions of handsome, functional, durable furniture: tables, chairs, wall cabinets, desks, a hall tree, and more. Construction plans with drawings, schematics, dimensions, and lumber specs reprinted from 1900s *The Craftsman* magazine. 128pp. 8⅛ x 11. 0-486-25000-8

MATHEMATICS FOR THE NONMATHEMATICIAN, Morris Kline. Erudite and entertaining overview follows development of mathematics from ancient Greeks to present. Topics include logic and mathematics, the fundamental concept, differential calculus, probability theory, much more. Exercises and problems. 641pp. 5⅜ x 8½. 0-486-24823-2

MEMOIRS OF AN ARABIAN PRINCESS FROM ZANZIBAR, Emily Ruete. This 19th-century autobiography offers a rare inside look at the society surrounding a sultan's palace. A real-life princess in exile recalls her vanished world of harems, slave trading, and court intrigues. 288pp. 5⅜ x 8½. 0-486-47121-7

THE RED BADGE OF COURAGE, Stephen Crane. Amid the nightmarish chaos of a Civil War battle, a young soldier discovers courage, humility, and, perhaps, wisdom. Uncanny re-creation of actual combat. Enduring landmark of American fiction. 112pp. 5³⁄₁₆ x 8¼. 0-486-26465-3

RELATIVITY SIMPLY EXPLAINED, Martin Gardner. One of the subject's clearest, most entertaining introductions offers lucid explanations of special and general theories of relativity, gravity, and spacetime, models of the universe, and more. 100 illustrations. 224pp. 5⅜ x 8½. 0-486-29315-7

REMBRANDT DRAWINGS: 116 Masterpieces in Original Color, Rembrandt van Rijn. This deluxe hardcover edition features drawings from throughout the Dutch master's prolific career. Informative captions accompany these beautifully reproduced landscapes, biblical vignettes, figure studies, animal sketches, and portraits. 128pp. 8⅜ x 11. 0-486-46149-1

THE ROAD NOT TAKEN AND OTHER POEMS, Robert Frost. A treasury of Frost's most expressive verse. In addition to the title poem: "An Old Man's Winter Night," "In the Home Stretch," "Meeting and Passing," "Putting in the Seed," many more. All complete and unabridged. 64pp. 5³⁄₁₆ x 8¼. 0-486-27550-7

ROMEO AND JULIET, William Shakespeare. Tragic tale of star-crossed lovers, feuding families and timeless passion contains some of Shakespeare's most beautiful and lyrical love poetry. Complete, unabridged text with explanatory footnotes. 96pp. 5³⁄₁₆ x 8¼. 0-486-27557-4

SANDITON AND THE WATSONS: Austen's Unfinished Novels, Jane Austen. Two tantalizing incomplete stories revisit Austen's customary milieu of courtship and venture into new territory, amid guests at a seaside resort. Both are worth reading for pleasure and study. 112pp. 5⅜ x 8½. 0-486-45793-1

THE SCARLET LETTER, Nathaniel Hawthorne. With stark power and emotional depth, Hawthorne's masterpiece explores sin, guilt, and redemption in a story of adultery in the early days of the Massachusetts Colony. 192pp. 5³⁄₁₆ x 8¼. 0-486-28048-9

THE SEASONS OF AMERICA PAST, Eric Sloane. Seventy-five illustrations depict cider mills and presses, sleds, pumps, stump-pulling equipment, plows, and other elements of America's rural heritage. A section of old recipes and household hints adds additional color. 160pp. 8⅜ x 11. 0-486-44220-9

SELECTED CANTERBURY TALES, Geoffrey Chaucer. Delightful collection includes the General Prologue plus three of the most popular tales: "The Knight's Tale," "The Miller's Prologue and Tale," and "The Wife of Bath's Prologue and Tale." In modern English. 144pp. 5³⁄₁₆ x 8¼. 0-486-28241-4

SELECTED POEMS, Emily Dickinson. Over 100 best-known, best-loved poems by one of America's foremost poets, reprinted from authoritative early editions. No comparable edition at this price. Index of first lines. 64pp. 5³⁄₁₆ x 8¼. 0-486-26466-1

SIDDHARTHA, Hermann Hesse. Classic novel that has inspired generations of seekers. Blending Eastern mysticism and psychoanalysis, Hesse presents a strikingly original view of man and culture and the arduous process of self-discovery, reconciliation, harmony, and peace. 112pp. 5³⁄₁₆ x 8¼. 0-486-40653-9

SKETCHING OUTDOORS, Leonard Richmond. This guide offers beginners step-by-step demonstrations of how to depict clouds, trees, buildings, and other outdoor sights. Explanations of a variety of techniques include shading and constructional drawing. 48pp. 11 x 8¼. 0-486-46922-0

THE TRIAL, Franz Kafka. Translated by David Wyllie. From its gripping first sentence onward, this novel exemplifies the term "Kafkaesque." Its darkly humorous narrative recounts a bank clerk's entrapment in a bureaucratic maze, based on an undisclosed charge. 176pp. 5³⁄₁₆ x 8¼. 0-486-47061-X

THE TURN OF THE SCREW, Henry James. Gripping ghost story by great novelist depicts the sinister transformation of 2 innocent children into flagrant liars and hypocrites. An elegantly told tale of unspoken horror and psychological terror. 96pp. 5³⁄₁₆ x 8¼. 0-486-26684-2

UP FROM SLAVERY, Booker T. Washington. Washington (1856-1915) rose to become the most influential spokesman for African-Americans of his day. In this eloquently written book, he describes events in a remarkable life that began in bondage and culminated in worldwide recognition. 160pp. 5³⁄₁₆ x 8¼. 0-486-28738-6

VICTORIAN HOUSE DESIGNS IN AUTHENTIC FULL COLOR: 75 Plates from the "Scientific American – Architects and Builders Edition," 1885-1894, Edited by Blanche Cirker. Exquisitely detailed, exceptionally handsome designs for an enormous variety of attractive city dwellings, spacious suburban and country homes, charming "cottages" and other structures — all accompanied by perspective views and floor plans. 80pp. 9¼ x 12¼. 0-486-29438-2

VILLETTE, Charlotte Brontë. Acclaimed by Virginia Woolf as "Brontë's finest novel," this moving psychological study features a remarkably modern heroine who abandons her native England for a new life as a schoolteacher in Belgium. 480pp. 5³⁄₁₆ x 8¼. 0-486-45557-2

THE VOYAGE OUT, Virginia Woolf. A moving depiction of the thrills and confusion of youth, Woolf's acclaimed first novel traces a shipboard journey to South America for a captivating exploration of a woman's growing self-awareness. 288pp. 5³⁄₁₆ x 8¼. 0-486-45005-8

WALDEN; OR, LIFE IN THE WOODS, Henry David Thoreau. Accounts of Thoreau's daily life on the shores of Walden Pond outside Concord, Massachusetts, are interwoven with musings on the virtues of self-reliance and individual freedom, on society, government, and other topics. 224pp. 5³⁄₁₆ x 8¼. 0-486-28495-6

WILD PILGRIMAGE: A Novel in Woodcuts, Lynd Ward. Through startling engravings shaded in black and red, Ward wordlessly tells the story of a man trapped in an industrial world, struggling between the grim reality around him and the fantasies his imagination creates. 112pp. 6⅛ x 9¼. 0-486-46583-7

WILLY POGÁNY REDISCOVERED, Willy Pogány. Selected and Edited by Jeff A. Menges. More than 100 color and black-and-white Art Nouveau–style illustrations from fairy tales and adventure stories include scenes from Wagner's "Ring" cycle, *The Rime of the Ancient Mariner, Gulliver's Travels,* and *Faust.* 144pp. 8⅜ x 11. 0-486-47046-6

WOOLLY THOUGHTS: Unlock Your Creative Genius with Modular Knitting, Pat Ashforth and Steve Plummer. Here's the revolutionary way to knit — easy, fun, and foolproof! Beginners and experienced knitters need only master a single stitch to create their own designs with patchwork squares. More than 100 illustrations. 128pp. 6½ x 9¼. 0-486-46084-3

WUTHERING HEIGHTS, Emily Brontë. Somber tale of consuming passions and vengeance — played out amid the lonely English moors — recounts the turbulent and tempestuous love story of Cathy and Heathcliff. Poignant and compelling. 256pp. 5³⁄₁₆ x 8¼. 0-486-29256-8

Violins, a simple *pizzicato* quaver figure on the Cellos, helped on the second half of the bar by the *divisi* Violas, a *pizzicato* Bass-note every other bar and a four-part Wood-Wind chord to set things going. As a miniature it is exquisite.

EXAMPLE 264.

The student would do well to compare *the sound* of this as played on the pianoforte with the intended sound in the orchestra. He would also do better to consider, not only the notes which Sullivan has written, but the many other notes which he might have written but didn't.

The type of Cello *pizzicato* seen in the last two examples is equally effective when the upper parts are played by the Wind. In the general *mf* ensemble of Strings, Wood-Wind, and Horns, the Cello part may be associated with the dry *staccato* of the Bassoon. In the latter case it is often wise, either to divide the passage up between two Bassoons, or, if the figures are allotted to a single instrument, to omit the bass-note. The lower *staccato* notes of the Bassoon are sometimes a little too heavy and the Double-Basses, of course, supply the omission. In addition this arrangement gives the Bassoonist regular places for breathing.

In the more serious forms of music the Cello *pizzicato,* without being bound down to a persistent figure of accompaniment, appears in delightful combinations with the Wood-Wind and Horns. Brahms often makes a very happy use of this method in his Allegrettos. Of these one cannot quote a better example than the opening of the 3rd Movement of his *Symphony in C minor.*

EXAMPLE 265.

Here the flowing Clarinet-tune and the easy upward movement of the Horn are charmingly contrasted and combined with the pointed Cello-bass. Notice also the unexpected and happy entry of the three upper String-parts, *p dolce* <>, and their no less unexpected and happy exit. The held Oboe-C with its little *crescendo*, followed by two bars of movement *diminuendo*, and then twelve bars rest, is well worth noting for its tiny perfection. The student should examine the whole of this movement in the full score, as the *pizzicato* Cello-bass plays quite a prominent part in it throughout.[1]

As with the other Strings there is a certain upward limit beyond which it is inadvisable to write the *pizzicato*. This limit, fixed by the shortness of the string and the consequent dryness of the tone, may be exactly illustrated by the little unaccompanied scale-passage which leads from Scene II. to Scene III. in Act III. of Humperdinck's *Hänsel und Gretel*. Anything higher than the last note of this passage—top B♭—is not very effective.

EXAMPLE 266.

Tone-Quality.

The Cello is, in the instrumental force, the vocal complement of the Violin. The one is the poet of the orchestra, the other the poetess. The one associates itself with our ideas of the Male-Voice, the other with those of the Female-Voice.

[1] The slow movement of the same Symphony contains a good example of the Cello *pizzicatos*. The triplet passage begins at the tenth bar before letter "D." The rest of the Strings, even the Basses, are *arco*, and there are Wood-Wind, Horns, Trumpets, and Drums in the score. Yet the Cello *pizzicatos* always "tell" well in performance.

[2] A Bassoon-fifth, B and F♯, is omitted from the first beat of this quotation.

It is scarcely necessary to describe the poignant aching quality of the Cello top-string, which, in the three semitones of *Tristan,* is able to foretell a drama. The use of this tone-colour for melodic purposes is so common nowadays that one may almost call it an abuse. It is wise to bear this point in mind. The singing ecstatic quality of the Cello top-string is not for all tunes. Unless they have something of grief, of passion, or of chivalry they will suffer from an excess of emphasis.

Some few examples of the Cello used on its top string have already been given.[1] The following extract, however, shows the somewhat unusual melodic unison of the Cellos with the 1st Violins and one Bassoon. The passage occurs at the extreme end of Tschaikowsky's Fantasy-Overture *Romeo and Juliet,* and is interesting, not only from the point of view of the String-ensemble, but as an example of a persistent Drum rhythm supported by the Bass *pizzicatos* and the *tenuto* of the Tuba.

EXAMPLE 267.

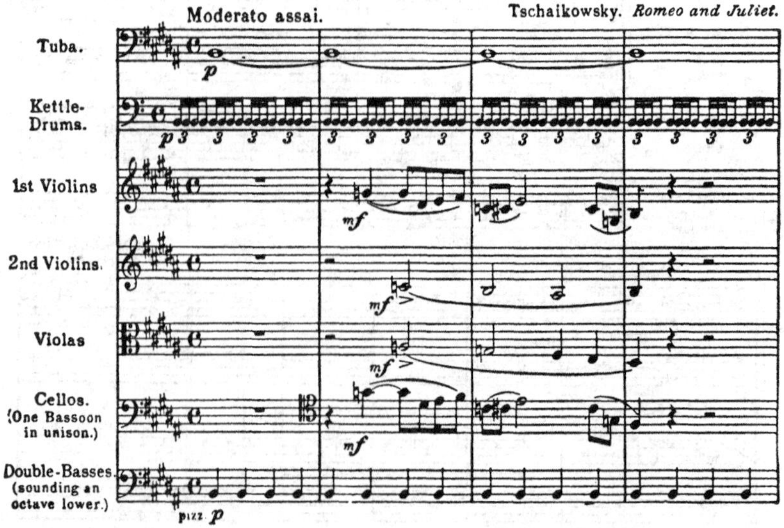

To the musical ear the "D" is probably the most beautiful string on the Cello. Its notes differ totally from the same notes when played on the Viola. The latter instrument has a certain hollow tragic sound on its C string, a sound that is easily capable of orchestral prominence. On the other hand, the Cello "D" is characterized by a sort of caressing reticence. In fact, it is not going too far to say that, of all the soft, silky sounds in the orchestra, it is the softest and silkiest. Forceful it cannot be called, but when unaccompanied, or only lightly accompanied, it is capable of expressing the most poetical feelings. For an example of its lovely tone-quality one need travel no further than Beethoven's

[1] See Exs. 43, 99, 137, 221, 247, 253-6, 258, 259, 261, 262.